Andrew V. Kudin

IN SEARCH OF THE PERFECT STATE:

FOUNDATIONS OF POLITICAL PHILOSOPHY

KUDIN & SONS

ACADEMIC PRESS

Published by Kudin & Sons Academic Press
Los Angeles, California, United States
ISBN: 979-8-9935342-0-6

Other editions:
Hardcover: 979-8-9935342-1-3
eBook (Kindle): 979-8-9935342-2-0
eBook (EPUB): 979-8-9935342-3-7
Audio: 979-8-9935342-4-4

Library of Congress Control Number: 2025922705

First Edition
Printed in the United States of America

CONTENTS

PREFACE

Every human being strives for well-being and happiness. This desire is woven into life itself; it lies at the core of our existence. From our first breath to our last, we long to feel the joy of living, to see the world in its brightness, and to feel the warmth of love and the nearness of those dear to us. We come from an ideal world into the earthly one not to suffer and endure pain, but to experience pleasure and joy. In our dreams, fragments of a lost paradise return to us. Upon waking, we strive to recreate that paradise here, in this world, and to be happy once again—as we once were long ago, before birth.

Through us, God knows Himself. We are His sense organs.

The pursuit of happiness is inseparable from the experience of freedom, for a person deprived of freedom cannot fully taste life or enjoy happiness. Without freedom, happiness becomes a phantom—appearing real, yet disappearing the moment one tries to hold it. An unfree person is like a bird in a cage that has never flown: it may have food, shelter, and safety, yet lacks the one essential thing—space and sky. Such a bird has never known the joy of flight—and may never know it.

Seeing others fly and flying yourself are profoundly different experiences. There is always a gulf between another's life and your own. It is one thing to watch birds soar, to admire their freedom and grace, and quite another to spread your own wings and rise into the air, feeling the exhilaration and lightness of flight.

The same world looks and feels completely different when viewed through the grimy window of a crowded bus or from the window of a private Rolls-Royce. And the difference is not merely about where one happens to be at a given moment. Too often, one person's freedom becomes another's enslavement. History is filled with examples in which the well-being of a small elite was built upon the suffering, deprivation, and oppression of vast numbers of people.

Human beings are social creatures. We realize our potential only through interaction with others. But how should such interaction be organized so that it respects the interests of every living being it touches? How can we build an ideal, harmonious, balanced society in which one person's freedom is not an obstacle to another's, but rather a foundation for shared prosperity and mutual harmony?

Throughout history, humanity has sought to create the perfect model of society.

If you wish to change the world, you must study the experience of past thinkers and understand what models have existed before and what models exist today. This knowledge can help you develop an effective strategy for building and governing a state.

If you are an ordinary citizen, it is essential to understand the nature of the society you live in, how it is structured, and the laws that govern its development.

If you are forced to leave your homeland and seek a new place to live and build a future for your family, it is crucial to know in advance what realities and difficulties you will encounter.

Unfortunately, the media and propaganda too often distort reality, presenting falsehood as truth. We are deceived again and again. Those at the top of power need people to give up their savings and pay taxes to sustain a regime or to finance war. We are told this is for noble causes—for the defense of freedom and democracy. But time passes, power changes hands, and the message on television shifts entirely. We discover that there was no struggle for freedom and democracy after all, and that our money served entirely different, far less noble ends.

Caligula and Hitler—like many other dictators—sincerely believed that under their leadership the state was the most democratic and free. But the only ones who truly felt free in such countries were they themselves and, perhaps, their closest circle—not the ordinary people. No dictator will ever admit to establishing a brutal tyranny or to grossly violating the rights and freedoms of citizens. The media, controlled by the dictator and by foreign allies pursuing their own geopolitical aims, will echo these lies, amplifying them until they dominate public discourse.

This is why it is so vital to recognize the key characteristics and indicators of a state's political structure. With such knowledge, you can analyze the situation in a country independently and reach sound conclusions without relying on external interpretations. You will be far less vulnerable to confusion or deception. This is especially true today, when everyone is under intense informational pressure from competing political forces seeking to manipulate public opinion for their own ends.

Such is the value of this book.

HOW IS THIS BOOK STRUCTURED

The book opens with a universal classification of models of government, past and present. This classification serves as a guide, helping the reader understand the variety of political systems and the links between them. The analysis is divided into nine main parts, each focusing on a particular dimension of state organization — from the form of government and political regime to the economic system, cultural and historical patterns, and the degree of protection of human rights and freedoms.

This structure allows for a systematic study of the subject: by moving from one dimension to another, the reader gains a multi-layered perspective that shows both the theoretical foundations and the practical workings of different models. Historical examples illustrate how these models arise, develop, and interact, while the comparative approach highlights their strengths and weaknesses.

The framework is not limited to the study of the past; it can also be applied to the analysis of current events worldwide. By identifying the features of a particular state within this classification, one can better interpret political developments, assess reforms, and anticipate possible shifts in governance.

To determine which model a given state corresponds to, the reader is invited to answer YES or NO to the questions in the final chapter — Questionnaire for Determining the State Model — and then, at the end of the book, use the key to apply the formula. This method turns abstract concepts into a practical tool for political analysis.

UNIVERSAL CLASSIFICATION

I. By Form of Government

1. **Monarchy** – a form of government in which supreme authority is vested in a single ruler, usually for life and often hereditary.
    • **Absolute Monarchy** – the monarch holds unrestricted political power, unconstrained by laws or constitutions.
    • **Constitutional Monarchy** – the monarch's powers are defined and limited by a constitution.
    • **Parliamentary Monarchy** – the monarch acts within a parliamentary system, with executive authority derived from the legislature.
    • **Elective Monarchy** – the monarch is chosen through an election process rather than hereditary succession.

2. **Republic** – a form of government in which the head of state is elected, directly or indirectly, for a fixed term.
    • **Presidential Republic** – executive power is vested in an elected president, separate from the legislature.
    • **Parliamentary Republic** – executive authority is vested in a cabinet that is accountable to the legislature.
    • **Mixed (Semi-Presidential) Republic** – executive power is shared between an elected president and a prime minister.

II. By Political Regime

1. **Democratic Regime** – a system in which political authority derives from the people, with institutions ensuring participation and accountability.
    • **Direct Democracy** – citizens directly participate in decision-making without intermediaries.
    • **Representative Democracy (Parliamentarism)** – citizens elect representatives who make decisions on their behalf within a parliamentary framework.
    • **Liberal Democracy** – a representative democracy that guarantees individual rights, the rule of law, and separation of powers.
    • **Limited (Electoral) Democracy** – a system with regular elections but significant restrictions on political rights or competition.

2. **Authoritarian Regime** – political power is concentrated in the hands of a leader or small elite, with limited political freedoms.
    • **Military Authoritarianism** – the armed forces control the state's political power.
    • **Personalist Authoritarianism** – authority is centered on an individual leader whose power is not effectively constrained.
    • **Bureaucratic Authoritarianism** – political control is exercised by state bureaucratic structures.
    • **Electoral (Hybrid) Authoritarianism** – elections are held but are neither free nor fair, serving to legitimize the regime.

3. **Totalitarian Regime** – an extreme form of authoritarianism with pervasive state control over all aspects of life.
   • **Ideological Totalitarianism** – governance based on an all-encompassing official ideology.
   • **Fascist Totalitarianism** – authoritarian nationalism promoting unity through strict control and suppression of dissent.
   • **Nazi (National Socialist) Totalitarianism** – authoritarian rule grounded in racial ideology and nationalist expansionism.
   • **Religious Totalitarianism** – political authority justified and enforced through religious doctrine.

III. By Administrative and Territorial Structure

   • **Unitary State** – a state governed as a single entity with centralized authority.
      o **Centralized** – decision-making power is concentrated in the central government.
      o **Decentralized** – local authorities have delegated powers within a unified framework.

   • **Federal State** – sovereignty is constitutionally divided between a central authority and constituent political units.
      o **Symmetrical Federation** – all constituent units have equal powers and status.
      o **Asymmetrical Federation** – constituent units have different powers or status.

   • **Confederation** – a union of sovereign states that retain primary authority and delegate limited powers to a central body.
      o **Union of Sovereign States** – the central authority exists only by agreement of the member states and has limited powers.

IV. By Economic System

   • **Market Economy** – resources are allocated through supply and demand with minimal state intervention.
      o **Liberal Capitalism** – economic activity is predominantly private and market-driven.
      o **State Capitalism** – the state plays a significant role as owner or controller of key industries.

   • **Planned Economy** – economic decisions are made centrally by the state.
      o **Socialist Planned Economy** – planning is based on socialist principles, emphasizing collective ownership.
      o **Non-Socialist Model of Planned Economy** – centralized planning without a socialist ideological framework.
   • **Mixed Economy** – a combination of market mechanisms and government regulation.
      o **Combination of Market and State Regulation** – the private sector operates alongside state-directed economic activities.

V. By Degree of Religious Influence

- **Secular State** – religion and government are institutionally separate.
  - o **Strictly Secular (Laïcité)** – religion is fully excluded from public and political life.
  - o **Moderately Secular** – religion may play a limited role in cultural or ceremonial contexts.

- **Religious State** – governance is based wholly or partly on religious principles.
  - o **Islamic State** – governance based on Islamic law (Sharia) and traditions.
  - o **Christian State** – political authority influenced by Christian doctrine and values.
  - o **Jewish State** – governance influenced by Jewish law (Halakha) and traditions.
  - o **Buddhist State** – governance influenced by Buddhist doctrine and ethics.
  - o **Hindu State** – political authority influenced by Hindu traditions and philosophy.
  - o **State with an Official Religion** – a specific religion is recognized and integrated into public life but does not control all aspects of governance.

VI. Special Historical and Cultural Models

- **Military Oligarchy** – political authority concentrated among a small group of military leaders.
- **Aristocratic Republic** – governance dominated by a hereditary elite or nobility.
- **Absolute Theocratic Monarchy** – the monarch holds supreme political and religious authority.
- **Caste-Based State** – political and social organization determined by hereditary caste divisions.

VII. Philosophical and Hypothetical Models

- **Ideal (Utopian) State** – a theoretical model of perfect governance.
- **Minimal State ("Night-Watchman")** – government limited to essential protective functions such as security and enforcement of contracts.
- **Technocratic State** – governance by technical and scientific experts.
- **Ecological State (Ecocracy)** – governance prioritizing environmental sustainability.
- **Digital State (Virtual Democracy)** – governance conducted primarily through digital technologies and platforms.
- **Transhumanist State** – governance adapted to the integration of advanced human enhancement technologies.
- **Cosmopolitan State (World Government)** – governance extending beyond national boundaries to a global authority.

VIII. Anti-State (Anarchist) Models

- **Anarcho-Syndicalism** – self-management of production and governance by workers' collectives.
- **Anarcho-Communism** – stateless society based on communal ownership and egalitarian principles.
- **Individualist Anarchism** – emphasis on individual autonomy and voluntary association without state authority.

IX. By the Level of Protection of Human Rights and Freedoms

- **Liberal State** – maximum legal and practical protection of rights and freedoms.
- **Non-Liberal State** – restrictions on rights and freedoms.
- **Intermediate or Hybrid Forms** – partial protection of rights and freedoms.
- **Declarative Model** – formal recognition of rights without effective enforcement.

PART I
CLASSIFICATION BY
FORM OF GOVERNMENT

SECTION 1. MONARCHY

Introduction

> **Monarchy** is a form of government in which a single individual—the monarch—serves as head of state, typically for life or until abdication, most often through hereditary succession, with powers that may range from absolute to largely ceremonial.

Monarchy, by its nature, entails the concentration of power in the hands of a king, emperor, sultan, or other sole ruler. The term "monarchy" derives from the Greek μοναρχία (monarchía), from μόνος (mónos, "alone") and ἄρχειν (árchein, "to rule"), literally "sole rule."

Monarchy is one of the oldest and most widespread forms of governance. Its origins cannot be confined to any single culture or corner of the world. Across continents and through the centuries, peoples have arrived at this system independently, seeing in it a way to organize political and social life. From the ancient realms of the East and Africa to the kingdoms of Medieval Europe and the civilizations of pre-colonial America, monarchies appeared in diverse forms almost everywhere. Their persistence suggests that monarchy rests not only on historical necessity but also on deeper patterns of human nature and the psychology of communities.

From a psychological perspective, monarchy appears both understandable and natural. Human beings instinctively seek order, clarity, and stability in political life. A single ruler—embodying the center of power and responsibility—offers a simple and recognizable image of governance in the public mind. People often find it easier to relate to an individual than to an abstract institution, and the figure of the monarch makes authority tangible and visible.

The presence of a ruler at the head of the state also satisfies a deep emotional need for continuity. Monarchs are not only political leaders but also symbols of tradition, linking past, present, and future. Their role provides a sense of permanence in a world of constant change. In this respect, monarchy mirrors family structures, where authority and protection are entrusted to a single parental figure.

Succession strengthens this continuity. Power passes from one generation to the next within the same dynasty, preserving accumulated experience and cultural traditions. In this way, monarchy becomes a thread between past and future, offering stability and a sense of unbroken heritage. For many, the monarch is more than a political figure: they embody national identity.

Even in countries where monarchy is largely ceremonial, the monarch remains central in public life. It is not only a political institution but also a social and cultural force. It embodies unity and gives citizens a sense of belonging to a shared history. That is why, after thousands of years, monarchy has not disappeared but continues to adapt to new eras and social realities, existing alongside other forms of government.

Chapter 1

Absolute Monarchy:
Centralized Authority Without Constitutional limits

Absolute monarchy is a form of government in which all state power—legislative, executive, and judicial—is concentrated in the hands of a single monarch, unconstrained by a constitution, laws, or representative bodies. In such a system, the ruler's decisions are not subject to challenge and carry the highest legal authority.

Characteristics

Absolute monarchy is a form of state in which all power—legislative, executive, and judicial—is held by a single ruler. The monarch exercises the full range of authority: issuing laws and decrees, forming the government, appointing and dismissing officials, directing the courts, commanding the armed forces and security services, and controlling the nation's finances. His will is not restrained by law, constitution, or parliament, and his decisions carry absolute force.

A defining feature of absolute monarchy is its highly centralized character. All authority flows from the ruler and rests on personal loyalty. State institutions exist only at the monarch's will and function according to his directives. This structure allows for swift decision-making, since approval from independent bodies or parliaments is unnecessary; such institutions either do not exist or are purely ceremonial.

In this system, court circles and the ruler's closest advisers play a pivotal role. Senior officials, ministers, and counselors are appointed directly by the monarch and act under his supervision. Their status, influence, and careers depend entirely on his favor, making the personal element decisive for the fate of the state and its people.

The ideological foundation of absolute monarchy is closely linked to the doctrine of the Divine Right of Kings—the belief that royal authority comes directly from God and cannot be challenged. This doctrine flourished in Europe between the sixteenth and eighteenth centuries, when rulers emphasized their divine status, presenting their power as both political reality and sacred truth. One of the most famous examples was the French king Louis XIV, the "Sun King," whose declaration L'État, c'est moi ("I am the state") became a symbol of absolute power, where ruler and state were inseparable.

In many ancient civilizations and traditional societies, monarchs went further, claiming descent from the gods and presenting themselves as divine or semi-divine beings. Such claims were thought to justify their right to rule and to make their authority sacred in the eyes of their subjects.

Historically, absolute monarchy was not only a political system but also an ideology of power, rooted in sacred justifications of the monarch's role. Around the ruler grew a carefully cultivated aura of mystique, reinforced by rituals and ceremonies that highlighted his exceptional place in the life of the state and society.

Strengths of Absolute Monarchy

1. Stability and Unity of Leadership

One of the main advantages of absolute monarchy is its capacity to ensure stability and unified governance. When authority is concentrated in the hands of a single ruler, the state avoids political infighting, partisan conflict, and rivalry among factions. The monarch serves as a national arbiter, able to reconcile divisions and restore order quickly in times of crisis or instability.

2. High Speed of Decision-Making

Another important strength of absolute monarchy is the speed of decision-making. The monarch does not need to coordinate with parliament or other representative bodies; ultimate authority rests with one person. Here, as the American saying goes, the buck stops with the monarch, who carries full responsibility for the final decision. This enables the state to respond quickly to threats, resolve emerging problems, and introduce reforms without delay.

3. Clear Hierarchy and Transparency in Governance

Absolute monarchy is defined by a clear hierarchy. Citizens know who makes decisions and who is responsible for them, which reduces bureaucratic confusion and removes uncertainty in governance. Officials at all levels know to whom they report and whose orders they follow, making the execution of decisions consistent and effective.

4. Continuity of Power and Long-Term Planning

Absolute monarchy secures continuity of power by passing the throne from one generation to the next within a single dynasty. This allows the state to plan long-term policies without the risk of sudden shifts in direction caused by frequent changes of leadership. As a result, the country can look decades ahead and carry out its goals steadily over time.

5. Symbolic Unity and the Monarch's High Authority

In an absolute monarchy, the ruler is not just a head of state but embodies the nation itself—its history, traditions, and culture. His authority, grounded in both political and symbolic power, allows decisions to be carried out effectively and internal conflicts to be resolved quickly.

6. Efficient Use of State Resources

The absolute monarch holds sole control over the state's resources and directs them where they are most needed. This removes bureaucratic delays and formal approvals, allowing resources—financial, human, and military—to be allocated quickly and effectively to priority tasks.

7. Centralization of Responsibility

In an absolute monarchy, responsibility for decisions rests with one person. The monarch is directly accountable for the outcome of every state initiative and cannot shift blame to other institutions. This concentration of responsibility forces the ruler to govern with caution, aware that the results of his actions shape both his authority and the legacy he leaves behind.

Weaknesses of Absolute Monarchy

1. Risk of Despotism and Arbitrary Rule

The most serious risk of absolute monarchy is that unchecked power can foster despotism and authoritarian rule. Without effective oversight, the monarch and his inner circle may suppress opposition, silence dissent, and stifle criticism. Power without limits also carries the temptation to use it for personal gain or to serve the interests of a narrow elite. Under such conditions, violations of rights, political persecution, and abuses by state agencies become likely.

2. Absence of Political Freedoms and Citizen Representation

Another serious problem of absolute monarchy is the absence of political freedoms and real ways for citizens to influence policy. People cannot freely express opinions, choose representatives, or take part in decision-making. This produces passivity and apathy, weakens civic involvement, and narrows participation in social life. A state cut off from feedback loses the capacity to respond to society's needs, which in turn fuels social tension.

3. Problems of Succession and Crises of Inheritance

In an absolute monarchy, succession is a critical issue, since the monarch usually rules for life. The death or abdication of a ruler without a clear heir often triggers a crisis of succession. Rivalries among heirs, struggles between claimants, and court intrigues can escalate into civil war and armed conflict, undermining stability and plunging the state into political turmoil.

4. Risk of Incompetence and Unfitness of the Monarch

Another drawback is that absolute power is inherited, which does not guarantee the competence of the next ruler. If the throne passes to an inexperienced or weak monarch, the state may face grave challenges. With no mechanism to remove an unfit ruler or limit his authority, the risks to the country and its people increase sharply.

5. Limited Adaptability and Flexibility of the Political System

Absolute monarchies are often slow to adapt to new conditions and social change. Because decisions are made unilaterally, without input from a wider circle of experts, they may be detached from reality and overlook shifts in public needs. The rigidity of the system hinders reform and weakens the state's capacity to respond to changing political and economic circumstances, which over time can lead to crisis and decline.

6. High Dependence of the State on the Monarch's Personal Qualities

Because all power in an absolute monarchy is concentrated in the hands of a single person, the ruler's personal qualities become the decisive factor in the country's rise or decline. The monarch's morality, intellect, education, and psychological state directly influence his decisions and, consequently, the fate of the entire state. This makes the political system extremely vulnerable to chance, where the nation's future depends entirely on the character and abilities of one individual.

Absolute monarchy is a spark in a dry forest — it carries with it risks that are neither few nor small. Hidden contradictions lie under the surface, waiting for the right spark to turn them into political, economic, or social earthquakes. And yet, for all its dangers, there is a quiet truth: in every leader — be it a monarch who wore a crown centuries ago, a modern president in a tailored suit, or the unassuming head of a small-town board — their lives the same dream. To hold all the cards. To be the single, unchallenged center of gravity where every decision begins and ends. The sole source of law. The final word.

This hunger for dominion is stitched into the very fabric of human nature. It runs through history like a scarlet thread, winding through the rise and fall of empires, whispered in palaces and shouted in the streets. Sometimes it wears a humble face. In some, the thirst for power is the quiet will to master their own fears, to keep the reins tight on their impulses, to wrestle their weaknesses to the ground. They see in this inner victory the real crown jewel of the spirit. For them, self-mastery is the only road to freedom worth walking.

Others carry the same thirst, but it burns in another way — hotter, louder, and outward. It's the unshakable urge to bend others to their will, to pull the strings of another's choices, thoughts, and even dreams. This instinct goads leaders and rulers alike, prodding them to push the edge of their authority further, and further still, until there's no horizon left. In absolute power, they see not just a prize, but the very point of existence. And for even one step closer to it, they'll pay any price, walk through fire, or burn bridges without a second thought.

Here lies the two-faced truth of power. Some turn inward, finding their kingdom within, building their freedom brick by brick through self-control. Others look outward, chasing the high of total command over people and events. And so long as this ancient hunger keeps beating in the human heart, absolute monarchy will be more than a system of rule. It will be a siren song — calling every ruler, in every age, to imagine themselves on the throne, no matter how far away it stands.

Historical Examples of Absolute Monarchy
France During the Reign of Louis XIV (1643–1715)

France under Louis XIV, the Sun King, is one of the most studied examples of absolute monarchy in European history. He ascended the throne in 1643 as a child after the death of his father, Louis XIII, and at first reigned under the regency of his mother, Queen Anne of Austria, with Cardinal Mazarin as chief adviser. The turning point came in 1661, after Mazarin's death, when Louis declared that he would govern personally. From that moment, power was concentrated in his hands to an unprecedented degree.

Louis XIV pursued a clear strategy of centralization. Local parliaments, once able to challenge royal edicts, were reduced to ceremonial bodies. The king himself appointed and dismissed ministers and generals, issued laws without parliamentary consent, oversaw judicial affairs, and controlled fiscal policy. This eliminated institutional checks and affirmed that sovereignty lay wholly with the monarch.

His famous declaration, L'État, c'est moi ("I am the state"), captured the essence of his rule. In the culture he created, the monarch's will and the state's authority were inseparable. Opposition to royal policy was treated not as debate but as disloyalty to the nation, making dissent both dangerous and unacceptable.

The Palace of Versailles became the most effective tool of control. More than a royal residence, it was designed as the symbolic and practical center of power. By requiring nobles to live at court and binding them to elaborate rituals, Louis ensured their dependence on royal favor. Versailles functioned as a theater of power where etiquette and spectacle reinforced his supremacy and prevented nobles from building independent influence in the provinces.

Foreign policy was another foundation of Louis XIV's rule. His reign was marked by major wars—the War of Devolution (1667–1668), the Dutch War (1672–1678), the War of the Palatinate (1688–1697), and the War of the Spanish Succession (1701–1714). These conflicts aimed not only at territorial expansion but also at projecting France as Europe's leading power, enhancing the monarchy's prestige at home and abroad. They also placed France at the center of European politics, making the kingdom both admired and feared by its rivals.

Yet the very methods that strengthened his rule also carried the roots of later instability. Unchecked military spending and the extravagance of Versailles strained the treasury. The burden of taxation fell heavily on the lower classes, while representative bodies were unable to voice grievances. Social discontent grew quietly but persistently.

By the end of his reign, France's standing in Europe was secure, but the monarchy's domestic foundations were fragile. Concentrating authority in one person brought unity but removed flexibility. The economic pressures and social tensions left unresolved under Louis XIV would, in the next century, help lead to the French Revolution of 1789.

The Russian Empire During the Reigns of Peter I and Catherine II

Another major example of absolute monarchy is the Russian Empire under Peter I (1682–1725) and Catherine II (1762–1796). Under their reigns, Russian autocracy took on the most complete form of European absolutism.

Peter the Great's rule was a time of radical change and the consolidation of central power. He came to the throne at the age of ten, at first ruling with his half-brother Ivan V under the regency of Tsarevna Sophia, and later as sole ruler after her removal. From the start of his independent reign, Peter held near-unlimited authority. His determination and ambition were directed at transforming what he saw as a backward and isolated state.

Centralization was the hallmark of his rule. He dismantled the old boyar institutions and created collegia—new administrative bodies answerable directly to the monarch. In 1711 he founded the Senate as the highest governing institution, but it functioned entirely under his command. Peter appointed officials, enforced decrees, and punished even minor breaches of discipline. A centralized bureaucracy took shape, extending through every level of government.

His reforms sought to modernize Russia. He built a standing army and navy, which secured victory in the Great Northern War (1700–1721) against Sweden, gave Russia access to the Baltic, and led to the proclamation of the Russian Empire in 1721. He introduced Western customs, reformed taxation and currency, promoted industry, founded factories, and created new cities, most notably the new capital, St. Petersburg.

After Peter's death, decades of instability followed until Catherine II seized power in 1762 after deposing her husband, Peter III. Born a German princess, she was well educated, influenced by Enlightenment thought, and corresponded with Voltaire, Rousseau, and Diderot.

Catherine II ruled as an absolute monarch. She decided policy herself, appointed and dismissed ministers and governors, and held direct control over finance, the military, and foreign affairs. Her reforms streamlined the legal system, created a unified provincial administration, and strengthened bureaucracy and policing.

Her foreign policy brought major gains. She fought two successful wars against the Ottoman Empire (1768–1774, 1787–1791), annexed Crimea in 1783, and expanded Russian territory through the three partitions of Poland (1772, 1793, 1795). By the end of her reign, Russia had become the leading power in Europe.

But the same concentration of power that brought achievements also created lasting problems. Political dissent was crushed, freedoms were absent, and corruption thrived in the bureaucracy. Social unrest erupted in the massive Pugachev Rebellion (1773–1775), suppressed with brutal force. Succession remained unresolved: after Catherine's death, the lack of a stable system of transfer of power once again led to political uncertainty.

The reigns of Peter I and Catherine II show the defining features of Russian absolutism. Both rulers transformed Russia into a major European power, but their rule also exposed the weaknesses of absolute monarchy—authoritarian governance, the lack of political freedoms, and the constant risk of succession crises.

Saudi Arabia: A Modern Absolute Monarchy

The Kingdom of Saudi Arabia is a modern state that has preserved the core traits of absolutism into the 21st century. All governing authority belongs to the Al Saud dynasty, which has ruled since the country's unification in 1932 by its founder, King Abdulaziz ibn Saud.

A defining feature of the Saudi model is the fusion of political and religious authority. The king is at once head of state and government, commander of the armed forces, and the highest religious authority. He approves laws and decrees, appoints ministers and governors, directs domestic and foreign policy, and carries full responsibility for state decisions.

Formally, Saudi Arabia has an advisory body, the Shura Council, whose members are appointed by the king. It has no legislative power and serves only in a consultative role. Recommendations may be issued, but final authority rests with the monarch. This highlights the absolute nature of royal power and its independence from other political institutions.

The ideological basis of Saudi absolutism differs from the European doctrine of the divine right of kings. In Saudi Arabia, legitimacy derives from Islam, where authority is seen as rooted in the will of Allah rather than in popular sovereignty. The Al Saud dynasty is regarded as guardian of Islamic tradition and custodian of Mecca and Medina. This religious legitimacy grants the ruling family near-unquestioned authority, making criticism of the king not just political dissent but a grave religious offense.

In practice, this system offers advantages of decisiveness and speed. Concentrated power enables rapid responses to challenges, large-scale infrastructure development, and economic modernization. Saudi Arabia's advances in oil, urban growth, transport, and technology are often credited to centralized rule.

Another advantage is internal stability. Acting as arbiter, the monarch mediates among tribal, religious, and social groups, maintaining cohesion and preventing open conflict.

Yet the weaknesses are familiar. Political freedoms and civil rights are largely absent: opposition is banned, public debate restricted, and the media censored. The judiciary applies conservative interpretations of Islamic law, often criticized by international human rights organizations.

Succession is another source of uncertainty. With hundreds of princes and an opaque process for choosing the next monarch, rivalries and intrigue within the royal family are inevitable. Though traditions and guidelines exist, the question of succession has often stirred competition.

Saudi Arabia remains a striking example of how absolute monarchy, grounded in religion and dynasty, can persist into the modern era—combining the strengths of centralized authority with the vulnerabilities of unchecked power.

Chapter 2
Constitutional Monarchy:
Monarch's Powers Defined and Restricted by a Constitution

> **Constitutional monarchy** is a form of government in which the powers of the monarch are clearly limited by law and the constitution, while actual political authority rests with elected bodies and is regulated by democratic institutions.

Characteristics

Unlike absolute monarchy, where the ruler holds nearly unlimited power, this form of government places the crown within a system where authority is defined and limited by law. At its core stands the principle of the rule of law: no individual, not even the monarch, may act outside established legal norms. In such a system, everyone is subject to the same legal standards, regardless of status or birth.

Another cornerstone is the separation of powers. Legislative authority belongs to parliament, formed through free elections. Executive power is carried out by the government and cabinet of ministers, who are accountable to parliament and, through it, to the citizens. Judicial authority rests with independent courts, ensuring justice without political interference.

Within this framework, the monarch has no direct political power and fulfills mostly ceremonial, representative, and symbolic roles. The crown embodies unity and continuity, carries historical traditions, and serves as a reminder of national identity. While the monarch may formally open parliament, sign laws, or appoint officials, these acts are performed strictly according to constitutional provisions and parliamentary will.

A defining aspect of this system is the recognition and protection of rights and freedoms enshrined in law. The state is responsible for safeguarding freedom of speech and conscience, freedom of the press and assembly, political participation and fair elections, as well as the right to a fair trial.

The monarchy also plays a symbolic role in moments of national crisis or celebration. Its presence at ceremonies, anniversaries, or times of mourning provides citizens with a sense of continuity that rises above party politics. It reassures society that beyond competition for power there exists a figure representing the state as a whole.

At the same time, this form of monarchy serves as a bridge between tradition and modern governance. It preserves rituals and historical symbols while fully integrating democratic institutions. This dual nature enhances political legitimacy: governments change through elections, but the crown endures as a constant point of reference.

In this way, constitutional monarchy combines the stability of dynastic tradition with democratic governance and the protection of citizens' rights. It demonstrates how an ancient institution can remain relevant in modern society, retaining its symbolic role while leaving political authority to elected representatives.

Strengths of Constitutional Monarchy

1. Harmonious Combination of Tradition and Democracy

Constitutional monarchy combines national traditions with modern democratic institutions. The monarch stands as a symbol of unity and continuity, while parliament and independent courts give citizens real means to take part in political life and protect their rights.

2. Limitation of Arbitrary Power

The monarch's powers are clearly limited by the constitution and laws, which prevents overreach and guards against authoritarian rule. A system of checks and balances ensures that no branch of government can fully dominate the others.

3. Political Stability and Continuity of Governance

The monarch, remaining outside party politics and daily conflicts, stands as a symbol of stability and continuity. This allows the country to handle changes of government and parliament calmly.

4. Neutral Arbiter in Times of Crisis

During political crises or deadlocks, the monarch can serve as a neutral figure standing above party struggles. This stabilizing role helps restore dialogue, mediate tensions, and prevent escalation.

5. Strengthening of National Identity

The monarch serves as a living symbol of the nation's history and culture, strengthening feelings of unity and belonging. Through both the person and the institution, the crown helps hold society together and creates a lasting bond between state and citizens.

6. Transparency and Predictability of Governance

Constitutional monarchy presupposes well-defined powers for all branches of government, including the monarch. This ensures clarity in governance and allows citizens to see who is responsible for specific decisions.

7. Encouragement of Long-Term Vision

Because the monarch is not subject to election cycles, the institution provides continuity that fosters long-term national projects. Governments may change, but the crown sustains a sense of strategic direction across generations.

8. Promotion of Charity and Social Causes

Royal patronage of cultural, educational, and charitable initiatives brings public attention and resources to important causes, strengthening civil society and supporting social cohesion.

9. High International Standing

By carrying out representative and ceremonial duties, the monarch strengthens the country's standing in international relations. Presence at global events highlights goodwill and stability, helping to shape a favorable image abroad.

Weaknesses of Constitutional Monarchy

1. Potential Conflicts Between the Monarch and Other Branches of Government

Even with clear constitutional rules, disputes may arise over the monarch's role. While parliaments and governments usually view it as ceremonial, a monarch may sometimes attempt to intervene in politics.

Crises expose these tensions most sharply. A refusal to approve a parliamentary bill, for example, can spark a clash in which parliament and government must balance respect for the crown with defense of their democratic mandate.

Ambiguities in the constitution add further risk. A coalition deadlock may force the monarch to appoint a prime minister, a decision that is inevitably political. Even brief episodes of this kind can undermine trust in both monarchy and parliament.

2. Limited Real Influence of the Monarch

In a constitutional monarchy, the monarch is head of state in name but holds mainly ceremonial powers. This prevents authoritarian rule but leaves little room to shape policy. Even with a personal vision, constitutional limits exclude the monarch from major decisions.

These limits are most evident in times of crisis, when swift action is needed. Bound by protocol and dependent on elected officials, the monarch often remains a passive figure—high in symbolic authority yet unable to act in practice.

3. Complexity of Crisis Management

The separation of powers, while providing stability in normal times, can slow decision-making in emergencies. Consultations between parliament, government, and the monarch prevent rash choices in calm periods, but during crises they may delay urgent measures.

In moments of economic shock, natural disaster, or sudden political conflict, swift action is essential. Yet checks and balances restrict unilateral steps: even necessary measures require debate and approval, consuming valuable time and weakening the state's response. This can lead to paralysis, as branches avoid responsibility for unpopular decisions. The monarch, though formally above politics, has no mandate to intervene, and any attempt to do so risks breaching constitutional limits.

4. High Cost of Maintaining the Monarchy

The monarchy can place a heavy financial burden on the state, even without real political power. Costs include the upkeep of the royal household, security, residences, and ceremonial events.

Such spending may be tolerated in prosperous times but often provokes discontent during economic downturns. Lavish allocations for royal functions can seem unjustified when public services are underfunded, fueling criticism and calls for greater financial transparency.

5. Legitimacy of Hereditary Succession in Modern Society

In modern democracies that value equality, freedom of choice, and merit, hereditary succession often appears outdated and at odds with contemporary principles. Democratic systems choose leaders based on competence and public trust, while monarchies pass power by birth. This can place unqualified individuals on the throne, raising doubts about fairness and legitimacy. Such concerns regularly fuel debate over the compatibility of monarchy with democratic values, especially in societies with strong civic traditions.

6. Risk of Obsolescence and Loss of Relevance

Traditions and rituals that once unified the nation may seem detached from modern life. Though culturally significant, they can appear excessive or irrelevant to citizens focused on practical governance and equality.

In societies that value openness and accessibility, the hierarchical customs of monarchy often clash with prevailing norms. Among younger generations, it is increasingly viewed as ceremonial and politically marginal, which over time can weaken public support.

7. Inflexibility of the Succession Process

Hereditary succession ties leadership change to birth and family tradition rather than merit or public need. This can place unsuitable individuals on the throne and prevents the timely removal of ineffective monarchs.

Regencies required for underage heirs add to instability, while personal scandals or unpopular royals can damage the monarchy's reputation and weaken public trust in the state.

8. Limited Accountability of the Monarch

The monarch holds symbolic authority but little direct responsibility. In democracies, senior officials are accountable to the public and subject to criticism, whereas in constitutional monarchies such scrutiny is often muted by tradition.

This lack of openness creates uncertainty about the monarch's powers and can weaken public trust. Without open discussion, the monarchy risks drifting away from the society it represents.

9. Potential for Abuse by the Monarch's Inner Circle

Advisers and relatives with privileged access to the monarch may wield influence without accountability, shaping decisions that serve private rather than public interests.

Such influence is hard to detect or restrain, since the monarch's inner circle lies beyond the oversight applied to official institutions. Even if the monarch is uninvolved, scandals around close associates can damage the institution's reputation.

10. Tensions Between Democratic and Monarchical Values

Democracy rests on equality before the law, while monarchy reserves the highest office for a single family by birth. This contradiction becomes sharper in times of social change, when citizens demand broader equality and participation.

Historical Examples of Constitutional Monarchy
Great Britain (from the 17th Century to the Present)

Great Britain offers one of the most enduring examples of constitutional monarchy. The British model developed gradually over centuries, shaped by conflict, compromise, and the adaptation of tradition to changing circumstances.

The first major attempt to limit royal power came in 1215 with the Magna Carta. Although not a constitution in the modern sense, it marked an early step in restraining monarchy and securing rights for subjects. Over time, additional charters and parliamentary acts further reduced the scope of royal prerogatives.

A decisive turning point came in the 17th century during the English Revolution (1642–1651), when King Charles I was executed and England briefly became a republic under Oliver Cromwell. The experiment failed to deliver stability, and the monarchy was restored in 1660.

The foundations of constitutional monarchy were firmly laid in 1688 with the Glorious Revolution. Parliament invited William III of Orange and Mary II to take the throne on condition of parliamentary supremacy. The Bill of Rights (1689) formalized this settlement, establishing that royal authority was subordinate to Parliament. Later, the Act of Settlement (1701) secured Protestant succession and gave Parliament control over the line of inheritance, further restricting monarchical independence.

The 18th and 19th centuries brought steady change. The Hanoverian kings relied heavily on ministers, and the office of prime minister emerged as the true head of government. By the time of Queen Victoria (1837–1901), the monarchy was widely recognized as a symbolic institution, while Parliament and Cabinet exercised effective power. The Reform Acts of the 19th century expanded suffrage, anchoring the system ever more firmly in democratic principles.

In the modern United Kingdom, the sovereign serves as head of state but fulfills mainly ceremonial and representational duties. The monarch formally opens Parliament, grants royal assent to legislation, receives foreign dignitaries, and undertakes state visits abroad. All political authority rests with the elected Parliament and the government led by the prime minister. In practice, royal assent is ceremonial: while the monarch must sign every law, refusal is not considered possible. As is sometimes said in Britain, the monarch "can say 'yes' or... say 'yes.'"

The monarchy today plays a cultural and unifying role. National ceremonies such as coronations, jubilees, and royal weddings attract worldwide attention and foster a shared sense of identity. The monarch also serves as a focus of continuity during times of crisis, embodying stability when governments change frequently.

The British model blends deep respect for historical tradition with strong democratic institutions. Its resilience lies in its ability to adapt to political, economic, and social change, surviving wars, revolutions, and crises while preserving constitutional stability.

Japan After World War II (Since 1947)

Japan's political system underwent a profound transformation after its defeat in World War II. In 1947, under Allied occupation led by the United States, the new Constitution of Japan (日本国憲法 — Nihon-koku Kenpō) came into effect, redefining the emperor's role in both society and the state.

Before the war, the emperor held a unique and sacrosanct position—regarded not only as sovereign ruler but also as a divine being, a descendant of the sun goddess Amaterasu. To the Japanese people, he embodied spiritual authority and national identity. Although policy was largely shaped by military and political elites, the emperor's symbolic power was immense, and in theory his authority was absolute.

Japan's surrender in 1945 and the Allied-led reforms ended this system. The new Constitution stripped the emperor of governing authority and recast him as "the symbol of the State and of the unity of the People." Sovereignty now resided with the people, and all acts of state performed by the emperor required cabinet approval.

Since 1947, the emperor has held no political power. His duties are purely ceremonial, carried out on the advice of Japan's elected government. These include opening sessions of the National Diet, attesting to the appointment of the prime minister and Supreme Court justices, awarding state honors, receiving foreign dignitaries, and presiding over national ceremonies.

The Japanese model represents a synthesis of ancient imperial tradition and modern democracy. The imperial institution preserves historical and cultural continuity, while the constitutional framework ensures its complete separation from political power. This arrangement prevents authoritarian concentration of authority and safeguards democratic governance.

Japan's post-war success illustrates the strength of this model. In the decades since 1947, the country has risen from wartime devastation to become one of the world's leading economies, combining prosperity with political stability. The emperor's symbolic role, alongside democratic institutions, has been a stabilizing force throughout this period of rapid modernization.

In recent years, the monarchy has shown its continued ability to adapt. Emperor Akihito's historic abdication in 2019—the first in over two centuries—was widely regarded as a gesture of responsibility, reflecting his concern over age and health. His son, Emperor Naruhito, ascended the throne that year, beginning the Reiwa era. The smooth transition reinforced the monarchy's symbolic role as a unifying presence, linking Japan's ancient imperial tradition with the realities of modern constitutional democracy.

Although debates occasionally arise over the relevance of the imperial institution, public opinion remains strongly supportive of its current non-political role. For most citizens, the emperor endures as a respected symbol of historical continuity, national pride, and cultural unity.

Sweden and Denmark (Modern Constitutional Monarchies)

Both Sweden and Denmark have centuries of monarchical tradition, but over the past two hundred years their political systems have changed profoundly. Royal authority has been steadily reduced, and democratic governance has been consolidated. This gradual evolution shows how long-standing institutions can adapt to modern democracy while the monarchy retains symbolic importance within a framework of full parliamentary sovereignty.

Sweden

The Swedish model was firmly defined by the 1974 Instrument of Government (Regeringsformen), which reduced the monarch's role to that of a symbolic head of state. King Carl XVI Gustaf, who ascended the throne in 1973, has presided over this modernized form of monarchy throughout his reign. His duties include opening the annual session of the Riksdag, presenting the Nobel Prizes, receiving foreign dignitaries, and representing Sweden on state visits abroad.

Political authority rests entirely with the elected parliament and government, keeping the crown outside party politics. The monarchy remains, however, an important cultural institution. The royal family is closely associated with national traditions, public celebrations, and charitable activities. Sweden has also maintained broad public support for the monarchy, with opinion polls regularly showing a majority in favor of retaining it, though debates about reform or abolition occasionally surface in political discourse.

A distinctive feature of the Swedish monarchy is its emphasis on simplicity and accessibility. Members of the royal family are expected to live in close contact with the public, participate in civic events across the country, and uphold a modest image in keeping with Sweden's egalitarian culture. This combination of formality and approachability has helped the monarchy maintain legitimacy.

Denmark

The Danish monarchy is based on the 1849 Constitution (Danmarks Riges Grundlov), substantially revised in 1953. The revision introduced important democratic reforms, including the transition to a unicameral parliament (the Folketing) and changes to succession law, which eventually allowed for absolute primogeniture in 2009, granting daughters and sons equal rights to inherit the throne.

Queen Margrethe II, who reigned from 1972 until her abdication in 2024, became Denmark's longest-serving monarch and a deeply respected cultural figure. Her official duties included promulgating laws, signing treaties, and representing Denmark internationally, always on the advice of the prime minister and cabinet. Beyond her constitutional role, she was known for her personal contributions to the arts, including painting, design, and translation, which helped strengthen her public popularity.

The monarchy in Denmark continues to enjoy widespread support, with the royal family often described as a unifying institution in a small country with strong democratic traditions. The succession of King Frederik X in 2024 further demonstrated the monarchy's adaptability and the stability of Denmark's constitutional framework.

Comparative Analysis: Modern Constitutional Monarchies

Modern constitutional monarchies—such as those in the United Kingdom, Japan, Sweden, and Denmark—show that monarchy can coexist with, and even reinforce, democratic governance. While each reflects its own history and culture, several shared principles define their role today.

1. Separation of Symbolic and Political Functions

In all four systems, the monarch is head of state but excluded from political authority. Executive power belongs to the elected government, and legislative authority rests with parliament. This separation prevents the monarchy from being used for political control while preserving its role as a neutral symbol above party politics.

2. Constitutional and Customary Restraints

The form of limitation differs. In Japan and Sweden, constitutions (the 1947 Constitution and the 1974 Regeringsformen) explicitly remove the monarch from political life. In the United Kingdom and Denmark, restrictions rest mainly on constitutional conventions, supplemented in Denmark by the Grundlov. In every case, monarchs act only on the advice of the government.

3. Ceremonial and Representational Duties

The monarch's work is almost entirely ceremonial: opening parliament, granting formal assent to laws, welcoming foreign leaders, representing the nation abroad, and presiding at state events. These duties keep the monarchy visible as a symbol of continuity and identity.

4. Historical Legitimacy and National Identity

Even without power, monarchs retain deep cultural weight. In Britain, the crown reflects centuries of constitutional development; in Japan, the imperial house links the present to ancient origins; in Sweden and Denmark, monarchy ties medieval traditions to modern democracy.

5. Stability Through Institutional Balance

These monarchies enjoy notable stability thanks to the balance between democratic institutions and a politically neutral head of state. The monarchy acts as a steady presence, giving continuity without interfering in governance.

6. Public Support

Although debates about their relevance recur, public opinion remains broadly favorable. Polls suggest that a non-political monarchy can strengthen trust in institutions and foster a shared sense of belonging.

Modern constitutional monarchies show that monarchy, once the hallmark of absolute rule, can be reshaped into an institution that strengthens democracy rather than threatens it. By preserving historical symbols while transferring real authority to elected bodies, they provide societies with both continuity and adaptability. This balance explains why, in an age defined by rapid change, the institution of monarchy endures—not as a relic of the past, but as a stabilizing force that connects tradition with modern democratic life.

Chapter 3
Parliamentary Monarchy:
Monarch Acting Within a Parliamentary System

> **Parliamentary monarchy** is a type of constitutional monarchy in which the monarch formally retains the status of head of state but exercises only representative and ceremonial functions, while actual political power rests with a democratically elected parliament and the government it forms.

Characteristics

Parliamentary monarchy is a form of constitutional monarchy in which the monarch formally remains head of state but performs only symbolic and representative functions. In practice, the sovereign embodies national unity, cultural identity, and historical continuity, while exercising no influence over political decision-making or daily governance.

The essential distinction between a parliamentary monarchy and other constitutional monarchies lies in the complete exclusion of the monarch from the sphere of executive authority. All acts attributed to the monarch—such as granting royal assent to legislation, appointing the prime minister, opening parliamentary sessions, or conferring honors—are performed strictly on the advice of the cabinet and parliament. The monarch is constitutionally bound to accept this advice and has no authority to withhold approval or act independently. In this way, the monarchy functions as the ceremonial crown of a system governed entirely by elected officials.

The essence of the system is best expressed in the well-known formula that the sovereign *"reigns but does not rule."* The monarch stands above party competition, refrains from expressing political opinions, and maintains strict neutrality in ideological debates. This impartiality allows the institution of monarchy to serve as a unifying symbol that can be respected by citizens across the political spectrum, regardless of their affiliations.

Historically, parliamentary monarchy emerged as the culmination of long struggles between monarchy and representative institutions. Over time, the balance of power shifted decisively toward parliaments and cabinets, with the monarch's prerogatives reduced to ceremonial and symbolic functions. Today, parliamentary monarchy represents the clearest and most fully realized version of constitutional monarchy, in which the sovereign's political powers are reduced to a minimum and democratic governance is entrusted entirely to representative institutions.

It is important to note that parliamentary monarchy rests not only on written constitutions but also on unwritten conventions and traditions. In some states, these conventions—such as the automatic approval of parliamentary decisions—are as binding as formal law. This reliance on both legal norms and constitutional customs underlines the flexibility of the system, allowing monarchies to adapt to modern democratic standards while preserving continuity with the past.

Strengths of Parliamentary Monarchy

1. High Degree of Democratic Accountability

Parliamentary monarchy establishes a clear framework of democratic oversight. The monarch has no political power and cannot intervene in the activities of parliament or government. This prevents the concentration of authority in one individual, safeguards against authoritarian tendencies, and reduces the risk of arbitrary decisions. Power is vested exclusively in elected representatives whose legitimacy is regularly renewed through free and competitive elections.

2. Preservation of Cultural and Historical Continuity

One of the key strengths of parliamentary monarchy is its ability to harmonize modern democratic institutions with respect for historical traditions and cultural heritage. The monarch, as a symbolic figurehead, embodies unity and continuity across generations, linking the nation's past with its present. This symbolic role fosters a sense of belonging among citizens, reinforces national identity, and contributes to long-term stability within society.

3. Effective Safeguard Against Authoritarianism

By removing all political authority from the monarch and limiting the crown to a purely symbolic function, parliamentary monarchy provides strong protection against the rise of dictatorship. The system makes both a return to absolute monarchy and the emergence of a "strongman" figure who could undermine civil rights highly unlikely. Authority is exercised through parliament and a government accountable to it, ensuring democratic development and the protection of fundamental freedoms.

4. Political Stability and Peaceful Transitions of Power

Because the monarch remains above political struggles, the institution provides a stabilizing effect during times of political change. The continuity of the crown guarantees that transitions of government, even after heated elections, take place within a framework of stability and national unity. This reduces the risk of political crises and ensures that citizens maintain trust in the legitimacy of democratic institutions.

5. Enhanced International Standing

Parliamentary monarchies often enjoy significant prestige in the international arena. The presence of a monarch as a non-partisan and respected head of state strengthens diplomacy, as royal visits and symbolic gestures foster goodwill between nations. At the same time, democratic governance guarantees that foreign policy is firmly in the hands of accountable, elected representatives. This dual structure enhances both stability and credibility on the world stage.

6. Neutral Head of State

The monarch, stripped of political power, can act as an impartial arbiter in moments of crisis. By remaining above party politics and factional disputes, the sovereign helps to prevent the escalation of conflicts and provides a nonpartisan point of reference that commands respect across the political spectrum.

Weaknesses of Parliamentary Monarchy

1. High Cost of Maintaining the Monarchy

Critics often point to the considerable expense of sustaining the royal household. Although monarchs play no role in actual governance, their representative functions require substantial funding. In difficult economic times, these costs are perceived as wasteful and can fuel public discontent.

2. Debate Over the Monarchy's Relevance

The purely symbolic role of the sovereign regularly sparks questions about whether the institution should continue to exist. Among younger citizens, the monarchy is frequently regarded as a relic of the past that no longer aligns with democratic values of equality and openness. Such debates resurface again and again, sometimes creating sharp divisions in society.

3. Bureaucratic and Slow Decision-Making

Parliamentary systems are designed to encourage debate and consensus. Yet this strength can become a weakness in emergencies, when swift action is required. Complex procedures and multiple layers of approval often slow the adoption of laws, leaving the state less agile in moments of crisis.

4. Visible Social Privilege

Even without political authority, a hereditary monarchy preserves social hierarchies that clash with the ideal of meritocracy. The image of inherited privilege can generate resentment and reinforce perceptions of inequality in a democratic society.

5. Risk of Politicization

Although expected to remain neutral, monarchs cannot always avoid being drawn into political controversy. A symbolic gesture, a public comment, or even silence on divisive issues may be interpreted as political, threatening the credibility of the crown as a unifying force.

6. Generational Divide

Public support for monarchy tends to decline among younger generations, who see it as outdated or unnecessary. This generational gap gradually undermines the institution's legitimacy and gives rise to recurring calls for abolition.

7. Vulnerability to Scandals

The reputation of the monarchy depends heavily on the conduct of the royal family. Personal scandals, perceived extravagance, or breaches of public trust can quickly damage the prestige of the institution as a whole, making it fragile despite its historical depth.

8. Democratic Deficit in Symbolic Terms

Even without governing power, the presence of an unelected head of state is seen by some as inconsistent with the principle of popular sovereignty. Critics argue that it creates a symbolic tension between the ideals of democracy and the realities of hereditary succession.

Historical Examples of Parliamentary Monarchy
Spain after 1978

Modern Spain illustrates how a country can move from dictatorship to a stable parliamentary monarchy without losing continuity or national identity. The turning point came in 1975 with the death of Francisco Franco, which opened the way for a period of profound political transformation known as the Transition (La Transición).

A cornerstone of this process was the democratic Constitution of 1978 (Constitución Española de 1978). It defined Spain as a parliamentary monarchy, assigning King Juan Carlos I the role of head of state while limiting his authority to ceremonial and symbolic functions. Real political power was placed in the hands of the elected parliament (Cortes Generales) and a government responsible to it, headed by the prime minister.

The Transition was not only a legal reform but also a carefully managed process of reconciliation. The legalization of political parties, the free elections of 1977, and agreements between reformers and former regime officials created the foundations for a democratic system. Within this fragile balance, the monarch became a unifying figure, embodying continuity and representing a nation marked by regional and cultural diversity.

The strength of this new order was tested on 23 February 1981 (23-F), when a group of military officers attempted to overturn democracy. In a decisive televised address, King Juan Carlos I defended the constitution and called on the armed forces to remain loyal to it. His intervention proved critical to the coup's failure and gave the monarchy new moral authority as a defender of democratic institutions.

Four decades later, Spain remains a parliamentary monarchy. After the abdication of Juan Carlos I in 2014, King Felipe VI has continued the tradition of political neutrality, performing only symbolic and representative duties. By staying outside daily disputes, he reinforces the impartiality of the crown and sustains public confidence in the democratic order, where real authority rests with parliament and government.

The Netherlands in the 20th and 21st Centuries

The Dutch monarchy in the 20th and 21st centuries shows how a traditional royal institution can adapt to the demands of a modern parliamentary democracy without rupture or revolution. Today the Netherlands stands as a prosperous democratic state, where the crown remains a symbol of continuity and national tradition but no longer holds real political authority.

Unlike some European neighbors, the Dutch path to constitutional monarchy was marked by gradual reform rather than abrupt crisis. By the early 20th century, legislative power had firmly shifted to the democratically elected parliament, while the royal house began to limit its role to representation and ceremony. This steady process of self-restraint allowed the monarchy to retain respect while aligning itself with democratic values.

Queen Beatrix, who came to the throne in 1980, embodied this balance. Her reign was distinguished by strict neutrality, a refusal to interfere in government, and a quiet authority built on personal integrity rather than formal power. She became a respected figure by maintaining tradition and offering continuity in a rapidly changing society. Her abdication in 2013, in favor of her son Willem-Alexander, reinforced the principle that the monarchy serves the state by ensuring stability, not by exercising power.

King Willem-Alexander continues this model. His duties are purely ceremonial: opening the parliamentary year, representing the Netherlands abroad, and lending support to cultural and charitable causes. The exercise of political power lies entirely with the parliament and the government, led by the prime minister.

Yet the role of the monarchy remains a subject of debate. Critics argue that it is an outdated and costly institution, while many citizens regard the royal family as a living emblem of Dutch identity and pride. For supporters, the monarchy embodies the cultural and historical heritage of the nation and offers a unifying presence in public life.

Belgium in the Modern Era

Belgium entered European history as a newly independent state in 1830, choosing a constitutional monarchy as its form of government. From the outset, the monarchy served as a stabilizing institution in a country divided by language, region, and religion. Over time, and especially in the 20th century, it adapted to the realities of parliamentary democracy, gradually limiting its powers and preserving mainly symbolic functions.

The evolution of the crown was not without challenges. King Leopold III's controversial decision to surrender to German forces in 1940 during the Second World War led to a severe political crisis known as the "Royal Question." His eventual abdication in 1951 in favor of his son Baudouin illustrated how the monarchy had to respond to public opinion and political pressures in order to survive. These episodes demonstrated that the Belgian monarchy, unlike its absolute predecessors in Europe, could endure only by reshaping itself within the boundaries of democracy and compromise.

The contemporary Belgian crown is symbolic in character. The king no longer holds political authority, refrains from daily involvement in government, and stands above party conflict. His role is to act as a bridge between Belgium's distinct communities— French-speaking Wallonia, Dutch-speaking Flanders, and the small German-speaking minority. In this capacity, the monarch embodies national unity and continuity, functions of particular importance in a state where linguistic and cultural divisions remain a central feature of political life.

The monarchy's capacity for adaptation was again evident in 2013, when King Albert II voluntarily abdicated in favor of his son Philippe. The smooth transition reinforced the institution's reputation as a source of stability in a democratic framework that relies on negotiation and compromise.

Belgium's political system, however, remains famously complex. Effective governance requires coalition-building across parties and regions, often producing delays and protracted talks. The most striking example came after the 2010 parliamentary elections, when Belgium went without an official government for more than 500 days. During such prolonged uncertainty, the monarch provides continuity and calm, even without participating directly in negotiations or exercising real authority.

Chapter 4
Elective Monarchy:
Monarch Chosen Through an Established Election Process

> **Elective monarchy** is a form of monarchical government in which the head of state—the monarch—does not inherit the throne but is chosen for the position through a vote conducted by specially authorized individuals or governing bodies in accordance with an established procedure.

Characteristics

Elective monarchy stands apart from hereditary kingship by the principle that the crown is granted through choice rather than inherited by birth. This model preserved the pageantry and symbolism of monarchy, yet placed succession in the hands of those deemed powerful or privileged enough to decide, giving the institution a hybrid and often paradoxical form.

Throughout history, this principle took strikingly different shapes. In the Holy Roman Empire, the emperor was chosen by a narrow college of prince-electors; in the Polish–Lithuanian Commonwealth, every noble theoretically had a vote; in medieval Hungary and Bohemia, assemblies of magnates and clergy determined who would wear the crown. Such procedures meant that legitimacy derived not only from bloodline but from the formal consent of influential groups acting on behalf of the polity.

The elections themselves rarely ran smoothly. Competing factions promoted rival candidates, foreign dynasties spent lavishly to influence outcomes, and deliberations could stretch on for months. Polish royal elections sometimes resembled vast political gatherings, full of fiery speeches, shifting alliances, and even outbreaks of violence. In the Holy Roman Empire, careful diplomacy and bargaining among electors shaped not just the identity of the new ruler but also the balance of power across Europe.

The monarch who emerged from these contests owed his throne as much to negotiation as to lineage. His authority rested on political bargains and the recognition of elites, giving elective monarchy the quality of a negotiated kingship rather than a simple dynastic inheritance. Yet this very process, which in theory could restrain absolutism, also carried structural weaknesses. Election brought openness, but it also invited instability, external interference, and long interregna that left states vulnerable.

At the same time, elective monarchy encouraged a distinctive political culture. Because succession depended on the will of influential groups, nobles and magnates developed habits of negotiation, coalition-building, and contractual politics that left a deep imprint on governance. Even when marred by corruption or foreign pressure, these practices accustomed elites to thinking of the crown as something to be bargained over, rather than a sacred inheritance beyond question. This legacy often outlived the elective monarchies themselves, shaping political traditions long after the crowns they contested had disappeared.

Strengths of Elective Monarchy

1. Ability to Select the Most Qualified Candidate

Elective monarchy allows for the deliberate choice of a ruler on the basis of personal qualities and competence. The crown does not pass automatically but is awarded to someone judged capable of guiding the state effectively.

2. Reduced Risk of an Incompetent Ruler

Because succession is not tied to birth alone, the system prevents the rise of weak or unprepared heirs. The requirement of election makes the process more selective and raises the standard for leadership.

3. Mutual Accountability Between Monarch and Electors

The bond between ruler and those who elect him or her creates obligations on both sides. The monarch cannot disregard the interests of the groups responsible for accession, which introduces an element of balance into governance.

4. Enhanced Legitimacy Through Deliberate Choice

An elected ruler carries authority not only as a monarch but also as one whose position results from conscious decision. This gives the crown additional weight and helps secure wider recognition.

5. Adaptability to Changing Circumstances

Since succession is not bound to a single dynasty, the state can choose a monarch suited to the needs of the moment. This flexibility allows quicker adjustment to new realities.

6. Avoidance of Dynastic Crises

The absence of automatic hereditary succession eliminates disputes that arise when heirs are lacking or contested. A regulated electoral process provides clarity and continuity.

7. Greater Sense of Responsibility

Knowing that legitimacy depends on election rather than bloodline, monarchs tend to approach their office more cautiously.

8. Broader Range of Candidates

The elective system opens the throne to a wider circle of potential rulers. Not confined to one family line, it broadens the pool of possible leaders and increases the chance of securing a capable sovereign.

9. Opportunity to Balance Competing Interests

The election of a monarch often required negotiation and compromise among influential groups. This process made it possible to reconcile diverse interests and prevented any one faction from exercising unchecked dominance.

10. Greater Political Participation for Elites

Although the electorate was narrow, the act of choosing a monarch involved elites directly in shaping the highest authority. This sense of participation strengthened cooperation between the crown and the social groups on which its rule depended.

Weaknesses of Elective Monarchy

1. Uncertainty and Intrigue in Succession

Every election of a monarch reopened the question of power. Rival factions competed openly, striking bargains and weaving intrigues behind the scenes.

2. Exclusion of the Wider Population

The right to vote for the monarch was reserved for a privileged few—aristocrats, clergy, or special councils. Ordinary citizens had no voice in the choice of the sovereign, which made the crown appear as the possession of elites rather than a national institution.

3. Exposure to Foreign Influence

Royal elections were rarely contained within national borders. Neighboring states sought to advance their own candidates, offering financial support or applying diplomatic pressure.

4. Instability in Succession

Without a clear hereditary line, each transition carried uncertainty. The absence of an accepted successor created political vacuums. Long-term planning became difficult, since the future hinged on an unpredictable election.

5. Dependence on Powerful Groups

An elected monarch owed his position to the factions that secured his throne. This dependence limited independence of action and forced the crown to prioritize the interests of a narrow circle rather than the needs of society as a whole.

6. Restricted Legitimacy

Because the king was chosen by a select minority, his authority did not always command the respect of the entire nation. For many, he symbolized privilege rather than unity, which fostered alienation and made the crown vulnerable to criticism.

7. Short-Term Orientation

Rulers chosen through election often shaped policies to satisfy the groups that had raised them to power. Such decisions brought immediate benefits to a few but neglected broader, long-term goals. This orientation toward political survival weakened reform and delayed development.

8. Corruption in the Election Process

The high stakes of royal elections made them fertile ground for bribery and corruption. A small electorate could be more easily swayed by financial inducements or promises of privilege, compromising both the fairness of the process and the authority of the victor.

9. Prolonged Power Vacuums

Deliberations sometimes stretched on for months or even years. During these interregna, the state lacked firm leadership, and institutions struggled to function. Defense, diplomacy, and administration all suffered from the absence of a clear sovereign.

Historical Examples of Elective Monarchy

The Holy Roman Empire (13th–18th Centuries)

The Holy Roman Empire offers one of the clearest examples of an elective monarchy. From the thirteenth century onward, the crown did not pass automatically by inheritance but was awarded through election by a group of powerful princes.

The principle was formally fixed in 1356, when Emperor Charles IV of Luxembourg issued the Golden Bull (Goldene Bulle). This constitutional document codified the process and confirmed the exclusive right of seven electors—three archbishops and four secular rulers—to choose the emperor. A majority of four votes was sufficient to secure the throne, and this framework remained in force for centuries, shaping the political life of Central Europe.

This arrangement gave the Empire the possibility of elevating rulers for their qualities rather than their birth. Charles IV himself, Sigismund of Luxembourg, and Maximilian I of Habsburg rose to power under this system, remembered as figures of lasting political and diplomatic significance. The practice also helped to maintain the prestige of the imperial office in the wider European balance of power, even when its practical authority was limited.

But the same framework opened the way to fierce contests. The election of 1519, when Francis I of France and Charles V competed for the imperial crown, became notorious for intrigue, bargaining, and lavish expenditure. Charles triumphed, supported by the vast resources of the Fugger banking house, which financed gifts and bribes to secure votes.

Foreign involvement was a recurring theme. Rival powers, especially France and Spain, sought to shape the outcome to their advantage. In 1658, Louis XIV attempted to block Leopold I's election, pressing instead for a candidate favorable to French interests. Such interventions undermined the Empire's sovereignty and added a layer of chronic instability to each succession.

The electoral system also reinforced internal divisions. Because emperors relied on the electors for their position, they seldom possessed the authority to centralize power. Over time, autonomy in states such as Bavaria, Prussia, and Saxony grew, while the emperor's role narrowed to that of a symbolic head of a fragmented realm.

By the late eighteenth century, these weaknesses had become stark. The system that once allowed flexibility now left the Empire vulnerable. During the Napoleonic Wars, pressure from France revealed the fragility of the imperial structure. In 1806, Francis II abdicated and dissolved the Empire, bringing to an end an institution that had survived for centuries but failed to achieve enduring cohesion.

The story of the Holy Roman Empire demonstrates both the promise and the peril of elective monarchy: its ability to elevate capable rulers, and its susceptibility to rivalry, corruption, and external manipulation, which in the end contributed to its downfall.

The Polish–Lithuanian Commonwealth (16th–18th Centuries)

The Polish–Lithuanian Commonwealth, created in 1569 by the Union of Lublin, became the stage for Europe's most radical experiment in elective monarchy. Nowhere else did the system reach such scale: in principle, every member of the szlachta had the right to cast a vote, making royal elections mass political events unprecedented for their time.

The end of the Jagiellonian dynasty in 1572 marked the decisive break. With the death of Sigismund II Augustus, the throne fell vacant, and in 1573 tens of thousands of nobles gathered near Warsaw to take part in the first wolna elekcja. The sight of entire fields filled with armed nobles debating, negotiating, and voting embodied the spirit of a system that merged aristocratic privilege with electoral procedure.

Candidates came from across Europe. Henry of Valois, elected in 1573, soon abandoned the throne to become king of France. Stephen Báthory, chosen in 1576, left a deeper mark, reforming the army and strengthening the Commonwealth's position abroad. Later elections brought rulers from the Swedish Vasa line—Sigismund III, Władysław IV, and John II Casimir—as well as Saxon princes from the Wettin dynasty, Augustus II and Augustus III. The open nature of the system made the throne a prize in European power politics.

But the process also bred conflict. The election of 1587 turned violent, as the candidacies of Sigismund Vasa and Archduke Maximilian of Habsburg sparked armed clashes, culminating in the War of the Polish Succession. Foreign powers repeatedly intervened: France backed its princes, the Habsburgs pushed imperial candidates, and Russia intruded ever more forcefully in the eighteenth century. The 1733 election, which secured Augustus III with Russian and Austrian backing, ignited yet another War of the Polish Succession.

Internal dysfunction compounded these pressures. From the mid-seventeenth century, the liberum veto allowed any single deputy of the Sejm to dissolve the session and nullify its acts. Parliaments collapsed in paralysis, and legislation—including the approval of monarchs—was repeatedly blocked. This chronic dysfunction hollowed out the Commonwealth's institutions and turned the promise of a broad political nation into stalemate.

The social order itself remained narrow. While the nobility claimed full political rights, townspeople and peasants were excluded entirely. The monarchy, beholden to noble interests, never became a truly national institution. Instead, it embodied the privileges of one estate, which left much of the population alienated from public life.

By the eighteenth century, intrigue, foreign manipulation, and legislative paralysis had pushed the Commonwealth into deep crisis. It could not defend its sovereignty, reform its institutions, or contain the ambitions of its neighbors. Between 1772 and 1795, Russia, Prussia, and Austria partitioned the state in three stages, erasing it from the European map.

The history of the Polish–Lithuanian Commonwealth shows both the reach and the ruin of elective monarchy. What began as a bold experiment in aristocratic self-rule ended in systemic collapse, undone by factionalism, corruption, and the relentless pressure of foreign powers.

Vatican City (Modern Elective Monarchy — The Papacy)

Vatican City remains the world's only surviving elective monarchy. Though its territory covers scarcely forty-four hectares, its political structure preserves traditions rooted in the Middle Ages. The Pope, who embodies this system, unites two roles in one person: he is the spiritual head of the Catholic Church and at the same time the sovereign of Vatican City. From the moment of his election he holds supreme authority in both capacities.

Unlike hereditary monarchies, the papacy is never passed from father to son. The choice belongs to the College of Cardinals, the highest body of the Catholic hierarchy. They gather in a conclave—a word derived from the Latin cum clave, "under key"—recalling the custom of locking the electors inside the Sistine Chapel until a decision is reached. The secrecy of the ritual, combined with its elaborate symbolism, gives the election of a pope a unique character unmatched by any other monarchy.

The procedure is defined by the Apostolic Constitution Universi Dominici Gregis, issued by John Paul II in 1996 and amended by Benedict XVI and Francis. Only cardinals under the age of eighty may vote, and their number is capped at 120. Ballots are cast in secret, and the candidate must secure a two-thirds majority. The smoke signals that rise above St. Peter's Square—black for no result, white for success—make the waiting of the faithful an integral part of the drama.

The system has often succeeded in elevating figures of wide respect and authority. John Paul II, chosen in 1978, brought extraordinary moral influence on the global stage, while Francis, elected in 2013, embodied the cardinals' wish for renewal and greater attention to social issues. Both men had entered the conclave with reputations for learning, leadership, and spiritual stature, qualities that the electors consciously weighed in their choice.

Yet conclaves have never been free of politics. Alignments along national, cultural, or theological lines shape the discussions, and in the twentieth century the divide between conservative and progressive currents was especially visible. The 1978 conclave that brought John Paul II marked a break in centuries of Italian dominance, producing the first non-Italian pope in 455 years after intense debate between different groups of cardinals.

In earlier times the papal election was even more vulnerable to outside influence. Monarchs of Spain, France, and the Holy Roman Empire sought to secure candidates favorable to their policies, sometimes through open pressure. The period of the Avignon Papacy (1309–1377) stands as the clearest example, when the French crown exerted such control that the papal court left Rome altogether and remained in Avignon for nearly seventy years.

The system also draws criticism for its exclusivity. Hundreds of millions of Catholics worldwide have no direct role in the election of their spiritual leader, as the decision rests solely with a small circle of cardinal electors. This has led to periodic debate over the democratic legitimacy of the process. Yet the weight of tradition, the authority of the cardinals, and the sacred symbolism of the office have preserved the system to the present day. Despite its limits, the papacy continues to exercise enormous influence, not only within the Church but also in global affairs, making Vatican City a unique and enduring example of elective monarchy.

Conclusion

Monarchy is among the oldest of political forms, and yet it has never been a fixed one. Across centuries it has worn many masks: the stern face of absolutism, the balanced countenance of constitutional rule, the ceremonial dignity of parliamentary crowns, and the shifting expressions of elective thrones. Each mask tells a story of how societies sought to concentrate, limit, or share power, and each reflects a dialogue between tradition and necessity, continuity and change.

The age of absolute monarchs revealed the brilliance and the danger of authority gathered into a single hand. Kings and emperors could move swiftly, reform boldly, and conquer widely. Yet behind their splendor lay fragility: silence where dissent should have spoken, instability where continuity was needed, and dependence on the fortune of one ruler's character. When such figures disappeared, the states they had built often trembled, like monuments with no foundation beneath their weight.

Constitutional monarchy emerged as a middle path, where crowns were kept but their power encircled by law. In these systems, the sovereign ceased to be a commander and became a symbol—an emblem of identity and continuity while elected bodies assumed real governance. In Britain, Japan, and Scandinavia, this balance gave tradition new life within democratic frameworks. But even here, questions whisper at the edges: how long can ceremony alone justify cost, and how much relevance remains when sovereignty rests with the people?

Parliamentary monarchy carried this evolution to its farthest point. The sovereign no longer rules but reigns, a figurehead above the political storm. In Spain, the Netherlands, and Belgium, the crown binds together lands of varied tongues and histories, offering an image of unity where politics divides. Yet its very emptiness of power fuels doubt: is such symbolism a living need, or is it the echo of an age that has already passed?

Elective monarchy was the boldest experiment, grafting choice onto tradition. The Holy Roman Empire and the Polish–Lithuanian Commonwealth revealed both its promise and its peril—elevating rulers of ability, but also unleashing rivalries, foreign meddling, and instability. Only Vatican City preserves the model today, the white smoke rising above St. Peter's Square a medieval sign to a modern world.

In our own age, monarchies live not by command but by symbol. They endure as guardians of memory, arbiters of continuity, figures above the contests of politics. Their survival will not depend on crowns or palaces but on adaptability—on finding ways to embody unity in societies that prize equality, openness, and democracy. Should they cling only to the past, they risk becoming relics, admired but irrelevant. But if they can weave tradition with renewal, dignity with responsiveness, they may continue to shine, not as rulers but as living emblems of nations, bridges between what was and what may yet be.

SECTION 2. REPUBLIC

Introduction

> **Republic** — a form of government in which supreme authority rests with elected representatives of the people, chosen by citizens for a fixed term and held accountable to them.

Few ideas in political history have traveled as far—or endured as long—as the republic. Born in the debates of the ancient world and refined over centuries, it remains one of humanity's boldest experiments in self-government.

The word republic comes from the Latin res publica, literally "public matter" or "commonwealth." The name itself underscores a central idea: the state belongs not to a ruling dynasty or a single sovereign, but to the people as a whole.

The concept of the republic has a history of more than two millennia, reaching back to the experiments of the ancient world. Among the most renowned examples are the Roman Republic and the classical Greek city-states. Athens in the 5th century BCE is often celebrated for pioneering direct democracy, where citizens gathered in the ekklesia to decide public affairs. Rome, after overthrowing its last king, Lucius Tarquinius Superbus, in 509 BCE, established a system in which elected magistrates shared power and were accountable to the citizen body. Roman political thought drew a sharp contrast between monarchy and the republican order, insisting that no individual should hold absolute authority.

The essential distinction between a republic and a monarchy lies in how supreme authority is obtained and exercised. In a monarchy, power is typically inherited and concentrated in one family or person. In a republic, by contrast, the highest offices—whether president, consul, or prime minister—are filled through elections for fixed terms. This principle of election ensures that leaders remain accountable to those who chose them and can be lawfully removed if they fail to meet public expectations.

Equally important, the republican model rests on the separation of powers and the regular renewal of mandates through free elections. These mechanisms are intended to prevent any single person or faction from monopolizing authority. The result is a system of checks and balances that guards against arbitrariness, corruption, and authoritarian rule.

In the modern era, the republic stands as the main alternative to monarchy because it is based on the rule of law, equality before the law, and the accountability of government to the governed. Today, the majority of the world's sovereign states function as republics, embracing this form of government as the one most consistent with democratic ideals and the protection of civil liberties.

Chapter 1
Presidential Republic:
Executive Power Vested in an Elected President

Presidential Republic — a form of republican government in which the head of state, the president, is elected directly by the citizens and simultaneously serves as the head of the executive branch. In this system, the president exercises broad constitutional powers and enjoys a significant degree of independence from the legislature.

Characteristics

The presidential republic is among the most widespread forms of government in the modern world. Its defining feature is that the president serves simultaneously as head of state and head of government, bearing direct responsibility to the citizens who elected him or her for the actions of the executive branch.

A core principle of the presidential republic is the strict separation of executive and legislative powers. Each branch operates independently, derives its legitimacy from separate elections, and cannot be dissolved or subordinated by the other under normal circumstances. The president is elected directly by the citizens in a nationwide vote, receiving a mandate from the people. This sharply distinguishes the presidential model from the parliamentary model, in which the head of government is appointed by a parliamentary majority rather than chosen through a direct popular vote.

The president in such a system is vested with extensive constitutional authority: appointing ministers and heads of state agencies, shaping the primary directions of domestic and foreign policy, and serving as commander-in-chief of the armed forces. Unlike in a parliamentary system, the president does not require the ongoing confidence of a parliamentary majority to implement policies or advance a political agenda. Legitimacy rests on the mandate granted directly by the electorate. In the United States—where this system first took shape—this independence has been vividly captured in the expression that the president does not "stand with an outstretched hand" before the legislature.

Another defining element of the presidential republic is the principle of mutual independence between the branches of government. The legislature cannot remove the president for purely political reasons; removal is possible only through the extraordinary process of impeachment, reserved for grave offenses such as serious crimes or violations of the Constitution. Conversely, presidents generally lack the authority to dissolve the legislature. This structural separation creates a system of checks and balances that limits the concentration of power and helps prevent authoritarian rule.

The first fully articulated model of a presidential republic was established in the United States with the adoption of the Constitution in 1787 and the election of George Washington as the nation's first president in 1789. The American model has demonstrated enduring effectiveness, maintaining governmental stability, ensuring clear accountability for decisions, and enabling swift responses in times of crisis. Over time, this model inspired other nations in the Americas and beyond to adopt presidential constitutions, though often with significant variations adapted to local political cultures.

Nevertheless, the successful operation of a presidential republic depends on more than constitutional design. It requires well-established democratic traditions, a politically engaged and informed citizenry, and consistent adherence to constitutional norms and procedures. Without these foundations, the system is vulnerable to institutional deadlock, deep political conflict, and systemic crisis. Where democratic institutions are weak, presidential republics have sometimes slid into authoritarianism, as leaders attempted to bypass constitutional limits by concentrating power in the executive.

Strengths of a Presidential Republic

1. Stability and Effectiveness of the Executive Branch

Because the president derives a direct mandate from the electorate, he or she is not required to seek the confidence of parliament or negotiate with shifting parliamentary majorities. This independence enables the consistent pursuit of a political agenda, fostering stability even in periods of crisis or turbulence.

2. Clear Division of Powers and Direct Accountability

In a presidential system, executive authority and political responsibility are vested in a single, identifiable figure—the president. Unlike in parliamentary models, where responsibility is dispersed among coalition partners, party leaders, and legislatures, the presidential republic offers clarity: citizens know who is responsible for policies and outcomes. This transparency enhances public oversight and strengthens accountability.

3. Speed and Decisiveness in Decision-Making

The presidential model allows the head of state to act swiftly, without the delays of prolonged parliamentary debate or coalition negotiations. In moments of crisis— domestic emergencies, economic shocks, or foreign policy challenges—this capacity for rapid decision-making can be crucial in limiting harm and restoring stability.

4. Immunity of the Executive from Parliamentary Deadlock

The executive branch continues to function even when parliament is paralyzed by partisan disputes or prolonged stalemates. The president and executive apparatus can operate effectively, reducing the risk of paralysis and ensuring continuity of administration.

5. Direct Electoral Connection Between Citizens and the Executive

Because citizens elect the president directly, the head of state's legitimacy rests on the will of the people rather than on negotiations among party elites. This relationship strengthens the bond between the presidency and the electorate, compelling the president to remain attentive to public opinion and voters' priorities.

6. Predictable and Transparent Transfer of Power

Presidential republics operate under constitutionally defined terms of office, with elections held at regular intervals. Citizens can anticipate electoral cycles and assess incumbents accordingly. This predictability fosters transparency, prevents indefinite retention of power, and encourages pluralism through competitive elections.

7. Capacity to Implement Reforms and Long-Term Projects

Presidents possess autonomy to initiate reforms and implement large-scale programs. Freed from the need for constant parliamentary approval, they can undertake ambitious, sometimes politically difficult measures serving long-term national interests. This decisiveness is especially valuable during economic restructuring, technological modernization, or broad policy reform.

8. Lower Susceptibility to Coalition-Driven Corruption

Because the president's authority does not depend on maintaining parliamentary coalitions, there is less incentive for backroom bargaining and informal deals among factions. This independence reduces avenues of corruption often associated with coalition-based governance.

Weaknesses of a Presidential Republic

1. Risk of Power Concentration and Authoritarianism

A major vulnerability of the presidential model is the potential concentration of power in the hands of a single individual. A president with broad constitutional authority and significant autonomy from the legislature may gradually erode legal constraints and democratic norms, moving toward authoritarian rule. This danger is especially acute in states with weak democratic institutions and underdeveloped civil society. History offers many examples of presidential systems that slid into highly personalized regimes under dominant leaders.

2. High Likelihood of Executive–Legislative Conflict

Because both the president and legislature are elected separately and draw legitimacy directly from the electorate, sharp disagreements are common. Such conflicts can produce paralysis when neither branch can advance its policies. In the United States, these standoffs are known as gridlock—deadlock between Congress and the president that blocks action even on urgent issues.

3. Inflexibility in Altering Political Direction

Presidential systems often make it difficult to adjust policies to changing political, economic, or social conditions. In parliamentary systems, a government that loses legislative confidence can be replaced immediately. In a presidential republic, however, the chief executive serves a fixed term, and the political agenda remains in place until the next election. This rigidity can prolong ineffective policies and delay reforms, even when public dissatisfaction grows.

4. Limited Accountability to the Legislature

In a presidential republic, the executive is not accountable to the legislature in the same way as in a parliamentary system. The president does not need legislative confidence or regular adjustment of policies to reflect parliamentary majorities. While this independence strengthens executive stability, it weakens legislative oversight and can allow decisions that diverge from the preferences of most citizens.

5. Weak Oversight and Transparency Mechanisms

Extensive presidential authority may reduce transparency, particularly in states without strong democratic safeguards. Oversight by parliament or the public can be minimal, enabling secrecy in decision-making and limiting accountability. This opacity creates opportunities for corruption, nepotism, and the pursuit of private interests, undermining public trust in institutions.

6. Risk of Populism and Over-Personalization of Power

Direct presidential elections can encourage populist appeals, with candidates making broad but unrealistic promises to win votes. This fosters over-personalization of politics, where a leader's image and charisma outweigh competence, policy expertise, or institutional strength. Over time, such dynamics can weaken governance and reduce the role of institutions.

7. Difficulty in Resolving Political Deadlock

In cases of severe conflict between the president and legislature, presidential systems often lack quick mechanisms for resolution. In parliamentary systems, early elections or government resignation can end an impasse. In presidential systems, by contrast, such conflicts may persist until the end of the president's term, undermining stability and slowing development.

Historical Examples of Presidential Republics

The United States of America (1789 – present)

The United States is the first and most influential example of a presidential republic, and the first state in history to define this form of government explicitly in a written constitution.

The U.S. Constitution, adopted in 1787 and entering into force in 1789, established a strict separation of powers, provided for the direct election of the head of the executive branch, and set out the president's powers in detail. George Washington, unanimously elected as the nation's first president in 1789, shaped the traditions of the American presidential model. Rejecting monarchical symbols, he emphasized the democratic and republican character of his office. His most important precedent was voluntary self-restraint: after serving two terms (1789–1797), he declined to seek a third. This custom was later codified in the 22nd Amendment to the Constitution (1951), which limits any individual to two presidential terms.

The U.S. president serves as head of state, head of government, and commander-in-chief of the armed forces. The president appoints cabinet members, nominates federal judges—including Supreme Court justices—directs foreign policy, and exercises executive authority without needing a legislative majority in Congress. This independence rests on the direct electoral mandate conferred by the people.

Strengths Demonstrated in American History

1. The Civil War and the Leadership of Abraham Lincoln (1861–1865)

During the gravest national crisis in U.S. history, President Abraham Lincoln acted decisively to preserve the Union. He mobilized resources, issued the Emancipation

Proclamation, and took extraordinary measures—including the suspension of habeas corpus—showing the capacity for strong and unified leadership in a time of existential threat.

2. The Great Depression and World War II: Franklin D. Roosevelt (1933–1945)

Elected at the height of the Great Depression, Franklin Delano Roosevelt launched the sweeping economic and social reforms of the New Deal, stabilizing the economy and restoring public confidence. During World War II, his ability to make rapid strategic decisions, combined with sustained leadership over four terms, highlighted the effectiveness of the presidential model in guiding the nation through prolonged crises.

Weaknesses Revealed in American Practice

1. Abuse of Power and the Limits of Oversight

The Watergate scandal (1972–1974) remains the most infamous case of presidential misconduct in U.S. history. President Richard Nixon's attempts to obstruct justice and misuse executive authority to cover illegal activities led to a constitutional crisis and his resignation. This showed that even in a mature democracy, strong presidential powers can be abused and that institutional checks, while effective in the long run, often act only after major damage has been done.

2. Legislative–Executive Gridlock

Because the president and Congress are elected separately and may be controlled by opposing parties, political stalemate—known as gridlock—is a recurring feature of U.S. politics. Notable examples include budgetary impasses and government shutdowns in 1995–1996, 2013, and 2018–2019. Such deadlocks hinder governance, delay urgent legislation, and weaken public confidence in government effectiveness.

3. Rigidity of Fixed Terms

The president serves a fixed four-year term, and there is no mechanism for replacing an unpopular or ineffective president between elections, short of impeachment. This rigidity can prolong policies that have lost public support. For example, unpopular wars or economic measures often continued until the end of a president's term, even when they no longer reflected the majority's will.

4. Weakness of the Impeachment Mechanism

Although impeachment exists as a constitutional tool, in practice it rarely removes a president. Andrew Johnson (1868), Bill Clinton (1998–1999), and Donald Trump (2019, 2021) were all impeached by the House of Representatives but acquitted by the Senate. Political polarization makes conviction unlikely, limiting impeachment as an effective safeguard against executive abuse.

5. The Role of Money in Elections

U.S. presidential campaigns are among the most expensive in the world, often costing billions of dollars. Dependence on donors, Political Action Committees (PACs), and, since *Citizens United v. FEC* (2010), unlimited corporate and union spending, raises concerns about the influence of moneyed interests on democratic outcomes.

Latin American Countries (Argentina, Brazil, Mexico)

Latin America is the region where the presidential republic became the dominant form of government. Countries such as Argentina, Brazil, and Mexico drew inspiration from the U.S. constitutional model but adapted it to their own historical, political, and cultural circumstances. The region's varied experience highlights both the potential strengths of presidential rule and the vulnerabilities inherent in this system.

Argentina

Argentina adopted the presidential form of government shortly after gaining independence from Spain in 1816, with the 1853 Constitution providing the framework for its political system. The President of Argentina serves as both head of state and head of government, appoints ministers and senior officials independently, and directs domestic and foreign policy.

Strengths

The concentration of executive authority has at times enabled decisive national reforms. In the late 19th and early 20th centuries, President Julio Argentino Roca (1880–1886; 1898–1904) led major programs of modernization, expanding infrastructure and stimulating economic development, which contributed to rapid national growth.

Weaknesses

The same concentration of power has also encouraged authoritarian tendencies. The presidency of Juan Domingo Perón (1946–1955; 1973–1974) illustrates this danger. Relying on personal popularity and political charisma, Perón built a regime with strong authoritarian features, including suppression of opposition, media control, and a pervasive cult of personality. The aftermath of his rule contributed to long-term political instability. Later, Argentina experienced periods of direct military rule, most notably the 1976–1983 dictatorship, marked by repression and severe human rights abuses. These episodes demonstrated how unchecked presidential authority, in the absence of strong democratic institutions, can lead to authoritarian breakdown.

Brazil

Brazil became a presidential republic in 1889 after the fall of the monarchy and the proclamation of the republic. The president was granted full executive authority, independent of parliament.

Strengths

The presidential system allowed for ambitious modernization efforts. President Juscelino Kubitschek (1956–1961) launched an industrialization program and oversaw the construction of Brasília, a project that came to symbolize a transformative stage in Brazil's national development.

Weaknesses

The broad powers of the presidency also fueled recurring conflicts with other political institutions. The military dictatorship (1964–1985) demonstrated the risks of concentrated executive authority: the presidency became the core of an authoritarian regime marked by repression, censorship, and systematic human rights violations. The restoration of democracy in the mid-1980s began a gradual rebalancing of the system, with new efforts to reinforce separation of powers and institutional checks.

Mexico

Mexico consolidated its presidential model after the Mexican Revolution (1910–1917) and the adoption of the 1917 Constitution. The president was granted sweeping powers, including broad control over political processes and state institutions.

Strengths

The concentration of authority enabled decisive governance and long-term policy implementation. Under President Lázaro Cárdenas (1934–1940), Mexico carried out major reforms, including agrarian redistribution and the nationalization of the oil industry, laying the foundations for modern economic and social policy.

Weaknesses

This system also fostered what scholars have called "authoritarian democracy." For much of the 20th century, the presidency operated within the framework of single-party dominance by the Institutional Revolutionary Party (PRI), which effectively eliminated political competition. Decision-making was concentrated in the hands of the president and his inner circle, political freedoms were curtailed, and systemic corruption took root. Economic crises, particularly the debt crisis of the 1980s, exposed the fragility of this model. Only in the late 20th century did Mexico begin meaningful democratic reforms, strengthening the independence of parliament and the judiciary, encouraging multiparty competition, and improving mechanisms of executive oversight.

Comparative Assessment

The experiences of Argentina, Brazil, and Mexico reveal the dual nature of the presidential republic in Latin America. While the system can deliver rapid reforms, strong leadership, and political stability, it also carries acute risks: excessive concentration of power, erosion of democratic norms, systemic corruption, and recurring political crises. Striking a balance between effective executive authority and resilient institutional safeguards remains the central challenge for presidential systems in the region.

South Korea (Modern Model)

Modern South Korea is a notable example of a presidential republic that combines advanced economic development with a consolidated democratic framework, yet remains prone to recurring political crises. The current system was firmly established with the 1987 Constitution, born out of the nationwide protests of the June Democratic Uprising. These events marked a decisive break from decades of authoritarian rule and ushered in a democratic order grounded in competitive elections, constitutional limits on executive authority, and expanded civil liberties.

Under the 1987 Constitution, the President of South Korea is elected by direct popular vote for a single, non-renewable five-year term. The president wields broad powers: appointing the prime minister (with the consent of the National Assembly), selecting cabinet ministers and senior officials, setting the domestic and foreign policy agenda, serving as commander-in-chief of the armed forces, and representing South Korea in international affairs.

Strengths

Efficiency and Speed in Decision-Making

In an era of rapid economic growth and global competition, South Korean presidents have shown the ability to make swift economic and strategic decisions. This decisiveness contributed to the country's rise as one of the world's largest economies, known for technological innovation, export-driven growth, and industrial modernization.

Clear Executive Accountability

The president's constitutional responsibilities are explicitly defined, concentrating executive authority in a single office. This provides citizens with clarity about who is ultimately responsible for national policy. Although the five-year term precludes re-election, the electorate can judge a president's leadership by evaluating their record at the conclusion of their tenure.

Weaknesses

High Incidence of Political Scandals and Executive Misconduct

Since democratization, South Korea has faced frequent scandals involving former presidents. Roh Tae-woo (1988–1993) was convicted in 1996 of corruption and complicity in the 1979 military coup. His predecessor, Chun Doo-hwan (1980–1988), faced similar charges. The most dramatic case was the impeachment and removal of Park Geun-hye (2013–2017), convicted in 2018 of bribery, coercion, and abuse of power—an event that sparked mass protests and deepened political polarization.

Persistent Executive–Legislative Conflict

When the National Assembly is controlled by opposition parties, confrontation with the president is frequent. These clashes often produce legislative gridlock, stalling or blocking major policy initiatives. This recurring pattern undermines political stability, delays reforms, and reduces the effectiveness of governance.

Chapter 2
Parliamentary Republic:
Executive Authority Formed Through Parliamentary Majority

Parliamentary Republic — a form of government in which supreme authority is vested in a parliament elected by the citizens. The parliament forms a government that is politically accountable to it, while the head of state performs primarily ceremonial and representative functions.

Characteristics

In a parliamentary republic, the legislature holds the central position in the political system and determines the overall direction of state policy. The executive depends directly on parliament and is fully accountable to it.

Unlike in a presidential republic, where the president is elected directly by citizens, the central political figure in a parliamentary system is the prime minister. The prime minister forms and leads the cabinet, bears responsibility for the government's performance before parliament, and must regularly maintain its confidence.

The government in a parliamentary republic is formed by the parliamentary majority that emerges from elections. The party or coalition securing a majority of seats nominates its candidate for prime minister and assembles the cabinet of ministers. The cabinet must obtain—and continually maintain—parliament's support. If the legislature passes a vote of no confidence, the government must resign. Parliament may then form a new government or call early elections, allowing the electorate to decide who will govern.

The president in a parliamentary republic generally performs ceremonial and representative functions. While formally serving as head of state, the president's powers are limited. Typical responsibilities include signing laws, approving the prime minister's appointment on parliament's recommendation, receiving foreign dignitaries, and taking part in official ceremonies. Day-to-day governance rests with the prime minister and cabinet.

A parliamentary republic is defined by the government's dependence on parliament and by strong legislative oversight of the executive. This model is often regarded as one of the most democratic and transparent, as it ensures close alignment between the executive and elected representatives, while providing a clear and regular mechanism for changing political direction through parliamentary votes.

Strengths of a Parliamentary Republic

1. High Degree of Democratic Representation

A parliamentary republic reflects the will of citizens more directly than other models. The government is formed by parliament, whose members are elected by the people. This ensures that the state's political course aligns with the preferences of the majority and that political power remains accessible and understandable to the public. Citizens can hold governments accountable through regular parliamentary elections, reaffirming or withdrawing support based on performance.

2. Flexibility and Ability to Adjust Political Course

Unlike the presidential model—where an elected president typically maintains a fixed course throughout the term—the parliamentary system allows for rapid policy changes. If a government no longer meets public expectations, parliament can remove it through a vote of no confidence and form a new cabinet better suited to current needs. This flexibility enables the state to adapt to changing circumstances and prevents prolonged crises or growing public dissatisfaction.

3. Reduced Risk of Authoritarianism and Power Concentration

One of the main strengths of the parliamentary republic is its ability to guard against authoritarianism. The executive operates under constant parliamentary oversight, and its powers are limited. The prime minister and cabinet depend on parliamentary confidence, which must be renewed regularly. This arrangement prevents the concentration of power in a single individual or small group and helps preserve democratic governance and a balanced distribution of authority.

4. Transparency and Accountability to Citizens

Governments in parliamentary systems must report regularly to parliament, explaining and justifying their actions. Through their elected representatives, citizens can monitor executive activity and receive timely, accurate information on national affairs. This transparency strengthens public trust in state institutions and reduces opportunities for corruption or abuse of power.

5. Effectiveness in Achieving Political Compromise

The parliamentary model fosters ongoing dialogue and negotiation among political forces. Cabinets often emerge from coalitions of multiple parties, requiring leaders to seek common ground and take into account the interests of diverse groups. As a result, policy decisions tend to be more balanced and broadly acceptable to society.

Weaknesses of a Parliamentary Republic

1. Political Instability and Frequent Changes of Government

Because the government depends on maintaining a parliamentary majority, it is vulnerable to even minor political shifts. Fragile coalitions can result in frequent cabinet changes—sometimes several times within a single electoral cycle. Such instability creates uncertainty, disrupts policy continuity, and undermines long-term planning, leaving important reforms and major projects delayed or unfinished.

2. Dependence on Party Coalitions and Compromises

Parliamentary republics often rely on coalition governments, where multiple parties with different platforms must cooperate to form a majority. These arrangements demand constant compromise, which can dilute the clarity of policy decisions. The more parties involved, the harder it becomes to reach consensus. This may lead to unclear political direction, a loss of voter confidence, and public frustration when firm electoral promises are replaced by vague compromise policies.

3. Slower Decision-Making in Crisis Situations

Another drawback is the difficulty of making rapid decisions during crises. Parliamentary governance is based on debate and negotiation, which take time. In urgent situations requiring swift action, prolonged deliberations and interparty bargaining can slow responses, reducing effectiveness and, in severe cases, threatening national security.

4. Diffuse Personal Responsibility Among Leaders

In a parliamentary system, responsibility for decisions is often spread across members of the governing coalition. This collective approach can make it difficult for citizens to identify who is accountable for policy failures or mismanagement. As a result, public oversight is weakened, and leaders may feel less direct responsibility, lowering public trust.

5. Heightened Risk of Political Corruption and Backroom Deals

The constant need to build and maintain coalitions increases the risk of corruption and informal agreements. Parties may engage in mutual concessions or political bargaining, producing behind-the-scenes deals and questionable practices. Such behavior fosters public disillusionment and undermines trust in democratic institutions.

Historical Example of a Parliamentary Republic

The Federal Republic of Germany (Post-1949)

In the Federal Republic of Germany, the parliamentary form of government was established after World War II with the adoption of the Basic Law (Grundgesetz) in 1949, which became the constitution of the new state.

The German model of parliamentary democracy clearly defines the powers of the federal parliament (Bundestag) and the executive branch, headed by the Federal Chancellor. The chancellor is the central figure of the political system, responsible for forming the cabinet, setting the main directions of domestic and foreign policy, and maintaining the confidence of the parliamentary majority. A chancellor remains in office as long as this support continues but must resign if it is withdrawn.

The Federal President of Germany, by contrast, performs largely ceremonial and representative functions. While formally serving as head of state, the president holds no real political power. The role is to symbolize national unity, embody democratic continuity, and represent Germany abroad, without involvement in daily governance or policymaking.

Strengths of the German Parliamentary Model

1. Stability of Democratic Institutions and Protection Against Authoritarianism

Postwar Germany shows how a parliamentary republic can preserve stability and prevent authoritarian rule. A system of strong parliamentary oversight over the government prevents power from being concentrated in one person or a small group.

2. Flexibility and Capacity for Political Adjustment

The German system has proven able to adapt quickly to changing circumstances and public demands. In 1982, when Chancellor Helmut Schmidt lost parliamentary support, power passed peacefully to Helmut Kohl without political upheaval. This flexibility also enabled Germany to manage reunification in 1990 and to carry out complex economic reforms in the early 21st century without destabilizing the political order.

3. Broad Representation of Societal Interests

Germany's multi-party system and the need to form coalition governments encourage inclusivity and ensure that diverse social groups are represented in policymaking. Coalition-building fosters compromise and consensus, which strengthens the legitimacy of political decisions.

Weaknesses of the German Parliamentary Model

1. Prolonged Coalition Formation

Despite its stability, the German system sometimes faces lengthy coalition negotiations. After the 2017 federal elections, for example, parties required several months to agree on a governing coalition. This delay created temporary uncertainty and slowed important decisions, raising the risk of political gridlock.

2. Complex Compromises and Loss of Policy Clarity

The need to form broad coalitions often dilutes policy positions. Governing programs shaped by compromise may force parties to scale back or abandon campaign promises to satisfy coalition partners. This can lead to voter disappointment and erode trust in political actors.

Italy (1946 – Present)

In June 1946, the Italian people voted in a nationwide referendum to abolish the monarchy. The following year, a new constitution was adopted and entered into force on January 1, 1948, formally establishing a parliamentary form of government.

The Italian Parliament, which holds supreme legislative authority, is bicameral, consisting of the Chamber of Deputies and the Senate. The parliamentary majority forms the government, which depends entirely on the confidence of the legislature. The central political figure is the prime minister, who leads the executive branch, oversees government policy, and bears direct responsibility to parliament.

By contrast, the President of Italy, while formally the head of state, exercises mainly ceremonial and representative functions. Although generally uninvolved in day-to-day politics, the president plays a unifying and stabilizing role in moments of national crisis.

Strengths of Italy's Parliamentary Republic

1. Democratic Restoration and Protection of Civil Liberties

The parliamentary model enabled Italy to rebuild democratic institutions after World War II and decades of fascist rule. It established mechanisms for safeguarding civil liberties, ensuring political pluralism, and protecting human rights.

2. High Degree of Representation and Responsiveness

Parliamentary governance has ensured broad representation, allowing diverse social groups to influence policy and participate in coalition-building. Frequent changes of government, while often seen as a weakness, have also demonstrated the system's ability to respond to shifting public sentiment and evolving priorities.

Weaknesses of Italy's Parliamentary Republic

1. Chronic Political Instability and Frequent Government Turnover

Italy is perhaps the clearest example of instability in parliamentary governance. Since 1946, the country has had more than 65 governments, many lasting less than a year. Between 1948 and 1994, the average government survived only 11 months. This instability made it difficult to pursue long-term planning or implement major reforms.

2. Political Fragmentation and Fragile Coalitions

Italy's multi-party system has often required coalitions of parties with very different ideologies and agendas. These alliances tend to be fragile, and the compromises needed to sustain them frequently weaken policy coherence. As a result, public frustration has grown when campaign promises could not be effectively fulfilled.

3. Difficulty Responding Rapidly to Crises

Instability has hampered Italy's ability to act swiftly in times of crisis. During the economic turmoil of the 1970s and the financial crises of the late 2000s and early 2010s, urgent measures were delayed by political conflict, parliamentary deadlock, and frequent government changes—sometimes for months or even years.

Italy's experience shows that while a parliamentary republic can foster democracy and pluralism, it requires mature institutions, a strong culture of compromise, and effective public oversight. Without these, the system risks generating political uncertainty and instability—problems that have recurred throughout Italy's postwar history.

India (Post-1950)

Modern India is one of the most prominent examples of a parliamentary republic built on the foundations of the British parliamentary tradition. This system was formally enshrined in the Constitution of India, which came into force on January 26, 1950—a date now celebrated annually as Republic Day.

India's political framework separates the legislative and executive branches, placing the central role in parliament and the government accountable to it. Supreme legislative authority rests with the bicameral Parliament, composed of the lower house—Lok Sabha ("House of the People")—and the upper house—Rajya Sabha ("Council of States").

The Lok Sabha is the more powerful chamber. Its members are directly elected in nationwide general elections every five years. It holds primary legislative authority, approves the national budget, and exercises oversight over the government. The Rajya Sabha, whose members are largely elected by the legislative assemblies of India's states, represents regional interests and ensures that diverse state and territorial perspectives are reflected in national decision-making.

Executive authority lies with the government, headed by the prime minister—the central political figure in India's system. The prime minister is formally appointed by the president but must command a majority in the Lok Sabha. The prime minister forms the Council of Ministers, directs domestic and foreign policy, and is accountable to parliament for the government's performance.

The president of India, by contrast, serves primarily as a ceremonial head of state. While responsible for signing parliamentary legislation, appointing the prime minister, and performing other constitutional duties, the president's role in day-to-day politics is minimal and exercised on the advice of the government.

Strengths of India's Parliamentary Republic

1. High Degree of Representation and Democratic Legitimacy

Through direct elections to the Lok Sabha and state representation in the Rajya Sabha, the Indian model reflects the interests of the country's vast array of ethnic, religious, and social groups. This inclusiveness has helped India maintain national unity and democratic governance despite immense cultural and regional diversity.

2. Flexibility and Political Adaptability

The parliamentary system has repeatedly demonstrated its ability to respond to shifts in public sentiment. The historic victory of the opposition Janata coalition in 1977—ending decades of uninterrupted rule by the Indian National Congress—showed the system's capacity to bring about rapid change in government when voter support shifts.

3. Strong Judicial and Constitutional Safeguards

India's parliamentary democracy is reinforced by the independent judiciary, especially the Supreme Court, which has the authority of judicial review. This safeguard has played a central role in protecting fundamental rights, checking executive overreach, and upholding the constitutional balance of power.

Weaknesses of India's Parliamentary Republic

1. Political Instability and Frequent Crises

Coalition governments have at times been fragile and short-lived. The 1990s in particular saw frequent changes of government, producing political uncertainty and complicating long-term reforms.

2. Complex and Slow Decision-Making

India's multi-party landscape and political fragmentation have often made swift action difficult, especially during economic or social crises. Negotiations among diverse coalition partners can delay urgent reforms and reduce policy efficiency.

3. Risks of Political Corruption and Clientelism

The competition for parliamentary majorities has often fostered patronage politics, with parties and leaders using state resources to reward supporters or secure coalition partners. This dynamic has contributed to corruption, weakened public trust, and at times distorted the priorities of policymaking

Chapter 3
Mixed (Semi-Presidential) Republic:
Executive Power Shared Between President and Prime Minister

Semi-Presidential Republic — a form of government in which executive authority is shared between a president, elected by direct popular vote, and a government accountable to parliament. This arrangement is designed to ensure a balance of powers and mutual oversight between the presidential and parliamentary branches of government.

Characteristics

A semi-presidential republic combines elements of both presidential and parliamentary government, with executive power divided between two principal figures: the president and the prime minister, who heads the government.

A defining feature of this system is the direct election of the president, who holds significant powers and bears political responsibility to the electorate. The president sets the strategic direction of domestic and foreign policy, oversees defense and national security, and represents the state in international affairs.

Unlike in a classical presidential republic, the president is not the sole center of executive authority. Daily administration is entrusted to the prime minister and cabinet, which are formed by—and dependent on—the support of the parliamentary majority. The government must maintain parliament's confidence, making the prime minister and cabinet directly accountable to the legislature.

This arrangement creates a balance of power between the president, the government, and parliament. The president may appoint the prime minister and, under certain conditions, dissolve parliament, but cannot fully control the cabinet without parliamentary support. Conversely, the prime minister and parliament cannot ignore the president's role, especially on major questions of state.

The semi-presidential model was first clearly formulated in France with the Constitution of the Fifth Republic (1958). Its design, shaped by Charles de Gaulle, aimed to combine the strengths of presidential and parliamentary systems while avoiding their weaknesses.

By nature, a semi-presidential republic fosters dialogue and negotiation between the president and parliament. On one hand, it provides stability, since executive authority does not rest entirely on shifting parliamentary coalitions. On the other, it ensures flexibility and democratic responsiveness, as the government must continually retain parliamentary support.

At times, this dual executive can lead to crises if the president and prime minister come from opposing political camps. This situation, known as cohabitation, forces both sides to compromise to prevent deadlock.

The semi-presidential republic is a complex form of government. Its success depends on clear constitutional boundaries, the strength of democratic institutions, and political culture.

Strengths of a Semi-Presidential Republic

1. Effective Balance of Powers and Protection Against Authoritarianism

One of the most significant strengths of the semi-presidential republic is its successful combination of presidential and parliamentary authority. The president, elected directly by the citizens, holds substantial powers and plays a central role in national politics. At the same time, the government, headed by the prime minister, is formed by and remains dependent on the support of parliament. This mutual oversight reduces the risk of power being concentrated in the hands of a single individual or institution, providing effective safeguards against authoritarian tendencies and abuse of power.

2. High Adaptability and Systemic Flexibility

The semi-presidential model is notable for its ability to adapt to changing political conditions and public sentiment. Depending on the circumstances, the balance of power may shift toward the president—particularly when swift and decisive action is needed during a crisis—or toward parliament and the government when society demands broader representation and participation. This flexibility allows the state to respond promptly to emerging challenges while preserving the stability of democratic institutions and constitutional procedures.

3. Moderate Stability and Capacity for Compromise

By dividing executive authority between the president and the prime minister, the semi-presidential republic promotes political stability while avoiding the extremes associated with purely parliamentary or purely presidential systems. The government is compelled to maintain dialogue both with parliament and with the president, encouraging compromise and reducing the likelihood of abrupt or unpredictable shifts in policy. As a result, the political system retains a degree of stability without sacrificing democratic openness or transparency.

4. Clarity of Responsibility and Transparency in Governance

A key advantage of the semi-presidential system is the clear delineation of political responsibility. The president is directly accountable to the electorate for strategic direction, foreign policy, and national security, while the government, led by the prime minister, answers to parliament for day-to-day administration, economic policy, and social affairs. This division allows citizens to identify clearly who is responsible for specific decisions and to hold leaders accountable through both parliamentary and presidential elections.

5. Enhanced Decision-Making Efficiency

The semi-presidential republic combines the strengths of both presidential and parliamentary systems. The president can act decisively in times of crisis or external threat, while the parliamentary-governmental framework ensures democratic debate and balanced decision-making on domestic matters. This combination allows for the timely adoption of strategic measures while maintaining democratic procedures and public oversight of government actions

Weaknesses of a Semi-Presidential Republic

1. Frequent Conflicts Between the President and Parliament (Cohabitation)

Paradoxically, the balance of powers that defines a semi-presidential system can itself become a source of conflict. This is especially evident when the president and the parliamentary majority belong to opposing political forces. Such situations, famously observed in France during the 1980s, are known as *cohabitation* ("living together"). Under these conditions, the president and government often compete for influence and control over key decisions. The result is political tension, difficulty in adopting major policies, and at times partial or complete paralysis of state institutions.

2. Ambiguity and Contradictions in the Distribution of Powers

In many semi-presidential systems, constitutions do not clearly specify who has the final say on contested issues, particularly during crises. This ambiguity frequently leads to disputes and power struggles between the head of state and the government, complicating governance and decision-making.

3. Risk of Political Deadlock in Cases of Severe Disagreement

The system is especially vulnerable to stalemate when the president and prime minister cannot reach a compromise. If consensus proves elusive, government functions may grind to a halt. Mutual obstruction between the president and the parliamentary majority can make urgent economic or social reforms impossible. This inability to respond effectively to crises undermines state institutions and erodes public confidence.

4. Difficulty in Assigning Political Responsibility

The president is directly elected and accountable to the people, while the government is appointed by and accountable to parliament. When policies fail or provoke dissatisfaction, citizens may struggle to determine whether the president, the government, or the legislature bears primary responsibility. This uncertainty blurs accountability and weakens public oversight.

5. Potential for Authoritarian Tendencies

Although designed to maintain checks and balances, the semi-presidential system can in practice allow an expansion of presidential power. A president with a strong popular mandate may seek to increase personal authority at the expense of parliament and the government, weakening democratic institutions. In extreme cases, this can lead to the concentration of power in the executive and even the dismantling of democratic governance.

A semi-presidential republic requires a well-crafted constitution with a clear division of powers, a strong culture of political dialogue, and a willingness to compromise. Without these conditions, the system risks becoming a source of constant conflict, making effective governance far more difficult.

Historical Examples of Mixed (Semi-Presidential) Republics

France (Since 1958, the Fifth Republic)

In 1958, under the leadership of General Charles de Gaulle, a new constitution was drafted and adopted, establishing the Fifth Republic. This constitution introduced a fundamentally new distribution of power, designed to combine the strengths of presidential and parliamentary government while correcting the weaknesses of the previous system.

Under the Constitution of the Fifth Republic, the President of France is elected by direct popular vote for a five-year term (previously seven years until 2002). The president holds extensive authority: appointing the prime minister, approving the composition of the government, setting foreign policy, serving as commander-in-chief of the armed forces, and overseeing national security. The president also has the significant power to dissolve the National Assembly and call early parliamentary elections.

The government, led by the prime minister, is formed on the basis of the parliamentary majority and is directly accountable to the National Assembly. The prime minister manages day-to-day administration, directing domestic policy, socio-economic reforms, and budgetary matters. This division of responsibilities creates conditions for both cooperation and oversight between the president, the government, and parliament.

The French semi-presidential model has demonstrated its effectiveness by providing stability to democratic institutions and to the functioning of the state—stability that had been elusive during the Fourth Republic (1946–1958). At that time, fragile multiparty coalitions produced frequent government changes and recurrent political crises, undermining the strength of the state.

Over time, however, the Fifth Republic has also faced challenges. The weaknesses of the semi-presidential model became most visible during periods of *cohabitation*—when the president and the parliamentary majority represented opposing political forces.

The first cohabitation occurred in 1986, when Socialist President François Mitterrand was compelled to appoint center-right leader Jacques Chirac as prime minister after the opposition won parliamentary elections. For two years, from 1986 to 1988, France experienced intense confrontation between a president and a government from different camps. Disputes over authority and policy priorities became routine, slowing decision-making and reducing the effectiveness of governance.

This scenario repeated twice more. From 1993 to 1995, Mitterrand again governed in cohabitation, this time with Prime Minister Édouard Balladur after the parliamentary majority shifted to the right. From 1997 to 2002, President Jacques Chirac was required to work with a left-wing government led by Prime Minister Lionel Jospin. Each of these periods was marked by political disagreements, uncertainty, and difficulties in implementing major reforms.

Nevertheless, the French experience also highlighted the resilience of the semi-presidential republic. Even during cohabitation, the political system remained stable and democratic, as the president and parliamentary majority were compelled to compromise, restrain each other's ambitions, and account for the interests of diverse groups in society.

To reduce the likelihood of future cohabitation, constitutional reform in 2000 shortened the presidential term from seven to five years, and since 2002 presidential elections have been held shortly before parliamentary elections. This synchronization has typically produced aligned mandates for president and parliament, making cohabitation far less common.

Portugal (Since 1976)

Portugal is a notable example of a semi-presidential republic that emerged after the fall of the authoritarian regime of António de Oliveira Salazar, known as the New State (*Estado Novo*). This regime ruled from 1933 until 1974, when the Carnation Revolution of April 25, 1974, brought about a profound transformation in Portuguese political life.

The Constitution of 1976 established the framework for a semi-presidential model of governance—a compromise between strong presidential authority and full parliamentary control over the executive branch. Unlike the unstable parliamentary system of the First Republic (1910–1926), the new model sought to ensure the stability of democratic institutions and a balanced distribution of political power.

Under the 1976 Constitution, authority is divided among three main institutions: the president, parliament, and the government. The president is elected by direct popular vote for a five-year term and wields significant powers, including the appointment of the prime minister (taking into account the parliamentary majority) and the right to dissolve the Assembly of the Republic and call early parliamentary elections. The president also serves as guarantor of the Constitution and democratic freedoms, helping to maintain stability in times of crisis.

Executive power rests with the government, headed by the prime minister, who directs the day-to-day administration of the country as well as economic, social, and domestic policy. The prime minister forms the cabinet and is politically accountable to parliament, on which the government depends for legislative support. Parliament holds the exclusive authority to oversee and, if necessary, dismiss the government.

Strengths of the Portuguese Semi-Presidential Model

1. Balance of Power and Protection Against Authoritarianism

The semi-presidential system has helped Portugal avoid a return to authoritarianism by maintaining an effective separation of powers among president, parliament, and government. The president plays a crucial role in the system of checks and balances, preventing excessive concentration of power in any single branch and safeguarding democratic institutions.

2. Flexibility and Crisis Responsiveness

The president acts as a stabilizing figure who can intervene during parliamentary or governmental crises. In times of political uncertainty or the collapse of a governing coalition, the president may dissolve parliament and call new elections to restore stability.

3. Preservation of Democratic Stability

This framework has enabled Portugal to navigate periods of economic and social upheaval—such as the 2008–2014 financial crisis and the subsequent era of austerity—while preserving stable democratic institutions and avoiding severe unrest.

Weaknesses of the Portuguese Semi-Presidential Model

1. Political Conflicts Between President and Parliament

Despite its relative stability, Portugal has experienced tensions when the president and the parliamentary majority represented opposing political forces. In the 1980s and 1990s, for example, Socialist President Mário Soares (1986–1996) worked with governments led by center-right parties, creating friction over policy direction and governance.

2. Ambiguity in Powers and Responsibilities

Although the Constitution defines the roles of president and government, certain provisions leave room for interpretation. This has at times resulted in disputes between president and prime minister over final decision-making authority on strategic issues, prolonging political conflicts and complicating governance.

Russian Federation (Since 1993)

The Russian Federation is a notable historical example of a mixed (semi-presidential) republic, established in the aftermath of the acute political crisis of the early 1990s. The Constitution of the Russian Federation was adopted on December 12, 1993, following dramatic events marked by a confrontation between President Boris Nikolayevich Yeltsin and the Supreme Soviet, the pre-reform national legislature. At that point, the country opted for a semi-presidential model intended to combine a strong presidency with mechanisms of parliamentary oversight and the political accountability of the government to the State Duma.

Under the Constitution, the president is elected by direct popular vote for a six-year term (prior to 2008, the term was four years). The president holds extensive powers and is the key figure in the political system. He determines the main directions of domestic and foreign policy, serves as commander-in-chief of the armed forces, appoints the chair of the government (prime minister) with the consent of the State Duma, and has the authority to dissolve the lower house of parliament under certain constitutional conditions.

Executive authority is exercised by the government, headed by the prime minister, which is responsible for the day-to-day administration of the state and for implementing economic, social, and administrative policy. Formally, the government is accountable to the State Duma, which has the right to pass a vote of no confidence. If the Duma repeatedly rejects the president's nominee for prime minister, the president may dissolve parliament and call new elections.

The functioning of Russia's semi-presidential model has varied considerably depending on the political context and the balance of power between the presidency and parliament.

In the 1990s, President Yeltsin's relationship with the State Duma was often tense and conflict-ridden, as the president and the parliamentary majority represented opposing political forces and interests. This frequently made it difficult to advance reforms or reach agreement on strategic decisions. A notable example was the repeated rejection by the Duma of presidential nominees for prime minister, as in 1998–1999 with Sergey Kiriyenko and later Viktor Chernomyrdin.

A different pattern emerged in the 2000s and 2010s, when the parliamentary majority in the State Duma became closely aligned with presidential authority, especially during the presidency of Vladimir Vladimirovich Putin (since 2000, with a break during the presidency of Dmitry Anatolyevich Medvedev from 2008 to 2012). Under these conditions, the semi-presidential model operated in a mode of pronounced presidential dominance, with parliament and the government functioning largely as allies and implementers rather than as independent political actors.

Strengths of the Russian Semi-Presidential Model

1. Stability and Capacity for Rapid Decision-Making

Strong presidential authority has provided a high degree of political stability and the ability to take swift, decisive action, especially during periods of political, economic, or security crises. This capacity has been particularly evident in situations requiring immediate responses, such as managing large-scale economic reforms, addressing security threats, or implementing nationwide policies without prolonged legislative delays.

2. Clarity of Political Responsibility

Unlike in purely parliamentary systems, Russia's semi-presidential framework makes it clear to the electorate who is responsible for major policy directions and national priorities.

3. Strong Centralized Leadership in a Large, Diverse State

Given Russia's vast territory, significant regional diversity, and complex federal structure, a strong presidency has helped maintain political cohesion and coordinate governance across different regions. The centralized leadership of the president allows for unified national policy-making, reducing the risk of fragmentation or inconsistent regional governance.

4. Ability to Pursue Long-Term Strategic Policies

The concentration of executive authority in the presidency allows for the initiation and continuation of long-term strategic projects, including infrastructure development, energy policy, and defense modernization. These initiatives can be pursued more consistently, even across changes in government or parliamentary composition.

5. Effective Crisis Management and Coordination of State Institutions

The Russian semi-presidential system enables the president to coordinate the work of various branches of government and state agencies during emergencies. In times of natural disasters, economic shocks, or national security threats, this capacity for centralized coordination can facilitate faster mobilization of resources and more coherent responses.

6. International Representation and Foreign Policy Consistency

By granting the president a leading role in foreign policy, the system ensures continuity and coherence in Russia's international relations. This centralized approach strengthens the state's ability to negotiate with other countries, represent national interests abroad, and respond promptly to changes in the global environment.

7. Reduced Risk of Legislative Deadlock

Compared with systems where the executive depends entirely on parliamentary majorities, the Russian semi-presidential model reduces the likelihood of prolonged legislative paralysis. Even when disagreements arise with the State Duma, the president retains significant constitutional powers to ensure that the executive branch continues to function and implement policy.

Weaknesses of the Russian Semi-Presidential Model

1. Risk of Power Concentration and Authoritarian Tendencies

The Russian version of the semi-presidential republic, with its extensive presidential powers, has frequently been criticized for enabling an excessive concentration of authority in the hands of the head of state. This imbalance can weaken democratic checks and balances, reduce the independence of other branches of government, and create conditions for the erosion of political pluralism.

2. Political Conflicts and Parliamentary Crises

When the president and the parliamentary majority represent opposing political forces—as in the 1990s—the political system has faced serious institutional conflicts. Such confrontations have often delayed the adoption of key legislation, hindered reform efforts, and contributed to governmental instability. In extreme cases, they have risked leading to constitutional crises, as political actors contested the boundaries of their authority.

3. Weak Parliamentary Oversight

Despite the formal accountability of the government to the State Duma, in practice parliamentary oversight over the executive branch has often been limited. The president's ability to dissolve parliament under certain circumstances, combined with strong control over key political appointments, can discourage legislators from challenging the executive, reducing the effectiveness of parliamentary scrutiny.

4. Dependence on Political Context and Leadership Style

The functioning of Russia's semi-presidential model has been highly dependent on the personal leadership style of the president and the prevailing political climate. In periods of strong presidential dominance, the balance intended by the constitution can shift toward a de facto presidential system, limiting the intended role of parliament and the prime minister.

5. Potential for Policy Inconsistency in Times of Political Division

When political power is more evenly divided between the president and parliament, the system can experience inconsistency in policy direction. Disagreements between the president and a parliamentary majority from a different political camp can lead to policy reversals, delays in implementation, and uncertainty in both domestic and foreign affairs.

6. Limited Opportunities for Political Competition

The combination of strong presidential authority and the centralization of political resources can limit opportunities for opposition parties to compete effectively.

The example of the Russian Federation since 1993 illustrates that the semi-presidential model can operate in different modes depending on the prevailing political context. The Constitution established the foundations of a strong presidency alongside certain mechanisms of parliamentary influence. In practice, the effectiveness of these constitutional principles depends heavily on political culture, the maturity of democratic institutions, and the current balance of political power.

Conclusion

This section has reviewed the three principal forms of republican government—presidential, parliamentary, and mixed (semi-presidential)—each offering distinct solutions for electing leaders, distributing powers, and ensuring accountability.

The presidential republic features a strict separation between the executive and legislative branches, with a directly elected president holding a broad mandate and significant independence. This enables decisive action in times of crisis but also carries risks of power concentration and institutional deadlock.

The parliamentary republic ties the government directly to parliament, ensuring broad representation and flexibility in responding to public sentiment. At the same time, frequent changes of government can undermine stability and complicate the pursuit of long-term reforms.

The semi-presidential republic seeks to combine the strengths of both systems by sharing executive power between a directly elected president and a parliamentary government. This arrangement can balance authority and increase adaptability, but periods of cohabitation often produce tension and slow decision-making.

Republican systems remain the most widespread form of government worldwide, valued for their adaptability to diverse historical, cultural, and social contexts. Their future stability will depend on how effectively they address global change, rising demands for transparency, and the active role of civil society. A republic must function not only as a formal structure but also as a responsive mechanism, one that reflects and adapts to the expectations of its citizens.

PART II

CLASSIFICATION BY

POLITICAL REGIME

SECTION 1. DEMOCRATIC REGIME

Democratic Regime — a type of political system in which state authority is formed and controlled by the people through free and regular elections, with the guarantee of civil rights and liberties, the preservation of political pluralism, the rule of law, and genuine accountability of government to society.

Introduction

Democracy is a political system in which the highest authority belongs to the people. The word *democracy* comes from the Greek *demos* ("people") and *kratos* ("power"), literally meaning "rule of the people." At its core lies the idea that citizens have the right to take part in political life and decide the future course of their society.

The roots of democracy reach back to Ancient Greece, above all to Athens in the 5th–4th centuries BCE, where a distinctive form of governance took shape. Here the principle of direct democracy was applied: citizens assembled in the *ekklesia* to debate and decide crucial matters of state—passing laws, declaring war, or concluding peace. Athenian democracy thus became the first practical example of direct citizen participation in public affairs.

Over time, this early democracy declined. In the Middle Ages, democratic practices disappeared from Europe, replaced by feudal and monarchical systems. The revival of democratic thought came only in the 18th century, during the Enlightenment, when thinkers such as Jean-Jacques Rousseau, John Locke, and Charles-Louis Montesquieu developed ideas that shaped modern democracy. They argued for popular sovereignty, civil liberties, and the separation of powers—principles that remain central today.

A new stage in democratic development began with the revolutions of the late 18th and early 19th centuries in the United States and France. The U.S. Constitution of 1787 and the French Declaration of the Rights of Man and of the Citizen of 1789 affirmed fundamental rights and freedoms and laid the foundations of modern liberal democracy. Both documents profoundly influenced the growth of democratic states worldwide and served as models for later constitutions and laws.

In the modern era, democracy exists in many forms, but all rest on several core principles:

- **Popular sovereignty** — political authority originates with the people. State power is legitimate only when based on the will of citizens, expressed through free and fair elections.

- **Elected and limited authority** — regular elections ensure peaceful transfers of power and allow government to reflect changes in public opinion.

- **Separation of powers** — dividing legislative, executive, and judicial authority protects society from arbitrary rule, with each branch operating within constitutional limits.

- **Guarantee of rights and freedoms** — democracy cannot exist without protecting basic liberties: freedom of speech, press, assembly, religion, the right to a fair trial, and personal security.

These principles have been tested through centuries of crises and transformations. Today, democratic systems make up the majority of developed states. Despite challenges and imperfections, democracy has proved to be the most effective form of political organization for maintaining stability, supporting development, and protecting human rights.

At the same time, democracy faces new pressures from globalization, digital technologies, and rising demands for transparency and accountability. The ability of democratic institutions to meet these challenges will determine how democracy evolves in the twenty-first century.

Chapter 1

Direct Democracy:
Citizens Participate Directly in Political Decision-Making

Direct Democracy — a form of democracy in which citizens participate directly, without elected representatives, in the deliberation and adoption of political decisions through voting, referendums, public assemblies, and other forms of direct expression of the popular will.

Characteristics

The defining feature of direct democracy is the immediate involvement of citizens in governing the state. In this model, the people do not simply elect representatives to make decisions on their behalf; they express their will directly by voting on specific issues and laws. In this way, direct democracy most fully realizes the principle of popular sovereignty, where the people themselves are the active source of authority.

In the modern world, the main forms of direct democracy include:

1) **Referendums** — nationwide votes on major state matters, the results of which are binding on public authorities. Referendums are used to decide critical issues such as the adoption of a new constitution, changes in territorial organization, or membership in international unions. Examples include the 2016 referendum on the United Kingdom's withdrawal from the European Union ("Brexit"); the 2014 referendum on Scottish independence; the 2017 Catalan independence referendum; and numerous referendums on EU membership, such as Poland's in 2003.

2) **Plebiscites** — also nationwide votes, but generally consultative in nature. A plebiscite is organized by the government to determine public opinion on policy questions, political leadership, or confidence in officeholders. Unlike a referendum, its results are not always legally binding but often carry significant political weight. Historical examples include plebiscites in France under Napoleon III (1852 and 1870) and the 1988 plebiscite in Chile, in which citizens voted against extending the presidency of General Augusto Pinochet.

3) **Popular assemblies** — the oldest form of direct democracy, in which citizens gather in person to deliberate and decide on important public issues. The best-known example is the *ekklesia* of ancient Athens in the 5th–4th centuries BCE, where citizens debated and voted on laws, elected military leaders, and discussed foreign policy. Today, this practice survives mainly in small communities, such as the Swiss cantons of Glarus and Appenzell Innerrhoden, where citizens meet in the town square to debate and vote on key local matters.

Despite its clear advantages—allowing citizens to shape state policy directly—direct democracy faces significant limitations. It is difficult to implement in large states with sizable populations, as it requires complex procedures for organizing votes and assemblies and a high level of civic engagement. Moreover, modern politics often demands rapid decision-making, and constant direct participation can slow the process and undermine effective governance.

Strengths of Direct Democracy

1. Maximum Citizen Involvement and Personal Responsibility for Political Decisions

In a direct democracy, citizens are not distant observers but active participants in public life. By taking part in votes and discussions themselves, people experience a direct connection between their choices and the consequences that follow. This fosters political literacy, civic awareness, and a shared sense of responsibility.

2. High Legitimacy of Adopted Decisions

Decisions made directly by the people carry the highest degree of legitimacy. Citizens tend to trust outcomes in which they have personally participated, even if the result does not match their own preference. This trust reduces the likelihood of unrest, protests, and political crises. Referendum results, for instance, are widely seen as the genuine expression of the majority's will, strengthening social unity and reinforcing the stability of institutions.

3. Reduced Risks of Corruption and Abuse of Power by Political Representatives

Another key advantage of direct democracy is that citizens do not hand over all decision-making authority to elected officials. This reduces the risk of corruption, misuse of public trust, or the pursuit of narrow personal interests. When crucial decisions are made by the people themselves, the space for political intrigue and backroom deals is greatly diminished. The result is greater transparency, stronger accountability, and increased public trust in the system.

4. Improved Quality of Decisions Through Broad Public Debate and Discussion

Direct democracy creates opportunities for open and wide-ranging debate on major issues. Citizens can hear arguments from both supporters and opponents, as well as receive input from experts. This process raises public awareness, improves the quality of decisions, and fosters broader consensus on matters of national importance.

Weaknesses of Direct Democracy

1. Organizational Complexity and High Costs in Large States

One of the main drawbacks of direct democracy is its organizational burden. The larger the population, the harder it becomes to arrange regular and fair participation of all citizens. Nationwide referendums and plebiscites demand significant financial resources, careful logistics, and reliable systems for secure vote counting. In large states, these procedures slow political processes and impose heavy costs on budgets and administrations.

2. High Risk of Populism and Emotion-Driven Decisions

Although direct democracy gives all citizens an equal voice, not everyone has the time or expertise to study complex issues in depth. This makes public opinion vulnerable to manipulation by leaders who rely on simple slogans and emotional appeals rather than sound arguments. History provides many examples of referendums where outcomes reflected temporary moods rather than long-term interests of society.

3. Low Responsiveness and Slow Decision-Making

Direct democracy is poorly suited to emergencies that require swift action. Each decision involves drafting a proposal, organizing debate, arranging the vote, and verifying results. This lengthy procedure makes the system cumbersome and unable to react quickly to crises. In urgent situations, such delays can seriously damage state effectiveness and public safety.

4. Limited Public Competence in Complex Issues

Modern governance often requires decisions based on advanced knowledge in economics, finance, environmental policy, or international relations. Most citizens cannot fully assess the long-term consequences of such measures, raising the risk of poorly informed outcomes. Even beneficial solutions may be rejected simply because their advantages are difficult to explain in simple terms.

Despite its appeal and the high legitimacy it gives to decisions, direct democracy faces serious limitations: organizational difficulties, vulnerability to populism, delays in decision-making, and the challenge of resolving highly technical issues through popular votes. These weaknesses explain why pure direct democracy is rare today and is usually combined with representative institutions, applied only to the most fundamental national questions.

5. Danger of the "Tyranny of the Majority"

Direct democracy can lead to situations where the rights of minorities are overridden by the will of the majority. Without institutional safeguards, decisions taken by popular vote may neglect or even harm vulnerable social groups, undermining the principles of equality and justice.

6. Risk of Voter Fatigue and Declining Participation

Frequent referendums or plebiscites can produce "democratic fatigue." Citizens may lose interest in constant voting, resulting in low turnout. Reduced participation undermines the legitimacy of decisions and weakens public trust in democratic procedures.

Historical Examples of Direct Democracy

Ancient Athens (5th–4th Centuries BCE)

The most famous and classical example of direct democracy is the system that flourished in Athens during the 5th–4th centuries BCE. In this Greek polis, the principle of direct citizen participation in governance was embodied for the first time in history.

At the heart of Athenian democracy stood the popular assembly, the ekklesia. It met regularly—about forty times a year—first in the marketplace, the agora, and later on the Pnyx Hill, arranged specifically for public debate and collective decision-making. Every male citizen over the age of eighteen had the right to attend. Wealth, lineage, or social standing made no difference: a poor craftsman or merchant could vote on equal terms with a wealthy aristocrat.

The ekklesia exercised legislative authority in its fullest sense. It passed laws, approved the budget, determined foreign policy, declared war and made peace. It also elected magistrates, judges, and military commanders, ensuring that officeholders remained accountable to the citizen body and that power could not be monopolized by a narrow elite.

A distinctive institution of Athenian democracy was ostracism, introduced to guard against tyranny. If citizens feared that a politician or general was becoming dangerously powerful, they could vote—by secretly writing a name on a shard of pottery (ostrakon)—to exile that individual from the city for ten years. In this way, potential threats to democracy were removed without bloodshed.

Another unique feature was the use of sortition, the random selection of officials by lot. Many administrative and judicial posts were filled in this way, reflecting the belief that chance embodied fairness more reliably than elections, which could favor wealth or influence. Sortition gave every eligible citizen an equal opportunity to hold office and reinforced the principle of political equality.

Yet participation in this democratic system was limited. Women, slaves, and resident foreigners (metics) were excluded, leaving only about 30,000–40,000 citizens—out of a population of more than 250,000—eligible to take part in the assembly.

Despite these restrictions, Athenian democracy laid the foundations of political thought. Its ideals of popular sovereignty, political equality, civic duty, and innovative practices such as ostracism and sortition became a source of inspiration for modern theories of democratic governance.

Switzerland (Modern Use of Referendums and Popular Initiatives)

Modern Switzerland is often regarded as the most successful example of how elements of direct democracy can be woven into a contemporary political system. Although the country functions as a representative democracy with a parliament and executive government, citizens play an unusually active role: through frequent referendums and popular initiatives, they are able to shape state policy directly.

The referendum is the central instrument of Swiss direct democracy. Several times a year, the electorate is called to vote on issues that may range from constitutional amendments and federal legislation to questions of social, economic, or environmental importance. In recent decades, ballots have included proposals to restrict immigration (2014), to introduce an unconditional basic income (2016, rejected by voters), to ban the construction of new minarets (2009), and to phase out nuclear energy (2017).

No less important is the right of citizens to launch popular initiatives. Any group that gathers 100,000 signatures within eighteen months can force a nationwide vote on a constitutional amendment. This mechanism allows ordinary citizens to set the political agenda independently of parliament or government. In recent years, such initiatives have frequently addressed issues of environmental protection, migration, social welfare, public health, and taxation.

Direct democracy in Switzerland extends beyond the federal level. Each of the country's twenty-six cantons has its own institutions of citizen participation, and at the municipal level local referendums are common. In the smaller cantons of Glarus and Appenzell Innerrhoden, the old tradition of the Landsgemeinde survives: citizens gather in the town square, raise their hands, and decide on local matters in full view of their neighbors.

The Swiss experience shows that direct democracy can function effectively even in a complex modern society with an advanced economy. Regular participation not only strengthens trust in political institutions but also enhances the legitimacy of government decisions.

Chapter 2
Representative Democracy (Parliamentarism): Governance Through Elected Representatives

> **Representative Democracy (Parliamentarism)** — a form of democracy in which citizens exercise their authority not directly, but through elected representatives chosen in free elections. Acting on behalf of the people, these representatives pass laws, form the government, and oversee its activities.

Characteristics

In a representative democracy, citizens exercise power through their elected representatives. These representatives form the legislative body—the parliament—which expresses the will of the people, enacts laws, and oversees the executive branch on behalf of the citizenry.

This model rests on the principle of delegating political authority from the people to members of parliament, chosen in regular, free elections. Representative democracy makes it possible to govern effectively even in large states, where the direct participation of every citizen in decision-making is practically impossible.

The main features of representative democracy include:

1) **Exercising Power Through Elected Representatives**

   Citizens entrust their authority to members of parliament, elected by universal, equal, and secret ballot. Elected representatives are expected to act in the public interest, conveying the will and perspectives of citizens on key matters of state policy. This enables citizens to participate indirectly in the political process while avoiding the logistical burden and cost of direct democracy, particularly in states with large populations.

2) **The Central Role of Parliament in the Political System**

   Parliament occupies a pivotal place in representative democracy. It is the primary forum for debating and passing legislation, adopting the national budget, and setting the direction of domestic and foreign policy. Parliament also plays a vital role in holding the executive accountable, regularly scrutinizing and evaluating the work of government.

   Parliamentary systems may be unicameral, with all legislative functions performed by a single chamber (as in Denmark, Sweden, and Israel), or bicameral, with upper and lower chambers (as in the United Kingdom, Germany, and the United States). Bicameral systems are especially common in federal states, where the upper chamber represents regional interests, and the lower chamber represents the population as a whole.

3) **Political Accountability of Elected Bodies to Citizens**

   Representative democracy is built on regular changes of government and the accountability of legislators to their constituents. Members of parliament are elected for a fixed term—typically four to five years—and are expected to report regularly on their work. If representatives or the government they support no longer reflect the will of the people, citizens can register their dissatisfaction at the next election by choosing others. This ensures the constant accountability and responsiveness of political authority.

4) **Capacity for Professional and Efficient Governance**

   Unlike direct democracy, representative democracy allows for professional governance. Elected representatives can specialize in particular areas, study complex political and economic issues in depth, and make informed decisions that would be difficult for ordinary citizens to evaluate without expertise. This raises the quality of legislation and improves the efficiency of political decision-making in modern, complex societies.

Today, representative democracy is the dominant form of democratic governance worldwide. It successfully combines citizen participation—through elections and public oversight—with the advantages of professional, stable, and effective state institutions.

Strengths of Representative Democracy

1. High Efficiency and Manageability of Political Processes

Representative democracy allows the state to respond quickly and professionally to new challenges and to make considered decisions. Authority is delegated to elected representatives—members of parliament—who have the qualifications, experience, and knowledge needed to deal with complex public issues. Unlike direct democracy, which requires lengthy organization of nationwide debates and votes, the representative model permits swift and decisive action, especially during crises, emergencies, or urgent reforms. This system is particularly well suited to large, multiethnic states, where convening mass assemblies on every policy question is impossible.

2. Broad and Continuous Citizen Participation Through Elections

Although citizens in a representative democracy do not decide policy directly, they remain actively engaged in political life by electing representatives. Elections are the primary instrument for expressing the public will, giving citizens a way to influence state policy through their chosen legislators. This fosters a sense of involvement in governance, raises political awareness, and strengthens civic responsibility. Regular elections also provide the means for peaceful change of government, allowing citizens to show confidence or disapproval toward political forces.

3. Stability of the Political System Through Regular Turnover of Representatives

Representative democracy promotes political stability by limiting the terms of office for legislators and governments, usually to four or five years. Regular, predictable elections ensure timely and orderly policy adjustments, reducing the likelihood of upheavals or revolutionary change typical of less stable systems. Citizens know they will be able to evaluate their representatives at fixed intervals and replace them if necessary. This reduces the danger of political stagnation, authoritarian consolidation, or violent conflict, strengthening both the stability and resilience of democratic institutions.

4. High Competence of Representatives and Quality of Decision-Making

Representative democracy also makes it possible to place well-qualified and prepared individuals in legislative and executive roles. Representatives can study complex policy issues in depth, consult with experts, and make informed decisions—something far harder to achieve in the mass deliberations typical of direct democracy. This approach improves the quality and effectiveness of legislation and governance while reducing the risk of errors or populist measures driven by emotion or temporary moods.

5. Flexibility and Adaptability of the System

Representative democracy combines citizen participation with the work of professional institutions, making it more adaptable to social change. Parliaments and governments can adjust policies in response to evolving circumstances without undermining the overall stability of the political system.

Weaknesses of Representative Democracy

1. Risk of Alienation Between Representatives and Citizens ("Crisis of Representation")

A major challenge for representative democracy is the risk of gradual detachment of elected officials from the needs and interests of their constituents. Once in office, representatives may lose their sense of direct connection with the electorate. They can become guided by personal ambitions, career goals, or the interests of narrow groups, neglecting the broader public good. This gap between government and society erodes trust. Citizens may withdraw from politics, dissatisfaction may grow, and in some cases this alienation can escalate into protests or political crises.

2. Dominance of Party Interests Over National Priorities

Parliaments often turn into arenas of intense party competition, where political advantage outweighs national priorities. Partisan rivalries and maneuvering can paralyze parliamentary work, delay crucial decisions, and push pressing social, economic, or environmental issues into the background.

3. Periodic Crises and Political Instability in Fragmented Parliaments

Representative democracies are prone to instability when no single party holds a majority. In such cases, forming governments and adopting key policies becomes a slow and contentious process. Coalition governments may prove fragile, vulnerable to internal disputes, and inconsistent in policy direction. Frequent changes of government undermine long-term stability and weaken institutional resilience.

4. Limited Influence of Citizens on Decision-Making Between Elections

Citizens exercise real influence primarily during elections. Between them, opportunities to hold representatives accountable are limited. If legislators fail to keep campaign promises or adopt unpopular policies, voters must wait until the next election to express dissatisfaction. This weakens the link between public sentiment and the daily work of governing institutions.

5. Influence of Money and Lobbying on Politics

Campaign financing and lobbying create risks of disproportionate influence by wealthy donors, corporations, or organized interest groups. Representatives may prioritize the agendas of these actors over the general public, undermining the democratic principle of equal political voice.

6. Risk of Political Apathy and Declining Participation

When citizens feel that their participation is confined to casting votes every few years—and that little changes regardless of the outcome—political apathy grows. Declining voter turnout and reduced civic engagement weaken the legitimacy of representative institutions.

7. Slowness of Parliamentary Decision-Making

Parliamentary debate and procedural rules improve the quality of decisions but make the process slow. In emergencies or during rapid crises, this lack of agility can impair effective governance and delay urgent measures.

Historical Examples of Representative Democracy (Parliamentarism)

United Kingdom (Parliamentary Tradition Since the 17th Century)

The British parliamentary tradition is often described as one of the oldest and most authoritative in the world. Its roots reach back to the Middle Ages, but its modern shape emerged in the 17th century during the events of the Glorious Revolution of 1688.

That revolution established the principle that parliament stands above the monarchy. In 1689, the Bill of Rights was adopted, curbing the powers of the crown and transferring real political authority to the elected assembly. From then on, monarchs retained largely ceremonial functions, while parliament became the central political body representing the will of the people.

Today, the British Parliament is composed of two chambers:

- **House of Commons** — the lower house, elected directly by citizens in general elections. It is the heart of political life in the United Kingdom, holding the power of legislative initiative and responsibility for forming the government. Members of Parliament are elected for a five-year term (though elections may be called earlier). It is here that decisions are made on domestic and foreign policy, the national budget, and legislation.

- **House of Lords** — the upper chamber, made up of life peers appointed by the monarch on the advice of the prime minister, along with a limited number of hereditary peers. The Lords act primarily as a revising chamber, reviewing and amending legislation from the Commons. While their powers have gradually declined, they still play an important role in scrutiny and delay, though the final word rests with the elected House of Commons.

The British model of representative democracy has shaped parliamentary traditions across the world. From the United Kingdom came such fundamental principles as the regular rotation of political power, the accountability of government to parliament, and strict oversight of the executive by elected representatives.

Federal Republic of Germany (Since 1949)

Modern representative democracy in Germany took shape after the Second World War, under the direct control of the United States, which designed a system to prevent instability and authoritarianism. On May 23, 1949, the Basic Law (Grundgesetz) was promulgated, creating the Federal Republic of Germany (FRG) with a parliamentary system of government. Conceived at first as a provisional constitution for West Germany, it became permanent after reunification on October 3, 1990.

At the heart of the system stands the Bundestag, Germany's federal parliament. Its members (Abgeordnete) are chosen in general, free, equal, direct, and secret elections, usually every four years, though early elections may be called under specific constitutional conditions. The electoral system is a distinctive mixed-member proportional model (personalisierte Verhältniswahl). Half of the seats are filled through first-past-the-post voting in single-member constituencies (Erststimme), while the other half are distributed to parties according to their share of the national vote, based on state lists (Zweitstimme). This design balances local representation with proportional fairness, limits domination by a single party, and avoids excessive fragmentation. To enter parliament, a party must either win at least five percent of the national vote or secure three constituency seats directly — a safeguard against splinter parties.

The Bundestag's responsibilities are wide-ranging: it passes federal laws, approves the budget, and oversees the executive branch. Sessions are public, with proceedings broadcast and published to ensure transparency.

Executive authority lies with the Federal Government (Bundesregierung), headed by the Federal Chancellor (Bundeskanzler), the central figure in German politics. The chancellor is elected by an absolute majority of Bundestag members, following a nomination by the Federal President (Bundespräsident). Once elected, the chancellor sets the overall direction of government policy (Richtlinienkompetenz) and appoints ministers to lead key departments such as finance, foreign affairs, and defense.

A unique safeguard of the Basic Law is the constructive vote of no confidence (konstruktives Misstrauensvotum). The Bundestag can remove a sitting chancellor only by simultaneously electing a successor with an absolute majority. This mechanism was a deliberate response to the Weimar Republic, where frequent no-confidence votes toppled governments without ensuring viable alternatives. In contrast, the postwar system secures stability by allowing change only when a new majority is ready to govern.

Alongside the Bundestag functions the Bundesrat, the chamber representing Germany's sixteen Länder (states). Its members are not elected by citizens but delegated by state governments, and each state must cast its votes as a block — between three and six, depending on population. The Bundesrat has a decisive role in legislation affecting state powers, such as education, policing, and regional infrastructure, where its approval is mandatory. In other matters it may propose amendments or delay bills, but the Bundestag has the final word.

Federalism and a strong system of checks and balances form another cornerstone of the Basic Law. The Länder retain wide authority in areas such as education, culture, and local policing. The Federal Constitutional Court (Bundesverfassungsgericht) in Karlsruhe stands as the guardian of the constitution. It can strike down laws, resolve disputes between federal institutions or between the federation and the states, and protect individual rights through the constitutional complaint procedure (Verfassungsbeschwerde).

Since 1949, Germany's parliamentary system has been marked by stability and continuity. Strong political parties, proportional representation tempered by the five-percent threshold, the constructive vote of no confidence, and cooperative federalism have combined to create one of the most resilient democracies in the world. This framework has guided the country through decisive moments: the economic recovery of the 1950s (Wirtschaftswunder), the social and political transformations of the late 1960s, Ostpolitik and Cold War diplomacy in the 1970s, reunification in 1990, and deep integration into the European Union's political and economic structures.

Japan (Since 1947)

Modern representative democracy in Japan was established with the adoption of the new Constitution, which came into force on May 3, 1947. Drafted under strong U.S. influence during the Allied occupation, the Constitution entrenched parliamentary government as the foundation of Japan's political order and created a firm framework for democratic governance.

At the heart of the system is the **National Diet** (*Kokkai*, 国会), a bicameral legislature composed of two chambers:

- **House of Representatives** (*Shūgiin*, 衆議院) — the lower house, elected directly by the population in general elections for a four-year term. It holds decisive authority in forming the government, approving the budget, and passing major legislation. Members of the House of Representatives also elect the Prime Minister, making this chamber the true center of political power.

- **House of Councillors** (*Sangiin*, 参議院) — the upper house, whose members serve six-year terms, with half the chamber renewed every three years. Its powers are more limited, functioning mainly as a reviewing and stabilizing body. It may delay legislation and propose amendments, but in cases of disagreement the lower house can override it with a two-thirds majority.

The executive branch is led by the **Prime Minister**, elected by a majority of the House of Representatives. The Cabinet, composed of ministers of state, is collectively responsible to the Diet, ensuring accountability and political turnover. Article 66 of the Constitution stipulates that the Prime Minister and most ministers must be civilians, reinforcing civilian control over government and the armed forces.

A distinctive feature of Japan's system is the blend of Western parliamentary principles with traditional Japanese political culture, which emphasizes consensus and collective decision-making. While its constitutional framework resembles other parliamentary democracies, in practice Japanese politics often relies on negotiation, incremental reform, and coalition-building. These habits have helped maintain stability and limit open political confrontation.

Japan's party system has for decades been dominated by the **Liberal Democratic Party (LDP)**, which has governed almost continuously since its creation in 1955, with only brief interruptions in the 1990s and early 2010s. This long period of dominance provided continuity in policymaking and contributed to Japan's postwar "economic miracle," turning the country into one of the world's leading industrial and technological powers.

Japan's representative democracy, as defined in the 1947 Constitution, rests on the principles of popular sovereignty, respect for fundamental human rights, and the pacifist renunciation of war in Article 9. The combination of institutional stability, regular electoral cycles, and a political culture favoring compromise has made Japan's parliamentary system one of the most durable and distinctive among modern democracies.

Chapter 3
Liberal Democracy:
Political Rights and Civil Liberties Guaranteed by Law

> **Liberal Democracy** — a form of democratic regime in which popular power, exercised through free elections and representative institutions, is combined with the guaranteed protection of human rights and freedoms, the rule of law, and an independent judiciary that limits the potential for arbitrariness and abuse of power.

Characteristics

In a liberal democracy, the authority of the state derives from the people and is exercised through representative institutions, but it is constrained by a constitutional framework that limits government power and safeguards minority rights. Liberal democracies operate on the basis of written constitutions or established legal traditions, uphold the separation of powers, and rely on an independent judiciary capable of reviewing the legality of legislative and executive actions.

Key Features of Liberal Democracy

1) **Constitutionally Protected Individual Rights and Freedoms**

Liberal democracy is founded on the recognition of inalienable civil liberties: the right to life and personal security, property rights, freedom of expression, freedom of assembly and association, freedom of conscience, and religious liberty. These rights are codified in constitutional provisions or legal instruments of equivalent authority. Crucially, they are protected even against majority decisions, preventing the "tyranny of the majority" and ensuring the political participation and protection of minority groups. Constitutional or supreme courts have the power to strike down laws and policies that violate these rights.

2) **Rule of Law and Judicial Independence**

The rule of law means that all individuals and institutions, including the head of state, members of parliament, and government officials, are subject to the same legal order. This principle is upheld by an independent judiciary, insulated from political interference and authorized to review legislative and executive acts for constitutionality. Judicial independence is supported through appointment procedures, tenure guarantees, and financial autonomy, which reduce the risk of political pressure on the courts.

3) **Freedoms of Speech, Assembly, Press, and Religion; Equality Before the Law**

Liberal democracies protect the freedom to speak, publish, assemble, and practice religion without interference. Equality before the law prohibits discrimination based on ethnicity, religion, gender, or social status. Independent media and freedom of information laws further reinforce transparency, accountability, and public oversight of government activity.

4) **Political Pluralism and Competitive Elections**

Liberal democracy requires genuine competition among political parties and movements in regular, fair, and transparent elections. Electoral systems may differ, but all must guarantee free public choice and peaceful alternation of power. Political pluralism also extends to trade unions, non-governmental organizations, and civic associations that influence policymaking and hold the government accountable.

5) **Checks and Balances Between Branches of Government**

Liberal democracies maintain a clear separation of legislative, executive, and judicial powers. Each branch is equipped with mechanisms to limit the others: legislatures control budgets and conduct inquiries, executives can veto or return legislation, and courts may declare executive actions unlawful. This balance prevents the concentration of power and ensures that no branch dominates the system.

Strengths of Liberal Democracy

1. High Level of Protection for Civil Rights and Freedoms

The greatest strength of liberal democracy lies in its ability to provide effective guarantees for fundamental rights. Citizens are protected from arbitrary interference by the state and enjoy freedom of opinion, religion, and peaceful assembly, as well as access to diverse and independent sources of information. Equality before the law ensures that no one is privileged or disadvantaged on the basis of gender, ethnicity, religion, or social status.

2. Effective Limitation of State Power

Liberal democracy establishes clear constitutional boundaries for political authority, reducing the risk of its abuse. The separation of legislative, executive, and judicial functions ensures that each branch serves as a counterbalance to the others, preventing the concentration of power. Independent courts, free from political interference, safeguard the rule of law and guarantee that even the highest officials remain accountable. Corruption, misuse of authority, and violations of rights can be investigated and punished within a transparent legal framework, reinforcing public confidence in the system.

3. Conditions for Political Pluralism and Civil Society

Liberal democracy creates an environment where pluralism can flourish. Citizens may form political parties, advocacy groups, and associations to defend their interests and express diverse viewpoints. Competitive multiparty elections allow society to evaluate different programs and change its political course when necessary. Beyond elections, a strong civil society—supported by independent media and non-governmental organizations—promotes oversight and dialogue between citizens and the state.

4. Stability and Predictability of the Political System

A further strength of liberal democracy lies in the stability it provides. Clearly defined constitutional procedures ensure the peaceful and regular transfer of power through elections, reducing the likelihood of radical upheavals or violent conflict. Predictability in political life fosters public trust, creates conditions for long-term development, and encourages compromise over confrontation. At the same time, the system allows for gradual reform and adaptation, ensuring that stability does not turn into stagnation but remains a framework for continuous democratic renewal.

Weaknesses of Liberal Democracy

1. Concentration of Power in Elites

Even where democratic procedures function properly, influence often gathers in the hands of a narrow elite. Wealth, control over information, and access to lobbying allow small groups to shape political life more than ordinary citizens. In such cases, the system may look democratic on paper, yet the reality is that decisions are made for the benefit of a few.

2. Dependence on Political Culture and Civic Responsibility

Institutions alone cannot sustain a democracy. The system relies on citizens who are ready to respect each other's rights, to compromise, and to hear opposing views. Where these habits are weak, polarization deepens and democratic institutions struggle to function. Instead of cooperation, politics becomes a battlefield, and stalemates or recurring crises can open the door to authoritarian or extremist alternatives.

3. Tensions Between Liberty and Security

Liberal democracies constantly wrestle with the need to protect rights while also guaranteeing safety. In moments of danger—terrorism, war, or national emergency—governments often expand surveillance, regulate information, or limit privacy. These steps may be justified as temporary safeguards, but citizens view them as infringements on freedoms. If restrictions last too long or go too far, they corrode the principles they were meant to defend.

4. Populism and Manipulation of Opinion

The competition for votes makes democracies vulnerable to populist appeals. Politicians may rely on easy slogans, sweeping promises, or emotional rhetoric detached from what can actually be achieved. Modern technologies and social media amplify these risks, spreading false or distorted information quickly and shaping moods on a mass scale.

5. Unequal Access to Political Participation

Formal rights do not always translate into equal opportunities. Groups with fewer resources—whether defined by income, education, or social position—often find it harder to make their voices heard. This weakens the representative character of democracy and leaves whole segments of society feeling overlooked or excluded.

6. Slowness and Complexity of Decision-Making

Because liberal democracy values discussion, oversight, and checks on authority, the process of decision-making can be slow. In times of crisis—economic collapse, natural disaster, or security threat—such delays frustrate citizens and fuel doubts about the effectiveness of institutions. Calls for more decisive, less democratic alternatives can grow louder in these moments.

7. Risk of Polarization and Social Fragmentation

Pluralism is the lifeblood of democracy, but when divisions harden and compromise is rejected, pluralism turns into paralysis. Groups retreat into camps that no longer speak to each other, and democratic institutions lose their capacity to mediate.

Historical Examples of Liberal Democracy

United States of America (Since 1789)

The United States became the first modern nation to build its political order on the principles of liberal democracy. At its heart stood the idea of popular sovereignty, limited government, and the safeguarding of individual rights. The Constitution, written in 1787 and taking effect in 1789, was the first document to serve as a binding fundamental law for a contemporary state. It created a federal union with a clear division of powers among three branches — legislative, executive, and judicial — each designed to restrain the others.

Constitutional Framework

Congress holds the legislative power. The House of Representatives, elected for two years, reflects population size, while the Senate, with two members from each state, serves staggered six-year terms. Together they pass laws, oversee the budget, regulate commerce, and supervise the executive branch.

The President, chosen every four years through the Electoral College, serves as both head of state and commander-in-chief. The office carries responsibility for implementing laws, directing foreign policy, and appointing key officials, subject to Senate approval.
The judiciary, headed by the Supreme Court, interprets the Constitution and ensures that laws and executive acts remain within its bounds. Federal judges serve for life, securing independence from political influence.

Bill of Rights and Civil Liberties

In 1791, the first ten amendments were added to the Constitution. They guaranteed freedoms that became defining features of American political life: speech, press, religion, assembly, and petition; security against unreasonable searches; due process, fair trial, and legal counsel; and protection from cruel or unusual punishment. These guarantees gained force through Supreme Court rulings. In *Brown v. Board of Education* (1954), segregation in schools was declared unconstitutional. In *New York Times v. United States* (1971), press freedom prevailed in the Pentagon Papers case.

Federalism

The Constitution reserved many powers for the states under the Tenth Amendment. Each state maintains its own constitution, legislature, governor, and courts, and regulates fields such as education, policing, and infrastructure. This balance allows local diversity while keeping the union intact.

Political System and Elections

The United States has a competitive party system long dominated by Democrats and Republicans. Presidential elections occur every four years, congressional elections every two. The Electoral College, intended to balance large and small states, sometimes produces results where the winner of the presidency does not carry the popular vote, as in 2000 and 2016.

Historical Resilience

The constitutional system has endured crises and transformations.

- The Civil War (1861–1865) preserved the Union and ended slavery with the 13th Amendment.
- Progressive reforms expanded democracy with direct election of Senators (17th Amendment) and women's suffrage (19th Amendment).
- The Civil Rights Movement secured the Civil Rights Act (1964) and Voting Rights Act (1965).
- Watergate exposed executive abuse and forced President Nixon to resign in 1974.

Civic Life and Media

American democracy has been shaped by an active civil society. Advocacy groups, non-governmental organizations, and community associations influence debate and policy. The press, protected by the First Amendment, has served as a watchdog, from traditional newspapers to modern digital platforms. Investigative journalism has kept government accountable and public life open to scrutiny.

This framework — a written constitution, strong institutions, and an engaged public — explains why the United States has remained one of the most durable liberal democracies in modern history.

United Kingdom (Contemporary Period)

A distinctive feature of the British system is the absence of a single written constitution. Instead, the framework of government rests on a blend of statutes, historic charters, judicial precedents, and long-standing political conventions. Among the most influential foundations are the Magna Carta of 1215, which bound the monarchy to the rule of law; the Bill of Rights of 1689, which confirmed Parliament's supremacy and secured freedoms such as free elections and free speech in Parliament; and the Parliament Acts of 1911 and 1949, which limited the veto powers of the House of Lords in favor of the elected House of Commons.

Parliament and the Government

Parliament is the central authority. The House of Commons, chosen in general elections under the first-past-the-post system, shapes national policy, approves budgets, and forms the government. Its electoral rules favor larger parties, often producing single-party governments. The Prime Minister is normally the leader of the majority party or coalition.

The House of Lords is unelected, consisting of life peers appointed by the monarch on the advice of the Prime Minister, 92 hereditary peers, and bishops of the Church of England. It revises and amends legislation but cannot ultimately block the will of the Commons.

The Monarchy

The monarch remains the head of state. Today this role is ceremonial, yet it carries constitutional weight. The sovereign opens and dissolves Parliament, gives royal assent to legislation, and represents the nation in ceremonial and diplomatic life. These duties are performed on the advice of elected ministers, making the Crown a visible symbol of continuity while executive authority rests with government.

Judiciary and the Rule of Law

The judiciary operates independently, applying the principle of equality before the law. Since 2009 the Supreme Court of the United Kingdom has exercised the highest judicial authority, taking over from the House of Lords. Courts may review government action for legality, though Parliament retains ultimate legislative sovereignty.

Parties and Elections

Britain has a multi-party system, but politics since the early twentieth century has been dominated by the Conservative and Labour parties. Other significant forces include the Liberal Democrats, the Scottish National Party, Plaid Cymru, and parties in Northern Ireland. The first-past-the-post system usually produces majority governments, which lends stability but often disadvantages smaller parties.

Civil Liberties

Fundamental rights — freedom of speech, press, assembly, and religion — are safeguarded through a mixture of statute, common law, and international commitments. The Human Rights Act 1998 gave domestic force to the European Convention on Human Rights.

Canada and Australia (Contemporary Liberal Democracies)

Canada and Australia successfully combined the parliamentary traditions inherited from Britain with strong protection of human rights, political pluralism, and active civic participation. Both states are notable for their high levels of civil liberties, the stability of democratic institutions, and strong public trust in their political systems.

Canada

Canada represents a modern liberal democracy shaped by both British parliamentary tradition and its own constitutional evolution. The foundations of Canadian statehood rest on two major constitutional milestones. The Constitution Act of 1867 (originally the British North America Act) created the federation and introduced a parliamentary system modeled on Westminster. More than a century later, the Constitution Act of 1982 gave Canada full constitutional independence and incorporated the Canadian Charter of Rights and Freedoms. The Charter remains the central guarantee of civil liberties, securing freedom of speech, assembly, and religion, equality before the law, and protection against discrimination.

Parliament consists of the House of Commons and the Senate. Members of the Commons are chosen through competitive elections, and the government is held accountable to Parliament, ensuring direct responsibility to the electorate.

An independent judiciary reinforces this framework. The Supreme Court of Canada, as the nation's highest court, has safeguarded constitutional rights in landmark rulings on Indigenous self-government, linguistic equality, and limits on state power. Through these decisions, the Court has confirmed its role as a guardian of the rule of law and a central pillar of Canadian democracy.

Australia

Australia developed its own version of parliamentary democracy while preserving the core features inherited from Britain. The Commonwealth of Australia Constitution, which took effect in 1901, created a federal system with a defined separation of powers.

Parliament is composed of the House of Representatives and the Senate, both directly elected by citizens. The government is formed by the party or coalition that secures a majority in the House of Representatives and remains accountable to Parliament, ensuring that executive authority is tied to electoral support.

The High Court of Australia stands at the top of the judiciary. It interprets the Constitution, settles disputes between the Commonwealth and the states, and has shaped Australian democracy through landmark rulings on federal authority and individual rights.

One distinctive feature of the Australian system is compulsory voting, introduced in 1924. This measure has kept voter turnout among the highest in the world, strengthening the legitimacy of democratic institutions. Freedoms of speech, press, and assembly are secured both in law and by the courts, while a vibrant civic culture sustains political pluralism and active participation

Chapter 4

Limited (Electoral) Democracy:
Competitive Elections Under Restricted Rights or Participation

> **Limited (Electoral) Democracy** — a form of democratic regime in which citizens formally participate in governing the state through elections, but their actual influence on political processes is restricted, and the full protection of civil liberties and the rule of law is not adequately guaranteed.

Characteristics

Limited democracy, often described as *electoral democracy*, is a system in which elections formally take place and institutions appear to follow democratic rules, yet the deeper foundations of democracy — civil liberties, real political competition, the rule of law, and effective checks on power — are only partly respected or openly undermined. In such regimes, elections are less a genuine contest of ideas than a ritual confirming the authority of those already in power.

Key Features of Limited Democracy

1) **Elections with predictable outcomes**

Ballots are cast at regular intervals, with registration lists, campaign periods, and official counts. Yet incumbents dominate the process through unequal access to resources, state-controlled media, restrictions on opposition, and manipulation of districts or results. Electoral commissions lack independence, and legal challenges rarely succeed, making political alternation in power unlikely.

2) **Restricted competition and a managed party system**

Several parties may exist on paper, but administrative hurdles, selective law enforcement, and funding imbalances tilt the field toward ruling elites. Opposition groups face legal harassment, deregistration, or marginalization in legislatures, leaving voters with few genuine alternatives.

3) **Civil and political rights curtailed in practice**

Constitutions may proclaim freedoms of speech, assembly, and association, yet governments impose restrictive laws, burdensome permits, and censorship. Independent media and NGOs encounter audits, registration barriers, or outright bans. Activists and journalists risk harassment or detention, creating a climate of intimidation.

4) **Executive dominance over the legislature**

Parliaments hold elections and sessions, but real authority lies with the executive. Legislators often approve government initiatives automatically, with little debate or oversight. Opposition proposals seldom reach the floor, and investigative powers are rarely used.

5) **Politicized judiciary and weak rule of law**

Courts operate, but independence is fragile. Appointments and rulings often follow political directives. Judiciaries may validate disputed elections or prosecute government critics. Legal protections exist on paper but are applied selectively, eroding trust in justice.

6) **Concentration of power and hollow checks and balances**

Institutions meant to restrain authority — constitutional courts, ombudsman offices, audit chambers — lack the strength to challenge the executive. Decision-making narrows to a small circle of political and economic elites, reducing accountability and silencing wider debate.

Strengths of Limited (Electoral) Democracy

1. Legitimacy Through Regular Elections

Even flawed elections provide governments with a formal claim to popular support. This appearance of legitimacy can calm social tensions, reduce the likelihood of unrest, and secure a degree of recognition abroad.

2. A Partial Barrier Against Absolute Rule

Restricted competition, though tightly controlled, prevents politics from becoming a pure monopoly of power. The presence of even a weak opposition and some space for criticism preserves minimal diversity and slows the slide into full authoritarianism.

3. A Possible Stage Toward Democratization

Limited democracy can, in certain contexts, serve as a transitional step. Institutions such as parliaments, parties, and periodic elections lay down a framework that may, over time, support liberalization and the strengthening of rights. Historical examples show that some states have moved from electoral democracy toward more open and competitive systems.

4. Decision-Making Stability Under Low Competition

When political rivalry is muted, governments can act quickly in times of crisis. The absence of sharp partisan deadlock allows unpopular reforms or urgent measures to be implemented without prolonged confrontation.

5. Minimal but Real Political Participation

Even controlled elections give citizens a channel — however limited — to express preferences. This preserves a basic level of civic involvement and political awareness, which can support gradual change in the long run.

6. Reduced Risk of Isolation Abroad

By holding elections and maintaining parliaments, states present themselves as at least nominally democratic. This image helps sustain diplomatic relations, attract investment or aid, and avoid the full weight of sanctions and exclusion.

7. Containment of Social Conflict

Periodic elections offer people a legal outlet for expressing dissatisfaction. The hope, however faint, of peaceful political change reduces the chance of radical protest and the escalation of violence.

8. Predictability of Political Life

With competition limited, the political system becomes more stable and predictable. This reduces the frequency of sudden government crises and provides a degree of continuity in governance.

9. Attractiveness to Investors

Compared with outright dictatorships, limited democracies appear more reliable to foreign partners and investors. Even weak institutions create a framework that reassures businesses and encourages cooperation.

10. Space for Gradual Reform From Above

Ruling elites in limited democracies sometimes use their position to introduce controlled reforms without risking immediate loss of power. Such top-down liberalization has, in certain cases, opened the way to broader political modernization.

11. Feedback From Society

Even tightly managed elections and parties provide a channel for authorities to gauge public mood. This feedback helps governments anticipate discontent and adjust policies before grievances erupt into open conflict.

Weaknesses of limited (selective) democracy

1. High Risk of Manipulated Elections

Although voting procedures are formally observed, elections are often shaped by the use of administrative resources, biased media coverage, and pressure on the opposition. These practices distort the will of the voters and turn elections into a predictable confirmation of power rather than a genuine contest.

2. Restrictions on Rights and Freedoms

Civil liberties are often declared but rarely respected. Independent media face censorship, activists encounter harassment, and opposition groups are subject to repression. Rights to assembly, speech, and association exist in law but are undermined in practice, preventing civil society from holding government accountable.

3. Erosion of Public Trust

When elections are manipulated and institutions ignore public opinion, citizens grow disillusioned. Many perceive state bodies as corrupt and biased. This alienation undermines legitimacy and weakens the relationship between government and society.

4. Rule by Narrow Elites

Power concentrates in the hands of small political and economic circles. These groups use state resources for private gain, deepen inequality, and block opportunities for social advancement, leaving the majority excluded from decision-making.

5. Lack of Renewal in Political Life

With genuine competition absent, the same leaders and parties dominate for decades. Political stagnation sets in, new ideas struggle to emerge, and ruling elites grow complacent, slow to respond to public needs, and reluctant to reform.

6. Weak Civil Society and Growing Apathy

Knowing that elections change little, citizens often disengage from politics. This passivity reinforces the position of those in power, who face no real pressure from below and can ignore public demands without consequence.

7. Risk of Authoritarian Drift

The greatest danger lies in the steady erosion of even nominal democratic features. When institutions exist without real checks, executive power expands unchecked. Over time, such regimes may shed their remaining democratic forms and slide fully into authoritarian rule.

8. International Vulnerability

Limited democracies often struggle with credibility abroad. Their flawed elections and rights violations invite criticism from international organizations, weaken diplomatic standing, and increase the risk of sanctions or reduced cooperation with democratic states.

9. Growth of Informal Practices

When institutions lack transparency and accountability, informal networks take hold. Corruption, patronage, and clan politics become normal tools of governance, further weakening institutions and widening the gap between rulers and citizens.

Varieties of Limited Democracy: Managed Democracy

Within the spectrum of limited regimes, *managed democracy* represents a particularly deliberate model of political control. Like electoral democracy, it preserves the outward forms of democratic life — elections, parliaments, and parties — but narrows pluralism and curtails liberties. What distinguishes it is the systematic way in which the authorities design and oversee the entire political field.

How Managed Democracy Differs

1) **Depth of control**: The authorities not only restrict competition but actively shape it, defining acceptable opposition and excluding unpredictable actors.
2) **Institutional design**: Laws on elections, media, and civil society are crafted to prevent genuine alternation of power.
3) **Elite unity**: The ruling circle acts in a coordinated manner, applying a consistent set of tools to maintain stability and dominance.

Mechanisms of Managed Democracy

1) **Elections Under Control.** Ballots take place regularly and resemble democratic contests, but results are largely predetermined. Candidate lists, electoral commissions, and campaign coverage are managed to ensure outcomes favorable to the incumbents.

2) **Regulated Opposition.** Parties and movements are allowed to exist but operate within tight boundaries. Independent forces are marginalized, while a loyal "systemic" opposition remains, giving the impression of pluralism without threatening the regime.

3) **Parliament Without Autonomy.** The legislature retains its formal appearance but functions mainly as a body that endorses executive decisions. It rarely becomes a genuine center of political debate.

4) **Media and Civil Society Under Guidance.** Non-governmental organizations and major media outlets operate, yet most align closely with state interests. They amplify official narratives and limit the reach of dissenting voices.

Why Managed Democracy Endures

1) **Procedural legitimacy**: Regular elections and the presence of a controlled opposition lend an image of democratic process, sustaining recognition at home and abroad.

2) **Conflict management**: By channeling rivalry into managed forms, the system avoids uncontrolled political crises.

3) **Control of institutions**: Security forces, courts, media, and financial resources remain firmly in the hands of the authorities, minimizing risks of losing power.

4) **Adaptability**: When pressured, the regime can adjust procedures or rhetoric to placate public opinion or international critics, while preserving the core structures of control.

Historical Examples of Limited (Electoral) Democracy

Mexico (1929–2000)

Although Mexico held regular nationwide elections for the presidency, parliament, and local governments, these processes were long dominated by the ruling elite. From the creation of the Institutional Revolutionary Party (PRI) in 1929 until the year 2000, a single party governed without interruption, shaping the entire political system to its advantage.

The PRI's dominance rested on its ability to mobilize state resources. Elections were managed through control of electoral commissions, pressure on local officials, and the use of patronage networks. State media gave little or negative coverage to rivals, while independent outlets faced censorship, harassment, or outright persecution. Other parties were permitted to run, but under conditions that left them little chance of winning.

This system is often described as electoral authoritarianism: democratic institutions such as elections and parliaments were preserved, but mainly as instruments of regime legitimacy. The PRI relied on practices ranging from vote-buying to "carousel voting" schemes and ballot fraud, ensuring decades of predictable victories and an image of democracy abroad.

Yet the very existence of these institutions created space for gradual change. Beginning in the 1980s, civil society grew stronger, and opposition parties such as the National Action Party (PAN) and the Party of the Democratic Revolution (PRD) gained influence. Rising civic engagement and political competition culminated in the presidential election of 2000, when Vicente Fox of the PAN defeated the PRI's candidate, ending seventy-one years of uninterrupted single-party rule.

Egypt under Hosni Mubarak (1981–2011)

Hosni Mubarak, leader of the National Democratic Party (NDP), ruled Egypt for three decades, repeatedly winning presidential elections with margins above ninety percent. Opposition parties and candidates were legally permitted but functioned under severe constraints, facing constant surveillance, administrative obstacles, and restrictions imposed by security services.

The state also exercised firm control over the media. Major outlets followed the government line, while independent journalists and publications encountered censorship, harassment, and repeated shutdowns. Political activists, opposition movements, and protest groups were subject to arrests, detentions, and bans on public gatherings, keeping organized dissent fragmented and weak.

This environment secured the NDP's dominance and Mubarak's uninterrupted rule. Though the outward form of multiparty democracy was preserved, in practice political life was orchestrated to prevent any real challenge to the regime.

In early 2011, however, mass demonstrations erupted as part of the wider Arab Spring. Protesters demanded political change, an end to corruption, and Mubarak's resignation. On February 11, 2011, Mubarak stepped down, bringing an end to thirty years of entrenched rule.

Indonesia under Suharto (1967–1998)

During the presidency of Suharto (1967–1998), Indonesia preserved the outward form of parliamentary democracy, with elections every five years and a multiparty system on paper. In reality, political life revolved around Golkar (Golongan Karya), the ruling organization closely tied to Suharto.

Only two other parties were permitted: the United Development Party (PPP) and the Indonesian Democratic Party (PDI). Their activities were tightly regulated, ensuring that none could mount a serious challenge.

Press freedom and public assembly were similarly constrained. Independent newspapers and political groups operated under censorship and constant surveillance, while critics of the regime faced harassment and interference.

Election results reflected this managed system. In 1971, Golkar won 62.8 percent of the vote, and in every subsequent election its share remained above 60 percent, culminating in 74.5 percent in 1997.

Suharto's rule ended abruptly in 1998 amid mass protests, political turmoil, and the economic collapse brought on by the Asian financial crisis.

Conclusion

Democracy is not a single, uniform model but a political tradition that has assumed different forms across time and societies. Each type reflects the historical context, social conditions, and cultural values of the community in which it develops. Political theory usually distinguishes several main models, each with distinctive advantages and limitations.

Direct democracy grants citizens the fullest role in shaping public life. Instead of delegating power, people themselves vote on laws and policies. This form, known from ancient Athens in the 5th century BCE, remains alive today in Switzerland, where referendums occur several times a year, and in U.S. states such as California, where ballot initiatives decide major issues. Direct democracy ensures broad participation but becomes difficult to manage in large, complex states, where it slows governance and complicates administration.

Representative democracy entrusts decision-making to elected officials, enabling governments to rule large and diverse societies more effectively. Britain's Westminster system of the 17th and 18th centuries established the foundations of parliamentary government, while the United States, through its written Constitution of 1787, pioneered presidential representation. This model allows professional and relatively efficient policy-making, but it also creates the risk that representatives may drift from their voters, prioritizing party or personal interests.

Liberal democracy strengthens representative structures with constitutional limits and guarantees of individual rights. Independent courts, separation of powers, and the rule of law prevent concentration of authority and protect freedoms. This model, consolidated in Western Europe and North America after World War II, expanded globally through mechanisms such as the European Court of Human Rights and the United Nations' human rights system. Its durability, however, depends on civic engagement: institutions remain strong only when citizens actively demand accountability and justice.

Limited or electoral democracy preserves outward democratic institutions — parliaments, political parties, and regular elections — but restricts real competition. The system maintains legality and procedure, while preventing alternation in power. Mexico under the Institutional Revolutionary Party (PRI), which ruled from 1929 to 2000, and Egypt under Hosni Mubarak are well-known examples. In such systems, elections serve as instruments of legitimacy rather than vehicles of genuine choice.

In the contemporary world, democratic regimes confront challenges that test both their adaptability and resilience. Populist leaders gain support by offering simplified solutions to complex social problems, while digital platforms accelerate the spread of disinformation and deepen political polarization. Globalization, meanwhile, brings cultural richness and social diversity but also heightens tensions as communities with different values and priorities struggle to coexist.

SECTION 2. AUTHORITARIAN REGIME

An authoritarian regime is a political system characterized by the concentration of power in the hands of a single individual, a group of individuals, or a ruling elite, in which political freedoms are restricted, political competition is absent or significantly weakened, and citizen participation in governance is largely formal in nature.

Introduction

A defining characteristic of an authoritarian regime is the restriction of political competition, the suppression of opposition, and the close control of society. Civil and political freedoms are drastically limited and remain only in the narrow forms tolerated by those in power.

Key Characteristics of Authoritarianism

1. Concentration of Power.

In authoritarian states, authority is centralized to such an extent that genuine separation of powers is absent. The executive branch dominates the legislature and judiciary, which retain formal structures but lack real independence or the ability to constrain the ruler's decisions.

2. Restriction of Political Freedoms.

Opposition parties, independent media, and civic organizations face tight control and frequent persecution. Political activity and criticism of the authorities may exist but only within boundaries set by the regime, and these boundaries are enforced with censorship, harassment, or repression.

3. Weak Civil Society.

An authoritarian regime actively obstructs independent civic engagement, preventing grassroots initiatives and associations from growing into alternative sources of influence. By controlling or eliminating autonomous social organizations, the state secures its monopoly over political life.

Origins and Conditions for the Rise of Authoritarian Regimes

Authoritarian systems often emerge when existing institutions cannot respond effectively to social, political, or economic challenges. Several recurring conditions explain their rise:

1. Political Instability and Crises.

Authoritarian regimes frequently appear after wars, revolutions, or prolonged unrest. In such moments, societies look to strong and centralized authority to restore order and stability.

2. Weak Democratic Institutions.

Fragile parliaments, partisan courts, and ineffective governments leave a vacuum that can easily be filled by concentrated power. When democratic mechanisms fail to address urgent problems, authoritarian solutions appear more effective.

3. Economic and Social Problems.

Severe economic collapse, unemployment, or widespread poverty create fertile ground for authoritarian promises of discipline and rapid recovery. In exchange for stability, citizens may accept restrictions on their freedoms.

4. Cultural and Historical Factors

In societies lacking a strong tradition of pluralism or democratic practice, authoritarian regimes face less resistance and can more easily consolidate control.

An authoritarian regime often emerges as a response to social, economic, and political challenges, particularly when democracy is seen—by the public or by the elite—as too weak or unreliable to govern effectively. Yet there is also an undeniable human factor: power is not taken in order to be relinquished. Power is like a drug. Any ruler dreams of concentrating it entirely in their own hands, of becoming the sole and absolute master of their country—and, if ambition allows, of the whole world.

Chapter 1
Military Authoritarianism:
Governance Controlled by the Armed Forces

Military authoritarianism is a form of authoritarian political regime in which state power is concentrated in the hands of military institutions, and the country is governed by members of the armed forces' leadership.

Characteristics

Military authoritarianism is a distinct form of authoritarian rule in which supreme power lies in the hands of the armed forces. Such regimes usually emerge through a coup d'état, a violent seizure of authority, or as an outcome of civil conflict. In these systems, senior officers occupy the highest posts in government and define the main directions of state policy.

Key Features of Military Authoritarianism

1) **Concentration of Power in the Military Elite**

    Political authority is exercised by a junta or by a single general who came to power through force. Civilian institutions may be abolished outright or reduced to empty shells under military oversight.

2) **Central Role of the Armed Forces**

    The army becomes the chief instrument of governance. Senior officers are placed at the head of ministries, state agencies, and regional administrations, ensuring that civilian structures operate under military priorities.

3) **Militarization of Public Life**

Military regimes infuse politics and daily life with symbols of discipline and strength. Propaganda glorifies the armed forces, defense spending rises, and parades and displays of power become central to state ritual.

4) **Suppression of Opposition and Freedoms**

Political parties, independent media, and civic organizations are banned or heavily restricted. Dissent is branded a threat to national security and punished through censorship, arrests, or exile.

5) **Reliance on Coercive Structures**

Beyond the regular army, the regime depends on security services, military police, and surveillance networks to maintain order and stifle protest.

6) **Absence of Separation of Powers**

Legislatures and courts remain under military control, stripped of independence and used to legitimize decisions already taken by the junta.

7) **Legitimation Through National Security**

Military rulers justify their dominance as essential for protecting the country from enemies or preventing chaos and institutional collapse.

8) **Control of Elections**

Elections are either suspended or conducted in a tightly managed way, ensuring that the military elite retains control without risk of losing office.

9) **Personalization of Authority**

Even where a junta exists, power often concentrates in the hands of a single leader. Around him a cult of personality may emerge, presenting the general as both protector and savior of the nation.

In such regimes, the armed forces dominate political life, subordinating state institutions and civil society to military command while leaving little space for freedom or genuine participation.

Strengths of Military Authoritarianism

1. Strict Control and Immediate Stability

Military regimes are capable of imposing order with unusual speed, especially after periods of political turmoil or civil strife. Concentrated authority and rigid methods of governance allow juntas to halt unrest and restore a sense of security. This stabilization is usually temporary, but it can provide societies exhausted by chaos with much-needed respite.

2. Capacity to Suppress Internal Conflicts

Armed forces possess the discipline, organization, and resources to act swiftly in the face of uprisings, mass protests, or clashes threatening public order. By responding decisively, military rulers reduce the risk of prolonged domestic conflicts that civilian governments often struggle to contain.

3. Organizational Discipline in Governance

The hierarchical structure of the military allows decisions to be made rapidly and executed uniformly. Clear chains of command eliminate the drawn-out bargaining and inter-agency disputes typical of civilian politics, enabling quick adaptation to emerging challenges.

4. Ability to Enforce Unpopular but Necessary Measures

Military authorities, unbound by the need to seek consensus or electoral approval, can adopt harsh policies that civilian governments might hesitate to implement. Structural reforms, emergency economic measures, or policies demanding strong political will can thus be carried out with greater speed and determination.

5. Concentration of Resources in Emergencies

Centralized control allows military regimes to channel resources quickly toward urgent priorities, whether in response to natural disasters, epidemics, or severe economic crises. This capacity to mobilize and direct national means can make crisis management more effective in the short term.

6. Temporary Curtailment of Civilian Corruption

In their early stages, military governments often dismantle entrenched civilian patronage networks and replace them with officers who embody military ideals of duty and obedience. Such changes can lead to short-term improvements in transparency and efficiency.

7. National Mobilization in the Face of External Threats

Military regimes present themselves as guardians of the nation, particularly during times of real or perceived external danger. By appealing to patriotism and collective defense, they can unite the population and enhance readiness to confront threats.

8. Accelerated Development of Strategic Sectors

Authoritarian military governments often prioritize investment in defense industries, infrastructure, and strategically vital fields. While primarily intended for military use, these efforts can indirectly stimulate technological growth and spill over into civilian sectors.

9. Strengthened Security and Border Control

Military authorities frequently place strong emphasis on internal security. Measures against smuggling, illegal migration, and terrorism are intensified, sometimes producing short-term gains in border protection and public safety.

Weaknesses of Military Authoritarianism

1. Suppression of Rights and Freedoms

Military regimes rely on silencing opposition and controlling civil life. Independent media are censored or shut down, public assemblies are banned, and dissent is criminalized. Any criticism is treated as treason, which deepens alienation between rulers and citizens.

2. Repression and Abuse of Power

Without civilian oversight, military leaders often resort to force as their primary instrument of rule. Security services, police, and the army itself use intimidation, arrests, and violence against opponents, activists, and ordinary citizens. Fear becomes the foundation of governance, yet it weakens the regime over time.

3. Weak Legitimacy and Cyclical Instability

Because most juntas come to power through coups or conflict, they lack genuine legitimacy. This fragile foundation breeds resistance: counter-coups, factional struggles, and popular uprisings. Instead of stability, the state enters a cycle of confrontation that undermines institutions and slows national development.

4. No Peaceful Mechanism of Power Transfer

Military rulers rarely step down voluntarily. Succession depends on force or internal bargaining rather than established rules. Each leadership change risks becoming a crisis, perpetuating the pattern of violent transitions instead of democratic renewal.

5. Weakness in Long-Term Economic Policy

Military governments often succeed in imposing short-term order but fail to sustain economic growth. Their focus on control, discipline, and defense diverts attention from modernization, social welfare, and innovation. As a result, development stalls, and opportunities for progress are lost.

6. Imbalance Between Military and Civilian Needs

Excessive military spending comes at the expense of education, healthcare, infrastructure, and other civilian priorities. This neglect weakens the social fabric and undermines human capital, leaving society less prepared for the future.

7. Stifling of Political Culture

By eliminating pluralism and restricting competition, military regimes reduce politics to obedience. Over time, citizens lose habits of participation and debate, and public life becomes passive, marked by apathy rather than engagement.

8. Dependence on Loyalty Instead of Competence

Appointments are made not on the basis of merit but of personal allegiance to the ruling clique. Such favoritism fosters corruption, weakens professional standards, and undermines administrative efficiency even within the armed forces themselves.

9. Internal Rivalries in the Military

Though united at first, armies are not monolithic. Rivalries between branches, units, or commanders can erupt into factional disputes, coups within coups, and leadership crises, destabilizing the regime from within.

10. International Isolation

Military takeovers and authoritarian practices rarely escape international scrutiny. Sanctions, suspension of aid, and loss of foreign investment follow, depriving the state of resources and access to global markets. What begins as a promise of strength often ends in isolation and economic weakness.

Historical Examples of Military Authoritarianism
Chile under General Augusto Pinochet (1973–1990)

Rise to Power

Pinochet assumed leadership of the country after the military coup of September 11, 1973, overthrowing the socialist government of President Salvador Allende. As a result of the assault on the presidential palace, La Moneda, Allende died, and power passed to a military junta composed of the commanders of the branches of the armed forces. General Pinochet quickly consolidated his personal position and, within a year, became the absolute leader of the junta and the de facto sole ruler of Chile.

Characteristics of the Regime

Pinochet's military regime was characterized by the concentration of power in the hands of the junta, the complete militarization of the political system, and brutal repression against the opposition. Political parties were banned, strict media censorship was introduced, and thousands of citizens were subjected to arrests, torture, and "disappearances." According to official data, during Pinochet's rule, about 3,200 people were killed or disappeared without a trace, while tens of thousands were tortured and repressed.

Political and Legal Changes during the Rule

From the very beginning, the junta implemented measures aimed at dismantling democratic institutions and concentrating authority in the hands of the military leadership. The National Congress was dissolved, and legislative powers were transferred to the junta. The 1925 Constitution was effectively suspended, and a system of military governance was created, with generals and admirals heading key administrative structures. In the regions, power was transferred to military governors, while the judiciary was placed under the strict control of the executive. Decrees and laws significantly expanded the powers of the military authorities and severely restricted civil rights and freedoms.

Role of the Army and Security Forces

The army and other security agencies played a decisive role in the country's governance. The commanders of the army, navy, air force, and police were part of the junta and held the highest state positions. The country was divided into military zones administered by regional military commanders. Particular importance was attached to the secret police — the Dirección de Inteligencia Nacional (DINA) and later the Central Nacional de Informaciones (CNI) — which were responsible for suppressing opposition, conducting political surveillance, and carrying out intimidation, arrests, and extrajudicial actions.

Economic Policy

In parallel with political repression, the junta carried out radical economic reforms. These were implemented by a group of economists known as the "Chicago Boys" (educated at the University of Chicago, USA). They introduced a free-market economy, privatization of enterprises, cuts in social spending, and liberalization of the economy.

Social Consequences of Economic Reforms

These reforms stabilized the economy after a severe crisis but at the same time led to a sharp increase in social inequality and the impoverishment of part of the population. Wealth became concentrated in the hands of a narrow elite, while reductions in social programs and the weakening of labor protections worsened living standards for many Chileans.

The 1980 Constitution and the Referendum

In 1980, Pinochet initiated the adoption of a new Constitution. It established the office of president with an eight-year term, and under its provisions, a national referendum was to be held in 1988 on whether to extend Pinochet's powers for the next presidential term. At that time, it seemed that the referendum would be a mere formality confirming Pinochet's rule.

However, by the late 1980s, Chilean society was growing increasingly dissatisfied with authoritarian rule, repression, and economic difficulties. Civil movements became significantly more active, support for the opposition grew, and the international community increased pressure on the regime, demanding a transition to democracy.

International Response beyond the United States

In addition to U.S. policy shifts, the Pinochet regime faced growing condemnation from the United Nations, which repeatedly passed resolutions denouncing human rights violations in Chile. Amnesty International and other human rights organizations documented torture, disappearances, and political repression, bringing worldwide attention to the regime's abuses. Several Latin American countries distanced themselves from Chile, and European nations applied diplomatic and economic pressure, including restrictions on trade and cooperation, to push for democratic reforms.

The 1988 Referendum and Pinochet's Defeat

The referendum took place on October 5, 1988. Citizens were to vote "Sí" ("Yes") or "No" on the question of extending Pinochet's presidency until 1997. The regime allowed relatively open campaigning before the vote, which enabled the opposition to unite and organize an effective campaign against extending Pinochet's rule.

To the surprise of many observers, the majority of Chileans (about 56%) voted "No." This result meant that democratic elections would be held in Chile, in which Pinochet could no longer run. In December 1989, presidential elections took place, in which the candidate of the united opposition, Patricio Aylwin, won.

Reasons Pinochet Failed to Retain Power

1. Growing public discontent

Citizens were tired of constant pressure, repression, and the lack of freedoms. The economic crisis of the early 1980s particularly deepened social divisions.

2. The rise of the opposition and civil society

The opposition managed to unite within the broad coalition of democratic parties — the "Concertación de Partidos por la Democracia" (Coalition of Parties for

Democracy) — and was able to effectively mobilize society to participate in the referendum.

3. International pressure

Loss of support from the United States and European countries. For a long time, the regime of Augusto Pinochet enjoyed active support from the United States, especially in the early stages of his rule. In the early 1970s, during the Cold War, the main reason for U.S. support for Pinochet was the fight against communism and leftist movements. President Salvador Allende was a socialist and pursued leftist policies, which the U.S. administration perceived as a threat to American interests in Latin America. The United States feared the nationalization of American enterprises and investments, which was carried out by Allende's government. The Pinochet regime, on the other hand, implemented liberal economic reforms beneficial to American companies and international financial organizations. Therefore, the United States closely cooperated with Pinochet and turned a blind eye to human rights violations.

<u>Forms of American support included:</u>

- Financial aid and economic cooperation
- Military and technical assistance
- Political and diplomatic recognition at the international level
- Support from international financial institutions (IMF, World Bank), which provided Chile with loans for economic reforms

However, by the late 1980s, the U.S. position had changed. With the weakening of the USSR and the decline of East–West confrontation, anti-communism ceased to be the main reason for supporting dictatorships. In the United States, criticism of Pinochet's policies increased, and public opinion demanded that the government stop supporting the dictatorial regime.

4. Mistakes of the regime itself

Pinochet and his inner circle underestimated the possibility of defeat in the referendum and allowed freer pre-election campaigning. The Concertación coalition of opposition parties took advantage of television debates, mass rallies, and door-to-door campaigns to mobilize support, while the government failed to suppress these initiatives as tightly as in previous years. After losing the referendum and the victory of democratic forces in the 1989 elections, Pinochet handed over power to the civilian president Patricio Aylwin in March 1990, ending the period of military authoritarianism in Chile. Although Pinochet retained his position as commander-in-chief of the army for several more years, the political transition marked the irreversible decline of his regime's dominance.

Argentina under the Military Junta (1976–1983)

The Argentine military dictatorship of 1976–1983, led successively by Generals Jorge Rafael Videla, Roberto Viola, Leopoldo Galtieri, and Reynaldo Bignone, is remembered as one of the darkest periods in modern Latin American history.

On March 24, 1976, the armed forces deposed President Isabel Perón in a coup organized by the high command of the army, navy, and air force. The coup was justified by references to hyperinflation (over 300% annually), a collapsing economy, political instability, and the growing influence of leftist guerrilla movements such as the Montoneros and the Ejército Revolucionario del Pueblo (ERP). Conservative sectors of society and major business associations supported the takeover, expecting the military to restore order.

The junta named its regime the *Proceso de Reorganización Nacional* (Process of National Reorganization). General Videla assumed the presidency, ruling alongside Admiral Emilio Massera and Brigadier Orlando Agosti. Congress was dissolved, constitutional guarantees suspended, trade unions banned, and all political activity prohibited.

Political and Legal Transformation

The junta concentrated authority in its own hands. Legislative powers were transferred to the military command, while the judiciary was placed under direct supervision. Regional governance was entrusted to military commanders who combined administrative, political, and security powers.

Freedoms of speech, assembly, and association were eliminated. Newspapers such as *Clarín* and *La Nación* were subjected to strict censorship, while dissident publications were closed outright. Universities were purged of "subversive" faculty and students.

Repression and the "Dirty War"

The most infamous aspect of the dictatorship was the large-scale campaign of state terror later known as the "Dirty War" (*Guerra Sucia*). Its declared purpose was to eradicate subversion, but in practice it became a system of systematic terror aimed at silencing all dissent.

Repressive methods included:

- **Mass arrests and illegal detentions**, often without charges.
- **Secret detention centers** (*centros clandestinos de detención*) such as ESMA (Escuela de Mecánica de la Armada) in Buenos Aires and Automotores Orletti.
- **Torture and inhumane treatment**, used both for information extraction and intimidation.
- **Extrajudicial killings and enforced disappearances** — thousands were abducted, never to be seen again.
- **"Death flights"**, in which prisoners were drugged and thrown into the sea or rivers from military aircraft.

According to CONADEP's *Nunca Más* report (1984), 8,961 cases of disappearance were officially documented, while human rights organizations such as the Mothers of the Plaza de Mayo estimate the number at up to 30,000. The term *desaparecidos* ("the disappeared") became the defining symbol of the regime's cruelty.

Role of the Armed Forces and Security Agencies

The armed forces and security services exercised complete control. The army, navy, and air force commanders were the core of the junta, while the federal police, the Gendarmería, and intelligence agencies carried out daily repression.

The state intelligence service SIDE (*Secretaría de Inteligencia del Estado*), in coordination with military intelligence, oversaw surveillance, infiltration of opposition networks, and kidnappings. Argentina also participated in **Operation Condor**, the transnational campaign of repression organized by South American military regimes, which coordinated assassinations and disappearances across borders.

Economic Policy and Social Consequences

Under Economy Minister José Alfredo Martínez de Hoz, the regime adopted neoliberal reforms: trade liberalization, financial deregulation, privatization of public enterprises, and cuts in social spending. Initially, these measures curbed inflation, but they also led to:

- rapid **deindustrialization** and the closure of thousands of factories,
- a surge in **foreign debt**, which grew from $7.8 billion in 1976 to more than $45 billion by 1983,
- a sharp rise in **inequality and poverty**, as public services were dismantled.

For many Argentines, daily life became harder not only because of repression but also because of economic decline.

The Falklands War and the Collapse of the Regime

By the early 1980s, the junta faced a crisis of legitimacy. To rally public support, General Leopoldo Galtieri launched an invasion of the Falkland (Malvinas) Islands on April 2, 1982. The move initially generated nationalist enthusiasm, but Britain responded with force, and after ten weeks of fighting Argentina suffered a humiliating defeat.

The war cost the lives of 649 Argentine soldiers and 255 British troops. Defeat destroyed the credibility of the armed forces, which had presented themselves as guardians of the nation. Instead of restoring legitimacy, the war exposed the regime's incompetence, eroded its last vestiges of popular support, and accelerated its downfall.

International Response

While the regime maintained some ties with the United States during the Cold War (particularly under President Carter's successor Ronald Reagan), European governments imposed diplomatic pressure, limited cooperation, and provided refuge to Argentine exiles. Latin American neighbors, especially Venezuela and Mexico, became vocal critics. This growing isolation, combined with internal crisis, further weakened the junta.

Fall of the Regime and the Return of Democracy

By 1983, Argentina was bankrupt, socially fractured, and internationally isolated. Protests intensified, with the Mothers of the Plaza de Mayo gaining global recognition for their weekly demonstrations demanding the truth about the disappeared.

In October 1983, the junta announced elections. Raúl Alfonsín of the Radical Civic Union won and assumed the presidency in December, marking Argentina's return to democracy.

Chapter 2

Personalist Authoritarianism: Concentration of Power in a Single Leader

> **Personalist authoritarianism** is a type of authoritarian regime in which political power is concentrated in a single individual who exercises absolute authority over the state and its principal institutions.

Characteristics

Personalist authoritarianism is defined by the deep and comprehensive domination of a single individual over the state, society, and political institutions. Such regimes are inherently unstable, as they depend entirely on the leader's personality and lack stable mechanisms for the transfer of power.

The Main Features of Personalist Authoritarianism

1) Concentration of Power in a Single Leader

In personalist regimes, authority is gathered in the hands of one figure whose decisions require neither approval nor debate. Institutions that could limit his will — government, parliament, or courts — become tools that merely enact his orders.

2) Control Over All Branches of Power

Though the separation of powers may exist on paper, in practice both legislature and judiciary serve the leader and his circle. Judges are appointed for loyalty, parliaments function as ceremonial bodies, and executive posts are distributed to clients who owe their careers to him. Security forces, police, and intelligence services are bound to his command, suppressing dissent and eliminating rivals.

3) Lack of Succession Mechanisms

Personalist leaders rarely prepare for their own replacement, seeing succession rules as a threat to their grip on power. Most remain until death, incapacity, or overthrow. When power finally changes hands, it does so in turmoil — through elite struggles, coups, or sudden collapse.

4) Cult of Personality

Propaganda and controlled media build an image of the leader as the nation's sole guide and savior. His face and name saturate public life — from schools to ceremonies — turning politics into a theater of personal glorification. Dissenting voices are silenced, while loyalty to the leader is equated with loyalty to the state itself.

5) Weakness of Institutions

State and party structures exist, but without autonomy. They are reshaped, merged, or dissolved according to the leader's needs, leaving no stable framework that might outlast him.

6) Patronage Networks

Careers and promotions depend less on merit than on loyalty. A network of clients and dependents ties the ruling elite directly to the leader, ensuring their obedience in exchange for resources, protection, and privilege.

7) Control of Media and Information

Independent voices are silenced through censorship, harassment, or bans. The official narrative dominates, narrowing public discourse to what the leader permits and shaping both domestic and foreign perceptions.

8) Suppression of Civil Society

Independent unions, associations, and human rights groups are stifled or eliminated. Collective action outside state control is treated as a danger, leaving society fragmented and vulnerable.

9) Leader-Centered Foreign Policy

Diplomacy reflects the ruler's personal goals — political, strategic, or ideological — even when these diverge from national interests. International decisions are guided less by long-term state needs than by the ambitions of a single individual.

Key Differences Between Personalist, Military, and Single-Party Regimes

1. **Source of Power**
   - *Personalist Authoritarianism* — Power is concentrated in a single individual, whose authority stems from personal dominance rather than from a collective body or institutional framework.
   - *Military Authoritarianism* — Power is held by a group of high-ranking officers or a junta, with legitimacy often based on control of the armed forces and claims of maintaining order and stability.
   - *Single-Party Authoritarianism* — Power is vested in one political party that dominates political life, claims ideological legitimacy, and controls the state apparatus through party structures.

2. **Decision-Making**
   - *Personalist* — Decisions are made unilaterally by the leader, without formal checks, and institutions exist only to implement his will.
   - *Military* — Decisions are made collectively by a small group of military leaders, though a strong commander may still dominate.
   - *Single-Party* — Decision-making follows party structures, with debates and internal negotiations occurring within the party elite.

3. **Succession of Power**
   - *Personalist* — Succession is highly uncertain; it often depends on the leader's personal choice or is resolved through elite struggle after his departure.

- *Military* — Leadership change tends to follow internal military procedures, though coups are common.
- *Single-Party* — Succession is more institutionalized, with leadership transitions managed through party rules and internal consensus.

4. **Stability**
   - *Personalist* — Typically the most unstable, due to overreliance on the leader's personal authority and lack of institutional resilience.
   - *Military* — Can be moderately stable if the armed forces remain united, but vulnerable to factionalism and coups.
   - *Single-Party* — Usually the most durable, as power is embedded in strong party institutions capable of surviving leadership changes.

Strengths of Personalist Authoritarianism

1. **High Speed of Decision-Making and Resource Allocation**

In a personalist regime, all crucial decisions are concentrated in the hands of one leader. The absence of parliamentary debate or institutional negotiation allows for immediate responses to crises. Resources can be redirected without delay, and policies imposed without compromise. In moments of natural disaster, war, or financial collapse, such rapid concentration of power can provide short-term stability and efficiency that democratic systems, with their checks and balances, often lack.

2. **Capacity to Preserve Unity and Quell Opposition**

The leader commands the full range of coercive institutions — the military, police, and security services. This allows him to silence protests or suppress uprisings quickly, ensuring the appearance of national unity. In fragmented or polarized societies, such dominance may prevent the state from splintering into competing groups or territories.

3. **Strict Hierarchical Chain of Governance**

Authority flows vertically, from the leader downward. Every official is directly accountable to superiors, and career survival depends on loyalty rather than independent initiative. This structure prevents the emergence of rival power centers, enforces strict discipline, and ensures that orders are carried out without delay.

4. **Flexibility in Policy Choices**

Free from institutional constraints, a personalist ruler can shift strategy rapidly to meet new circumstances. Laws, regulations, and foreign policy directions can be adjusted at will, allowing adaptation to sudden international or domestic challenges.

5. **Continuity of Leadership and Long-Term Projects**

The long tenure of a personalist leader reduces the risk of abrupt changes in national strategy. Infrastructure, ideological programs, or foreign alliances can be pursued over decades without the interruptions caused by electoral cycles or coalition governments.

6. Symbolic Cohesion and National Identity

The figure of the leader often becomes synonymous with the state itself. Through propaganda and state-controlled media, he embodies national independence, strength, or revival. In times of external threat or reconstruction, this symbolism can unify the population and create a sense of collective destiny.

7. Ability to Avoid Institutional Deadlock

Where democratic systems may stall in conflict between branches of power, personalist rule cuts through with unilateral decisions. This prevents prolonged paralysis and provides swift resolutions to urgent problems.

8. Direct Control of Security and Order

Concentrated command over armed and security forces enables rapid suppression of insurgencies, organized crime, or terrorism. This capacity may foster a perception of safety and order, at least in the short run, especially in unstable or divided societies.

9. Mobilization of Mass Support

Charismatic leaders can call for national campaigns and quickly orchestrate them through state-controlled media and administrative networks. Whether for war efforts, economic initiatives, or ideological projects, this capacity for rapid mobilization strengthens their authority.

10. Personalized Diplomacy Abroad

Personalist rulers often cultivate direct ties with foreign leaders, bypassing complex diplomatic procedures. This personalization of foreign policy can sometimes yield favorable deals, foreign aid, or symbolic recognition that reinforces their domestic legitimacy.

Weaknesses of Personalist Authoritarianism

1. Arbitrariness, Corruption, and Abuse of Power

Concentrating authority in one person inevitably fosters arbitrariness and systemic corruption. Without oversight, state resources are diverted for the enrichment of the leader, his family, and loyal clients. Contracts, privileges, and positions become rewards for obedience rather than merit.

2. Instability After the Leader's Departure

Because the entire system is built around the leader, his death, illness, or overthrow creates a political vacuum. Rivalries erupt among the military, security services, and elite factions. In the absence of succession rules, transitions often descend into violent conflict, coups, or even state collapse.

3. Repression and Weak Civil Liberties

Personalist regimes rely on coercion to silence dissent. Criticism of the ruler is treated as betrayal; opposition parties, media, and civic organizations are harassed, banned, or placed under surveillance. Fear and censorship stifle civic life, isolating citizens and preventing peaceful expression of grievances. Over time, this breeds hidden anger and erodes the regime's social foundations.

4. Dependence on the Leader's Personal Competence

The system's stability rests on one individual. A single miscalculation, poor judgment, or declining health can destabilize the entire state. Because institutions are weak, they cannot correct errors or cushion crises, turning personal weakness into national vulnerability.

5. Policy Volatility and Lack of Institutional Memory

Without strong institutions, policy shifts follow the leader's moods and personal interests. Long-term planning is undermined, investment is discouraged, and citizens lose trust in governance. The state becomes reactive rather than strategic, unable to sustain coherent development.

6. Suppression of Initiative and Innovation

Excessive centralization discourages officials from taking initiative. Fear of deviating from the leader's directives fosters stagnation, poor problem-solving, and reduced adaptability in crises. Over time, the bureaucracy becomes rigid and incapable of reform.

7. Economic Fragility

Personalist rulers often use the economy to consolidate power: distributing subsidies to supporters, neglecting structural reforms, or exploiting resources for short-term political gain. This weakens the foundations of sustainable growth and leaves the state exposed to economic shocks.

8. Degradation of the Leadership Cadre

Promotions are based on loyalty rather than competence. As unqualified allies fill key posts, the professional capacity of government and military institutions declines. This erosion of expertise makes the regime brittle in moments of crisis.

9. Legitimacy Bound to the Leader's Image

Because legitimacy depends on the leader's charisma and propaganda, it fades as his appeal weakens. With no institutional or ideological alternative to sustain authority, the regime becomes fragile once the leader's image loses credibility.

10. Risk of Radicalized Protest

By eliminating legal avenues of dissent, the regime leaves citizens with no peaceful way to express opposition. When frustration erupts, it often takes explosive and violent forms, destabilizing the system more abruptly than gradual democratic opposition would.

11. International Condemnation and Isolation

Human rights abuses and authoritarian practices provoke criticism, sanctions, and diplomatic exclusion.

12. Elite Rivalries and Coup Attempts

With no institutions to regulate competition, loyalty among elites is temporary and self-serving. Ambitious generals or security chiefs may plot against the leader or each other, leading to intrigue, coups, or factional conflict.

Historical Examples of Personalist Authoritarianism

Spain under Francisco Franco (1939–1975)

Francisco Franco (1892–1975) dominated Spain's political and social life for nearly four decades, ruling from the end of the Civil War in 1939 until his death in 1975.

Rise to Power (1936–1939)

Franco emerged as the central figure of the nationalist uprising during the Spanish Civil War. With the support of the army, monarchists, the Catholic Church, and conservative elites, he forged a coalition against the Republican government. The victory of the nationalists in 1939 established a military dictatorship with Franco as *Caudillo* — Leader of Spain.

Concentration of Power

After victory, Franco concentrated authority in his hands. The parliament (*Cortes*) became a ceremonial body, approving decisions already made. Political parties were banned, leaving only the Falange Española as the official state party. Yet the Falange was never autonomous; it existed as an instrument to sustain Franco's power and propagate the ideology of Francoism.

Army and Security Services

The army was the backbone of the regime. Senior officers occupied key administrative posts, while Franco controlled all top appointments to ensure loyalty. Security services and the Political-Social Brigade functioned as instruments of repression: monitoring citizens, dismantling opposition networks, and persecuting "anti-state activities." Thousands were executed or imprisoned, and repression became a permanent feature of public life.

Repression and Civil Liberties

The years immediately following the war were marked by mass trials and executions of Republican sympathizers. Between 1939 and 1945, tens of thousands were executed and hundreds of thousands imprisoned. Throughout the dictatorship, censorship was total, trade unions were banned, and civic organizations operated only under close surveillance. Freedom of speech, assembly, and political participation existed only in name.

Economic Policy

Franco's economic policies passed through two distinct phases.

- In the 1940s and 1950s, Spain pursued autarky — an attempt at self-sufficiency that produced stagnation, shortages, and widespread poverty.
- In the late 1950s, facing crisis, Franco permitted reforms that liberalized trade, attracted foreign investment, and encouraged tourism. The result was rapid growth, known as the "Spanish Economic Miracle." Living standards improved, but inequality widened, and modernization was uneven.

Social Policy and Ideology

Franco built his rule on nationalist and conservative foundations, with the Catholic Church as a central ally. Catholicism was declared the state religion, divorce and contraception were prohibited, and religious education was compulsory.

Education and culture were tightly controlled: curricula emphasized Francoist ideology, regional languages were banned, and art and literature were censored.

National identity was cultivated through propaganda and symbols. The slogan *España, una, grande y libre* ("Spain, united, great, and free") became the regime's central motto, echoed in parades, ceremonies, and media that glorified Franco as *Caudillo* and equated dissent with treason against the nation

Social Policy and Ideology

Franco built his rule on nationalist and conservative foundations. The Catholic Church, declared the official religion of the state, became a central ally. It supported the regime in return for extensive privileges, while schools, media, and cultural institutions promoted values of patriotism, obedience, and traditional family order.

Foreign Policy

Spain was isolated after World War II, excluded from the Marshall Plan and shunned by the Allies. Yet the Cold War changed its fortunes. By 1953, Franco secured a military and economic cooperation agreement with the United States — the so-called *Pact of Madrid*. Under this agreement, Washington obtained the right to use and modernize several strategic bases in Spain: Torrejón (near Madrid), Zaragoza, and Morón for the U.S. Air Force, and Rota in Cádiz for the U.S. Navy. In exchange, Spain received more than $1.5 billion in economic and military assistance over the following decade.

This partnership marked the beginning of sustained American support for Franco's dictatorship. The presence of U.S. forces and aid flows stabilized Spain's economy, integrated it into Western defense structures, and gradually lifted its international isolation. In 1955, Spain entered the United Nations, formally ending its diplomatic quarantine.

Longevity of the Franco Regime

Franco's regime endured longer than those of Hitler or Mussolini due to a combination of factors. Spain remained officially neutral during World War II, avoiding the fate of Axis powers. Franco refrained from foreign wars, sparing Spain military defeat. With the onset of the Cold War, Western powers — above all the United States — came to see him as a useful ally. American economic aid, military cooperation, and diplomatic recognition provided the regime with external legitimacy and financial resources that helped consolidate its rule.

At home, Franco relied on the loyalty of the army, the Catholic Church, and conservative elites, while harsh repression and censorship kept opposition fragmented. Economic liberalization in the 1960s, backed in part by foreign investment facilitated through U.S. cooperation, strengthened the regime further by raising living standards. In his final years, limited easing of repressive policies reduced international criticism and gave the appearance of gradual change.

Zaire (now the Democratic Republic of the Congo) under Mobutu Sese Seko (1965–1997)

On 24 November 1965, Mobutu seized power in a coup that overthrew the country's first president, Joseph Kasa-Vubu. Declaring himself head of state, he established a regime in which his personal authority overshadowed all other institutions.

Concentration of Power

In 1967 Mobutu created the Popular Movement of the Revolution (MPR), which by 1974 was enshrined in the constitution as the only legal party. The distinction between party and state disappeared. Parliament, the courts, and the army served as extensions of the presidency, their function reduced to carrying out the leader's directives.

Cult of Personality

Few postcolonial rulers cultivated so elaborate a personal image. In 1972 Mobutu adopted the grandiose name Mobutu Sese Seko Kuku Ngbendu wa za Banga — often translated as "the all-powerful warrior who, because of his endurance and inflexible will, goes from conquest to conquest, leaving fire in his wake." His Authenticité campaign sought to break with colonial traditions: Western suits were replaced with the *abacost*, European place names vanished, Léopoldville became Kinshasa (1966), and in 1971 the country itself was renamed Zaire.

Corruption and Economic Decline

Mobutu's regime was marked by extreme corruption. State resources — copper, diamonds, gold — were diverted into private fortunes. His wealth reached into the billions of U.S. dollars while ordinary citizens faced poverty, inflation, and mounting debt.

Repression and Civil Liberties

Political rivals were arrested, tortured, or assassinated; many went into exile. Independent media did not exist, and criticism of the regime was criminalized. Fear and surveillance became the norm of political life.

Cold War Support

Despite repression and economic decay, Mobutu secured strong external support during the Cold War. For the United States and its allies he was a reliable anti-communist partner. In return for political loyalty, Zaire received aid, investment, and diplomatic backing, which helped sustain Mobutu's power for decades.

Collapse of the Regime

The end of the Cold War removed this external shield. As domestic crises intensified, legitimacy evaporated. The First Congo War (1996–1997), led by Laurent-Désiré Kabila with regional backing, swept across the country. On 17 May 1997, rebels captured Kinshasa. Mobutu fled into exile, dying a few months later in Rabat, Morocco. The speed of the collapse revealed how entirely the system had rested on a single ruler.

Haiti under François "Papa Doc" Duvalier and Jean-Claude "Baby Doc" Duvalier (1957–1986)

The rule of François Duvalier ("Papa Doc") and his son Jean-Claude Duvalier ("Baby Doc") from 1957 to 1986 stands as a classic example of a personalist authoritarian regime with elements of a family dictatorship. It combined extreme concentration of power, a pervasive cult of personality, systematic repression, and endemic corruption.

François Duvalier's Rise to Power (1957)

François Duvalier, a physician by training, won the 1957 presidential election and quickly consolidated personal rule. After suppressing an attempted coup in 1958, he purged the army and security services to neutralize rivals. In 1959 he created the paramilitary Tonton Macoutes (later formalized as the Volontaires de la Sécurité Nationale, VSN), which became the backbone of repression.

Political-Legal Architecture of the Regime

In 1964 a new constitution, confirmed by a tightly controlled referendum, declared him President-for-Life and codified sweeping executive powers. It also laid the foundation for dynastic succession. In 1971, another referendum lowered the presidential age limit and enabled the succession of his 19-year-old son Jean-Claude Duvalier.

Concentration of Power and Cult of Personality

All branches of government were subordinated to the presidency. Parliament became a rubber stamp, while propaganda fused politics with religion, turning Duvalier into a figure of mystical authority — "voodoo politics." Portraits, slogans, and rituals reinforced a cult of personality, and Haiti functioned as a police state built on fear and surveillance.

Role of the Army, Secret Police, and Parallel Forces

The Tonton Macoutes operated outside the law, conducting arrests, torture, disappearances, and executions. They infiltrated rural communities, extorted citizens, and enriched themselves through contraband. Their presence weakened the regular army, which Duvalier had purged of potential rivals. Direct presidential control of military command in the capital ensured loyalty at the top.

U.S. Support and Cold War Context

During the Cold War, Washington regarded Haiti as a strategic ally against communism, especially after the Cuban Revolution. The United States provided political backing, economic aid, and military assistance.

- **Geopolitical motives**: to prevent Cuban and Soviet influence in the Caribbean.
- **Economic aid**: through USAID, Haiti received $20–25 million annually in the early 1970s for roads, ports, electricity, and food shipments under *Food for Peace*.
- **Military assistance**: the U.S. supplied light weapons, vehicles, communications equipment, and training, including at the School of the Americas in Panama.

- **Diplomatic support**: American diplomats shielded Haiti from international isolation and softened criticism in the UN and OAS.

This support modernized some infrastructure and public health but simultaneously entrenched the dictatorship.

Economic Policy and Performance

Haiti's economy deteriorated throughout the Duvalier era. While aid built some infrastructure, much was siphoned off by elites. The 1973 oil crisis and falling commodity prices aggravated decline. By the mid-1980s, GDP per capita had fallen to one of the lowest in the hemisphere, unemployment hovered above 30 percent, and more than two-thirds of the population lived in poverty. Chronic food shortages led to widespread malnutrition.

Social and Cultural Policy

Propaganda portrayed Duvalier as the nation's guardian against internal and external enemies. Vodou symbolism reinforced his aura of mystical authority. Education and culture were subordinated to state control, with censorship stifling dissent. Social control was so coercive that thousands of professionals — doctors, teachers, engineers — emigrated, creating a long-term *brain drain*. By the early 1980s, an estimated 500,000 Haitians had fled abroad, many as "boat people."

Scale and Pattern of Repression

Both Duvaliers used systematic repression: arbitrary arrests, torture, and executions claimed thousands of lives. Human rights organizations estimate that more than 30,000 people were killed or disappeared between 1957 and 1986. Trade unions, independent media, and civic organizations were banned or tightly controlled.

Family Succession and Jean-Claude Duvalier's Rule (1971–1986)

At 19, Jean-Claude Duvalier inherited the presidency. Initially portrayed as less severe, his regime deepened corruption and failed to address economic collapse. International pressure over human rights mounted. By the mid-1980s, mounting debt, declining exports, and rampant poverty eroded legitimacy. Protests spread across cities and rural communities, involving students, workers, and the Catholic Church, which became a vocal critic.

Fall of the Regime and Aftermath (1986)

On 7 February 1986, amid mass protests and violence, Jean-Claude Duvalier fled Haiti aboard a U.S. Air Force aircraft to exile in France. A military-led National Governing Council under General Henri Namphy assumed power, but Haiti entered a prolonged period of instability. Attempts to dismantle the authoritarian legacy faced resistance from entrenched elites and remnants of the Macoutes.

Long-Tail Accountability and Legacy

Jean-Claude Duvalier's return in 2011 reignited demands for accountability. Human rights groups filed cases against him for crimes against humanity. He died in 2014 before most cases were resolved. The Duvalier era left behind hollow institutions, a culture of fear, mass poverty, and a fractured society. Its legacy still shapes Haiti's political fragility and democratic struggles today.

Chapter 3

Bureaucratic Authoritarianism:
State Administration as the Primary Political Authority

> **Bureaucratic authoritarianism** is a type of authoritarian regime in which state power is concentrated in the hands of a bureaucratic apparatus led by a narrow group of technocrats, military officers, or government officials.

Characteristics

Bureaucratic authoritarianism is a distinct form of nondemocratic rule in which real authority is concentrated not in a charismatic leader or a military junta, but in the administrative apparatus of the state. The bureaucracy becomes both the main engine of governance and the ultimate arbiter of political decisions, while citizens are almost entirely excluded from meaningful participation.

Core Characteristics

1) Power Rooted in the Bureaucracy

Senior administrators and civil servants occupy the central position in this system. Their authority stems less from personal charisma or military strength than from stable positions inside a vast administrative network. Decisions reflect the internal priorities of this apparatus, meaning that changes in individual leaders rarely alter the overall course of policy.

2) Formal Institutions with Hollow Authority

Parliaments, courts, law enforcement agencies, and local governments continue to function outwardly, but they no longer exercise independence. Elections are held, laws are passed, and rulings are issued, yet these processes serve mainly to validate decisions already shaped within the bureaucracy. The system projects legality and order while masking the absence of genuine political competition.

3) Restricted Representation

Political parties, civic associations, and social movements may be allowed, but their role is minimal. Elections become ritualized events, opposition is constrained by administrative barriers, and parliaments simply endorse bureaucratic directives. Civil liberties are nominally guaranteed, but in practice curtailed by regulations, permits, and administrative surveillance.

4) Technocratic Style of Rule

Leadership posts are filled by technocrats and career administrators rather than mass politicians. The emphasis lies on management, efficiency, and measurable outcomes. Ideological debates and popular mobilization are pushed aside in favor of pragmatic goals.

5) Economic Stabilization Over Political Reform

Bureaucratic authoritarian regimes often justify limits on rights and pluralism as the price of economic growth and national stability. Order and predictability are presented as prerequisites for development, while liberalization is portrayed as a dangerous source of instability.

6) **Weak Ideological Basis**

Unlike personalist or one-party systems, bureaucratic authoritarianism does not rely on a grand ideology. Instead, it legitimizes itself with pragmatic slogans — "order," "efficiency," "rule of law" — that emphasize stability over vision.

7) **Closed Decision-Making**

Political choices are made within small circles of high-level administrators. Policy deliberations are opaque to the public and often even to lower levels of bureaucracy, ensuring central control and limiting accountability.

8) **Institutional Inertia and Durability**

The strength of the regime comes from institutions rather than personalities. Even as top officials come and go, the system reproduces itself, maintaining continuity of policies and priorities.

9) **Selective Repression**

Coercion exists, but it is typically administrative rather than overtly violent. Licensing rules, audits, and targeted legal cases serve to discipline opponents. Mass terror is unnecessary when bureaucratic tools can silence dissent quietly and effectively.

Bureaucratic authoritarianism can provide stability and continuity, but at the cost of political vitality. By replacing civic participation with formal procedures and by elevating administration above representation, it creates a rigid order where efficiency and control prevail over freedom and accountability.

Strengths of Bureaucratic Authoritarianism

1. **Stability and Predictability of Governance**

In bureaucratic authoritarian systems, authority lies not with a charismatic leader or shifting political coalitions but with a professional administrative machine. Decisions are made within established procedures, giving government a steady rhythm and reducing the likelihood of sudden upheavals. Policies unfold incrementally, and even in moments of crisis the system tends toward continuity rather than rupture.

2. **Professionalism of the State Apparatus**

Governance is carried out by trained officials and experts whose careers advance through competence and experience rather than rhetoric or electoral popularity. Policies reflect analysis and technical knowledge rather than crowd-pleasing slogans. This reliance on professional judgment reduces the risk of major errors and lends government action a more rational, measured character.

3. **Capacity for Long-Term Projects**

Concentrated authority within the bureaucracy allows for the mobilization of resources toward large-scale goals. Without constant partisan conflict, disputes, or electoral turnover, administrators can sustain long-term economic, infrastructural, and social programs. Such regimes are therefore able to pursue projects that require consistent attention across decades, from industrial modernization to nationwide infrastructure building.

4. Institutional Continuity

Because power resides in the apparatus rather than in individual leaders, changes in the top ranks rarely alter the broader course. Policy continuity across different administrations strengthens strategic planning and reassures both domestic actors and foreign partners that the rules of the game remain stable.

5. Technocratic Problem-Solving

Bureaucratic authoritarianism privileges expertise. Public health campaigns, financial reforms, or infrastructure planning are shaped by specialists rather than populist politicians. In fields where technical knowledge is crucial, this can produce effective solutions and consistent outcomes.

6. Insulation from Populist Pressures

With limited public participation, bureaucratic regimes are shielded from short-term demands of mass politics. Freed from the need to cater to electoral cycles, administrators can give priority to long-term goals such as fiscal stability, technological development, or institutional consolidation, even when these policies are unpopular in the short run.

Weaknesses of Bureaucratic Authoritarianism

1. Alienation of Power from Society

In bureaucratic authoritarian systems, decision-making becomes detached from ordinary citizens. Politics is conducted behind closed doors, through procedures opaque to the public. As people lose any influence over policies that shape their lives, they come to see the state as distant and indifferent. Over time, mistrust and apathy erode legitimacy, and what begins as quiet disillusionment can erupt into protests and social unrest.

2. Corruption and Administrative Arbitrariness

Without oversight or transparency, bureaucracies tend to serve themselves. Officials exploit privileged positions, distributing posts to loyal associates and diverting resources for private gain. The system's closed nature shields misconduct from scrutiny. This corrodes the efficiency of government, undermines trust, and fosters the view that state institutions exist not for the public good but for the enrichment of insiders.

3. Restricted Mobility and Social Stagnation

Bureaucratic authoritarian regimes offer little room for new talent. Advancement depends less on merit than on loyalty to entrenched rules and networks. As elites become self-contained, innovation withers. The result is a conservative governance structure that reacts slowly to change, producing economic stagnation and leaving society ill-prepared for global competition.

4. Institutional Rigidity and Resistance to Reform

Deeply rooted bureaucratic interests create formidable barriers to change. Even when inefficiencies are obvious, internal resistance slows or blocks reform. Protecting the status quo becomes more important than pursuing adaptation, locking the system into patterns of inefficiency.

5. Policy Inertia and Weak Crisis Response

The same procedural discipline that gives bureaucracies stability often makes them clumsy in emergencies. Reliance on elaborate regulations and consensus delays decisive action. In crises, this inertia prevents innovation and risks turning manageable problems into systemic breakdowns.

6. Suppression of Political Pluralism

Parties and civic associations may formally exist, but their role is largely symbolic. By excluding alternative viewpoints and neutralizing dissent, bureaucratic regimes deprive themselves of constructive criticism. Over time, the absence of pluralism narrows the policy horizon, weakens governance quality, and deepens the sense of exclusion within society.

Historical Examples of Bureaucratic Authoritarianism

Brazil during the Military Regime and Bureaucratic Authoritarianism (1964–1985)

The Coup and the First Years of Military Rule

In the last days of March 1964, tanks rolled through Rio de Janeiro and São Paulo. Within hours President João Goulart was gone, replaced by the generals who promised to restore order. Behind them stood not only Brazil's conservative elites and the Catholic hierarchy, but also Washington. Declassified records later revealed Operation Brother Sam: a U.S. naval force waiting off the coast, ready to supply the coup with fuel and ammunition if resistance broke out.

General Humberto de Alencar Castelo Branco took office, and the long night of military rule began. Civil liberties were curtailed at once. More than 400 politicians lost their mandates, professors were expelled from universities, and a torrent of decrees known as Institutional Acts replaced the 1946 Constitution.

Institutional Acts and the Machinery of Control

Each Institutional Act pulled Brazil further from democracy.

- **AI-1 (1964)** suspended political rights on a massive scale.
- **AI-2 (1965)** dissolved the existing party system, replacing it with two creations of the regime: the loyalist ARENA and the docile opposition MDB.
- **AI-5 (1968)** was the decisive blow. It empowered the president to shut down Congress, suspend habeas corpus, and rule by decree. From that moment censorship, arbitrary arrests, and torture became permanent features of the political landscape.

From Military Dictatorship to Bureaucratic Authoritarianism

At first the generals appeared to hold power directly. But as the years passed, governance shifted into the hands of technocrats: economists, engineers, administrators trained abroad.

The Ministry of Planning, the BNDES development bank, and state companies in oil, steel, and energy became the true engines of policy. Budgets were long-term, leadership stable, and projects insulated from politics. Here, in the web of ministries and councils, lay the essence of what political scientist Guillermo O'Donnell would call *bureaucratic authoritarianism*: a system where technocratic order replaced democratic debate, and modernization outweighed participation.

The "Brazilian Miracle"

Between 1968 and 1973, Brazil lived through what seemed like a miracle. GDP rose by 10–11% a year. Steel plants multiplied, petrochemical complexes appeared, and car factories expanded. The state poured money into giant infrastructure projects: the Trans-Amazonian Highway, intended to open the rainforest, and the colossal Itaipu Dam, for a time the largest in the world.

But this miracle was built on debt. External borrowing jumped from $3 billion in 1964 to $55 billion in 1979, and by 1982 it crossed $90 billion. The dream collapsed into the nightmare of the 1980s: inflation surged beyond 200% a year, foreign creditors dictated terms, and growth evaporated.

Repression and Fear

Economic progress went hand in hand with repression. The SNI intelligence service and DOPS police watched every movement. DOI-CODI interrogation centers became synonymous with torture. According to Brazil's National Truth Commission, more than 20,000 people were imprisoned for political reasons and at least 434 were killed or disappeared.

Censorship muzzled the press and even popular music. Artists like Caetano Veloso and Gilberto Gil were forced into exile. Fear became part of daily life, and silence often the safest form of survival.

Society Pushes Back

By the late 1970s, the regime's armor began to crack.

- Workers in São Paulo's industrial belt launched strikes of historic scale, led by Luiz Inácio Lula da Silva, the future president.

- The Catholic Church, inspired by liberation theology, gave shelter to activists and denounced torture and inequality.

- Civil society found its voice through underground newspapers, human rights lawyers, musicians, and filmmakers who challenged the official narrative.

The International Setting

For Washington in the 1960s, Brazil was a cornerstone against communism. The U.S. supplied training (including at the School of the Americas) and diplomatic cover. But by the late 1970s the tone had changed. President Jimmy Carter's emphasis on human rights increased pressure on Brasília, even as the 1973 oil crisis and global recession forced Brazil to borrow ever more abroad. By the early 1980s, soaring U.S. interest rates pushed Brazil into full-blown debt crisis.

The Long Road to Democracy

President Ernesto Geisel (1974–1979) understood the regime could not last unchanged. He began the slow abertura — loosening censorship, curbing the security services, and allowing more political activity. His successor João Figueiredo (1979–1985) went further: a 1979 Amnesty Law allowed exiles to return, and the two-party system was abolished.

By the early 1980s, the Diretas Já movement brought millions into the streets demanding direct elections. Though Congress blocked immediate reform, the tide could not be turned. In January 1985, the electoral college chose civilian politician Tancredo Neves as president, ending 21 years of military rule. His sudden death placed José Sarney in office, ushering Brazil back to democracy.

Why the Regime Became Bureaucratic Authoritarian

Brazil's dictatorship illustrates O'Donnell's model:

1. **Technocrats at the Helm** — civilian experts guided economic and social modernization.
2. **Institutionalized Planning** — agencies and state firms executed long-term projects shielded from politics.
3. **Continuity Across Presidents** — five generals came and went, but the bureaucratic structure endured.
4. **Controlled Politics** — ARENA and MDB gave a façade of democracy without real competition.
5. **Economic Strategy** — rapid industrialization required centralized planning, strengthening bureaucratic power.
6. **Public Alienation** — society was excluded, and by the 1980s discontent broke the regime's legitimacy.

Distinction from Classical Military Dictatorship

Brazil's generals retained veto power, but everyday governance belonged to the bureaucracy. This gave stability for grand projects but silenced the nation's voice. Unlike Chile or Argentina, where juntas ruled directly, Brazil's regime became a *machine of administrators*. That machine built highways and dams, but it also created distance, repression, and debt. When society rose in the 1980s, the technocratic shell proved too rigid to adapt — and it crumbled.

South Korea under Park Chung-hee (1961–1979)

Rise to Power

On 16 May 1961, tanks entered Seoul under the command of General Park Chung-hee. The short-lived democratic government of Prime Minister Chang Myon collapsed overnight. Park stood at the center of the new order, yet the strength of the regime did not rest solely on his will or on the generals who backed him. It was anchored in a powerful administrative–technocratic machine: economists, engineers, and planners who gave the state a new sense of purpose. Park provided the political shield, the bureaucracy drew the blueprint.

Bureaucratic and Technocratic Governance

From the beginning, institutions were reshaped to serve a single mission — development. In 1961, the regime created the Economic Planning Board (EPB), the command post of national modernization. It designed five-year development plans, coordinated ministries, and set industrial priorities. Ministries, staffed by university-trained technocrats, carried out targeted policies in infrastructure, finance, and trade. Many officials had studied in the United States or Japan and returned with both technical skills and a sense of urgency. Decision-making became centralized and methodical, insulated from the turbulence of public politics.

The "Korean Economic Miracle"

The bureaucracy's central task was to transform South Korea from a war-ravaged, agrarian society into an industrial nation. Through state-directed credit, export promotion, and protection for infant industries, the transformation was breathtaking.

- **GDP growth** averaged more than 8% per year between 1962 and 1979.
- The **Gyeongbu Expressway** (1970) stitched together Seoul and Busan, moving goods and people with unprecedented speed.
- The **Heavy and Chemical Industry Drive** of the 1970s expanded steel, shipbuilding, petrochemicals, and automobiles.
- Chaebol conglomerates — **Hyundai, Samsung, Daewoo** — flourished under state guidance, receiving cheap credit and privileged access to contracts.

The state–business alliance was run less by patronage than by institutions. Success or failure was measured in export figures and production quotas, reinforcing the bureaucratic nature of the regime.

Political Repression and Authoritarian Control

Economic growth came with a price. Political life was suffocated. Opposition parties were harassed, labor unions tightly controlled, and the press censored. The Yushin Constitution of 1972 effectively crowned Park as president for life, allowing him to dissolve the National Assembly, appoint a third of its members, and govern by decree. Surveillance was constant, arrests routine, and imprisonment the fate of those who resisted. Civil freedoms were sacrificed on the altar of development.

Assassination of Park Chung-hee

The end came abruptly on 26 October 1979. At a dinner in a KCIA safe house in Seoul, Park sat with his security chief Cha Ji-chul and KCIA director Kim Jae-gyu. An argument flared over repression and Cha's heavy-handed methods. Kim left the room, returned with a pistol, and shot Cha before turning the gun on Park. The president died instantly.

Kim later claimed he acted to prevent the dictatorship from tightening further and to open the way for democracy. Instead, his act plunged South Korea into another cycle of military rule. Arrested and executed in 1980, Kim did not live to see the reforms he imagined.

Aftermath and Continued Authoritarianism

After Park's death, South Korea entered turmoil. Martial law was imposed, and General Chun Doo-hwan seized power in 1980. Authoritarianism endured, culminating in the bloody suppression of the Gwangju Uprising. Only with the June Democracy Movement of 1987 did South Korea finally embark on a sustained transition to democracy.

Park Chung-hee's Regime as Bureaucratic Authoritarianism

Park's system was neither a pure personalist dictatorship nor a simple military junta. It was a hybrid where authoritarian leadership rested on the shoulders of a disciplined, professional bureaucracy.

1. **Delegation to Technocrats** – The EPB institutionalized planning, empowering economists and administrators to design national development.

2. **Centralized State Planning** – Five-year plans set long-term goals, from heavy industry to infrastructure, ensuring consistency.

3. **State–Business Alliance** – Bureaucrats directed the chaebol through credit and protection, steering them toward exports.

4. **Military in the Background** – The generals guaranteed security, but civilian ministries ran daily governance.

5. **Controlled Politics** – The Yushin Constitution kept the façade of institutions while eliminating real competition.

6. **Legacy** – GDP per capita rose more than fourfold during Park's rule, but the exclusion of pluralism created tensions that exploded after his death.

Difference from Classical Military Dictatorships

In Chile under Pinochet or Argentina under the junta, officers dominated both security and economic policy. In South Korea, the military guaranteed regime survival, but it was technocrats and bureaucrats who steered the economy and built institutions. The result was the Korean economic miracle, achieved at the cost of suppressed freedoms and a rigid, authoritarian order.

Chapter 4
Electoral (Hybrid) Authoritarianism:
Elections Without Genuine Political Competition

> **Electoral (Hybrid) Authoritarianism** is a type of political regime in which democratic institutions — such as regular elections, a multiparty system, a parliament, and an independent judiciary — formally exist, but in practice their functioning is severely constrained by authoritarian power.

Characteristics

Electoral authoritarianism is a political model that stands between democracy and authoritarian rule, blending features of both.

Key Features

1) Formal Institutions without Real Autonomy

The state retains the outward structure of democracy: elections are held, parties are registered, parliaments convene, and courts exist. Yet these institutions lack genuine independence. The executive dominates them, preventing legislatures and courts from exercising oversight. Political parties and civic organizations face restrictions that limit their ability to act freely.

2) Restricted Competition and Manipulated Elections

Elections serve as the main instrument of legitimacy, but they are shaped by administrative pressure, censorship, and intimidation of the opposition. Results are frequently manipulated, making a change of power through the ballot box nearly impossible. The opposition is allowed to exist but remains politically powerless.

3) A Dual Character

What defines electoral authoritarianism is its mixed nature. It preserves the image of democracy, which helps secure internal stability and maintain a measure of credibility abroad. At the same time, it relies on authoritarian practices—suppressing civic activism, weakening the opposition, and controlling the political sphere. This balance enables ruling elites to hold power without resorting to open repression.

4) Legal Mechanisms of Control

Instead of naked coercion, these regimes often use laws to restrict opponents. Rules on party registration, campaign financing, and media regulation are formally legal but designed to disadvantage challengers.

5) Management of International Reputation

Because they cannot afford to appear as outright dictatorships, such regimes invest in carefully staged reforms and controlled liberalization. These measures are meant to reassure foreign observers without loosening the ruling elite's hold on power.

Strengths of Electoral (Hybrid) Authoritarianism

1. Legitimacy through Elections

Regular elections give the regime a formal right to rule. They preserve the outward image of democracy and allow leaders to claim the consent of the people. This appearance of popular approval lowers the risk of mass unrest and reduces the danger of isolation abroad. With a democratic façade in place, the regime maintains stable relations with the international community.

2. Controlled Space for Opposition

Although political life is tightly restricted, opposition parties, civic groups, and independent media are not entirely silenced. Their limited presence creates an impression of pluralism and eases social tension. Allowing measured criticism keeps frustration from building into large-scale protest.

3. Adaptability under Pressure

When faced with demands for reform—whether from citizens or foreign actors—the system shows flexibility. Electoral rules may be amended, censorship slightly relaxed, or observers invited. Such steps meet external expectations without loosening the ruling elite's control. This ability to bend without breaking helps the regime defuse criticism, avoid sanctions, and survive political crises.

4. Shaping an International Image

Credibility abroad is vital. To preserve it, regimes introduce selective reforms and symbolic gestures designed to reassure foreign partners. These moves help secure economic ties, foreign aid, and diplomatic support while leaving the foundations of power untouched.

5. Balancing Stability and Change

The strength of electoral authoritarianism lies in its balance. It mixes limited openness with firm control, avoiding both the stagnation of total repression and the chaos of uncontrolled democratization. This capacity to steer change without losing stability makes the system durable over time.

6. Distribution of Resources and Patronage

Control of state resources allows ruling elites to build loyalty. Jobs, subsidies, and public programs are often directed to supportive regions or groups, rewarding compliance and discouraging dissent. Patronage networks turn economic dependency into political support.

7. Durability of Rule through Institutions

By combining regular electoral procedures with tight control, these regimes create an appearance of predictability. The rhythm of elections and parliamentary sessions provides stability, while manipulation ensures continuity of rule. This blend reduces the shocks typical of openly repressive dictatorships and helps the regime endure for decades.

Weaknesses of Electoral (Hybrid) Authoritarianism

1. Fragile Legitimacy

Elections are held, but their fairness is widely doubted. Manipulated results, pressure on voters, and persecution of opponents create mistrust among citizens and criticism from abroad. This fragile legitimacy weakens public support and steadily erodes the authority of the ruling elite.

2. Risk of Social Upheaval

With no genuine competition and few legal avenues to influence power, frustration grows beneath the surface. Excluded from normal political life, people are more likely to take to the streets. Protests can swell rapidly, sometimes turning into unrest or fueling radical opposition. Each eruption forces the regime to suppress dissent at high political and economic cost.

3. Suppression of Rights and Freedoms

Maintaining control demands constant restrictions on liberty. Independent media are censored, civic groups harassed, and opposition movements silenced. These measures instill fear, but they also deepen resentment. Over time, repression erodes social trust, radicalizes protest, and destabilizes the political order itself.

4. Erosion of Institutions

The repeated manipulation of democratic procedures destroys faith in state institutions. Electoral commissions, courts, and parliaments are seen less as neutral arbiters than as tools of the regime. Once stripped of credibility, they lose their capacity to stabilize political life.

5. Exposure to International Pressure

Hybrid regimes depend on a democratic façade to maintain foreign partnerships. When abuses become too visible, pressure mounts in the form of sanctions, reduced investment, and diplomatic isolation. If the pretense of reform cannot be sustained, their international position becomes precarious.

6. Internal Elite Conflicts

These systems rely on the cohesion of the ruling circle. Yet competition for resources, offices, and influence often sparks rivalries among elites. Such internal fractures may destabilize the regime from within, posing a greater threat than street protests.

7. Economic Vulnerability

The survival of electoral authoritarianism rests on access to resources that sustain patronage networks and repressive structures. Economic crises, declining revenues, or loss of foreign aid undermine this foundation. Without steady resources, the regime's ability to buy loyalty and suppress dissent weakens sharply.

Historical Examples of Electoral (Hybrid) Authoritarianism

Peru under Alberto Fujimori (1990–2000)

Alberto Fujimori rose to power in 1990 through democratic elections, carried by a population exhausted by economic collapse, political turmoil, and the threat of insurgency. His victory inspired hope for decisive reform. Yet within two years, the democratic framework began to unravel.

In 1992, Fujimori staged a self-coup, dissolving parliament and suspending the constitution. He claimed these steps were needed to defeat terrorism and corruption, but in practice they concentrated power in the executive. The legislature was later restored, though firmly under government control, while the judiciary lost its independence and became an instrument of presidential authority.

Elections continued on schedule, but they no longer offered real competition. State resources funded campaigns, opposition parties were harassed, and the media was censored or co-opted through financial pressure. These measures deprived rivals of a fair chance to contest power.

Over the decade, the regime grew increasingly personal. Fujimori relied heavily on his intelligence chief, Vladimiro Montesinos, whose network penetrated the military, security services, and press. Corruption became entrenched, with public funds diverted for political and personal ends.

The turning point came in 2000, when videotapes revealed Montesinos bribing politicians and journalists. The scandal ignited mass protests, cost Fujimori his international backing, and left him isolated. In November of that year, he fled to Japan. His later attempt at a political return ended in extradition from Chile in 2007. In 2009 he was convicted of human rights violations, corruption, and authorizing death squads, receiving a 25-year prison sentence.

Though pardoned briefly in 2017 on humanitarian grounds, legal reversals returned him to prison. Released again in 2023 due to ill health, he died in Lima in 2024 at the age of 86.

Fujimori's Regime as Electoral Authoritarianism

Fujimori's decade in power shows how democratic procedures can be preserved in form yet stripped of substance. His system combined elections, parties, and formal state institutions with authoritarian control.

1. **Controlled Institutions** – Parliament and courts retained their formal structures but operated without independence, subordinated to presidential authority.

2. **Elections as Instruments of Power** – Voting took place regularly but was marred by manipulation, biased media coverage, and the use of state resources in favor of the incumbent.

3. **Restricted Political Space** – Opposition parties faced legal, financial, and administrative obstacles that curtailed their ability to campaign effectively.

4. **Media Capture and Censorship** – Independent outlets were silenced through intimidation or financial pressure, while major networks were brought under government influence.

5. **Personalized Rule** – Decision-making centered on Fujimori and Montesinos, whose influence extended across military, security, and media structures.

6. **Collapse of Legitimacy** – Corruption scandals exposed the regime's manipulation, sparking public mobilization, defections within the elite, and ultimately Fujimori's downfall.

Fujimori's Peru illustrates the fragile nature of electoral authoritarianism: a system that preserves the rituals of democracy, while ensuring that power remains tightly in the hands of the incumbent.

Philippines under Ferdinand Marcos (1965–1986)

Ferdinand Marcos came to power in 1965 through democratic elections. In his early years, he launched ambitious social and economic reforms. Yet by the late 1960s, his leadership was turning toward authoritarianism.

Imposition of Martial Law and Concentration of Power

In 1972, Marcos declared martial law, officially as a response to communist insurgency and social unrest. In practice, it became the instrument for consolidating personal control. Democratic structures continued to exist in name: parliament convened, courts issued rulings, and elections were held. But their independence was dismantled. The legislature was reduced to ceremony, and the judiciary lost its autonomy, serving instead as an obedient arm of the regime.

Elections, Media Control, and Suppression of Opposition

Elections remained on the calendar, but they lost credibility. Fraud, intimidation, and the use of state resources guaranteed Marcos' dominance. Independent journalism disappeared under strict censorship. Television, radio, and newspapers turned into platforms of official propaganda, silencing critical voices. Opposition leaders faced harassment, imprisonment, or exile. The 1983 assassination of Benigno "Ninoy" Aquino Jr., the country's most prominent opposition figure, shocked the nation and became a catalyst for mass protest.

Corruption and Elite Enrichment

Marcos' presidency was deeply marked by corruption. His family and closest allies amassed enormous wealth through the illegal diversion of public resources. Patronage networks tied political elites, military leaders, and business groups to the regime, rewarding loyalty with privilege. The contrast between the luxury of the ruling elite and the poverty of most citizens intensified public resentment.

The People Power Revolution and the Fall of the Regime

By the mid-1980s, economic decline, corruption, and political repression had eroded the regime's foundations. Aquino's assassination accelerated the breakdown of public trust. In February 1986, millions filled the streets of Manila in the peaceful demonstrations known as the People Power Revolution. The loss of support from the military and the international community sealed Marcos' fate. Forced from office, he fled with his family to Hawaii, where he died in 1989.

The Marcos Regime as Electoral Authoritarianism

Marcos' two decades in power preserved the outward symbols of democracy while steadily stripping them of substance.

1. **Formal Institutions as Ornaments**

   After martial law in 1972, the structures of constitutional rule remained but functioned without autonomy. Parliament and courts continued to exist, yet their decisions merely ratified presidential authority.

2. **Elections Without Real Choice**

   Voting became a managed performance. Results were shaped by fraud and vote-rigging. Opposition candidates were harassed, intimidated, or arrested. Media coverage favored the ruling camp, while state resources ensured electoral dominance. These elections provided international legitimacy but denied citizens any real opportunity for change.

3. **Controlled Pluralism and Censored Media**

   A multiparty system survived in form, but opposition groups were fragmented, co-opted, or weakened by legal restrictions. Independent journalism was extinguished under censorship, and investigative reporting vanished from public life.

4. **Authoritarian Suppression of Dissent**

   Political opponents were silenced through arrests, imprisonment, or exile. The murder of Aquino in 1983 revealed the regime's readiness to use violence as a last resort to preserve power.

5. **Personalized Power and Patronage Networks**

   Real authority centered on Marcos and his wife Imelda. Patronage bound the political elite, military, and business leaders, trading loyalty for wealth and influence.

6. **The Façade of Democracy as Legitimacy**

   Maintaining democratic forms — elections, parties, courts — gave the regime international credibility, securing aid and diplomatic support, particularly vital during the Cold War.

7. **Collapse of the Hybrid System**

   By the mid-1980s, economic decline, entrenched corruption, and public outrage over Aquino's assassination shattered the regime's legitimacy.

Distinction from Full Autocracy

The Philippines under Marcos never abolished elections, parties, or institutions. Instead, it retained them as instruments of control and legitimacy. This duality — preserving democratic rituals while denying their essence — places the regime squarely within the model of electoral authoritarianism.

Conclusion

Authoritarian regimes, despite their variety, share the same foundation: power gathered into the hands of a few, the curtailment of political freedoms, and the weakening of civil society. Yet within this shared design, each type of authoritarianism follows its own script, with distinctive strengths and built-in limits.

Military regimes rely on discipline and speed. They can impose order swiftly, like a commander barking commands on the parade ground. But their strength is also their weakness: rivalries inside the officer corps and the constant specter of a coup mean the regime lives in permanent unease, never far from implosion.

Personalist regimes place everything on a single figure. Decisions come quickly, crises are confronted head-on, and challenges met with immediate force. Yet when the entire machine runs on one person's energy, it becomes brittle. Once the leader falters, the system, like a tent without its central pole, risks collapsing overnight.

Bureaucratic authoritarianism entrusts the state to technocrats and administrators. At first, it resembles a well-oiled machine, steady and predictable. Over time, however, the gears begin to rust: corruption creeps in, the gap between rulers and society hardens into a wall, and the system slows until it risks seizing up altogether.

Electoral, or hybrid, authoritarianism plays a double game. Ballot boxes are displayed, parliaments meet, and courts issue rulings, yet the outcome is written before the first vote is cast. Elections turn into stagecraft, a theater of choice without the substance of real competition. Gradually, the façade cracks, and cynicism erodes what legitimacy remains.

The staying power of any authoritarian order rests on its ability to control institutions, silence opponents, dominate information, and manage public expectations. In moments of crisis, authoritarianism may appear to offer the quickest route to stability, a promise to restore order when democracy falters. But repression accumulates pressure, and no grip is strong enough to hold forever; eventually, the strain breaks through.

In today's interconnected world, globalization, digital technology, and the reach of social media make it ever harder to keep truth under lock and key. Every smartphone is a camera, a microphone, and a rallying point. Faced with this reality, authoritarian regimes confront a choice: to seal themselves into fortress-like isolation, or to take the slower but more sustainable path toward openness and reform. That decision will determine not only their survival, but the future of the societies they govern.

SECTION 3. TOTALITARIAN REGIME

> **A totalitarian regime** is a political system characterized by the state's complete control over every sphere of public and private life, the dominance of a single mandatory ideology, and the total absence of political and civil freedoms.

INTRODUCTION

The term "totalitarianism" comes from the Latin *totalis*, meaning "complete" or "all-encompassing." The defining feature of such a regime is that power is not limited to controlling political or economic institutions but actively intrudes into the personal lives of citizens, regulating their behavior, beliefs, values, and even private thoughts.

The Main Characteristics of a Totalitarian State

1) A Single Mandatory Ideology

At the heart of a totalitarian state lies an officially sanctioned ideology declared to be absolute and the only correct worldview. This ideology becomes the foundation for all state decisions and dictates societal norms and codes of conduct. The state tolerates no dissent and ruthlessly suppresses any challenge to the official doctrine. Through education, propaganda, and mass events, totalitarian regimes aim to embed the ideology deeply in the consciousness of every citizen.

2) Monopoly on Power and a Cult of Personality

Totalitarian regimes concentrate all political power in the hands of a single party, one leader, or a small ruling elite. Other political parties or movements are banned and eliminated. Often, a central leader emerges as the embodiment of the regime, wielding virtually unlimited authority. Around this figure, a cult of personality is built, portraying the leader as possessing superhuman qualities, wisdom, and unquestionable authority. This cult is sustained through constant propaganda, portraits, monuments, and ceremonial acts of reverence, reinforcing control over society.

3) Complete State Control Over All Spheres of Society

A totalitarian state seeks to dominate not only the political and economic life of society but also every other aspect — culture, art, science, education, religion, and even family life. The state dictates the content of books, films, theater productions, and scientific research. Education is shaped to instill loyalty to the regime and devotion to the state ideology from early childhood. Private life is subject to scrutiny, with the state intervening in daily behavior, personal relationships, and moral values.

4) Mass Terror and Repression

Systematic mass terror is a core instrument of a totalitarian state. To eradicate dissent and ensure absolute obedience, the regime employs arrests, torture, executions, exile, and imprisonment in labor camps. These repressive measures are deliberate, far-reaching, and affect vast segments of the population. An atmosphere of fear and suspicion is deliberately cultivated and maintained by state security agencies to prevent any attempt at resistance or criticism.

5) All-Encompassing Propaganda and Strict Censorship

Totalitarian regimes operate a powerful machinery of propaganda and censorship to create a unified public opinion and secure support for their policies. All mass media — press, radio, television, and later the internet — are entirely state-controlled, transmitting only information aligned with the state ideology. Alternative viewpoints, criticism, or discussion of sensitive issues are strictly censored and immediately suppressed. This enables the regime to construct a single, officially approved worldview for its citizens.

6) Militarization and Societal Mobilization

A common feature of totalitarian states is the militarization of public life and the mobilization of the population for mass campaigns. The state promotes the cult of strength, discipline, and military achievement, urging citizens to be ever-ready to confront external and internal "enemies." People are organized into mass associations — youth movements, professional unions, sports societies, paramilitary groups — enabling the authorities to keep constant watch over the population and direct their energy toward regime goals.

7) Centralized Economy and State Planning

Many totalitarian regimes operate a command economy in which the state fully controls production, distribution, and pricing. Private enterprise is either heavily restricted or eliminated entirely. Economic decisions are made to serve ideological objectives rather than efficiency, and central planning is used as a political tool.

8) Use of Mass Organizations as Instruments of Control

Beyond political and military structures, the state creates mass organizations — women's associations, professional guilds, cultural societies — that operate as extensions of government authority. Through them, the regime monitors and influences all aspects of social activity.

9) Historical Revisionism and Control Over Collective Memory

The regime actively rewrites history, removing inconvenient facts and glorifying its own achievements and leadership. This version of history is reinforced through school curricula, monuments, films, and official holidays, ensuring that the state's narrative becomes the only accepted one.

10) Suppression or Co-optation of Religion

Religious institutions are either placed under complete state control or replaced with a form of "civil religion" centered on the ideology and the leader. Independent religious activity is banned or heavily restricted to prevent alternative sources of authority or loyalty.

11) Comprehensive Surveillance System

In addition to official security services, a network of informants, agents, and collaborators is established to monitor private conversations, relationships, and behavior. Surveillance becomes a permanent feature of daily life, eroding trust among citizens and ensuring that dissent is detected and crushed at its earliest stages.

Totalitarianism is the most rigid and intrusive form of political organization. Under it, individual freedoms and rights are entirely subordinated to the state's interests, and every sphere of public and private life is regulated and controlled to preserve absolute power. This model relies not only on overt repression but also on reshaping society's beliefs, memories, and institutions to align completely with the will of the regime.

Chapter 1

Ideological Totalitarianism:

Absolute Control Based on a Single State Ideology

> **Ideological totalitarianism** is a form of totalitarian regime in which the state exercises absolute control over society and the personal lives of citizens through the imposition of a single official ideology — mandatory for all and allowing no dissent.

Characteristics

In ideological totalitarianism, an official state ideology stands at the very core of the political system. It is declared the absolute, universal, and mandatory truth, regulating not only the political order but also the everyday life of citizens. This ideology sets uniform standards of behavior, shapes a common system of values and worldview, and leaves no room for alternative opinions or perspectives.

Main Features of Ideological Totalitarianism

1) **Absolute Dominance of a Single Ideology**

The official ideology is proclaimed as the ultimate truth that defines the worldview of all citizens. The state works to implant it into every sphere of life — from politics and the economy to private relationships, daily routines, and even family matters. Alternative beliefs, religions, or philosophies are categorically rejected and treated as threats to social unity and state stability.

2) **Total State Control over Information, Education, and Culture**

All mass media are fully subordinated to the state and serve solely to disseminate the official ideology and propaganda. The information space is tightly controlled, leaving no platform for dissenting voices. Educational institutions become tools for ideological indoctrination, instilling uniformity of thought from an early age. Cultural institutions and artistic expression are permitted only within the boundaries defined by the state, suppressing any freedom of creative expression.

3) **Systematic Persecution and Suppression of Dissent**

Any deviation from the official ideology is treated as a direct threat to the regime. Dissent is met with harsh repression: opposition figures, critics, and those expressing independent views may face arrest, exile, internment in labor camps, or even physical elimination. A powerful network of secret police and security services is maintained to detect and neutralize "enemies of the people."

4) Cult of Personality and Mass Mobilization

Ideological totalitarianism often builds an elaborate cult of personality around the leader, portraying them as the living embodiment of the official ideology and endowing them with superhuman qualities. State-organized mass events, rituals, and propaganda campaigns reinforce the image of unity and loyalty. This emotional engagement makes citizens more politically compliant and easier to mobilize.

5) Militarization of Society and the Perpetual Search for Enemies

The regime sustains constant mobilization by portraying internal and external "enemies" as ongoing threats. Citizens are drawn into military and paramilitary organizations, as well as mass political campaigns. The militarization of public life not only promotes discipline and unity but also serves as a means to suppress dissatisfaction and protest.

6) Historical Revisionism and Control Over Collective Memory

The state rewrites history to suit the needs of the regime, erasing inconvenient facts and glorifying its achievements and leadership. This official narrative is enforced through school curricula, monuments, cultural productions, and national holidays, ensuring that the regime's version of history becomes the only accepted one.

7) Control Over Religion and Spiritual Life

Independent religious organizations are banned or placed under strict state control. Religion is either adapted to serve the ideology or replaced with a "civil religion" centered on the leader and the state's doctrine, eliminating any competing sources of moral authority.

8) Comprehensive Surveillance System

Beyond official security forces, the regime develops a dense network of informants and collaborators to monitor ideological conformity in both public and private life. This constant surveillance erodes trust among citizens and deters any form of dissent.

9) Mandatory Participation in Mass Organizations

Citizens are required to join state-controlled youth groups, professional associations, cultural societies, and other mass organizations. These bodies act as channels for ideological indoctrination and tools for close monitoring of the population.

10) Ideological Control of Economic Policy

Economic decisions are made in accordance with the principles of the official ideology, even when this contradicts considerations of efficiency. The economy is often centrally planned and subordinated to political and ideological priorities.

Strengths of Ideological Totalitarianism

1. High Level of Societal Mobilization Toward Common Goals

The dominance of a single state ideology allows the regime to mobilize society with exceptional efficiency to address complex and large-scale challenges. With clear ideological unity and centralized control, the state can direct the resources and efforts of all citizens in a single direction. People act in coordination, like parts of a single organism, achieving set objectives quickly and with minimal effort spent on reconciling competing interests.

2. Capacity for Centralized Planning and Execution of Major Projects

Full state control over political, economic, cultural, and social life enables the rapid and effective planning, organization, and implementation of large-scale economic, military, scientific, and infrastructure projects. Decisions are made centrally and executed with high discipline and organizational precision. This proves especially effective for industrialization, the construction of massive infrastructure, the implementation of ambitious scientific programs, or military mobilization.

3. Rapid Decision-Making and Operational Efficiency

In an ideological totalitarian system, there are no protracted political debates, partisan rivalries, or parliamentary stalemates typical of democratic societies. This allows decisions to be made swiftly and implemented immediately. The ability to respond quickly to crises or emergencies is a significant advantage compared to slower, more bureaucratic systems.

4. Provision of Social and Political Stability (Short-Term)

Strict ideological discipline, centralized control, and the complete suppression of opposition make society stable and predictable in the short run. The outward social uniformity, shaped by official ideology and mass propaganda, reduces the risk of internal conflicts and fragmentation. This fosters public order and predictability in state actions, especially in the short term.

5. Effective Resource Mobilization in Extreme Situations

Ideological totalitarianism demonstrates particular strength in times of war, large-scale economic downturns, or natural disasters. Thanks to centralized governance and powerful ideological propaganda, the state can swiftly mobilize resources, manpower, and production capacity to address emerging threats. In such circumstances, society often exhibits a high degree of obedience and willingness to sacrifice for the common cause.

6. Long-Term Consolidation of Power

A unified ideology helps maintain political dominance over decades, fostering a public perception that the existing regime is the natural and only legitimate order. This deep-rooted acceptance can delay or weaken challenges to authority.

7. Unified Value System and Collective Identity

Official ideology shapes a shared sense of belonging among citizens, strengthening national unity and cohesion. This collective identity can serve as a stabilizing force in the face of external pressure or internal unrest.

8. High Level of Social Manageability

Through control over information, education, and cultural life, the state can easily shape public opinion and mass behavior, adjusting them to its strategic objectives.

9. Integration of All Spheres into a Single Strategic Plan

Political, economic, military, cultural, and educational policies are interlinked and aligned with a unified ideological strategy, eliminating conflicts between different sectors of governance.

10. Potential for External Ideological Influence

In certain cases, a state can use its ideology to exert influence beyond its borders — for example, by engaging diaspora communities or exporting ideological narratives to other countries to expand its sphere of influence.

Weaknesses of Ideological Totalitarianism

1. Complete Suppression of Freedom of Thought and Expression

One of the central weaknesses of ideological totalitarianism is the rigid suppression of intellectual freedom, free speech, and creativity. The state's absolute monopoly on ideology leaves no room for alternative opinions or independent viewpoints. Any expression of individuality or criticism is treated as hostile and is immediately silenced through repression.

These conditions lead to intellectual and creative stagnation. Citizens are deprived of the opportunity to voice their own ideas, develop original projects, or engage freely in scientific and artistic work. Over time, cultural life declines, and society as a whole loses its creative and intellectual potential.

2. Mass Repression and a Climate of Fear

Constant state control over citizens' lives requires the regular use of mass repression against any form of dissent. Security services, secret police, networks of informants, and systems of punishment create an atmosphere of pervasive fear and mutual suspicion. People live in constant expectation of punishment or persecution, leading to deep psychological trauma and moral degradation.

As trust erodes, citizens avoid close relationships, minimize contact with others, and withdraw into themselves. This breaks traditional social bonds and produces an atomized society incapable of healthy communication or collective action.

3. Social Stagnation and Cultural Isolation

The drive to control all information and block outside influences results in the cultural and intellectual isolation of society. Strict censorship limits access to new knowledge, ideas, and global achievements. Without the exchange of views and contact with other cultures, intellectual and cultural stagnation sets in.

A closed society loses the ability to evolve and adapt to change. In the long run, this leads to systemic crisis, as the state becomes incapable of responding to external challenges or carrying out effective modernization.

4. Inefficient Economic and Social Planning

Total state control over the economy and social life eliminates feedback mechanisms and free exchange of information. Decisions are made exclusively from the top down, based on ideological priorities rather than actual needs and objective conditions.

Inevitably, this produces inefficiencies — shortages of goods, resource misallocation, breakdowns in production chains, and a declining quality of life. Over time, these distortions develop into systemic crises and trigger social unrest.

5. Instability and Vulnerability During Leadership Changes or Ideological Crises

An ideological totalitarian regime built on the absolute authority of a leader and rigid dogma is extremely vulnerable to moments of crisis, the leader's death, or weakening ideological control. The absence of institutional mechanisms for peaceful power transfer often leads to sharp political conflict and internal struggles for leadership. The sudden departure or death of a leader can trigger events that destabilize the entire regime. If the ideology loses its persuasive power and the repressive apparatus weakens, the system may collapse abruptly and disintegrate entirely.

6. Overdependence on Propaganda and Indoctrination

Sustaining control requires constant propaganda, which becomes less effective over time as the gap between official narratives and lived reality grows. This erosion of credibility can accelerate public disillusionment and make the regime's fall more sudden and severe.

7. Suppression of Innovation and Adaptability

By stifling alternative thinking and discouraging risk-taking, ideological totalitarianism hampers technological progress and problem-solving capacity. In a rapidly changing global environment, this inability to innovate makes the regime increasingly outdated and uncompetitive.

Historical Examples of Ideological Totalitarianism
China During the Cultural Revolution (1966–1976)

In the late 1950s and early 1960s, China was reeling from the catastrophic aftermath of the "Great Leap Forward" (1958–1962). The campaign's failed economic policies, forced collectivization, and unrealistic production targets had led to a severe famine, causing the deaths of an estimated 20 to 30 million people. The country faced an economic crisis, agricultural decline, and deep disillusionment among the population. Within the Chinese Communist Party (CCP), political rivalries were intensifying between Mao Zedong's radical supporters and more moderate factions, who advocated pragmatic reforms to restore economic stability. Mao, perceiving these moderates as a threat to his ideological vision and personal authority, decided to "relaunch" the revolution through a sweeping cultural and ideological purge.

In 1966, Mao initiated the Great Proletarian Cultural Revolution, presenting it as a campaign to root out "bourgeois elements" that had allegedly infiltrated the party, government, culture, and education. At the heart of this campaign was Maoism — a uniquely Chinese adaptation of Marxism-Leninism that emphasized the revolutionary role of the peasantry and the necessity of permanent class struggle. Maoism was declared the sole political, moral, and cultural foundation of society, and adherence to it became obligatory for every citizen.

Mechanisms of Ideological Control and Mass Mobilization

The Cultural Revolution quickly transformed into the most intense period of ideological totalitarianism in modern Chinese history. Mao called upon millions of young people to form units of "Red Guards" (*hongweibing*), tasked with defending the revolution by identifying and persecuting anyone suspected of ideological deviation. The Red Guards destroyed temples, libraries, museums, and countless artifacts — estimates suggest that over 4,000 historical sites in Beijing alone were damaged or destroyed. Traditional customs, religious practices, and Confucian values were branded as "feudal" or "bourgeois" remnants to be eradicated.

Mao's "Little Red Book" — a collection of his quotations — became the ultimate moral and political guide. Distribution was massive: hundreds of millions of copies were printed and circulated, often mandatory for every household and workplace. Citizens were expected to study it daily, recite passages in workplaces, schools, and public rallies, and demonstrate loyalty through public declarations of faith in Mao's thought.

Public "struggle sessions" became a hallmark of the era: mass gatherings where accused individuals — intellectuals, teachers, former officials — were subjected to verbal abuse, humiliation, and sometimes physical violence until they confessed to "crimes" against the revolution. Revolutionary committees, often led by radical students or junior cadres, replaced existing administrations in schools, factories, and local governments, ensuring that ideological purity was enforced at every level.

Repression and Human Cost

During the decade of the Cultural Revolution, an estimated 1 to 2 million people died as a result of executions, beatings, and persecution. Tens of millions more were subjected to harassment, imprisonment, or forced relocation to rural areas for "re-education" through manual labor. Many prominent figures of Chinese intellectual and cultural life — such as philosopher Li Zehou, playwright Wu Han, and Marshal Peng Dehuai — were purged, imprisoned, or driven to suicide.

Collapse of Education and Culture

Educational institutions at all levels were shut down for years. Universities suspended academic programs, and students spent much of their time in political rallies, ideological study sessions, or traveling the country to spread revolutionary fervor. Formal education was replaced with "revolutionary practice," severely undermining the professional training of an entire generation. The arts and sciences were subordinated entirely to ideological goals, producing a cultural landscape dominated by propaganda operas, politically approved plays, and didactic literature.

Atmosphere of Fear and Fanaticism

Society was gripped by a climate of suspicion and ideological zeal. Friendships, family bonds, and professional relationships could be destroyed overnight by accusations of ideological impurity. Loyalty to Mao became the supreme measure of a citizen's worth, and any deviation — real or imagined — could result in arrest, exile, or death.

Long-Term Consequences and Lessons

The Cultural Revolution left China in deep economic, social, and cultural crisis. While the regime demonstrated its ability to mobilize vast segments of the population for short-term ideological campaigns, the long-term effects were devastating: scientific research stalled, the education system deteriorated, and cultural heritage suffered irreparable losses.

As a case of ideological totalitarianism, the Cultural Revolution illustrates how a regime with total mobilization capacity and absolute ideological control can, in its pursuit of purity and unity, generate chaos, self-destruction, and long-lasting harm to the very society it seeks to shape.

The Soviet Union (1917–1991)

The central pillar of the Soviet political system was the official state ideology of Marxism-Leninism. Regarded as the only correct and universally binding worldview, it permeated every sphere of public life and shaped the consciousness of every citizen.

From the very outset of the October Revolution in 1917, the Bolshevik government began building a society based on communist ideology. All alternative political views, parties, and movements were outlawed, and their members faced repression and persecution. The state assumed complete control over the mass media, education, science, and culture, aiming to embed Marxist-Leninist ideas into every area of public life. Schools, universities, theaters, publishing houses, and the press became powerful instruments of ideological indoctrination and propaganda.

The period of Joseph Stalin's rule (1924–1953) marked the height of ideological control. State ideology regulated not only the political behavior of citizens but also their private lives, family relations, moral norms, and even scientific research. Millions of people were arrested and sent to the GULAG labor camps for "ideological deviations" or suspected disloyalty.

Under Nikita Khrushchev (1953–1964), the regime experienced a partial liberalization, yet the state ideology remained mandatory for all citizens. While censorship eased somewhat and certain political prisoners were released, Marxism-Leninism continued to serve as the foundation of governance and social order.

During Leonid Brezhnev's tenure (1964–1982), ideological control shifted into a phase of conservative stagnation. The official ideology remained unchanged, and any attempt to criticize or revise it was immediately suppressed. The mass media operated under strict censorship; literature and the arts were tightly controlled, and access to foreign sources of information was extremely limited. This led to intellectual and cultural isolation, gradual social stagnation, and an erosion of the state's capacity to respond effectively to new challenges.

By the late 1980s, under Mikhail Gorbachev's policies of *perestroika* and *glasnost*, ideological control began to loosen. Harsh censorship was lifted, public debate was permitted, and open criticism of the official ideology became possible. However, this liberalization triggered a rapid crisis of legitimacy for the entire regime, contributing directly to its dissolution in 1991.

The Soviet case stands as a prime historical example of ideological totalitarianism: a system that, at its height, sought to regulate every aspect of life through a rigid doctrine, and which ultimately collapsed when that doctrine could no longer command the loyalty or belief of its people.

Chapter 2

Fascist Totalitarianism:
Authoritarian Nationalism as the Organizing Principle

> **Fascist totalitarianism** is a type of totalitarian political regime based on the ideology of fascism. It is characterized by extreme nationalism, militarism, a cult of the leader, and the all-encompassing control of the state over society.

Characteristics

Fascist totalitarianism is a system built on an ultranationalist ideology, rigid centralization of power, pervasive control over the economy and society, the cult of a leader, and an aggressive foreign policy. While such a regime can demonstrate efficiency in solving short-term goals, it inevitably leads to brutal repression, suppression of freedoms, and, in the long term, deep social crisis and eventual collapse.

Main Features of Fascist Totalitarianism

1) Ideology of Ultranationalism, Corporatism, and Authoritarianism

Fascist regimes are founded on extreme nationalism, promoting the belief in the exclusivity and superiority of their nation over others. The nation is portrayed as a single organic whole whose interests override personal rights and freedoms. Corporatism envisions a tightly regulated society in which economic and social groups are subordinated to the state, and private or corporate interests are directed toward national objectives. Any dissent or criticism of the official ideology is suppressed, and citizens are expected to sacrifice personal interests for those of the state and nation.

2) Strong Role of the State in the Economy and Public Life

The state actively intervenes in economic and social life, controlling key industries, financial flows, and resources. The economy becomes a tool for implementing state objectives, particularly militarization and strengthening national power.

Public life is strictly regulated: trade unions, civic organizations, and cultural associations are integrated into a unified system of state oversight. Private life, personal beliefs, and daily routines are aligned with state ideology.

3) Centralization of Power under a Strong Leader

Authority is concentrated in the hands of a single charismatic, authoritarian leader who embodies the nation and the state. A powerful cult of personality surrounds the leader, reinforced by propaganda, state symbols, and public rituals. The leader's decisions are unquestionable, and state institutions function entirely according to his directives, ensuring unity, discipline, and swift decision-making.

4) Militarism and Aggressive Foreign Policy

The military occupies a central place in national life, with expansion of armed forces and armaments treated as top priorities. Citizens are educated in a spirit of militarism, heroism, and readiness to sacrifice for the nation.

Foreign policy is characterized by expansionism, territorial conquest, and confrontations with other states. War is seen as a natural and necessary means to achieve national ambitions and prove the state's strength.

5) Mass Propaganda, Repression, and Suppression of Opposition

The state fully controls the media, spreading official ideology and shaping a uniform worldview. Alternative opinions and opposition movements are ruthlessly suppressed; their supporters face arrest, persecution, and even physical elimination. Security services and secret police maintain total control and a pervasive climate of fear.

6) Mass Mobilization and Political Indoctrination

Citizens are constantly engaged in state-controlled organizations — youth movements, labor unions, women's associations — which act as channels for political indoctrination and loyalty reinforcement.

7) Integration of Party and State

The ruling party is inseparable from the state apparatus. Party structures penetrate all government institutions, and party membership often becomes a prerequisite for career advancement.

8) Economic Autocracy with Controlled Private Property

Unlike communist regimes, fascist systems usually retain private property, but it is strictly regulated and subordinated to state interests. Business owners are compelled to align with state policies and serve national goals.

9) Cult of National Symbols and Mythologized History

National flags, emblems, slogans, parades, and monumental architecture are omnipresent. The regime creates a heroic myth about the nation's past and destiny, using it to inspire unity and justify policies.

10) Control over Culture, Art, and Science

All cultural expression serves propaganda purposes. Art is used to glorify the regime, while science is directed toward military and ideological goals.

11) Xenophobia and Discrimination

Fascist regimes deliberately foster hostility toward certain ethnic, religious, or political groups, using them as "internal enemies" to consolidate public support.

12) Patriarchal Social Model

Traditional gender roles are promoted, with women often encouraged to focus on motherhood and domestic responsibilities, and their participation in politics or business restricted.

13) Police State and Constant Surveillance

An extensive security apparatus monitors citizens' political loyalty, with networks of informants used to detect and suppress dissent.

14) Permanent State of Emergency

The regime frequently invokes internal or external threats to justify exceptional powers, restrict freedoms, and further militarize society and the economy.

Strengths of Fascist Totalitarianism

1. Effective Mobilization in Times of Crisis

A fascist regime's rigid, centralized power structure and clearly defined ideology allow for rapid mobilization of the population during deep political, economic, or social crises. Orders from the top are carried out swiftly and without challenge, enabling the state to channel resources and societal effort toward specific national objectives. This capacity can be seen in the rapid implementation of large-scale projects, post-crisis economic recovery, or military preparation.

2. High Degree of National Unity and Public Order

The ultranationalist foundation of fascism fosters a strong sense of solidarity and collective identity. Public interest is placed above individual rights, temporarily reducing internal conflict and social tension. The state's strict controls effectively suppress instability, crime, and dissent, creating a visible sense of order and stability — particularly appealing in societies emerging from economic turmoil, political disorder, or social fragmentation.

3. Centralized Planning and Rapid Implementation of Major National Programs

Significant state involvement in the economy and society allows decisions to be made and executed without prolonged political debate or bureaucratic delay. This enables swift completion of major infrastructure projects, industrialization, military modernization, and the expansion of armaments industries. All available resources can be concentrated on priority goals, producing substantial short-term results.

4. Operational Speed in Decision-Making and Reform

The absence of political competition and parliamentary deadlock means that decisions can be taken and enacted immediately. In times of crisis, such speed can be decisive, allowing the regime to implement necessary reforms or emergency measures without obstruction, even if they require significant sacrifices from the population.

5. Strong Leadership and Clear Accountability

Fascist regimes are centered around a charismatic leader who holds absolute authority. This structure creates a clear line of responsibility for decisions and offers the population a sense of strong guidance. The leader serves as a symbol of national strength and unity, bolstering public confidence in the government — particularly in difficult times — and facilitating rapid stabilization.

6. Integration of Society Through State-Controlled Organizations

Citizens are actively engaged in state-run youth, labor, and cultural organizations, which serve as vehicles for political indoctrination and national mobilization. This creates a highly organized, disciplined society where the regime can easily communicate directives and rally support for state initiatives.

7. Efficient Coordination Between Party and State

The fusion of the ruling party and the state apparatus eliminates policy conflicts and ensures unified direction in governance. Party structures penetrate all levels of administration, allowing for efficient top-down control and consistent implementation of policies.

8. Retention of Private Property Under State Direction

While the regime tightly controls the economy, it often allows private enterprise to exist under state oversight. This hybrid model can harness entrepreneurial skills and industrial capacity while ensuring they serve national and military priorities.

9. Cultivation of National Pride and Collective Purpose

The glorification of national history, culture, and symbols generates pride and a shared sense of mission, which can strengthen societal cohesion and inspire public participation in state-led projects.

10. High Level of Social Discipline

The combination of strict laws, pervasive propaganda, and visible state authority fosters discipline in daily life, reducing certain types of crime and promoting punctuality, obedience, and conformity — qualities that the regime channels into national objectives.

Weaknesses of Fascist Totalitarianism

1. Aggressive Foreign Policy and Militarism

Fascist ideology's emphasis on national superiority, expansion, and territorial conquest inevitably drives the state toward militarism and war. This results in frequent confrontations with other nations, international isolation, and the breakdown of diplomatic relations. Long wars drain resources, cause massive human losses, and often end in the regime's defeat — as historical examples from the 20th century clearly demonstrate.

2. Harsh Internal Repression and Suppression of Freedoms

Fascist regimes maintain strict systems for eliminating political opposition and dissent. Secret police, mass arrests, censorship, and brutal repression are used to crush any disagreement with official policy or ideology. The resulting climate of fear and total control strips citizens of basic rights and freedoms, stifles creative, scientific, and civic life, and over time leads to intellectual decline, cultural stagnation, and social atomization.

3. High Risk of Catastrophic Wars

The ideological focus on national supremacy and expansionism almost guarantees involvement in large-scale wars. Such conflicts bring catastrophic consequences — massive casualties, destruction of infrastructure, economic collapse, and social chaos. Historically, most fascist regimes have ended in defeat in wars they themselves initiated.

4. Economic Instability and Long-Term Inefficiency

While fascist regimes can deliver rapid economic growth in the short term by mobilizing all available resources, in the long term this model is highly unstable. Centralized state control suppresses healthy competition, flexibility, and innovation. Resources are often funneled into militarization and propaganda rather than sustainable development. Over time, stagnation and decline set in, undermining legitimacy and fueling public discontent.

5. Vulnerability During Leadership Transitions

Built around the absolute authority of a single charismatic leader, fascist systems are fragile in moments of the leader's weakness, illness, or death. The absence of institutional mechanisms for peaceful power transfer or collective leadership leads to instability, factional struggles, and governance crises. Such periods often accelerate the regime's collapse.

6. Overdependence on Propaganda

The regime's control over public opinion relies heavily on propaganda. Over time, the gap between official narratives and lived reality erodes credibility. When propaganda loses its persuasive power, public trust in the government can collapse rapidly.

7. Suppression of Innovation and Adaptability

The rigid control of political and economic life discourages creativity, experimentation, and technological advancement. In rapidly changing global conditions, this inability to adapt leaves the regime outdated and uncompetitive.

8. Polarization and Persecution of Targeted Groups

Fascist regimes often build unity by targeting minority groups as "internal enemies." While this can rally support in the short term, it fosters deep divisions in society and can lead to acts of mass violence that permanently damage national cohesion.

9. Long-Term Social and Moral Degradation

The culture of obedience, fear, and unquestioning loyalty corrodes moral standards, personal responsibility, and civic engagement. Citizens accustomed to authoritarian rule may struggle to participate constructively in democratic governance after the regime's fall.

Historical Examples of Fascist Totalitarianism

Fascist Italy under Benito Mussolini (1922–1943)

Italy under Benito Mussolini was the first fully realized fascist totalitarian state in modern history. Mussolini came to power in October 1922 through the "March on Rome" — a mass demonstration by the National Fascist Party that pressured King Victor Emmanuel III to appoint him Prime Minister. Post–World War I Italy was in deep political and economic turmoil: war debts, high unemployment, social unrest, and fear of socialist revolution created fertile ground for Mussolini's promises of national revival, order, and strength.

Consolidation of Power (1922–1928)

Mussolini moved quickly to dismantle parliamentary democracy. The Acerbo Law of 1923 guaranteed two-thirds of parliamentary seats to the party with at least 25 % of the vote, paving the way for Fascist dominance in the 1924 elections — marred by intimidation and violence. The assassination of socialist leader Giacomo Matteotti in 1924 triggered a political crisis, after which Mussolini openly assumed dictatorial powers in 1925–1926. All opposition parties were banned, press freedoms curtailed, and political freedoms abolished.

State Ideology and Institutions

The regime's foundation rested on ultranationalism, militarism, and corporatism. Italy was portrayed as a unified, disciplined body with the state supreme over the individual. Mussolini's title, *Il Duce* ("The Leader"), became central to a cult of personality: his image filled coins, stamps, monuments, posters, and newsreels.

All branches of government were subordinated to Mussolini. In December 1928, the *Grand Council of Fascism* — created in 1922 — became the supreme constitutional authority, formalizing the merger of party and state.

Propaganda, Censorship, and Indoctrination

Press, radio, and cinema were placed under strict state control. The Ministry of Popular Culture (*Ministero della Cultura Popolare*, or *MinCulPop*) was established as a ministry in 1935, and the name was formalized on 27 May 1937; it coordinated censorship and propaganda in all media. Schools were restructured to instill Fascist ideology. Youth organizations such as the Opera Nazionale Balilla (1926–1937) and its successor, the Gioventù Italiana del Littorio (1937–1943), enrolled millions of young people in programs blending physical training, political indoctrination, and military preparation — participation was effectively compulsory by the late 1930s.

Foreign Policy and Expansionism

Mussolini sought to restore the grandeur of a "new Roman Empire." Defense spending grew steadily; by 1939, military expenditures consumed roughly one-third of the national budget.

- In October 1935, Italy invaded Ethiopia in the Second Italo-Ethiopian War. The campaign, completed by May 1936, saw the use of chemical weapons — notably mustard gas — in quantities estimated from about 100 tons to as much as 300–500 tons, in violation of international law. The League of Nations condemned the aggression and imposed sanctions, though these proved ineffective.

- From 1936 to 1939, Italy intervened in the Spanish Civil War, sending at least 50 000 troops by early 1937; some estimates place peak involvement at 70–75 000 when auxiliary units are included.

- In April 1939, Italian forces invaded and annexed Albania within days — King Zog fled on 9 April, and by 12 April formal annexation was declared.

Alliance with Nazi Germany and World War II

In 1936, Italy joined Germany in the Rome–Berlin Axis, reinforced by the Pact of Steel in 1939. Mussolini kept Italy out of the war until 10 June 1940, when he declared war on Britain and France. The poorly prepared Italian military suffered defeats in Greece (1940–1941), North Africa (1940–1943), and East Africa (1941).

By 1942, Allied bombings devastated cities such as Milan, Turin, and Genoa, while blockades and shortages eroded civilian morale.

Downfall of the Regime (1943)

Following the Allied invasion of Sicily in July 1943, the Grand Council of Fascism voted to remove Mussolini on 25 July; King Victor Emmanuel III ordered his arrest. Marshal Pietro Badoglio formed a new government and signed an armistice with the Allies, announced on 8 September 1943.

On 12 September 1943, German commandos rescued Mussolini in the Gran Sasso raid and installed him as head of the Italian Social Republic (Repubblica Sociale Italiana) — a German puppet state in the north. It survived until April 1945.

Attempting to flee toward Switzerland, Mussolini was captured by Italian partisans on 27 April 1945 and executed the next day near Lake Como. His body, along with other Fascist leaders, was displayed publicly in Milan's Piazzale Loreto.

Legacy

Mussolini's 21-year rule left Italy politically fractured, economically weakened, and socially scarred. Early public works and infrastructure projects could not offset the long-term damage caused by repression, militarization, and catastrophic war policies. Fascist totalitarianism in Italy collapsed completely with the end of World War II in 1945, leaving a lasting historical warning about the dangers of ultranationalist dictatorship.

A Study of Fascist Propaganda in Mussolini's Italy

The Italian fascist propaganda poster depicting a soldier of the *Milizia Volontaria per la Sicurezza Nazionale* (MVSN) standing before the monumental figure of Julius Caesar is more than an artistic work — it is a condensed manifesto of the regime's ideological and psychological arsenal. Created during the years when Benito Mussolini sought to cement his vision of the *Terza Roma* (Third Rome), this image functions simultaneously as a visual appeal, a historical appropriation, and an emotional command.

Historical Context

In the interwar period, Mussolini's government systematically cultivated the idea that Fascist Italy was the legitimate heir to the Roman Empire. This was not mere nostalgia, but a deliberate political project: the *Romanità* campaign aimed to weave the glories of ancient Rome into the fabric of modern Italian identity. The MVSN, or "Blackshirts," served as the regime's paramilitary arm, enforcing political loyalty and eliminating opposition. Placing an MVSN soldier alongside the revered image of Julius Caesar symbolically fused the modern fascist state with the imperial past.

Visual Composition and Symbolism

The composition of the poster is calculated for psychological effect. Caesar's figure, rendered in monumental stone, towers above the soldier, bathed in light as if illuminated by history itself. The soldier stands in the foreground, holding a flag marked *MVSN*, angled towards Caesar in a gesture that can be read as both offering and oath. This spatial relationship is not accidental: the leader of antiquity literally and symbolically overshadows the modern fighter, implying that service to the state is service to the eternal Roman ideal.

The use of Latin — *Nihil adeo arduum quod virtute constantiaque non possit* — operates as a seal of authenticity. Even for those unable to translate it, the script signals tradition, authority, and sacredness. For those who understand it, the meaning — "Nothing is so difficult that it cannot be achieved through valour and constancy" — reinforces the moral imperative of endurance and sacrifice.

Propaganda Techniques

The poster employs several classic propaganda strategies:

1. Historical Appropriation

By aligning Mussolini's forces with Caesar's legions, the regime rewrites history to place itself within a continuous, glorious lineage. This transforms political obedience into historical destiny.

2. Cult of the Leader

Although Mussolini is not pictured, his presence is implied. The soldier stands not only under Caesar's gaze but under the Duce's, as the inheritor of Caesar's mantle. The message is clear: loyalty to Mussolini is loyalty to Rome itself.

3. Sublimation of the Individual

The soldier is deliberately generic, without distinctive facial features. This anonymity invites the viewer to imagine himself in the same role, subsuming personal identity into the collective mission.

4. Moral Absolutism

The virtues of *virtus* and *constantia* are presented as unquestionable. They bypass debate on the justice of the cause, framing victory as a matter of personal worthiness rather than political legitimacy.

Psychological Impact

The image functions on multiple emotional levels. It inspires pride through association with imperial Rome, guilt at the thought of failing to live up to ancestral greatness, and aspiration to embody the soldier's unwavering stance. The physical upward gaze towards Caesar mirrors the internal submission to an idealized authority. The fusion of ancient and modern imagery blurs temporal boundaries, creating the illusion of an unbroken national mission that demands the viewer's participation.

This poster exemplifies the potency of fascist propaganda in Mussolini's Italy. It does not simply advertise an ideology; it constructs a worldview in which the individual's value is measured solely by service to the state, and the state's legitimacy is anchored in a mythic past. Through careful visual design, selective historical reference, and moral absolutism, the image transforms political obedience into an act of historical and even sacred continuity. In the theatre of Fascist Italy's visual culture, the soldier before Caesar is not merely a figure — he is the viewer's own shadow, called to step forward into the ranks of history.

Nazi Germany under Adolf Hitler (1933–1945)

Nazi Germany under Adolf Hitler (1933–1945) became the most striking and tragic embodiment of fascist totalitarianism. The regime was founded on the racial theory of National Socialism, aggressive militarism, and the absolute power of the Führer. The state carried out large-scale repression against political opponents, unleashed the Second World War, and perpetrated the genocide of millions. Its defeat in 1945 led to the complete collapse of the Nazi system and cemented the condemnation of fascist ideology in world history.

Chapter 3

Nazi (National Socialist) Totalitarianism:

Authoritarian Rule Grounded in Racial Ideology

Nazi (National Socialist) totalitarianism is the most aggressive and radical form of totalitarian regime, founded on the ideology of National Socialism. It is characterized by racism, extreme nationalism, a cult of personality surrounding the leader, and the state's total control over society.

Characteristics

Nazi (National Socialist) totalitarianism is a political system that fully subordinates society to a rigid, centralized state, aiming to construct a "racially pure" and ideologically uniform community. It fuses radical nationalism with authoritarian control, militarism, and a single, dominant ideology, eliminating all space for dissent or independent thought.

Its defining features include:

1) **Racial ideology and hierarchical social order**

The system is founded on the belief in the inherent superiority of a particular "master" race and the necessity of its dominance over others deemed "inferior." This racial doctrine is embedded into law, policy, and public life, producing systematic discrimination, segregation, and persecution of groups classified as undesirable.

2) Absolute monopoly of power in one party and leader

All political and state authority is concentrated in a single party, headed by a leader presented as the embodiment of the national will. The leader holds unrestricted power, and all state institutions — including the legislature, judiciary, armed forces, and administrative bodies — are subordinated to the party structure and execute directives without challenge.

3) Mass repression, terror, and organized violence

The regime maintains extensive mechanisms of surveillance, coercion, and punishment to eliminate opposition and enforce ideological conformity. Secret police, paramilitary organizations, detention facilities, and execution systems operate systematically, targeting political opponents, dissenters, and groups deemed racially or socially undesirable.

4) Militarism and permanent mobilization

Military preparedness is central to the system's structure. The economy, education, and culture are directed toward building military strength, fostering a martial spirit, and sustaining a state of permanent mobilization for expansion or conflict.

5) Aggressive expansionism

The ideology incorporates a doctrine of territorial conquest — often framed as the pursuit of "living space" — to secure resources and assert dominance over other nations and peoples. Foreign policy is shaped by the aim of extending control and influence through force.

6) Total control over information, education, and culture

All mass media, educational institutions, scientific research, and cultural production are subordinated to official ideology. Strict censorship eliminates alternative viewpoints, while propaganda saturates public life, shaping attitudes and behaviors in line with state objectives.

7) Indoctrination of youth

Children and adolescents are systematically drawn into state-controlled organizations designed to instill ideological loyalty from an early age. Education and extracurricular activities are structured to replace independent moral development with unconditional adherence to the state's worldview.

8) Militarization of society and paramilitary structures

In addition to the formal armed forces, the state maintains paramilitary organizations that enforce discipline, intimidate opponents, and deepen public participation in militarized culture.

9) Centralized economic direction for political and military goals

While private property may formally exist, economic activity is directed by the state to serve rearmament, autarky, and ideological objectives. Independent enterprise is permitted only insofar as it aligns with state priorities.

10) **Use of political ritual, symbols, and mass spectacle**

Orchestrated rallies, parades, and symbolic displays reinforce ideological unity and emotional attachment to the regime. Visual symbols, uniforms, and ceremonial events create an atmosphere of collective identity and discipline.

11) **Legal subordination of the individual to the state**

Law is reshaped to reflect and enforce ideological principles, discarding traditional protections of individual rights. Courts act as political instruments, punishing dissent and legitimizing discriminatory policies.

12) **Suppression or co-optation of religion**

Religious institutions are either brought under state control or suppressed if they conflict with the official ideology. Where possible, religious influence is redirected to support the regime's objectives.

13) **Culture of surveillance and mutual denunciation**

Networks of informants and an atmosphere of suspicion are cultivated to ensure conformity. Citizens are encouraged — or coerced — to monitor and report on one another, preventing the formation of opposition networks.

Strengths of Nazi (National Socialist) Totalitarianism

1. Rapid consolidation of power and effective suppression of opposition

One of the most notable strengths of this system is its ability to seize and consolidate power quickly, decisively eliminating any alternative political forces. Harsh repressive measures, coupled with absolute control over the security apparatus, allow the regime to suppress opposition in the shortest possible time, establishing strict order and unquestioned authority over society and all state institutions.

2. Highly effective propaganda machinery and control over mass consciousness

Nazi totalitarianism is characterized by an exceptionally developed propaganda system capable of reaching all layers of society. State control over the media, education, culture, and public organizations enables the regime to shape a uniform perception of reality and secure broad popular support, especially in its early stages. This control provides the ability to launch large-scale national projects and mobilize society effectively to meet the regime's objectives.

3. High degree of organization and public discipline

This political model imposes strict social and political order, significantly increasing discipline and organization across society. Citizens follow state-imposed rules precisely, while any form of anarchy or social instability is swiftly suppressed. In the short term, such an approach creates a sense of safety and stability, appealing to populations that have experienced economic turmoil or political upheaval.

4. Centralized economic management and rapid execution of national projects

Centralized authority and full control over economic resources enable the regime to plan and implement large-scale infrastructure, economic, and military projects efficiently. The absence of bureaucratic delays and political disputes allows for the rapid mobilization of resources for militarization, infrastructure development, industrial growth, and the execution of critical state initiatives, often leading to short-term industrial and economic surges.

5. Capacity for effective mobilization in extreme or crisis situations

In times of war, economic crisis, or natural disaster, Nazi totalitarianism demonstrates a high capacity to mobilize both the population and state resources swiftly. Rigid ideology, absolute discipline, and strict state control allow society to organize rapidly in pursuit of a common goal, making the regime particularly effective in managing urgent situations.

6. Clear and straightforward ideological goals

The ideology offers a simplified, easily understood worldview based on national and racial superiority. This clarity and accessibility make it appealing to broad segments of the population, facilitating acceptance of state objectives and encouraging mass support. In the short term, this contributes to social consolidation around shared goals and priorities.

7. Creation of a strong sense of collective identity and belonging

National Socialist ideology actively cultivates feelings of collective identity, pride, and belonging to a "superior" nation or "chosen" race. This sense of unity helps reduce internal divisions and conflicts, creating a temporary perception of solidarity. Such cohesion enables the regime to mobilize people effectively and direct their energy toward state objectives, particularly in times of crisis.

Weaknesses of Nazi (National Socialist) Totalitarianism

1. Crimes against humanity and moral condemnation by the international community

Rooted in racial supremacy and extreme nationalism, this system perpetrates grave crimes against humanity, including mass repression, genocide, and persecution based on racial and ethnic identity. Such actions provoke unequivocal condemnation from the global community, lead to severe international confrontation, and cause irreparable reputational damage on a worldwide scale. Inevitably, these policies draw the regime into global conflicts, sharply worsen diplomatic relations, and generate lasting hostility from other states.

2. Profound moral degradation of society and destruction of fundamental human values

Tight state control over public consciousness and the imposition of an aggressive racist ideology result in deep moral decay. Citizens gradually lose the capacity for empathy, justify cruelty and violence, and become indifferent to the repression or destruction of entire population groups. The systematic dehumanization of individuals and large-scale crimes leave deep psychological scars and severe social consequences that persist for generations after the regime's collapse.

3. High risk of global conflict and the inevitability of long-term defeat

An ideology oriented toward territorial expansion and conquest inevitably drives the regime toward aggression on the international stage and warfare with other states. While short-term tactical successes or temporary alliances may occur, such conflicts typically escalate to global proportions, producing massive human casualties, physical devastation, and socio-economic catastrophe. In the long run, this path tends to end in strategic defeat and systemic collapse.

4. Economic instability and depletion of state resources

Although the system can temporarily mobilize resources to achieve military and national objectives, over time such policies exhaust economic capacity and lead to deep structural crises. The absence of market mechanisms, excessive centralization, and wasteful allocation of resources toward militarization and aggressive wars undermine the economic foundation of the state, making it increasingly vulnerable to prolonged conflicts and internal crises.

5. Lack of stable mechanisms for succession and political instability

Built around the absolute authority of a single leader, this political model becomes extremely fragile during leadership transitions. The death, removal, or incapacitation of the leader triggers acute political crises, internal power struggles, and the breakdown of state institutions. The absence of institutionalized succession processes accelerates political disintegration, generating chaos and undermining stability.

6. Cultural and intellectual stagnation

Harsh censorship and strict control over education, science, and the arts suppress independent thought, free creativity, and scientific inquiry. This results in cultural and intellectual isolation, a lack of innovation, and a deep intellectual crisis. Over time, society loses its ability to adapt to global changes, leading to economic and technological backwardness in comparison to other nations.

Historical Example of Nazi (National Socialist) Totalitarianism
Germany under Adolf Hitler (1933–1945)

The Nazi regime in Germany under Adolf Hitler stands as the most vivid and tragic embodiment of Nazi totalitarianism. Rising to power in 1933, Hitler moved swiftly and decisively to establish an absolute dictatorship, concentrating all authority in the hands of the National Socialist Party and himself alone.

The Hitler phenomenon demands careful and objective analysis, yet it is often obscured by familiar clichés and stereotypes that depict him solely as a monster or a deranged individual. Such views fail to explain how a destitute artist, once living in severe poverty and sleeping on a bench in Vienna, ultimately rose to lead the Third Reich.

Despite the vast number of books written about him, we know surprisingly little about this man. Some demonize him, others glorify him. Even after Germany's denazification following its defeat in World War II, by 1952 half the population of West Germany viewed Hitler's rule positively, and a third regarded him as an outstanding political figure. Today, he remains one of the most revered figures among Nazis in various countries — including those that once suffered under fascism and the atrocities committed by the Nazi regime.

For example, during World War II, one in every four inhabitants of Ukraine was killed at the hands of the Nazis, and about 2.5 million people were forcibly deported to Germany for slave labor. Nevertheless, in modern Ukraine, Nazi ideology has found renewed popularity among the younger generation, intertwining with the official ideology of the current Ukrainian state. The glorification of Nazi collaborators and torchlight processions through the streets of Kiev (capital of Ukraine) have become a routine spectacle. The slogan of the far-right Ukrainian nationalists "Україна понад усе" ("Ukraine above all") is in essence, a local adaptation of the Nazi motto "Deutschland über alles," taken from the opening line of the song Das Lied der Deutschen (The Song of the Germans), written by August Heinrich Hoffmann von Fallersleben in 1841. This song became Germany's national anthem in 1922 and remained so throughout the Nazi regime (1933–1945). During that period, the first verse, opening with the words Deutschland, Deutschland über alles ("Germany, Germany above all"), was widely used. After World War II, this verse was removed from the official anthem, as its content was viewed as nationalistic and chauvinistic.

The difference between modern forms of Nazism and Adolf Hitler's regime lies chiefly in the fact that his rule was grounded in the most radical form of National Socialist ideology, one that preached the racial superiority of the so-called "Aryan race" and embraced extreme nationalism. The state ruthlessly persecuted all groups it deemed "racially inferior" — Jews, Roma, Slavs, and members of many other peoples. This policy culminated in horrific crimes and the establishment of concentration camps, where millions of innocent people were systematically exterminated.

However, alongside its obvious weaknesses, the regime possessed a number of strengths that were particularly evident in its early years:

Strengths of Adolf Hitler's Regime

1) Effective consolidation of power and rapid restoration of state order

After coming to power in 1933, Hitler and the National Socialist Party displayed remarkable determination and the ability to swiftly and decisively suppress any internal opposition. This enabled them to eliminate political rivals in short order and establish one-man rule. The regime restored strict state order, reinforcing discipline and control across all public and state institutions.

The Nazi government implemented effective administrative reforms, cutting through bureaucratic delays and ensuring centralized oversight of state bodies and institutions. This significantly accelerated decision-making and improved the efficiency of public administration — an achievement that, in the early years, was widely regarded by the population as a major advantage.

These measures found support among a significant portion of German society, weary of the prolonged period of political instability, economic crisis, social unrest, and ineffective governance that had characterized the Weimar Republic.

2) Rapid economic stabilization and effective mobilization of resources

One of the most notable early achievements of the Nazi regime was its rapid resolution of the economic crisis and mass unemployment that had plagued Germany during the final years of the Weimar Republic. In early 1933, unemployment stood at roughly six million people — about one-third of the working population. Upon taking power, Hitler and his government immediately launched a program of economic recovery and national development, which dramatically reduced joblessness. By 1936–1937, Germany had come close to achieving full employment. In the regime's early years, wages stabilized, working conditions improved, and by 1937 average incomes for workers and employees had risen by approximately 10–15%.

Nazi economic policy rested on large-scale state projects and the intensive militarization of the economy. The government invested heavily in infrastructure, launching ambitious programs to build highways (autobahns), public buildings, industrial plants, housing, and transportation networks. These projects not only provided mass employment but also stimulated growth in key sectors such as metallurgy, construction, mechanical engineering, and the chemical industry.

Special emphasis was placed on expanding the military-industrial base and modernizing the armed forces. The economy was deliberately restructured to serve military objectives, enabling a rapid increase in the production of weapons, ammunition, and military equipment within a short period. Strict centralized control of economic resources ensured that all activity and financial flows were regulated by the state. Specialized agencies coordinated economic processes, allocated raw materials, and oversaw production and consumption. This structure allowed resources to be concentrated quickly in priority areas, ensuring the swift execution of key state programs and objectives.

Together, these measures produced significant economic growth, stabilized the national economy, and raised the standard of living. German industry received a powerful boost, rapidly regaining its position after years of stagnation and decline.

3) Improving working conditions and social guarantees for workers

The Nazi regime implemented a system of social protection and support aimed at the working class, most notably through the creation of the German Labor Front (DAF), which replaced the former trade unions. The DAF provided workers with regular paid vacations, improved workplace conditions, and organized affordable leisure activities — most famously through the *Strength Through Joy* (*Kraft durch Freude*) program. These initiatives

were designed to raise worker morale, promote loyalty to the regime, and enhance the social standing of the labor force.

4) Highly effective propaganda and mass mobilization

One of the most striking and influential features of the Nazi regime was its exceptionally effective and all-encompassing propaganda apparatus. The leadership understood the central role of mass media as a tool for shaping and directing public consciousness. Upon taking power in 1933, the Nazis quickly seized complete control over all channels of information — the press, radio, cinema, literature, and the arts — transforming them into powerful instruments of state propaganda.

At the core of this system stood the newly created Ministry of Public Enlightenment and Propaganda, headed by Joseph Goebbels. This ministry developed and coordinated all propaganda efforts, tightly controlling the flow of information to ensure uniformity and consistency. Through carefully crafted, emotionally charged, and easily understood messages, propaganda shaped public opinion and steered mass behavior with remarkable precision.

A central theme was the portrayal of national unity and the revival of Germany after years of crisis. Nazi propaganda emphasized pride, solidarity, and patriotism, presenting Hitler's government as the embodiment of the German people's longing for order, strength, and greatness. These narratives resonated deeply in a society still burdened by the trauma of defeat in World War I, the humiliation of the Treaty of Versailles, and the hardships of economic collapse.

The cult of Adolf Hitler was a key component of this strategy. He was depicted not merely as a political leader, but as a savior of the nation endowed with exceptional qualities. His image appeared everywhere — on posters, in newspapers and magazines, in newsreels, on radio broadcasts, and in films. Mass rallies, parades, and public celebrations were orchestrated to display unity and reinforce the image of universal support for the regime.

Special emphasis was placed on youth indoctrination. From an early age, children were immersed in the ideals of National Socialism and taught unconditional loyalty to Hitler. Organizations such as the Hitler Youth fostered patriotism, discipline, and a readiness to serve the state.

This powerful and meticulously organized propaganda machine enabled the Nazi regime not only to secure widespread public support but also to mobilize the population for large-scale state initiatives. Its impact was particularly evident during the preparations for war and in the early years of World War II, when German society displayed a remarkable degree of unity and discipline — a direct result of the regime's mastery of mass persuasion.

5) Creation of an organized and disciplined society

One of the most visible and widely acknowledged strengths of the Nazi regime was its ability to forge an exceptionally organized, disciplined, and tightly controlled society in a remarkably short period. This was achieved through an unprecedented combination of ideological indoctrination, state oversight of daily life, and the relentless suppression of resistance, crime, and civil disobedience.

After seizing power in 1933, the Nazi government introduced stringent measures to strengthen public discipline. Criminal laws were tightened, penalties became harsher, and oversight of public safety and street order intensified. Police forces and security services were granted broad powers to combat crime, often using repressive methods that swiftly reduced crime rates and fostered an atmosphere of order and security, particularly in major cities.

At the same time, the regime established total ideological control, actively regulating and directing the behavior of citizens. Strict rules and norms governed not only public life but also private conduct. Society was steeped in values of discipline, responsibility, hard work, and collectivism, with a constant emphasis on sacrifice and personal service to state and national goals. This rigid social regulation enabled the regime to effectively channel the population's energy toward fulfilling state objectives.

Mass organizations played a crucial role in maintaining discipline and integration. Groups such as the Hitler Youth, the League of German Girls, the National Socialist Women's League, the German Labor Front, and other state-sponsored associations were designed to incorporate every segment of the population into a single, centrally controlled system. Citizens were systematically engaged in events, activities, and programs that reinforced a shared identity and a sense of personal duty to the state.

For many Germans, these measures were seen as a significant improvement, especially when contrasted with the chaos and instability of the Weimar Republic. The strict order and structure imposed by the Nazi regime fostered a sense of stability and security — something deeply sought after by a society emerging from years of political upheaval and economic hardship.

6) Active development of science, technology, and engineering

The Nazi regime placed significant emphasis on advancing scientific and technological progress, particularly in fields that could directly serve state and military objectives. Substantial support was provided for both fundamental and applied research, with notable breakthroughs in rocket engineering — including the development of the V-2 rocket — as well as in aviation technology, chemistry, and physics. Despite strict ideological controls and the suppression of certain areas of inquiry, Nazi Germany achieved remarkable results in military-industrial and technical innovation. Many of these advances had a lasting influence, shaping the post-war development of science and technology in both Europe and beyond.

7) Development of healthcare and social protection systems

The Nazi state pursued an active policy of expanding medical care and improving public health, with a particular focus on strengthening the health of the so-called "Aryan" population. Effective sanitary services were established, an extensive network of hospitals and clinics was developed, and large-scale programs for disease prevention, vaccination, and routine medical examinations were implemented.

Special attention was devoted to supporting motherhood, childhood, and young families. State programs offered financial incentives to increase the birth rate and reduce infant mortality. Between 1933 and 1939, the natural population growth of Germany (excluding territorial annexations) reached approximately 2.5–3 million people. Including newly acquired territories, the total population rose from about 66 million to roughly 79 million by 1939.

These demographic changes were partly the result of deliberate state policy, which included:

o   financial assistance to families with children;
o   benefits and allowances for large families;
o   the creation of a comprehensive social support system for mothers and children;
o   the promotion of traditional family values and the elevation of motherhood as a social ideal.

8) Improvement of the physical education and sports system

The Nazi regime attached great importance to the physical health of the nation, integrating physical education and sports into its broader ideological and social programs. Sports clubs were organized nationwide, while stadiums, sports facilities, and dedicated training institutions were built or expanded.

The 1936 Olympic Games in Berlin served as a high-profile showcase of German athletic achievement and organizational capability, significantly boosting interest in physical culture.

9) Support and development of culture, art, and architecture

The cultural policy of Nazi Germany was marked by deliberate state sponsorship of artistic and cultural forms that aligned with the regime's official ideology and aesthetic principles. Large-scale architectural projects were undertaken, museums and galleries were established, and major cultural events were organized to promote a sense of national pride and unity.

The regime favored classical art forms and works emphasizing patriotic and heroic themes, positioning them as embodiments of "true" German culture. These were deliberately contrasted with what the Nazis labeled "degenerate art" — modernist, avant-garde, or politically subversive works — which were banned, confiscated, and often publicly denounced. Through this selective promotion and suppression, the state sought to shape cultural life as a direct instrument of propaganda and ideological influence.

However, despite these achievements, Adolf Hitler's regime harbored deep structural weaknesses that ultimately led to its collapse and one of the most catastrophic chapters in modern history.

Weaknesses of Adolf Hitler's Regime

1) Crimes Against Humanity and Genocide

The Nazi regime carried out the mass extermination of people on racial, ethnic, and ideological grounds. Between 1941 and 1945, approximately six million Jews, hundreds of thousands of Roma, millions of Soviet prisoners of war, Poles, and members of other nationalities deemed "racially inferior" by the Nazis were murdered. To implement this policy, death camps such as Auschwitz, Treblinka, Majdanek, Sobibor, and Chelmno were established, where victims were systematically killed in gas chambers, by firing squads, and through deliberately imposed starvation.

One of the most brutal manifestations of Nazi terror was the mass execution of civilians in occupied territories. For example, in September 1941, at Babyn Yar (Kyiv, Ukraine), more than 34,000 Jews were murdered in just two days. Similar mass shootings of civilians took place in Minsk, Riga, Lviv, and other cities across Eastern Europe.

The Nazis also targeted people with physical and mental disabilities under the so-called "euthanasia program" (Aktion T4). From 1939 onward, at least 70,000 German citizens deemed "unfit" by the authorities were killed by lethal injection or in special gas chambers.

Particularly notorious were Nazi doctors who conducted inhumane medical experiments on concentration camp prisoners. At Auschwitz, Dr. Josef Mengele performed experiments on twins in an attempt to study heredity and alter human traits. In Dachau and Buchenwald, prisoners were subjected to hypothermia and high-altitude pressure tests, while in Ravensbrück, inmates were deliberately infected with bacteria to study the progression of gangrene.

Millions of concentration camp inmates and prisoners of war were held in conditions deliberately designed to cause slow death: constant starvation, brutal punishments, and exhausting forced labor. In the final months of the war, as German forces retreated, prisoners were forced on so-called "death marches" — long treks over vast distances during which tens of thousands died from exhaustion, disease, and violence.

The Nazis also routinely executed hostages in occupied territories. In retaliation for acts of local resistance, occupation authorities killed hundreds or even thousands of randomly chosen civilians, fostering an atmosphere of terror and crushing the will to resist.

After Germany's defeat, these atrocities became widely known to the world. They were meticulously examined at the Nuremberg Trials (1945–1946). Many of the organizers and perpetrators of the genocide were sentenced to death or long prison terms, and the Nazi regime was formally declared criminal and condemned by the international community.

2) Aggressive Foreign Policy and the Outbreak of World War II

Nazi Germany pursued an expansionist course aimed at enlarging its territories at the expense of neighboring states through aggressive actions. In March 1938, in violation of the Treaty of Versailles, Germany annexed Austria (the *Anschluss*). This was followed by the annexation of the Sudetenland from Czechoslovakia in September 1938 under the Munich Agreement, and by March 1939, German troops had occupied the entirety of Czechoslovakia. On September 1, 1939, Germany's invasion of Poland became the immediate trigger for World War II. Later, on June 22, 1941, Germany launched its military campaign against the Soviet Union (*Operation Barbarossa*).

Initially, the German state reaped tangible benefits from conquered territories. From occupied France, Belgium, the Netherlands, and other Western European countries, the regime extracted food, raw materials, manufactured goods, and cultural and material assets. These were used to supply the German military and civilian population during wartime. From Eastern Europe—particularly occupied areas of the Soviet Union such as Ukraine, Belarus, and the Baltic states—Germany seized vast quantities of grain, meat, coal, oil, and other resources, temporarily improving domestic supply.

Additionally, Nazi Germany extensively exploited forced labor, with around 7.5 million prisoners of war and civilians from Poland, the USSR, Czechoslovakia, and other countries compelled to work in hazardous industries, agriculture, and construction. This workforce replaced German laborers mobilized for the front, allowing the regime in the early years of the war to maintain steady civilian supply levels and sustain relatively high industrial output.

During the initial war years (1939–1941), these seizures of goods, resources, and property—particularly from persecuted groups such as Jews—helped Germany partially offset wartime economic pressures and maintain a degree of material comfort for the so-called "Aryan" population.

3) Suppression of Free Speech and Critical Thinking

The Nazi regime eliminated freedom of expression and independent journalism. Censorship and harsh reprisals against any form of dissent destroyed the public's ability to think critically or objectively assess the government's actions. This suppression of open discourse made it impossible for German society to challenge or avert the catastrophic decisions taken by Nazi leadership during the war.

4) Intellectual and Cultural Brain Drain from Germany

With the Nazi rise to power and the imposition of racial and ideological restrictions, Germany experienced a mass exodus of scientists, writers, and artists—particularly Jews and political opponents of the regime. Estimates suggest that around 500,000 intellectuals left the country.

Among them were physicists Albert Einstein and Max Born, writer Thomas Mann, filmmaker Fritz Lang, and philosophers Theodor Adorno and Hannah Arendt. This wave of emigration meant not only the loss of prominent individuals but also the collapse of entire academic schools: German universities lost an estimated 20–25% of their faculty. With the departure of key figures, Germany relinquished its leadership in fields such as quantum physics and mathematics.

Many of these émigré scholars and artists relocated to the West, especially the United States and the United Kingdom. Their migration had a measurable impact on innovation abroad: in the U.S., the number of patents in areas connected to the work of émigré scientists increased by approximately 31%.

5) Profound Moral Degradation of Society

The vast Nazi propaganda machine, built on racial supremacy and hatred toward specific peoples and groups, drove German society into a deep moral crisis. Citizens gradually became accustomed to viewing violence, brutality, and mass repression as part of everyday life. Accepted moral standards and traditional human values eroded over time. The active participation of millions of Germans in crimes—or their passive acceptance of them—produced severe psychological consequences that affected several generations. After the war, German society was confronted with the heavy legacy of guilt, trauma, and the loss of moral bearings brought on by the Nazi regime's mass atrocities.

6) Economic Exhaustion and Long-Term Collapse

Despite the impressive successes of its early years, Nazi Germany's economy was highly unstable and vulnerable. The militarization of production and vast spending on armaments created chronic shortages of raw materials and resources, which the regime sought to offset through the plunder of occupied lands. The absence of a functioning market economy, extreme centralization, and rigid state control deprived the system of flexibility and resilience. By 1943, Germany was facing a deepening crisis: shortages of goods and inflation were rising, consumption was falling, and Allied bombing raids had severely undermined industrial capacity.

7) Destruction of Infrastructure and Cities

As a result of military operations, mass bombings, and fierce fighting on German soil, major cities such as Berlin, Hamburg, Dresden, and Cologne were heavily damaged or destroyed. Entire industrial regions, transportation networks, and communication lines were devastated. The economic losses were enormous, and Germany faced decades of reconstruction in the postwar period.

8) Political Instability and Collapse After Military Defeat

The political system of the Nazi regime rested entirely on the authority and personal power of Adolf Hitler, who made all major state decisions himself. The absence of genuine institutions capable of ensuring stability and continuity made the regime extremely vulnerable. As Germany began to suffer major defeats on the battlefield, by 1944 it became clear that the Nazi system was incapable of functioning effectively in a wartime crisis. Following the final collapse of German forces in the spring of 1945 and Hitler's death, the entire political structure disintegrated.

9) Loss of Sovereignty and Occupation of Territory

Defeat in the war resulted in the complete loss of German sovereignty. In 1945, the country was fully occupied by Allied forces and divided into occupation zones, later becoming two separate states—the Federal Republic of Germany (FRG) and the German Democratic Republic (GDR). This marked the total loss of Germany's political, economic, and military independence.

Chapter 4
Religious Totalitarianism:
Political Authority Justified by Religious Doctrine

> **Religious totalitarianism** is a form of totalitarian political regime in which state power exercises complete control over society, relying on a single mandatory religious ideology. It harshly suppresses any form of dissent and enforces strict control over all spheres of citizens' lives in accordance with religious laws and prescriptions.

Characteristics

In religious totalitarian states, power is entirely concentrated in the hands of a religious elite and rests exclusively on a single doctrinal foundation. There is no separation between the secular and the spiritual: religion becomes the sole source of law, morality, and social order. Both political life and the daily existence of citizens are completely subordinated to strict religious norms, and any departure from the official faith is treated as a grave offense against the state.

Key Features of Religious Totalitarianism

1) **Absolute power of the religious elite**

All political and administrative authority lies in the hands of spiritual leaders. These figures govern state institutions, make political decisions, and set the overall course of society. Their authority derives from sacred texts, and their rulings are regarded as binding, often justified as the will of a higher power. Political directives are framed as divinely sanctioned, making them virtually immune to challenge.

2) **Legislation and norms based solely on religious texts**

Laws are not created through democratic processes, nor do they reflect the will of the people. Instead, they follow directly from religious doctrines and sacred writings. Religious canons replace civil legal codes, regulating every sphere of life—from family relations and personal conduct to economic activity and judicial practice. Matters such as marriage, child-rearing, inheritance, dietary rules, dress codes, and even leisure are dictated by religious law. Violations are punished harshly, often as criminal acts against public order.

3) **Suppression of dissent and strict censorship**

Criticism of the official doctrine, expressions of doubt, or discussion of alternative beliefs are strictly forbidden. To enforce conformity, the state imposes comprehensive censorship: books, newspapers, television, and online content are monitored and filtered. All publications undergo prior review to ensure alignment with religious orthodoxy. Those who voice dissent face arrest, severe punishment, or other forms of repression.

4) **Total control over education and youth upbringing**

The state monopolizes education to ensure total loyalty to the official creed. Curricula at all levels are shaped entirely by religious doctrine, with no tolerance for alternative viewpoints. From early childhood, students are taught the tenets of the state religion, instilling unquestioning obedience to spiritual authority and rejection of all competing perspectives. The goal is to produce generations fully loyal to both faith and state.

5) **Religious police and enforcement bodies**

Special agencies—often called "religious police"—are tasked with monitoring citizens' daily lives for compliance with prescribed norms. They patrol public spaces, inspect private homes, and enforce rules governing dress, diet, public behavior, family life, and religious rituals. Penalties for violations range from fines and imprisonment to corporal punishment or even execution.

6) **No separation between state and religious institutions**

Government and religious structures merge into a single power system. The state ideology is identical to the official religion, and all state ceremonies are infused with religious rites and symbolism. Religious leaders hold top political positions and wield decisive influence over governance. National symbols, emblems, and mottos take on explicitly religious meanings, underscoring the subordination of politics to faith.

7) **Severe restrictions on the rights of women and minorities**

Such regimes often impose strict limits on women, barring them from senior positions, higher education, or participation in political life. Women's behavior, dress, and private lives are closely regulated according to religious prescriptions. Minority groups— whether defined by religion, ethnicity, or belief—are systematically discriminated against, with members facing ongoing persecution and repression.

Strengths of Religious Totalitarianism

1. High Level of Social and Ideological Cohesion

One of the main advantages of a religious totalitarian regime is its ability to unite society quickly and effectively around a single, absolute system of religious values and norms. People bound by a shared worldview, clearly defined moral rules, and a unified doctrine develop a strong sense of community and solidarity. This greatly strengthens social bonds and helps prevent serious internal conflicts and divisions. Society becomes predictable, with citizens' behavior strictly regulated and clearly understood by all. This creates an atmosphere of stability and internal order, highly valued after periods of crisis and uncertainty.

2. Full Integration of Religious and State Institutions, Enabling Efficient Governance and Control

In a religious totalitarian state, religious and governmental structures operate as a single, coordinated system. This ensures exceptional efficiency in governance, rapid decision-making, and prompt implementation. The absence of separation between secular and religious authority removes bureaucratic barriers, speeds up administrative processes, and makes the system highly centralized. With close coordination between religious leaders and state institutions, the authorities maintain absolute control over society and can respond quickly to threats, changes, or challenges. In the short term, this results in high governability and stability, often viewed by citizens as a significant advantage.

3. Low Crime Rates and High Public Discipline

Religious totalitarian regimes typically maintain very low levels of crime, due to strict adherence to moral norms and harsh punishments for violations. Citizens view the law not only as a state requirement but also as a divine commandment, which significantly reduces the likelihood of criminal behavior. This creates an atmosphere of discipline, order, and safety, often seen by the population as a major benefit of such a system.

4. Strong Motivation and Ability to Mobilize Society in Times of Crisis

A unified religious ideology and spiritual leadership can effectively mobilize the population in times of crisis, war, or external threats. Religious faith and a sense of shared mission make citizens more willing to act selflessly, accept sacrifices, and demonstrate solidarity. In wartime or other emergencies, this motivation becomes a key factor in the state's strength and resilience.

5. Clear Moral Guidelines and Predictability of Social Life

In such a state, all norms of behavior and moral standards are clearly defined and unchanging, as they are based on religious canons and traditions. This eliminates moral uncertainty, ambiguity, and ethical chaos. Citizens receive clear guidance and life rules, contributing to social stability and preventing deep moral conflicts.

6. Effective System of Social Support and Mutual Aid

Religious regimes often place great emphasis on social justice and mutual aid, viewing them as a religious duty of every citizen. This fosters the development of active charitable systems and support for the poor and needy. These states often maintain effective networks of social institutions, hospitals, and charitable organizations, supported not only by the state but also by citizens themselves, driven by religious conviction.

7. High Levels of Loyalty and Trust Toward the Authorities

Because political power is perceived as spiritual and divinely sanctioned, citizens in such regimes tend to show strong loyalty and trust toward the state and its leadership. Belief in the fairness and infallibility of religious leaders strengthens the authority of the government, ensures political stability, and reduces the likelihood of internal opposition.

Weaknesses of Religious Totalitarianism

1. Suppression of Freedom of Conscience

Religious totalitarianism denies citizens the right to spiritual choice. Any belief that diverges from the official doctrine is forbidden. Individuality is stifled, freedom of thought is curtailed, and personal spiritual exploration becomes impossible.

2. Intolerance and Discrimination Against Minorities

When one faith is declared the sole truth, all others are treated as false. Religious minorities, dissenters, and secular-minded citizens face discrimination, repression, and exclusion from public life. Denied equal access to education, employment, and political participation, they live on the margins of society. The result is growing division, social tension, and, at times, violent conflict.

3. Cultural and Intellectual Stagnation

Rigid dogma leaves little room for creativity, science, or cultural exchange. Innovation is treated with suspicion, often branded as heresy. Over time, societies that reject new ideas fall behind, closing themselves off from global progress and drifting into cultural decline.

4. Weak Economic Performance

Restrictions on intellectual freedom, censorship, and hostility toward innovation undermine productivity and competitiveness.

5. Hypocrisy and Double Standards

Strict moral codes and constant surveillance encourage outward conformity but private disobedience. Citizens may publicly display loyalty to doctrine while privately disregarding its rules.

6. Limits on Women's Rights

Grounded in conservative interpretations of religion, these regimes impose strict barriers on women. Education, careers, and political participation are restricted.

7. Conflict with the Outside World

Religious totalitarianism, uncompromising in its ideology, often collides with external forces. Attempts to export its doctrine or to insulate itself from foreign influence create friction with other states. The result is isolation, sanctions, and a constant risk of confrontation.

8. Instrumentalization of Religion

When religion is used primarily as a political instrument, its spiritual meaning erodes. Faith becomes a tool of control rather than a source of moral authority. This undermines trust not only in the state but also in the religious tradition itself, creating a long-term legitimacy crisis.

9. Radicalization and Internal Instability

Harsh repression of dissent frequently fuels underground radical movements. Suppressing moderate opposition creates space for more extreme voices, turning the regime into a generator of instability. What begins as control often ends in cycles of unrest and repression.

10. Economic Dependence on Resource Rent

Many religious authoritarian states survive not through efficient governance but through resource wealth, particularly oil and gas. This dependence makes them highly vulnerable to fluctuations in global markets. Economic shocks quickly translate into political crises, exposing the fragility of the system.

11. Suppression of Civil Society

Independent associations, labor unions, and human rights organizations are either tightly controlled or eliminated. Without such institutions, society becomes atomized, leaving citizens without peaceful channels to voice concerns or protect their rights. This absence of civil society weakens resilience and deepens authoritarian control.

Historical Examples of Religious Totalitarianism
Geneva under John Calvin (1541–1564)

John Calvin, a French theologian and leading figure of the Protestant Reformation, had first arrived in Geneva in 1536 at the invitation of reform-minded citizens who wished to transform their city into a bastion of the new faith. His uncompromising vision and strict doctrinal demands soon provoked resistance, and in 1538 he was expelled.

Three years later, in 1541, political circumstances changed. Facing internal discord and fearing the influence of Catholic neighbors, Geneva's authorities invited Calvin back, this time granting him sweeping powers to shape both the spiritual and civic life of the city. From that moment, Calvin began building what he envisioned as a model Christian commonwealth, governed entirely by the principles of Scripture and a rigorous moral code. The result was a theocratic system in which no line divided church from state, and where every aspect of public and private life was subject to religious oversight.

Absolute Power of the Religious Elite and the Consistory

Calvin established the Consistory — a powerful church tribunal composed of pastors and lay elders — which quickly became the central organ of governance in Geneva. Its authority extended far beyond theological matters. It investigated citizens' conduct, summoned them to account for breaches of moral and religious norms, and imposed punishments ranging from public admonitions and fines to imprisonment and corporal punishment. Attendance at church services was mandatory, and absence or tardiness could lead to penalties. Even private quarrels, domestic disputes, or excessive merriment could come under its scrutiny.

Strict Regulation of Daily Life

Under Calvin's rule, daily life in Geneva was minutely regulated. Theatrical performances, dancing, and the singing of secular songs were banned. Gambling and drunkenness were punished severely. Clothing was subject to sumptuary laws: citizens were required to dress modestly, avoiding bright colors and luxurious fabrics that might be seen as signs of vanity or moral decline. Festivities deemed inconsistent with Calvinist morality were prohibited, and even family celebrations were monitored — the number of dishes served at a wedding or banquet could be restricted to discourage excess. Women who appeared in "immodest" attire or elaborate hairstyles could face fines or even imprisonment.

Religious Intolerance and Persecution of Dissenters

Any deviation from Calvin's doctrine was treated as a grave offense. Religious pluralism had no place in Geneva; the preaching of other confessions was forbidden, and theological dissent was equated with sedition. The most infamous example was the trial and execution of the Spanish physician and theologian Michael Servetus, who rejected the doctrine of the Trinity. Arrested while passing through Geneva, Servetus was condemned by the city council, with Calvin's full approval, and burned at the stake in 1553. Voltaire, writing nearly two centuries later, remarked that Servetus's execution horrified him more than all the burnings of the Inquisition — a reflection of how deeply this act shocked even those critical of Catholic persecution.

Nor was Servetus the only victim. During Calvin's tenure, around 60 people were executed for religious or moral offenses, while several hundred more were banished or otherwise punished for views or behaviors deemed incompatible with the strict Calvinist order.

Total Control over Education and Youth Formation

Calvin believed that education was the cornerstone of a godly society. He instituted a comprehensive system of schooling under strict church supervision, ensuring that from childhood citizens were molded in the spirit of Calvinist orthodoxy. Teachers were required to adhere to approved religious curricula, and no alternative viewpoints were tolerated. In 1559, Calvin founded the Geneva Academy (today's University of Geneva), which became a major training center for Protestant pastors and a hub for spreading Calvinist theology across Europe.

Discipline, Order, and Economic Stability

Despite — or perhaps because of — its severe moral code, Calvin's Geneva was noted for its low crime rate, high degree of social order, and efficient administration. Vices such as prostitution, gambling, and public drunkenness were outlawed. The city attracted Protestant refugees from across Europe, bringing new skills, trades, and commercial connections. Geneva grew into a prosperous center of printing, watchmaking, and finance, admired by some for its stability and feared by others for its rigid orthodoxy.

For Calvin and his supporters, this was the realization of a moral ideal; for dissenters, it was a suffocating regime that punished thought and behavior alike. Its legacy remains complex — admired by some for discipline and moral rigor, condemned by others as a warning of what happens when faith becomes law.

Florence under Girolamo Savonarola (1494–1498)

At the close of the fifteenth century, Florence stood at a crossroads. Once a beacon of Renaissance culture, wealth, and artistic brilliance under the patronage of the Medici, the city was shaken by political upheaval. In 1494, the French invasion of Italy forced the Medici family into exile, creating a sudden vacuum of power. Into this turbulent void stepped a Dominican friar — Girolamo Savonarola — whose fiery sermons, delivered for years in the pulpits of Florence, had already condemned the moral corruption of the ruling elite, the vanity of secular pleasures, and the spiritual decay of Christendom.

Savonarola declared that Florence had been chosen by God to become a "New Jerusalem," a model Christian republic purified of sin and worldly vice. Within months, he rose to the position of the city's unchallenged moral and political authority, uniting spiritual power with civic control and transforming Florence into a city-state governed by an uncompromising religious code.

Seizing power and establishing a theocratic regime

With the Medici gone, Savonarola gained dominance through his charisma, his prophetic warnings of divine judgment, and his promise to restore Florence's covenant with God. A new republican government emerged, but behind its formal structures stood Savonarola's will. He became the city's guiding force, shaping both policy and morality. The political vision he advanced was inseparable from the spiritual — a state fully subordinated to religious authority.

Rigid moral censorship and daily life under surveillance

Savonarola imposed a strict moral order enforced through sweeping bans and unyielding religious discipline. Theaters, carnivals, gambling, and public dancing were prohibited. Music was confined to sacred hymns; secular songs vanished from the streets. Citizens were expected to dress in plain, modest garments — bright colors and luxurious fabrics were forbidden as signs of vanity and moral corruption.

Attendance at church services was compulsory, and private life fell under public scrutiny. To enforce these decrees, Savonarola relied on patrols of zealous youths — the *Piagnoni*, or "Weepers" — who acted as a kind of moral militia. They patrolled the streets, inspected homes, confiscated "sinful" objects, and reported offenders to the authorities, subjecting them to public humiliation, fines, or imprisonment.

The Bonfire of the Vanities

The most infamous act of Savonarola's rule came on 7 February 1497. On Florence's central square, the Piazza della Signoria, thousands of objects deemed immoral or decadent were piled high and set aflame in what became known as the "Bonfire of the Vanities." Fine clothing, mirrors, cosmetics, playing cards, musical instruments, and books of secular poetry went into the flames. Works of art — including paintings and drawings by Sandro Botticelli and other masters — were destroyed.

To Savonarola, these sacrifices were purifications of the soul; to others, they were acts of cultural vandalism. The event shocked Europe and came to symbolize the destructive potential of religious extremism when wielded with political power.

Religious intolerance and repression of dissent

Savonarola's Florence left no room for alternative faiths or divergent opinions. Preaching outside the official doctrine was forbidden, and those who defied his authority faced exile, imprisonment, or even execution. The friar wielded the threat of excommunication against opponents, silencing both common citizens and influential patrician families. Many of Florence's most prominent figures either fled the city or submitted in silence to the new moral order.

Conflict with Rome and the downfall of the regime

Savonarola's growing influence and his denunciations of corruption in the Roman Curia brought him into direct confrontation with Pope Alexander VI. In 1497, the pope excommunicated Savonarola, cutting him off from the Church he claimed to defend. This weakened his standing in Florence, where resistance to his rule began to swell.

Public discontent boiled over in 1498. Citizens, weary of prohibitions, fearful of papal wrath, and resentful of constant moral policing, turned against the friar. He was arrested, tortured, and charged with heresy and sedition. On 23 May 1498, Girolamo Savonarola and two of his closest followers were hanged and their bodies burned in the Piazza della Signoria — the very square where, a year earlier, his own followers had consigned the treasures of Florence to the flames.

Saudi Arabia

Saudi Arabia offers one of the clearest modern examples of a state shaped by religious authoritarianism.

The Dominance of Wahhabi Islam

In the kingdom, Sunni Islam in its Wahhabi interpretation stands as the foundation of law, morality, and governance. Sharia is recognized as the supreme law of the land, shaping family relations, personal conduct, criminal justice, and economic life. Civil law and religious doctrine are inseparable, interpreted through a conservative lens that reinforces the unity of religion and state.

The Religious Establishment as a Pillar of Power

The authority of the monarchy rests on religious legitimacy. Senior scholars (ulama) endorse royal authority and, through fatwas and religious oversight, influence both social life and political decisions.

Limits on Religious Freedom

Saudi Arabia prohibits public worship outside Islam. Non-Muslims may practice their faith privately, but under strict control. Public displays of worship, proselytizing, or criticism of the official faith are banned, with penalties that may include imprisonment, corporal punishment, or even capital punishment in cases of apostasy and blasphemy.

The Religious Police

For decades, the Committee for the Promotion of Virtue and the Prevention of Vice — widely known as the mutawa — enforced Islamic codes in public life. They monitored women's dress, ensured prayer attendance, and banned activities deemed immoral. Since 2016, their powers have been curtailed, but they remain a potent reminder of the state's reach into daily conduct.

Restrictions on Women's Rights

Until recently, women in Saudi Arabia lived under one of the world's strictest guardianship systems. They required permission from a male guardian to travel abroad, marry, or make major personal decisions, and until 2018 were barred from driving. Reforms introduced in the late 2010s — such as lifting the driving ban and easing guardianship rules — marked important change, yet sharia-based constraints still limit women's autonomy in both public and private spheres.

Why Saudi Arabia Is Not Fully Totalitarian

Despite the depth of religious control, Saudi Arabia diverges from fully totalitarian models. The Vision 2030 program, spearheaded by Crown Prince Mohammed bin Salman, seeks to diversify the economy away from oil — once responsible for more than 80 percent of state revenues — by developing tourism, technology, renewable energy, finance, manufacturing, health, and education. The kingdom also preserves elements of a market economy, protects private property, and participates actively in global trade and diplomacy. These features distinguish it from closed and self-isolated regimes, placing it instead in the category of religious authoritarianism with hybrid characteristics.

CONCLUSION

Totalitarianism represents the most rigid and uncompromising form of political organization, a system in which the state seeks absolute control not only over public life but also over the inner world of its citizens — their thoughts, feelings, and convictions. At its core lie several defining traits: a single obligatory ideology, the concentration of power in the hands of one party or leader, the suppression of dissent, and pervasive censorship. Yet within this common framework, different models of totalitarianism bear distinctive features.

Ideological totalitarianism rests on the absolute dominance of a political doctrine that seeks to regulate every dimension of human and social existence. In the Soviet Union and Maoist China, ideology became inseparable from daily life, shaping work, family, education, and private belief alike.

Fascist totalitarianism was built on ultranationalism, the cult of strength, militarism, and the unification of society around a single leader who promised to restore national greatness. National Socialism pushed these principles to their most radical and destructive form, grounding the state in racial theory and pursuing genocide as official policy. It became the most brutal and inhumane variant of totalitarian rule in history.

Religious totalitarianism differs in that absolute authority rests with spiritual elites, while sacred texts and dogmas serve as the exclusive source of law and morality. Under such regimes, censorship is justified in the name of faith, dissent is branded as heresy, and clerical power extends deep into both public institutions and private life.

The historical record of the twentieth century — and of earlier epochs — shows the destructive legacy of totalitarianism. Millions perished in repression, genocide, and wars of aggression. Entire generations bore lasting psychological scars. Freedom of thought was extinguished, creativity suppressed, and cultural as well as intellectual heritage destroyed. Intellectual elites fled abroad, human capital was squandered, and societies paid not only in lives lost but also in potential never realized.

To study totalitarianism is therefore more than an inquiry into the past. It is a necessary safeguard for the future. Understanding its logic and its consequences allows humanity to resist repeating the same path. At stake are the fundamental values of freedom, dignity, and respect for the individual — values that stand as the only true antidote to the legacy of totalitarian rule.

PART III
CLASSIFICATION BY ADMINISTRATIVE AND TERRITORIAL STRUCTURE

INTRODUCTION

> **The administrative and territorial structure of a state** is the system by which its territory is organized, divided into distinct units, and governed.

Like a circulatory system, the territorial structure of a state permeates society, shaping its internal order and the efficiency of interactions between different regions. The way a state's territory is organized determines much. Above all, it influences the stability of society and the effectiveness of governance. A clear, well-designed territorial framework allows emerging issues to be addressed swiftly and with minimal disruption, helps prevent conflicts, and fosters economic growth. By contrast, a chaotic or ill-defined division can become a constant source of tension and social destabilization.

In political philosophy, two primary models of territorial organization are recognized: the unitary state and federalism.

A unitary state is a unified system of governance in which all key decisions are made by the central authorities. Local governments generally have limited powers and are subordinate to the center. This model ensures cohesion and centralized control, yet it requires a high level of competence and accountability from the central government.

Federalism, by contrast, is built on the union of several relatively autonomous territorial units, each possessing its own powers and governing institutions. The federal model makes it possible to address the interests of diverse regions, particularly in large and multiethnic states. However, it also demands a complex system of coordination between central and regional authorities—one that can at times lead to political disagreements and reduced administrative efficiency.

Each of these models has its advantages and drawbacks, and the choice between them depends on historical circumstances, cultural characteristics, and the geographic realities of the state.

SECTION 1. UNITARY STATE — A FORM OF STATE STRUCTURE WITH CENTRALIZED SOVEREIGNTY

> **A unitary state** is a form of state structure in which authority is concentrated in the hands of a single center.

Characteristics

The defining feature of a unitary state is the absence of any sovereign or politically independent entities within its territory. Administrative divisions — such as provinces, regions, or districts — hold no inherent authority in either foreign or domestic affairs. Their powers, boundaries, and status are determined entirely by the central government, which may revise them at any time. The state functions as a single political organism, with authority concentrated in the center.

Fundamental Features of a Unitary State

1) Absence of Internal Sovereignty of Territorial Units

In a unitary state, administrative divisions do not possess political autonomy and are fully subordinate to the central authorities. Their powers are delegated rather than inherent and may be modified or revoked at any moment. Local administrations cannot adopt laws or regulations that contradict national legislation. Their role is to carry out the decisions of the central government and ensure effective local administration.

2) Unified Legislative and Legal System

A unitary state is governed by a single body of law that applies equally across the entire territory. All legislative acts are adopted by central institutions — parliament and government — and are binding on citizens as well as local authorities. Legal uniformity simplifies oversight, prevents contradictions, and minimizes the risk of disputes between regions.

3) Centralized Public Administration

Decision-making in a unitary state is highly centralized. The central government not only makes key decisions but also supervises the work of local authorities and their officials. Such centralization enables rapid responses to crises, ensures effective coordination between regions, and allows the state to pursue a consistent policy in areas such as taxation, education, defense, and foreign affairs.

4) Absence of the Right to Secession

The territory of a unitary state is regarded as indivisible. Regions and provinces have no legal right to secede or proclaim independence. By denying such a possibility, the unitary system reduces the risks of separatism and strengthens territorial integrity and internal stability.

5) Unified Citizenship and National Identity

Inhabitants of a unitary state share a single form of citizenship. This fosters a common national identity, reinforces solidarity between regions, and promotes cultural cohesion.

Advantages of a Unitary System

1. Simplicity and Efficiency of Governance

Concentrating authority in the central government makes decision-making more direct and less burdened by bureaucratic layers. Policies can be adopted and implemented without delay, allowing the state to respond swiftly to challenges and crises.

2. Stability and National Unity

By denying regions sovereign rights, the unitary model minimizes the risk of separatism and internal conflict. It safeguards the territorial integrity of the state and reinforces a strong sense of cohesion across the population. A single political framework strengthens solidarity between regions, reduces the possibility of fragmentation, and fosters the perception of a shared national destiny.

3. A Unified Legal System

A single body of law applies equally to all citizens and regions. This uniformity prevents contradictions between national and local legislation, reduces disputes, and strengthens confidence in the rule of law. It creates clear legal standards across the entire country, ensuring that rights and obligations are interpreted consistently. Such coherence reinforces stability and allows the state to govern with predictability and authority.

4. Cost-Effectiveness of Administration

The absence of overlapping layers of authority reduces administrative expenses. Resources can be allocated more efficiently, avoiding unnecessary bureaucracy and channeling funds into essential public needs.

5. Clarity of Responsibility

In a unitary state, accountability is concentrated in the central government. Citizens know which institutions are responsible for policy decisions, avoiding disputes over jurisdiction that often arise in federations.

6. Uniform Policy Implementation

National standards in areas such as education, healthcare, taxation, and environmental protection can be applied consistently across the country. This reduces regional inequalities and ensures a more even distribution of public goods.

7. Stronger International Representation

A unitary state speaks with one voice in foreign policy. The absence of competing regional positions strengthens its diplomatic leverage and enhances its ability to act coherently on the global stage.

8. Administrative Flexibility

The central government retains the authority to alter regional boundaries or redistribute powers when necessary. This flexibility allows the system to adapt to changing political, social, or economic conditions without requiring complex constitutional reform.

Disadvantages of a Unitary System

1. Insufficient Consideration of Regional Specificities

A highly centralized system frequently overlooks local needs. Policies designed in the capital fail to capture the economic, cultural, or social realities of peripheral regions, leading to dissatisfaction among the population. Over time, this gap between national policy and local conditions erodes trust in government institutions, deepens regional inequalities, and fuels protest movements or demands for greater autonomy.

2. Limited Initiative of Local Authorities

When power is concentrated in the center, local administrations may act as passive executors rather than proactive managers. This discourages initiative and innovation, slowing the effective development of individual territories.

3. Risk of Overconcentration of Power

Excessive centralization without proper oversight leads to abuse. Corruption, arbitrariness, and inefficiency thrive when accountability is weak and decision-making remains unchecked. Power concentrated in too few hands isolates the ruling elite from society, erodes institutional balance, and ultimately undermines both the effectiveness and the legitimacy of governance.

4. Difficulty in Accommodating Diversity

In large or multiethnic states, a unitary framework may struggle to recognize cultural, linguistic, and ethnic differences. The lack of space for diversity fosters alienation and deepens regional discontent.

5. Democratic Deficit

Citizens in remote regions may feel disconnected from national politics, as decisions are made exclusively by central institutions. Limited opportunities for participation at the local level weaken public engagement and reduce the legitimacy of governance.

6. Policy Rigidity

Uniform decisions imposed from the center are not always well suited to local conditions. Reforms that ignore regional variation can lead to inefficient outcomes and poor implementation.

7. Slower Local Response to Crises

Because authority rests with the center, local governments may lack the flexibility to respond quickly to emergencies or unique regional challenges. Delays in decision-making can worsen crises and damage public trust.

8. Overburdening of the Central Government

When the center is responsible for every major issue, national institutions risk being overwhelmed. This overconcentration of responsibility breeds inefficiency and hampers effective governance.

Chapter 1

Centralized Unitary State:
Political Authority Concentrated at the National Level

> **A centralized unitary state** is a model of territorial organization in which power is concentrated to the greatest extent in the hands of the central governing institutions. Regions and local structures possess only minimal autonomy, since all key matters are decided exclusively by the central authorities.

Characteristics

In a centralized unitary state, political, administrative, and economic power is concentrated in the hands of the central governing institutions. In such a system, regions, provinces, or other territorial units possess no real autonomy in making key decisions.

Fundamental Features of a Centralized Unitary State

1) Maximum Concentration of Power in the Center

In a centralized unitary state, the central government holds exclusive authority over major political, economic, social, and cultural decisions. Regional and local administrations are not permitted to chart independent development strategies. Their role is confined to the faithful implementation of directives issued from the center and the enforcement of these policies at the local level.

2) Minimal Autonomy of Local Authorities

Administrative units are fully subordinate to the central government and cannot independently determine their economic or social policies. They lack the authority to enact legislation or regulate essential aspects of local life. Regional and municipal bodies serve as executors of central decisions, which ensures consistency of governance across the entire country.

3) Strict Oversight by Central Authorities

A defining characteristic of this model is the constant oversight exercised by the center over local administrations. Regular inspections, obligatory reporting, and close monitoring of compliance are the mechanisms through which central leadership maintains control.

4) A Unified and Standardized Legal System

The centralized state preserves a single legal framework with no regional variations. All laws are enacted by central institutions, are universally binding, and apply equally to all citizens. The absence of regional distinctions reinforces stability, guarantees equality before the law, and provides a coherent foundation for national policy.

5) A Unified Budgetary and Tax Policy

The financial system is likewise concentrated in the hands of the central government. Regional budgets are planned at the national level, and the allocation of financial resources reflects state priorities. Local administrations lack independent taxing authority and cannot freely dispose of revenues without central approval.

Strengths of a Centralized Unitary State

1. A High Degree of National Unity and Political Stability

A centralized unitary state strengthens the unity and integrity of the country. By concentrating power in the hands of the central authorities, it minimizes the risk of regional conflict and separatist movements. Local administrations lack independent political authority and therefore cannot challenge the center or undermine territorial integrity. This ensures stability and allows the state to pursue a consistent set of priorities across the whole territory.

2. Efficiency of Governance and Speed in Crisis Decision-Making

Centralization gives the state the ability to act quickly and decisively in times of crisis — whether in response to natural disasters, economic shocks, or threats to national security. Decisions do not require lengthy negotiations with regional authorities or the reconciliation of competing local interests. The central government can mobilize resources swiftly, direct them to where they are needed, and ensure that measures are implemented promptly at every level of administration.

3. Uniformity of Legislation and Public Policy

In a centralized state, legal norms and standards are unified across the entire country. Citizens, regardless of where they live, enjoy equal rights, obligations, and social guarantees. The absence of regional legal variation prevents jurisdictional conflicts and secures equality before the law.

4. A Clear and Transparent Vertical of Power

A centralized system provides a clearly defined chain of authority, extending from the central government to local administrations. This makes governance simple, predictable, and comprehensible for both citizens and officials.

5. Simplified Control and Supervision of Policy Implementation

Strong centralization facilitates effective monitoring and enforcement of state decisions. Regular inspections, reporting requirements, and close supervision allow the central government to detect and correct errors quickly, while also combating corruption and inefficiency.

6. Symbolic Cohesion and Nation-Building

The centralized model strengthens national identity by promoting shared symbols, common institutions, and unified state policies. This fosters a sense of belonging to a single nation and reinforces the cultural cohesion of society.

7. Ease of Reform Implementation

Reforms introduced at the central level can be applied uniformly throughout the entire country. This accelerates modernization, prevents uneven development, and avoids the patchwork of regional differences that often complicates reform in federal systems.

Weaknesses of a Centralized Unitary State

1. Insufficient Consideration of Local Characteristics and Interests

One of the clearest weaknesses of a centralized unitary system is its inability to reflect the diversity of regions. A country usually includes territories with distinct economic, cultural, ethnic, and social conditions. Excessive concentration of power in the center leads to decisions that disregard these differences.

2. Restriction of Local Initiative and Suppression of Innovation

When local governments function only as executors of central directives, their ability to take initiative and seek creative solutions is steadily diminished. Over time, officials grow passive, conservative, and reluctant to accept responsibility for regional development.

3. Overload of Central Authorities and Bureaucratization

Central institutions become burdened with a massive volume of decisions, ranging from strategic priorities to minor administrative details. This overload creates delays, generates red tape, and slows the government's response to pressing issues. Citizens and local administrations are forced to wait for instructions even on routine matters, which undermines efficiency and fuels dissatisfaction with the system as a whole.

4. Low Flexibility and Slow Response to Local Problems

A centralized model is poorly equipped to respond quickly to local challenges. The time lag between the emergence of a problem and the adoption of a central decision erodes public trust and amplifies frustration. In emergencies or crises, this lack of flexibility can cause real harm, leaving communities vulnerable and deepening social discontent.

5. Absence of Political and Administrative Competition at the Local Level

In a centralized state, local governance depends not on the choice of citizens but on appointments and instructions from above. Without competition or electoral accountability, regional leaders lack incentives to improve their performance or to respond to the concerns of the population. Over time, this weakens the quality of governance, distances authorities from society, and worsens the conditions of local communities.

6. Democratic Deficit and Weak Public Participation

The concentration of decision-making in the center reduces opportunities for citizens to influence politics at the local level. People in the regions feel excluded from governance, which undermines engagement, weakens civic responsibility, and erodes the legitimacy of central institutions.

7. Regional Alienation in Multinational States

In countries with strong ethnic, linguistic, or cultural diversity, a rigidly centralized model often deepens the sense of marginalization among minority regions. When their identities and interests are ignored, tensions grow, fueling mistrust, separatist tendencies, and sometimes open conflict.

Historical Examples of Centralized Unitary States
France before the 1982 Reform

France has long been regarded as one of the clearest historical examples of a centralized unitary state. From the nineteenth century through much of the twentieth, political, economic, and administrative authority was concentrated almost entirely in the hands of the central government in Paris.

The French Revolution of 1789 and, later, the reforms of Napoleon Bonaparte reinforced this centralization. The revolutionaries sought unity and predictability in governance, while Napoleon built a strong administrative vertical in which Paris exercised control over every level of the state. Prefects, appointed by the central government and accountable to the Ministry of the Interior, embodied this principle. They executed directives from above, supervised compliance with state decrees, and curtailed any local initiative not sanctioned by the center.

Strengths of the Centralized Model

Maximum centralization provided France with a high degree of unity and stability. A single legal system, a standardized approach to education and healthcare, and a uniform administrative apparatus made the country cohesive and governable. The government could quickly mobilize resources, implement nationwide reforms, and respond effectively to crises. For decades, this model was seen as a hallmark of discipline and administrative efficiency.

Weaknesses and the Push for Reform

By the mid-twentieth century, however, the limitations of rigid centralization had become clear. French regions differed sharply in economic resources, cultural traditions, and historical identity, yet Paris imposed standardized policies with little regard for these differences. This created discontent in places such as Brittany, Corsica, Alsace, and Provence.

The central government was also overburdened, as nearly every matter — large or small — required national decision-making. The result was inefficiency, bureaucratic delay, and slow responses to local issues. Over time, strict centralization stifled initiative at the regional and municipal levels. Local administrations grew dependent on Paris, losing both responsibility and incentive to pursue independent development.

The Decentralization Reform of 1982

By the early 1980s, reform was inevitable. In 1982, under President François Mitterrand, France adopted sweeping decentralization measures. Significant powers were transferred to regional and municipal governments, giving them authority in economic, social, and cultural affairs. Prefects lost much of their former dominance, while elected regional councils and city mayors gained real decision-making authority.

France remained a unitary state, but abandoned extreme centralization. The reform created a more balanced system, in which central authority continued to guarantee unity while local governments acquired the ability to address the needs and identities of their own territories.

Turkey

The Republic of Turkey, founded in 1923 by Mustafa Kemal Atatürk, was conceived from the outset as a strongly centralized state. Atatürk sought to build a modern, homogeneous nation, and to achieve this he created a system in which political authority was concentrated firmly in the capital. This rigid centralization continues to shape Turkey's governance today.

Main Features of Centralized Governance in Turkey

Power in Turkey is concentrated in Ankara. Although the country is formally divided into provinces and districts, these territories possess no real political autonomy. Legislative, executive, and judicial authority rests entirely with central institutions, enabling national leaders to direct political, economic, and social policy across the whole territory.

Local administrations are tightly controlled by the central government. Provincial governors (vali) are appointed rather than elected, report directly to the Ministry of the Interior, and are obliged to enforce central directives. In practice, this leaves little scope for local initiative, as governors serve primarily as extensions of Ankara's authority.

Uniform legislation reinforces this model. Laws passed by parliament and confirmed by the president apply nationwide, without exceptions or special provisions for particular regions. This guarantees legal consistency and administrative uniformity, but it leaves little room to adapt policies to regional needs.

Centralization also extends into education and culture. Curricula, textbooks, and teaching standards are defined exclusively by the Ministry of Education.

Strengths of the Turkish Model

Centralization has made the Turkish state highly manageable, allowing it to maintain effective control across its territory and respond quickly to crises. National standards ensure uniformity in social and economic policy, simplifying implementation and oversight. The model also strengthens territorial integrity and national cohesion, reducing the risk of separatism or fragmentation.

Weaknesses of the Turkish Model

At the same time, rigid centralization has exposed its limitations. Many regions — particularly in the east and southeast, where much of the Kurdish population resides — continue to face chronic economic and social problems that centralized policies fail to resolve. National institutions are often overburdened with administrative tasks, generating bureaucratic delays and reducing the efficiency of decision-making.

The Balance Between Centralization and Decentralization

Turkey's model has succeeded in safeguarding national unity and governability, but it has struggled with the challenge of insufficient sensitivity to regional differences and limited local autonomy. Like other states governed through rigid centralization, Turkey continues to face the task of finding a sustainable balance between strong central authority and meaningful decentralization of powers.

Japan

Japan has historically been regarded as a classic example of a centralized unitary state. The country's political history is a long process of reinforcing central unity, which has shaped the way governance is organized to this day.

Centralization in Japan reaches back to the early state of Yamato in the 6th–7th centuries, when the imperial court in Kyoto issued decrees for the entire country. During the Tokugawa era (1603–1868), this tendency reached new heights: the shogunate exercised strict control over the provinces, maintaining political unity and administrative discipline across the islands.

The Meiji Restoration of 1868 launched a new phase. Power shifted from the shogunate back to the emperor, and the central government in Tokyo introduced sweeping reforms. Prefectures were created as purely administrative units without political or economic autonomy. All major decisions—whether industrial development, infrastructure, education, or healthcare—were made exclusively by the central authorities. This model enabled Japan to modernize rapidly and build the foundations of a modern state.

After World War II, Japan underwent deep reforms, but its centralized system remained intact. The 1947 Constitution established a unitary framework in which prefectures continued to operate under strong central oversight, especially in finance, economic policy, and social programs. Local officials are formally elected, yet their work remains closely tied to directives from Tokyo.

Strengths of Japan's Centralized Model

Centralization gave Japan remarkable administrative capacity and discipline. A unified framework ensured consistency in education, healthcare, and social policy, providing equality of opportunity and high living standards across all regions. Central authority also allowed Japan to implement reforms swiftly, laying the foundation for rapid technological progress and long-term economic development.

Weaknesses of the Model

Rigid centralization often failed to account for regional needs. Rural and remote areas struggled with funding and infrastructure, while prefectures had little power to address these challenges independently. Limited autonomy stifled initiative and innovation at the local level, discouraging self-driven development. At the same time, concentrating nearly all decisions in Tokyo placed a heavy administrative burden on the central government, slowing policy adaptation and creating bureaucratic delays.

Trends Toward Decentralization

In recent decades, Japan has begun cautiously transferring some powers to prefectural and municipal authorities. Reforms have expanded their financial and administrative responsibilities, giving local governments more room to respond to their communities. Yet central authority remains dominant, and Japan continues to stand as one of the clearest textbook examples of a centralized unitary state.

Chapter 2

Decentralized Unitary State:
Local Governments with Delegated Powers
Under a Unified Framework

A decentralized unitary state is a form of government in which the single and indivisible territory of the state is divided into administrative units that are granted a certain degree of autonomy by the central authority in resolving local matters, while centralized control is maintained over key national policies and legislation.

Characteristics

In a decentralized unitary state, the central authority retains supremacy in governing the country but significantly expands the powers of regional and local governments. The central government continues to set the main directions of domestic and foreign policy and ensures compliance with national legislation and standards, yet many specific matters of territorial administration are delegated to regional and municipal bodies.

Fundamental Features of a Decentralized Unitary State

1) Combination of Centralized Control and Local Autonomy

The essence of this model lies in combining two principles: strong central direction and genuine local autonomy. The central government defines the overall course and provides the legal framework, while regional and local administrations are given the authority to adapt implementation to their own conditions and the needs of their citizens.

2) Expansion of Powers of Regional and Local Administrations

Local and regional governments manage their own budgets, organize economic activity, regulate social welfare, develop infrastructure, and oversee education and healthcare. This enables them to respond quickly and flexibly to local challenges, set development priorities independently, and allocate resources in line with the specific characteristics of their territories.

3) Clear Division of Competences between Center and Regions

Responsibilities are distributed transparently between central and regional authorities. The center retains control over defense, foreign policy, law enforcement, and strategic economic planning. Regional administrations, in turn, are entrusted with areas that shape daily life — from schools and hospitals to housing, utilities, cultural programs, and local social policy.

4) Balance of Responsibility and Autonomy

Decentralization implies not only granting rights but also assigning clear responsibility. Local governments receive powers and resources but are fully accountable for how effectively they use them. The central government maintains supervisory functions, intervening only when necessary to safeguard national interests or correct serious failures.

5) **Encouragement of Local Initiative and Stimulation of Regional Development**

Decentralization fosters creativity and initiative at the local level. Regional authorities can launch their own projects, attract investment, and pursue strategies tailored to their communities. This strengthens accountability, unlocks regional potential, and contributes to the balanced social and economic development of the entire country.

Strengths of a Decentralized Unitary State

1. **Flexibility and High Adaptability of Governance**

Decentralization gives the state the ability to respond quickly to changing conditions and local needs. Regional and local administrations, being closer to the daily lives of citizens, can detect and address problems more effectively.

2. **Effective Consideration of Regional Characteristics and Interests**

Local governments have a direct understanding of the economic, social, geographic, and cultural features of their communities. This makes it possible to plan budgets, set development priorities, and design social programs and infrastructure projects with greater accuracy.

3. **Encouragement of Local Initiative and Creativity**

When entrusted with real powers and resources, local administrations feel a stronger sense of responsibility and are motivated to seek innovative approaches. This fosters greater activism, independence, and creativity among regional leaders, leading to new projects that directly improve the lives of citizens. Decentralization strengthens the link between responsibility and initiative, encouraging confidence and accountability at the local level.

4. **Development of Civil Society and Local Self-Government**

Decentralization creates opportunities for citizens to influence decision-making through local elections and civic participation. It strengthens the mechanisms of local self-government and allows communities to oversee the performance of their leaders more directly. As a result, civic responsibility deepens, trust between citizens and the state grows, and democratic institutions become more resilient.

5. **Reduced Burden on the Central Government**

By transferring responsibility for routine matters to the local level, decentralization frees the center from the need to manage everyday issues. Central authorities can then concentrate on strategic tasks such as national security, foreign policy, macroeconomic planning, and major reforms. This division of labor enhances the effectiveness of central institutions while leaving local matters in the hands of those closest to them.

6. **Promotion of Balanced Regional Development**

Decentralization encourages more even development across the country. Regional governments can attract investment, launch economic programs, and design projects suited to their own needs. This helps reduce disparities between prosperous and underdeveloped regions, stimulates local growth, and contributes to a fairer distribution of national resources.

Weaknesses of a Decentralized Unitary State

1. Risk of Conflicts between Central and Regional Authorities

When regions are granted broad powers, disagreements with the center become more likely. Regional governments may adopt policies that contradict national priorities, creating tensions that escalate into open confrontation. Over time, such conflicts undermine national unity, complicate the implementation of state programs, and may even trigger political crises.

2. Erosion of Cohesion and Intensification of Regional Differences

Excessive decentralization weakens the integrative role of the state. Different regions begin to follow their own standards in education, healthcare, or social protection, eroding the sense of shared citizenship. The result is a fragmented political space, where regional disparities deepen and civic unity becomes harder to sustain.

3. Uneven Economic and Social Development

Decentralization often sharpens inequalities between regions. Wealthier areas, rich in resources and infrastructure, move ahead quickly by attracting investment and launching ambitious projects. Poorer regions, lacking resources or administrative capacity, lag further behind. The widening gap fuels dissatisfaction and internal tensions, sometimes spilling over into political conflict.

4. Difficulties in Control and Coordination

The wider the scope of powers delegated to the local level, the more difficult it becomes for the center to maintain coherence. Independent-minded administrations are reluctant to follow national directives, preferring their own approaches. Central authorities must then spend time and resources on monitoring and alignment, which increases the administrative burden and weakens efficiency.

5. Increased Risk of Corruption and Abuse of Power

When significant powers and financial resources are devolved without strong oversight, opportunities for corruption multiply. Local administrations gain control over substantial funds but are often subject to weaker checks by the center and civil society. This fosters clientelism, misuse of public money, and declining trust in both regional leaders and the decentralization process itself.

6. Shortage of Qualified Personnel

Decentralization requires skilled and responsible administrators at the local level. Yet many regions lack professionals capable of handling complex governance tasks. This shortage leads to mistakes, inefficiency, and uneven performance, slowing development and undermining the credibility of local self-government.

7. Risk of Inequality in Rights and Services

When regions receive greater powers, differences emerge in the quality of healthcare, education, and social protection. Citizens in wealthier territories enjoy better services and opportunities, while those in poorer areas are left behind.

Historical Examples of Decentralized Unitary States

The United Kingdom after the Devolution Reforms (Late 20th Century)

For centuries, the United Kingdom was regarded as a classic example of a centralized unitary state. Real political and economic power was concentrated in London, with Parliament and the government holding authority over England, Scotland, Wales, and Northern Ireland alike. By the close of the twentieth century, however, rigid centralization no longer suited the realities of a multinational and multicultural society. It was generating discontent and sharpening regional tensions.

The Beginning of Devolution

Between 1997 and 1999, Britain undertook far-reaching constitutional reforms known as devolution — literally, the transfer of power downward. The aim was to shift part of the authority from London to regional parliaments and governments in Scotland, Wales, and Northern Ireland. This redistribution of powers granted these territories far greater autonomy and enabled their institutions to respond more effectively to regional concerns.

The Nature of Devolution in the UK's Regions

Scotland received the broadest powers. A parliament was created in Edinburgh, elected by the Scottish people, and authorized to legislate in areas such as education, healthcare, justice, culture, infrastructure, and regional development. Scotland also obtained partial control over taxation, including the right to introduce supplementary local taxes.

Wales established the National Assembly (later renamed the Senedd, or Welsh Parliament). Its authority covered healthcare, education, culture, agriculture, and environmental protection. Though narrower than Scotland's, these powers nevertheless allowed Welsh institutions to tailor policy to local needs.

Northern Ireland formed its own Assembly and devolved government with powers over healthcare, education, agriculture, social policy, transport, and housing. Devolution there had special significance: it helped ease long-standing conflict by accommodating the interests of divided communities and reducing political tensions.

Retention of Central Authority

Even with wide powers devolved, the London government retained control over the fundamental levers of sovereignty: foreign policy and international relations, defense and national security, immigration, monetary and fiscal policy, and constitutional matters. These safeguards maintained national unity and prevented fragmentation, while still leaving ample space for regional self-government.

Strengths of Devolution in the United Kingdom

Devolution eased tensions in historically divided regions. By granting institutions in Edinburgh, Cardiff, and Belfast real powers, local grievances were better addressed and the risks of separatism reduced, especially in Scotland and Northern Ireland. Regional governments were able to act with greater flexibility, taking into account specific economic, social, and cultural conditions. Citizens, in turn, gained a stronger voice in governance, which encouraged civic engagement, fostered local initiative, and strengthened democratic accountability.

Weaknesses of Devolution in the United Kingdom

At the same time, decentralization introduced new challenges. Coordination between central and regional institutions became more complex, often requiring careful negotiation and producing administrative disputes. Development proceeded unevenly: some regions advanced more quickly than others, deepening inequalities in welfare and living standards.

Italy after World War II

At the end of the Second World War, Italy was confronted with profound challenges: a devastated economy, sharp regional disparities, and deep social divisions. These conditions forced the country to reconsider its traditionally centralized model of governance and to move gradually toward decentralization.

The Beginning of Decentralization

The Italian Constitution of 1947, which came into force in 1948, laid the foundation for a new system. While affirming the unity of the state, it also acknowledged the need to transfer significant powers to the regions so that local authorities could better address the concerns of their populations. Italy was divided into regions (*regioni*), each with its own elected council and executive government.

The Scope of Regional Powers

Regional administrations were entrusted with broad authority across many spheres of public life. They were empowered to shape economic development, design programs tailored to local priorities, and allocate resources to attract investment. Responsibility for hospitals, healthcare, and welfare was also devolved, allowing policies to be adapted more closely to the needs of communities. In education and culture, regions could oversee schools, vocational training, and cultural institutions, while also promoting local traditions. Infrastructure and transport became another important domain, as regions planned and modernized roads, bridges, and municipal networks. At the same time, the central government retained responsibility for matters of national importance such as foreign policy, defense, taxation, macroeconomic planning, and the judiciary.

Strengths of Italian Decentralization

Decentralization made it possible to consider regional needs more accurately, since local authorities were closer to the population and could respond more quickly to emerging challenges. It also encouraged initiative and creativity in the regions, improving the quality of governance and strengthening civic engagement. By giving communities a greater role in managing sensitive social issues, the new system helped reduce public dissatisfaction and eased social tensions.

Weaknesses of the Italian Model

Yet decentralization also exposed its limitations. The most visible problem was uneven development: northern regions such as Lombardy, Piedmont, and Veneto prospered, while southern areas including Calabria, Sicily, and Apulia continued to struggle with chronic economic difficulties and weak institutional capacity. Coordination between the center and the regions also proved difficult. Wide regional autonomy produced a complex administrative system that increased bureaucratic costs and slowed effective oversight. Finally, decentralization led to recurring disputes between the central government and the regions, particularly over taxation, financial regulation, and the distribution of budgetary resources.

Sweden

The Swedish model of governance is built on a carefully balanced combination of centralized oversight and broad autonomy for regional and municipal authorities.

Main Characteristics of Swedish Decentralization

Sweden is divided into 21 regions (*län*) and more than 290 municipalities (*kommuner*), each enjoying extensive autonomy. They are responsible for social policy, healthcare, education, transportation infrastructure, housing, and local economic development. Local councils and executive bodies are elected by the population and are directly accountable for their decisions and results.

A cornerstone of the Swedish model is the principle of subsidiarity: authority should rest at the level of government closest to the citizens. The central government in Stockholm intervenes only when national interests are at stake or when local decisions contradict national law. This principle allows municipalities and regions to respond flexibly and promptly to challenges, applying solutions best suited to local circumstances.

Responsibilities are clearly divided between levels of government. Central authorities manage foreign policy, defense, financial regulation, and set nationwide standards in healthcare and education. Yet their role is limited to defining principles and objectives. Implementation rests with regions and municipalities, which independently manage their budgets and resources in pursuit of these goals.

Strengths of the Swedish Model

This system makes it possible to take regional needs into account with great precision. Regions and municipalities can adapt policies to their own conditions and respond quickly to local concerns. Decentralization also stimulates initiative and strengthens accountability, while enhancing civic participation in decision-making. With financial and administrative independence, local governments actively work to improve the quality of life for citizens, ensuring consistently high standards in education, healthcare, and social protection across the country.

Weaknesses and Risks

Yet decentralization also presents challenges. Broad autonomy requires constant coordination from the center, which complicates the management of nationwide policies and increases the complexity of governance. In addition, despite Sweden's overall balance of development, differences persist between urban and rural municipalities. Smaller or less wealthy communities sometimes struggle to provide services at the same level as larger cities, which necessitates additional oversight and support from the central government.

Conclusion

A comparison of centralized and decentralized models of unitary states clearly reveals both their strengths and weaknesses. Each model carries its own advantages and specific risks, making it well-suited in some contexts and less effective in others.

A centralized unitary state resembles a finely tuned mechanism with a strict vertical of authority. It can respond decisively and swiftly to crises, while ensuring a high degree of unity and political stability. A unified legislative and administrative system simplifies enforcement and guarantees equal conditions of life for all citizens. Yet such a model often lacks the flexibility and sensitivity required to address regional differences.

A decentralized model, by contrast, is marked by adaptability and the ability to take regional conditions and community interests into account. The transfer of significant powers to lower levels stimulates local initiative, strengthens civil society, eases the burden on central institutions, and allows regions to chart their own paths of development. However, this flexibility comes at a cost: decentralization heightens the risk of conflict between center and regions, complicates policy coordination, and makes oversight more difficult. Moreover, regions with unequal starting conditions develop at different rates, producing economic inequality and social tensions.

The choice between these models depends on numerous factors. Historical experience, geography, economic structure, national and ethnic composition, and the degree of social and cultural homogeneity all play a decisive role in shaping the appropriate balance between centralization and decentralization. States with diverse populations, strong regional identities, and significant economic disparities often favor decentralization, as it allows for effective accommodation of local interests, conflict prevention, and more sustainable development. By contrast, states with a high degree of homogeneity and a long tradition of centralized rule are more inclined to maintain a centralized model, prioritizing stability and unity.

In today's world, the boundary between these two models is becoming increasingly blurred. The twenty-first century is defined by rapid social and economic change, globalization, and technological advancement. Modern states increasingly seek to combine the advantages of both models through hybrid forms of territorial organization. Such systems unite centralized control in strategic matters with significant regional autonomy in local governance.

Looking ahead, the future of state territorial organization is likely to be shaped by the continued development of hybrid governance models, in which centralized and decentralized elements are combined in the most rational way. In an era of constant change, a state's ability to adapt flexibly and efficiently has become a crucial factor of its resilience and success. For this reason, the search for an optimal balance between unity and autonomy, centralization and local initiative, remains one of the foremost tasks of governance in the twenty-first century.

SECTION 2. FEDERAL STATE — DIVISION OF POWERS BETWEEN NATIONAL AND REGIONAL GOVERNMENT

> **A federal state** is a form of government in which the territory of the country is composed of several relatively autonomous entities—such as states, provinces, or republics—each possessing its own system of government, legislative powers, and authority to make decisions on certain matters of domestic policy, while the supremacy of federal authority is maintained in all affairs of national importance.

Characteristics

A federal state is composed of relatively autonomous territorial units — states, provinces, Länder, cantons, or republics — each with its own system of government, legislative assembly, and judicial structures. These entities exercise authority over many issues independently of the central government, yet remain bound together by a single federal constitution. This constitution defines the scope of their powers and guarantees the supremacy of federal authority in matters of national importance.

Fundamental Features of a Federal State

1) **Clear Division of Powers between Center and Regions**
   - The federal constitution specifies which powers belong exclusively to the central government (foreign policy, defense, monetary system, customs).
   - It also defines the competences of constituent units (local legislation, education, healthcare, culture, infrastructure).
   - Shared responsibilities, such as taxation or law enforcement, require coordination between center and regions.

2) **Independent Systems of Government in the Constituent Units**
   - Each region has its own elected parliament, government, and judicial system.
   - These bodies independently govern their territories and enact laws, provided they do not contradict federal legislation.
   - This arrangement reflects cultural and historical traditions and allows for local specificity in governance.

3) **Supremacy of the Federal Constitution**
   - The unity of the state is preserved by the federal constitution, which is the highest law of the land.
   - It regulates conflicts of competence, defines mechanisms of coordination, and ensures the coherence of federal policy across all regions.

4) **Representation of Constituent Units at the Federal Level**
   - Federations establish special institutions to represent the interests of regions in national decision-making (e.g., the U.S. Senate, the German Bundesrat).

- o Through these institutions, constituent units actively participate in shaping federal policy, reinforcing both unity and legitimacy.

Historical Origins of Federal States

- **Voluntary Union of States or Territories**:

  For example, the United States was formed when former British colonies united to better address defense, foreign policy, and economic challenges.

- **Preservation of Unity in Multinational States**:

  In countries with diverse ethnic, linguistic, or cultural groups, federalism helps prevent disintegration by granting autonomy. Canada, for instance, adopted a federal structure to balance the interests of its French- and English-speaking populations.

Comparison with the Unitary State

- In a **unitary system**, regions possess no sovereignty and remain subordinate to the central government.

- In a **federation**, constituent units enjoy constitutionally guaranteed autonomy and broad powers.

- Federal states are more adaptable to diversity but require complex mechanisms to coordinate policies and resolve conflicts between the center and the regions.

For this reason, the federal model is most often adopted by large and diverse states, where no other arrangement can simultaneously preserve unity, ensure stability, and respect the interests of different communities.

Chapter 1

Symmetrical Federation:
Equal Rights and Powers Among Constituent Units

> **A symmetrical federation** is a form of federal organization in which all constituent units possess the same constitutional and legal status, hold an equal scope of powers, and enjoy the same rights and responsibilities in relation to the federal government, without any privileges or special conditions granted to particular territories.

Characteristics

A symmetrical federation is a model of territorial organization in which all constituent units of the federation possess an absolutely equal legal status and hold an identical set of powers, rights, and responsibilities in their relations with the federal center. In such a system, there are no territories or regions endowed with special privileges, exceptional rights, or extended autonomy compared to other constituent units.

Fundamental Features of a Symmetrical Federation

A symmetrical federation is defined by the strict legal equality of all its constituent units. Whether they are called states, provinces, Länder, or republics, each enjoys the same rights and competences as laid down in the federal constitution or legislation. No territory is granted a privileged status or exceptional arrangements in its relationship with the center. This principle secures the uniformity of the state's structure and guarantees equal political and legal opportunities for citizens throughout the federation.

1) Equality of Constituent Units

The hallmark of a symmetrical federation is that all territorial entities stand on equal footing. Their constitutional powers are identical, and none enjoys privileges or special prerogatives in its relations with the federal government. This ensures that citizens across the country live under the same institutional framework, with equal rights and opportunities regardless of their region of residence.

2) Unified System of Legislation and Administration

Another defining characteristic is the standardization of legislative and administrative principles. Federal laws apply uniformly throughout the entire state, and all regions operate within the same framework. The constitution clearly establishes the boundaries of federal and regional competences, leaving little room for ambiguity or selective interpretation. This guarantees transparency and predictability in governance, while also creating equal living conditions for citizens across the federation.

3) Clear Division of Powers

The constitution sets out a strict division of authority between the federal center and the constituent units. The central government is responsible for matters of strategic and national significance, such as:

- defense and national security,
- foreign policy and international relations,
- the national tax system,
- financial, banking, and monetary policy,
- nationwide standards in law, human rights, healthcare, and education.

The constituent units, by contrast, govern issues of regional and local concern, including:

- the development of local infrastructure (roads, utilities, housing),
- regional economic development and social policy,
- education, healthcare, and culture at the regional level,
- environmental protection and resource management.

Such a framework allows both levels of government to act effectively within their own sphere, avoiding duplication of powers and minimizing conflict. The result is a political system that combines national unity with regional autonomy, while maintaining equality across all constituent units.

Strengths of a Symmetrical Federation

1. A High Level of Political and Social Unity

The central advantage of symmetrical federalism lies in its ability to foster strong national unity. Full equality among constituent units removes privileged regions or territories with special status, thereby reducing the risk of interregional tensions, conflicts, or separatist movements. By treating all units equally, the system strengthens national identity, nurtures a shared civic consciousness, and harmonizes relations between the regions and the federal center.

2. Transparency and Predictability of Governance

Symmetrical federations are built on a unified system of law and administration. The constitution clearly defines the competences of both the federal center and the constituent units, preventing duplication of functions and jurisdictional disputes. Citizens can easily see which level of authority is responsible for particular decisions, which makes governance straightforward, transparent, and more accountable.

3. Ease of Coordination between Center and Regions

Because constituent units enjoy equal powers and operate under the same framework, coordination between the center and the regions becomes far less complicated. Nationwide programs are easier to implement, since regions follow common standards without exceptions or special arrangements. This uniformity increases efficiency and ensures coherence of governance, particularly in times of crisis, when swift and unified action is essential.

4. Equal Opportunities and Fairness in Regional Development

Symmetrical federalism ensures that no region enjoys special privileges, which makes the distribution of resources more equitable. Equal conditions for economic growth and social development reduce the likelihood of deepening disparities, limit public dissatisfaction, and promote balanced prosperity across the country. This fairness strengthens trust in federal institutions and supports long-term stability.

5. Strengthening of National Identity

The equal status of all regions and the existence of a unified legal system help cultivate a strong sense of belonging to one nation. Common standards in education, cultural policy, and social programs create a shared civic space in which citizens identify not only with their local community but also with the federation as a whole.

6. Simplified Oversight and Supervision

The clear division of competences makes it easier for federal institutions to monitor the work of regional governments. Because all units operate under the same legal framework and possess no exceptional rights, compliance with federal laws can be enforced more effectively. This reduces the risks of violations, strengthens accountability, and upholds the integrity of the system.

Weaknesses of a Symmetrical Federation

1. Insufficient Consideration of Regional Specificities

The greatest limitation of symmetrical federalism is its inability to reflect the diversity of its regions. Legal equality does not erase real differences in economic development, geography, demographics, or cultural traditions. Uniform laws and standards often force territories with very different conditions to follow the same rules, even when they are poorly suited to local realities. This reduces the effectiveness of governance, lowers the quality of life, and generates dissatisfaction among the population.

2. Limited Flexibility in Governance and Adaptation to Change

Because all constituent units operate within the same legal framework, their ability to respond quickly to local challenges is restricted. Standardized rules devised at the federal level rarely correspond to the varied realities of regions, especially in times of crisis, when urgent and unconventional measures may be required. The result is slower adaptation to new circumstances and reduced efficiency in administration.

3. Risk of Progressive Centralization of Power

Although regions formally retain autonomy, the symmetrical model carries the danger of creeping centralization. By imposing uniform norms and standards, the federal center can gradually expand its influence, reducing genuine independence to a formality. Over time, this tendency erodes regional autonomy and provokes resentment, particularly if the center begins to interfere in local affairs without regard to specific needs and interests.

4. Stifling of Local Initiative and Regional Development

Rigid uniformity weakens the motivation of local administrations to pursue innovation. When all territories are bound by identical competences and rules, regions lose the ability to design tailored programs or experiment with solutions suited to their own development. This uniformity fosters passivity, limits creativity, and in the long run risks stagnation in economically or socially vulnerable areas.

5. Potential Growth of Regional Inequality

Finally, symmetrical federalism does not eliminate the risk of inequality. Formally equal conditions benefit stronger regions, which possess greater resources and administrative capacity, while poorer territories fall behind. Instead of narrowing disparities, uniform standards can widen them, since weaker regions lack the means to meet the same requirements as their more prosperous counterparts.

6. Absence of Mechanisms for Exceptional Cases

A symmetrical federation is poorly adapted to situations in which particular regions objectively require special arrangements — whether because of their ethnic composition, geopolitical position, exposure to natural disasters, or persistent economic weakness. Lacking flexible mechanisms for such cases, the system forces all territories into identical frameworks. This rigidity not only prevents the resolution of pressing local problems but also risks intensifying conflicts and deepening crises.

Historical Examples of Symmetrical Federations
The United States of America

Since the adoption of the Constitution in 1787, the United States has preserved the foundations of its federal system, built on the principle of complete legal equality among all states. The framers of the Constitution saw this equality as a safeguard against regional conflict and as a guarantee of unity for the new nation, created by the voluntary union of thirteen former colonies. Today, the federation includes fifty states, each with identical legal status and none enjoying special rights or privileges.

System of Governance and Division of Powers

Every state has its own constitution, legislature, governor and executive branch, and an independent judiciary. Within their competences, states exercise broad autonomy: they regulate local self-government, law enforcement, civil and criminal law at the state level, the organization of healthcare and education, social policy, infrastructure development, and the regulation of business.

At the same time, the Constitution clearly delineates the authority of the federal government, which retains exclusive control over areas of national and strategic importance:

- national defense and security,
- foreign policy and international relations,
- issuance of currency and monetary policy,
- regulation of interstate and international trade,
- protection of constitutional rights and freedoms.

The principle of division of powers is reinforced by the Tenth Amendment (1791), which specifies that all powers not explicitly delegated to the federal government are reserved to the states. This constitutional guarantee preserves the balance between the center and the regions and prevents unlimited interference of federal institutions in state affairs.

Strengths of the American Model

- **Political Stability.** Equality of the states and the clear delineation of competences prevent systemic conflict between the center and the regions, maintaining national unity.

- **Equal Conditions for Development.** Uniform legal status excludes privileges for particular states, promoting balanced development and reducing inequality.

- **Transparency of Governance.** Citizens clearly see where the authority of state governments ends and federal authority begins, which strengthens trust in institutions and simplifies interaction with them.

Weaknesses of the Model

- **Limited Flexibility.** Formal equality sometimes fails to reflect the real differences among states with very different economic and social contexts — for example, between California, Alaska, and Mississippi.

- **Disparities in Quality of Life.** Despite equal status, differences in economic capacity and development create significant variation in public services and living standards across states.

Contemporary Trends

For more than two centuries, the American federal system has shown remarkable resilience. In recent decades, the scope of federal authority has expanded in areas such as healthcare, counterterrorism, and economic regulation. Yet the principle of legal equality among states and the clear constitutional division of powers remain unchanged.

The Federal Republic of Germany

After the end of World War II and the adoption of the Basic Law in 1949, Germany deliberately chose the federal model, based on the principle of complete legal equality among all its constituent units — the federal states (*Bundesländer*). Today, the Federal Republic consists of sixteen Länder, each enjoying the same legal status, equal powers, and identical responsibilities in relation to the federal center.

Constitutional Guarantee of Equality

The Basic Law ensures that all federal states possess the same constitutional rights. It precisely defines the competences of the federal government (*Bundesregierung*) and those of the Länder (*Landesregierungen*). This uniform framework rules out special privileges and secures equal opportunities for all regions, reinforcing both fairness and unity within the federation.

Division of Powers between the Center and the Länder

The constitution sets a strict and detailed allocation of competences:

- **Federal authorities** are responsible for matters of nationwide significance, such as foreign policy, defense and security, taxation and macroeconomic regulation, monetary policy, and federal legislation, which establishes uniform standards across the country.
- **The Länder** exercise authority in most areas of daily life, including education policy, culture and heritage, healthcare and social protection, infrastructure development, management of territorial resources, law enforcement, and local self-government.

This distribution allows the federal government to preserve coherence in key strategic areas while leaving broad autonomy to the states in governing local affairs.

The Role of the Bundesrat

A distinctive feature of the German model is the Bundesrat (Federal Council), the legislative chamber representing the Länder at the national level. Each state sends its delegates, who participate directly in the adoption of federal legislation. Through the Bundesrat, the Länder influence national policy on equal terms, ensuring that regional interests are incorporated into federal decisions and preserving the balance of the system

Chapter 2

Asymmetrical Federation:
Unequal Distribution of Powers Among Constituent Units

> **An asymmetrical federation** is a form of federal organization in which the constituent units possess different constitutional and legal statuses, exercise unequal scopes of authority, and enjoy varying degrees of autonomy in their relations with the federal center, depending on the historical, ethnic, cultural, or political characteristics of the regions.

Characteristics

An asymmetrical federation typically emerges in states with pronounced regional differences rooted in historical, cultural, national, or economic factors. To preserve stability and unity, the central government deliberately grants certain constituent units special powers, rights, or even privileges that reflect their specific needs and distinctive interests.

Fundamental Features of an Asymmetrical Federation

1. Inequality of Status and Powers among Constituent Units

The defining and most visible feature of an asymmetrical federation is the existence of substantial differences in the rights and autonomy of its territorial entities. Some constituent units may enjoy a special status expressed in additional powers, such as:

- the right to adopt their own regional constitution,
- special economic and taxation regimes,
- an enhanced degree of political autonomy,
- their own judicial systems and law enforcement bodies,
- special cultural, linguistic, and educational rights.

Other constituent units, by contrast, possess only standard competences and considerably more limited autonomy. Such inequality is not arbitrary but reflects the real historical, national, or cultural needs of particular regions.

2. Flexible and Differentiated Distribution of Powers

In an asymmetrical federation, the federal center retains authority over key national functions, such as:

- foreign policy and international relations,
- defense and national security,
- nationwide tax policy,
- macroeconomic and financial regulation.

At the same time, specific constituent units are granted authority to regulate a wide range of important issues according to their own circumstances. Such autonomy may include:

- language and cultural policy,
- education and social programs,

- control over local natural resources,
- special conditions for business and economic activity.

This makes the federal structure highly flexible and enables the accommodation of particular regional interests that cannot be effectively addressed under a system of uniform rules.

3. Individualized Approach of the Central Government toward Each Constituent Unit

A defining characteristic of asymmetrical federalism is the need for the central government to adopt an individualized approach to each region. Relations between the center and the constituent units are established on a case-by-case basis, reflecting the unique conditions and needs of every territory. This requires the federal authorities to exercise a high degree of flexibility, attentiveness to regional differences, and constant balancing of the interests of diverse constituent units.

Strengths of an Asymmetrical Federation

1. Flexible Accommodation of Regional Specificities

The principal advantage of an asymmetrical federation lies in its ability to address regional differences with precision and effectiveness in large and diverse states. In countries where regions vary significantly in economic conditions, historical traditions, and national or cultural composition, a uniform model of governance inevitably generates tensions. An asymmetrical federation, by contrast, allows each constituent unit to receive the set of rights and competences best suited to its unique characteristics and needs. This provides the state with a high degree of flexibility, enabling it to respond to local conditions and regional challenges in a timely and effective manner.

2. Prevention of Interethnic Conflicts

An asymmetrical model is particularly valuable in states marked by pronounced ethnic and cultural diversity. Regions populated by national minorities or indigenous peoples gain the ability to regulate independently the most sensitive aspects of their lives: language and cultural policy, education, preservation of traditions, and local self-government. This reduces tensions caused by attempts to impose uniform standards, which minorities often perceive as a threat to their cultural identity. In this way, asymmetry helps prevent interethnic conflicts and sustain internal stability and peace within society.

3. Minimization of the Risk of Separatism

Asymmetry can serve as an effective mechanism for reducing separatist pressures. Regions striving for greater independence can satisfy their aspirations within the framework of the federation by receiving an enhanced degree of autonomy. This reduces incentives for secession and decreases the likelihood of open confrontation or state disintegration. Granting special rights to regions demanding greater autonomy creates a compromise between regional and national interests, thereby maintaining the stability and integrity of the federation.

4. Improved Efficiency of Regional Governance

Granting regions the authority to regulate key matters according to local conditions significantly enhances the efficiency of governance. Regional authorities, vested with appropriate powers and resources, are able to address local problems more effectively, as they are closer to the population and its needs. This encourages initiative, responsibility, and accountability at the local level, leading to improved quality of life for citizens in specific regions.

5. Preservation and Promotion of Cultural and Linguistic Diversity

Another strength of an asymmetrical federation is its ability to safeguard and foster cultural and linguistic diversity. Regions with a distinct ethnic composition are granted special conditions in areas such as education, media, culture, and administration. This allows different cultures and languages not to be suppressed but to coexist and develop harmoniously. As a result, the federation becomes a political framework that respects and acknowledges the cultural identities of all peoples residing within its territory, thereby strengthening national unity.

Weaknesses of an Asymmetrical Federation

1. Complexity of Governance and Coordination

One of the most evident shortcomings of an asymmetrical federation is the substantial complication of governance and coordination. When constituent units hold different powers, privileges, and degrees of autonomy, the federal center must establish individualized mechanisms of interaction with each region. This demands constant additional effort from federal authorities, complicates decision-making, and requires far greater resources for oversight and regulation. As a result, administrative processes become not only less transparent but also more costly in terms of time and resources.

2. Increased Risk of Conflicts and Interregional Tensions

Another serious drawback of the asymmetrical model is the heightened risk of conflict both between the central government and particular regions and among the constituent units themselves. Regions with less autonomy often feel disadvantaged and express dissatisfaction with the unequal distribution of powers and privileges. This can lead to ongoing political disputes, diminished trust in the federal center, and the emergence of separatist sentiments in less autonomous units. The central government is forced to continuously balance competing demands from different regions in order to minimize tensions and preserve national unity.

3. Deepening Socioeconomic Inequality among Regions

A further problem of asymmetrical federalism is the uneven pattern of socioeconomic and political development. Regions endowed with broader powers and special conditions are often able to attract more investment, foster business activity, and advance infrastructure projects. Meanwhile, less autonomous regions lag behind, leading to widening gaps in development. This disparity fuels regional inequality, social discontent, and frustration in territories without such privileges. In the long term, it may pose a serious threat to social stability and national cohesion.

4. Risk of Weakening National Unity and Territorial Integrity

Granting certain regions special privileges and extensive autonomy carries the risk of eroding national unity and weakening central authority. Regions with significant rights and competences may begin to perceive themselves as entities separate from the rest of the country. Such tendencies can loosen ties with the center, encourage local nationalism, and foster separatism or even aspirations for full independence. Under these conditions, the central government must constantly take measures to curb separatist pressures and safeguard the territorial integrity of the state.

5. Difficulty in Maintaining Uniform Legal Standards

The uneven distribution of powers and rights among constituent units can result in a fragmented and complex legal system. Within an asymmetrical model, different regions are granted varying degrees of legislative and administrative authority, which complicates the establishment of uniform legal norms. For citizens and businesses, this creates additional challenges, as the legal environment becomes inconsistent, confusing, and difficult to navigate.

Historical Examples of Asymmetrical Federations

The Russian Federation

The Russian Federation is one of the most prominent examples of an asymmetrical federal system in the modern world. As a state marked by exceptional national, cultural, and economic diversity, Russia adopted an asymmetrical model of federalism after the dissolution of the Soviet Union in order to accommodate the historical and national particularities of its constituent units.

Constitutional Basis of Asymmetry among Federal Subjects

According to the 1993 Constitution of the Russian Federation, the country is composed of 89 constituent units (later consolidated), divided into several categories:

- **Republics** – national-state entities with the right to adopt their own constitutions, establish official languages alongside Russian, and regulate cultural and educational matters tied to the ethnic and national identities of their populations.

- **Krais and oblasts (territories and regions)** – administrative units with fewer powers, governed by charters rather than constitutions, and without the right to declare their own national languages.

- **Autonomous okrugs and the autonomous oblast** – territories with special status, usually incorporated into larger regions but granted certain additional rights.

- **Federal cities (Moscow, St. Petersburg, Sevastopol)** – subjects with a special legal status and expanded competences due to their strategic importance for the state.

This diversity of constitutional statuses makes Russian federalism asymmetrical by nature.

Reasons for Adopting an Asymmetrical Model

The chief reason for introducing asymmetry in Russia was the country's multiethnic composition and the existence of regions with strong cultural, historical, and economic particularities. In the early 1990s, after the collapse of the USSR, there was an urgent need to curb separatist tendencies, especially in national republics such as Tatarstan, Bashkortostan, Chechnya, and Yakutia. Granting these territories extended powers and greater autonomy was a conscious decision by the federal center, designed to preserve territorial integrity and national unity.

The Special Position of Republics within the Federation

The republics occupy a unique position among Russia's federal subjects. Each republic has the right to adopt its own constitution, establish official languages (in addition to Russian), and regulate matters of culture, education, and national traditions.

For example:

- **The Republic of Tatarstan** has its own constitution, recognizes Tatar as an official language alongside Russian, and maintains an educational system that actively supports Tatar language and culture.

- **The Chechen Republic**, with its special status, has been allowed to establish distinctive forms of governance and legal arrangements that differ substantially from those of other regions.

These measures were taken to address regional demands and to prevent conflicts rooted in ethnic and cultural divisions.

Strengths of Russia's Asymmetrical Federal Model

- **Prevention of Separatism.** By granting autonomy and special arrangements to certain regions, the federal center significantly reduced separatist pressures and helped prevent state disintegration in the 1990s.

- **Accommodation of Regional Diversity.** The asymmetrical model enabled Russia to preserve cultural, linguistic, and national pluralism, creating conditions for the coexistence of many peoples within a single state.

Weaknesses of the Russian Asymmetrical System

- **Tensions among Federal Subjects.** Unequal distribution of rights and powers often creates dissatisfaction in regions without the privileges granted to republics. Territories such as oblasts and krais have at times considered this asymmetry unfair and called for revisions.

- **Complexity of Governance.** Managing a large number of entities with differing legal statuses complicates administration, oversight, and coordination. The federal center must adopt a highly individualized approach to different regions, which requires significant additional resources.

In recent decades, Russia has attempted to mitigate this asymmetry by strengthening the role of the federal center and unifying legislation. Nevertheless, asymmetry remains a fundamental characteristic of the Russian Federation, reflecting its multiethnic and diverse composition.

Despite the challenges posed by unequal statuses and complex governance, this model allowed Russia to maintain unity and stability during the difficult internal conflicts of the late twentieth and early twenty-first centuries.

India (Before 2019)

For many decades, India was regarded as a classic example of an asymmetrical federation. After achieving independence in 1947, the Indian government faced the challenge of accommodating profound regional, cultural, and religious differences within the country. As a result, a federal model was adopted under which certain states were granted special rights and privileges that went far beyond the autonomy of most other territories.

The Special Status of Jammu and Kashmir

The clearest manifestation of asymmetry in India was Article 370 of the Constitution, which granted Jammu and Kashmir a unique autonomous status. Under this article, the state had the right to:

- adopt its own constitution to regulate internal matters,
- establish special property laws restricting land ownership to residents of the state,
- independently legislate on issues such as local governance and education,
- use its own flag and symbols to emphasize regional identity.

These privileges reflected the distinctive historical, cultural, and religious features of the region, whose population is predominantly Muslim in contrast to the largely Hindu majority in the rest of India.

Strengths of India's Asymmetrical Model

- **Reduction of Interethnic Tensions.** Granting special rights to Jammu and Kashmir helped mitigate religious and ethnic conflicts for many years.

- **Prevention of Separatism.** Broad regional autonomy reduced separatist pressures, allowing aspirations for self-rule to be accommodated within the Indian state and preserving territorial integrity.

- **Recognition of Regional Diversity.** The asymmetrical approach enabled the state to account flexibly for the historical and cultural diversity of India's many regions.

Weaknesses of India's Asymmetrical Model

- **Inequality among States.** The privileged position of Jammu and Kashmir caused dissatisfaction in other states, which viewed such asymmetry as unjust.

- **Political Controversy.** The state's special status became a constant source of dispute, fueling political conflicts and complicating national governance.

- **Growth of Separatism and Terrorism.** In later decades, Jammu and Kashmir's autonomy was increasingly exploited by separatist and terrorist groups, leading to escalating violence, instability, and a serious threat to India's national security.

The Abolition of Asymmetry and the Move toward Symmetry (2019)

In August 2019, the Indian government revoked Article 370 of the Constitution, stripping Jammu and Kashmir of its special privileges and autonomous status. The principal justification for this decision was the sharp rise in separatist movements, instability, and terrorist activity in the region. According to the government, the state's autonomy had created conditions in which separatist and militant groups could operate freely and obstruct integration into the wider Indian polity.

As a result, Jammu and Kashmir was reorganized into two union territories — Jammu and Kashmir, and Ladakh — administered directly by the federal government. Since 2019, India has ceased to be an asymmetrical federation. All states now enjoy equal legal status, equal rights, and identical competences, making the federal structure of India predominantly symmetrical.

Canada (The Special Status of Quebec)

Canada is an example of a state that has deliberately chosen an asymmetrical federal model. The special status of the French-speaking province of Quebec is one of the most prominent and illustrative cases of asymmetry in practice. The rationale for granting Quebec this status lay in the need to take account of the province's cultural, linguistic, and historical distinctiveness and to prevent potential separatism.

Distinctive Features of Quebec

Quebec differs significantly from the other Canadian provinces in its linguistic and cultural composition: more than 80 percent of its population speaks French, in contrast to the English-speaking majority elsewhere in Canada. Historically, Quebec has been the center of French influence and culture in North America, which made a special federal approach to its autonomy necessary.

Asymmetry and its Constitutional Foundations

The Canadian constitutional framework grants Quebec substantial autonomy in education, culture, and language policy. Among the province's key rights and privileges are:

- **Broad autonomy in education.** Quebec independently regulates its education system, where French is the primary language of instruction. The province maintains a unique system of secondary and higher education, distinct from the standards applied in other provinces.

- **Cultural policy and protection of the French language.** Quebec determines its own cultural and linguistic policies. For instance, the *Charter of the French Language* (Bill 101), adopted in 1977, established French as the sole official language of the province, setting it apart from the rest of Canada, where English holds equal or dominant status.

- **Autonomy in immigration policy.** Quebec has authority over certain aspects of immigration, including the right to select immigrants based on linguistic and cultural criteria.

Objectives of Asymmetry in Canada

- **Prevention of Separatism.** By granting Quebec extensive rights, the federal government mitigated tensions between the center and the French-speaking population, reducing calls for independence.

- **Preservation of Cultural and Linguistic Diversity.** The special framework safeguarded the French language and culture in North America, protecting the province's unique identity.

- **Political Stability and Territorial Integrity.** Asymmetry preserved Canada's unity by lowering the risk of state fragmentation arising from ethnic and linguistic divisions.

Challenges of Canadian Asymmetry

- **Inequality among Provinces.** Other provinces have often expressed discontent over Quebec's privileges, viewing such arrangements as unfair.

- **Political Disputes and Public Tensions.** Quebec's special status remains a subject of recurring debate at both federal and provincial levels, contributing to political instability and complicating governance.

- **Persistent Risk of Separatism.** Despite its autonomy, separatist movements continue to surface in Quebec, as illustrated by the independence referendums of 1980 and 1995, when the issue of secession was put to a provincial vote.

Today, Canada's federation continues to preserve elements of asymmetry, with Quebec maintaining special rights in cultural and linguistic matters. At the same time, federal authorities consistently strive to balance the protection of provincial autonomy with the principle of equality among all constituent units.

Conclusion

The choice of a particular model of territorial organization depends on many factors: historical circumstances, the national composition of the population, and the economic and cultural characteristics of the state. The two most widespread federal models are symmetrical and asymmetrical federations, each with its own strengths and weaknesses.

A **symmetrical federation** ensures a high level of political unity and stability, since all of its constituent units have equal legal status and identical powers. Such a uniform model allows for:

- political stability and clarity of governance,
- simplicity in coordinating actions between the center and the regions,
- equality among constituent units and the absence of grounds for interregional tensions.

Yet this model has a significant limitation: it is not always capable of adapting flexibly to the specificities and diversity of regions. A standardized approach may hinder the recognition of local needs and lead to dissatisfaction and internal tensions.

An **asymmetrical federation**, by contrast, is characterized by a high degree of flexibility and enables the state to account for regional diversity, especially in multinational and culturally heterogeneous societies. Among its chief advantages are:

- the ability to address effectively the problems of regions with unique cultural, historical, and national features,
- the reduction of separatist pressures through the granting of special status and broad autonomous rights,
- the preservation and development of cultural and linguistic diversity.

At the same time, the asymmetrical model presents significant difficulties for the central government:

- governance, coordination, and decision-making at the national level become more complex,
- the likelihood of conflicts between the center and the regions increases,
- inequality and the risk of interregional rivalry and tensions grow.

In general, the **federal model of governance** offers a number of important advantages that make it especially attractive for large and multinational states. Among these are:

- recognition of regional differences and local specificities,
- provision of autonomy for local governments, encouraging initiative and responsibility,
- the creation of conditions for political pluralism and the strengthening of democratic institutions.

Nevertheless, federalism is not without its weaknesses. The complexity of governance, inevitable conflicts between the federal center and the regions, and the potential danger of separatism demand constant attention, considerable effort, and political wisdom from state leadership to preserve unity and stability.

The modern world is shaped by globalization, regionalization, and the desire of peoples to preserve their identities. Under globalization, the need for a strong central government to address issues of national security, international policy, and economic development is increasing. At the same time, regions seek to preserve their cultural distinctiveness and expand their autonomy.

In these conditions, **federalism** stands out as the most promising and effective model of governance, capable of simultaneously meeting two fundamental needs:

- maintaining territorial unity and political stability,
- respecting and safeguarding regional, cultural, and national diversity.

In the twenty-first century, federalism not only retains its relevance but acquires special significance, emerging as the optimal solution for modern multinational states striving for stability, prosperity, and internal cohesion.

"*Several sovereign and independent states may unite themselves together by a perpetual confederacy, without each in particular ceasing to be a perfect state. They will together constitute a federal republic: their joint deliberations will not impair the sovereignty of each member.*"

— Emer de Vattel, *The Law of Nations* (1758), Book I, §10

SECTION 3. CONFEDERATION — A UNION OF STATES RETAINING SOVEREIGN AUTHORITY

> **A confederation** is a union of independent states that come together on a contractual basis, retaining their sovereignty while delegating limited powers to central institutions for the achievement of common objectives.

A confederation is the only relevant type of union of independent states in the classification of state forms, because it represents an intermediate arrangement between fully sovereign states and a more centralized federation. Other types of unions—such as international organizations, military-political alliances, or personal and real unions—do not qualify as forms of state structure. They belong instead to the sphere of international cooperation rather than the territorial organization of a state.

Characteristics

A confederation is a union of fully sovereign and independent states brought together by common interests, aims, and objectives. Unlike a federation, where the central authority holds supremacy and governs most spheres of public life, a confederation leaves the primary powers with its member states. The participants delegate to central bodies only limited functions necessary to achieve common goals. A confederation does not create a new state entity; rather, it constitutes a form of close interstate cooperation based on equality and the preservation of sovereignty.

Fundamental Features of a Confederation

1) Full Sovereignty and Independence of Members

Each state within a confederation retains complete independence and control over its territory, domestic affairs, and foreign policy. The central institutions cannot intervene in the internal matters of member states without their explicit consent. This guarantees the full autonomy of each participant, enabling them to preserve their traditions, laws, and institutions intact.

2) Voluntary Nature of Union and Right of Secession

A confederation is established by voluntary agreement among its members. States are free to join or to withdraw from the union. The right of withdrawal is one of the most important attributes of a confederation, underscoring its voluntary rather than compulsory character. This sharply distinguishes a confederation from a federation, in which the right of secession is limited or entirely absent.

3) Limited Powers of Central Institutions

The central bodies of a confederation hold minimal, clearly defined competences. These are most often confined to foreign policy, collective defense, or shared economic matters. Even in these areas, central institutions act only by consensus and do not possess independent legislative authority. This arrangement prevents excessive concentration of power and safeguards the interests of each member state.

4) Absence of a Unified Legal System and Common Citizenship

In a confederation, there is no single legal or legislative system binding upon all members. Each state continues to function under its own laws, and citizens retain only the citizenship of their respective states. The absence of common citizenship underscores the independence of members and highlights the fact that a confederation is a union of states, not a single state entity.

Reasons for the Formation of Confederations

Confederations generally arise in specific historical circumstances, when states must unite their efforts in the face of an external threat, an economic crisis, or an urgent need to address common problems while maintaining their full independence. This arrangement allows for coordinated action in critical situations without endangering the sovereignty or internal order of member states.

Historical experience shows that confederations are most often temporary and transitional in nature. Over time, they tend either to dissolve or to evolve into a more stable federal structure, marked by the strengthening of central authority.

Strengths of a Confederation

1. Preservation of Full Sovereignty and National Identity

The principal strength of a confederation lies in the fact that each member state fully retains its sovereignty, independence, and national identity. Domestic and foreign policy remain entirely under the authority of national governments, which independently regulate social, economic, cultural, and legal life. This is particularly valuable for states with distinctive national characteristics, unique cultural traditions, and historical legacies. Within a confederation, there is no forced "dilution" of identity, since member states are not compelled to adopt uniform laws or follow a single policy in all areas of public life.

2. Flexibility and Voluntary Participation

A confederation is marked by a high degree of voluntarism and flexibility. States join solely on their own initiative by signing a treaty, the terms of which may later be revised by mutual consent. If participation ceases to serve national interests or creates internal contradictions, a state may freely withdraw from the union without significant political, economic, or legal consequences. This voluntary character minimizes the risks associated with more rigid forms of statehood, such as federations, where secession by regions is generally restricted or entirely prohibited.

3. High Efficiency in Clearly Defined Areas

A confederation is most effective in addressing a limited set of clearly defined tasks. These typically include collective defense against external threats, the pursuit of a common foreign policy, or the creation of a shared economic space and free trade zone. Because the central organs of a confederation have minimal and precisely outlined competences, they can act quickly and without excessive bureaucracy, enabling states to reach agreements on matters of shared importance without the protracted procedures characteristic of federations or unitary states.

4. Accommodation of the Specificities of Member States

A confederation allows for the preservation of regional, cultural, economic, and social diversity among its members. In the absence of rigid unification, each state is free to pursue internal policies that reflect the interests of its citizens. This is especially important for countries with heterogeneous populations, where the imposition of uniform standards could generate tensions and conflicts.

5. Reduction of Internal Tensions

The confederative structure significantly reduces the risk of ethnic, religious, or cultural conflict. Since states are not required to submit to a centralized policy and can govern their domestic affairs independently, the likelihood of internal tensions or separatist pressures diminishes. This ensures long-term stability and peaceful coexistence among diverse peoples and cultures within the union.

6. Minimization of Bureaucratic Costs

Because the powers of central institutions are minimal and clearly delimited, a confederation does not require a large bureaucratic apparatus. This reduces financial expenditures on administrative structures and increases the efficiency of decision-making. Member states are not burdened with maintaining a costly federal administration or numerous agencies.

7. Facilitation of Joint Projects

Thanks to its voluntary character and limited scope, a confederation provides a straightforward framework for launching joint initiatives, particularly in infrastructure, economic development, and defense. Member states find it easier to reach agreements on specific projects and initiatives, since they are not required to coordinate all aspects of governance but can instead focus on the most pressing common objectives.

Weaknesses of a Confederation

1. Low Efficiency in Decision-Making

One of the principal shortcomings of a confederation is the slow and often ineffective nature of decision-making. Central institutions hold only minimal powers, and all key matters require the consent and approval of every member state. Even minor disagreements among members can completely block the adoption of important decisions, making it extremely difficult to respond swiftly to crises, external threats, or economic challenges.

2. High Risk of Internal Instability and Dissolution

Confederations usually unite states with divergent or even conflicting interests, cultures, levels of economic development, and political priorities. The absence of a strong central authority capable of regulating disputes and managing conflicts effectively often leads to persistent internal contradictions. Over time, these disputes intensify, producing recurring crises and, ultimately, the withdrawal of individual states or the disintegration of the entire confederation.

3. Lack of Capacity for Long-Term Planning

The weakness of central authority and the limited scope of its competences make it nearly impossible to pursue unified, consistent, and long-term policies. A confederation lacks the necessary instruments to implement strategic programs and sustained projects, since every initiative depends on the current agreement of its member states. This severely restricts the ability of a confederation to plan effectively for the future and undermines its capacity for development.

4. Inability to Enforce Compliance with Decisions

Central institutions in a confederation often lack mechanisms of enforcement. Their resolutions typically carry only a recommendatory character, leaving each member state to decide whether or not to implement them. As a result, many decisions of confederal bodies remain merely on paper, and their practical realization becomes extremely difficult.

5. Limited Economic Capacity and Absence of a Unified Financial Policy

Confederations generally lack a common financial, tax, or budgetary system. The absence of a shared currency, a unified budget, and a coordinated economic strategy weakens economic integration and impedes effective cooperation. Each member state conducts its own fiscal policy, which significantly reduces the prospects for large-scale joint economic projects.

Historical Examples of Confederations

The Confederate States of America (1861–1865)

The Confederate States of America (CSA) embodied a classical example of confederal organization: the member states retained full sovereignty and voluntarily delegated only limited powers to central institutions, primarily in the fields of defense and foreign policy.

Each state preserved its own internal structures, laws, army, and police forces, in line with the principles of confederal governance.

Strengths of the CSA:

- **Full Independence and Preservation of Internal Orders.**

Each member state of the Confederacy maintained complete control over its domestic policy, legislation, and social system. This enabled the southern states to defend their economy and preserve their cultural and social identity.

- **Capacity for Collective Defense.**

Pooling the resources and armies of individual states enabled the CSA to establish a common defensive strategy, organize centralized command, and mount effective resistance during the early stages of the war.

- **Coordinated Foreign Policy.**

The Confederacy conducted its own foreign policy. Despite international isolation and economic blockade, it actively employed diplomatic channels in efforts to secure recognition and economic ties.

- **Strong Regional Solidarity.**

A shared identity and common cultural and historical traditions among the southern states fostered high levels of regional cohesion at the outset of the conflict.

- **Minimal Bureaucratic Structures.**

The absence of an expansive central administration reduced bureaucratic overhead. This allowed for the swift mobilization of local resources and kept administrative costs relatively low.

Weaknesses of the CSA:

- **Ineffectiveness of the Central Government.**

The extremely limited powers of central institutions severely hindered effective governance during wartime. The Confederate government was unable to mobilize financial resources and manpower quickly.

- **Difficulties in Coordinating State Actions.**

Since each state retained full control over its internal affairs, the Confederate authorities constantly struggled to coordinate military and economic efforts. States often prioritized local interests over collective goals, resulting in delays in mobilization, financing, and supply.

- **High Risk of Instability and Dissolution.**

The lack of a strong central authority fueled disputes among the states. Continuous disagreements over army funding, resource allocation, and military strategy weakened unity and created internal frictions.

- **Absence of Long-Term Planning and Strategy.**

The confederal framework made it nearly impossible for central institutions to design or implement long-term strategies. Strategic plans were consistently obstructed by disagreements and the lack of unity among states.

- **No Unified Financial System or Currency.**

Each state maintained its own approach to taxation and currency, producing economic disorder, inflation, and weakening the Confederacy's wartime capacity.

- **Weakness of Central Executive Authority.**

Confederal institutions lacked the ability to enforce their own decisions. Without real executive power to compel compliance, many policies remained unimplemented, rendering the central government largely ineffective.

The experience of the Confederate States of America demonstrated that, despite advantages such as the preservation of sovereignty, regional identity, and efficiency in narrowly defined areas, the confederal model carried structural weaknesses. These shortcomings proved critical in the context of large-scale conflict and ultimately led to the defeat and collapse of the Confederacy.

Switzerland before the Federal Constitution of 1848

Until the adoption of the Federal Constitution in 1848, Switzerland was a classical example of a confederation.

Strengths of the Swiss Confederation

- **Flexibility and Full Autonomy of the Cantons.**

Each canton maintained full sovereignty and internal autonomy.

- **Effective Cooperation in Defense and Trade.**

The Swiss cantons successfully established cooperation in vital areas such as collective defense and foreign trade.

- **Preservation of Cultural Diversity and Local Traditions.**

The confederal structure allowed each canton to maintain its cultural, linguistic, and religious distinctiveness.

- **Minimal Bureaucracy and Administrative Costs.**

Cantonal governments managed their resources independently, avoiding the bureaucratic burdens and inefficiencies characteristic of more centralized systems.

Weaknesses of the Swiss Confederation

- **Low Governability and Difficulty of Decision-Making.**

The requirement of unanimous consent and the minimal powers of central institutions made governance inefficient.

- **Frequent Internal Disputes and Conflicts among Cantons.**

Differences in the interests, cultures, religions, and economies of the cantons produced recurring tensions and conflicts. The absence of a strong central authority left the confederation vulnerable to domestic crises and instability.

- **Need for Reform and Limitations of the Model.**

By the mid-nineteenth century, the confederal system had reached its limits. The lack of centralized authority hindered reforms and long-term projects, while the absence of a unified tax and economic policy obstructed national economic development. This ultimately led to the adoption of the Federal Constitution in 1848 and the transition to a federal system.

- **Absence of a Unified Economic Policy and Currency.**

Each canton regulated its own finances, taxation, and currency. The lack of a common monetary system created serious obstacles to trade, weakened internal economic ties, and limited the overall economic potential of the confederation.

- **Lack of a Unified Legal Space.**

Because each canton maintained full legislative autonomy, significant differences in legal norms emerged. This complicated inter-cantonal relations, hindered commerce, and caused frequent legal disputes, weakening social and economic integration across Switzerland.

The German Confederation (1815–1866)

The German Confederation was established in 1815 at the Congress of Vienna as a confederal union of numerous German states.

Strengths of the German Confederation

- **Preservation of State Independence.**

Member states of the Confederation retained complete sovereignty, internal autonomy, and political self-determination.

- **Flexibility of Structure and Voluntary Participation.**

Each member state joined voluntarily and could freely express its position on matters debated at the confederal level.

- **Capacity for Coordinated Defense.**

The Confederation allowed states to coordinate their military efforts in the face of external threats.

- **Diplomatic Unity and International Influence.**

On the international stage, the Confederation presented itself as a unified diplomatic bloc.

Weaknesses of the German Confederation

- **Low Effectiveness of Central Governance.**

The severely limited competences of the central organs (the Bundestag) hindered effective administration. Major decisions required unanimity or broad consensus.

- **Internal Contradictions and Conflicts of Interest.**

The Confederation comprised states of vastly different size, power, and economic and political interests. This produced continual disputes, political tensions, and instability within the union.

- **Absence of a Unified Economic and Customs Policy.**

The lack of a common economic and customs framework led to disputes among member states. Without a unified economic space, the Confederation struggled to secure free trade.

- **Limited Capacity for Strategic Planning.**

Member states often pursued short-term interests, disregarding the collective long-term needs of the Confederation.

- **Weakness in the Face of External Threats.**

Due to internal divisions and the weakness of its central institutions, the Confederation could not respond effectively to external military or political challenges. This vulnerability was most evident during the Austro-Prussian War of 1866, after which the Confederation collapsed, unable to defend its interests.

COMPARATIVE ANALYSIS OF CONFEDERAL AND FEDERAL MODELS

Federation and confederation represent two fundamentally different models of state organization. Their differences are determined primarily by the degree of centralization of authority and the nature of relations between the central institutions and the constituent units (or member states).

Key Differences between a Federation and a Confederation

1. **Nature of the Union**

- **Federation:** A federation is a single state in which constituent units transfer a substantial portion of their sovereignty to the central government. Sovereignty belongs to the federation as a whole, rather than to its individual subjects.

- **Confederation:** A confederation is a voluntary union of fully sovereign states that retain complete independence. It does not create a new state but functions as a form of interstate alliance.

2. **Degree of Centralization of Authority**

- **Federation:** Central institutions possess broad and constitutionally defined powers, including legislation, the economy, finance, defense, and foreign policy. Federal decisions are binding throughout the entire territory.

- **Confederation:** Central institutions have only minimal powers, generally confined to defense, diplomacy, or limited areas of economic coordination. Their decisions are usually recommendatory and require the consent of all member states.

3. **Decision-Making Process**

- **Federation:** Decisions are adopted by majority vote at the federal level. Central institutions do not require unanimous approval from all constituent units, which allows decisions to be made efficiently even amid disagreements.

- **Confederation:** Decisions require the full consent or consensus of all member states. A single disagreement can block decision-making, greatly reducing the effectiveness of governance.

4. **Common Legal and Economic System**

- **Federation:** Characterized by a unified legal framework, a single economic policy, a common currency, and a uniform tax system. These features ensure internal integration and the free movement of people and goods.

- **Confederation:** Lacks a unified legislative and economic system. Each state retains full control over its laws and financial policies, which complicates integration and interstate cooperation.

5. **Citizenship**

- **Federation:** Provides for common federal citizenship, extending equally to all residents of constituent units, who enjoy the same rights throughout the state.

- **Confederation:** Does not establish common citizenship. Citizens retain only the citizenship of their own states and do not acquire additional rights in other member states.

6. **Stability and Durability of the Union**

- **Federation:** Represents a stable and enduring form of state organization. Strong central authority and a unified legal system allow federations to preserve unity even in the face of deep internal conflicts.

- **Confederation:** Often temporary or transitional in nature, marked by instability and a high risk of disintegration when confronted with serious internal disputes.

The key distinction between a federation and a confederation lies in the degree of concentration of power and the nature of interaction between the central institutions and the constituent units. A federation is oriented toward long-term and stable unity under a strong central authority, whereas a confederation guarantees maximum independence for its member states with only minimal centralization of power—a feature that significantly limits its effectiveness and durability in the long run.

PART IV

CLASSIFICATION BY ECONOMIC SYSTEM

INTRODUCTION

> **An economic system** is the aggregate of economic relations and institutions that determine the ways in which economic activity is organized within a state, including the production, distribution, exchange, and consumption of goods and services.

Types of Economic Systems

The type of economic system determines the standard of living, the stability of the political order, and the trajectory of social development. The choice of a specific economic system depends largely on historical circumstances, the political structure of the state, the level of economic development, natural resources, and cultural traditions. In economic science, several main types of economic systems are traditionally identified, each with its own characteristics, strengths, and weaknesses. Understanding these systems allows us to evaluate how societies allocate scarce resources and balance efficiency with fairness.

Traditional Economy

The traditional economy is the oldest form of economic organization, rooted in customs and long-established practices. Economic activity is oriented primarily toward subsistence and the satisfaction of basic needs. Decisions are made collectively, relying on the experience of previous generations. This system was widespread in antiquity and the Middle Ages but today survives only in limited forms within small traditional communities, mainly in remote and isolated regions of the world. Its stability comes from continuity, but its weakness lies in its inability to adapt quickly to technological change or external shocks.

Command (Planned) Economy

The command, or planned, economy is characterized by centralized management of all economic processes by the state. Government institutions design and approve production plans, set prices, and determine norms of consumption and resource distribution. The means of production are owned by the state, while private property is either absent or severely restricted. This model became widespread in the twentieth century in the socialist bloc, including the USSR, Eastern Europe, and China prior to its market reforms. Its main advantages lie in the state's ability to mobilize resources quickly for large-scale projects and to guarantee social stability. Its weaknesses, however, include inefficiency in resource use, lack of incentives for innovation, slow responsiveness to changing social needs, and restrictions on individual economic freedoms. In practice, this often led to shortages of consumer goods, the emergence of shadow markets, and a gap between official economic indicators and the actual standard of living.

Market Economy

The market economy is based on private property, free enterprise, and competition. Economic and production decisions are made independently by entrepreneurs and consumers, guided by the mechanisms of supply and demand. The state plays only a limited role, focusing mainly on maintaining a legal framework and safeguarding competition. This model encourages innovation, rapid technological and industrial development, entrepreneurial initiative, and adaptability to changing economic conditions. It is the dominant system in most developed states, including the United States, the United Kingdom, Australia, and Canada. Yet an uncontrolled market may lead to economic crises, sharp social inequality, and high unemployment. For this reason, even states with primarily market systems rely on some degree of government regulation.

Mixed Economy

The mixed economy combines elements of the market and command models. The state actively regulates certain areas of economic life to achieve social goals while preserving private property and economic freedoms. Government institutions play a key role in healthcare, education, social welfare, infrastructure, environmental protection, and labor market regulation. This system avoids the extremes of purely planned or purely market economies, providing a balance between economic freedom and social protection. Today, the mixed economy is the most common form of economic organization worldwide.

The Political Role of Economic Systems

An economic system shapes not only the economic sphere but also the political structure of society. The type of economic system directly affects the distribution of political power, the degree of state intervention, the level of civic and economic freedoms, and the nature of social relations. Authoritarian regimes tend to adopt planned economies because they allow for strict state control. Democratic regimes are more likely to adopt market or mixed models, as these are compatible with political pluralism and individual liberty.

In the modern world, understanding the characteristics and consequences of different economic systems has particular importance. Such awareness enables states to design effective economic policies that secure stability and promote the prosperity of society.

SECTION 1. MARKET ECONOMY AND ITS MODELS — SYSTEMS BASED ON MARKET MECHANISMS

> **A market economy** is an economic system based on the principles of free competition, private ownership, and minimal state intervention.

Characteristics of a Market Economy

A market economy is an economic system founded on the principles of free enterprise, private ownership of the means of production, competition, and minimal state intervention in economic activity. Within this system, the market itself serves as the primary regulatory mechanism: it determines prices, sets production levels, allocates resources, and shapes patterns of consumption.

In a market economy, economic actors—producers and consumers—make decisions independently, guided by their own interests and preferences. The state plays only a supporting role by creating the necessary legal and institutional framework for market functioning, ensuring the protection of property rights, the enforcement of contracts, and the preservation of free competition, without directly interfering in business activity or market decision-making.

Core Principles of a Market Economy

1) Free Competition

Enterprises and entrepreneurs compete freely for consumers. Competition serves as the main driver of efficiency, improved product quality, technological innovation, and cost reduction—factors that contribute to lower prices for goods and services.

2) Private Ownership

Private property is a cornerstone of the market economy. It guarantees individuals and enterprises the right to own, control, and use economic resources and means of production at their discretion. Private ownership provides strong incentives for efficient resource management and the realization of entrepreneurial potential.

3) Minimal State Intervention

In a market economy, the role of the state is limited to regulatory and protective functions. It ensures the stability of the monetary system, safeguards property rights, enforces contractual obligations, and prevents monopolization, while refraining from direct control over production and distribution.

4) Consumer Sovereignty

Consumers, through their purchasing choices, determine what goods and services are produced. Producers must respond to consumer demand in order to remain competitive, which makes the consumer the ultimate arbiter of market outcomes.

5) **Profit Motive**

The pursuit of profit serves as the primary incentive for producers and entrepreneurs. It encourages efficiency, cost reduction, and innovation, driving overall economic growth and technological advancement.

6) **Freedom of Choice**

Both producers and consumers enjoy broad freedom in economic decision-making. Consumers decide how to spend their income, while producers choose what to produce and how to allocate resources. This freedom fosters diversity in goods and services and stimulates competition.

Strengths of a Market Economy

1. Efficiency and Dynamism

Free competition compels enterprises not to stand still but to refine their technologies, reorganize their processes, and raise productivity. It is this relentless pressure that drives efficiency forward and fuels technological progress.

2. Flexibility and Adaptability

A market economy has the gift of quick adjustment. It responds almost organically to changes in demand and production, restoring balance without the need for rigid directives. This quality makes the market resilient to shocks and capable of turning crisis into renewal.

3. Freedom of Enterprise and Individual Initiative

Here lies one of its greatest strengths: the freedom to choose, to risk, and to create. With property rights secured and state interference minimal, individuals are free to pursue their ideas. This liberty nurtures initiative, innovation, and the spirit of entrepreneurship that gives the system its vitality.

4. Encouragement of Innovation

The pursuit of profit becomes a call to constant renewal. Firms innovate, not as a matter of charity, but as a matter of survival. They bring forth new technologies, refine their products, and seek better ways of doing business—thereby advancing society as a whole.

5. Efficient Allocation of Resources

Through the mechanism of supply and demand, resources are quietly but effectively guided to where they are most valued. What might seem like chaos from outside reveals itself as a hidden order, channeling labor, capital, and knowledge into their most productive uses.

6. High Degree of Consumer Satisfaction

In the end, it is the consumer who rules. By choosing what to buy, citizens decide what will be produced. This sovereignty of the consumer ensures that the economy listens to real needs and desires, offering variety and abundance.

7. Incentives for Labor and Income Growth

Competition does not allow complacency. It pushes people to learn, to improve, to seek better opportunities. In doing so, it raises productivity and, with it, the standard of living.

8. Promotion of International Trade and Openness

The market looks outward. It connects nations through trade, exchange, and cooperation. This openness accelerates development, spreads knowledge, and strengthens the bonds between economies across the world.

Weaknesses of a Market Economy

1. Social Inequality

Unregulated markets tend to concentrate wealth in the hands of a minority, leaving large groups with limited access to education, healthcare, and housing. This widening gap fosters resentment and exclusion, increasing the likelihood of social tension and unrest. Over time, such inequality can weaken trust in institutions and erode the sense of shared citizenship that holds society together.

2. Economic Cycles and Instability

The market breathes in rhythms of expansion and contraction. Periods of prosperity are followed by downturns, crises, inflation, and unemployment. These cycles expose the fragility of a system driven by competition alone and demonstrate the need for stabilizing mechanisms beyond the market.

3. Insufficient Provision of Public Goods

The logic of profit does not naturally extend to all that society requires. Infrastructure, education, healthcare, and environmental protection are often underfunded because they do not promise immediate returns. Without state intervention, essential public goods risk neglect.

4. Risk of Market Monopolization

Unchecked competition can paradoxically destroy itself. Over time, resources may concentrate in the hands of a few corporations. Monopolies emerge, competition fades, and consumers are left with fewer choices and higher costs.

5. Negative Externalities

Markets tend to overlook costs imposed on society as a whole. Pollution, resource depletion, and environmental degradation are classic examples of externalities left unaddressed when firms focus solely on profit.

6. Short-Term Orientation

Firms frequently aim at quick financial results, prioritizing quarterly earnings over long-term growth. This approach reduces incentives to fund renewable energy projects, advanced research, or infrastructure that would strengthen competitiveness for future generations.

7. Exploitation of Labor and Natural Resources

Without regulation, markets may exploit workers and overuse natural resources. This leads to poor working conditions, widening inequality, and ecological damage, all of which undermine social stability.

8. Underprovision of Merit Goods

Markets underprovide goods and services that are beneficial to society but less profitable to supply—such as universal education, preventive healthcare, or cultural development—leaving gaps that only government action can fill.

Conditions for the Effective Functioning of a Market Economy

For the advantages of the market system to be realized and its weaknesses minimized, several fundamental conditions must be met:

1) **A Stable Legal System and Reliable Protection of Property Rights**

   Economic actors must have confidence that their property and rights are safeguarded against unlawful interference. Secure property rights create a favorable climate for investment, entrepreneurship, and long-term economic growth.

2) **A Well-Developed Competitive Environment**

   Government institutions must guarantee and protect competition, preventing monopolies and cartels that restrict freedom of action and undermine consumer welfare. A healthy competitive environment ensures efficiency, innovation, and fair prices.

3) **Flexible and Moderate Government Regulation**

   State intervention should be limited to essential measures aimed at maintaining economic stability, preventing crises, and mitigating the impact of economic cycles. At the same time, regulation must avoid excessive restrictions that could stifle entrepreneurship and economic freedoms.

4) **Transparency and Accessibility of Economic Information**

   Markets function effectively only when participants have open and equal access to information about prices, product quality, contract terms, and economic opportunities. Transparency fosters trust in market mechanisms and reduces risks of fraud and inefficiency.

5) **A Well-Developed Market Infrastructure**

   Modern infrastructure—financial, transport, digital, and informational—facilitates transactions, supports trade and exchange, accelerates economic processes, and increases the overall efficiency of the system.

6) **Macroeconomic Stability**

   A market economy requires low and predictable inflation, sustainable public finances, and a stable currency. Macroeconomic stability ensures confidence among investors and consumers and reduces uncertainty in decision-making.

7) **A Fair and Independent Judicial System**

Effective enforcement of contracts and impartial resolution of disputes are vital for market efficiency. Without an independent judiciary, property rights and competition cannot be reliably protected.

8) **Investment in Human Capital**

A well-educated and skilled workforce enhances productivity and ensures that individuals can adapt to changing labor market conditions. Investment in education, training, and health is indispensable for long-term economic performance.

Chapter 1

Liberal Capitalism:
Market-Driven Economy with Minimal State Intervention

Liberal capitalism is an economic system founded on the principles of a free market, minimal state intervention in the economy, full freedom of private enterprise, and the protection of private property.

Characteristics of Liberal Capitalism

Liberal capitalism represents a model of market economy built on the principles of maximum freedom of enterprise, a free market, and minimal state involvement in economic processes. Within this system, economic activity is regulated primarily by market mechanisms of supply and demand, while government institutions perform limited functions directed mainly toward ensuring the conditions necessary for the proper functioning of the market.

Fundamental Features of Liberal Capitalism

1) **Minimal State Intervention**

In liberal capitalism, the role of the state is restricted to maintaining legal order, protecting private property, enforcing contracts, and safeguarding competition. The government does not take part in economic activity, regulate prices, or intervene in the production decisions of companies. This provides economic actors with broad opportunities for independent decision-making and the free development of business.

2) **Maximum Freedom of Enterprise**

Freedom of enterprise is a cornerstone of liberal capitalism. Every market participant has the right to choose their field of economic activity, determine methods of production, and sell goods and services independently, while also setting prices and defining the terms of competition and cooperation. This fosters entrepreneurship, innovation, technological progress, and higher efficiency.

3) **Free Pricing and Competition**

Prices are determined exclusively by market forces of supply and demand. State price regulation is either absent or minimized. Free competition becomes the chief instrument of regulation, ensuring efficient resource allocation and encouraging firms to improve products, reduce costs, and enhance quality.

4) **Private Property as the Basis of Economic Relations**

Liberal capitalism rests on the principle of private property, giving individuals and companies the right to own, use, and dispose of assets and means of production at their discretion. Property rights provide strong incentives for efficient resource management, long-term investment, and entrepreneurial activity.

5) **Primacy of Individual Responsibility and Initiative**

In this model, success or failure depends directly on the efficiency of decisions and the willingness of individuals to assume risks. Such responsibility encourages initiative, independence, and the development of an entrepreneurial culture.

6) **Rule of Law**

The system depends on a stable legal framework that guarantees equality before the law, impartial enforcement of contracts, and protection against arbitrary government interference. The rule of law is what sustains confidence in the functioning of markets.

7) **Freedom of Contract**

Market actors are free to negotiate and conclude agreements without restrictive state intervention. This principle strengthens voluntary exchange and trust among economic agents.

8) **Profit Motive**

The pursuit of profit is recognized as the primary driver of economic activity. It motivates efficiency, encourages innovation, and sustains growth, channeling resources into their most productive uses.

9) **Consumer Sovereignty**

Consumers, by expressing their preferences through demand, guide production decisions. Producers must adapt to consumer choices in order to remain competitive, which makes the consumer the ultimate regulator of the market.

10) **Open Markets and Free Trade**

Liberal capitalism is outward-looking, emphasizing open markets, free trade, and integration into the global economy. This promotes specialization, international cooperation, and broader opportunities for growth and innovation.

Strengths of Liberal Capitalism

1. High Efficiency and Innovation

Liberal capitalism fosters a high level of efficiency through free competition. Firms are compelled to refine production processes, adopt advanced technologies, and improve the quality of goods and services. This constant drive for improvement fuels innovation and enables rapid adaptation to technological change.

2. Rapid Market Response to Shifts in Supply and Demand

With minimal government regulation, market mechanisms adjust quickly to changes in consumer preferences and economic conditions. This ensures timely reallocation of resources across sectors, flexible adjustment of production levels, and pricing that reflects real demand, thus efficiently meeting societal needs.

3. Stimulation of Individual Initiative and Entrepreneurship

The extensive economic freedoms of liberal capitalism create fertile ground for entrepreneurial activity. With few administrative barriers, individuals are encouraged to take initiative, assume risks, and develop new ideas. This unleashes entrepreneurial potential, driving both economic growth and social development.

4. Efficient Allocation of Resources

The market mechanism directs scarce resources to their most productive uses. Guided by supply and demand, capital and labor flow toward the sectors most valued by society, maximizing overall economic returns and productivity.

5. Flexibility and Adaptability of the Economic System

Minimal state involvement allows for rapid adjustment to internal and external shocks. Whether facing crises, shifting consumer preferences, or technological breakthroughs, market forces facilitate quick adaptation, supporting long-term stability and resilience.

6. Strong Motivation of Economic Actors

Because incomes and profits are directly tied to performance, firms and individuals in a liberal capitalist system have strong incentives to act efficiently. This creates a culture of responsibility, ambition, and accountability, which sustains productivity and innovation.

7. Attraction of Investment and Development of Financial Markets

Clear property rights and a predictable legal framework make liberal capitalist economies highly attractive to both domestic and foreign investors. This accelerates the development of financial markets, increases the availability of capital, and stimulates entrepreneurial activity.

8. Reduction of Bureaucratic Costs

The limited role of government reduces administrative burdens on business. With fewer regulatory hurdles and lower bureaucratic costs, firms operate more efficiently and maintain greater competitiveness in both domestic and global markets.

9. Consumer Sovereignty and Choice

In liberal capitalism, the consumer is the ultimate regulator. Producers must respond to consumer demand to survive. This ensures a wide variety of goods and services, constant improvements in quality, and better alignment with the needs of society.

10. Promotion of Global Integration

By emphasizing open markets and free trade, liberal capitalism fosters international cooperation and exchange. This encourages specialization, technological transfer, and deeper integration into the global economy, amplifying growth opportunities.

11. Wealth Creation and Rising Living Standards

The dynamism of liberal capitalism tends to generate significant wealth and raise average living standards over time. Although inequality may persist, overall prosperity typically expands, providing more opportunities for social mobility.

12. Cultural and Social Dynamism

The emphasis on individual freedom, innovation, and competition nurtures a culture of creativity and openness. This dynamism influences not only the economy but also the broader social and cultural environment, encouraging diversity of thought and progress.

Weaknesses of Liberal Capitalism

1. Inequality of Income Distribution and High Levels of Social Stratification

One of the defining weaknesses of liberal capitalism is its tendency to generate significant disparities in wealth and income. Because the free market does not entail active state redistribution, large differences emerge between social groups. This fuels high levels of inequality, which in turn create risks of social discontent, polarization, and instability.

2. Vulnerability to Economic Crises and Cyclical Instability

Liberal capitalist economies are subject to recurrent business cycles, marked by booms followed by recessions or depressions. In the absence of effective government regulation, these crises can become severe and prolonged, leading to mass bankruptcies, unemployment, declining household incomes, and intensified social hardship.

3. Weak Protection of Low-Income and Vulnerable Groups

Minimal state intervention often results in insufficient protection for disadvantaged populations such as low-income households, pensioners, and people with disabilities. Market forces do not automatically provide social safety nets, leaving these groups highly vulnerable during downturns or market disruptions.

4. Underfunding of Public Goods and Infrastructure

Private enterprise in liberal capitalism prioritizes profitability. As a result, areas critical for society—education, healthcare, infrastructure, and environmental protection—tend to be underfunded. Since they do not generate immediate profits, their quality and accessibility often suffer, undermining long-term development and social cohesion.

5. Risk of Monopolization and Decline in Competition

Without effective antitrust regulation, liberal capitalism risks concentration of wealth and power in a small number of large corporations. This reduces competition, lowers quality, raises prices, and restricts consumer choice, eroding the very market dynamics the system is based on.

6. Insufficient Environmental Responsibility

The profit motive often leads to the neglect of ecological standards and overexploitation of natural resources. Without proper state regulation, environmental degradation intensifies, threatening ecosystems, public health, and long-term sustainability.

7. Short-Term Orientation in Economic Planning

The pursuit of quick profits drives firms to prioritize short-term gains over long-term investments. This discourages commitment to areas such as research and development, sustainable energy, and infrastructure projects, which require high upfront costs and lengthy payback periods.

8. Weak Oversight of Financial Markets

Minimal regulation of financial markets fosters excessive speculation and the formation of economic "bubbles." When left unchecked, these bubbles eventually burst, causing large-scale financial crises that reverberate throughout the global economy.

9. Lack of Strategic Economic Planning

Liberal capitalism does not naturally provide mechanisms for long-term strategic coordination. Vital areas such as scientific research, energy security, and national infrastructure may remain underdeveloped, limiting the state's ability to respond effectively to external shocks and long-term challenges.

10. Consumer Vulnerability and Market Failures

Markets do not always ensure that consumer interests are protected. False advertising, unsafe products, and information asymmetries can undermine consumer rights, requiring intervention to guarantee transparency and fairness.

11. Cultural and Social Fragmentation

The emphasis on individual gain and competition may weaken social solidarity. Rising inequality and consumerism can erode community ties and collective values, increasing the risk of alienation within society.

Historical Examples of Liberal Capitalism

Great Britain during the Industrial Revolution (late 18th – mid-19th century)

During the Industrial Revolution, Britain's economy rested on free enterprise, limited state regulation, and the dominance of private property.

Key Features of Liberal Capitalism in Britain

1. Minimal State Intervention

From the eighteenth into the nineteenth century, the British government embraced economic liberalism, most clearly expressed by Adam Smith in *The Wealth of Nations* (1776). Smith argued that markets achieve the greatest efficiency when freed from direct interference. The repeal of the Corn Laws in 1846, which ended protectionist tariffs on grain, became a turning point, signaling Britain's commitment to free trade.

2. Private Initiative and Entrepreneurship

Industrialization advanced through individual enterprise rather than state planning. The government safeguarded contracts and property rights but left business decisions to entrepreneurs. Figures such as Richard Arkwright, James Watt, and George Stephenson transformed textiles, steam power, and rail transport through private investment and innovation.

3. Competition and Market Prices

In the emerging industrial economy, prices were shaped directly by supply and demand, without government regulation or fixed tariffs. Intense competition among manufacturers forced them to improve machinery, adopt new production techniques, and cut expenses to remain profitable. Between 1770 and 1850, output in the cotton textile industry increased fortyfold, while the price of cotton cloth fell by roughly 90 percent, making once-luxury fabrics accessible to ordinary households.

Consequences of Liberal Capitalism

1. Industrial Expansion

Britain became the first fully industrialized nation and the leading economic power of the early nineteenth century. Factories, mills, and railways reshaped the landscape. By 1850, the railway network exceeded 9,000 kilometers, linking domestic markets and accelerating overseas trade, which reinforced Britain's role as the "workshop of the world."

2. Social Inequality

Rapid growth brought severe human costs. Factory labor meant exhausting schedules, unsafe conditions, and meager pay. The Sadler Report of 1832 revealed the extent of exploitation: child labor, diseases, and 14–16 hour shifts. These realities fueled early labor protests, union activity, and reform movements.

3. Economic Crises

The liberal order was prone to instability. The crisis of 1825, caused by speculation and reckless credit, led to widespread bankruptcies and mass unemployment. Cyclical downturns exposed the fragility of a system with little state oversight.

Britain's path showed both the energy of liberal capitalism—industrial growth, technological advance, global reach—and its costs: social inequality, labor exploitation, and recurring crises.

The United States in the Late 19th and Early 20th Centuries

The late nineteenth and early twentieth centuries marked the height of liberal capitalism in America. The economy rested on entrepreneurial freedom, minimal state oversight, and unrestrained competition. This model, consolidated after the Civil War (1861–1865), defined what became known as the Gilded Age.

Main Features of Liberal Capitalism

1. Minimal State Intervention

Until the 1890s, federal institutions limited their role to protecting property rights and enforcing contracts. They neither regulated production nor set prices. The first real challenge to laissez-faire came with the Sherman Antitrust Act of 1890, aimed at curbing monopolistic power.

2. Freedom of Enterprise

With few restrictions, business leaders expanded industry on a massive scale. Decisions about investment, technology, and markets were left to private initiative. John D. Rockefeller's Standard Oil, Andrew Carnegie's steel empire, and Cornelius Vanderbilt's railroads grew into giants under this environment of almost complete economic freedom.

3. Industrial and Infrastructural Growth

By 1900, the United States had become the world's foremost industrial nation. Heavy industry, mining, and transport expanded at remarkable speed. The railroad system, stretching over 300,000 kilometers, unified the national market and accelerated the circulation of goods and capital.

Consequences of Liberal Capitalism

1. Industrial Expansion and Innovation

Between 1870 and 1900, American industrial output increased sixfold, and the country's share of world production rose from 23 to 36 percent. Steel, coal, and oil placed the United States at the forefront of global industry.

2. Inequality and Labor Unrest

Economic growth was accompanied by deepening inequality. By the 1890s, the richest 1 percent controlled nearly half of the nation's wealth. Workers faced long hours, unsafe conditions, and little protection. Strikes such as the Pullman Strike of 1894 exposed the growing conflict between capital and labor.

3. Recurring Crises

The liberal order proved highly unstable. The Panic of 1893, sparked by financial speculation and banking failures, drove unemployment to nearly 18 percent. The downturn lasted until 1897, making it the most severe crisis before the Great Depression.

4. Rise of Monopolies

Concentration of capital produced vast trusts that limited competition. By the 1880s, Standard Oil controlled about 90 percent of the American oil market. Such dominance alarmed the public and spurred the first wave of antitrust reforms.

The Gilded Age revealed both the energy and the fragility of liberal capitalism. It propelled the United States to global industrial leadership, yet it also brought extreme inequality, labor conflict, recurrent crises, and the unchecked growth of monopolies.

Chapter 2

State Capitalism:
Market Economy with Significant State Ownership and Control

> **State capitalism** is a type of economic system in which the state acts not only as the regulator of economic processes but also as an active participant in economic activity.

Characteristics of State Capitalism

State capitalism is an economic system in which the government owns or controls a substantial share of resources and enterprises, directing key sectors to serve national and political goals.

Core Features

1. Dominant Role of the State

The state does not merely regulate the economy but acts as a direct participant. It creates enterprises, allocates resources, and makes investment decisions that shape the course of national development.

2. Ownership of Strategic Sectors

Energy, heavy industry, transport, finance, defense, and infrastructure often fall under state control, either fully or in part. This allows the government to secure stability, manage critical resources, and pursue long-term priorities.

3. Planning and Regulation

Economic activity is frequently guided by strategic plans. Authorities set priorities, channel investment into key industries, and supervise corporate operations to align business activity with broader social and economic goals.

4. Economic Instruments for National Objectives

Public investment, subsidies, tax measures, and price policies are used to safeguard economic security, strengthen competitiveness, protect jobs, and cushion the impact of crises.

5. Integration of Politics and Economics

Decisions are driven not only by markets but also by national ambitions such as geopolitical influence, technological independence, and social cohesion.

6. Hybrid System

Private enterprise operates alongside public ownership, yet the state retains decisive influence in strategic areas. The result is a mixed system, where market incentives coexist with centralized control.

Strengths of State Capitalism

1. Capacity for Large-Scale Reforms

Because the state controls major resources and enterprises, it can concentrate funds quickly and direct them toward ambitious projects. Centralized decision-making enables rapid construction of infrastructure such as roads, railways, power plants, and industrial complexes—especially valuable in periods of accelerated modernization.

2. Fairer Income Distribution and Social Protection

Through active regulation, governments can channel resources toward vulnerable groups, improve social infrastructure, and raise living standards. This reduces inequality and provides stronger safety nets for the population.

3. Short-Term Economic Stability

Direct state intervention allows rapid responses to crises. Authorities can stabilize banks, curb inflation, and prevent mass bankruptcies or surges in unemployment. This makes the system resilient in the face of shocks.

4. Long-Term Strategic Planning

Control of key sectors allows governments to set priorities that extend beyond market cycles. Projects in energy, resource extraction, science, and technology—often requiring decades of investment—become possible under this model.

5. Economic Security and Sovereignty

When industries such as energy, transport, finance, and defense remain under state control, the economy is less dependent on foreign capital or corporate monopolies. This strengthens independence and reduces external vulnerability.

6. Balanced Regional Development

Governments can direct resources into lagging areas, narrowing regional disparities. Such redistribution promotes national cohesion and prevents destabilizing imbalances.

7. Support for Strategic Industries

States often protect and invest in industries considered essential for global competitiveness or technological sovereignty. These "national champions" help maintain leadership in critical sectors.

8. Insulation from Global Volatility

Acting as both regulator and owner, the state can soften the impact of international crises. Tools such as stabilization funds, trade policies, or currency controls protect domestic industries from sudden global shocks.

Weaknesses of State Capitalism

1. Risk of Lower Efficiency

Strong state control often weakens competition. Without pressure to innovate or cut costs, state-owned enterprises may lag behind private firms, leading to slower technological progress and reduced competitiveness.

2. Corruption and Bureaucracy

When resources are concentrated in government hands, corruption becomes more likely. Bureaucratic agencies, burdened with lengthy procedures and poor accountability, often misallocate resources and respond slowly to economic needs.

3. Limits on Entrepreneurship

Excessive regulation restricts private initiative. Entrepreneurs face fewer chances to act independently, which discourages creativity and weakens the growth of a dynamic private sector.

4. Lack of Flexibility

Centralized planning adapts poorly to rapid changes in demand, technology, or global markets. This rigidity makes it difficult to restructure industries quickly or to adjust to external shocks.

5. Financial Risks

Governments may pour money into unprofitable projects for political reasons. Subsidies to inefficient enterprises strain public finances and expose the economy to long-term risks.

6. Crowding Out the Private Sector

Preferential treatment of state firms often sidelines private companies. This reduces competition and discourages private investment in key industries.

7. Distorted Market Signals

Price controls, subsidies, and similar interventions interfere with supply and demand. Distorted signals lead to poor allocation of resources and weaken the transparency of the market system.

8. Politicization of the Economy

Economic decisions are frequently driven by political goals—such as winning elections or maintaining social stability—rather than by long-term economic logic.

9. Risk of Isolation

Heavy protection of domestic industries can limit trade and foreign investment. Reduced access to global markets and technologies makes the economy less competitive on the international stage.

Historical Examples of State Capitalism

The People's Republic of China (from the late 20th century to the present)

Since the late 1970s, following the economic reforms initiated under Deng Xiaoping, China's economy has transformed from a classical command system into a mixed model in which active state involvement coexists with market mechanisms. This system has come to be widely described as state capitalism, combining centralized state power with the dynamics of a partially liberalized market.

Key Features of State Capitalism in China

1. **State Control over Strategic Sectors**

   The Chinese government either controls or fully owns enterprises in strategically vital sectors such as energy, banking, telecommunications, transportation, metallurgy, oil and gas, and defense. State-owned assets and enterprises are administered through the State-owned Assets Supervision and Administration Commission (SASAC).

According to SASAC data from the end of 2022, the agency managed 98 major state-owned corporations, including PetroChina, Sinopec, China Mobile, the Industrial and Commercial Bank of China (ICBC), the China Construction Bank (CCB), and the Bank of China (BOC).

2. **Active State Planning and Regulation**

   Despite the expansion of market forces, China continues to rely heavily on centralized planning. Five-Year Plans set strategic directions, development priorities, and the scale of public investment.

For example, in March 2021 the government adopted the official 14th Five-Year Plan (2021–2025), which prioritized innovation in biotechnology, artificial intelligence, renewable energy, and modern infrastructure.

3. **Massive State Investment in Strategic Projects**

   The state plays a leading role in financing large infrastructure and technology projects, including highways, bridges, ports, energy facilities, high-speed railways, and high-tech industries.

By the end of 2023, China's high-speed rail network exceeded **42,000 kilometers**, the largest in the world, according to official data from the China State Railway Group Co.

Strengths of China's State Capitalism

- **High Rates of Economic Growth**

  For four decades, China has sustained some of the world's fastest growth rates. According to World Bank data, between 1980 and 2020, annual GDP growth averaged around 9 percent, lifting hundreds of millions out of poverty and transforming China into the world's second-largest economy.

- **Efficient Implementation of Infrastructure Projects**

  Centralized planning enabled rapid completion of massive infrastructure projects, laying the foundation for industrial and economic expansion. Highways, ports, airports, and high-speed rail networks became symbols of China's state-led development model.

- **Maintenance of Social and Economic Stability**

  Strong state involvement helped cushion the effects of global crises, ensuring social stability and avoiding large-scale upheaval. Both IMF and World Bank reports highlight the Chinese state's ability to stabilize employment and growth during turbulent global economic periods, including the 2008 financial crisis and the COVID-19 pandemic.

Weaknesses of China's State Capitalism

- **High Levels of Corporate and Regional Debt**

  Extensive state investment and credit expansion fueled rapid growth but also raised debt levels. According to the IMF's 2022 report, China's combined corporate and regional non-financial debt reached approximately 280 percent of GDP. However, since most of this debt is domestic and held by state banks, the risks of external financial dependency remain limited.

- **Corruption and Bureaucratic Inefficiency**

  The Chinese leadership itself acknowledges corruption as a systemic challenge. In 2012, the government launched a far-reaching anti-corruption campaign. According to official reports by the Central Commission for Discipline Inspection (CCDI), more than 600,000 officials were disciplined in 2022 alone—evidence both of the scale of the problem and the state's attempt to address it.

The Russian Federation (2000s – Present)

Since the early 2000s, the Russian Federation has combined elements of state capitalism with market mechanisms. The state has significantly expanded its role in the economy, maintaining predominant influence over strategic sectors and enterprises.

Key Features of State Capitalism in Russia

1. **Significant Role of the State in Strategic Sectors**

   The state owns or controls a large share of assets in vital industries such as energy (oil, gas, and electricity), transportation, the defense-industrial complex, and banking. Control is exercised primarily through large state-owned enterprises and corporations.

According to official data from the Russian government and the Accounts Chamber (2023), the state's share in the economy is estimated at **40–50 percent**. Major state-owned companies include:

- **Gazprom** – Russia's largest natural gas company, with a majority stake (over 50%) owned by the state.

- **Rosneft** – the country's largest oil company, with controlling shares held by the state corporation Rosneftegaz.

- **Rostec** – a state corporation overseeing a substantial portion of defense and high-technology enterprises.

- **Sberbank** and **VTB** – the largest Russian banks, with controlling stakes held by the Central Bank of Russia (Sberbank) and the Russian government (VTB).

2. **State Regulation and Implementation of Major Projects**

   The government plays an active role in economic management through state programs, large-scale projects, and direct regulation. This includes national infrastructure development, support for priority industries, subsidies, and state-led investment initiatives.

Since 2018, Russia has implemented national projects approved by presidential decree, covering infrastructure modernization, transportation, healthcare, and digitalization. For example, the Comprehensive Plan for Modernization and Expansion of Main Infrastructure provides for massive state investment in railways, highways, ports, and airports through 2024, with extensions planned until 2030.

3. **Active State Participation in the Financial Sector**

The state, through the Central Bank of Russia and other institutions, regulates and supervises the banking system while owning major stakes in leading financial institutions. According to Central Bank data (2023), state-owned banks—primarily Sberbank, VTB, Gazprombank, and Rosselkhozbank—control over 60 percent of national banking assets.

Strengths of State Capitalism in Russia

- **Stability in Strategic Sectors**

State control helps maintain stability and security in critical industries such as energy, defense, and transportation, ensuring resilience against external shocks and safeguarding independence.

- **Capacity to Mobilize Resources for Major Projects**

Russia's state capitalism enables the rapid mobilization of resources for infrastructure and social projects of national significance, including regional development, industrial modernization, and transport expansion.

- **Support for Social and Economic Stability**

Active state involvement allows for the provision of social support, reducing risks of unrest and maintaining stability during crises.

- **National Security and Sovereignty**

Control over the defense-industrial complex and energy resources strengthens national security and sovereignty. This is reflected in official programs such as the State Armament Program and the Energy Strategy of the Russian Federation to 2035.

- **Support for High-Technology Sectors**

Government investment is directed toward advanced industries, such as aviation, space exploration, nuclear energy, and digital technologies. Key examples include:

  o **Rostec** – supporting aviation clusters and high-tech equipment,
  o **Rosatom** – building nuclear power plants and advancing atomic technology,
  o **Roscosmos** – implementing state space programs.

- **Implementation of Long-Term Strategic Programs**

Centralized state planning allows for the development of national projects and long-term strategies, such as *Digital Economy of the Russian Federation*, *Ecology*, *Healthcare*, and *Science and Universities*. These programs are intended to foster modernization and sustainable growth.

Weaknesses of State Capitalism in Russia

- **Bureaucratization and Reduced Efficiency**

Heavy state involvement often results in bureaucratic delays, slower decision-making, and weaker adaptability to market changes. This challenge is acknowledged in reports from the Accounts Chamber and the Center for Strategic Research.

- **High Risk of Corruption**

  The concentration of state resources in large corporations and administrative bodies creates opportunities for corruption and misuse of public funds. Reports from the General Prosecutor's Office and official anti-corruption campaigns regularly highlight this issue.

- **Constraints on Small and Medium-Sized Enterprises (SMEs)**

  Dominance of state corporations restricts opportunities for private business growth, limits competition, and reduces entrepreneurial activity. These concerns are reflected in official documents from the Ministry of Economic Development.

- **Exposure to External Sanctions and Global Pressures**

  Because state capitalism ties key sectors to government policy, strategic industries such as energy and banking are especially vulnerable to international sanctions and geopolitical shocks, which directly impact economic performance.

Singapore

Singapore's economy combines strong state involvement with open-market principles. The government invests, regulates, and plans strategically, while also fostering private enterprise and welcoming foreign capital.

Core Features

1. **State Ownership of Strategic Assets**

Through sovereign wealth funds, the state holds significant stakes in leading firms across finance, transport, telecommunications, energy, real estate, and infrastructure. Temasek Holdings, with assets of about USD 382 billion in 2023, owns shares in Singapore Airlines, DBS Bank, SingTel, PSA International, and CapitaLand. GIC Private Limited, managing over USD 700 billion, focuses on global investments to safeguard long-term financial stability.

2. **Strategic Planning**

Authorities direct resources into priority areas such as finance, biotechnology, digital technologies, and logistics. The Singapore Green Plan 2030, launched in 2021, illustrates this approach with goals for renewable energy, sustainable infrastructure, and innovation-driven growth.

3. **Business-Friendly Climate**

Low taxes, minimal bureaucracy, and a stable legal framework make Singapore attractive to investors. In the World Bank's *Doing Business 2020* report, it ranked 2nd worldwide; in the 2024 Heritage Foundation Index of Economic Freedom, it placed 3rd.

Strengths

- **Effective Governance**

Low corruption, strong legal institutions, and efficient public administration ensure that state-managed resources are used productively.

- **Long-Term Orientation**

Government planning channels funds into future-oriented sectors, supporting steady growth and high living standards.

- **Global Investment Appeal**

Political stability, advanced infrastructure, and predictable rules have made Singapore a favored base for international business.

- **Crisis Management**

Strong state involvement in finance and infrastructure has enabled Singapore to weather global downturns with relative stability.

Weaknesses

- **Inequality**

Despite high prosperity, income gaps persist. In 2022, Singapore's Gini coefficient stood at 0.41 before taxes and transfers—higher than the OECD average.

- **High Cost of Living**

Housing, healthcare, and education are expensive. In 2023, the Economist Intelligence Unit ranked Singapore the world's most costly city to live in. Social protections exist but remain limited compared to welfare states.

- **Dependence on Global Trade**

Singapore's reliance on trade and foreign capital makes it sensitive to supply chain disruptions and geopolitical tensions.

- **Dominance of State-Linked Companies**

Although Temasek and GIC have been successful, their scale risks overshadowing smaller private firms and limiting entrepreneurial diversity at home.

Comparative Analysis of Liberal and State Capitalism:
Differences in Ownership Structure and Regulatory Role

Liberal and state capitalism reflect two different logics of economic organization. Neither model is universally effective, as their outcomes depend on national development, political institutions, cultural traditions, and external conditions such as globalization, competition, and technological change.

Liberal Capitalism

Liberal capitalism rests on private ownership, limited government intervention, and competition as the central mechanism of efficiency. It thrives in contexts where innovation, adaptability, and entrepreneurial activity are crucial. The strengths of this model lie in its capacity to generate productivity, stimulate creativity, and encourage rapid technological progress. Yet these very advantages often come with costs: minimal regulation tends to widen inequality, create social tensions, and expose economies to cycles of boom and crisis.

State Capitalism

State capitalism emphasizes active government involvement, combining market exchange with centralized control and planning. It is particularly effective in contexts that require rapid mobilization of resources, coordination of large-scale projects, or protection from economic shocks. Its strengths include stability, the ability to redistribute income, and the safeguarding of strategic sectors. However, heavy state dominance may foster bureaucracy, encourage corruption, and restrict private initiative, which limits long-term efficiency and innovation.

Hybrid Approaches

In the contemporary world, neither pure laissez-faire liberalism nor rigid state control can function in isolation. Most economies adopt hybrid systems, seeking to balance competition with regulation, and market incentives with state direction. Such arrangements attempt to protect strategic interests, support innovation, and ensure social stability, while preserving an environment in which private enterprise can thrive.

Balancing Efficiency and Equity

The key challenge is not choosing one model over the other, but reconciling their strengths while minimizing their weaknesses. Liberal capitalism prioritizes efficiency and innovation but risks instability and inequality. State capitalism prioritizes stability and long-term planning but risks inefficiency and stagnation. Sustainable development in the twenty-first century requires frameworks that combine growth with fairness, adaptability with security, and innovation with social cohesion.

The future of capitalism depends on balance. Economic systems that succeed will be those capable of blending efficiency with equity, market vitality with social responsibility, and openness with resilience.

SECTION 2. PLANNED ECONOMY —
CENTRALIZED ECONOMIC DECISION-MAKING

A planned economy is an economic system in which the fundamental questions of production, distribution, and consumption of goods and services are determined through centralized state planning rather than the mechanisms of market demand and supply.

Characteristics of a Planned Economy

A planned economy is an economic system in which economic life is directed almost entirely by the state through centralized planning. Unlike a market system, where supply and demand guide decisions, in a planned system central authorities determine what will be produced, in what quantities, and at what prices.

In this model, the state assumes the leading role in organizing and coordinating economic activity. It sets production targets, fixes prices, allocates resources, and directs investment across industries and enterprises. Market mechanisms are largely absent, and decisions follow political or social priorities rather than competition.

Core Principles and Mechanisms of a Planned Economy

1) Centralized Decision-Making

A single, binding plan covers every sector of the economy. Multi-year programs set goals and quotas that are mandatory for all enterprises and institutions. Firms operate without autonomy, carrying out assigned targets under state directives.

2) State Ownership of the Means of Production

Land, natural resources, major industries, transportation networks, and infrastructure belong almost entirely to the state. This ownership gives the government full control over productive assets and makes comprehensive coordination possible.

3) Administrative Regulation of Prices and Production

Prices are fixed not by supply and demand but by government authorities, who base them on calculated costs, social priorities, or political aims. Output levels are likewise imposed from above, and enterprises are expected to meet assigned figures. Competition is absent, and incentives are created by administrative pressure rather than market signals.

4) Norm-Based Allocation of Resources

Resources, raw materials, and finished goods are distributed according to state norms and quotas. Scarce items are directed to priority sectors so that national objectives receive concentrated support. This often produces shortages of consumer goods and persistent imbalances between supply and demand.

5) Primacy of Social and Political Goals over Profitability

Planned economies are designed to meet collective objectives—industrial growth, defense, or social welfare—rather than private profit. Efficiency is frequently subordinated to political directives or social obligations.

6) Elimination of Market Competition

Rivalry between enterprises is either minimal or absent. Since production, pricing, and distribution are dictated from above, competition no longer serves as the mechanism for efficiency or innovation.

Causes and Historical Conditions for the Emergence of Planned Economies

Planned economies usually appeared in periods of extraordinary pressure, when societies faced urgent needs for rapid transformation, large-scale mobilization of resources, or survival in times of crisis. Centralized planning was adopted as a way to channel national energy toward industrialization, modernization, or recovery under conditions where market mechanisms were considered inadequate.

Key Conditions that Led to the Rise of Planned Economies

1. Industrialization and Overcoming Backwardness

In countries that lagged behind the leading capitalist powers, planning was introduced as a means to speed up industrial development. The intention was to close the technological gap, establish heavy industry, and build the foundations of a modern economy within a condensed period of time.

2. Wartime Mobilization and Postwar Reconstruction

During war and in the years of recovery that followed, strict centralization allowed governments to direct resources toward defense, survival, and the rebuilding of devastated industries and infrastructure. Planning served as a way to concentrate national effort under conditions of extreme strain.

3. Response to Deep Economic Crises

In moments of severe economic breakdown, such as the Great Depression, elements of planning were employed to stabilize production, restore employment, and strengthen confidence. Centralized control was viewed as a safeguard against the volatility of unregulated markets.

4. Social Transformation and the Pursuit of Equality

Planned economies were often tied to ambitious social projects that sought to create greater equality and social justice. Through centralized redistribution, governments aimed to reduce exploitation, narrow income disparities, and ensure fair access to essential goods and services.

Historical Examples of Planned Economies

- **The Soviet Union (1928–1991)**

With the launch of the first Five-Year Plan, the USSR created a fully centralized system. Planning was used to industrialize at unprecedented speed, turning a predominantly agrarian country into a global power.

- **Eastern Europe (1945–1989)**

After World War II, socialist governments in Eastern Europe established centrally planned economies as part of their integration into the Soviet sphere.

- **China before the Reforms of Deng Xiaoping (late 1970s)**

In its early decades, the People's Republic of China adopted a rigid planned model to consolidate socialist transformation, mobilize rural labor, and push for rapid industrialization.

- **Cuba, Vietnam, and Other Socialist States**

These countries relied on planning to secure independence from capitalist economies, redistribute resources, and strengthen social systems.

Indicative Planning in Mixed Economies

Planning mechanisms were not limited to socialist systems. After World War II, several market economies—among them France and Japan—experimented with indicative planning. In this model, the state guided investment priorities, coordinated industrial policy, and supported strategic sectors, while private ownership and market exchange continued to operate. This hybrid approach enabled rapid reconstruction and modernization without undermining the vitality of the market.

Chapter 1

Socialist Planned Economy:
State Control of Production Based on Socialist Principles

> **A socialist planned economy** is an economic system in which state ownership of the means of production dominates, and all major economic decisions are made through centralized planning rather than market mechanisms.

Characteristics of a Socialist Planned Economy

A socialist planned economy is an economic system in which the state assumes a dominant role in nearly every sphere of economic life. Production, distribution, and consumption are directed through centralized planning rather than the spontaneous interaction of supply and demand. Unlike a market economy, where decisions are made by independent producers and consumers pursuing their own interests, a planned system operates according to priorities set by the government, often linked to broader social, political, or national aims.

The foundation of this model is state or collective ownership of the means of production, natural resources, and essential infrastructure. Such ownership gives the government direct control over resource allocation, investment, and economic mobilization in pursuit of strategic goals—industrialization, defense, or wide-reaching social programs. While the system aspires to ensure equality and social protection, it often does so at the cost of efficiency, adaptability, and consumer choice.

Core Features of a Socialist Planned Economy

1) State Ownership of Production and Resources

In socialist economies, land, factories, mines, transport, and energy resources are owned and managed by the state on behalf of society. Private ownership in large-scale industry or natural resources is heavily restricted or eliminated. This arrangement is meant to prevent monopolies, secure equal access to resources, and allow governments to launch large projects without dependence on private capital.

2) Centralized Planning

The defining feature of the system is the national economic plan. Central planning bodies set binding targets for enterprises, decide the volume and variety of goods, and allocate raw materials, labor, and capital. Plans typically cover long periods—most famously the Soviet Five-Year Plans—and extend beyond industry to agriculture, transport, housing, and social services. Prices are also set by state decision, often shaped by political aims such as keeping basic goods artificially cheap.

3) Administrative Control of Production and Distribution

Enterprises do not compete on open markets but follow administrative commands. Factories and collective farms work under quotas, while ministries and planning committees direct the flow of goods from producers to consumers. Profit plays little role; success is measured instead by fulfilling the targets of the plan.

4) Limited Space for Private Activity

Although planning dominates, some socialist economies permitted small-scale private activity in trade, services, or handicrafts. These sectors filled consumer gaps but were tightly regulated, licensed, and taxed to prevent the rise of independent capitalist enterprises.

5) Absence of Competition and Use of Non-Market Incentives

Without profit-based competition, enterprises lacked the usual market pressures to innovate or cut costs. To motivate workers and managers, states introduced alternative incentives: bonuses for exceeding quotas, public awards, or social prestige for "heroes of labor."

6) Social Orientation and Redistribution

A central aim of the socialist planned economy was social equality. The state sought to narrow income differences, guarantee universal employment, and ensure access to education, healthcare, housing, and other essential services. Redistribution was deliberate, carried out through planning rather than left to the market, reflecting the ideological goal of reducing class divisions and raising the common standard of living.

7) Strategic National Priorities

With full command of resources, the state could concentrate effort on projects deemed vital for development or security. Industrialization drives, heavy industry expansion, defense programs, and nationwide infrastructure could be pursued on a massive scale. This ability to mobilize quickly was especially evident during wartime and in periods of technological catch-up.

Strengths of a Socialist Planned Economy

1. Concentration of Resources on Strategic Goals

A key advantage of the socialist planned model is its ability to mobilize and concentrate national resources on major social, economic, and strategic objectives. Centralized management makes it possible to direct funds into education, healthcare, infrastructure, research, defense, and heavy industry. Even under conditions of scarcity, governments can carry out ambitious projects such as rapid industrialization, universal literacy, or nationwide healthcare.

2. High Social Stability and Full Employment

Because employment is planned in advance, jobs are provided for virtually all citizens of working age. This eliminates the risk of mass unemployment and the instability that often accompanies it. At the same time, the state ensures extensive social protections—free education, healthcare, and affordable housing—creating a strong sense of security and reinforcing social cohesion.

3. Reduction of Inequality and Poverty

Planned economies are designed to minimize social and economic disparities. Wages are regulated and resources distributed in ways that prevent extreme poverty and limit inequality. Wealth may not be abundant, but access to essential goods and services is broad and relatively equal, securing a basic level of material well-being for the population.

4. Capacity to Withstand Crises

Centralized control enables rapid responses to war, natural disasters, or global economic shocks. Resources can be redirected immediately toward essential production and crisis management, allowing the system to absorb external pressures more effectively than decentralized models.

5. Long-Term Orientation

Unlike market economies, which are often driven by short-term profitability, planned systems can sustain capital-intensive projects that require decades of investment. Fields such as nuclear energy, space exploration, or fundamental science can flourish because long-term planning shields them from the volatility of markets.

6. Economic and Social Security

Strict regulation of production and pricing ensures stable living conditions. Inflation, speculative surges, and sudden price hikes are largely prevented. Citizens benefit from predictability in access to goods and services, while essential items remain available even in turbulent times.

7. Primacy of Collective over Individual Interest

Economic activity is directed toward public welfare rather than private profit. This orientation allows the state to prioritize social infrastructure—roads, power stations, housing—that private capital might overlook, ensuring collective benefits take precedence.

8. Rapid Industrial and Infrastructural Transformation

Planned economies are able to accelerate modernization through massive national projects. Centralized mobilization of resources makes it possible to expand heavy industry and infrastructure in a relatively short time, achieving progress that would be slower under purely market-driven systems.

9. Price Stability and Protection from Speculation

With the state controlling prices, planned economies avoid inflationary spirals and speculative manipulation. Citizens benefit from stable pricing and the assurance that essential goods remain accessible, free from shortages created by profiteering.

10. Support for Fundamental Science and Research

Planned systems can sustain large-scale scientific initiatives that private investors might neglect because of long payback periods. Projects in nuclear physics, space exploration, and basic research in mathematics and natural sciences have historically thrived under this model, supported by deliberate state investment.

Weaknesses of a Socialist Planned Economy

1. Low Efficiency and Weak Incentives

The absence of competition diminishes both efficiency and motivation. Enterprises fulfill quotas regardless of demand or quality, while workers and managers lack personal incentives to improve results. Over time, productivity falls, technical progress slows, and product quality deteriorates.

2. Chronic Shortages and Limited Choice

Central planning cannot keep pace with changing consumer needs. Everyday shortages, poor assortments, and long queues become common. Citizens face rationing and limited access to consumer goods, which lowers living standards and undermines satisfaction with the system.

3. Rigidity and Poor Adaptability

Plans are drawn up for long periods and offer little room for revision. This rigidity prevents quick responses to crises, external shocks, or technological change. As a result, mismatches between planned output and actual needs accumulate, producing inefficiencies and distortions.

4. Bureaucracy and Administrative Inefficiency

Managing an entire economy centrally demands an enormous bureaucracy. Such structures are costly, slow, and vulnerable to corruption. Delays, rigid adherence to outdated directives, and misallocation of resources further weaken efficiency.

5. Weak Innovation in Civilian Sectors

While planned economies often succeed in strategic projects such as defense or space exploration, innovation spreads poorly in consumer industries. Without competitive pressure, producers lack incentives to modernize, diversify, or improve quality, leaving everyday goods stagnant.

6. Distorted Information and Planning Errors

Without price signals and free market feedback, planners work with incomplete or inaccurate data. This leads to systematic errors: surpluses of unwanted goods appear alongside shortages of essentials, reflecting the limits of centralized decision-making.

7. Low International Competitiveness

Socialist economies could produce heavy machinery and industrial goods but struggled with consumer products. Lacking variety, quality, and modern design, such goods were less competitive on global markets, limiting exports and reducing access to foreign currency.

8. Restricted Private Initiative

Private enterprise was eliminated or tightly controlled. With the state monopolizing resources and production, citizens had little opportunity for independent economic activity. The absence of entrepreneurship deprived the system of innovation, flexibility, and responsiveness to consumer demand.

Historical Examples of Socialist Planned Economies

The Soviet Union (1922–1991)

After the end of the New Economic Policy (NEP, 1921–1928), the Soviet Union moved toward strict centralized planning, launching rapid industrialization and the collectivization of agriculture. The central institution responsible for coordinating economic planning was the State Planning Committee (Gosplan), which drafted the binding *Five-Year Plans*.

The Soviet model of a planned economy was defined by complete state ownership of the means of production, the elimination of private enterprise, centralized allocation of resources, and state-determined prices for goods and services.

Strengths of the Soviet Planned Economy

1. Accelerated industrialization and rapid economic growth

Centralized planning enabled the Soviet Union to transform in a remarkably short time from a largely agrarian society into a leading industrial power. During the first two Five-Year Plans (1928–1937), roughly 9,000 large industrial enterprises were built, including the DniproHES hydroelectric station, the Magnitogorsk Iron and Steel Works, and major tractor and automobile plants.

2. Major scientific and technological achievements

Planned allocation of resources allowed vast investments in science, technology, and infrastructure, particularly in strategic sectors.

- In 1957, the USSR launched the world's first artificial satellite, *Sputnik-1*.

- In 1961, Yuri Gagarin became the first human to travel into space.

- Soviet researchers made significant advances in nuclear physics, aviation, and missile technology, including the development of the atomic bomb (1949), the hydrogen bomb (1953), and the first intercontinental ballistic missiles (1957).

3. Full employment and social stability

The Soviet economy guaranteed employment for virtually all working-age citizens. Alongside job security, the state provided free education, healthcare, housing, and pensions. Unemployment was officially close to zero.

4. Relatively low inequality and widespread social protections

The state-controlled wage and income system limited socio-economic stratification. According to international research, the Soviet Union's Gini coefficient in the 1970s and 1980s was among the lowest in the world (around 0.25–0.28).

5. Rapid recovery after wars and crises

Centralized control allowed the Soviet Union to mobilize resources quickly for reconstruction after devastating conflicts such as the Civil War (1918–1922) and World War II (1941–1945). By the end of the first postwar Five-Year Plan (1946–1950), industrial output exceeded prewar levels by 73% (official Central Statistical Administration data).

6. Expansion of universal education and workforce training

The Soviet Union developed a vast system for training highly qualified specialists in technical, scientific, and humanitarian fields. By the 1970s, literacy rates were nearly universal, and the country ranked among world leaders in access to higher education.

7. Access to basic goods and services for the population

Although shortages persisted, basic goods such as food staples, housing, utilities, and public transport were widely accessible at low, stable prices. Housing and utilities rarely consumed more than 5% of household income.

Weaknesses of the Soviet Planned Economy

1. Chronic shortages of consumer goods

Fixed prices and rigid planning led to persistent shortages of consumer products, particularly in the 1970s and 1980s. Citizens often faced queues for everyday goods such as appliances, cars, clothing, and even food staples.

2. Low efficiency and lagging productivity

Without competition or profit incentives, labor productivity at many enterprises was significantly lower than in advanced capitalist economies. By the 1980s, Western economists estimated Soviet industrial productivity at only 40–60% of U.S. levels.

3. Bureaucratization and administrative inefficiency

The sheer scale of centralized planning created a bloated bureaucracy. By the late 1980s, Gosplan and related agencies were processing more than 20 million economic indicators annually, slowing decision-making and increasing inefficiency.

4. Weak adaptability to global change

Rigid plans prevented rapid responses to technological advances or shifts in the global economy. This led to growing technological lag, especially in consumer and civilian industries.

5. Disproportional development across sectors

Prioritizing heavy industry and defense came at the expense of consumer goods, agriculture, and services. By the early 1980s, military spending and investment in heavy industry vastly exceeded allocations for consumer needs.

6. Environmental degradation and wasteful resource use

The drive to meet quantitative targets often produced ecological damage and resource inefficiency. Problems such as severe urban pollution and the ecological disaster of the Aral Sea reflected the environmental costs of the system.

7. Limited consideration of regional diversity

Centralized planning rarely accounted for the specific needs of the Soviet republics and regions. This created economic imbalances and fueled political and social tensions among different parts of the Union.

8. Lack of consumer feedback

Because consumer demand played little role in production decisions, enterprises often produced goods that failed to meet actual needs. This disconnect reduced satisfaction with the quality and variety of products available to the population.

East Germany (GDR) before Reunification (1949–1990)

In 1949, the German Democratic Republic (GDR) was established, and its economy was organized according to the Soviet model, based on state ownership of the means of production and strict centralized planning.

The key institution responsible for economic planning was the State Planning Commission (Staatliche Plankommission), which developed five-year and annual plans mandatory for all enterprises and institutions. Industrial enterprises were consolidated into state-owned combines and production associations, known as Volkseigene Betriebe (VEB, People's Own Enterprises).

Strengths of the Socialist Planned Economy in the GDR

1. Social stability and near-full employment

Centralized planning ensured virtually universal employment. Throughout the existence of the GDR, unemployment remained below 0.5 percent.

2. Strong social protection and equal distribution of income

The state controlled wages and prices for essential goods and services, maintaining one of the lowest levels of inequality in the world. The Gini coefficient in East Germany was estimated at 0.20–0.22, far lower than in most Western economies.

3. Well-developed education, healthcare, and social services

The GDR provided universal access to free education and healthcare. Citizens were guaranteed professional training, medical care, and social benefits. Among socialist countries, East Germany ranked highly in terms of the quality of its education and health systems.

4. Expansion of infrastructure and housing construction

Centralized planning enabled large-scale housing projects and infrastructure development. According to the **Statistical Yearbook of the GDR (1988)**, more than two million apartments were built between 1971 and 1988.

5. Highly skilled workforce

The GDR invested heavily in vocational and technical training, producing a qualified labor force to meet the needs of its industrial sector.

6. Advanced performance in selected industrial sectors

East Germany achieved notable success in industries such as optics (Carl Zeiss Jena), chemicals (Leuna Works), electrical engineering, precision instruments, and machine tools. Products from these sectors were competitive and exported to Western Europe as well as to the Soviet Union.

Weaknesses of the Socialist Planned Economy in the GDR

1. Low competitiveness and technological lag

The absence of market competition and limited integration with the global economy led to growing technological backwardness. By the late 1980s, labor productivity in the GDR was estimated at only 40–50 percent of West German levels (DIW, 1990).

2. Chronic shortages of consumer goods

Centralized planning failed to respond effectively to consumer demand, resulting in persistent shortages and limited variety of everyday goods throughout the GDR's history.

3. Rigid and inflexible economic system

The GDR economy lacked the ability to adapt to external shocks such as the oil crises of the 1970s, global technological innovation, and economic globalization. Scholars argue that systemic rigidity was a major factor behind the economic crisis of the late 1980s.

4. Bureaucratization and inefficiency

Centralized decision-making created a cumbersome bureaucracy, slowed policy implementation, and restricted enterprise autonomy, reducing overall efficiency.

5. Dependence on the Soviet Union

The GDR relied heavily on Soviet supplies of energy and raw materials, limiting its economic independence. This dependency deepened as the Soviet economy entered crisis in the 1980s.

6. Emigration of skilled labor ("brain drain")

Economic and political constraints triggered the emigration of highly qualified workers and specialists. Before the construction of the Berlin Wall in 1961, more than two million citizens left East Germany, according to data from the German Federal Archives (Bundesarchiv, 1989).

7. Severe environmental degradation

The emphasis on heavy industry without regard for environmental costs resulted in serious ecological problems, especially in Saxony and Saxony-Anhalt. According to the German Environment Agency (Umweltbundesamt, 1991), air and water pollution levels in the GDR during the 1980s far exceeded West German and European standards.

8. Inefficient agriculture and reliance on imports

Collectivized agriculture, organized in agricultural production cooperatives (LPG, Landwirtschaftliche Produktionsgenossenschaften), failed to ensure sufficient productivity. By the late 1980s, the GDR relied heavily on food imports from the USSR, Poland, and Hungary (Statistical Yearbook of the GDR, 1988–1989).

Cuba (1960s – Present)

After the victory of the Cuban Revolution in 1959, Fidel Castro's government nationalized major industries, agriculture, banking, and trade. By the mid-1960s, Cuba had completed its transition to centralized planning and state ownership of the means of production, modeled closely on the Soviet system.

The main planning institutions were the Ministry of Economy and Planning (*Ministerio de Economía y Planificación*) and the Central Planning Board (*Junta Central de Planificación*, JUCEPLAN). These bodies set production targets, allocated resources, and determined prices for goods and services.

Strengths of Cuba's Socialist Planned Economy

1. Comprehensive Social Guarantees

Cuba offers universal access to free healthcare and education of high quality. According to the World Health Organization (2020), life expectancy stood at 78.9 years, one of the highest in Latin America, while infant mortality was just 4.6 per 1,000 live births—among the lowest in the region.

2. Low Economic Inequality

Wage regulation and subsidies for basic goods have maintained relatively equal income distribution. The World Bank notes that Cuba's Gini coefficient has historically ranged between 0.25 and 0.30, far below the regional average.

3. Near-Universal Employment

The state guarantees work for nearly all citizens of working age. Data from Cuba's National Office of Statistics and Information (ONEI) show unemployment levels consistently between 1 and 3 percent.

4. Strategic Investment in Priority Sectors

Centralized planning allows the concentration of resources in areas such as biomedicine, healthcare, and international tourism. Cuban biotechnology firms export vaccines and medicines to dozens of countries.

5. **Subsidized Food and Housing**

A rationing system (*Libreta de Abastecimiento*) ensures access to essential food and goods at low prices, keeping them affordable for most households.

6. **Public Safety**

Cuba maintains comparatively low crime rates. The UN Office on Drugs and Crime (UNODC) reports that levels of violent crime are significantly lower than the regional average.

7. **Effective Disaster Preparedness**

Centralized coordination has produced one of the most effective disaster management systems in Latin America. The United Nations often cites Cuba's hurricane response model as exemplary.

Weaknesses of Cuba's Socialist Planned Economy

1. **Chronic Shortages**

Centralized planning has led to persistent shortages of consumer goods and poor service quality. The UN Economic Commission for Latin America and the Caribbean (ECLAC) has documented long-standing deficits in essential items.

2. **Low Labor Productivity**

Lack of competition and rigid wage structures weaken incentives for workers and managers. The World Bank reports that Cuba's productivity lags well behind most Latin American economies.

3. **Dependence on External Aid and Imports**

The Cuban economy has long depended on external support—first from the Soviet Union, later from Venezuela—alongside reliance on tourism and imported food, fuel, and medicine.

4. **Rigid Planning and Weak Adaptability**

The centralized model makes it difficult to adjust to global market shifts, technological change, or external shocks, reducing flexibility.

5. **Inefficient Agriculture**

Despite favorable conditions, agriculture remains unproductive and underfunded. According to the World Food Programme (WFP), Cuba imports 70–80 percent of its food supply.

6. **Underdeveloped Private Sector**

Reforms in recent years have legalized limited private enterprise, but regulatory barriers continue to restrict entrepreneurship. The International Labour Organization (ILO) notes that small and medium-sized enterprises remain marginal.

Chapter 2

Non-Socialist Models of Planned Economy: Central Planning Without Socialist Ideology

> **A non-socialist planned economy** is an economic system based on centralized state planning and regulation, which allows private ownership and limited use of market mechanisms but does not rely on socialist principles or state monopoly over the means of production.

In this model, the state not only regulates economic activity but also shapes the strategic direction of development by allocating resources and setting national priorities. The private sector functions within the framework of centralized state plans and strategies.

Non-socialist planned economies usually emerge in situations demanding rapid development, recovery from crisis, wartime mobilization, or large-scale modernization. Unlike socialist systems, they combine state planning with the preservation of private ownership and market mechanisms.

Main Forms of Non-Socialist Planned Economies and Their Characteristics

1. State Dirigisme (Dirigiste Economy)

The concept of *dirigisme* (from the French *diriger* — "to direct, to guide") represents a model of non-socialist planned economy in which the state plays an active role in directing economic activity through centralized planning, regulation, subsidies, and direct investment. Within dirigisme, government agencies not only regulate key industries and distribute resources but also set strategic goals and define the trajectory of national economic development.

At the same time, the private sector retains a significant role, operating under clearly defined state frameworks. Entrepreneurial initiative and competition are combined with strong state support and oversight.

Key features of state dirigisme include:

- Centralized strategic planning and regulation of the economy;
- State financing and subsidization of priority industries;
- The use of state-owned enterprises and banks to steer economic development;
- Preservation of private property, competition, and market mechanisms under strong state regulation;
- Institutionalized cooperation between state agencies and large private corporations.

Strengths of State Dirigisme

1. Implementation of Large-Scale Projects and Reforms

Dirigisme allows governments to mobilize resources quickly and direct them toward national priorities and major infrastructure projects. Centralized coordination reduces uncertainty for private actors, ensures consistency in long-term initiatives, and accelerates the execution of complex reforms. Organized allocation of resources lowers the risks often associated with market-driven development and supports sustained national goals.

2. Accelerated Growth Through Strategic Investment

By channeling financial and material resources into priority sectors—such as energy, transportation, automotive production, aviation, and high technology—the dirigiste model stimulates rapid industrial expansion. State-backed modernization enables the rise of advanced industries, allowing economies to narrow the gap with or even surpass global competitors in relatively short periods.

3. Balance Between State and Market

A central advantage of dirigisme is its hybrid nature. The state defines strategic objectives and maintains regulatory oversight, while the private sector retains the ability to innovate, compete, and expand. This balance creates a dynamic interplay between stability and flexibility: entrepreneurship flourishes, but the volatility of unregulated markets is kept in check.

4. Support for Strategic Industries and Market Protection

Through subsidies, preferential credit, and selective tariff protection, the state can sustain critical industries and shield them from external competition until they become internationally competitive. This targeted support helps preserve jobs, secure technological independence, and strengthen sectors of long-term importance.

5. Guided Structural Transformation

Dirigisme provides the means to direct structural change by reallocating resources from declining industries toward those with stronger growth potential. This managed transformation encourages diversification, reduces reliance on unstable primary sectors, and promotes balanced, forward-looking development.

6. Macroeconomic Stability

By influencing investment flows, directing credit, and shaping industrial priorities, the state can reduce the severity of boom-and-bust cycles typical of liberal capitalism. This capacity helps maintain steadier growth and reduces the risk of systemic crises.

Weaknesses of State Dirigisme

Although dirigisme can accelerate modernization and guide strategic development, it also reveals structural weaknesses that limit its long-term effectiveness. Most of these stem from the dominant role of the state in economic decision-making and the restricted autonomy of market mechanisms.

1. Bureaucratization and Administrative Inefficiency

Heavy state involvement often creates a large and rigid bureaucracy. Multiple layers of administration slow decision-making, increase costs, and reduce efficiency. Implementation becomes formalistic, delaying projects and discouraging initiative at the enterprise level.

2. Corruption, Lobbying, and Favoritism

The concentration of authority in state agencies opens opportunities for rent-seeking. Corporations may lobby for favorable regulations, subsidies, or privileged access to resources, distorting competition and undermining fairness and transparency.

3. Limited Flexibility and Adaptability

Dirigiste systems adjust slowly to shifts in consumer demand, technological change, or global competition. Long-term state plans constrain rapid adaptation, leaving the economy less responsive to shocks and innovation trends. This rigidity reduces competitiveness in fast-changing markets.

4. Resource Misallocation and Inefficient Investment

Strategic priorities are not always aligned with economic efficiency. Governments may direct resources to politically favored industries rather than those with the greatest potential for productivity or innovation. This often results in overfunding unviable projects and wasting capital.

5. Suppression of Small and Medium Enterprises

Large state-backed corporations tend to dominate, leaving limited space for small and medium-sized firms. Barriers to entry, scarce financing, and restricted market access discourage entrepreneurship, reduce economic diversity, and weaken bottom-up innovation.

6. Fiscal Burden and Risk of Overinvestment

Extensive state intervention requires high levels of public spending, subsidies, and directed credit. Over time, this can create heavy fiscal pressure and rising debt. Investments may also overshoot real demand, producing overcapacity and inefficiencies in industries such as steel, shipbuilding, or infrastructure.

7. Dependence on State Support and Weak Private Initiative

Enterprises accustomed to subsidies and protection often lack incentives to cut costs, improve efficiency, or innovate. This dependency makes the economy vulnerable when state support declines and limits the growth of an independent private sector. Managers focus on lobbying for continued aid instead of improving competitiveness, which entrenches inefficiency. Over time, this creates a culture of reliance where initiative, risk-taking, and entrepreneurship are suppressed, leaving the economy stagnant and unprepared for global competition.

8. Political Interference in Economic Priorities

Dirigisme blurs the line between economic and political goals. Governments may channel resources not only for economic development but also to secure legitimacy, satisfy interest groups, or pursue geopolitical aims. This politicization of strategy undermines efficiency and diverts resources from sectors crucial for long-term competitiveness.

Historical Examples of State Dirigisme
France under Charles de Gaulle (1958–1969)

In the aftermath of World War II, and particularly under the leadership of Charles de Gaulle, France embraced a dirigiste model to rebuild its economy and strengthen key industries. The state assumed a decisive role in strategic sectors such as energy, metallurgy, and transportation, while channeling substantial investment into new technological and industrial frontiers.

Major initiatives included the expansion of the aerospace sector (Airbus), the development of nuclear energy through Électricité de France (EDF), and the modernization of the automobile industry with companies such as Renault and Citroën. The dirigiste approach fueled a period of extraordinary growth known as Les Trente Glorieuses ("The Thirty Glorious Years," 1945–1975), during which France emerged as one of Europe's leading industrial powers.

South Korea (1960s–1980s)

Beginning in the early 1960s, the government assumed direct control over financial flows, channeling credit and subsidies to large family-owned conglomerates (chaebols) such as Hyundai, Samsung, and LG.

The state set explicit development targets and prioritized export-oriented industrialization in sectors including shipbuilding, automobiles, and electronics. This strategy generated remarkable economic growth, transforming South Korea from a poor agrarian society into a newly industrialized economy—an achievement often referred to as the "Korean economic miracle."

Japan (1950s–1980s)

After its defeat in World War II, Japan embraced a dirigiste approach to accelerate reconstruction and modernization. The Ministry of International Trade and Industry (MITI) became the key institution for shaping long-term strategies, coordinating private corporations, and directing credit and investment into priority sectors such as automobiles, electronics, and steel.

The Japanese state also shielded strategic industries from foreign competition until they were strong enough to succeed internationally. This state-guided model powered what became known as the "Japanese economic miracle," allowing Japan to emerge by the late twentieth century as one of the world's leading industrial and technological powers.

2. The Military–Mobilization Model

The military–mobilization economy is a distinctive form of non-socialist planned system in which the state centrally directs economic activity with the overriding purpose of concentrating resources on military, political, and strategic objectives. Its defining feature is the subordination of the entire economy to defense and security needs, underpinned by strict state regulation of production, distribution, and investment.

Unlike socialist command economies, the military–mobilization model usually preserves private property and retains some market mechanisms, but the autonomy of private actors is severely restricted. Private firms and entrepreneurs must comply with state production targets and strategic directives, especially in sectors tied to armaments, infrastructure, and logistics. Market exchange continues but functions entirely within priorities established by the state.

Key Features of the Military–Mobilization Economy

- **Centralized Planning and Control**: Decision-making is concentrated in government hands, which issue binding quotas and directives to industries and firms.

- **Primacy of Military Objectives**: Civilian goals are subordinated to defense needs, with substantial resources diverted to weapons, equipment, and military infrastructure.

- **Regulation and Rationing of Resources**: Raw materials, labor, and capital are distributed through state quotas, often accompanied by rationing systems for consumer goods.

- **Private Property Under Regulation**: Enterprises may remain privately owned, but their freedom of decision is limited by state contracts and strategic requirements.

- **Industrial Conversion to Military Production**: In wartime or periods of geopolitical tension, industries are reoriented—sometimes temporarily, sometimes permanently—toward producing weapons, equipment, and supplies.

Strengths of the Military–Mobilization Economy

1. Rapid Resource Mobilization in War or Crisis

Centralized planning allows labor, capital, and raw materials to be mobilized swiftly and directed toward urgent military needs. In wartime or acute crises, this model ensures the maximum concentration of national effort and rapid decision-making.

2. Execution of Large-Scale Military and Infrastructural Projects

State-directed planning enables the rapid launch of massive initiatives such as building bases, expanding arms production, and developing transport and logistical infrastructure for military use. Government authorities can act immediately, allocate resources, and enforce compliance with strategic objectives.

3. Unified Strategic Coordination

With centralized control, economic activity follows a single strategic direction. Enterprises and industries are closely coordinated, allowing resources to be deployed in line with military priorities and making it possible to respond effectively to sudden shifts in the security environment.

4. Reduction of Fragmentation and Duplication

By removing competition between firms and eliminating overlapping production, the state streamlines industries for maximum efficiency. Redundant activities are minimized, and resources are concentrated in sectors critical to defense.

5. Maximization of Output in Critical Sectors

Through binding quotas and centralized resource allocation, production in armaments, transportation, and energy can be dramatically increased, sustaining prolonged military campaigns.

6. Capacity to Foster National Unity and Discipline

By aligning economic life with defense priorities, the military–mobilization economy cultivates a sense of collective purpose. Citizens, enterprises, and institutions operate under shared objectives, strengthening morale, discipline, and political cohesion in times of existential threat.

Weaknesses of the Military–Mobilization Economy

1. Shortages of Consumer Goods

The diversion of resources to military priorities sharply reduces the supply of food, clothing, and other essentials. Chronic shortages, rationing, and a decline in the quality and availability of everyday goods become common features of the system.

2. Falling Civilian Living Standards

Strict rationing of non-military goods and services restricts consumption and access to basic comforts. Citizens face economic hardship, and the overall standard of living for the civilian population steadily declines.

3. Suppression of Entrepreneurship and Freedoms

Private enterprise is tightly constrained by state planning and compulsory directives. Competition and innovation are suppressed, and economic actors operate within rigid state frameworks. These restrictions often coincide with broader limitations on civil liberties and individual freedoms.

4. Inefficiency and Misallocation of Resources

Prioritizing defense distorts the balance of the economy, leading to underinvestment in civilian sectors such as agriculture, housing, healthcare, and consumer technology. Once the immediate military need has passed, correcting these structural distortions proves difficult.

5. Lack of Long-Term Sustainability

While effective in emergencies, a mobilization model is too costly and disruptive to sustain in peacetime. Chronic underproduction of consumer goods, combined with the heavy fiscal burden of military spending, undermines economic development over the long run.

6. **Innovation Limited to Defense**

Technological progress is concentrated in military industries, while consumer-oriented innovation stagnates. Advances in weaponry and defense systems rarely spill over into the civilian economy, leaving productivity and modernization lagging behind.

7. **Risk of Isolation and Dependency**

A mobilized economy often turns inward, emphasizing military self-sufficiency over international trade. This can produce economic isolation, limit access to foreign technologies, and increase vulnerability if external supply chains are disrupted.

8. **Social and Psychological Strain**

The militarization of daily life imposes a constant burden on society. Austerity, enforced discipline, and sacrifice erode personal well-being, weaken morale, and may eventually spark public discontent, resistance, or unrest.

Historical Examples of a Military–Mobilization Economy

Germany during the First and Second World Wars

In both World Wars, Germany shifted its economy entirely to military needs. Civilian industry was redirected to weapons and equipment, while food and consumer goods were rationed through a strict coupon system. Major private companies such as Krupp, Siemens, IG Farben, and BMW formally remained private but operated entirely under state control, producing what the government demanded. By 1944, nearly 75% of Germany's industrial output was dedicated to armaments. This rapid militarization allowed for massive weapons production in the short term but left the civilian population facing chronic shortages and declining living standards.

The United States and the United Kingdom during World War II (1939–1945)

When the war began, both the United States and Britain transformed their economies almost overnight. In America, civilian factories stopped making cars and refrigerators and started building tanks, aircraft, and ships. Between 1940 and 1945, the U.S. produced over 300,000 aircraft, 88,000 tanks, and thousands of naval vessels, turning the country into the so-called "Arsenal of Democracy." Britain followed the same path. The government introduced ration books for food, clothing, and fuel, ensuring that resources were directed to the military. Nearly every factory in Britain was tied in some way to the war effort, whether in steel, chemicals, or textiles.

Japan during World War II (1941–1945)

Japan also adopted a rigid war economy. The state seized control of resource allocation and ordered leading industrial groups—Mitsubishi, Mitsui, Sumitomo—to prioritize weapons and military technology. Consumer goods disappeared almost entirely from the market. By the last years of the war, Japan's economy was fully devoted to sustaining the military, even as the civilian population struggled with scarcity and widespread deprivation.

These cases show the double-edged nature of a military–mobilization economy. In the short run, such systems can concentrate resources and achieve astonishing levels of military production. Germany's rapid rearmament, America's industrial surge, and

Japan's ability to maintain its war machine all demonstrate this. Yet the long-term costs are severe: shortages, falling living standards, mounting debt, and eventual economic exhaustion. War economies succeed only as temporary measures; over time, they undermine both social stability and economic resilience.

3. The Planned-Corporatist Model

A planned–corporatist economy is a form of non-socialist planned system in which the state regulates economic life through close cooperation with large private corporations and industry associations. In this model, government agencies do not merely intervene in the market; they work directly with corporate structures to define strategic goals, allocate resources, and guide private-sector activity. Private ownership remains, and companies continue to operate within a market framework, but their actions are closely aligned with national economic priorities.

Core Features of the Planned–Corporatist Model

- Strong state regulation combined with active coordination of private business.
- Establishment of industry-wide associations that manage production, pricing, and investment jointly with the state.
- Preservation of private property, provided its use serves national economic objectives.
- Institutionalized cooperation between government agencies and large corporations.
- Market mechanisms continue to function, but they are constrained and directed through centralized agreements.

Strengths of the Planned-Corporatist Economy

1. **Efficiency in Large-Scale Projects**

Close cooperation between the state and major corporations enables the rapid realization of national infrastructure and industrial programs. The state mobilizes resources, while corporations provide technical expertise and capital, creating an effective partnership for development.

2. **Coordination of Public and Private Initiatives**

By aligning government priorities with corporate strategies, this model reduces uncertainty and ensures that resources are allocated with greater precision. Economic actors work together toward shared objectives, improving coherence in long-term development.

3. **Stability Through Corporatist Mechanisms**

Regular consultations and negotiated agreements between the state, industry associations, and sometimes labor unions establish predictability in policy. This institutionalized dialogue helps prevent major disruptions and supports steady, long-term growth.

4. Reduction of Social Conflict

Because the interests of the state, business, and organized labor are formally coordinated, the system tends to reduce social tensions and limit the risk of strikes or political unrest.

5. Support for Strategic Industries

The corporatist model allows governments to direct investment into sectors considered vital—such as energy, transportation, and advanced technologies—ensuring their development even in the face of international competition.

6. Long-Term Orientation

Unlike purely market-driven systems, which often prioritize short-term profits, corporatist planning promotes sustained investment in infrastructure, education, and research, guided by strategic national objectives.

7. Predictability for Business

Corporations benefit from clear state signals about long-term priorities and are less exposed to the volatility of unregulated markets. This stability encourages investment and strategic planning.

8. Institutionalized Partnership

The establishment of permanent mechanisms of negotiation—sectoral committees, tripartite councils, and joint boards—builds trust between the state and business, facilitates compromise, and accelerates decision-making.

Weaknesses of the Planned-Corporatist Economy

1. Risk of Monopolization by Large Corporations

Because governments tend to rely on the largest and most established firms, monopolies or oligopolies may emerge. Such concentration of power weakens competition, limits consumer choice, and reduces incentives for innovation.

2. Restrictions on Competition and Market Entry

Heavy regulation and centralized agreements constrain small and medium-sized enterprises. Barriers to entry discourage entrepreneurship, limit market dynamism, and make it difficult for new firms with innovative potential to grow.

3. Bureaucracy and Corruption Risks

The close relationship between state institutions and corporate elites often leads to bureaucratic expansion and opens opportunities for corruption. Firms with privileged access can influence regulations in their favor, undermining fairness and eroding efficiency.

4. Reduced Economic Flexibility

When business decisions are bound to long-term state–corporate agreements, economies become less responsive to sudden changes in technology, global markets, or consumer demand. This rigidity can slow adaptation and weaken competitiveness.

5. **Risk of Policy Capture by Corporate Interests**

Large corporations may come to dominate the policy-making process, shaping national strategies to serve their own goals rather than the broader public interest. Over time, this blurs the line between public regulation and private lobbying.

6. **Neglect of Consumer Interests**

Because strategic priorities are often defined at the state–corporate level, consumer needs and preferences may be sidelined. This can lead to inefficiencies, reduced product variety, and weaker incentives to improve quality.

7. **Potential for Social Exclusion**

While the corporatist model integrates big business into policy-making, it often excludes smaller firms, labor unions, or civil society groups from meaningful participation. This imbalance can generate inequality in influence and foster social tensions.

Historical Examples of the Planned-Corporatist Economy

Italy under Benito Mussolini (1922–1943)

During Mussolini's rule, the Italian economy was organized into sectoral corporations where state officials, business leaders, and union representatives sat together to decide on production quotas, wages, and working conditions. In practice, these institutions were not genuine arenas of negotiation but instruments of state control.

The government imposed binding directives on production and investment, subordinating economic life to political goals—above all, militarization and the pursuit of autarky. Private property formally remained, but its use was tightly bound to the dictates of the regime and aligned with the strategic objectives of the Fascist Party.

This corporatist system projected an image of harmony among labor, capital, and the state. In reality, it suppressed independent unions, banned strikes, and curtailed market freedom.

Spain under Francisco Franco (1939–1975)

After the Spanish Civil War, Franco established a corporatist economy modeled in part on Mussolini's system but adapted to Spain's conditions. The regime introduced vertical syndicates that brought together employers, workers, and the state under the supervision of the Falange. Working closely with major corporations and banks, the government concentrated authority over industry, agriculture, construction, and finance.

In the early decades, this model restricted growth and left Spain economically isolated. The situation began to change in the 1960s with partial liberalization and the inflow of foreign capital. During the so-called Spanish Miracle, the country modernized industry, expanded infrastructure, and became more integrated into global markets.

Even so, the economy retained strong corporatist features: competition remained limited, small and medium-sized enterprises had little room to grow, and the state continued to exercise decisive influence over national priorities.

Portugal under António de Oliveira Salazar (1933–1974)

Salazar's Estado Novo created one of the most enduring corporatist systems in Europe. The regime organized the economy into guild-like sectoral associations, where production, prices, and investment were coordinated under state supervision. Private ownership continued, but its use was strictly regulated to serve national priorities, especially political stability and financial conservatism.

This model ensured continuity and shielded Portugal from the turbulence experienced by other Southern European economies. Yet stability came at the expense of growth and innovation. The country remained heavily rural and underdeveloped, with limited industrialization and persistent poverty.

Compared to Italy and Spain, Salazar's corporatism placed greater emphasis on austerity and stability rather than modernization, leaving Portugal among the poorest countries in Western Europe until the fall of the regime in 1974.

Comparative Perspective

The three cases illustrate different variations of the planned–corporatist model. Mussolini's Italy employed corporatism primarily as an instrument of ideological control, subordinating economic life to the political and military ambitions of the Fascist state. Franco's Spain blended authoritarian corporatism with gradual liberalization, eventually opening to foreign investment and modernization while still keeping labor and capital under tight state oversight. Salazar's Portugal placed less emphasis on industrial growth and more on preserving stability and order, maintaining corporatist structures but failing to generate dynamic development.

Taken together, these examples show that corporatism could deliver short-term stability, infrastructure expansion, and some industrial progress, yet at the price of restricted competition, curtailed freedoms, and weaker long-term performance compared with liberal market economies.

4. The Mixed Model with Active Industrial Policy

The mixed model with active industrial policy represents a variant of a non-socialist planned economy in which the state plays a significant role in strategic planning and regulation while preserving market mechanisms and private ownership of the means of production. Its defining feature is the active use of industrial policy tools—targeted programs, subsidies, tax incentives, and public investment—to support and stimulate key sectors of the economy.

Core Characteristics

- Combination of state planning and market mechanisms;
- Strategic support for priority sectors through targeted programs and public investment;
- Preservation of private ownership and a vibrant private sector;
- Use of market-based incentives (tax benefits, subsidies, access to credit) to guide economic activity;

- Partnership between the state and private businesses in research, development, and infrastructure.

Strengths of the Mixed Model with Active Industrial Policy

1. Economic Dynamism and Technological Progress

Targeted state support for innovative industries stimulates the growth of advanced technologies and emerging sectors. This strengthens national competitiveness and sustains long-term economic expansion.

2. Balance Between Regulation and Flexibility

The state sets a strategic framework without suppressing private initiative. This balance keeps the economy adaptable, innovative, and responsive to both global and domestic challenges.

3. Capacity to Realize Large-Scale Projects

Public investment makes it possible to carry out ambitious initiatives that private capital alone might not finance—such as renewable energy systems, nationwide transport networks, or high-tech clusters.

4. Resilience in Times of Crisis

The ability of the state to direct investment and intervene selectively provides stability during downturns. Strategic programs can safeguard critical industries, preserve employment, and maintain social cohesion.

5. Promotion of Long-Term Development

Industrial policy allows governments to prioritize sectors essential for national security, energy independence, and global competitiveness. This ensures continuity and progress beyond short-term market fluctuations.

6. Investment in Human Capital

State-led initiatives in education, vocational training, and research strengthen the foundations for innovation and sustainable growth, equipping the workforce with skills needed in advanced industries.

7. Reduction of Regional Disparities

Government programs can channel resources into underdeveloped regions, stimulating balanced development and reinforcing national cohesion.

8. Collaboration Between State, Business, and Science

Institutionalized cooperation fosters partnerships between government, corporations, and research institutions, accelerating technological progress and the diffusion of innovation.

9. Social Stability Through Redistribution

By supporting strategic sectors and creating jobs, the state contributes to reducing inequality and strengthening public trust, making economic modernization more socially inclusive.

Weaknesses of the Mixed Model with Active Industrial Policy

1. Risk of Misallocation of Resources

Poorly designed strategies can channel funds into uncompetitive sectors, distorting market signals and locking resources in inefficient activities.

2. Bureaucratic Expansion and Inefficiency

Active state involvement may create excessive administrative layers, delays in decision-making, and politicization of economic choices, reducing overall efficiency.

3. Difficulty in Balancing Public and Private Interests

Maintaining cooperation requires careful governance. Too much intervention discourages private initiative, while weak oversight limits the effectiveness of industrial policy.

4. Dependence on State Support

Firms accustomed to subsidies and protection may lose incentives to innovate or cut costs, weakening their long-term competitiveness once support is withdrawn.

5. Corruption and Rent-Seeking

Close ties between government and corporations create opportunities for lobbying, favoritism, and capture of resources by politically influential groups, undermining fairness and efficiency.

6. Fiscal Burden

Large-scale subsidies, tax breaks, and directed credit place heavy pressure on public finances. Sustaining such measures over time risks budget deficits and mounting public debt.

7. Risk of Protecting Inefficient Firms

Industrial policy may shield declining sectors or so-called "national champions" beyond what is economically justified, delaying structural transformation and wasting resources.

8. Reduced Market Dynamism

By steering investment and limiting competition, the state may suppress the entry of new firms and reduce diversity, stifling bottom-up innovation.

9. Vulnerability to Policy Shifts

Industrial policy depends on continuity. Changes in government, shifting political priorities, or external shocks can disrupt long-term programs, leaving unfinished projects and stranded investments.

10. International Trade Tensions

State subsidies and protectionist measures can provoke disputes with trade partners and lead to retaliatory barriers, limiting access to global markets.

11. Innovation Bias

While targeted policies may boost certain strategic sectors, they risk neglecting other areas of potential growth, creating technological imbalances across the economy.

Historical Examples of the Mixed Model with Active Industrial Policy

Singapore (1960s – present)

Singapore stands as one of the clearest examples of a successful mixed model guided by active industrial policy. After independence in 1965, the government under Lee Kuan Yew built a centralized system of strategic planning and directed resources into infrastructure, education, and emerging industries. Sovereign wealth funds such as Temasek Holdings and GIC Private Limited became key instruments for supporting national enterprises, attracting foreign investment, and fostering high-tech sectors including electronics, biotechnology, and pharmaceuticals.

What distinguished Singapore's model was the balance between strong state direction and a dynamic private sector. The state invested in priority industries and offered long-term guidance, but at the same time encouraged foreign corporations to establish operations and promoted local entrepreneurship. This combination produced a business environment marked by transparency, efficiency, and global competitiveness.

As a result, Singapore transformed from a small port economy into one of the world's most prosperous nations, consistently ranking near the top in global competitiveness indexes and maintaining one of the highest GDP per capita levels in Asia.

United Arab Emirates (late 20th century – present)

The United Arab Emirates illustrates how a mixed economy shaped by active industrial policy can evolve from a resource-based foundation into a diversified system. From the late twentieth century onward, the government combined state-led planning with market openness to reduce dependence on oil. Large-scale public investment reshaped national infrastructure, building modern airports, seaports, and logistics networks that support both regional and global connectivity.

Alongside this, the UAE established free trade zones, tax incentives, and liberal investment laws to attract foreign capital and encourage private enterprise. Strategic sectors such as finance, tourism, renewable energy, and advanced technologies have been promoted in parallel with oil and gas. Flagship initiatives—including Masdar City, focused on renewable energy and sustainability, and Expo 2020 in Dubai—reflect the state's role in steering innovation while leaving room for competitive market forces.

The result has been a diversified economy and a high standard of living by regional measures. By combining state intervention with openness to global capital and entrepreneurship, the UAE has shown how industrial policy can support long-term growth in a resource-rich yet forward-looking context.

Final Characteristics of Non-Socialist Planned Economies

A non-socialist planned economy is distinct in that it seeks to guide development through state direction while still preserving private ownership and market exchange. Its hallmark is the attempt to combine long-term national strategies with the innovative capacity of private enterprise.

Unlike socialist command systems, where markets are replaced, or liberal models, where the state retreats, this approach relies on a structured partnership: governments define priorities, create incentives, and establish regulatory frameworks, while private firms remain central actors in production and trade.

The challenges are significant. If state planning becomes too rigid, policy may favor politically chosen sectors over competitive ones, weakening efficiency. If intervention is too weak, coordination collapses and the model loses coherence. Success therefore depends not only on striking a balance but also on the quality of governance—professional administration, effective institutions, and credible oversight.

Main Causes of the Crisis and Decline of Planned Economies in the 20th Century

In the second half of the twentieth century, many states that relied on centralized planning—both socialist and non-socialist—encountered deep structural problems. Systems that had once delivered rapid industrialization, postwar recovery, and large-scale mobilization of resources began to reveal fundamental flaws that led to stagnation, crisis, and eventual retreat from rigid planning.

1. Weak Market Incentives and Limited Competition

Centralized planning undermined the role of markets. In socialist systems, this meant the elimination of free pricing and competitive pressure; in dirigiste or corporatist economies, it often meant heavy regulation and protection of large enterprises.

Consequences:

- Declining productivity and systemic inefficiency.
- Persistent technological lag compared with market economies.
- Loss of competitiveness in global trade.

Examples: By the 1980s, industries in the USSR and Eastern Europe had clearly fallen behind technologically. Even in France, highly regulated state industries struggled to compete internationally.

2. Rigidity and Low Adaptability

Long-term plans, often fixed for years, proved incapable of responding to new technologies, shifting consumer demand, or changing world markets. Whether guided by ideology or corporatist planning boards, such systems locked resources into outdated priorities.

Consequences:

- Failure to redirect production toward global demand.
- Structural imbalances and resource misallocation.
- Slower growth compared with flexible market economies.

Examples: Italy under Mussolini's corporatism and socialist states of Eastern Europe in the 1970s–80s both failed to modernize in step with global economic change.

3. Neglect of Consumer Needs

Planned economies prioritized defense, heavy industry, or large national projects at the expense of household consumption. Everyday goods were scarce, often of low quality, and distributed through rationing or queues.

Consequences:

- Declining living standards and growing public dissatisfaction.
- Expansion of black markets and informal economies.
- Erosion of trust in state institutions.

Examples: In Nazi Germany and wartime Japan, resources were concentrated on military production, leaving civilians with severe shortages. In the USSR and Eastern Europe, long queues for basic products became a defining feature of daily life.

4. Bureaucratization, Inefficiency, and Corruption

The machinery of central planning demanded vast administrative structures. Decision-making was slow, rigid, and often detached from economic reality. Close ties between political authorities and corporate elites encouraged favoritism and corruption.

Consequences:

- Rising administrative costs.
- Waste and mismanagement of resources.
- Entrenched corruption that undermined fairness and efficiency.

Examples: In Spain under Franco and Portugal under Salazar, corporatist planning was weighed down by bureaucracy and clientelism, preventing sustained modernization.

5. Strategic Misjudgments and Planning Failures

Planners often overestimated their capacity to foresee future needs. Large investments were directed toward sectors later shown to be uncompetitive or technologically obsolete. When global trends shifted, economies found themselves locked into costly mistakes.

Consequences:

- Loss of credibility of planning institutions.
- Misallocation of public investment.
- Long-term stagnation and erosion of economic legitimacy.

Examples: In the late stages of French dirigisme (1970s–80s), state-directed industrial projects frequently missed global shifts, forcing painful reforms.

Overall Assessment

Despite their different ideological foundations, both socialist and non-socialist planning models revealed similar weaknesses: lack of competitive incentives, rigidity, inefficiency, neglect of consumer needs, bureaucratic overload, and flawed long-term strategies. By the end of the twentieth century, most countries had abandoned rigid planning in favor of more flexible mixed systems, combining state guidance with the dynamism of market economies.

Comparative Analysis of
Socialist and Non-Socialist Planned Economies:
Differences in Goals and Methods of Implementation

Planned economies in the twentieth century developed in two broad forms: socialist planned economies, based on the principle of collective ownership and central command, and non-socialist planned economies, which combined state planning with the preservation of private property and limited market mechanisms. Although both models relied on centralized state intervention, they diverged significantly in their ideological foundations, institutional frameworks, and social outcomes.

1. Forms of Ownership and Control

- **Socialist Planned Economy:**

  Ownership of the means of production, natural resources, and infrastructure is vested almost exclusively in the state. Private property is either eliminated or confined to marginal areas (small-scale farming, handicrafts, or household goods). State-owned enterprises (SOEs) form the backbone of the economy, and their activity is strictly subordinated to centralized plans. This approach was designed to abolish class distinctions and create an egalitarian structure of production and distribution.

- **Non-Socialist Planned Economy:**

  Private property remains legally protected, but its use is aligned with state-defined strategic priorities. Large corporations, financial institutions, and industrial groups operate under significant state guidance. While they retain formal autonomy, their investment decisions, production targets, and pricing strategies are often influenced or dictated by state plans. This balance preserves entrepreneurial initiative while subjecting it to national objectives.

2. Ideological Foundations and Objectives

- **Socialist Planned Economy:**

  Grounded in Marxist–Leninist ideology, the system sought to abolish capitalist relations of production and replace them with collective ownership and centrally determined economic goals. The emphasis was placed on achieving social equality, eliminating exploitation, and ensuring universal access to essential goods and services. Long-term objectives included industrialization, rapid modernization, and the creation of a classless society.

- **Non-Socialist Planned Economy:**

  Lacking an explicit socialist ideology, this model was pragmatic and often arose in response to crises, postwar reconstruction, or the need for rapid modernization. The objective was not to transform social relations but to strengthen national competitiveness, achieve industrial self-sufficiency, and coordinate private enterprise with state-defined national priorities. Planning was thus viewed as a tool of development rather than as an ideological imperative.

3. Role of Market Mechanisms and Competition

- **Socialist Planned Economy:**

  Markets and competition were marginalized or abolished. Prices were set administratively, not through supply and demand. Enterprises operated according to production quotas rather than profit incentives. The absence of competition limited innovation and responsiveness to consumer needs, though it allowed for stability in employment and the elimination of price fluctuations.

- **Non-Socialist Planned Economy:**

  Markets retained a supporting role. Competition continued to exist, though constrained by state regulation and industrial policy. Strategic sectors—such as energy, transport, or defense—were often subject to heavy state oversight, while other sectors operated under relatively freer market conditions. This hybrid arrangement preserved at least some of the dynamism of market economies while ensuring state control over critical resources.

4. Mechanisms of Distribution and Resource Allocation

- **Socialist Planned Economy:**

  Distribution was organized through administrative mechanisms such as rationing, state quotas, and fixed pricing. Consumer choice was restricted, and shortages were common. The guiding principle was equality of access rather than efficiency or consumer preference. Although basic needs such as food staples, housing, education, and healthcare were usually met, the range and quality of consumer goods lagged behind that of market economies.

- **Non-Socialist Planned Economy:**

  Distribution combined state regulation of key goods with market-based allocation for consumer products. The state intervened heavily in strategic industries (steel, energy, defense) but allowed consumer markets to function with relative freedom. As a result, shortages were less severe, and consumer choice was generally broader, though still subject to distortions from industrial policy and protectionist measures.

Strengths of Socialist Planned Economies

a) Strong social stability, with relatively low levels of inequality.
b) Universal employment and guaranteed access to housing, education, and healthcare.
c) Ability to concentrate resources rapidly on strategic projects such as industrialization, defense, or space exploration.
d) Protection from extreme market fluctuations and speculative crises.

Weaknesses of Socialist Planned Economies

a) Chronic shortages of consumer goods and services, leading to rationing and long queues.
b) Weak incentives for productivity, innovation, and efficiency due to lack of competition.

c) Bureaucratic inefficiency and excessive administrative control.

d) Rigid structures that could not adapt to technological change or shifting global markets.

Strengths of Non-Socialist Planned Economies

a) High efficiency in mobilizing resources for large-scale industrial and infrastructural projects.

b) Ability to coordinate state goals with private initiative, combining central planning with entrepreneurship.

c) Greater adaptability to technological change compared to socialist systems.

d) Potential for higher productivity and global competitiveness in export-oriented sectors.

Weaknesses of Non-Socialist Planned Economies

a) Risk of monopolization, with large corporations benefiting disproportionately from state support.

b) Persistent problems of bureaucracy, corruption, and corporate lobbying.

c) Vulnerability to state policy failures—misallocation of resources, industrial overcapacity, or unsustainable investment strategies.

d) Social inequality remained high, since redistribution was not the primary objective of non-socialist planning.

Long-Term Consequences and Historical Outcomes

Both socialist and non-socialist planned economies achieved early successes—socialist systems in rapid industrialization (USSR, China) and non-socialist systems in postwar reconstruction and modernization (France, Japan, South Korea). However, over time, structural weaknesses became increasingly visible. Socialist economies struggled with stagnation, inefficiency, and consumer dissatisfaction, ultimately contributing to the collapse of the Soviet bloc in the late 20th century. Non-socialist planned economies, though more flexible, often required liberalization and deregulation to remain competitive in the global economy, as seen in France's turn away from dirigisme in the 1980s or South Korea's gradual liberalization from the 1990s.

"The important thing for Government is not to do things which individuals are doing already, and to do them a little better or a little worse; but to do those things which at present are not done at all."

— John Maynard Keynes, *The End of Laissez-Faire*

SECTION 3. MIXED ECONOMY — COMBINING MARKET AND STATE MECHANISMS

> **A mixed economy** is an economic system that combines elements of both market freedom and government regulation.

The mixed economy rests on the integration of market mechanisms—entrepreneurial initiative, private property, and competition—with state intervention aimed at correcting imbalances and pursuing socially important goals.

The idea gained wide recognition in the twentieth century as a response to the shortcomings of two opposing models:

- **The pure market model**, where economic life was left entirely to free competition. While dynamic, it produced deep social inequality, recurring crises, and the rise of monopolies that undermined fair competition.

- **The centrally planned model**, where the state directed all aspects of economic activity. This system lacked flexibility, discouraged innovation, and generated inefficiencies, resulting in persistent shortages and weak incentives for productivity.

The mixed economy emerged as an alternative, based on the search for equilibrium. Market forces drive efficiency, adaptability, and innovation, while state mechanisms secure stability, fairness, and long-term development. By combining these elements, the mixed economy seeks to preserve the dynamism of private enterprise while limiting its social costs, and to employ state coordination without the rigidity of full central planning.

Chapter 1

Nature and Principles of a Mixed Economy: Balancing Public and Private Sectors

Core Characteristics of a Mixed Economy

1. **Pluralism of Property Forms**

A central feature of the mixed economy is the coexistence of different types of ownership.

- Private property dominates in most sectors, sustaining entrepreneurial initiative, competition, and innovation.

- Public ownership is preserved mainly in strategic areas—defense, infrastructure, healthcare, education, and basic research—where private capital is less effective. In these fields, state control ensures reliability and broad access.

2. Combination of Market and State Regulation

In a mixed economy, the state complements rather than replaces the market. Prices, production, and resource allocation are primarily shaped by market forces, while government intervention corrects failures, curbs monopolization, and addresses inequality or environmental challenges. State influence usually operates through taxation, subsidies, preferential credit, and regulation rather than direct management of enterprises.

3. Flexibility and Adaptability

Markets provide dynamism and rapid adjustment to shifts in consumer demand, technological change, and global trends. At the same time, public policy cushions cyclical downturns, mitigates crises, and upholds macroeconomic stability. This dual structure combines responsiveness with resilience.

4. Balance Between Freedom and Social Responsibility

Individual initiative and private enterprise remain central, but they are paired with collective responsibility for social well-being. The state secures universal education, healthcare, social insurance, and public safety, ensuring that economic freedom is compatible with fairness and inclusion.

5. Institutional Diversity and Cross-Sector Cooperation

Mixed economies rely on interaction among private firms, public enterprises, and non-profit institutions. Cooperation across these sectors aligns market efficiency with public objectives, supporting innovation while maintaining social stability.

Reasons for the Global Spread of Mixed Economies

The spread of mixed economies in the twentieth century reflects their ability to combine the dynamism of markets with the coordinating role of the state. This synthesis helped overcome the weaknesses of pure laissez-faire capitalism and rigid central planning, making the mixed model the dominant form of economic organization worldwide.

1. Addressing Market Failures

Unregulated markets often generate monopolies, financial instability, unemployment, and social unrest. Mixed economies enable governments to act through antitrust policy, financial regulation, and labor protections, ensuring that competition remains open and that markets function in the interests of society as a whole.

2. Correcting the Shortcomings of Centralized Planning

Command economies proved vulnerable to inefficiency, shortages, and technological stagnation. Mixed systems preserve the flexibility of markets while allowing governments to coordinate investment and long-term development in areas where private initiative is insufficient.

3. Providing Social Protection

Mixed economies reduce poverty and inequality by combining private initiative with public welfare systems. Universal healthcare, pensions, unemployment insurance, and subsidized education create a safety net that shields citizens from market volatility without undermining economic freedom.

4. Ensuring Long-Term Sustainability

Beyond immediate growth, mixed economies integrate environmental standards, renewable energy programs, and regulations on resource use into national policy. Governments guide technological development in directions that protect future generations, distinguishing this model from both laissez-faire and centralized planning.

5. Balancing Freedom and Responsibility

Private enterprise drives innovation and productivity, but governments ensure that gains are more evenly shared. By preventing extreme inequality, mixed economies help sustain political legitimacy and strengthen social stability.

6. Adaptability in a Globalized World

Global integration demands resilience as well as flexibility. Mixed economies are well suited to these conditions: they harness private initiative while deploying state resources strategically, allowing them to manage competition, absorb external shocks, and adjust to rapid technological change.

Contemporary Approaches to the Concept of a Mixed Economy

In contemporary economic thought, the concept of the mixed economy is interpreted broadly. Most scholars agree that every real economy is mixed to some degree. Pure free-market systems and fully planned economies remain theoretical constructs; in practice, all nations combine elements of both.

What varies are the proportions. In some countries, markets are the primary force, with government intervention limited to maintaining competition and providing basic social protection. In others, the state takes a more active role—shaping industrial policy, investing in strategic sectors, or redistributing income to reduce inequality. These differences reflect not only stages of development but also cultural traditions, historical experience, and national policy choices.

The mixed economy should be understood not as a halfway point between two extremes, but as an evolving synthesis. It integrates the capacity of markets to allocate resources efficiently and adapt quickly with the ability of governments to pursue stability, equity, and long-term priorities. This interplay enables societies to grow, preserve cohesion, and adjust flexibly to both domestic and global challenges.

Core Principles of a Mixed Economy

The mixed economy is built on principles that reconcile market efficiency with state responsibility. Together they define a system that is both dynamic and socially sustainable.

1. Pluralism of Property Forms

A defining trait of the mixed economy is the coexistence of multiple ownership structures, each with its own role:

- Private property sustains entrepreneurship and innovation by linking initiative to profit and growth.

- State property is concentrated in sectors requiring large-scale capital and long-term strategy—energy, defense, major infrastructure—where public control secures continuity.

- Municipal and cooperative property addresses local needs, from public transport to housing, while cooperatives enable citizens to manage shared assets collectively.

This pluralism combines efficiency with collective responsibility.

2. Freedom of Enterprise and Protection of Competition

Private initiative flourishes only when competition is safeguarded by law:

- Secure property rights, contract enforcement, and intellectual property protection uphold entrepreneurship.

- Antitrust regulation curbs monopolies and cartels, protecting consumers.

- Equal access to markets ensures that small and medium firms can compete alongside large corporations, preserving diversity and innovation.

3. Targeted and Selective State Regulation

Unlike centrally planned systems, regulation in a mixed economy is selective and corrective:

- Indirect tools—taxation, subsidies, credit incentives—shape behavior without direct control.

- Targeted programs support start-ups, vocational training, or regional development.

- Limited direct intervention preserves the role of supply and demand as the main driver of economic life.

This approach avoids excessive bureaucracy while guiding development.

4. Social Orientation and Redistribution

Markets generate unequal outcomes, and the mixed economy corrects them through social policy:

- Progressive taxation and transfers reduce poverty and inequality.

- Safety nets—pensions, healthcare, education, unemployment benefits—ensure basic standards for all.

- Public investment in human capital strengthens mobility and opportunity.

Here, efficiency is paired with fairness to sustain social stability.

5. Sustainability and Long-Term Balance

Mixed economies emphasize resilience and forward-looking investment:

- Countercyclical fiscal and monetary policies moderate recessions and booms.

- Public funding for science, technology, and infrastructure maintains competitiveness where private capital is insufficient.

- Environmental standards, renewable energy, and green technologies anchor ecological responsibility.
- Investment in education, research, and healthcare provides continuity across generations.

By aligning short-term responsiveness with long-term priorities, the mixed economy avoids the extremes of laissez-faire instability and rigid central planning.

Core Functions of the State in a Mixed Economy

In a mixed economy, the state is neither absent, as in pure laissez-faire systems, nor dominant, as in fully planned economies. Instead, it operates in partnership with markets—correcting failures, setting long-term priorities, and ensuring that growth is compatible with equity and sustainability. Its functions are interdependent and reinforce one another.

1. **The Regulatory Function**

The state provides the legal and institutional framework within which markets operate:

- **Safeguarding competition** through antitrust laws that prevent monopolies, cartels, and price fixing. U.S. legislation such as the Sherman and Clayton Acts illustrates this role.
- **Protecting property rights** by ensuring secure ownership, transparent courts, and predictable rules, which encourage investment and innovation.
- **Setting standards** for labor conditions, product safety, and the environment, aligning economic activity with broader social and ecological priorities.

2. **The Stimulating Function**

Beyond regulation, the state actively promotes economic development and innovation:

- **Strategic public investment** in infrastructure, research, and education—areas often neglected by private capital due to long payback periods. Examples include Japan's MITI policies after World War II and U.S. federal funding of space and defense projects.
- **Targeted incentives** such as subsidies or tax breaks for key sectors (renewables, biotechnology, digital technologies) that accelerate modernization.
- **Support for SMEs** through soft loans, credit guarantees, and incubators, ensuring that entrepreneurship is not limited to large corporations.

3. **The Social Function**

Mixed economies commit to social inclusion and redistribution:

- **Income redistribution** through progressive taxation and transfers (welfare benefits, child allowances, unemployment insurance).
- **Universal access** to healthcare, education, and housing, securing minimum living standards.
- **Insurance schemes**—pensions, disability coverage, health programs—protect citizens from risks that markets alone cannot address.

These mechanisms sustain political stability and social trust by moderating the inequalities of unregulated capitalism.

4. The Stabilization Function

Economic cycles require active management to preserve stability:

- **Fiscal policy**: deficit spending in recessions to stimulate demand, and restraint during booms to curb inflation.

- **Monetary policy**: central banks adjust interest rates, manage liquidity, and stabilize credit flows.

- **Labor market measures**: employment programs, retraining, and unemployment benefits that cushion shocks and support adaptation.

This function reflects Keynesian insights that markets alone cannot secure full employment or steady growth.

5. The Environmental Function

In the 21st century, sustainability has become a central state responsibility:

- **Environmental regulation** sets binding limits on emissions, waste, and pollution.

- **Green incentives** encourage adoption of renewable energy, circular production, and eco-innovation.

- **Public investment** in clean infrastructure—from transit systems to energy grids—guides the ecological transition.

- **International cooperation** through agreements like the Paris Accord addresses global environmental challenges.

The state in a mixed economy acts not as an absolute controller but as a strategic partner to markets. Through regulation, stimulation, social protection, stabilization, and environmental stewardship, it ensures that efficiency is matched by fairness and that short-term growth is reconciled with long-term sustainability.

Advantages of a Mixed Economy

1. Balance Between Efficiency and Equity

The strength of the mixed economy lies in its capacity to combine market incentives with social policy.

- **Efficiency** is promoted by private property, competition, and entrepreneurship, which encourage rational resource use, technological progress, and productivity growth.

- **Equity** is advanced through progressive taxation, social programs, and transfers that reduce poverty and inequality. The Nordic states illustrate this balance, pairing competitive markets with strong redistribution to maintain both high productivity and relatively low inequality.

2. Adaptability to External Change

Mixed economies adjust more effectively to global and domestic shocks.

- Market pricing and competition allow resources to shift rapidly toward sectors with high demand.
- State tools—fiscal stimulus, subsidies, emergency programs—stabilize the economy in crises. During the 2008 financial downturn, governments in the United States and Europe injected liquidity and expanded fiscal spending to prevent collapse.
- The coexistence of private, public, and cooperative ownership ensures continuity while accommodating change.

3. **Innovation and Entrepreneurship**

The mixed model creates conditions where innovation thrives under both market pressure and public support.

- Competition pushes firms to improve products and adopt new technologies.
- Public policies—research grants, tax credits, and innovation clusters—reinforce the innovative ecosystem. Silicon Valley in the United States demonstrates this synergy, where private entrepreneurship has been supported by sustained federal research funding.
- State investment in education, training, and infrastructure enhances the quality of labor and the capacity for technological breakthroughs.

4. **Economic and Social Stability**

Unlike pure market economies, which experience sharp cycles, or planned economies, which risk stagnation, mixed systems integrate stabilizing mechanisms.

- Countercyclical fiscal and monetary policy smooths fluctuations and reduces the risk of deep recessions.
- Safety nets—pensions, health care, unemployment benefits—limit social conflict and support political stability.
- Long-term public investment in infrastructure, science, and education reinforces growth and secures improvements in living standards.

5. **Efficient and Sustainable Resource Use**

Regulation in mixed economies helps allocate resources more effectively.

- Antitrust policies prevent monopolization and safeguard competition.
- Environmental measures—carbon pricing, emission limits, and subsidies for clean energy—encourage energy efficiency and renewable technologies.
- Public investment in energy, transport, and digital infrastructure ensures that resources flow into sectors critical for long-term development.

Limitations of a Mixed Economy

1. Excessive Intervention and Bureaucratization

One central risk is that the state may extend its role too far, undermining market efficiency.

- **Reduced efficiency**: Heavy regulation can weaken competition, discourage entrepreneurship, and lower firms' motivation to improve productivity.

- **Slower innovation**: Excessive controls reduce willingness to take risks and adopt new technologies, entangling innovation in administrative procedures.

- **High administrative costs**: Expanding programs and agencies create bureaucratic overhead, slowing decisions and lowering efficiency.

2. Corruption and Corporate Lobbying

The state's role as regulator and allocator of resources makes it vulnerable to capture by vested interests.

- **Corruption**: Agencies distributing subsidies, licenses, or contracts may face bribery and abuse of power.

- **Distorted competition**: Large firms can lobby for privileges, subsidies, or exemptions, disadvantaging smaller businesses.

- **Erosion of trust**: Persistent corruption undermines public confidence in government and weakens investor confidence.

3. The Challenge of Optimal Regulation

Finding the right balance between markets and the state is complex and context-dependent.

- **Over-regulation**: Excessive intervention restricts entrepreneurship, reduces innovation, and discourages investment.

- **Under-regulation**: Insufficient oversight permits monopolies, rising inequality, and environmental harm.

- **Contextual variation**: Because no universal formula exists, governments must continually adjust policies to domestic and global conditions, creating the risk of inconsistency or short-termism.

4. Policy Inconsistencies

Because mixed economies pursue multiple objectives—growth, stability, equity, and innovation—policy conflicts often emerge.

- **Fragmentation**: Ministries and agencies may adopt measures that contradict one another.

- **Competing demands**: Governments must reconcile the interests of business, labor, and society, often through compromises that satisfy none fully.

- **Short-term bias**: Electoral pressures may lead to strategies that prioritize immediate gains over long-term stability.

5. High Fiscal Costs

The extensive functions of the state require significant public spending.

- **Tax burden**: Funding welfare programs and regulation often requires high taxation, which can discourage enterprise and reduce investment.

- **Deficits and debt**: Sustained expenditure on welfare, infrastructure, and subsidies risks chronic deficits and rising public debt.
- **Political constraints**: Attempts to reduce spending—such as cutting welfare—can provoke unrest, limiting fiscal flexibility.

Historical Examples of a Mixed Economy

The mixed economy has repeatedly proven its effectiveness and resilience across different regions of the world.

The Nordic Countries (Sweden, Denmark, Norway, Finland)

Northern Europe is often cited as the most consistent example of a mixed economy with a strong social orientation, commonly referred to as the Nordic Model.

- **Efficient Market Foundation.** The Nordic economies remain strongly market-based, characterized by open competition, transparency, and support for entrepreneurship. Innovation and private enterprise play a central role, and international rankings such as the World Bank's *Doing Business Index* regularly place these countries among the global leaders in business climate.

- **Comprehensive Social Protection and Redistribution.** A robust welfare state guarantees universal access to healthcare, education, housing assistance, and social security. Progressive taxation and redistributive policies reduce inequality and keep poverty levels low. On the United Nations *Human Development Index (HDI)*, the Nordic countries consistently occupy top positions in health, education, and overall quality of life.

- **Active State Involvement in Key Sectors.** Governments invest heavily in infrastructure, renewable energy, education, and research. Public support for innovation—from green technologies to digital transformation—has sustained competitiveness and fostered long-term growth.

- **High Levels of Trust and Social Cohesion.** The Nordic Model rests on a strong social contract. Citizens display high trust in institutions and in one another, which reinforces political stability, effective governance, and cooperative labor relations.

The distinctive strength of the Nordic Model lies in its balance: open and competitive markets ensure efficiency and innovation, while comprehensive welfare policies promote equity and cohesion. This equilibrium has enabled the Nordic countries to achieve both high living standards and enduring social stability.

Germany: The Social Market Economy

The model of the *Soziale Marktwirtschaft*—the social market economy—was introduced in West Germany after World War II under the leadership of Ludwig Erhard, often described as the architect of this system. It combined market competition with a strong social framework and continues to shape Germany's economic policy today.

- **Rapid Recovery and Growth.** By embracing market principles, Germany achieved the *Wirtschaftswunder* ("economic miracle"). Industrial output expanded quickly in the 1950s and 1960s, exports grew, and the country became a leading economy, particularly in manufacturing, engineering, and advanced technologies.

- **Active State Role in Regulation and Redistribution**. While markets functioned freely, the state guaranteed fair competition through antitrust legislation, limited monopolistic practices, and developed an extensive welfare system. Investment in education, healthcare, pensions, and infrastructure created a durable social safety net that complemented the market.

- **Tripartite Cooperation**. A distinctive element of the German model is the institutionalized partnership among the state, employers, and trade unions. This system of social dialogue fostered consensus, reduced labor conflicts, and promoted stability in economic and social policy.

- **Balance of Freedom and Solidarity**. The guiding principle was that economic liberty had to be matched by social responsibility. Profits and productivity gains were balanced by redistribution, ensuring broad access to social goods and limiting inequality.

The *Soziale Marktwirtschaft* enabled West Germany to rebuild after the war, sustain prosperity, and maintain high living standards while avoiding sharp social divisions. It remains a cornerstone of the German economic model and a prominent example of a mixed system aligning market efficiency with social welfare.

France: The Dirigiste Model of a Mixed Economy

The French variant of the mixed economy—*dirigisme*—emerged after World War II, when the state assumed an active role in reconstruction and modernization. Unlike a fully planned economy, it preserved private ownership and entrepreneurship but combined them with strong state intervention and centralized coordination.

- **Industrial Policy and State Planning**. From the late 1940s to the 1970s, France pursued ambitious strategies, nationalized strategic sectors, and launched major infrastructure programs. Energy, transportation, aviation, and defense became priorities of national planning, supported through public investment and long-term programs.

- **Public Enterprises**. State-owned companies such as Électricité de France (EDF), Société Nationale des Chemins de fer Français (SNCF), and later Airbus symbolized the dirigiste approach. They secured continuity in essential services and enhanced France's competitiveness in global markets.

- **Modernization Through State Leadership**. Institutions like the *Commissariat général du Plan* coordinated economic policy by setting targets and guiding private firms toward national priorities. This framework fostered modernization, technological progress, and the re-emergence of France as an industrial power.

- **Social Protection and Redistribution**. Dirigisme also integrated a strong social dimension. Public healthcare, pensions, and unemployment insurance were expanded, while progressive taxation and redistribution contributed to reducing inequality and improving living standards.

- **Balance of State and Market**. Government guidance coexisted with private initiative. The combination of state leadership and a dynamic private sector produced a distinctive hybrid model.

This system enabled France to rebuild after the war, modernize rapidly, and consolidate its position among Europe's leading economies. Although subsequent decades brought liberalization and a reduction of state control, the legacy of dirigisme remains visible in France's enduring tradition of close interaction between public authority and private enterprise.

Japan and South Korea: Active Industrial Policy and State-Led Development

The postwar experiences of Japan (1950s–1990s) and South Korea (1960s–1990s) illustrate how mixed economies with strong state direction can achieve rapid industrialization and sustained growth. Both countries relied on strategic planning, targeted support for selected industries, and close cooperation between government and business.

- **Support for Priority Sectors and Corporate Groups**. In Japan, the *keiretsu*—networks of interlinked firms supported by state policy—were central to industrial modernization. In South Korea, large family-owned conglomerates (*chaebols* such as Hyundai, Samsung, and LG) grew into pillars of national development under state guidance and incentives.

- **Targeted Financial Policies**. Preferential credit, tax incentives, and government programs attracted investment and promoted export-oriented industries. Sectors such as electronics, automobiles, shipbuilding, and heavy machinery expanded rapidly, securing leading positions in world trade.

- **Investment in Human Capital and Infrastructure**. Both governments prioritized education, research, and modern infrastructure. This not only enhanced industrial capacity but also facilitated the diffusion of new technologies across the economy.

- **Export-Led Growth**. By combining domestic industrial policy with integration into global markets, Japan and South Korea established themselves as highly competitive manufacturing economies. Advanced technologies and strong export performance underpinned long-term growth and rising living standards.

Through these strategies, Japan and South Korea moved in a relatively short time from largely agrarian or semi-agrarian economies to major industrial nations.

The Contemporary Significance of the Mixed Economy

The historical cases discussed above illustrate the diverse forms a mixed economy can take. Despite institutional differences, successful versions share a defining characteristic: they reconcile market initiative with effective state policy. This interplay has allowed them to maintain prosperity, stability, and broadly shared living standards over time.

In today's world, the mixed economy has become the prevailing model of economic organization. Its strength lies not in simple compromise but in integration—bringing together the adaptability of markets with the capacity of governments to provide direction, correct imbalances, and pursue long-term objectives. As a result, the mixed economy remains uniquely suited to address the challenges of globalization, technological change, and social inequality.

Key Conditions for the Success of a Mixed Economy

1. Balance Between Markets and the State

The success of a mixed economy depends on the government's ability to align market incentives with effective public policy. Excessive state control reduces initiative and innovation, while weak regulation allows inequality, instability, and market distortions to spread.

2. Flexibility and Adaptability of Policy

Public intervention must be precise and responsive to both domestic needs and global changes. This requires institutions with expertise, accountability, and transparency. Ongoing evaluation of programs ensures that state action reinforces rather than undermines market efficiency.

3. Social Orientation and Equity

A defining condition of the mixed model is its commitment to fairness. Redistribution mechanisms, comprehensive welfare systems, and universal access to healthcare and education strengthen social cohesion. By reducing poverty and inequality, the state builds public trust and consolidates the legitimacy of the system.

4. Sustainability and Long-Term Planning

The mixed economy integrates short-term efficiency with strategic objectives. Investment in education, research, infrastructure, and environmental protection supports balanced development and prepares societies for future challenges.

5. Checks on State Power and Anti-Corruption Safeguards

Because active government involvement can foster bureaucratization or corruption, safeguards are essential. Equal access to markets, independent oversight of public programs, and strict enforcement of anti-corruption rules help maintain efficiency and preserve confidence in state institutions.

6. Institutional Strength and Rule of Law

A durable mixed economy requires strong institutions. Independent courts, protection of property rights, and predictable legal frameworks ensure stability for both citizens and investors, reducing uncertainty and encouraging long-term commitment.

7. Citizen Participation and Social Dialogue

Effective systems include mechanisms for negotiation and cooperation among government, employers, and labor organizations. Such dialogue fosters compromise, prevents social conflict, and helps align economic strategies with the needs of society.

8. Fiscal Responsibility and Efficiency of Public Spending

Social programs and state investments are sustainable only when supported by sound public finances. Avoiding excessive debt and ensuring efficient use of tax revenues are critical to long-term stability and credibility.

Chapter 2

State Regulation in a Mixed Economy: Government's Role in Stabilizing and Guiding the Economy

Goals and Objectives of Government Regulation in a Mixed Economy

In a mixed economy, government regulation plays a vital role in ensuring the effective and stable functioning of the national economy. Its primary purpose is to address the shortcomings of market mechanisms—often described as market failures—and to achieve broader economic and social goals that markets alone cannot secure.

Government intervention in a mixed economy pursues several interrelated objectives:

1. Ensuring Macroeconomic Stability

Macroeconomic stability is a core responsibility of the state, since markets cannot always contain inflation, unemployment, or recurring crises on their own.

- **Inflation control** is carried out through monetary policy, including interest rate adjustments, money supply regulation, and fiscal measures.

- **Reducing unemployment** relies on public employment programs, retraining and upskilling initiatives, and targeted support for small and medium-sized enterprises that create jobs.

- **Managing business cycles** is achieved through counter-cyclical fiscal and monetary policies designed to mitigate recessions and prevent overheating.

2. Supporting Competition and Preventing Monopolization

Markets often tend toward concentration, which undermines efficiency and raises prices. Safeguarding open and fair competition is therefore a central regulatory task.

- **Antitrust enforcement** prevents abuse of dominance, monitors mergers and acquisitions, and combats collusion.
- **Support for small and medium enterprises** ensures equal entry conditions, access to resources, and financing opportunities.
- **Regulation of natural monopolies** (e.g., electricity, railways, utilities) establishes transparent pricing rules and service standards where competition is structurally limited.

By preserving competition, the state promotes efficiency, innovation, and consumer welfare.

3. Addressing Social Needs and Ensuring Equity

Left unregulated, markets tend to widen inequality and leave vulnerable groups unprotected. State intervention mitigates these effects by:

- **Redistributing income** through progressive taxation, social transfers, pensions, and welfare programs.
- **Expanding access** to healthcare, education, and housing, thereby improving equality of opportunity and social mobility.
- **Reducing social risks** by protecting disadvantaged groups and maintaining social stability.

4. Promoting Sustainable Growth and Innovation

Long-term economic development requires state involvement in areas where private incentives are insufficient.

- **Financing education and basic research** establishes the foundation for innovation and competitiveness.
- **Supporting technological development** through subsidies, grants, and tax incentives fosters emerging industries, innovation hubs, and research clusters.
- **Investing in infrastructure**—roads, ports, energy systems, and telecommunications—creates the framework for productivity gains and economic expansion.

5. Ensuring Environmental Protection and Sustainable Development

In the 21st century, environmental responsibility has become a key function of the state in mixed economies.

- **Environmental regulation** sets binding standards for emissions and industrial practices.
- **Green incentives and penalties**—pollution taxes, fines for violations, and subsidies for clean technologies—encourage environmentally responsible behavior.
- **Public investment in sustainability** supports renewable energy, sustainable agriculture, waste recycling, and other eco-friendly sectors.

By integrating environmental goals into economic regulation, governments safeguard public health and preserve resources for future generations.

Government regulation in a mixed economy does not replace market mechanisms but complements them. The state assumes responsibility for areas where markets are ineffective—macroeconomic stability, fair competition, social equity, innovation, and environmental sustainability—while avoiding excessive administrative control.

Methods of Government Regulation in a Mixed Economy

In a mixed economy, government regulation is carried out primarily through indirect methods, which influence economic processes without replacing or suppressing market mechanisms. These methods are designed to form an institutional environment that directs private actors' decisions toward alignment with the state's strategic priorities. By relying on financial instruments, social policies, competition law, and environmental standards, governments balance efficiency with equity and long-term sustainability.

a) Financial and Credit Regulation

Financial and credit policies are among the most important tools for stabilizing the economy and guiding its development. They affect inflation, employment, investment, and overall demand.

- ❖ **Monetary policy:**
  - Central banks regulate the money supply, interest rates, and access to credit, directly influencing inflation, consumer demand, and investment activity.

- Key instruments include open market operations (buying and selling government securities), adjustments to reserve requirements for banks, and the setting of discount rates.

❖ **Fiscal policy**:

- Through taxation, public spending, and budgetary investment, governments influence aggregate demand and correct economic imbalances.
- Tax incentives, subsidies, and preferential credit schemes encourage investment in strategic industries such as renewable energy, infrastructure, and technology.
- Management of public debt and budget deficits ensures financial stability and reduces the economy's vulnerability to systemic risks.

b) Regulation of Foreign Economic Activity

In a globalized economy, trade and investment policies are central to protecting national interests and enhancing competitiveness.

❖ **Tariff and non-tariff measures**:

- Customs duties, import and export tariffs, and quotas are used to protect sensitive domestic industries and regulate trade balances.
- Licensing systems and trade restrictions help manage the flow of strategic goods.

❖ **Support for exports and domestic producers**:

- Governments provide export guarantees, preferential export credits, and insurance against trade risks.
- Subsidies, tax benefits, and technical assistance help firms expand into foreign markets.

c) Social Regulation

Social regulation ensures stability by addressing inequality, protecting vulnerable groups, and maintaining trust in government institutions.

❖ **Social transfers and welfare programs**:

- Public pensions, disability benefits, unemployment assistance, and targeted support for low-income households reduce poverty and inequality.
- Special programs provide additional aid for children, the elderly, and disabled citizens.

❖ **Labor market regulation**:

- Employment promotion programs, vocational training, and retraining initiatives improve workforce adaptability.
- Unemployment benefits, temporary public works, and direct job-creation measures reduce social tensions during downturns.

d) Price Regulation and Antitrust Policy

Maintaining a competitive environment and preventing excessive market concentration are essential tasks of the state in a mixed economy.

❖ **Antitrust policy:**

- Oversight of mergers and acquisitions prevents monopolization and cartel behavior.
- Investigations and penalties target abuses of dominant market positions.

❖ **Price regulation for essential goods and services:**

- Governments may set price caps or regulate tariffs in critical sectors such as utilities, energy, public transport, and pharmaceuticals.
- Subsidies to producers help stabilize prices and prevent inflationary shocks in socially sensitive markets.

e) Environmental Regulation

Sustainable development requires governments to ensure that economic growth does not come at the expense of ecological well-being.

❖ **Standards and compliance mechanisms:**

- Binding environmental norms govern emissions, waste management, and resource use.
- Licensing and certification systems promote the adoption of safe production methods.

❖ **Economic incentives and sanctions:**

- Green taxes, fees, and penalties discourage polluting activities and encourage conservation.
- Subsidies, tax exemptions, and grants support companies investing in eco-friendly technologies and renewable energy.

Government regulation in a mixed economy relies less on direct administrative control and more on indirect, market-compatible methods. The goal is not to suppress entrepreneurial initiative but to guide market mechanisms toward national priorities such as macroeconomic stability, social equity, and ecological sustainability.

By combining financial instruments, trade policies, social protection measures, antitrust laws, and environmental standards, governments create a balanced framework that corrects market failures while preserving innovation and competition. This balance has turned the mixed economy into one of the most resilient and adaptable models in the modern world.

Policy Instruments of Government Regulation in a Mixed Economy

In a mixed economy, regulation is implemented through a variety of policy instruments that influence the economic environment, support strategic sectors, and maintain social and economic stability. These tools combine market-compatible incentives with targeted intervention, enabling governments to guide development while preserving the efficiency of private enterprise.

1. Tax Incentives and Preferences

Tax instruments are among the most widely applied tools of state regulation, used to stimulate investment, innovation, and socially significant activity:

- **Tax credits** lower taxable income for businesses and individuals investing in areas such as research and development, environmental protection, education, and social programs.
- **Reduced tax rates** encourage the growth of strategically important industries, innovative start-ups, and small and medium-sized enterprises.
- **Tax holidays and exemptions** provide temporary relief to investors in underdeveloped regions or high-risk industries, supporting regional development.

Through these measures, governments channel resources into priority sectors, enhance competitiveness, and encourage technological advancement.

2. Public Investment Programs

Public investment is a key instrument for implementing long-term development strategies, particularly in areas less attractive to private capital due to high risks or long payback periods:

- **Infrastructure development and modernization**—including roads, railways, telecommunications, and energy systems—strengthens economic capacity and connectivity.
- **Support for priority industries**—direct subsidies and public investment in manufacturing, agriculture, and information technology—accelerates structural transformation.
- **Grants and subsidies for innovation** finance research, development, and high-tech start-ups, ensuring participation in global technological change.

Public investment makes it possible to realize projects that private financing alone would not sustain.

3. Regulatory and Supervisory Agencies

Regulatory bodies are responsible for ensuring that markets function fairly and within established legal and social frameworks:

- **Antitrust authorities** oversee mergers and acquisitions, investigate cartel activity, and prevent abuse of dominant positions.
- **Consumer protection agencies** monitor product quality, defend consumer rights, and address unfair practices.
- **Environmental regulators** enforce compliance with environmental standards, conduct inspections, and impose sanctions for violations.

These institutions maintain the conditions necessary for competition, consumer protection, and environmental responsibility.

4. Targeted Government Programs

Targeted programs focus resources on specific economic or social priorities:

- **Support for SMEs** includes subsidies, preferential credit, and advisory services to strengthen entrepreneurship and employment.
- **Housing programs** address affordability, particularly for young families and low-income households, while improving housing stock.

- **Technology and innovation initiatives** promote the development of biotechnology, information technology, renewable energy, and other advanced sectors.

By concentrating resources on selected areas, targeted programs enhance long-term structural development.

5. Public-Private Partnerships (PPP)

PPP mechanisms combine public authority with private investment to deliver large-scale projects:

- **Joint investment projects** distribute costs and risks between government and private firms, especially in infrastructure and innovation.
- **Concession agreements** grant private companies the right to operate public assets such as highways, ports, or airports, with obligations for maintenance and modernization.
- **Life-cycle contracts** extend responsibility to include long-term operation and upkeep, improving quality and efficiency over time.

These arrangements enable governments to mobilize private capital for essential infrastructure and services while retaining oversight of strategic assets.

Features of Instrument Application in a Mixed Economy

The effectiveness of regulatory instruments depends on their transparent and balanced use. In contemporary mixed economies, governments aim to:

- Ensure openness of information regarding the allocation of public resources and incentives.
- Apply clear and accountable decision-making procedures, supported by independent audits and parliamentary oversight.
- Encourage public participation in the design and monitoring of economic policies, which strengthens legitimacy and limits corruption risks.

The purpose of these instruments is not to replace market dynamics but to channel them toward socially and strategically significant objectives. When applied consistently and transparently, they allow governments to:

- foster technological progress and sustainable growth,
- maintain social cohesion, and
- integrate environmental considerations into economic policy.

A coherent combination of tax incentives, investment programs, regulatory oversight, social initiatives, and public-private partnerships creates a stable framework that supports the long-term development of mixed economies.

The Interaction Between Government and Business in a Mixed Economy

The distinctiveness of a mixed economy lies not only in its combination of market and state mechanisms but also in the special character of the relationship between government and business. Unlike a purely planned economy, where business is fully subordinated to the state, or a laissez-faire market economy, where government intervention is minimal, the mixed model is built upon partnership and shared responsibility. Its foundation is a collaborative effort between the public and private sectors to achieve long-term strategic objectives that serve both economic growth and social stability.

Principles of Government–Business Interaction

The relationship between government and business in a mixed economy rests on several key principles:

- **Partnership and shared responsibility**

  Government and business act as partners rather than adversaries, jointly bearing responsibility for economic development and the pursuit of socially significant goals. Cooperation is based not on coercion, but on alignment of interests and mutual obligations.

- **Stability and transparency of conditions**

  The state commits to ensuring stable and predictable economic conditions—clear legislation, consistent taxation, and reliable regulatory policies—that allow businesses to engage in long-term planning and investment.

- **Openness and public accountability**

  Policy decisions that affect business and the economy are developed through consultation with the private sector and made public through forums such as business associations, advisory councils, and expert panels.

These principles establish the groundwork for constructive dialogue, strengthen trust between the state and entrepreneurs, and ensure that strategic development goals are met collaboratively.

Mutual Interests of Government and Business

The effectiveness of mixed economies stems from the degree to which public and private interests converge:

- **Business priorities**:
  - Stable and predictable conditions for entrepreneurship.
  - Transparent and fair regulation free from corruption or arbitrary state interference.
  - Access to high-quality infrastructure and public services such as transport, communications, education, and healthcare.
  - State support for innovation, protection of intellectual property, and assistance in entering international markets.

- **Government priorities**:
  - Expanding tax revenues through steady business growth.
  - Maintaining high levels of employment and job creation.
  - Enhancing the efficiency and competitiveness of the national economy.

o Ensuring business transparency, reducing the shadow economy, and minimizing corruption risks.

This overlap of interests creates fertile ground for constructive cooperation that benefits both economic actors and society at large.

Forms of Government–Business Cooperation

In practice, collaboration between the state and the private sector in a mixed economy takes multiple forms:

1. **Public–Private Partnerships (PPPs)**
   o Joint investment in large-scale infrastructure projects such as highways, airports, and rail networks.
   o Concession agreements and life-cycle contracts that balance risks and rewards between government and private investors.

2. **Business participation in policymaking**
   o Structured consultations with trade associations and chambers of commerce in drafting key legislation.
   o Advisory and expert councils within ministries and agencies that institutionalize private-sector input into decision-making.

3. **Joint programs for business support**
   o Subsidized credit programs for small and medium-sized enterprises (SMEs).
   o State co-financing of innovative or export-oriented projects run by private firms.
   o Tax incentives and preferential policies designed to stimulate investment in priority sectors.

These mechanisms combine state resources and private expertise, enhancing competitiveness and accelerating national development.

Outcomes of Effective Government–Business Interaction

When managed effectively, the partnership between government and business produces a series of important outcomes:

- **Growth of investment activity**

  Predictable conditions and state-backed incentives build investor confidence and attract both domestic and foreign investment.

- **Strengthening national competitiveness**

  Joint efforts in innovation, technology adoption, and productivity improvements bolster the country's position in global markets.

- **Social stability and sustainable development**

  Job creation and rising incomes, fostered through effective cooperation, contribute to broad-based prosperity and public trust.

- **Reduction of corruption and conflict risks**

  Transparent, structured, and institutionalized forms of cooperation reduce opportunities for favoritism or administrative abuse, promoting greater trust in both economic and political institutions.

Regulation of Innovation and Technological Development in a Mixed Economy

In a mixed economy, the regulation of innovation and technological development takes on special significance. Innovation and technology are not peripheral, but central drivers of long-term economic growth, global competitiveness, and the ability to address pressing social and environmental challenges.

Unlike a purely market-driven economy, where innovation depends almost entirely on private investment and profit incentives, the mixed economy framework assigns government an active and guiding role. The state does not replace market mechanisms, but supplements and strengthens them—helping reduce risks, directing resources into strategic areas, and ensuring that innovation serves the broader public good.

Core Objectives of Innovation Policy

Government regulation of innovation in a mixed economy is directed toward several interconnected goals:

- Stimulating scientific, technological, and innovative development across the national economy.

- Creating favorable conditions for the adoption of advanced technologies in industry, services, and everyday life.

- Enhancing the global competitiveness of domestic firms and integrating them into international production and technology chains.

- Addressing social, environmental, and economic challenges through the application of cutting-edge technologies.

Methods and Instruments of State Support for Innovation

Governments employ a broad set of tools to encourage innovation and technological progress. These include institutional, financial, fiscal, and cooperative measures.

1. **Building Innovation Infrastructure**

- **Innovation clusters and technology parks**: Dedicated spaces where innovative firms gain access to advanced infrastructure, shared services, and collaboration opportunities. These hubs foster knowledge exchange and accelerate commercialization.

- **Business incubators and accelerators**: Programs providing early-stage companies with mentorship, training, networking, and assistance in securing investment.

- **Centers of excellence and technology platforms**: Joint initiatives involving universities, research institutes, and industry to tackle major technological challenges and promote the diffusion of breakthroughs.

2. Direct Financing of Research and Innovation

- **Grants and subsidies for start-ups and research teams**: Direct public funding for high-risk projects that private investors are reluctant to support.

- **National technology programs**: Large-scale initiatives in fields such as digitalization, artificial intelligence, biotechnology, renewable energy, and advanced manufacturing.

- **Public procurement of innovative products**: Using government purchasing power to create demand for novel technologies and support domestic innovators.

3. Tax and Financial Incentives

- **Preferential tax regimes**: Reduced corporate tax rates, tax credits, and exemptions for companies that invest in R&D and innovation.

- **Support for venture capital and high-risk investment**: Tax breaks, guarantees, and co-financing mechanisms that encourage venture funds and private investors to channel resources into innovative projects.

4. Fostering Science–Business–Government Collaboration

- **University–industry partnerships**: State programs that link academic research with commercial applications, promoting knowledge transfer and joint innovation.

- **Technology transfer offices and commercialization centers**: Institutions that help transform scientific discoveries into market-ready products, safeguard intellectual property, and facilitate licensing agreements.

Outcomes of Effective Innovation Regulation

When properly implemented, state regulation of innovation in a mixed economy yields multiple long-term benefits:

- **Acceleration of technological progress and modernization**: Raising productivity, lowering production costs, and improving the quality of goods and services.

- **Global competitiveness**: Strengthening the ability of domestic firms to compete internationally and participate in global supply chains.

- **Creation of high-quality jobs**: Expanding employment opportunities in advanced sectors and raising overall wage levels.

- **Social and environmental solutions**: Supporting innovations in healthcare, education, clean energy, and sustainable practices that improve quality of life.

Distinctive Features of Innovation Policy in a Mixed Economy

A defining characteristic of innovation policy in mixed economies is its dual reliance on market incentives and active government participation. The state does not crowd out private enterprise, but instead lowers risks and provides targeted support, enabling businesses to innovate more aggressively.

Transparency and accountability are also crucial. Governments in mixed economies increasingly use open calls for proposals, public registries of grants and subsidies, and regular reporting mechanisms to ensure that funds are spent effectively. This not only strengthens efficiency but also builds public trust, minimizing the risks of corruption or favoritism.

The Role of Social Policy in a Mixed Economy

Social policy holds a central place in the framework of a mixed economy. It is not a marginal supplement, but an integral part of economic regulation. Its primary goal is to harmonize economic and social processes, offset the negative effects of market mechanisms, and ensure both social justice and social stability.

Unlike a purely market economy, where social issues are addressed mainly through individual initiative, or a centrally planned economy, where the state assumes full responsibility for welfare provision, the mixed model pursues a balanced approach. The state plays an active role in the social sphere, yet it does not fully replace private initiative or individual responsibility.

Core Objectives of Social Policy

In a mixed economy, social policy is oriented toward specific socio-economic outcomes, including:

- **Reducing poverty and inequality**: Redistribution of income and the implementation of targeted social programs are designed to lower poverty rates and reduce disparities in wealth, promoting fairness and stability.

- **Ensuring quality of life and access to social services**: Public investments in education, healthcare, housing, transport, and related sectors guarantee that these services remain accessible to the entire population, regardless of income or location.

- **Building a flexible and responsive system of social protection**: Modern systems of welfare and support are structured to respond quickly to economic shifts such as rising unemployment, financial crises, or demographic changes, providing timely and adequate assistance to citizens.

Guiding Principles of Social Policy

Social policy in a mixed economy rests on several interrelated principles:

- **Targeted assistance**: Public resources are directed to those who need them most, ensuring efficient allocation and tangible improvements in living conditions.

- **Differentiated approach**: Support programs are tailored to the needs of specific groups—pensioners, families with children, people with disabilities, the unemployed—enhancing the effectiveness of assistance.

- **Shared responsibility**: While the state guarantees a baseline of social protection, it also encourages private initiative, philanthropy, and social entrepreneurship. Cooperation between government and the private sector is seen as essential for expanding the reach and quality of services.

- **Systemic and long-term orientation**: Social policy is not limited to short-term relief. It is structured as a comprehensive and forward-looking strategy aimed at sustained social stability and predictable support.

Key Instruments of Social Policy

To achieve these aims, governments in mixed economies employ a variety of tools:

1. **Social transfers and direct payments**
   - Pensions for old age and disability.
   - Unemployment benefits, allowances for low-income families, support for vulnerable groups such as veterans, orphans, and people with disabilities.

2. **Employment and labor market programs**
   - Professional retraining and skills development initiatives.
   - Support for small and medium-sized enterprises to foster job creation.
   - Public works and temporary employment schemes to reduce joblessness during downturns.

3. **Public provision of social services**
   - State-funded education at all levels.
   - Public healthcare systems and medical insurance programs.
   - Housing initiatives and affordable housing projects.

4. **Tax incentives for social programs**
   - Tax benefits for firms engaged in socially oriented or charitable projects.
   - Tax deductions for individuals investing in education and healthcare.

5. **Public–private partnerships (PPPs) in the social sphere**
   - Private sector participation in the delivery of education, healthcare, and social care services.
   - Concession agreements and joint projects for the construction of social infrastructure.

Outcomes of Effective Social Policy

When properly implemented, social policy in a mixed economy delivers a wide range of benefits:

- **Reduced poverty and inequality**: Redistribution and targeted aid lower the share of people living below the poverty line and foster greater equity.

- **Improved living standards**: Equal access to quality education, healthcare, and housing enhances human capital and raises overall quality of life.

- **Stronger social cohesion and trust**: Reliable social programs reduce social tensions and build confidence in public institutions.

- **Greater social and economic mobility**: Opportunities for retraining, employment, and education enable citizens to improve their personal and professional standing.

Social policy in a mixed economy is best understood as a systematic and purposeful activity of the state. It is not simply about welfare provision, but about maintaining the delicate balance between efficiency and fairness, individual freedom and collective responsibility.

The Role of Environmental Policy in a Mixed Economy

In a mixed economy, environmental policy becomes an essential dimension of state regulation. This is largely due to the growing scale of global environmental challenges, climate change, and the urgent need to secure the long-term sustainability of economic development. Unlike a purely market system, where environmental issues are often neglected, or a centrally planned system, where the state fully controls ecological matters, the mixed model seeks a balanced approach. It combines the responsibility of the state, business, and society, ensuring that environmental protection is not an afterthought but a structural element of economic policy.

Core Objectives of Environmental Policy

Environmental policy in a mixed economy is designed to achieve several interconnected goals:

- **Sustainable and balanced growth**

  Aligning economic development with the preservation of natural resources and the reduction of environmental risks.

- **Reduction of pollution and environmental harm**

  Minimizing the ecological footprint of production and consumption while protecting ecosystems and biodiversity.

- **Promotion of green production and consumption models**

  Encouraging the transition to eco-friendly industries, renewable energy, clean technologies, and sustainable agriculture.

Key Principles of Environmental Policy

Environmental policy in a mixed economy rests on the following guiding principles:

- **The "polluter pays" principle**

  Firms and individuals responsible for environmental damage bear the cost of prevention, mitigation, or restoration, which motivates the adoption of cleaner technologies.

- **Incentivized voluntary action**

  Economic incentives such as tax benefits, subsidies, or preferential loans are used to encourage environmentally responsible behavior by businesses and households.

- **Systemic and integrated approach**

  Environmental policy considers the interconnection between different sectors and regions, ensuring long-term and holistic results rather than fragmented measures.

- **Transparency and public participation**

  Open discussion of environmental policies and public involvement in their design and monitoring builds trust and accountability.

Methods and Instruments of Environmental Policy

To achieve these goals, mixed economies employ a combination of regulatory, financial, and institutional tools.

1. **Regulatory standards and legal frameworks**
   - Binding limits on emissions, waste disposal, and resource use.
   - Licensing and certification of environmentally safe production methods and technologies.

2. **Economic and financial instruments**
   - Environmental taxes and fees: levies on emissions, resource extraction, and excessive pollution, alongside fines for regulatory violations.
   - Subsidies and tax relief for green industries: support for companies adopting clean energy, sustainable farming, or eco-friendly manufacturing.
   - Green investment programs: state funding for renewable energy, clean transport, waste recycling, and other areas of the green economy.

3. **Public procurement and state investment**
   - Government preference for purchasing environmentally sustainable goods and services, thereby stimulating demand for green technologies.
   - Large-scale public investment in green infrastructure such as renewable energy facilities, modern waste management systems, and sustainable transport networks.

Outcomes of Environmental Policy in a Mixed Economy

When applied effectively, environmental regulation in a mixed economy produces a range of positive outcomes:

- **Improved environmental quality**

  Cleaner air, water, and soil, along with reduced biodiversity loss and more responsible use of natural resources.

- **Development of a green economy**

  Expansion of eco-friendly industries that combine economic growth with ecological sustainability, creating new jobs and markets.

- **Enhanced international competitiveness**

  Leadership in environmental technologies strengthens national economies in global competition and supports export-oriented industries.

- **Greater social trust and quality of life**

  Environmental safety, improved health outcomes, and visible improvements in living conditions foster stronger public confidence in state institutions and their policies.

In a mixed economy, environmental policy serves as a bridge between growth and sustainability. By combining regulation with incentives, the state ensures that economic progress does not come at the expense of ecological balance. This integrated approach allows nations to confront climate change, preserve resources for future generations, and at the same time, remain competitive in the global economy.

Final Characteristics of Regulation in a Mixed Economy

State regulation in a mixed economy is defined by a comprehensive, balanced, and systemic approach. Its goal is to harmonize market mechanisms with public governance, drawing on the strengths of both while minimizing their weaknesses and risks.

A Comprehensive Scope of Regulation

Regulation in a mixed economy covers nearly every dimension of social and economic life, allowing governments to address complex challenges in an integrated way:

- **Economic regulation** ensures macroeconomic stability, fosters a competitive environment, protects consumers and entrepreneurs, and stimulates investment and innovation.

- **Social regulation** reduces poverty and inequality, expands access to quality social services, and builds an effective system of social protection.

- **Innovation policy** supports technological progress, develops research and innovation infrastructure, promotes the adoption of advanced technologies, and strengthens global competitiveness.

- **Environmental regulation** minimizes ecological damage, enforces sustainability standards, and guides the transition toward a "green economy."

This multi-layered approach gives mixed economies the capacity to pursue economic efficiency, social fairness, technological progress, and environmental sustainability simultaneously.

Partnership Between State and Business

One of the defining features of a mixed economy is the partnership model of state–business relations. Unlike command economies, where the state dominates, or laissez-faire systems, where it withdraws, here both sectors share responsibility for development:

- The state creates favorable conditions rather than suppressing private initiative.

- The private sector is recognized as a key partner in advancing national economic and social goals.
- Joint projects and public–private partnerships (PPPs) are widely used to implement large-scale infrastructure, innovation, and social programs.

This cooperative model builds trust, reduces risks of administrative arbitrariness and corruption, and lays the foundation for long-term, sustainable growth.

Predominantly Indirect Methods

Regulation in a mixed economy relies primarily on indirect, incentive-based tools that guide private-sector behavior without heavy-handed intervention:

- **Financial and credit measures** such as tax incentives, monetary policy, budgetary spending, and state investment programs support growth while preserving flexibility.
- **Regulatory and control measures** include antitrust enforcement, certification, licensing, and oversight of environmental and social standards.
- **Economic incentives**—grants, subsidies, preferential loans, and tax relief— encourage innovation, small business development, socially important projects, and eco-friendly production.

Flexibility and Adaptability

A hallmark of mixed economies is the capacity of regulatory systems to adapt to changing conditions:

- Rapid responses to crises, technological shifts, demographic change, or fluctuations in global markets.
- Adjustments in the intensity and direction of regulation depending on evolving national priorities.
- Consideration of the needs of different social groups and regions, ensuring balanced territorial and social development.

Flexibility makes regulation a stabilizing force, allowing economies to weather shocks while pursuing long-term objectives.

Transparency and Public Accountability

Another key feature of mixed-economy regulation is its emphasis on transparency and openness:

- Broad public debate on economic, social, innovation, and environmental policy.
- Easy access to information about government programs, funding, tax benefits, and support mechanisms.
- Active involvement of civil society and expert communities in policy design and oversight.

Such openness reduces corruption risks, strengthens public trust, and enhances the effectiveness of regulation.

Chapter 3

Role of the Market in a Mixed Economy:
Market Mechanisms within a Regulated Framework

The Market as the Foundation of a Mixed Economy

In a mixed economy, the market remains at the heart of economic life, providing the framework within which production and exchange take place. The state takes part in these processes, but its role is supportive rather than directive. It sets the rules, stabilizes conditions, and directs resources toward goals that exceed the logic of profit alone.

This model stands between two extremes: the planned economy, where the state monopolizes decision-making, and the laissez-faire system, where intervention is minimal. In a mixed economy, the initiative of entrepreneurs and the self-regulation of markets are preserved, while government action ensures that economic growth serves social needs and long-term priorities.

The market fosters entrepreneurship by distributing resources efficiently and creating incentives for innovation. Competition compels producers to adapt quickly to technological advances, shifting consumer demands, and external shocks. In this way, the market becomes a source of dynamism, constantly renewing production and encouraging progress.

It also weaves horizontal connections between industries and regions, strengthening interdependence and shaping an integrated economic space. Such linkages matter even more in the context of globalization and rising international competition.

Competition itself is the engine of efficiency. It raises productivity, improves the quality of goods and services, and broadens consumer choice. By giving individuals and businesses the freedom to act according to their interests, it sustains motivation and engagement across society.

The strength of the mixed economy lies in this balance: markets remain the leading mechanism, while government regulation refines their operation. Together they provide stability, transparency, and social responsibility, ensuring that economic forces serve both growth and the public good.

Core Functions of the Market in a Mixed Economy

In a mixed economy, the market remains central by carrying out a set of key functions that secure both everyday efficiency and long-term development. Through these functions, it helps society respond to change, satisfy consumer needs, and sustain growth.

1) Informational Function

The market operates as an information network where prices act as signals. They show the state of supply and demand, direct producers toward goods and services most valued, and allow consumers to compare options and make choices.

This function makes it possible to:

• detect shifts in consumer preferences as they occur;
• track the availability of resources and production capacity;
• coordinate the actions of producers and consumers with minimal delay.

By transmitting clear signals, the market reduces uncertainty and strengthens the adaptability of the economic system.

2) Regulatory Function

The market balances supply and demand and channels resources where they are most useful. This mechanism prevents persistent shortages or surpluses and keeps production aligned with real demand.

It enables the economy to:

• use limited resources more effectively;
• maintain equilibrium between demand and supply;
• adjust output rapidly when conditions change.

3) Stimulating Function

Competition and the pursuit of profit create strong incentives for innovation and efficiency. Businesses are pushed to cut costs, raise productivity, and improve the quality and variety of their products.

This function is expressed in:

• encouraging entrepreneurship and technological progress;
• raising labor productivity and resource efficiency;
• broadening consumer choice and improving product quality.

Through this dynamic, the market becomes a constant driver of progress and modernization.

4) Corrective Function

The market also disciplines participants. Inefficient firms lose ground, while resources move toward stronger and more innovative enterprises. In a mixed economy, this process ensures renewal and resilience.

It makes it possible to:

• withdraw resources from outdated or unproductive sectors;
• channel capital and labor to more competitive firms;
• keep the economy open to restructuring and adaptation.

Together, these functions show why the market remains the foundation of self-regulation in a mixed economy.

Features of the Market Mechanism in a Mixed Economy

In a mixed economy, the market operates under conditions different from those of a completely free system. The principles of supply, demand, and price formation remain in force, yet they unfold within a framework shaped by government regulation. This balance makes it possible to preserve the advantages of competition while addressing social and economic challenges more effectively.

1. Controlled Competition

Competition in a mixed economy does not proceed unchecked. The state monitors the market to prevent the concentration of power in a few hands and to protect the integrity of economic life.

This is achieved through:

• **Antitrust policy**: laws and agencies designed to curb monopolies and cartels, with the authority to investigate and sanction violations.

• **Protection against unfair practices**: restrictions on predatory pricing, deceptive advertising, and other methods that distort competition and harm both consumers and smaller firms.

2. Regulated Pricing of Essential Goods and Services

Governments intervene in price formation when social stability or access to basic needs is at stake. Most prices are left to the market, but key areas remain under oversight:

• **Basic necessities**: food staples, medicines, fuel, and other goods essential for daily life.

• **Utilities and housing services**: tariffs for electricity, heating, water, and sanitation often require state approval.

• **Strategic industries**: sectors such as energy, transportation, and defense-related enterprises are subject to regulation to ensure security and reliability.

This framework shields society from extreme price swings and secures affordable access to vital goods.

3. State Intervention in Economic Cycles

Governments in mixed economies do not attempt to control the entire course of economic life. Instead, they moderate cyclical fluctuations, supporting stability while preserving market flexibility.

Such intervention takes several forms:

• **Fiscal policy**: public investment and social spending during downturns, and restraint in times of rapid growth.

• **Monetary policy**: central banks adjust interest rates and credit supply to balance inflation and stagnation.

• **Tax measures**: temporary reductions, credits, or subsidies stimulate investment and encourage entrepreneurship in difficult periods.

This stabilizing role does not replace market forces but complements them, softening volatility and sustaining steady development.

Market Mechanisms and Entrepreneurial Initiative in a Mixed Economy

Entrepreneurship is one of the central forces of growth and renewal in a mixed economy. The market provides the space where initiative takes shape, while the state ensures stability, reduces risks, and protects the rules of fair play. Regulation here is not a constraint but a complement, allowing entrepreneurial energy to serve both efficiency and wider social goals.

1. Competition as a Stimulus

Competition compels firms to refine production, cut costs, and raise quality. Rivalry becomes a constant pressure that fuels innovation and broadens consumer choice.

It leads to:

• higher productivity through new technologies and better organization;
• improved standards of goods and services;
• diversification as firms explore new niches and respond to shifting demand.

2. Pricing Freedom

Prices remain a flexible instrument of decision-making. In a mixed economy, firms adjust prices to reflect demand, costs, and competition.

Free pricing allows:

• rapid adaptation to market shifts;
• efficient movement of capital and labor toward profitable sectors;
• incentives for risk-taking and product differentiation.

3. Innovation Incentives

The pursuit of profit drives investment in research and new technologies. Open markets and competition speed up the spread of successful innovations, ensuring that knowledge does not remain confined to a single firm or sector.

Innovation is shaped by:

• profit motives that reward successful advances;
• quick diffusion of technologies across industries;
• consumer demand for better and more diverse products.

4. The State's Role

The state strengthens, rather than restrains, entrepreneurial activity. Its role is to secure the framework within which initiative can flourish.

Key contributions include:

• clear laws, property rights, and contract enforcement;
• infrastructure and digital systems that reduce business costs;
• support for small and medium-sized enterprises through credit, tax relief, and grants;
• promotion of innovation through research funding, technology clusters, and links between universities and industry.

The Interaction of Market and State in a Mixed Economy

In a mixed economy, the market and the state are not adversaries but partners. The market provides the arena where resources are exchanged and value is created, while the state secures stability, fairness, and continuity. Together they shape a balance that neither unregulated capitalism nor centralized planning can deliver.

1. **The State as Guarantor of Stability**

Markets depend on reliable rules and institutions. It is the state that establishes these foundations, giving private enterprise the confidence to operate.

• **Protection of property rights**: secure ownership encourages investment and long-term planning.

• **Judicial independence**: impartial courts resolve disputes, reduce risks, and strengthen trust among participants.

• **Antitrust regulation**: oversight prevents monopolization and keeps competition alive, sustaining efficiency and diversity.

By upholding these frameworks, the state allows markets to flourish while safeguarding public interests.

2. **The Market as a Guide for Policy**

The state not only regulates but also learns from the market. Prices, demand, and production trends act as signals that direct policy choices.

• **Policy orientation**: market dynamics indicate where investment is most needed.

• **Risk detection**: shifts in supply and demand reveal inflationary pressures, shortages, or threats of concentration.

• **Efficient public spending**: by responding to market signals, governments can design infrastructure, innovation, and social programs that match real needs.

The market thus provides feedback not only for firms but also for public institutions.

3. **State Action in Times of Crisis**

The partnership between market and state is most visible in moments of turbulence. Recessions, financial shocks, or global disruptions often demand public intervention.

• **Sustaining demand**: transfers, benefits, and public spending preserve household purchasing power.

• **Protecting jobs**: targeted investments, tax relief, and employment programs maintain income and stability.

• **Securing liquidity**: credit support and monetary easing keep firms solvent during downturns.

Such measures do not replace the market. They reinforce it, allowing recovery to proceed more quickly while protecting society from heavy social costs.

In a mixed economy, state and market form a durable partnership: the state provides rules and safeguards, while the market supplies signals and incentives. In times of crisis, government action stabilizes the system and restores confidence.

Advantages of the Market in a Mixed Economy

The integration of market mechanisms into a mixed economy brings not only dynamism but also resilience. The market, with its capacity for self-regulation and competition, creates conditions for efficiency, innovation, and freedom of choice.

When balanced by state regulation, these qualities translate into tangible economic and social benefits, raising productivity, expanding opportunity, and improving daily life.

1. **Economic Efficiency**

Efficiency remains one of the clearest strengths of the market. Competition forces resources toward their most productive use, while waste is steadily reduced.

• capital and labor move into sectors and firms where they achieve the highest return;
• rivalry compels businesses to cut costs, raise productivity, and refine their methods;
• inefficient firms leave the market, while stronger ones expand, renewing the structure of the economy.

2. **Responsiveness to Consumer Demand**

The price system serves as a language of signals, guiding producers to align with the needs of consumers.

• production adjusts quickly to changes in demand;
• shortages and surpluses are corrected before they become entrenched;
• constant adaptation keeps consumers satisfied and markets dynamic.

3. **Incentives for Innovation and Technological Progress**

The search for profit and survival under competition makes innovation a necessity.

• firms invest in research and development to gain an edge;
• new technologies spread rapidly across industries, increasing productivity and accessibility;
• startups and high-tech enterprises emerge, diversifying the economic landscape.

4. **Improvement of Consumer Welfare**

Consumers are the immediate beneficiaries of competition.
• higher standards of quality as firms strive to earn trust;
• broader product ranges that expand choice;
• competitive pricing that increases affordability.

5. **Economic Freedom and Individual Choice**

Markets create space for initiative and independence.

• entrepreneurs can establish businesses, innovate, and contribute to growth;
• consumers influence production priorities through their decisions, reinforcing sovereignty of demand;
• individuals gain greater control over careers, investments, and lifestyles.

6. **Social Mobility and Opportunity**

The market also plays a role in shaping society. By rewarding initiative and effort, it can expand opportunities for upward mobility.

• entrepreneurship provides channels for advancement regardless of background;
• competition rewards talent and creativity, not only inherited position;
• access to goods, services, and employment broadens participation in economic life.

7. Integration into the Global Economy

Markets connect nations to the wider world, creating channels for exchange and cooperation.

- international trade diversifies exports and links domestic firms to global networks;
- open markets attract foreign capital, expertise, and technology;
- cross-border flows of knowledge and innovation enrich national economies.

8. Environmental Incentives

Although markets often overlook external costs, they can also support ecological progress when demand and competition align with sustainability.

- consumer preference for green products stimulates eco-friendly production;
- firms adopt energy-saving and cleaner technologies to reduce costs and win markets;
- competition accelerates the spread of sustainable practices.

9. Institutional Support and Reliability

Markets operate effectively only within strong institutional frameworks. Their advantages depend on clear rules, secure rights, and social trust.

- protection of property rights encourages long-term investment;
- contract enforcement reduces risks and increases cooperation;
- transparency and accountability strengthen confidence among participants.

10. Long-Term Development Effects

Beyond immediate efficiency, markets contribute to deeper forms of growth.

- the accumulation of knowledge and skills enhances human capital;

- entrepreneurial culture fosters creativity and adaptability;
- the constant renewal of enterprises creates conditions for durable progress.

11. Self-Regulation and Coordination

Through prices and competition, the market coordinates countless actions without central command.

- price signals reveal scarcity and demand;
- supply and demand adjust continuously, maintaining balance;
- reliance on decentralized coordination reduces the need for direct intervention.

In this way, the market within a mixed economy is more than an instrument of allocation. It is a dynamic system that fosters efficiency, innovation, mobility, and integration, while remaining anchored in legal and institutional safeguards. Its strengths are multiplied when paired with state regulation, producing not only growth but also fairness, resilience, and sustainability.

The Limitations of Market Mechanisms and the Necessity of State Regulation

Markets, though powerful, have inherent weaknesses that require the corrective hand of the state. Left alone, they generate efficiency and wealth, yet also inequality, instability, and social costs. For this reason, regulation and public policy become indispensable.

1. **The Drift toward Monopoly**

Markets often tend toward concentration of power. Large corporations expand, absorb smaller firms, and reduce competition. This weakens innovation, narrows consumer choice, and raises prices. Antitrust policy and active oversight are essential to keep competition alive.

2. **Inequality of Outcomes**

The market rewards resources and position rather than fairness. Wealth accumulates at the top, while poverty persists at the bottom. Social mobility slows, and unrest grows. Through taxation, redistribution, and investment in public services, governments mitigate these divides and preserve social cohesion.

3. **Cycles of Expansion and Decline**

Unregulated markets move in cycles of rapid growth and sudden downturn. Booms often end in crises, with unemployment and declining incomes as their legacy. Fiscal and monetary policies, together with social safety nets, act as stabilizers, softening the shocks and limiting wasted potential.

4. **Externalities and Hidden Costs**

Markets do not account for environmental and social damage. Pollution, deforestation, and overuse of natural resources create costs borne by society, not producers. Governments respond by setting environmental standards, taxing emissions, and supporting clean technologies.

5. **Public Goods and Collective Needs**

Certain goods and services—national defense, infrastructure, scientific research, and universal healthcare—cannot be provided adequately by markets alone. Their cost is high, their benefits shared, and the free-rider problem prevents private provision. Here the state assumes responsibility.

6. **Short-Term Orientation**

Markets often prioritize immediate profits over long-term investments in education, infrastructure, and research. Governments, with longer planning horizons, fill this gap by supporting projects essential for future generations.

7. **Information Asymmetry**

Market exchange presumes equal knowledge, but in reality sellers, corporations, and financial actors often hold decisive advantages. Such imbalances can lead to exploitation and crises. Consumer protection, financial regulation, and transparency laws help restore fairness.

Taken together, these limitations reveal that the market excels at efficiency but falters in equity and foresight. State regulation does not negate market strengths; it complements them.

Modern Trends and the Role of the Market in the Context of Globalization

Globalization — the growing interdependence of national economies — has transformed the conditions in which mixed economies evolve. Markets today extend beyond national borders, creating new pressures and opening new horizons. They demand higher efficiency, faster innovation, and greater flexibility, while at the same time exposing societies to fresh risks.

1. Global Markets and Intensified Competition

One of the central features of contemporary development is the expanding role of global markets for goods, services, capital, and technology. International competition compels firms and nations alike to sharpen their competitive edge.

• enterprises must raise efficiency, cut costs, and improve quality to remain viable;
• global rivalry accelerates technological progress and the spread of innovations;
• economies must adapt rapidly, reshaping production to meet fluctuating world demand.

2. Market Mechanisms as a Channel of Integration

Market forces are the primary medium through which economies enter global value chains. They facilitate trade, attract investment, and spread new knowledge across borders.

• international trade diversifies exports and links domestic firms to global production networks;
• open markets create conditions for inflows of capital, expertise, and advanced technologies;
• competition fosters the rapid exchange of practices and innovations, enriching national economies.

3. The Rising Demand for State Regulation

Globalization strengthens markets but also magnifies risks. National governments must therefore expand their regulatory role.

• safeguarding strategic sectors and industries from destabilizing competition and crises;
• stabilizing economies during global downturns with fiscal, monetary, and social policies;
• addressing inequality, unemployment, and social disruption through redistribution and public investment.

4. New Directions of Regulation in the Global Era

Modern states respond to globalization with policies aimed at reinforcing its benefits while controlling its costs.

• investment in research, infrastructure, and innovative enterprises to sustain competitiveness;
• education, continuous training, and reskilling to prepare citizens for shifting demands;
• flexible trade and industrial policies to help domestic firms withstand global pressures;
• environmental regulation to encourage green technologies and sustainable growth.

Globalization amplifies the strengths of the market within the mixed economy: it raises the tempo of competition, spreads innovation, and accelerates technological change. Yet it also heightens vulnerability, making state action indispensable. The modern mixed economy succeeds when it balances the dynamism of markets with the guiding role of the state, combining openness with stability, and integration with social responsibility.

Concluding Characteristics of the Role of the Market in a Mixed Economy

In a mixed economy, the market is not a secondary instrument but the foundation of economic life. It channels resources, stimulates enterprise, fosters innovation, and provides national economies with the flexibility to withstand constant shifts at home and abroad. Yet its role extends beyond efficiency: the market shapes social structures, connects countries to the global system, and challenges governments to balance growth with justice and sustainability.

1. **Market Mechanisms as the Basis of Development**

The market forms the backbone of the mixed economy by ensuring resource allocation, free pricing, and the preservation of competition. Through the price system, entrepreneurs read signals of supply and demand, which guide rational planning, business decisions, and rapid adjustment to changing conditions.

2. **The Market as a Stimulus for Innovation and Technological Progress**

Competition transforms innovation from a choice into a necessity. Firms invest in technology, improve quality, reduce costs, and raise productivity to survive and expand. Market pressure thus becomes a constant driver of technological change and a key force of national development.

3. **Flexibility and Adaptability in Shifting Conditions**

One of the market's greatest strengths lies in its responsiveness. Demand, global shifts, and new technologies redirect resources quickly to where they are needed most. This adaptability reduces imbalances, sustains stability, and proves indispensable in the era of globalization and accelerating change.

4. **The Market's Social Dimension**

The market not only drives economic performance but also shapes society. It influences employment, social mobility, and the distribution of opportunities. Left unchecked, it may widen inequality; with regulation, it can support inclusive growth and reinforce the cohesion of social structures.

5. **The Market and International Integration**

Markets extend beyond national borders, linking economies to global production chains and trade networks. They enable the flow of goods, capital, and knowledge, but also expose nations to external shocks. This dual role makes the state's responsibility to safeguard national interests while enabling openness all the more critical.

6. **Environmental Limits of Market Mechanisms**

The market excels at efficiency but often neglects long-term ecological costs. Pollution, overuse of natural resources, and climate risks remain outside the calculus of profit. This is why regulation must include environmental standards, carbon taxation, and incentives for clean technologies, ensuring that growth is compatible with sustainability.

7. The Market within the Institutional Framework

Markets cannot function in isolation. Their effectiveness depends on the strength of legal and cultural institutions — property rights, contract enforcement, and trust. The state provides these foundations, enabling market exchange to remain predictable, fair, and transparent.

8. The Limitations of the Market and the Need for Regulation

Despite its many advantages, the market shows clear weaknesses: it tends toward monopoly, generates inequality, and remains vulnerable to cycles and crises. Purposeful regulation is required to keep competition alive, mitigate social costs, stabilize fluctuations, and protect national economies from global turbulence.

9. Balance as the Foundation of Sustainable Development

The mixed economy achieves its greatest strength through balance. The state sets rules, safeguards property, ensures fair competition, and invests in long-term priorities such as education, infrastructure, and ecological protection. The market, in turn, provides signals, incentives, and adaptability that guide effective policy.

When this partnership is preserved, the mixed economy ceases to be a compromise and becomes a deliberate model: one that unites efficiency with justice, innovation with stability, and growth with sustainability, securing the foundations of development for generations to come.

Comparative Analysis of the Roles of the Market and the State in a Mixed Economy: Differences in Functions and Impact

A mixed economy is built upon the interaction and mutual complementarity of two essential elements — market mechanisms and state regulation. While the market and the state pursue different goals and employ distinct instruments, it is their optimal combination that ensures efficiency, stability, and social justice within the economic system.

1. Main spheres of influence of the market and the state

The Market:

• Regulation of prices and resource allocation through supply and demand.
• Stimulation of innovation through competition.
• Enhancement of productivity and economic efficiency.
• Adaptation to changing consumer preferences and needs.
• Formation of economic incentives for entrepreneurial initiative.

The State:

• Establishment of the rules of economic activity and the legal framework.
• Correction of "market failures" (monopolization, inequality, unemployment).
• Provision of social stability and fair redistribution of income.
• Implementation of large-scale infrastructure projects and public goods (education, healthcare, security, transportation).
• Support of economic stability by smoothing cyclical fluctuations.

2. Principles of Market and State Activity

Principles of Market Activity	Principles of State Regulation
Self-regulation	Goal-oriented management
Decentralization of decisions	Centralization of strategic decisions
Private initiative	State programs and priorities
Free pricing	Regulation of prices for essential goods and services
Profit maximization and competition	Social responsibility and fairness

The market and the state operate according to different principles, yet they complement one another.

3. Advantages of the Market and the State in a Mixed Economy

Advantages of the Market:

• High adaptability to changes in the economic environment.
• Efficient allocation of scarce resources through competition.
• Strong stimulation of entrepreneurial initiative and innovation.

- Flexibility and dynamism of economic processes.

Advantages of the State:
- Mitigation of the negative effects of market mechanisms (unemployment, poverty, social inequality).
- Maintenance of economic stability and prevention of major crises.
- Implementation of long-term and large-scale projects (infrastructure, social, technological).
- Protection of national interests in the context of globalization.

4. Limitations of the Market and the State in a Mixed Economy

Limitations of the Market Mechanism:
- A high degree of uncertainty and cyclical fluctuations in development.
- Unequal distribution of income, leading to social stratification.
- A tendency toward monopolization of markets and restrictions on competition.
- Insufficient provision of public goods (such as infrastructure, healthcare, and education).

Limitations of State Regulation:
- The risk of excessive bureaucratization and administrative interference in the economy.
- Vulnerability to corruption and lobbying by narrow interest groups.
- Restriction of private initiative and weakening of market incentives under excessive regulation.
- The danger of misguided decisions, resulting in inefficient allocation of resources and wasteful public investment.

5. Conditions for Effective Interaction Between Market and State

The successful functioning of a mixed economy depends on maintaining a delicate balance between market mechanisms and government intervention. The key conditions for this interaction include:

- **Clear boundaries of state intervention.** The state must complement rather than suppress market mechanisms, preserving the incentives for entrepreneurship, competition, and innovation.
- **Transparency and openness of government regulation.** Public accountability and openness of state institutions reduce the risks of corruption and excessive bureaucratization.
- **Sound antitrust policy.** Ensuring fair competition through effective monitoring of dominant market actors safeguards the integrity of the market environment.
- **Targeted social policy.** Directing support toward the most vulnerable groups in society ensures efficient use of public resources while avoiding unnecessary intrusion into market dynamics.

- **Active participation of civil society.** Oversight of government decisions by citizens and independent institutions strengthens transparency and enhances the effectiveness of economic governance.

6. Examples of a Successful Balance Between Market and State in a Mixed Economy

- **Germany (Social Market Economy):** A well-established model that combines competitive market forces with robust state regulation of labor relations and social welfare, ensuring both efficiency and equity.

- **Scandinavian countries (Sweden, Denmark, Norway):** Known for their comprehensive welfare systems and high living standards, supported by dynamic market economies and strong competition.

- **Japan and South Korea:** Illustrations of successful state-led planning and innovation policies paired with vibrant market systems, high levels of competition, and rapid technological advancement.

7. Contemporary Trends and Future Perspectives on the Balance Between Market and State

Digitalization, environmental challenges, globalization, and pandemic crises demand a rethinking of the roles of the market and the state:

- **The growing role of the state in times of crisis alongside the preservation and strengthening of market mechanisms as drivers of recovery and innovation.** Governments increasingly act as guarantors of stability through fiscal and monetary measures, while the market provides the flexibility and competition necessary for long-term recovery and technological renewal. This partnership has shown its value in financial crises and public health emergencies.

- **State support for digital technologies and the green economy, provided that competition and entrepreneurial freedom remain intact.** Public investment in infrastructure, research, and incentives for clean energy or digital transformation is most effective when it complements private entrepreneurship. In this way, regulation shapes priorities, while the market translates them into practical innovation and consumer choice.

- **Expansion of international cooperation between states and markets to address global challenges such as climate change, pandemics, and migration.** These issues cannot be solved by isolated action, as they require harmonized standards, coordinated investments, and shared technological solutions. Markets link economies together, but effective international agreements give this interdependence a stable and fair foundation.

- **Smart regulation as a guiding principle of modern governance.** Rather than excessive control, contemporary regulation emphasizes flexibility, efficiency, and transparency. It reduces bureaucratic barriers, adapts quickly to new realities, and combines classical instruments—taxation, standards, oversight—with modern tools such as incentives, partnerships, and innovation-driven policies.

CONCLUSION

The classification of economic systems demonstrates the diversity of ways in which societies address their most fundamental economic questions: what to produce, how to produce, and for whom. These systems—market, planned, and mixed—are not static categories but historically evolving models shaped by geography, culture, ideology, and levels of development.

The market economy represents the logic of decentralized decision-making, where private ownership and competition form the central mechanisms of coordination. It achieves efficiency in resource allocation, rapid adaptability to technological and consumer change, and strong incentives for innovation. Yet market economies also face recurring challenges: cycles of expansion and crisis, persistent inequality, and a tendency toward monopolization that threatens competition.

The planned economy, developed most prominently in the twentieth century, embodies the opposite principle: centralized coordination of production and distribution. By concentrating economic power in state institutions, planned systems can mobilize resources for large-scale projects, reduce unemployment, and pursue more equal distribution of wealth. However, rigid planning often undermines efficiency, producing shortages, misallocation of resources, and weak adaptability to change.

The mixed economy arises as an attempt to combine the strengths of both systems while reducing their weaknesses. By weaving together market dynamism with state regulation, it allows competition and innovation to flourish while public policy addresses inequality, provides essential goods, and stabilizes fluctuations. Mixed economies differ widely, but all recognize that neither unregulated markets nor rigid planning can by themselves ensure efficiency, justice, and stability.

Seen historically, the evolution of systems reflects adaptation to changing circumstances. The Great Depression of the 1930s exposed the vulnerabilities of unregulated markets, leading to new forms of intervention in capitalist countries. The collapse of centrally planned economies in the late twentieth century revealed the limits of rigid coordination, paving the way for reforms and hybrid models. In today's global economy, the mixed system dominates in diverse forms—Nordic social democracies, East Asian developmental states, and liberal capitalist economies with regulatory frameworks.

No universal or "perfect" system exists that can function equally well across nations and conditions. Each country shapes its own variant, influenced by history, traditions, and political choices. The real value of classification lies not in rigid categories but in recognizing the continuing search for balance—between efficiency and fairness, growth and stability, freedom and responsibility.

PART V
CLASSIFICATION BY
DEGREE OF RELIGIOUS INFLUENCE

SECTION 1. SECULAR STATE — SEPARATION OF RELIGION FROM POLITICAL AUTHORITY

> **A secular state** is a form of government in which religion is separated from state authority.

Introduction

In such a state, there is no official religion, and religious organizations hold no direct influence over political decision-making. The state guarantees freedom of conscience and religion, as well as equality for all citizens regardless of their religious affiliation.

Causes and Historical Context of the Separation of State and Religion

The separation of state and religion was the outcome of a long process of historical development. Several key factors contributed to this transformation:

- the need to prevent religious conflicts and wars fueled by intolerance and sectarian rivalry;
- the aspiration to guarantee equality and protect human rights regardless of religious belief;
- the emergence of rationalist and Enlightenment principles, which affirmed the primacy of reason, individual freedom, and civic equality under the law.

The idea of secularism found its most vivid expression during the Enlightenment, particularly in the wake of the French Revolution at the end of the eighteenth century. The Revolution not only dismantled the privileged position of the Catholic Church in France but also established a model of secular governance that influenced much of Europe. At the same time, across the Atlantic, the United States enshrined the principle of separation of church and state in the First Amendment to the Constitution in 1791, guaranteeing freedom of religion and prohibiting the establishment of an official church.

From these turning points, the gradual disentanglement of religious institutions from political authority spread throughout Europe and the Americas, shaping the foundations of modern secular states.

The Impact of Secularization on Politics and Public Life

Secularization has had a profound impact on political structures and social life, leading to:

1) **the emergence and consolidation of democratic institutions founded on the principles of civic equality.** In the United States, the First Amendment (1791) guaranteed freedom of religion and prohibited the establishment of an official church, laying the groundwork for a democratic system independent of ecclesiastical authority. In France, the legacy of the Revolution further reinforced the principle of laïcité, ensuring that political authority was grounded in civic, rather than religious, legitimacy.

2) **the development of religious pluralism and tolerance within society.** Throughout the nineteenth and twentieth centuries, many Western countries

moved away from confessional states toward systems that allowed multiple religions to coexist. The United States became a particularly striking example, where waves of Catholic, Jewish, and later Muslim immigrants found legal protection for their religious practices alongside Protestant traditions.

3) **the gradual decline of religious influence on education, culture, and legislation.** One of the clearest illustrations is France's Jules Ferry laws of the 1880s, which established free, mandatory, and secular primary education, removing the clergy from the school system. Similar reforms spread throughout Europe, ensuring that public education and civic culture were no longer shaped exclusively by religious institutions.

4) **the expansion of individual freedoms and human rights, including freedom of speech, freedom of conscience, and the right to choose one's religion.** This development was codified in international legal frameworks such as the Universal Declaration of Human Rights (1948), which enshrined freedom of thought, conscience, and religion as fundamental rights for all.

At the same time, secularization does not eliminate religion from public life altogether. Rather, it restricts its authority over state institutions and political decision-making, while allowing religion to remain a meaningful element of cultural identity and personal belief.

Characteristics of a Secular State

In a secular state, there is no official religion, and religious organizations do not participate in the governance of the country. The defining features are:

1) **Legal and institutional separation of religion from the state**

   The constitution and statutory law draw a clear boundary between the competencies of public authorities and religious institutions. This separation prevents ecclesiastical doctrines from determining public policy and shields religious bodies from political capture.

2) **Equality of all religions—and non-religion—before the law**

   The state guarantees equal civil and political rights to all confessions and to those who profess no religion. Legal protections apply uniformly, without privileges or penalties tied to belief or non-belief.

3) **State neutrality in matters of religion and worldview**

   Public authorities neither endorse nor disparage any faith or comprehensive doctrine. Neutrality governs legislation, administration, and public services, ensuring that citizens are treated as equals regardless of their convictions.

4) **Non-interference of religious organizations in state institutions**

   Religious bodies have no direct role in exercising public power, drafting state decisions, or directing government agencies. Participation in public debate is protected, but decision-making authority remains exclusively within secular institutions.

5) **Freedom of conscience and religion as an individual right**

Individuals are free to adopt, change, or reject religious beliefs, to practice a religion privately or in community, and to refrain from religious observance. Limitations, if any, must be prescribed by law and justified by compelling public interests in a democratic society.

6) **Secular foundations of public education**

Public schooling is organized on non-confessional principles to protect the neutrality of the classroom and the equal dignity of students. Where religious instruction is offered, it is voluntary, provided without coercion, and structured so as not to compromise the secular character of the curriculum.

7) **Judicial guarantees and constitutional review**

Independent courts, including constitutional jurisdictions where they exist, enforce the boundary between church and state, protect equal treatment of confessions and non-religion, and remedy violations of freedom of conscience and religion.

8) **Financial arrangements consistent with neutrality and equality**

The state does not establish or favor a particular church. Public funds may not be used to advance a specific creed; where legal systems allow indirect or neutral mechanisms (for example, generally available benefits or church-tax schemes administered under public law), these operate under strict conditions of voluntariness, transparency, and equal access for all recognized communities.

Philosophical Rationale

1) **John Locke** argued that civil government exists to secure civil interests—life, liberty, and property—while matters of salvation lie beyond the magistrate's competence. Coercion cannot produce genuine belief; toleration preserves civil peace and individual conscience.

2) **Voltaire** defended religious toleration as an antidote to fanaticism, contending that a plurality of sects restrains domination by any single one and stabilizes civic life.

3) **Thomas Jefferson and James Madison** grounded disestablishment in natural rights: freedom of conscience is inalienable, and any state preference for a church violates equal citizenship.

4) **John Stuart Mill** linked liberty of thought and discussion to social progress, arguing that a neutral state protects the open contest of ideas from which truth and improvement emerge.

5) **Immanuel Kant** tied secular public order to autonomy and the public use of reason: the state safeguards external freedom while citizens, as rational agents, deliberate under laws they can will for themselves.

Chapter 1

Strictly Secular State: Complete Exclusion of Religion from Governmental Institutions and Policy

> **Strict secularism**—often referred to by the French term laïcité—is a form of state organization in which religion is completely separated from political authority and exerts no influence on public policy, legislation, or education.

Strict Secularism (Laïcité)

In a strictly secular state—commonly referred to by the French term *laïcité*—all religious institutions are deprived of political privileges, and public authorities strictly adhere to principles of neutrality and equal treatment of all confessions. Religious norms and traditions are excluded from governance and public life. The defining characteristics of this model include:

1. **Rigid separation of religion and the state, with an absolute prohibition on religious influence in politics and education**

The boundary between governmental and religious institutions is drawn clearly and without exceptions. All decisions of public authorities are based exclusively on secular law and procedures. Religious leaders are barred from political intervention, just as political figures are prohibited from invoking religious dogma as justification for policy.

This principle is particularly evident in education. Curricula are designed without religious content, avoiding references to religious doctrines or values even in cultural contexts. Schools and universities remain neutral spaces where scientific methods and objective knowledge take precedence, and any attempt to introduce religious elements into the learning process is prohibited by law.

2. **Ban on religious symbols in public institutions**

State institutions—such as schools, universities, courts, police stations, and administrative offices—are entirely free from religious images, statues, or emblems. The ban extends to the appearance of public officials, who must maintain neutrality in dress and symbols, avoiding garments or accessories that reveal religious affiliation.

3. **Active protection of freedom from religion (not only freedom of religion)**

Citizens are guaranteed not only the right to practice any faith but also the right to live without religion. State institutions safeguard individuals from pressure, proselytism, or indirect influence by religious organizations. Freedom from religion is upheld as a value equal to freedom of religion.

4. **Exclusion of religious organizations from public funding**

Religious groups receive no financial support from the state budget. Expenses for worship, clergy, or places of worship are covered solely through private contributions. This ensures both financial independence and the neutrality of public resources.

5. **Equal treatment of all religions**

The state recognizes no religion as official or dominant. All faith communities that operate within the law are treated identically, without privileges or discrimination.

6. **Prohibition of religious rhetoric in official discourse**

Public officials, including presidents, ministers, judges, and civil servants, are forbidden to use religious references, symbols, or quotations in their speeches or official statements. Political discourse remains strictly secular, avoiding any impression of state endorsement of religious views.

7. **Exclusion of religious holidays from the official calendar**

National holidays are based solely on civic or historical events. Religious holidays are not recognized as public holidays; citizens may celebrate them privately but without state endorsement.

Laïcité draws its intellectual roots above all from the French Enlightenment and the political upheavals of the late eighteenth century. Unlike moderate secularism, which emphasizes freedom of religion, laïcité stresses freedom from religion in the public sphere. This principle was crystallized in the French Revolution and later codified in the 1905 Law on the Separation of Churches and the State.

While thinkers such as Jean-Jacques Rousseau argued that civic unity requires a "civil religion" grounded in shared civic values rather than confessional dogmas, French republican thought went further: it insisted that political legitimacy must be derived exclusively from reason and the general will, not from divine authority. This radical strand of secularism thus aims not merely to limit religious influence but to construct a public order entirely independent of it.

Strengths of Strict Secularism (Laïcité)

1. **Maximum equality of citizens regardless of religious belief**

In a state founded on strict secular principles, all citizens enjoy equal rights and obligations regardless of their faith—or their decision not to adhere to any faith. No one receives advantages or restrictions on account of religious conviction, and dominant confessions are granted no privileges. The neutrality of the state assures citizens that they will be treated fairly and impartially by public authorities and institutions.

2. **Complete independence of state policy from religious organizations**

The laïc model eliminates every form of religious influence on state decision-making. Policy is shaped exclusively on secular norms and rational criteria, without direct or indirect intervention by clergy or religious institutions. This guarantees that political processes remain objective, transparent, and free from manipulation through religious rhetoric, enabling government to act solely in the interests of society as a whole.

3. **Effective protection of individual freedom from religious pressure**

One of the greatest strengths of strict secularism is its active protection of both freedom of religion and freedom from religion. Citizens are guaranteed the right to live without being subjected to imposed religious practices, doctrines, or values. State institutions intervene where necessary to prevent coercion or proselytism, safeguarding each individual's freedom of conscience and autonomy of choice.

4. **Social stability and prevention of religious conflict**

The sharp separation of religion from state affairs reduces the likelihood of sectarian tension and conflict. By refusing to take sides in religious disputes, the state serves as a neutral arbiter, lowering the risk of confrontation along religious lines. Citizens learn to coexist on the basis of secular values of mutual respect and tolerance, which contributes to social stability and security.

5. **Scientific objectivity in education**

In a strictly secular system, education is freed from religious influence, fostering critical and scientific thinking among the younger generation. Schools and universities become spaces dedicated to objective knowledge, verifiable facts, and tested methods of inquiry. This strengthens the intellectual potential of society, preparing citizens to think rationally, independently, and creatively.

6. **No public expenditure on religion and financial transparency**

Under laïcité, religious institutions receive no state funding. All expenses for worship, clergy, or religious facilities are covered exclusively by voluntary contributions. This ensures both the financial independence of religious groups and the fair use of public resources, while eliminating any suspicion of misuse of taxpayers' money.

7. **Equal protection of religious minorities**

The rigor of secular principles provides reliable protection for minorities against discrimination or pressure from dominant religions. Even small confessions and non-believers are guaranteed equal treatment and legal protection. This strengthens mutual respect and promotes tolerance within society.

Weaknesses of Strict Secularism (Laïcité)

1. **Potential restriction of freedom to express religious identity and traditions**

A rigidly secular approach, designed to enforce neutrality and remove religion from the public sphere, inevitably raises questions about the boundaries of individual liberty. Strict regulations may be perceived by believers as an unfair limitation on their right to express religious identity. For example, bans on wearing religious symbols in public institutions are sometimes viewed not only as constraints on personal expression but also as infringements on cultural and family traditions. Such measures may provoke discontent among those for whom religiosity is an integral part of personal and social life.

2. **High risk of conflict with religious communities**

Radical secularism can trigger direct confrontation between the state and powerful religious organizations with deep social roots. The stricter the effort to remove religion from public life, the more likely believers are to perceive such measures as a threat to their identity and interests. This may result in protests, mass demonstrations, lawsuits, and other forms of conflict, undermining social integration and disturbing the balance of society.

3. Difficulties in societies with high levels of religiosity

Enforcing strict secular policies is particularly challenging in societies where religion is historically intertwined with political, cultural, and social life. Efforts to exclude religion from public space may appear artificial or alien to national traditions. The state must constantly overcome resistance from public opinion and religious institutions, which slows reforms and consumes significant resources.

4. Risk of secularism becoming a rigid ideology

Paradoxically, the uncompromising enforcement of strict secularism can lead to the emergence of a quasi-religious ideology of its own. Secularism ceases to function as a principle of neutrality and instead becomes a dogma that allows no compromise or alternative perspectives. In this case, the state risks becoming as restrictive of freedom as the religious authorities it originally sought to limit.

5. Alienation and marginalization of religious minorities

Excessively strict secularism may contribute to the marginalization and social isolation of religious minorities. Believers who cannot openly express their identity in public may begin to feel estranged from society and its institutions. This can lead to the formation of closed communities detached from the wider cultural and social context, which in turn may heighten social tensions.

6. Underestimation of religion as a social resource

In pursuing strict separation, the state may neglect the constructive role that religious institutions often play in society. Religious communities frequently support vulnerable populations through charity, solidarity, and the cultivation of moral values. By excluding religious organizations from the public sphere, the state risks losing an important channel of social engagement and diminishes its own capacity to address social challenges effectively.

Historical Examples of Strict Secularism (Laïcité)

France (since 1905 to the present)

France is widely regarded as the classical and most consistent example of strict secularism. The decisive turning point was the Law of 1905 on the Separation of Churches and the State, which formally and permanently established the independence of secular state institutions from all religious organizations. Since then, the French Republic has adhered to a strict policy of neutrality, prohibiting religious influence on politics, education, and public administration. Schools, universities, courts, and government offices are entirely free of religious symbols, and teaching is conducted exclusively on secular and scientific principles, without reference to religious doctrines.

French laïcité is not merely a formal declaration of neutrality but an active state policy designed to protect citizens from religious pressure. At the same time, this uncompromising stance has repeatedly led to tensions with religious communities—Catholic, Jewish, and especially Muslim—most notably following the 2004 law banning conspicuous religious symbols in schools and public institutions. Despite ongoing controversies, laïcité remains a cornerstone of French republican identity and is widely regarded as a guarantee of civic equality and social cohesion.

Turkey under Mustafa Kemal Atatürk

After the proclamation of the Turkish Republic by Mustafa Kemal Atatürk in 1923, the country adopted a model of strict secularism inspired by French laïcité. Religion was removed from politics and state administration. Sharia courts were abolished in 1924 and replaced with a secular legal system modeled on European codes, most notably the Swiss Civil Code of 1926. Strict prohibitions were introduced against the use of religious symbols and attire in government offices and educational institutions.

This radical rupture with tradition, however, provoked deep social divisions. Large segments of the population remained committed to Islamic norms and perceived Atatürk's reforms as excessive and even hostile to their way of life. These tensions shaped Turkish politics for decades, producing recurring struggles over the role of religion in public life and leaving a legacy of conflict between secularist and religious forces.

The state's uncompromising stance was reinforced by the military, which regarded itself as the guardian of secularism and intervened repeatedly in politics throughout the twentieth century—in coups of 1960, 1971, 1980, and the so-called "post-modern coup" of 1997. Each intervention was justified as a defense of Atatürk's legacy against what the generals saw as the growing influence of political Islam. Yet despite these measures, Islamic identity and practice continued to shape society, especially in rural areas and among conservative groups, laying the groundwork for the eventual rise of parties such as the Justice and Development Party (AKP) in the early twenty-first century.

Mexico (from 1917 onwards)

Mexico represents another notable case of strict secularism, established by the revolutionary Constitution of 1917. Article 130 codified the separation of church and state in particularly uncompromising terms. Religious institutions were stripped of legal personality, denied the right to own property beyond places of worship, and prohibited from engaging in political activity or education. Clergy were barred from voting or holding public office, and the formation of monastic orders was forbidden.

The anticlerical provisions were enforced with particular rigor under President Plutarco Elías Calles in the 1920s, culminating in the Cristero War (1926–1929), an armed uprising of Catholic groups against the secular state. Although the rebellion was eventually suppressed, it left a lasting scar on Mexican society and highlighted the intense conflict that radical secularism could provoke.

Over the course of the twentieth century, Mexico gradually moderated its policies, restoring limited rights to religious institutions. Yet the constitutional principle of secularism remained firmly in place, and public education and state institutions continue to operate on a strictly secular basis.

Chapter 2

Moderately Secular State:
Limited Religious Influence within a Primarily Secular Framework

> **Moderate secularism** is a form of state organization in which religion is institutionally separated from political authority, yet continues to be recognized as an important element of cultural and social life.

Characteristics of a Moderately Secular State

A moderately secular state maintains neutrality toward religious communities while allowing cooperation with them in areas such as education, social welfare, culture, and moral life. In such a system, religion is not a source of law or political authority, yet religious traditions and values may exercise a limited influence on public policy and government decisions.

Moderate secularism is characterized by a flexible and balanced approach to the separation of religion from state power. This model permits religion to contribute to cultural life, public events, and educational programs, while the state firmly preserves its neutrality and prevents any single faith from dominating or enjoying exclusive privileges.

Main Features of a Moderately Secular State

1) Flexibility and moderation in the separation of religion and state

Unlike the strict model of laïcité, moderate secularism permits limited but explicit interaction with religious organizations. The state recognizes the social importance of religion without removing it entirely from public life. At the same time, it maintains neutrality and prevents any one religion from dominating. Constructive and mutually beneficial partnerships may therefore exist between state institutions and religious communities.

2) Allowance for moderate religious influence on public life, culture, and education

Religious values and traditions may find expression in public life through holidays, national celebrations, and social initiatives. In education, religion may be taught as part of cultural and historical heritage, and elective courses on world religions may be included in school programs. However, the direct promotion of any particular faith is excluded. Public schools must ensure objectivity, equal treatment, and respect for all students regardless of belief.

3) State neutrality with limited support for traditional religions

Government institutions avoid interfering in the internal affairs of religious organizations. Nevertheless, moderate financial or organizational support may be provided to traditional religions that are historically linked to national culture. This support is strictly regulated by law and conditioned on equality and non-discrimination toward all other religions and non-believers.

4) No strict prohibition on public displays of religiosity

Citizens may wear or display religious attire and symbols in public spaces, including schools and state institutions, as long as this does not infringe on public order or the rights of others. This principle balances freedom of religious expression with the broader commitment to secular governance.

5) Recognition of religious holidays at the state level

Some traditional religious holidays may be granted the status of official public holidays, reflecting their cultural significance and preserving national identity. Such recognition affirms the role of religion as part of the historical and cultural heritage of the nation.

6) Permissibility of religious symbols in public institutions under conditions of neutrality

Religious symbols may be displayed in public institutions when they are understood primarily as cultural or historical emblems rather than instruments of religious propaganda. No single religion is favored, and all displays are subject to the principle of neutrality.

7) Cooperation with religious organizations in social and charitable spheres

The state collaborates with religious groups in areas such as welfare provision, healthcare, humanitarian aid, and community service. This cooperation allows governments to harness the resources and networks of religious institutions while maintaining neutrality and equality in public policy.

8) Recognition of religion as a source of moral and cultural authority

Moderate secularism accepts that religious organizations may contribute to public debates as moral voices on issues such as social justice, bioethics, or the environment. While they do not legislate, their perspectives are considered part of a pluralistic civil discourse.

9) Symbolic role of religion in national identity

In some moderately secular states, religion retains a symbolic function—for example, the coronation of the British monarch in Westminster Abbey or references to God in American oaths. Such elements are treated as traditions of national heritage rather than confessional impositions.

10) Legal guarantees of freedom of religion and belief

Moderate secularism emphasizes not only state neutrality but also the active legal protection of freedom of conscience. Laws explicitly prohibit discrimination on religious grounds and safeguard both the right to practice religion and the right not to practice any religion.

11) Institutionalized cooperation between state and religious organizations

Many moderately secular systems establish formal agreements with religious communities—for example, concordats in Italy or church treaties in Germany—regulating matters such as religious education, healthcare chaplaincy, or marriage law.

These arrangements are legally framed to ensure equality, transparency, and respect for pluralism.

Strengths of a Moderately Secular State

1. Maintaining balance between religious traditions and secular values

A moderate model of separation allows the state to preserve a careful equilibrium between secular principles and the religious traditions of society. This balanced stance avoids the extremes characteristic of more radical approaches and creates conditions for the peaceful coexistence of citizens with diverse beliefs. It enables society to integrate religious elements naturally into cultural and public life while preventing coercion or dominance by either religious organizations or the state.

2. Reducing the risk of conflict with religious communities

By adopting a flexible and open approach to cooperation, the state reduces the likelihood of tension with religious groups. Believers do not perceive government as a hostile force intent on expelling religion from public life. Instead, constructive dialogue and partnership between state institutions and religious organizations foster trust, stability, and social peace.

3. Acknowledging historical and cultural traditions

Moderate secularism allows the state to respect and incorporate long-established religious and cultural practices. This helps preserve national identity and continuity across generations, while maintaining social stability and cultural cohesion.

4. Enhancing social integration and civic unity

Allowing moderate religious influence in public life strengthens the inclusion of diverse groups, including minorities, in civic life. Citizens feel that their cultural and religious roots are respected, which increases loyalty to the state and encourages active participation in public and political life.

5. Effective use of the social resources of religious organizations

Cooperation with religious groups enables the state to mobilize their resources and networks in addressing social challenges. Religious communities often maintain extensive infrastructures and hold moral authority among the population, which can amplify the effectiveness of welfare programs, charity, and humanitarian aid.

6. Ensuring a high level of religious freedom

The flexibility of moderate secularism guarantees citizens broad opportunities to express their religious convictions without compromising the state's neutrality. Citizens do not feel restricted in meeting their religious needs and may manifest their beliefs in public, provided this does not infringe on the rights of others or disrupt public order.

7. Fostering tolerance and mutual respect

Because religious communities are recognized as equal participants in public life, society develops an atmosphere of respect, openness, and interfaith tolerance. This reduces the likelihood of sectarian hostility and supports peaceful coexistence and dialogue between believers of different faiths as well as non-believers.

8. Strengthening national identity through symbolic traditions

Moderate secularism makes it possible to preserve symbolic religious elements—such as traditional ceremonies, national holidays, or cultural symbols—without compromising neutrality. These traditions reinforce collective identity and cultural continuity while avoiding religious dominance.

9. Adaptability in diverse societies

Unlike strict secularism, the moderate model adapts more easily to pluralistic societies with multiple religious and ethnic groups. By respecting diversity while maintaining neutrality, the state creates an inclusive framework suitable for multicultural contexts, as seen in countries like India.

Weaknesses of a Moderately Secular State

1. Unclear boundaries between state and religion

The very flexibility that defines this model can also become its weakness, leading to ambiguity in distinguishing the roles of state and religious institutions. Since cooperation and interaction are permitted, the precise limits of influence may be blurred. This often results in difficulties of legal interpretation, disputes about the permissible scope of religious involvement, and recurring court cases.

2. Risk of discrimination against minority religions

By extending moderate recognition or support to religions with deep historical and cultural roots, the state may inadvertently privilege dominant traditions. Smaller or less established religious communities can feel marginalized or unfairly treated, perceiving government actions as biased. This dynamic may produce social tension, weaken trust in public institutions, and foster resentment among minorities.

3. Potential politicization of religion

Allowing moderate religious influence increases the risk of religion being used as a tool of political competition. Politicians and public figures may instrumentalize religious issues to gain electoral support, which invites religious organizations into the political process. In such cases, state policy risks losing its objectivity, eroding public trust, and fueling conflict along political and religious lines.

4. Possibility of expanding religious influence

The absence of strict restrictions may encourage religious organizations to gradually expand their role in education, culture, and social institutions. Over time, this incremental influence could weaken the secular character of the state and its institutions.

5. Limited protection of freedom from religion

In a moderately secular state, the rights of non-religious citizens may receive less protection than in a strictly secular model. Because public manifestations of religion are generally tolerated, individuals who do not adhere to any religion may feel discomfort or experience subtle pressure from traditions indirectly endorsed by public authorities or society at large.

6. Persistent disputes over the meaning of moderation

The flexibility of moderate secularism makes it inherently contested. Societies continually debate what constitutes an acceptable level of state–religion interaction. Disagreements about neutrality, fairness, and the boundaries of moderation often give rise to political conflicts, public controversies, and social polarization.

7. Dependence on historical and cultural context

The effectiveness of moderate secularism relies heavily on national traditions and historical legacies. A model that functions in Britain—where the Anglican Church is institutionally established yet coexists with pluralism—can produce instability in India, where extreme religious diversity generates persistent tension. Moderate secularism is therefore difficult to transplant and vulnerable to shifts in demographic or political conditions.

8. Uneven application of principles

In practice, the balance between religion and state may be implemented inconsistently across regions or institutions. In some areas, religion plays a minimal role, while in others it exerts disproportionate influence. Such asymmetry creates perceptions of double standards and undermines the credibility of secular neutrality.

9. Soft legitimization of religious norms

Because religious traditions are permitted a cultural role, there is a risk that specific religious norms may gradually come to be perceived as shared social values. Even without legal codification, this process can lead to the informal institutionalization of religious practices within public life.

10. Challenges in protecting the rights of women and vulnerable groups

When moderate secularism defers to cultural or religious traditions, it may struggle to safeguard the rights of women and minorities, particularly where religious norms conflict with principles of equality. Balancing respect for tradition with the protection of individual rights can become a persistent challenge.

Historical Examples of Moderately Secular States

Germany (contemporary period)

The German constitution formally guarantees the separation of state and church. In practice, however, Germany has developed a cooperative and pragmatic form of secularism. Its legal foundations rest on the Weimar Constitution of 1919, later carried into the Basic Law of 1949. After the collapse of National Socialism, the new state placed particular emphasis on safeguarding both freedom of religion and democratic pluralism.

This spirit of moderation is most visible in relations with the Catholic and Protestant churches. Through the Kirchensteuer, the state collects a church tax via its fiscal offices, channeling stable resources to the churches while refraining from interference in their internal affairs. Citizens remain free to end their membership and thus their obligation to pay the tax.

Federalism further shapes the religious landscape. Each Land sets its own rules for religious education: Bavaria maintains a strong Catholic tradition; Lower Saxony offers both Catholic and Protestant instruction; Berlin places the emphasis on secular ethics. In every case, participation is optional, and families or students may decide between religion and ethics.

The presence of Muslim communities has brought new discussions about recognition of Islamic organizations, including proposals for introducing Islamic education in public schools. These debates show how the German model adjusts to demographic change.

Religious institutions also serve as major actors in social welfare. Catholic Caritas and Protestant Diakonie stand among the largest providers of health care, education, and humanitarian aid. Although they receive public funds, their work is subject to legal oversight that protects equality and ensures that non-Christian groups are not disadvantaged.

The United States

The First Amendment to the U.S. Constitution (1791) established a strict separation of church and state. Its "no establishment" clause forbids the government from endorsing any religion, while its "free exercise" clause guarantees the right to practice—or not practice—faith. Thomas Jefferson described this principle as a "wall of separation between church and state" in his 1802 letter to the Danbury Baptists. James Madison, in his 1785 Memorial and Remonstrance, argued that liberty of conscience is an inalienable right.

In reality, American secularism has never been absolute. Religion continues to shape culture and politics. Churches and faith-based groups have long been active in education, social services, and civic causes. The civil rights movement of the 1960s, led by Reverend Martin Luther King Jr., remains a striking example of religion as a moral force in public life.

The Supreme Court has drawn the legal boundaries. In Engel v. Vitale (1962), it banned school-sponsored prayer. In Lemon v. Kurtzman (1971), it set criteria—the "Lemon test"—to judge government actions in church–state matters. Yet later rulings, such as Town of Greece v. Galloway (2014), upheld certain religious expressions in public ceremonies, including legislative prayer. These cases show that the line between religion and state is defined through ongoing judicial interpretation.

Education reflects this balance. Public schools exclude confessional instruction but allow the study of world religions and religious history as academic subjects. Private religious schools and universities, meanwhile, are free to shape their curricula according to denominational principles, though without direct state support.

Religion also plays a visible role in politics. Presidents often invoke God in inaugural speeches, and debates on social policy frequently include appeals to moral values rooted in faith. Still, the Constitution ensures neutrality: the state does not favor any belief and protects both religious practice and the choice to live outside religion.

Conclusion
Comparative Analysis of Strict and Moderate Secular Approaches

Strict and moderate forms of secularism differ above all in the role they assign to religion in public life.

The strict model, often called laïcité, demands a complete separation of state and religion. Faith is kept outside politics, education, and civic institutions. The state goes beyond neutrality: it actively safeguards every citizen's right to live free from religious pressure. In this framework, religious groups hold no sway over decision-making, and all citizens stand equal regardless of belief.

The moderate model takes a different path. It permits measured cooperation between state and church, so long as neutrality and equal treatment remain intact. Religious traditions may appear in public ceremonies, cultural events, or even school programs. The state refrains from interfering in church affairs yet may give limited support to religions tied to national history and culture. This arrangement is less rigid, more attuned to context, and often helps to ease social tensions.

These models grew out of distinct histories. French laïcité, codified in the 1905 Law on the Separation of Churches and the State, emerged from fierce battles against clerical privilege and became a safeguard of republican identity. The American approach, anchored in the First Amendment of 1791, was designed to secure freedom of religion while shielding citizens from an official state church. Each reflects a unique answer to the political challenges of its time.

The contrast remains clear. The strict approach guards most firmly against religious influence, but in devout societies it can breed resistance. The moderate approach, by contrast, adapts more readily to cultural realities and tends to preserve stability, even if it risks loosening the boundary between religion and state.

Consequences of Secularization and Religious Neutrality for Society and Politics

Secularization and the principle of religious neutrality have shaped modern societies in several decisive ways:

- they reinforced civic equality, making legal or political discrimination on religious grounds unacceptable;

- they broadened individual freedoms, guaranteeing the right of every person to choose a faith—or to reject religion entirely;

- they eased interconfessional tensions, markedly reducing the frequency of religious conflict in secular states;

- they encouraged tolerance, pluralism, and cultural diversity, supporting the growth of open and inclusive civic life.

Yet in societies with deep-rooted religious traditions, strict secularization has often produced friction. When religion is abruptly excluded from public life, many perceive it as a threat to collective identity. This has led to dissatisfaction and even open conflict between governments and religious communities, forcing state authorities to approach reform with caution and sensitivity.

The contemporary landscape adds further complexity. Migration has introduced new layers of religious diversity, creating challenges of integration and equal treatment. Populist movements increasingly use religious rhetoric for political gain, blurring the line between faith and neutrality. Globalization intensifies cultural encounters, at times fueling renewed religious tensions. These dynamics make clear that secularism is not a fixed formula but a principle that must be continually adjusted to shifting social realities.

Prospects for the Development of Secular States

Most secular states today seek a balance between strict and moderate approaches, shaped by their historical experiences and cultural traditions. Their central task is to uphold the core values of secularism—equality, freedom of conscience, and state neutrality—while also recognizing the religious legacies that have contributed to national identity.

Such a balance is intended to minimize social tensions and lessen the risk of conflict, thereby reinforcing civic stability. At the same time, the protection of individual freedoms and human rights remains a defining priority. This requires states not only to preserve equality and neutrality in religious matters but also to strengthen the guarantees behind them, addressing with care the diversity of both religious and non-religious worldviews. Safeguarding the rights of minorities on equal terms with those of majorities will continue to pose a central challenge.

Looking forward, several trends stand out. Multiculturalism will demand new forms of accommodation between secular institutions and a wide range of faiths. The rise of religious individualism—more people identifying outside traditional confessions—will push states to reconsider how freedom of conscience is secured. Digitalization opens new arenas for religious expression and debate, enriching public discourse yet sometimes deepening divisions. And the growing weight of international human rights norms will place additional pressure on states to guarantee freedom of religion and belief while ensuring equality across society.

SECTION 2. RELIGIOUS STATE — POLITICAL AUTHORITY SHAPED BY RELIGIOUS DOCTRINE

> **Religious state** — a form of government in which religion occupies a central place in the political system, defines legislative norms, and exerts dominant influence over public life.

Introduction

A religious state is characterized by the absolute dominance of a single religion in political, social, and cultural life. In such a system, political and legal decisions are based on religious dogmas and sacred texts, while religious institutions are closely intertwined with organs of power, exerting significant influence on education, culture, and the everyday lives of citizens.

Main Features of a Religious State

1) An official state religion with privileged status

In a religious state, one particular religion is formally recognized as the state religion. It enjoys a dominant position in society, receives institutional support and funding, and often plays a decisive role in shaping national identity, cultural norms, and social traditions.

2) Strong influence of religious institutions and leaders on politics

Religious leaders and organizations hold significant authority, often participating directly in policymaking. Their views can shape legislation, foreign policy, and internal governance. In some systems, religious figures are granted official or informal powers that allow them to intervene in crucial matters of state.

3) Integration of religious law into the legal system

Religious texts, commandments, and doctrines become the foundation of the legal order. Family law, criminal law, and civil codes are shaped by religious prescriptions. As a result, everyday life is governed by rules drawn directly from sacred sources.

4) Mandatory teaching of the state religion in education

Schools and universities are required to include instruction in the official religion as a core component of their curricula. Educational standards are shaped by religious principles, and the state ensures that religious knowledge is passed on to younger generations. In practice, this often means compulsory courses, examinations on religious texts, and close supervision by state-appointed clerics to guarantee uniformity of teaching..

5) Restrictions on freedom of conscience and belief

While freedom of religion may be declared in theory, in practice religious minorities and non-believers face legal or social restrictions. Their rights are often limited compared to adherents of the state religion, and they may experience discrimination or pressure to conform.

6) Direct state financing of religious institutions

Religious organizations receive significant support from the state budget, including funds for the construction and maintenance of places of worship, salaries for clergy, religious schools, charitable programs, and religious festivals. In many cases, this financial backing gives religious authorities a privileged status in society, reinforcing their influence over politics, education, and public life.

7) Use of religious symbols in government institutions

Courts, schools, administrative offices, and other public buildings prominently display the symbols of the dominant religion. These symbols often become part of national emblems and state ceremonies, reinforcing the fusion of religion and political authority.

8) Mandatory observance of religious norms in public life

Citizens are required to follow religious rules in their daily behavior. Dress codes, dietary restrictions, and gender relations in public may all be enforced by law. Violations can result in legal penalties or social condemnation, with the state acting as guardian of religious orthodoxy.

9) Fusion of political and religious legitimacy

Political authority is often justified through religious doctrine. Leaders may claim divine sanction for their rule, and legitimacy is tied not only to legal institutions but also to adherence to religious principles.

10) Suppression of secularism and alternative worldviews

Religious states typically view secular ideologies, humanism, or competing belief systems as threats to their authority. As a result, freedom of expression and academic inquiry may be curtailed whenever they conflict with the official faith.

The Influence of Religion on Law, Politics, and Social Life in a Religious State

In a religious state, religion becomes the central organizing principle that permeates virtually every sphere of public life. Its influence is especially visible in the legal, political, and social domains, shaping the relationship between citizens and the state, defining social norms, and reinforcing cultural traditions.

1. Religious influence on the legal system

The legal system of a religious state is largely based on religious norms, sacred texts, and theological teachings. Religious commandments provide the foundation of legislation, regulating key aspects of social relations such as marriage and family law, inheritance, property rights, criminal justice, and standards of moral behavior. Religious courts are often employed, and judges drawn from the clergy or religious authorities interpret and apply the law. As a result, religious morality is transformed into legally binding norms that govern the daily lives of all citizens.

2. Religious influence on politics

Religion and religious institutions play a decisive role in political life. Policy decisions and legislative initiatives are shaped in accordance with religious principles and values. Clergy may exert direct influence through holding official positions in government or indirect influence by serving as powerful advisors to political leaders. In this way, the direction of state policy is aligned with religious doctrines and the interests of dominant religious communities.

3. Religious influence on social life and culture

Religious values and traditions define the everyday life of citizens. Social relations, moral standards, and patterns of behavior are drawn from religious teachings. Rules concerning family life, personal conduct, and public interaction are often strictly regulated. Dress codes, dietary restrictions, and gender relations may all be enforced by law or social custom. Cultural life is infused with religious festivals, rituals, and traditions, which serve both to strengthen social cohesion and to reinforce a shared cultural identity.

4. Religious influence on education and upbringing

Mandatory religious education is a hallmark of religious states. Curricula at schools and universities are shaped by sacred texts and religious teachings. Education is not only about knowledge but also about cultivating moral character in accordance with religious principles. The state strictly supervises religious instruction, ensuring the transmission of religious values to younger generations and reinforcing the religious identity of society. In addition, teachers are often required to undergo special training in theology, and textbooks must be approved by religious authorities before they can be used in classrooms.

5. Religious influence on social institutions and charity

Religious organizations often control large parts of the welfare system, including schools, hospitals, and charitable institutions. Governments delegate authority and resources to them, further enhancing their social role. Charity and assistance to the poor are regarded not merely as civic duties but as religious obligations of both citizens and the state. This strengthens solidarity and social stability, while also consolidating the influence of religious institutions in everyday life. In many cases, religious charities operate with tax exemptions and state subsidies, allowing them to expand their reach and become indispensable providers of social support.

6. Religion as the foundation of national and cultural identity

Religion serves as the bedrock of national identity and historical continuity. State symbols, public ceremonies, and national holidays frequently derive from religious traditions. Religious heritage is presented as part of the nation's cultural DNA, linking past and present and fostering collective consciousness. In this sense, religion functions not only as a spiritual authority but also as a powerful instrument of cultural integration and national unity. In many states, this connection is institutionalized through constitutional references to the dominant faith, mandatory oaths taken on sacred texts, and the use of religious rituals to inaugurate political leaders.

Chapter 1

Islamic State:
Governance Based on Islamic Law (Sharia) and Principles

An Islamic state is a political system in which the entire structure of governance, law, and public life is grounded in Islamic law (Sharia).

Main Features of an Islamic State

1) Supremacy of Islamic law (Sharia)

The foundation of an Islamic state is the primacy of Sharia as the highest source of law and governance. Drawn from the Qur'an and the Sunnah—the recorded traditions of the Prophet Muhammad—Sharia regulates legal, social, and moral life: family law, inheritance, criminal justice, economic transactions, banking, and codes of conduct. In such a system, Sharia serves as the binding authority for legislation, judicial decisions, and the daily obligations of citizens.

2) Authority of religious leaders (the ulama) in governance

Religious scholars and clerics hold decisive influence over political life. This role may be formal, as in the Islamic Republic of Iran where the Supreme Leader has ultimate authority, or informal, through sustained influence on policymaking. The ulama act as guardians of religious compliance, shaping legislative, executive, and judicial practice.

3) Social and legal norms shaped by Islamic tradition

Standards of behavior and legal codes reflect Islamic prescriptions. Public morality is closely regulated: religious rules guide dress codes, gender relations, social interaction, and family upbringing. Religious teachings therefore define both private conduct and the public sphere.

4) Compulsory Islamic education

Religious instruction is obligatory at all stages of schooling. Curricula emphasize the Qur'an, Islamic doctrine, and moral principles, with the aim of instilling faith, reinforcing religious values, and strengthening Islamic identity among younger generations.

5) State support of Islamic institutions

The state funds and protects mosques, madrasas, Islamic universities, and charitable organizations. Supporting these institutions is regarded as both a religious and civic duty, integrating religion into governance and consolidating collective identity.

6) Use of Islamic symbols in state institutions

Government offices, courts, schools, and national ceremonies frequently display Islamic symbols and rituals. Public holidays and ceremonies follow religious patterns, reinforcing the identity of the state as distinctly Islamic and linking political authority with religious heritage.

7) Restrictions on other religions

Religious minorities may be recognized legally but usually face limitations. Their activities are monitored, missionary work is forbidden, and the construction of non-Muslim places of worship may be restricted. Religious pluralism exists within boundaries set and controlled by the state.

8) Enforcement of Islamic norms

Institutions such as Sharia courts and religious police ensure compliance with Islamic codes. Violations—ranging from dress requirements to dietary rules—can result in legal penalties. Moral precepts thus carry the force of law.

9) Fusion of political and religious legitimacy

Political leadership is closely tied to religious authority. Leaders may claim—or be perceived as holding—divine sanction, presenting themselves as protectors of the faith. Legitimacy rests not only on constitutional law but also on religious adherence.

10) Religion in foreign policy

Foreign relations often reflect religious identity and solidarity. Islamic states may align with other Muslim-majority countries, support pan-Islamic causes, or frame diplomacy in religious terms, extending Islamic principles beyond domestic governance to the international sphere.

Strengths of an Islamic State

1. Social cohesion rooted in shared faith

Grounded in a common religion and spiritual values, an Islamic state fosters strong solidarity and collective identity. Citizens see themselves as part of a single community, united by belief. Religion thus works as a powerful force of cohesion, reinforcing stability and reducing the risk of division.

2. A clear moral and legal framework

Sharia provides a comprehensive code governing both private and public life. By setting clear boundaries of what is allowed and forbidden, it reduces uncertainty, discourages unlawful conduct, and sustains order in society.

3. Perceived legitimacy of the judiciary

Courts that apply religious law enjoy broad acceptance among the faithful. Since Sharia is regarded as divinely inspired, judicial rulings are viewed as fair and authoritative. This perception enhances respect for the law and strengthens the authority of the courts.

4. Legitimacy of political authority

Rulers who ground their authority in religion are often seen as protectors of the community's spiritual values. This religious foundation builds trust in government and lends weight to its decisions.

5. Extensive welfare and charity networks

Islamic states maintain strong traditions of social support rooted in religious duty. Obligations such as zakat (alms tax), along with voluntary charity (sadaqah), provide assistance for the poor and vulnerable. This institutionalized solidarity alleviates poverty and reinforces social bonds.

6. Moral regulation in public life

By enforcing Islamic codes of conduct—such as modest dress, bans on alcohol, and restrictions on corrupt practices—the state promotes discipline and seeks to limit crime or harmful behavior. These standards aim to safeguard community values and public order.

7. Preservation of cultural and historical identity

Anchoring social and political life in Islam helps preserve long-standing traditions and protect national heritage. Religious rituals, festivals, and values secure cultural continuity across generations.

8. A shared sense of mission

An Islamic state often frames its community as united by a higher spiritual and political calling. This collective purpose strengthens motivation, mobilization, and common effort.

9. Discipline and solidarity

Religious principles, combined with the authority of the state, foster not only compliance with the law but also voluntary adherence to moral norms. This promotes trust among citizens and encourages a cooperative ethos.

10. Economic principles aimed at justice

Islamic economic teachings—such as the prohibition of usury (riba) and the encouragement of fair trade and redistribution—seek to prevent exploitation and promote equity. Advocates argue that these principles can support a more balanced and responsible economy.

Weaknesses of an Islamic State

1. Restricted freedoms for minorities

In states that apply Sharia strictly, personal freedoms and civil rights are curtailed, especially for those outside the dominant religion. Religious and cultural minorities often face limits on worship, public rituals, and cultural expression, resulting in marginalization and discrimination.

2. Risks to human rights

The dominance of religious law creates vulnerabilities for fundamental rights. Freedom of speech, conscience, and belief is often curtailed. Criticism of religious authorities may be criminalized, and dissenting voices suppressed.

3. Limited pluralism

Built around one dominant faith, Islamic states tend to exclude or downplay minority perspectives. This restricts pluralism, undermines intercultural dialogue, and complicates inclusive citizenship in diverse societies.

4. Dependence on religious authorities

Clerics and scholars wield strong influence over politics and law. This dependence can weaken secular institutions, restrict civil society, and block reforms toward more democratic or pluralist governance.

5. Rigidity of traditional norms

Because many Sharia rules stem from centuries-old texts, they may be hard to align with modern realities. A lack of mechanisms for reform often leaves states caught between strict adherence, which can hinder progress, and efforts at change, which meet resistance from conservatives.

6. Economic constraints

Restrictions on banking and commerce based on religious norms complicate integration into global markets. These limitations reduce competitiveness and make adaptation to modern financial systems difficult.

7. Social tensions

Strict enforcement of religious codes can provoke unrest, particularly among younger or more secular citizens seeking personal freedom. Conflicts between conservatives and progressives may escalate, undermining cohesion.

8. Suppression of intellectual freedom

Scholarship, philosophy, and the arts are often subject to censorship. Limits on critical inquiry stifle innovation, slow scientific progress, and reduce exposure to alternative ideas.

9. Strained international relations

Reliance on religious law frequently clashes with international legal norms, especially human rights standards. This complicates diplomacy, reduces cooperation, and may lead to isolation.

10. Risk of radicalization

When religion dominates politics and education, conditions can arise that foster fanaticism. Extremist movements may gain ground, threatening internal security and regional stability.

11. Economic dependence on resources

Because financial restrictions limit diversification, many Islamic states rely heavily on resource exports, particularly oil and gas. This dependence leaves them vulnerable to global price fluctuations and long-term instability.

12. Gender inequality

In many Sharia-based systems, women face restricted access to education, politics, and economic life. Unequal treatment in inheritance or legal testimony perpetuates systemic inequality and limits human capital.

13. Obstacles to modernization

Rigid adherence to traditional norms, combined with restrictions on intellectual freedom, hinders adaptation to technological and social change. This slows cultural development and reduces global competitiveness.

<u>Historical Examples of an Islamic State</u>

Iran (1979–Present)

The Islamic Republic of Iran emerged from the 1979 Revolution, which overthrew the Pahlavi monarchy of Shah Mohammad Reza. Led by Ayatollah Ruhollah Khomeini, the movement blended religious, political, and anti-imperialist elements, rejecting Western influence and establishing a new government rooted in Islamic principles.

At the heart of the republic lies the doctrine of Wilayat al-Faqih (Guardianship of the Jurist). This principle grants ultimate authority to a qualified Islamic jurist, who acts as guardian of both state and religion. It sets Iran apart from other Islamic states by institutionalizing direct clerical rule.

The Supreme Leader (Rahbar) occupies the highest position, combining spiritual and political power. Selected by the clerical Assembly of Experts, he holds sweeping authority: appointing senior officials, overseeing the armed forces, directing the judiciary, supervising state media, and guiding religious institutions.

Iran's political structure combines elected and clerical bodies. Institutions such as the president and parliament (Majlis) operate alongside the Guardian Council and the Assembly of Experts. The Guardian Council—half of whose members are appointed by the Supreme Leader—reviews all legislation for compliance with Sharia and the constitution. Without its approval, no law takes effect. This dual system ensures that clerical authority prevails over democratic institutions.

Coercive power rests not only in traditional state organs but also in revolutionary structures. The Islamic Revolutionary Guard Corps (IRGC) functions as both a military and political force, charged with defending the system and maintaining order. Alongside it stands the Basij militia, a mass volunteer organization enforcing moral codes and suppressing dissent. Together, these bodies secure the regime's control.

Iran's legal order is firmly grounded in Sharia. Family, criminal, and civil law are derived from Islamic sources, and Sharia courts handle most cases. Punishments prescribed by religious law are applied in criminal justice, while regulations shape family life, gender relations, and public morality. Mandatory dress codes, including the hijab for women, are legally enforced.

Religion permeates social and cultural life. Media, literature, cinema, and the arts are censored when judged contrary to Islamic principles. Education is infused with religion: Qur'anic studies, Islamic ethics, and Islamic history are compulsory at all levels, with curricula tightly supervised to maintain doctrinal conformity.

Religious institutions benefit from state patronage. Mosques, madrasas, and charities receive government funding and play a central role in welfare, healthcare, and social services. Religious symbols mark state institutions, ceremonies, and public events, reinforcing the Islamic identity of the republic.

In foreign policy, Iran positions itself as the leader of the global Shi'a community. It supports movements abroad, including Hezbollah in Lebanon and Shi'a groups in Iraq, Syria, and Yemen. This orientation has brought Tehran into confrontation with the United States, Israel, and Sunni-majority states in the Gulf.

The constitution recognizes certain religious minorities—Christians, Jews, and Zoroastrians—but their rights are restricted. Missionary work is banned, the construction of new non-Islamic places of worship is limited, and minorities face systemic discrimination.

Despite its theocratic framework, Iran has witnessed repeated waves of protest: student demonstrations in 1999, the Green Movement of 2009, economic protests in 2019–20, and the mass uprising in 2022 after the death of Mahsa Amini, sparked by opposition to compulsory hijab laws and broader repression. These movements reveal the gap between the state's religious order and the aspirations of a younger, more secular generation.

Economically, Iran remains heavily dependent on oil and gas exports. International sanctions imposed by the United States, the European Union, and the United Nations have severely constrained growth, exacerbating economic challenges.

Iran today stands as the most prominent modern example of an Islamic state, where Sharia serves as supreme law, clerical authority dominates politics, and religion shapes culture, education, and social order.

Saudi Arabia

In Saudi Arabia, Sharia is codified as the supreme source of law and forms the foundation of the legal system, shaping both public and private life.

The King serves simultaneously as secular and religious leader, combining political authority with responsibility for enforcing Islamic law. The monarchy derives its legitimacy from strict adherence to Sharia and the support of the religious establishment. Policies and legislation are adopted in consultation with clerics, ensuring alignment with Islamic principles.

Religious institutions and scholars (ulama) hold decisive influence. They advise the king and government, oversee the judiciary, and issue fatwas that guide both state policy and social behavior. The courts apply Sharia in criminal, family, and civil law, enforcing moral codes, dress regulations, and gender relations. Their rulings carry ultimate legal authority, confirming the primacy of religion in governance.

Social and cultural life reflects Islamic prescriptions. The state regulates expression in media, literature, and the arts, requiring conformity with religious rules. Public morality is mandatory for all residents, and violations may bring legal or social sanctions.

Education is likewise shaped by Islam. Qur'anic studies, Islamic ethics, and history are compulsory in schools and universities, with curricula closely supervised by religious authorities to maintain doctrinal conformity.

The state actively supports mosques, madrasas, universities, and charities, funding religious, educational, and welfare activities. This patronage consolidates the monarchy's authority and fosters stability by reinforcing religious identity. Islamic symbols mark official institutions, ceremonies, and public spaces, embedding religion into the fabric of governance.

Other religions are strictly restricted. Missionary activity is banned, non-Islamic worship is not permitted in public, and freedom of conscience for minorities or non-religious citizens is severely limited.

Historical foundations. The Saudi state traces its identity to the eighteenth-century alliance between the House of Saud and Muhammad ibn Abd al-Wahhab, founder of Wahhabism. This partnership created a compact in which the monarchy ruled with clerical support, while the religious establishment legitimized authority by insisting on strict observance of Islam. This alliance remains central to the Saudi political order.

Modern reforms. Under Crown Prince Mohammed bin Salman, the kingdom has introduced limited changes through the Vision 2030 program. While Sharia remains the basis of law, reforms have reduced the power of the religious police, expanded women's rights—including the right to drive and broader participation in public life—and reopened cultural spaces such as cinemas and concerts. These steps aim to diversify the economy and present a more moderate image abroad, while remaining within the framework of Islamic governance.

International role. Saudi Arabia enjoys unique authority as custodian of Islam's two holiest cities, Mecca and Medina. This role grants the monarchy immense symbolic weight in the Muslim world. The annual Hajj pilgrimage, organized by the state, demonstrates both religious duty and Saudi Arabia's central position in global Islam. Combined with its vast oil reserves and leadership within the Organization of Islamic Cooperation (OIC), the kingdom wields both religious and geopolitical influence worldwide.

Chapter 2

Christian State:
Governance Influenced by Christian Traditions and Moral Teachings

A **Christian state** is a political system in which the legal and social order is grounded in Christian values, traditions, and principles.

Main Features of a Christian State

1) Law and society shaped by Christian principles

The legal and social order of a Christian state rests on Christian moral values. Legislation reflects ideals of justice, mercy, and family life rooted in Christian teaching. Laws on marriage, family, and child-rearing are presented as expressions of the nation's moral foundation.

2) State support for churches and institutions

Christian states grant official recognition and material support to churches and religious organizations. Governments may fund the upkeep of cathedrals, monasteries, and historic sites, while extending privileges such as subsidies or tax exemptions. This backing secures the church's role in society and preserves religious infrastructure.

3) Clergy in public and political life

Religious leaders often act as advisors to state officials, shaping legislation, social policy, and moral debate. They serve as public voices on key issues, guiding opinion and reinforcing shared values within society.

4) Christian education as state policy

Schools and universities may include courses on Christian doctrine, ethics, and history. The state also supports Christian schools and universities, providing funding or legal advantages. Education thus seeks not only to impart knowledge but also to instill Christian values in younger generations.

5) Christian symbols in institutions and ceremonies

Crosses, icons, and other religious images appear in courts, schools, and government offices. National holidays, official ceremonies, and public events incorporate Christian rituals, emphasizing the religious character of the state.

6) Recognition of Christian holidays

Major holy days such as Christmas and Easter are observed as national holidays, underscoring their civic importance and ensuring participation across society.

7) Privileges over other religions

Although freedom of religion may be declared, Christianity typically enjoys a privileged position. Minority religions often face legal or administrative barriers to building places of worship, registering communities, or practicing openly.

8) National identity tied to Christian heritage

In many Christian states, national symbols, cultural traditions, and historical narratives are interpreted through a Christian lens. Citizenship and faith are closely linked, reinforcing loyalty to the state while often marginalizing non-Christian citizens.

Strengths of a Christian State

1. Cultural unity and shared moral vision

A Christian state fosters cohesion by grounding society in common spiritual and cultural traditions. Shared values and ethical principles provide citizens with a unifying worldview, reinforcing solidarity and strengthening national identity. With common moral reference points, internal disagreements are easier to manage and divisions are less likely to escalate.

2. Legitimacy of law and institutions

When legislation and social norms are anchored in Christian traditions, institutions gain durability and public trust. Laws informed by Christian morality are widely regarded as fair and authoritative, which strengthens confidence in governance and supports social order.

3. Commitment to welfare and charity

Christian states often integrate social care with religious duty. Governments and churches cooperate to provide assistance for the poor, the elderly, and the sick. These efforts, understood as both civic responsibility and religious obligation, reduce poverty, ease inequality, and enhance the quality of life.

4. Promotion of personal responsibility and morality

Christian ethics emphasize honesty, diligence, compassion, and mutual respect. Policies inspired by these principles encourage responsible conduct in both private and public life, improving civic culture and interpersonal relations.

5. Preservation of heritage

States rooted in Christianity invest in maintaining their religious and cultural heritage. Funding is directed toward the restoration of churches, monasteries, and historic monuments. These projects preserve traditions, reinforce continuity, and nurture a shared cultural identity.

6. Consistency and predictability of policy

Policies guided by long-standing moral standards tend to be stable and coherent. Decisions appear reasonable and fair to citizens, reducing uncertainty and contributing to political stability.

7. Community-oriented ethics

Beyond state structures, Christian principles encourage solidarity, mutual assistance, and service to others. This culture of care fosters trust among citizens and strengthens bonds between communities and institutions.

Weaknesses of a Christian State

1. Restrictions on minorities and secular citizens

When public policy rests on Christian traditions, conditions become less favorable for citizens of other faiths or with secular views. These groups may feel excluded from cultural and political life, leading to inequality and discrimination. Over time, such marginalization can erode trust in state institutions and deepen divisions within society.

2. Risk of religious conflict

Visible state support for Christian institutions can appear unjust to followers of other religions, who may interpret such policies as clear signals of exclusion. These perceptions often foster alienation and resentment, gradually weakening the bonds of mutual trust that hold diverse societies together. In some cases, dissatisfaction remains silent but pervasive, while in others it escalates into open conflict, eroding the stability of the political system itself.

3. Politicization of religion

Active involvement of clergy in politics carries the danger of religion being used as an instrument of power rather than a source of moral guidance. Political leaders may employ Christian rhetoric to bolster their authority, manipulate public opinion, or delegitimize their opponents under the guise of defending faith. Over time, this instrumentalization erodes the moral standing of the church itself, turning spiritual authority into a political tool.

4. Resistance to social change

Reliance on traditional Christian values can hinder the processes of modernization and adaptation. Conservative religious institutions frequently resist reforms that challenge established doctrines, slowing down society's response to new cultural, scientific, and technological realities. Such resistance not only delays necessary social change but also restricts the state's ability to address urgent challenges—ranging from human rights to bioethics and digital innovation.

5. Limits on pluralism

Favoring a single religion narrows opportunities for diversity. Over time, society may grow less open to alternative perspectives, weakening its resilience and limiting cultural innovation.

6. Erosion of boundaries between church and state

Close ties between political authority and religious institutions can compromise the independence of both. Blending sacred and secular authority reduces accountability, weakens democratic freedoms, and risks binding the church to the struggles of state power. In the long run, this entanglement can damage the credibility of religion and the legitimacy of the state alike.

Historical Examples of a Christian State

The Vatican

The Vatican City is the smallest state in the world, yet a unique embodiment of a Christian polity in the modern age. Its sovereignty was secured by the Lateran Treaty of 1929, which resolved the long-standing "Roman Question" and granted the Holy See full independence after the Papal States were lost in 1870. Within its 44 hectares live fewer than a thousand residents, almost all directly engaged in service to the Catholic Church.

At the center of this city-state stands the Pope, elected for life by the College of Cardinals in conclave. He unites spiritual leadership of the universal Church with temporal authority as sovereign of the Vatican. His powers are extensive: he enacts laws, appoints officials, directs diplomacy, and safeguards Catholic doctrine. The Fundamental Law of Vatican City State, most recently revised in 2023, outlines the structure of this distinctive theocratic monarchy.

The legal system rests entirely on canon law. Regulations concerning governance, the duties of clergy, and the moral life of residents derive directly from Catholic teaching. State institutions such as the Secretariat of State and the Roman Curia are staffed by clergy, reflecting the complete fusion of religious and political authority.

Catholic ritual and symbolism define the rhythm of public life. Religious festivals and ceremonies mark the calendar, education is shaped by theology, philosophy, and church history, and culture reflects the spiritual heritage of Catholicism. Beyond its walls, the Vatican speaks as the center of faith for over 1.3 billion Catholics, organizing events such as the Second Vatican Council (1962–1965) and major canonizations with global resonance.

The Vatican is also a repository of art and learning. St. Peter's Basilica, begun in 1506 and consecrated in 1626, rises above the traditional tomb of the Apostle Peter. The Sistine Chapel, where popes are elected, preserves Michelangelo's ceiling (1508–1512) and his Last Judgment (1536–1541). In 2024, more than 6.8 million visitors came to the Vatican Museums, placing them among the most visited in the world. The Vatican Library, founded in the 15th century, holds one of the richest manuscript collections, while the Vatican Observatory underscores the Church's engagement with science.

The Vatican's influence reaches far beyond its territory. Since 1964, the Holy See has been a Permanent Observer at the United Nations and today maintains diplomatic relations with more than 180 states, often serving as a mediator in international disputes.

Economically, the Vatican does not rely on taxation but on donations from the faithful—including Peter's Pence—as well as revenue from its museums, publishing, postage, and coinage. Since 2002, it has used the euro, issuing limited-edition coins that are highly valued by collectors.

The Vatican stands as a monument of faith and history, where spiritual authority and temporal power are fused in a single center of governance. Its voice, rising from the heart of Rome, continues to resonate across the Catholic world and the global stage.

The Byzantine Empire (4th–15th centuries)

The Byzantine Empire inherited the structures of Rome while reshaping them on Christian foundations. In 313 CE, the Edict of Milan issued by Constantine the Great legalized Christianity, and in 330 he founded a new imperial capital, Constantinople, the "New Rome." Christianity gained official supremacy after the Edict of Thessalonica in 380, when Theodosius I declared Nicene Christianity the sole religion of the empire. From that point, Byzantium became the first enduring Christian commonwealth.

The emperor was regarded not only as a ruler but as the "anointed of God." His authority carried both political and spiritual weight: he defended the faith, protected the Church, and was expected to embody Christian morality in governance. Patriarchs and bishops acted as imperial advisors, shaping policy, diplomacy, war, and the great councils that defined Christian dogma.

The principle of symphonia—harmony between Church and state—structured the Byzantine order. Emperor and Church cooperated in maintaining a unified Christian society, though the emperor retained ultimate supremacy in both secular and religious matters.

The empire became the stage for decisive theological debates. Emperors convened many ecumenical councils, from Nicaea in 325 CE to Chalcedon in 451 CE, where controversies over Christology and heresy were addressed. These decisions shaped Christian theology for East and West alike.

Law and governance reflected Christian ideals. Justinian I (527–565) codified Roman law in the Corpus Juris Civilis, preserving Roman jurisprudence while infusing it with Christian ethics. Legislation on marriage, inheritance, and care for widows, orphans, and the poor showed how law became an instrument of justice and moral duty before God.

Ritual and symbolism defined public life. Festivals, liturgies, and ceremonies structured the calendar. Hagia Sophia, built between 532 and 537 under Justinian, embodied imperial piety and architectural ambition. Icons and mosaics filled churches and palaces, though their place in worship was fiercely disputed during the Iconoclast Controversy (726–843), which ultimately reaffirmed the veneration of holy images.

Education and culture were grounded in Christian tradition. The University of Constantinople, founded in 425 CE, trained scholars in theology, philosophy, law, and classical literature. Monasteries preserved manuscripts and transmitted both sacred texts and the intellectual heritage of antiquity.

Yet the fusion of religion and politics carried costs. Pagans, heretics, Jews, and later Muslims often faced discrimination. Theological disputes—such as the Monophysite controversy—divided society, while tensions with Western Christendom culminated in the Great Schism of 1054. Later, the Fourth Crusade and the sack of Constantinople in 1204 inflicted deep wounds, weakening the empire and altering its course permanently.

England under the Tudors (16th century)

Tudor England exemplified the model of a Christian state in which crown and church were inseparable. This transformation unfolded under Henry VIII (1509–1547) and Elizabeth I (1558–1603).

Henry VIII, once honored by the Pope as Defender of the Faith for opposing Luther, broke with Rome after his request for annulment was denied. The Act of Supremacy (1534) declared him Supreme Head of the Church of England, merging secular and spiritual authority. The Dissolution of the Monasteries (1536–1541) transferred vast church lands to the crown, reshaping society and strengthening royal power. From this point, the king ruled with both political and religious authority.

The state church demanded conformity. Attendance at Anglican services was compulsory, and refusal was punished with fines or imprisonment. Priests and bishops functioned as political actors as well as religious leaders. Dissent was dangerous: the northern uprising known as the Pilgrimage of Grace (1536) was suppressed with force.

Edward VI (1547–1553) advanced reform further. The Book of Common Prayer (1549) standardized worship across the kingdom. Under Mary I (1553–1558), however, Catholicism was restored, and Protestant leaders faced execution, earning her the epithet "Bloody Mary."

Elizabeth I sought a middle course when she came to the throne in 1558. The Elizabethan Settlement (1559) reaffirmed royal supremacy and gave the Church of England a distinctive identity—Catholic in form, Protestant in doctrine. The Thirty-Nine Articles (1563) defined its lasting structure. Enforcement was strict: recusancy fines targeted those who refused attendance at services, and Catholic priests risked death as traitors.

Religion shaped education and culture. Schools and universities trained clergy, and doctrine was a compulsory subject. Writers and theaters, including Shakespeare's, worked in a world where faith and conscience were matters of public concern.

Henry VIII's break with Rome ended centuries of papal influence, setting England at odds with Catholic Europe. Elizabeth I's excommunication by Pope Pius V in 1570 deepened this divide, portraying her rule as illegitimate in Catholic eyes. Tensions with Spain, the leading Catholic power, culminated in the Armada of 1588, when Philip II launched a naval campaign to overthrow Elizabeth. The English victory secured the Protestant monarchy and symbolized England's emergence as a distinct religious and political power in Europe.

Beneath the official unity, divisions persisted. Catholics who rejected royal supremacy and radical Protestants—Puritans and Presbyterians—who sought deeper reform, were persecuted. Many practiced in secret or went into exile. These conflicts nurtured underground Catholic networks and Puritan movements that later contributed to the English Civil War (1642–1651) and drove dissenters across the Atlantic in search of religious freedom.

Under the Tudors, England created not only a national church but also enduring conflicts over authority and belief—struggles whose consequences extended far beyond the 16th century.

The Russian Empire (18th – early 20th centuries)

In the Russian Empire, Orthodoxy formed the official foundation of state and society. Beginning with the reforms of Peter the Great, the Church was subordinated to imperial authority. In 1721 the tsar abolished the patriarchate and created the Holy Synod, a state body directly answerable to the emperor. The Synod was overseen by the Ober-Procurator, a lay official who represented the tsar and controlled religious affairs.

In 1833, Minister of Education Sergei Uvarov formulated the doctrine of "Orthodoxy, Autocracy, and Nationality." This triad defined Orthodoxy as the spiritual basis of Russian identity and one of the main pillars of imperial power. Loyalty to the Church became inseparable from patriotism and allegiance to the crown.

Imperial law reinforced this privileged status. Conversion from Orthodoxy was forbidden, and missionary activity by Catholics, Protestants, and other confessions was tightly restricted. Old Believers, who had rejected the church reforms of the 17th century, faced harassment. At the same time, Orthodoxy served as an instrument of imperial expansion. Missionaries worked in Siberia, the Caucasus, and Central Asia, where the baptism of local peoples was linked to the broader project of political and cultural integration.

The state devoted vast resources to the Church. Treasury funds financed the building and maintenance of churches and monasteries, along with seminaries and theological academies. Major feasts such as Christmas, Easter, and Epiphany were both liturgical and public holidays. Members of the imperial family often attended liturgies and processions, displaying the close alliance between throne and altar.

The Church exerted wide influence over education, particularly in the countryside. Until the reforms of the 1860s, it controlled most elementary schools, where parish priests introduced children to reading, writing, and catechism. Beyond the classroom, ecclesiastical authorities supervised religious censorship, reviewing books, journals, and even theatrical productions to ensure their conformity with Orthodox teaching and loyalty to the monarchy.

In villages, the parish church shaped the rhythm of life. The priest was not only a spiritual guide but also a representative of the state: he conducted worship, registered births, marriages, and deaths, and reminded peasants of their duty to obey the tsar. Through sermons and rituals, the Church reinforced loyalty to authority and wove Christian symbolism into every stage of the life cycle—baptism, marriage, and burial. The parish thus became both a religious and a civic institution, anchoring the peasant community.

The upheavals of 1905 and 1917 shattered the old balance between throne and altar. The Revolution of 1905 brought the first real limits on state control of religion, loosening the grip of Orthodoxy as the exclusive faith of the empire. In the spring of 1917, the Provisional Government restored the patriarchate abolished two centuries earlier by Peter I, but the gesture came too late. The centuries-old alliance of monarchy and Church had already collapsed, and with the fall of the Romanov dynasty the entire religious-political order that had defined imperial Russia vanished into history.

"There is no nation like Israel where the contrast between the desire for peace and the lack of security is so acute."

— David Ben-Gurion

Chapter 3

Jewish State:
Governance Based on Jewish Law (Halakha) and Principles

> **A Jewish state** is a polity in which political and social life is grounded in Jewish religious traditions and laws.

Main Features of a Jewish State

1) Jewish Law as the Foundation

The legal and social framework rests on Jewish religious law (Halakha). It regulates family relations, inheritance, business ethics, dietary rules (kashrut), and observance of the Sabbath and festivals. Rabbinical courts interpret and apply Halakha, preserving continuity with tradition while also shaping the limits of civil life.

2) Religious Authority in Public Affairs

Rabbis and religious institutions influence both politics and everyday practice. Leading rabbis advise lawmakers, public institutions follow religious norms, and political parties rooted in Judaism take part in elections and parliamentary debates. Through these channels, religion remains an active force in shaping policy.

3) State Funding of Religious Life

Government resources support synagogues, rabbinical courts, yeshivas, ritual baths (mikva'ot), kosher facilities, and other communal institutions. Public backing gives these organizations financial stability and secures their role in society.

4) Education Grounded in Tradition

Schools emphasize Jewish history and sacred texts. Public education includes courses on the Torah and Talmud, while yeshivas and religious academies dedicate themselves fully to training rabbis, teachers, and spiritual leaders. This structure ensures the transmission of identity and values to new generations.

5) Religious Symbols in Civic Culture

Jewish rituals and symbols mark the rhythm of public life. State offices, transportation, and many businesses close on the Sabbath and during major festivals. Official ceremonies often incorporate religious rites, making faith visible in civic space.

6) Challenges for Non-Jews and Secular Citizens

Matters of personal status, such as marriage and divorce, remain under rabbinical jurisdiction, creating difficulties for citizens outside the Jewish faith. Religious minorities may face limits on building places of worship or conducting rituals independently.

7) Religion and National Identity

The identity of the state is closely tied to Judaism. National holidays follow the Jewish calendar, Hebrew carries biblical associations, and the collective narrative draws on sacred history. This fusion of religion and nationhood strengthens unity while marking clear boundaries for those outside the dominant tradition.

Strengths of a Jewish State

1. Preservation of Identity

Grounding institutions in Jewish tradition and Halakha allows the state to preserve the historical memory and cultural identity of the Jewish people. Observance of the Sabbath, celebration of festivals, and daily practice of religious law keep heritage alive and transmit it from one generation to the next.

2. Tradition of Mutual Aid

Jewish teaching emphasizes tzedakah (charity) and communal responsibility. In practice, this takes shape in networks of welfare and charity run by religious institutions. These structures support the poor, the elderly, and other vulnerable groups, embedding mutual assistance in public life.

3. Stable Legal Framework

Religious law gives citizens clear guidance on rights and obligations. Because Halakha is regarded as divinely sanctioned, judicial rulings carry moral as well as legal authority. This perception reduces uncertainty and reinforces respect for courts and institutions.

4. Education as a Vehicle of Values

Placing Jewish texts and traditions at the center of the curriculum ensures that values and historical memory are passed on. Schools and yeshivas prepare new generations with a shared cultural background and moral outlook.

5. Religion as National Purpose

Religion and national identity are closely connected. This linkage inspires citizens to see themselves as part of a collective mission, reinforcing resilience in times of external threat and nurturing pride in belonging to a community bound by faith and history.

6. Continuity and Historical Legitimacy

The reliance on centuries-old traditions gives the state a sense of historical depth and legitimacy. Citizens perceive their institutions not as recent constructs but as an extension of ancient law and heritage.

7. Cohesion through Ritual Life

Regular participation in communal rituals—daily prayers, annual festivals, and cycles of fasting—creates shared experiences that integrate individuals into the wider community and foster a sense of belonging.

8. Moral Resilience in Times of Crisis

Religious teachings provide stable moral reference points that guide behavior in times of uncertainty. This collective framework strengthens society's resilience in the face of external pressure or internal upheaval.

9. Intellectual and Cultural Vitality

The Jewish textual tradition encourages study, commentary, and debate. This culture of learning nurtures intellectual creativity, sharpening critical thought and reinforcing respect for knowledge.

Weaknesses of a Jewish State

1. Limited Rights for Secular Citizens

Strict application of Halakha creates challenges for those outside religious life. Marriage and divorce are handled only by rabbinical courts, with no civil alternative. Public observance of the Sabbath halts transportation, commerce, and many government services, imposing religious practice on citizens who may not share it.

2. Tension Between Religious and Secular Communities

The political weight of religion fuels disputes between observant and secular groups. Religious parties press to expand Halakhic authority, while secular movements call for freedom of choice and clearer separation of religion and state.

3. Constraints on Religious Minorities

Although minority faiths may be recognized, their freedom is limited in practice.

4. Religion in Politics

Close ties between faith and governance expose religion to political use. Leaders and parties may employ religious authority to rally voters or marginalize opponents, eroding the distinction between spiritual guidance and political competition.

5. Gender Inequality

Traditional Halakha places women at a disadvantage in matters such as divorce, inheritance, and religious participation. This imbalance conflicts with contemporary principles of equality and women's rights.

6. Division Within Judaism

Orthodox, Conservative, and Reform traditions interpret Jewish law differently. A state privileging Orthodox practice risks alienating Jews of other affiliations, creating tension within the Jewish majority itself.

7. Limits on Academic and Cultural Freedom

Heavy reliance on religious norms may curb the growth of science, arts, and culture. Research or creative works that question tradition can encounter restrictions, slowing intellectual and artistic development.

8. Economic Constraints

Mandatory observance of the Sabbath and dietary laws limits economic flexibility. The suspension of commerce and transportation on holy days can reduce efficiency and weaken competitiveness in international markets.

9. Political Dependence on Religious Authorities

Governance becomes tied to rabbinical leadership. Disputes among rabbis or religious parties may provoke crises, and disrupt the functioning of state institutions.

10. Risk of Radicalization

The prominent role of religion in politics and education may encourage fundamentalist interpretations.

Historical Example of a Jewish State

Israel

The State of Israel, founded in 1948, offers a distinctive case of a country that defines itself as both democratic and explicitly Jewish. The Declaration of Independence affirmed Israel as the state of the Jewish people, while promising equality of rights for all citizens regardless of religion or ethnicity. This dual commitment—to democracy and to Judaism—has shaped Israeli law, politics, and society in ways that continue to spark debate.

A key illustration is the absence of civil marriage. Marriage and divorce remain under rabbinical jurisdiction, and Halakha governs these matters exclusively. For secular citizens, interfaith couples, and individuals not recognized as Jewish by religious authorities, this creates significant barriers. The issue remains highly contested, and rulings of the Supreme Court often stand in tension with rabbinical interpretations, particularly in relation to the Law of Return.

Israel's legal framework has further strengthened its Jewish identity. The Law of Return (1950) grants every Jew the right to immigrate and obtain citizenship, though the question of "who is a Jew" has never been fully resolved. The Nation-State Law (2018) enshrined the special status of the Jewish people and Judaism as the foundation of the state, reinforcing its character but also generating domestic debate and international criticism.

Demographic diversity adds complexity. Roughly 74 percent of Israel's citizens are Jewish, 21 percent are Arab (predominantly Muslim, with Christian minorities), and around 5 percent belong to other groups. This pluralism intensifies discussions about minority rights, citizenship, and the meaning of equality within a state officially defined as Jewish.

Religion also intersects with national defense. Military service is compulsory for most citizens, yet exemptions for ultra-Orthodox Jews engaged in Torah study have long been a point of contention. Many secular Israelis view these exemptions as unequal, and protests frequently erupt over the demand for universal obligations.

The observance of the Sabbath deeply shapes public life. On Shabbat, public transportation, government offices, and most businesses close. While observant Jews see this as affirming tradition, secular citizens often view it as limiting personal freedom and economic activity..

Education reflects the same divisions. Israel supports both secular and religious school systems, including a large ultra-Orthodox sector. While religious schools emphasize Torah and Talmud study, critics argue that limited training in mathematics, science, and languages hampers the integration of ultra-Orthodox youth into the modern workforce.

On the international stage, Israel's Jewish identity is a source of both support and criticism. Advocates see the Jewish state as essential for preserving Jewish heritage. Critics argue that the intertwining of religion, national identity, and security policy complicates relations with Palestinians and hampers peace efforts.

Chapter 4

Buddhist State:
Governance Influenced by Buddhist Doctrine and Ethical Principles

> **A Buddhist state** is a polity that grounds its politics and social institutions in the principles and values of Buddhism.

Main Features of a Buddhist State

1) Policy Shaped by Buddhist Principles

Legislation and social norms are grounded in Buddhist teachings such as non-violence (ahimsa), compassion, and the pursuit of harmony. These values often lead to humanized criminal law, limited use or rejection of capital punishment, investment in welfare programs, and protections for animals and the environment.

2) Role of the Sangha in Public Life

Monastic communities serve as guardians of ethical principles and often advise political leaders. In some states, monks hold advisory or official roles, shaping legislation and public policy. Monasteries also run schools, charities, and welfare programs, reinforcing the social role of the sangha.

3) Support for Buddhist Institutions

Governments fund monasteries, stupas, temples, and Buddhist schools, while also preserving religious monuments as part of national heritage. This support secures the transmission of Buddhist traditions across generations.

4) Buddhist Symbols in Civic Space

Rituals and symbols mark the rhythm of public life. National holidays feature Buddhist ceremonies, and stupas, prayer flags, and images of the Buddha are prominent in civic spaces, linking identity and tradition.

5) Education in Buddhist Philosophy and Ethics

Schools and universities typically include courses on Buddhist philosophy, ethics, and history. Monasteries act as centers of advanced learning, preparing monks, teachers, and community leaders. In this way, moral discipline remains embedded in education and public culture.

6) Constitutional Status of Buddhism

In many Buddhist states, constitutions give Buddhism either official standing (Sri Lanka) or special protection (Thailand, Bhutan, Cambodia). This legal framework elevates Buddhism in public life.

7) Legal Position of the Sangha

Monastic orders often enjoy a distinct legal status. State laws regulate their property, education, and responsibilities, making the sangha both a spiritual and semi-political institution.

8) Monks in State Ceremonies

From coronations to national holidays, monks offer blessings to rulers, the military, and the public. Their ritual presence reinforces the legitimacy of political authority through religious sanction.

9) Buddhism in Foreign Policy

Religion is frequently used as a form of soft power. States present themselves abroad as advocates of peace, meditation, and harmony, using Buddhism to shape their international image.

10) Moral Regulation of Society

Some states codify Buddhist ethics into law, limiting gambling, alcohol consumption, or prostitution. These measures reflect efforts to align daily life with moral norms.

11) Buddhism and National Identity

Festivals, rituals, and education reinforce the idea that belonging to the nation means sharing in a common Buddhist heritage. In this way, Buddhism becomes a defining element of national identity.

Strengths of a Buddhist State

1. Governance Shaped by Non-Violence

Grounding politics in the ideals of ahimsa (non-violence), compassion, and harmony leads to an emphasis on dialogue and reconciliation. Criminal law often favors rehabilitation over severe punishment.

2. Social Cohesion Through Shared Ethics

Values such as mutual respect and compassion provide a common moral framework. Collective rituals and festivals bring together people from different backgrounds, while monasteries function as community centers that strengthen bonds and reduce tension.

3. Charity and Social Support

Monasteries and Buddhist organizations take responsibility for the vulnerable, offering food, shelter, education, and basic healthcare. In Thailand, for example, monastic schools and clinics complement state welfare programs, helping to reduce poverty and inequality.

4. Preservation of Cultural Heritage

Temples, monasteries, and stupas are maintained as symbols of national identity and historical memory.

5. Moral Legitimacy of Leadership

When rulers embody Buddhist virtues, their authority is seen as both political and moral. This dual legitimacy strengthens public trust, stabilizes governance, and reduces reliance on coercion.

6. Spiritual Values in Daily Life

Respect for monks, observance of precepts, and participation in rituals integrate spirituality into ordinary routines, ensuring that religion is not confined to sacred spaces but present in everyday life.

7. Environmental Awareness

Buddhist philosophy stresses interdependence and reverence for nature. Bhutan's concept of Gross National Happiness, which includes ecological balance as a measure of prosperity, reflects how these principles inform state policy.

8. Education and Ethical Training

Monasteries and Buddhist schools serve as centers of both learning and moral formation. Young people study Buddhist philosophy alongside general subjects, cultivating discipline, responsibility, and compassion.

9. Diplomacy Grounded in Peace

Buddhist states often draw on values of harmony and reconciliation in foreign relations. By presenting themselves as mediators, they employ religion as a form of soft power in regional and international diplomacy.

Weaknesses of a Buddhist State

1. Political Passivity

The focus on non-violence, contemplation, and self-perfection can reduce civic engagement. Citizens may prioritize spiritual practice over political participation, which limits reform and weakens state capacity. In premodern Burma (Myanmar), the sangha maintained distance from politics, preserving moral authority but slowing institutional development and modernization.

2. Tensions with Non-Buddhists and Secular Groups

The privileged position of Buddhism may create friction with religious minorities and secular citizens. In Sri Lanka, constitutional protection of Buddhism reinforced divisions between the Sinhalese Buddhist majority and the Tamil Hindu minority, contributing to decades of civil conflict. In Myanmar, political activism by monks and nationalist groups has deepened tensions with the Muslim Rohingya population, leading to violence and mass displacement.

3. Restrictions on Individual Freedoms

Where Buddhist norms dominate public life, non-Buddhists may feel constrained. Laws regulating alcohol sales, gambling, or entertainment in countries such as Thailand and Bhutan aim to uphold morality but also limit freedom of expression and reduce economic diversity.

4. Excessive Authority of the Sangha

When monks play a central role in politics, religious influence can overshadow secular expertise in areas like economics, science, and foreign policy. This politicization of the sangha risks undermining democratic institutions and eroding its spiritual credibility.

5. Obstacles to Modernization

Strict reliance on traditional codes may hinder adaptation to contemporary needs. In some Buddhist-majority states, balancing rapid industrial and technological development with traditional values has proven difficult, creating cultural and generational divides.

6. Religion as a Basis for Nationalism

Buddhism has sometimes been used to support nationalist ideologies. In these cases, a religion associated with compassion and tolerance becomes tied to exclusivist politics, marginalizing minorities and fueling social conflict.

Historical Example of a Buddhist State

Bhutan

Buddhism reached Bhutan from Tibet between the 7th and 8th centuries, during the reign of the Tibetan king Songtsen Gampo, who is credited with constructing some of the first Buddhist temples in the region. Over the following centuries, Buddhist practices spread gradually across the valleys, shaping local culture and beliefs.

A decisive transformation came in the 17th century under Shabdrung Ngawang Namgyal (1594–1651), a Tibetan lama who fled sectarian conflicts in Tibet and consolidated Bhutanese territories. He established a dual system of governance (chösi nyidhen) in which secular and monastic institutions shared authority. This framework placed the monarch and the sangha as interdependent pillars of the state and laid the institutional foundations of Bhutanese national identity.

Constitutional and Legal Status

Bhutan remained an absolute monarchy until the early 21st century. In 2008, the country adopted its first written Constitution, transforming into a constitutional monarchy. The document recognizes Buddhism as the nation's "spiritual heritage" and obliges the state to preserve and promote its values. At the same time, it guarantees freedom of religion and the protection of minority rights.

The monarchy retains strong symbolic and practical authority. King Jigme Khesar Namgyel Wangchuck, the current Druk Gyalpo ("Dragon King"), is widely respected as both a political leader and a cultural guardian, often portrayed as embodying Buddhist virtues of compassion and humility.

Social Policy and Gross National Happiness

Bhutan is internationally known for its development philosophy of Gross National Happiness (GNH), introduced by King Jigme Singye Wangchuck in the 1970s. Unlike conventional economic models, GNH evaluates progress through four pillars: sustainable development, environmental conservation, cultural preservation, and good governance. These pillars are assessed by nine domains, including health, education, community vitality, and psychological well-being.

This framework is guides state policy in health, education, and environmental management. Bhutan consistently ranks high on global happiness and well-being indexes relative to its GDP, which remains one of the lowest in Asia.

Environmental Policy

Bhutan is unique in its constitutional requirement that at least 60 percent of its territory remain forested at all times. As of 2024, more than 70 percent of the country is under forest cover, and over 50 percent of land area falls within protected national parks and biological corridors.

The government has pursued an ambitious policy of maintaining carbon negativity. Bhutan produces around 2.2 million tons of carbon annually but absorbs over 6 million tons through its forests. The country exports hydropower to India, which both sustains its economy and offsets regional carbon emissions. This makes Bhutan one of the only carbon-negative countries in the world.

Education, Health, and Social Services

Healthcare and education are provided free of charge, reflecting Buddhist principles of compassion and care. Literacy rates have improved dramatically: from below 20 percent in the 1970s to over 70 percent today. The state invests heavily in bilingual education, with English and Dzongkha (the national language) used side by side in schools.

Monasteries continue to serve as centers of social welfare. They provide shelter for orphans, food for the poor, and act as informal community centers.

Role of the Sangha and Monastic Institutions

The Je Khenpo, Bhutan's chief abbot, is appointed by the king and remains the highest spiritual authority in the country. Together with the Dratshang Lhentshog (Monastic Affairs Commission), he supervises the training of monks, management of monasteries, and the preservation of Buddhist teachings.

Monasteries (dzongs and gompas) are not only religious centers but also architectural landmarks and repositories of art, manuscripts, and ritual practices. Dzongs such as Punakha Dzong and Paro Dzong serve as both administrative headquarters and monastic institutions, symbolizing the unity of state and religion.

Symbols and Traditions in Daily Life

Bhutanese identity is expressed through cultural policies designed to preserve tradition. Citizens are required to wear national dress—gho for men and kira for women—during official events, in schools, and in government offices. This policy is part of Bhutan's strategy of "cultural fortification," intended to protect heritage from globalization.

Festivals (tsechu) are major social events, drawing entire communities to watch ritual cham dances, receive blessings, and participate in communal prayer. These festivals not only affirm Buddhist faith but also reinforce social cohesion and national identity.

Chapter 5

Hindu State: Governance Influenced by Hindu Traditions and Philosophical Principles

> **A Hindu state** is a state in which public life and government policy are organized on the basis of Hindu religious and cultural traditions.

Key Features of a Hindu State

1) Law and Social Order Based on Dharma

The foundation of legal and moral life rests on Hindu texts. These works regulate marriage, inheritance, family obligations, and moral conduct, framing law as an expression of *dharma*—the duty to maintain cosmic and social order.

2) Recognition of Hindu Festivals and Traditions

The state supports major Hindu festivals and rituals as part of national culture. Holidays such as Diwali, Holi, and Navaratri are marked by public celebrations, official holidays, and ceremonies that reinforce shared cultural identity.

3) Political Authority Linked to Religion

Historically, Hindu kingship (*raja dharma*) was based on the principle that rulers protected *dharma* and were divinely sanctioned to uphold order. In modern contexts, political leaders often use Hindu texts, rituals, and symbols to strengthen their legitimacy and connect governance with religious tradition.

4) Influence of Religious Leaders and Institutions

Priests, gurus, and Hindu organizations have historically shaped law, education, and policy. Their authority extends into both spiritual and social domains, influencing moral values, legal norms, and cultural practices.

5) Hindu Symbols in State Institutions

Religious symbols are integrated into public life, appearing in national emblems, courtrooms, and official ceremonies. Priestly blessings and the use of sacred texts often accompany major state events.

6) Education Rooted in Hindu Learning

School curricula may include Hindu philosophy, Sanskrit, and classical texts. Traditional *gurukuls*—residential schools where pupils studied under teachers—remain part of cultural heritage, alongside modern institutions supported by the state.

7) The Caste System in Legal and Social Structures

Historically, Hindu states incorporated the *varna-jati* (caste) hierarchy into law and society. Rights and duties were distributed by caste, regulating marriage, occupation, and social status. Although modern states often reject caste discrimination legally, its legacy continues to influence politics and society.

8) Ritualization of Public Life

Major political functions and ceremonies are often intertwined with Hindu ritual practices. Coronations, inaugurations, and legislative openings may involve sacred texts, offerings, or blessings from priests, reinforcing the link between political authority and religion.

9) Regulation of Public Morality

Hindu ethical norms shape civic life through laws and customs. Prohibitions on cow slaughter, restrictions on trades such as beef production or alcohol sales, and mandatory observance of religious holidays reflect the influence of religious morality on public order.

10) Hinduism as Cultural Identity

Hinduism is presented not only as a religion but also as a civilizational heritage. Temples, epics, and rituals serve as unifying symbols, and political leaders frequently invoke Hindu heritage as central to national identity and cultural pride.

Strengths of a Hindu State

1. Cultural Preservation

A Hindu state has the ability to safeguard religious practices and cultural traditions, keeping them visible in public life. Temples, processions, and annual festivals embody the continuity of memory across generations. This continuity allows citizens to see themselves as inheritors of an ancient culture that still has meaning in the present.

2. Social Unity

Shared rituals and sacred festivals serve as powerful forces of cohesion. When entire communities participate in Diwali, Holi, or Ganesh Chaturthi, people from different regions and castes stand side by side in common celebration. In times of national strain, these festivals create collective symbols of resilience and solidarity. They transform private devotion into public life, allowing the state to draw on religion as a resource for unity.

3. Reform Through Tradition

Far from being a static system, Hindu ethics have often been reinterpreted to justify reform. The idea of *dharma*—duty and justice—gave reformers moral language to advocate for change. Leaders such as Jyotirao Phule could promote education for women and marginalized groups while rooting their appeals in Hindu values. By doing so, reform avoided appearing alien or imposed, instead gaining acceptance as a natural extension of cultural tradition.

4. Integration of Diversity

India's linguistic and ethnic variety has always posed challenges for governance, but Hindu states developed ways to integrate this diversity. Shared pilgrimage sites, temple networks, and sacred geography provided spaces where communities interacted across regional boundaries. The Vijayanagara Empire is a classic example: Kannada, Telugu, Tamil, and Malayali groups were held together by a religious-cultural order that transcended language. This integration allowed states to survive despite immense internal variety.

5. Religious Economy

Devotion has always been intertwined with economy. Sacred cities such as Varanasi demonstrate how pilgrimage sustains entire networks of trade, crafts, and hospitality. Pilgrims create demand for food, lodging, ritual items, and local arts, stimulating economic life for both urban and rural areas. The Banarasi silk industry, world-renowned for its beauty, owes its survival to centuries of religious tourism. In this way, religion supports not just the spirit but also the livelihoods of countless families.

6. Governance and Dharma

Political power in Hindu states is legitimized by its connection to *dharma*. A ruler is not only a king but also a guardian of moral order, expected to protect the weak, punish corruption, and ensure fairness. Historical examples such as Shivaji's *Adnyapatra* show how laws framed in ethical terms created discipline among soldiers and officials, while also protecting peasants and artisans. When governance is linked to moral duty, authority becomes more trusted and less dependent on coercion.

7. Education and Morality

Learning in Hindu society has always been tied to ethical training. The *gurukul* system placed students under close supervision of teachers, emphasizing discipline, respect, and devotion to study. Great centers of learning such as Nalanda and Takshashila expanded this model into advanced education, combining philosophy, law, astronomy, and medicine with moral guidance.

8. Resilient Identity

Hindu culture has endured despite centuries of foreign rule and external pressure. Temples, festivals, and rituals continued even under regimes that did not share Hindu values. In South India, the Vijayanagara Empire preserved ritual and temple life despite invasions from the Delhi Sultanate and later the Mughals. This resilience demonstrates how cultural practices can outlast political upheavals, giving people a steady sense of belonging when states rise and fall.

9. Philosophical Depth

Philosophy in the Hindu world was never a purely abstract pursuit; it was a guide for law, ethics, and governance. The six classical schools—Vedānta, Nyāya, Sāṃkhya, Yoga, Mīmāṃsā, and Vaiśeṣika—each addressed practical concerns of public life. Mīmāṃsā developed methods of interpreting sacred texts that informed jurisprudence and the understanding of duty (*dharma*). Nyāya trained scholars in logic and debate, skills essential for courts and councils, while Vaiśeṣika offered frameworks for analyzing the natural world and its categories. Sāṃkhya and Yoga shaped ideas of discipline, responsibility, and the psychology of action, providing models for personal and civic conduct. Vedānta, in its diverse forms, offered metaphysical horizons that linked governance to ultimate values of justice and liberation. By supporting these traditions through schools and patronage, Hindu states ensured that philosophy enriched not only intellectual culture but also the daily practice of governance, law, and education.

10. Architecture and Arts

Temples in Hindu states were not only sacred spaces but also civic centers. They housed schools, supported artists, and brought entire communities together through festivals. Magnificent complexes such as Khajuraho or Madurai testify to the role of architecture in embodying shared values and cultural memory. Supported by rulers and patrons, temples became symbols of continuity that tied artistic beauty to communal life.

11. Flexibility of Tradition

A notable strength of Hinduism is its capacity to integrate local customs and devotional movements into a broader religious framework. The Bhakti movement, carried by poet-saints across India, allowed people to express devotion in vernacular languages and through personal worship. This inclusivity reduced barriers of caste and region, weaving diversity into unity without destroying local distinctiveness. Such adaptability enabled Hindu states to hold together populations that were varied yet interconnected.

12. Cultural Diplomacy

Hinduism's influence extended far beyond India's borders. Across Southeast Asia, Indian epics, religious symbols, and temple architecture shaped kingdoms from Cambodia to Indonesia. The temple of Angkor Wat, originally dedicated to Vishnu, stands as a visible reminder of this cultural exchange. Through religion, art, and literature, Hindu states projected soft power, extending their influence not by conquest alone but through shared culture.

13. Legal Continuity

The Dharmashastras, including the Manusmriti, provided rulers with structured codes on family law, inheritance, and moral duty. These texts established a predictable framework that shaped justice for centuries. Although interpretations evolved, the idea that law was anchored in *dharma* reinforced both stability and legitimacy. People look to law not only as rules imposed by rulers but as expressions of cosmic and social order.

14. Charity and Public Welfare

Hindu political thought emphasized the ruler's duty to protect and provide for his subjects. The principle of *dāna*, or generosity, meant that kings were expected to support temples, feed the poor, and protect farmers and artisans. Welfare was not an optional gesture but part of the very definition of good rule. By linking political authority to social responsibility, Hindu states strengthened the bond between rulers and the people.

Weaknesses of a Hindu State

1. Military Limitations under the Caste System

One of the structural weaknesses of Hindu states lay in their restricted approach to military organization. Warfare was traditionally confined to the kshatriya varna, excluding brahmins, vaishyas, and shudras from formal service. This reduced the available pool of defenders and limited collective resistance in times of crisis. Historical invasions—such as the Muslim conquests of northern India in the 12th–13th centuries—took advantage of fragmented and weakened Hindu polities. Later, British colonial rulers in the 18th–19th centuries exploited caste divisions to consolidate control.

2. Restricted Access to Education and Healthcare

Caste hierarchy shaped not only politics but also access to learning and medicine. Brahmins and kshatriyas dominated education, while lower castes were often barred from studying Sanskrit or sacred texts, as reflected in the Manusmriti. This exclusion curtailed intellectual growth and reduced opportunities for scientific advancement. Healthcare was also stratified: members of lower castes could be denied treatment by higher-caste physicians on grounds of ritual purity. As a result, entire communities relied on folk remedies, suffered higher rates of illness, and remained trapped in systemic inequality.

3. Limits on Religious and Cultural Minorities

The privileged status of Hinduism often restricted the freedoms of minority faiths. In Nepal, before the adoption of the 2008 constitution, conversion away from Hinduism was legally prohibited. In parts of India today, state governments led by Hindu nationalist parties have enacted anti-conversion laws. These measures are defended as protection against "forced conversions".

4. Interreligious Conflict and Social Tensions

When the state openly favors one faith, it unsettles the balance between communities and turns difference into division. In India, for example, tying politics too closely to Hindu identity has repeatedly sparked unrest and sharpened lines between religious groups. Instead of protecting all citizens equally, power becomes a tool for exclusion, and everyday coexistence gives way to suspicion and hostility.

5. Gender Inequality and Women's Rights

Hindu law codes placed women in subordinate roles for much of history. The Manusmriti described women as under the guardianship of father, husband, or son, limiting independence throughout life. Property rights were especially restricted: land passed to sons, while daughters and widows held only narrow claims, usually limited to dowry or temporary use. Regional legal traditions reinforced these inequalities, and child marriage remained widespread until the 20th century. Reform came slowly—the Child Marriage Restraint Act of 1929 set minimum ages, and inheritance rights improved only with the Hindu Succession Act of 1956, fully equalized for daughters and sons only in 2005. These reforms reveal how deeply entrenched inequality was, and how much legislative correction was required to establish gender balance.

6. Economic and Social Stratification

By embedding the varna and caste system into law and custom, Hindu states entrenched rigid hierarchies. Dalits and lower castes were excluded from land ownership, education, and access to political power. This created deep economic and social divides that weakened cohesion and limited mobility.

Historical Examples of a Hindu State

Nepal before the Secular Republic (before 2008)

Until 2008, Nepal stood as the world's only country to officially define itself as a Hindu state. Both the 1962 constitution of the kingdom and the democratic charter of 1990 enshrined Hinduism as the state religion. In this framework, politics and faith were inseparable: monarchy, law, and culture all drew authority from religion.

The legal foundation of this order was the Muluki Ain of 1854, issued under Prime Minister Jung Bahadur Rana. This national code inscribed caste hierarchy into law, regulating marriage, inheritance, property, and access to temples and education. Inter-caste marriage was forbidden; Dalits were excluded from public spaces and penalized for entering shrines. Even after a revision in 1963 softened some provisions, caste distinctions continued to shape daily life well into the modern period.

The monarchy itself carried sacred legitimacy. The Shah dynasty, rulers since 1768, claimed descent from Hindu warrior lineages. Each coronation took place at the great Pashupatinath Temple in Kathmandu, where priests blessed the new monarch and recognized him as an incarnation of Vishnu Narayan. Festivals such as Dashain and Tihar were celebrated as state holidays, with kings taking part in public rituals, binding royal power to religious devotion.

State patronage reinforced this religious order. Temples like Pashupatinath, Changu Narayan, and the Bhaktapur complexes received direct financial support; priests were salaried by the crown. Hindu schools, monasteries, and Sanskrit colleges were funded through public revenue, while the official calendar followed the rhythm of the ritual year—from Maha Shivaratri to Krishna Janmashtami.

Education and administration reflected the same priorities. Until the mid-20th century, Sanskrit schools formed the backbone of elite learning. Even after Tribhuvan University was established in 1959, Hindu philosophy and law remained central in curricula, with the Ministry of Education working closely with religious authorities.

Yet this tight union of state and religion came at a cost. Nepal's population is multiethnic and multireligious—Buddhists, Muslims, Christians, and indigenous groups such as the Tharu and Magar all lived within the kingdom. These communities often found themselves excluded from state service, denied recognition, or restricted in building their own places of worship. Even Buddhists, though Nepal is the birthplace of the Buddha, were treated as secondary in a polity that gave preference to Hinduism.

By the late 20th century, discontent grew. The 1990 People's Movement introduced constitutional monarchy but left Hindu privilege intact. The Maoist insurgency of 1996–2006 drew strength from Dalits, ethnic minorities, and secular activists demanding an end to caste discrimination and religious inequality. The civil war claimed more than 13,000 lives and destabilized the country. In 2006, the monarchy was stripped of its powers, and in 2008 Nepal was declared a secular republic. For the first time, the constitution guaranteed equal rights to all religions, ending centuries of Hindu dominance in public life.

India and the Politics of Hindu Nationalism (20th–21st Centuries)

Although India has been constitutionally defined as a secular republic since 1947, Hinduism has never been absent from its public life. Over 80 percent of the population identify as Hindu, and symbols, festivals, and rituals drawn from Hindu tradition remain part of national culture. The national flag itself carries the Ashoka Chakra—a wheel of law first associated with the Buddhist emperor Ashoka but equally interpreted in Hinduism as the Sudarshana Chakra of Vishnu, symbol of cosmic order and justice. Its presence signals that Indian identity blends secular ideals with religious symbolism.

From independence through most of the twentieth century, India's leaders worked to preserve a secular balance. Jawaharlal Nehru and the Congress Party promoted pluralism, protecting the rights of Muslims, Christians, Sikhs, and others. Yet religion remained embedded in law: Hindu personal law continued to regulate marriage, inheritance, and family life, while other communities followed their own "personal codes." This arrangement revealed the persistence of religion even within a secular system.

By the late twentieth century, Hindu nationalism had become a growing force. The Rashtriya Swayamsevak Sangh (RSS), founded in 1925, and its affiliates such as the Vishwa Hindu Parishad (VHP) mobilized Hindus around the vision of India as a Hindu nation. Their political wing, the Bharatiya Janata Party (BJP), rose to prominence in the 1980s. In 1992 Hindu activists demolished the Babri Mosque in Ayodhya, claiming it stood on the birthplace of Lord Rama. The destruction triggered riots across the country, making clear the power of religion in political life.

Since 2014, under Prime Minister Narendra Modi, Hindu nationalism has become central to government policy. Modi has repeatedly used religious symbols in state ceremonies, from presiding over nationwide rituals to laying the foundation stone of a Ram temple in Ayodhya in 2020. BJP-led states have expanded funding for temples, tightened cow-protection laws, and enacted anti-conversion legislation.

Public culture reflects these changes. Diwali, Holi, and Navaratri are celebrated as national holidays with state support. Sanskrit mottos appear on government seals, and political speeches often cite Hindu scriptures. Recent education reforms have emphasized Hindu philosophy and ancient texts, prompting debate over historical interpretation and concern among minority groups.

Critics argue that this trajectory erodes India's secular foundations, reducing space for pluralism. Supporters call it a cultural revival, restoring Hindu identity after centuries of Mughal and British dominance. They claim it brings moral clarity, cohesion, and pride in national heritage. Repeated BJP electoral victories show that this vision resonates with large parts of society.

Chapter 6

State with an Official Religion: Governance under Formal Recognition and Legal Endorsement of a Single Faith

> **A state with an official religion** is one in which a particular faith holds official status and receives state support, yet its influence on public life and politics remains limited and does not extend to all aspects of governance.

Key Features of a State with an Official Religion

1) Constitutional recognition of a single faith

The constitution or a fundamental law proclaims one religion as "official," "established," or "prevailing." This act seals a formal bond between state and church, granting the recognized body defined privileges and responsibilities.

2) State support and institutional privileges

Public resources may sustain the clergy, preserve houses of worship, and cover administrative needs. The official church is often endowed with legal standing in public law, given access to national platforms, and entrusted with an advisory voice in ministries.

3) Integration into civic ritual

Religion flows into public life through oaths, inaugurations, memorials, and national holidays. Prayers, blessings, or sacred texts become part of these ceremonies, weaving faith into the symbolic fabric of the nation without granting it political command.

4) Primacy of secular law

However honored, the official religion does not shape the legal system. Civil and criminal codes hold authority, while religious norms influence culture and tradition but remain subordinate to constitutional rights.

5) Limits on clerical influence

Parliamentary supremacy, judicial review, and administrative law stand as barriers to clerical power. Decisions of government must be justified on grounds accessible to all citizens, not only to the faithful.

6) Religious symbols in the public sphere

The imagery of the official faith may appear on state holidays, insignia, or public addresses. These symbols serve to affirm identity and continuity, yet they do not bind citizens in law or conscience.

7) Education and cultural heritage

Schools may include teaching about the official religion, and the state may fund the preservation of sacred buildings, manuscripts, and music. Where instruction is confessional, students are free to opt out or choose an alternative path, preserving freedom of conscience.

8) Guarantees of religious freedom

Minority traditions and non-believers enjoy the right to worship, organize, educate, and express their convictions. Public benefits and services remain open to all, regardless of faith.

9) Separation of jurisdictions

Marriage, family, property, and criminal justice fall under civil law. Religious rites have legal effect only when explicitly recognized by statute, while coercive authority belongs solely to the state.

10) Equal public administration

Recruitment and promotion in the civil service rest on merit and equality. Officials neither compel participation in religious acts nor deny accommodations for individual conscience.

11) Transparent financial arrangements

State transfers, grants, or tax measures related to the official religion are governed by law and subject to public scrutiny. Citizens retain avenues to dissent or opt out in ways consistent with fairness and rights.

12) Dialogue and conflict resolution

Institutional channels of consultation link government and the official church, complemented by independent courts or ombudsmen to resolve disputes. This balance honors tradition while safeguarding constitutional order.

13) Recognition of pluralism

Public discourse acknowledges the historical role of the official faith but affirms equal dignity for all beliefs. Shared symbols aim to foster unity, not uniformity, offering cohesion without coercion.

Strengths of a State with an Official Religion

1. Preservation of heritage alongside personal freedom

A state with an official religion offers a framework where historic traditions are preserved without erasing individual choice. The recognized faith provides continuity of national culture, yet citizens remain free to follow other beliefs—or none at all. This balance protects both memory and liberty.

2. Mediation between sacred and secular spheres

By linking the official church with civic authority, such a state creates channels of cooperation. The faith offers cultural grounding, while secular institutions safeguard pluralism. Together they form a structure that can temper conflicts and foster social peace.

3. National unity and shared identity

Common rituals, festivals, and sacred symbols remind citizens of a heritage larger than themselves. These moments strengthen bonds across classes and regions, nurturing an emotional sense of belonging to one community.

4. Moral legitimacy of authority

When political institutions stand in visible connection with the official faith, they often gain an added layer of trust. Rulers are seen not only as administrators of law but also as guardians of cultural and moral order, which reinforces the dignity of the state.

5. Stability of norms and law

The presence of an official religion gives legislation an ethical anchor. Laws echo familiar moral standards, making them easier to accept and respect. This shared foundation sustains discipline in public life without excessive reliance on coercion.

6. Social support through religious institutions

Churches, monasteries, and religious charities have long provided education, healthcare, and aid for the poor. When backed by the state, their reach expands, lightening the burden on public systems and weaving stronger bonds of solidarity within society.

7. Transmission of culture across generations

Through schools, the arts, and public ceremonies, states with an official religion nurture continuity of values. The preservation of sacred sites and traditions is not only a matter of history but also of living culture, ensuring that each generation inherits a sense of rooted identity.

Weaknesses of a State with an Official Religion

1) Unequal treatment of minorities

Privileging one faith often leaves others at a disadvantage. Religious minorities may find their schools, institutions, or places of worship denied equal recognition. Non-believers, too, can feel like second-class citizens when the state appears to honor only one worldview.

2) Tensions between church and state

Democratic institutions move toward broader rights, while religious authorities often stand guard over tradition. Disputes on marriage, education, or freedom of expression expose this fault line, polarizing society and delaying reform.

3) Strain on public finances

Maintaining churches, paying clergy, and sponsoring ceremonies requires steady funding. For taxpayers outside the official faith, such expenses may seem unfair, stirring resentment and questions of justice.

4) Religion as a political instrument

When faith becomes a tool for power, its spiritual voice is weakened. Politicians may invoke sacred authority to legitimize their rule or rally voters, erasing the boundary between pulpit and parliament. Trust in both state and church erodes in the process.

5) Pressure on conscience and choice

Even where freedom is guaranteed by law, the dominance of one creed can push individuals to conform. Alternative beliefs may be stigmatized, discouraging genuine diversity of thought and weakening the spirit of pluralism.

6) Resistance to change

Close ties between church and state can slow social progress. Rooted in tradition, religious institutions may oppose reforms in gender equality, civil rights, or education, holding back adaptation to modern realities.

7) Deepened divisions in diverse societies

In multiethnic or multifaith states, favoring one religion can widen existing rifts. Minority groups may read it as state-sanctioned exclusion, responding with protest or withdrawal. Instead of harmony, the system risks sowing polarization and mistrust.

Comparative Analysis
of the Strengths and Weaknesses of States with an Official Religion

Strengths	Weaknesses
Preserves cultural and religious traditions, reinforcing national identity.	Can marginalize or discriminate against religious minorities and non-religious citizens.
Strengthens social cohesion by uniting the majority around shared values and practices.	Risks creating social divisions, as minorities may feel excluded or second-class.
Provides stability and continuity by grounding law and culture in long-standing traditions.	Can slow social and legal reforms, making adaptation to modern values more difficult.
Offers state support for religious institutions, education, and heritage protection.	Imposes financial burdens on taxpayers, including those who do not share the official faith.
Creates moral and ethical guidance for society, helping to frame public debates.	Leads to conflicts between religious authorities and secular institutions over issues like gender equality, minority rights, and individual freedoms.
Enhances national unity through shared religious holidays, symbols, and ceremonies.	May politicize religion, turning faith into a tool for political agendas and fueling social tensions.

Historical Examples of States with an Official Religion

United Kingdom (Anglicanism as the Official Religion)

Since the sixteenth century, the Church of England has held the status of the established church, formally anchored in law. The monarch serves as its Supreme Governor—a title created by the Act of Supremacy of 1534 under Henry VIII and reinforced through later acts of Parliament and constitutional custom. This union of crown and church has long stood as a symbol of English identity.

The state continues to support the church materially and institutionally. Public funds sustain the hierarchy of bishops and archbishops, finance the preservation of historic cathedrals such as St. Paul's in London and Canterbury, and assist Anglican schools and charities. Twenty-six bishops, known as the Lords Spiritual, sit in the House of Lords, giving the church a voice in parliamentary debate and ensuring its presence in the nation's political architecture.

Yet the church's influence remains largely ceremonial. It presides over great moments of national life—coronations, jubilees, royal weddings, and funerals—but it does not shape the course of legislation. In 2013, Parliament legalized same-sex marriage despite the church's opposition, a decision that revealed the clear boundary between symbolic authority and political power. More recently, the rituals surrounding the death of Queen Elizabeth II in 2022 displayed the church's role in embodying continuity and unity, while the coronation of King Charles III in 2023, carried out with Anglican rites and broadcast worldwide, showed how its traditions still mold cultural identity even as direct governance lies firmly in secular hands.

Denmark and Norway (the Official Role of the Evangelical Lutheran Church)

Denmark and Norway illustrate how the Evangelical Lutheran Church long stood at the heart of national life.

In Denmark, the Constitution names the Lutheran Church the People's Church (Folkekirken), sustained by state funds and embraced by the monarchy. The sovereign must be Lutheran and serves as the church's protector. Members of the royal family take part in public worship—Christmas and Easter services, baptisms, and coronations—all celebrated in Lutheran rites and supported through public resources.

In Norway, the Lutheran Church retained its formal status as the state church until constitutional reforms in 2017. The king stood as its patron, while the state financed church life, from parish activity to the preservation of great monuments such as Nidaros Cathedral in Trondheim. For generations, the church was inseparable from civic festivity; even Constitution Day on May 17 carried a strong liturgical dimension.

Yet in both countries, secular governance remains firm. Parliament and civil law operate independently of ecclesiastical authority. Religious freedom is protected not only in principle but in practice: Copenhagen and Oslo host thriving mosques, synagogues, and diverse congregations. Thus, while the Lutheran Church still enjoys ceremonial privilege, modern Denmark and Norway reveal how constitutional monarchies can uphold tradition without restricting pluralism.

Conclusion

Comparative Analysis of Different Types of Religious States

Religious states differ widely in how deeply faith shapes their political and social order.

At one extreme stand Islamic states, where religion penetrates nearly every sphere of life. Law is grounded in sharia, and clerical authorities exercise direct influence over governance and justice. Contemporary Iran and Saudi Arabia embody this model, in which politics and religion are inseparable.

Christian and Jewish states follow another path. In the Vatican or modern Israel, religion stands at the center but does not govern every domain. Ecclesiastical or rabbinical courts oversee family law, marriage, and inheritance, while most civic and political affairs remain under secular authority. Here, faith provides identity and regulates particular areas of life without dominating the whole of government.

Buddhist states such as Bhutan or Thailand, and Hindu Nepal before 2008, rely less on codified religious law than on ethical ideals. Teachings of compassion, nonviolence, and social duty inform education, policy, and cultural life. Religion here serves as a guiding ethos, while day-to-day governance remains largely pragmatic and secular.

A different model appears in states with an established church, such as the United Kingdom or Denmark. Religion in these cases holds constitutional recognition and ceremonial prominence. The Church of England and the Lutheran churches of Scandinavia take part in state rituals, preserve traditions, and strengthen national identity, yet they wield little influence over legislation or political outcomes.

Viewed together, these cases reveal the many ways faith and power can meet. Some states fuse them completely; others grant religion a privileged but limited role; still others confine it to ritual and symbolism. Comparative study of these forms highlights not only the variety of religious states but also the different balances they strike between belief, authority, and individual freedom.

Consequences of Religious Influence on Governance and Society

The influence of religion on the state and public life has historically produced both positive and negative outcomes.

Positive Consequences of Religion in Public Life

1. Preservation of stability

A common faith can supply shared rules of conduct—honesty, family duty, respect for authority—that give society order and predictability. Such expectations work as informal restraints, reinforcing discipline through moral obligation rather than coercion. In states where religion permeates daily life, from Saudi Arabia to Bhutan, this shared framework has long underpinned continuity across generations.

2. National identity and unity

Religion often serves as a cornerstone of belonging. In Israel, Judaism has been both a spiritual foundation and a source of collective resilience for a people once dispersed. In Greece, Orthodoxy binds citizens through common feasts, rituals, and memories that shape the national story. In each case, faith helps knit disparate lives into a shared cultural fabric.

3. Endurance of moral and legal traditions

Religious institutions can preserve principles of justice and obligation even when political regimes fall. In Britain or Norway, churches transmitted ethical and legal norms that later shaped democratic institutions. Such continuity anchors societies in times of transition, offering stability where purely political structures may falter.

4. Charity and solidarity

Long before the rise of modern welfare states, churches, mosques, temples, and monasteries provided education, medical care, food, and shelter. These traditions of generosity endure. Even today, religious institutions remain central to supporting the poor and reminding society of its collective duty to care for its most vulnerable members.

5. Moral guidance for rulers

Faith traditions place ideals of justice, fairness, and compassion before those in power. When leaders take these principles seriously, religion can restrain excess and encourage policies aimed at the common good. Though no system guarantees justice, the presence of moral benchmarks can temper politics driven only by interest or ambition.

6. Cohesion across diversity

In societies divided by ethnicity, language, or region, religion can provide a common ground. Shared rituals and festivals allow people to see themselves as part of a larger whole. Hindu pilgrimages in India or Buddhist monasteries in Southeast Asia historically created spaces where communities met within a sacred framework, strengthening solidarity beyond local ties.

Negative Consequences of Religion in Public Life

1. Restrictions on personal freedom

When religious codes become state law, individual rights often contract. Marriage, inheritance, and family life may be governed by rules that privilege some while excluding others. Women in particular have faced limits on education, property, and mobility under systems justified by doctrine. Such inequalities erode the principle of universal rights.

2. Discrimination and conflict

States that elevate one faith risk alienating others. Minorities may be denied equal recognition, and resentment can harden into open hostility. From sectarian clashes in South Asia to tensions between Buddhists and Muslims in Southeast Asia, favoritism has too often ignited enduring cycles of mistrust and violence.

3. Obstacles to reform

Deeply rooted conservatism may stall social progress. Efforts to advance women's rights, improve education, or broaden civil liberties frequently encounter opposition when perceived as challenges to tradition. Laws and policies then lag behind lived reality, widening the gap between official norms and daily life.

4. Religion as a political weapon

When leaders use sacred language to secure power, faith itself is diminished. Religious symbols become instruments of partisanship, and the line between pulpit and parliament fades. This practice grants disproportionate influence to clerics or organizations, weakens democratic institutions, and erodes public trust in religion's moral voice.

5. Suppression of thought

Where orthodoxy is enforced as doctrine of state, inquiry in science, philosophy, and the arts can wither. Dissenting scholars may face censorship or exile, and entire disciplines can be delayed for generations. The result is not only intellectual loss but cultural stagnation, as creativity yields to conformity.

6. Sanctifying absolute power

Political rulers have often claimed divine sanction for their authority. Opposition is cast not merely as treason but as blasphemy. This fusion of throne and altar narrows pluralism and suppresses dissent, fostering authoritarian habits and leaving little room for democratic governance.

7. Marginalization of non-believers

In states where religion dominates public life, secular citizens may feel excluded from full participation. Ceremonies, schools, and laws often presume adherence to the dominant faith, leaving unbelievers without equal standing. Over time, this exclusion sharpens divides between religious and secular communities, weakening the sense of common citizenship.

Prospects for Religious States in the Contemporary World

In an age of global exchange and growing diversity, religious states face a central dilemma: how to preserve their spiritual traditions without compromising equality and universal rights. The tension between faith and modernity is especially acute in societies where religion is not only a private conviction but also a foundation of law, culture, and collective identity.

Rigid theocracies often encounter unrest at home, criticism abroad, and barriers to economic integration. Strict enforcement of one doctrine risks alienating minorities and undermining social cohesion. At the same time, international organizations and global markets exert pressure to respect human rights and guarantee freedoms. Failure to adapt can isolate such states diplomatically and economically, leaving them vulnerable to internal stagnation and external sanction.

By contrast, states that hold to a religious identity while allowing space for pluralism adapt more easily and endure more securely. They find ways to balance reverence for tradition with respect for difference, ensuring that religious heritage coexists with civic equality. Such states often present themselves as cultural bridges, able to participate fully in global institutions without erasing their spiritual roots.

The most promising future lies in moderate models. Here, religion continues to shape culture and offer moral orientation, yet civil liberties remain safeguarded by secular law and democratic institutions. Faith provides cohesion and ethical depth, but without restricting freedom of belief. Citizens may participate in rituals, draw inspiration from shared traditions, and still retain autonomy in matters of conscience.

Handled with care, such an arrangement can sustain stability, foster inclusion, and ensure fair treatment across diverse communities. Religious values can be translated into ethical guidelines for public life rather than rigid codes of law. In this way, spiritual traditions may evolve from instruments of exclusion into sources of shared identity. Instead of dividing, they can unify—strengthening national solidarity while leaving open channels for dialogue with the wider world.

Religious states that succeed in this transformation will not be those that abandon their faith, but those that reinterpret it in light of universal principles of dignity and justice. Continuity and openness, sacred memory and democratic freedom—only together can these elements form a foundation for resilience in a rapidly changing world.

.

PART VI

SPECIAL HISTORICAL AND CULTURAL MODELS

INTRODUCTION

> **Special historical and cultural models of the state** are political systems and forms of governance that emerged under the influence of the unique historical, cultural, and social conditions of particular countries and regions.

These models differ from classical forms of government because they grow out of a people's own history, character, and traditions. They cannot be reduced to standard classifications, for each reflects a distinct path of development and a particular way of shaping political life. To study them properly, one must approach each case on its own terms, attentive to the cultural memory and historical experience that sustain it.

The Influence of Historical, Cultural, and Social Conditions on the Formation of Unique Models of Governance

The bond between power and society is always shaped by context—geography, climate, faith, memory of war, and inherited traditions. Each leaves its mark, producing distinctive ways of organizing authority and ruling communities.

China's model, for example, grew under the imprint of Confucian philosophy and centuries of centralized bureaucracy. India followed another course, molded by extraordinary cultural diversity, the coexistence of many languages and religions, and the enduring weight of the caste order.

The Importance of Studying Historical and Cultural Models for Understanding the Diversity of Political Systems

Exploring distinctive historical and cultural models is essential for grasping the true variety of modern political systems. No universal scheme can be applied without regard to context, for every nation follows its own trajectory, shaped by history, tradition, and experience. Political forms emerge not in a vacuum but out of centuries of struggle, adaptation, and cultural memory.

Recognizing this uniqueness reduces the risk of misjudgment in international relations and makes dialogue across cultures more productive. It tempers the temptation to impose ready-made frameworks and instead encourages attentive listening, mutual respect, and creative compromise. For diplomats, it means fewer blind spots; for scholars, it offers a richer, more nuanced map of political life.

It also deepens respect for political pluralism, reminding both analysts and policymakers that effective strategies must be flexible—anchored in principles yet responsive to circumstance. Acknowledging diversity does not weaken the search for common ground; rather, it strengthens it, for genuine cooperation can only rest on an honest appreciation of difference.

In this light, political systems appear not as rigid blueprints but as living organisms. Each adapts to its environment, balancing local identity with the pressures of globalization. The task of statesmen and thinkers alike is to honor these distinct roots.

"...to have neither the wish nor the ability to live for themselves ... and to belong wholly to their country."

— Plutarch, *Life of Lycurgus* 25.3

"...there is no state in the world in which greater obedience is shown to magistrates, and to the laws themselves, than Sparta."

— Xenophon, *Constitution of the Lacedaemonians* 8

SECTION 1. MILITARY OLIGARCHY: POLITICAL AUTHORITY CONCENTRATED AMONG A SMALL GROUP OF MILITARY LEADERS

> **A military oligarchy** is a distinctive model of state governance in which political power is concentrated entirely in the hands of a narrow group of military elites.

A military oligarchy emerges in situations where the army ceases to function merely as an instrument of national defense and instead becomes the primary political actor, taking control of all key spheres of societal life.

Main Features of a Military Oligarchy

1) Power in the hands of the few

In a military oligarchy, authority is concentrated within a narrow circle of senior generals and high-ranking officers. These figures dominate political life: they appoint civilian officials, control the legislative process, and direct the executive branch without checks or balances. Civilian politicians become subordinate actors, while the ultimate power remains firmly in military hands.

2) Rule through the armed forces

The army and security services form the backbone of governance. Courts, ministries, and administrative structures operate under military supervision, leaving no space for institutional independence. Intelligence agencies monitor society with vigilance, suppressing dissent and neutralizing opposition before it can become a threat.

3) Stability through coercion

The regime maintains order not by consent but by force. Military discipline and a strict chain of command ensure obedience, while protest and resistance are met with repression. Stability exists, but it is imposed from above, silencing alternative voices and creating a rigid atmosphere of control.

4) Militarization of society

Symbols of the armed forces permeate everyday life. Parades, uniforms, and the glorification of military heroes dominate public culture. Citizens undergo compulsory service or training, and schools are tasked with instilling loyalty to the armed forces. Civic identity becomes inseparable from obedience to the military and devotion to the state.

5) Curtailment of freedoms

Civil liberties are sharply curtailed. Freedom of speech, press, assembly, and political activity is restricted or abolished. Media outlets operate under strict censorship, spreading only official narratives. Independent voices are silenced, and alternative channels of communication vanish.

6) Absence of democracy

Genuine elections and popular representation do not exist. Political parties and civic groups are dissolved, subordinated, or reduced to ceremonial functions.

7) Authoritarian leadership

Decision-making rests in the hands of commanders. Policies are dictated unilaterally, without debate or consultation. Public opinion plays no role in governance, and citizens are expected to obey rather than participate.

8) Permanent emergencies

States of emergency and martial law are declared frequently, often prolonged indefinitely. These measures allow the suspension of rights and justify rapid mobilization, giving the regime extraordinary powers to silence dissent and consolidate authority.

9) Economic dominance of the military

The military elite extends its control into the economy. Natural resources, defense industries, and infrastructure fall under their authority. Economic privilege becomes a tool of political loyalty: allies are rewarded with contracts and access, while opponents are excluded from economic life.

10) Legitimation through nationalism

The regime justifies its rule by appealing to national unity, external threats, and the defense of sovereignty. Military leaders present themselves as guardians of the nation, turning patriotism into a political shield. This rhetoric narrows the space for freedom and fosters conformity under the banner of survival and security.

11) Civil institutions reduced to symbols

Parliaments, ministries, and courts may remain in form but lose real autonomy. Their role is purely symbolic—providing the appearance of governance while the true power lies entirely with the military hierarchy.

12) Cult of the commander

A personal cult often grows around the supreme leader or a small circle of generals. They are portrayed as national saviors and guarantors of stability. Public rituals, propaganda, and iconography elevate their authority, discouraging criticism and demanding loyalty.

13) Opacity of rule

Political decisions are made behind closed doors. Secrecy replaces accountability, and the public is excluded from meaningful participation. Citizens live in uncertainty, unable to know how or why crucial decisions are made.

14) Reign of fear

Surveillance, intimidation, and repression serve as the everyday instruments of power. Citizens live under constant observation—by secret police, informants, or neighbors pressed into collaboration. People learn to censor themselves in speech, writing, and even thought, never certain who might be watching or listening. Public silence becomes a survival strategy, while trust between individuals erodes.

Fear itself turns into the regime's strongest weapon: it secures obedience more effectively than ideology, weakens solidarity among citizens, and prevents the emergence of organized resistance.

Strengths of a Military Oligarchy

1. Strict organization

Modeled on the army, the state follows a rigid chain of command. Officials know their duties, and hierarchy reduces internal conflict, creating an orderly system—especially valuable in times of turmoil.

2. Swift crisis response

Centralized authority allows decisions to be made without delay. In war, disaster, or economic crisis, the regime can act immediately, mobilizing men and resources without parliamentary deadlock.

3. Guarantee of security

Strong armed forces suppress rebellion and unrest. By keeping tight control, the military ensures domestic order and shields society from chaos.

4. Capacity for long-term projects

Stable leadership makes it possible to complete large undertakings—roads, industry, or military reform—without fear of political turnover or shifting coalitions.

5. Deterrence of corruption

Harsh penalties and constant oversight reduce petty corruption. Officials under surveillance hesitate to abuse their position, raising efficiency in administration.

6. Rapid mobilization

With command centralized, the state can redirect resources quickly and deploy them where needed, whether for war or emergency relief.

7. Clear national priorities

Defense, security, and infrastructure dominate the agenda. Resources are not scattered across rival political programs but focused on agreed strategic goals.

8. Political stability

Without competing parties or unstable coalitions, governance avoids paralysis. Policy remains consistent, and disputes that divide civilian politics are muted.

9. Enforcement of discipline

Patriotism and loyalty are elevated as core virtues. Society is bound together through shared symbols and the authority of the armed forces.

10. Push for modernization

Military elites channel resources into technology, defense, and infrastructure, often accelerating industrialization and strategic development.

11. Continuity of rule

With no frequent elections or fragile coalitions, leadership remains predictable. This continuity enables long-term planning and reduces abrupt policy reversals.

.

Weaknesses of a Military Oligarchy

1. Suppression of freedoms

Under military rule, society lives under constant surveillance. Any expression of dissent is branded subversion, and freedoms of speech, press, assembly, and political activity are silenced. Civic organizations are either dissolved or placed under tight control, leaving citizens excluded from genuine public life.

2. Authoritarianism and repression

Power concentrated in a narrow circle soon becomes coercive. Security agencies intrude into daily existence, and repression settles into routine. With no oversight, commanders use state resources for personal gain. Fear may silence protest for a time, yet beneath the calm resentment accumulates, gradually corroding the regime.

3. Lack of legitimacy

Military governments usually come to power through coups rather than consent. Deprived of real participation, citizens regard them as imposed and unjust. With no broad support, rulers lean on coercion instead of legitimacy, which fosters protest and persistent hostility.

4. Blocked political development

By suppressing competition and preventing leadership turnover, military regimes halt the growth of political institutions and civic culture. Over time, state administration weakens, living standards decline, and discontent deepens. With reform denied, society drifts into stagnation.

5. No peaceful succession

In the absence of elections or constitutional procedures, power passes through conspiracies or internal conflict. Each transfer risks turmoil, as leadership struggles destabilize institutions and endanger society.

6. International isolation

Authoritarian regimes often encounter sanctions, trade restrictions, and reduced diplomatic engagement. Such isolation undermines investment, weakens the economy, and narrows foreign policy options.

7. Resistance to change

Military rulers prize stability over reform. Scientific progress slows, innovation withers, and skilled professionals leave in search of freedom and opportunity. The resulting loss of talent weakens the prospects for modernization.

8. Militarized economy

Defense absorbs a disproportionate share of national wealth. Education, healthcare, infrastructure, and social programs are neglected, lowering living standards and intensifying social tensions.

9. Economic fragility

Mobilization may project strength in the short term, but structural weaknesses remain. Heavy defense spending, reliance on monopolies, and fragile civilian institutions lead to debt, stagnation, and long-term imbalance.

10. Dependence on leaders

Authority often rests on one or a few commanders whose personal prestige holds the system together. When such figures weaken or disappear, the regime faces crisis. Vacuums at the top encourage rivalries, coups, or even collapse.

11. Suppression of cultural and intellectual life

Patriotism, militarism, and obedience are exalted as guiding values, while independent art, scholarship, and alternative worldviews are suppressed. Writers, teachers, and artists lose their space for expression, leaving society culturally impoverished and intellectually stagnant.

12. Factionalism within the elite

Behind the façade of discipline, rival groups of generals and officers compete for influence and resources. Such struggles erode cohesion, weaken the state, and often open the way for further coups.

Historical Examples of Military Oligarchy

Sparta

The Political System of Sparta

Sparta's political system combined elements of monarchy, oligarchy, and limited popular participation, all embedded within a rigidly militarized and hierarchical society. Authority rested in the hands of the Spartiates, a narrow elite of full citizens who formed only a small minority of the total population. From early childhood, every male citizen was trained for war, ensuring that the state was governed by soldiers as much as by laws. This unique mixture of institutions and values produced stability for centuries, but also sowed the seeds of eventual decline.

The Kings (Basileis)

Sparta's dual monarchy (diarchy) was a rare institution in antiquity. Two hereditary kings ruled simultaneously: one from the Agiad dynasty and the other from the Eurypontid line. This unusual arrangement balanced rival houses and prevented the emergence of a single monarch with absolute power.

In wartime, the kings acted as supreme commanders. Normally, one king led the army on campaign, while the other remained in Sparta to guard internal order. Kings enjoyed great prestige in the army: they led the first battle line, performed sacrifices before combat, and were entitled to a double share at communal meals. Yet their power was not unchecked. Kings were accompanied by Ephors, who monitored their actions, and they could be held accountable for military failures.

In peacetime, royal functions were largely ceremonial and religious. Kings presided as high priests at public sacrifices and festivals such as the Carneia. They also exercised limited judicial powers, mainly in family law, inheritance, and adoption. In political affairs, however, they were overshadowed by the Gerousia and the Ephors, both of which could overrule their decisions. The Ephors even held the extraordinary right to fine, prosecute, or depose a king if he acted against the state's interests.

The Council of Elders (Gerousia)

The Gerousia was the heart of Spartan politics and the principal check on royal power. It consisted of 28 aristocrats over the age of 60, elected for life by the Apella, together with the two kings, making 30 members in total. Membership was a lifelong honor, reserved for men of outstanding reputation, military service, and noble lineage.

The Gerousia drafted laws, acted as the highest court in cases of homicide and treason, and judged even the kings themselves. It also prepared motions to be presented to the popular assembly, giving it control over the legislative agenda. Its conservatism was legendary: composed of elder statesmen, it tended to resist innovation and uphold traditional values, ensuring continuity in Spartan politics.

The Ephors

Perhaps the most powerful institution in Sparta was the college of five Ephors. Elected annually from among the Spartiates, they exercised extensive powers that touched almost every aspect of life. Unlike the Gerousia, the Ephors represented the principle of rotation: each year five new officials took office, preventing the accumulation of long-term power.

Their responsibilities were wide-ranging. They supervised the education system (*agoge*), oversaw military discipline, managed foreign policy in consultation with the kings, and controlled taxation and finances. They could summon the Gerousia and the Apella, and presided over trials.

Checks and Balances

Sparta's constitution was famous for its internal equilibrium. The dual monarchy provided continuity and leadership, but it was balanced by the Gerousia, which gave stability through lifelong membership, and by the Ephors, who guaranteed annual oversight. The Apella, though limited, symbolized the role of the people.

This balance prevented tyranny: no single office could dominate for long. Yet the same system also curtailed flexibility. The Gerousia's conservatism and the Ephors' vigilance ensured stability, but they also blocked innovation.

The Popular Assembly (Apella)

The Apella was composed of all male Spartiates over the age of thirty. In theory, it was the supreme legislative body, but in practice its powers were limited. The assembly could only accept or reject proposals submitted by the Gerousia; it had no right to introduce new legislation.

Voting was conducted by **acclamation**: citizens shouted their approval or disapproval, and the loudest response determined the outcome. This method emphasized unity rather than debate. While the Apella gave citizens a sense of participation, it lacked real decision-making power. Its existence, however, reinforced the principle that political legitimacy rested on the collective voice of the citizen body, even if that voice was tightly controlled.

The Social Order

Sparta's political system was inseparable from its rigid social structure. Full rights belonged only to the Spartiates, who devoted their lives to military service.

- **Perioeci** were free non-citizens who lived in surrounding communities. They handled trade, craftsmanship, and agriculture not entrusted to the Helots. They also served as hoplites in the army and provided vital logistical support, but had no political rights.

- **Helots** were state-owned serfs, primarily of Messenian origin, who worked the land and sustained the Spartan elite. They outnumbered the Spartiates many times over, making them a permanent threat. To control them, the Spartans relied on intimidation and the krypteia, a practice in which young men patrolled the countryside to terrorize or kill Helots suspected of plotting revolt.

This hierarchy freed the Spartiates for war, but created deep instability. Spartan politics could not be separated from the constant fear of Helot uprisings.

The Economic Base

Unlike Athens, Sparta had little interest in trade or maritime power. Its economy was based almost entirely on agriculture and the labor of the Helots. Coinage was deliberately limited: iron bars served as currency instead of silver or gold, discouraging accumulation of wealth and reinforcing the ethos of austerity.

This closed, agrarian system produced stability but also rigidity. By rejecting commerce and naval power, Sparta isolated itself economically and politically. While Athens grew into a dynamic maritime empire, Sparta remained rooted in its agrarian base, unable to adapt to wider Mediterranean trade networks.

The Agoge

From the age of seven, Spartan boys were enrolled in the agoge, a state-run system of education and training. They lived in communal barracks, enduring strict discipline, physical hardship, and meager rations. The purpose was to instill obedience, resilience, and loyalty to the state.

The *agoge* was not limited to combat training. Boys studied music, poetry, and choral performance, which fostered unity and collective identity. Gymnastics and athletics cultivated physical excellence, while constant competition sharpened discipline. By the time they reached adulthood, Spartans were molded into warriors completely devoted to the commonwealth.

The Syssitia

Participation in the **syssitia**, or communal meals, was mandatory for adult male citizens. Each man contributed food from his land, worked by Helots, to support the mess. At these gatherings, warriors ate simple fare together, reinforcing solidarity, equality, and a shared martial ethos.

Failure to contribute or refusal to participate could result in loss of citizenship. The syssitia embodied the collective spirit of Spartan society: wealth and privilege mattered less than loyalty to one's peers and to the state.

The Role of Women

Spartan women held a position unparalleled in the Greek world. They could inherit and own property, sometimes amassing significant estates. They received physical training in running, wrestling, and throwing the discus, preparing them to bear strong children.

While women had no formal political role, their influence was substantial. They managed estates in the absence of men, commanded domestic slaves, and encouraged martial values. Ancient sources describe them as outspoken, even bold, reflecting their unique role in a society that depended on their strength to sustain its warrior ethos.

Ideology and Values

Sparta's political order was legitimized by the legendary lawgiver **Lycurgus**, who was credited with establishing the constitution. His laws were revered as sacred, never to be altered. The central ideal was **eunomia**—good order—embodying stability, discipline, and obedience to law.

Spartans cultivated austerity, courage, and devotion to the state above all. Poetry and ritual reinforced collective values. The myth of Lycurgus and the cult of tradition gave legitimacy to a system that prized continuity and rejected innovation.

Foreign Policy and the Peloponnesian League

Sparta's military ethos made it the dominant land power of Greece. It organized the Peloponnesian League, a coalition of city-states bound by treaties of mutual defense. While Sparta remained the hegemon, allies were compelled to follow its lead in war and peace.

This alliance allowed Sparta to rival Athens and eventually defeat it in the Peloponnesian War (431–404 BCE). Yet Sparta's reliance on land forces limited its reach: without a strong navy or commercial empire, its influence rarely extended far beyond the Peloponnese.

Decline

Despite its power, the Spartan system carried within it the seeds of collapse. The number of full citizens steadily declined due to demographic crises, war losses, and economic inequality. Land became concentrated in the hands of a few, undermining the basis of the citizen army.

Heavy dependence on Helot labor bred constant instability. Spartan conservatism, rooted in reverence for tradition, blocked adaptation to new conditions. Isolation from trade and unwillingness to reform further weakened the state.

The decisive blow came at the Battle of Leuctra in 371 BCE, when Thebes shattered Sparta's army. This defeat exposed the fragility of its institutions and marked the beginning of its irreversible decline. By the fourth century BCE, Sparta had lost its position as the leading power in Greece.

Argentina under the Military Junta (1976–1983)

The military oligarchy in Argentina was established after a coup d'état on March 24, 1976. Power was seized by three generals—Jorge Rafael Videla, Emilio Eduardo Massera, and Orlando Ramón Agosti—who formed the ruling junta. Immediately after the takeover, the constitution was suspended, Congress dissolved, and political parties banned.

The period from 1976 to 1983 became known as the *Dirty War* (*La Guerra Sucia*). Human rights organizations documented more than 30,000 cases of forced disappearances, alongside thousands of instances of torture, extrajudicial executions, and illegal detentions. Across the country, over 300 secret detention centers were established, where suspected opponents of the regime were tortured and killed.

In its early years, the junta received support from the United States, framed by Cold War fears of communism. Yet the systematic use of terror and mass violations of human rights soon provoked strong international condemnation, severely isolating Argentina and damaging its reputation abroad.

Economically, the military government sought to stabilize the country through foreign investment and the privatization of state enterprises. These measures, however, quickly backfired: external debt rose sharply, inflation spiraled, living standards declined, and social unrest intensified.

The junta's downfall was accelerated by Argentina's defeat in the Falklands War in 1982. The military failure destroyed what remained of the regime's legitimacy, sparking mass protests and fueling demands for a return to democracy.

In 1983, the generals relinquished power, opening the way for democratic elections and the presidency of Raúl Alfonsín. One of his first initiatives was the creation of the National Commission on the Disappearance of Persons (CONADEP), which documented the crimes of the dictatorship in its landmark report *Nunca Más* (*Never Again*), a lasting testimony to the brutality of the regime.

Chile under General Pinochet (1973–1990)

The military oligarchy in Chile was established after the coup d'état of September 11, 1973, when the armed forces, led by General Augusto Pinochet, overthrew the democratically elected president Salvador Allende. Almost immediately, the United States recognized and supported the new junta, having long viewed Allende's leftist government as a threat during the Cold War. The coup suspended the constitution, dissolved Congress, and banned political parties, placing all power in the hands of the military, with Pinochet quickly concentrating authority in himself.

From the very outset, Chile entered one of the darkest chapters of its history. Mass repression targeted supporters of leftist parties and movements, trade union leaders, journalists, students, and intellectuals. According to later official investigations, more than 3,000 people were killed or disappeared, over 28,000 were imprisoned and tortured, and tens of thousands were driven into exile.

The most notorious instrument of repression was the *Dirección de Inteligencia Nacional* (DINA), Pinochet's secret police, later replaced by the *Central Nacional de Informaciones*

(CNI). With financial and logistical backing from U.S. intelligence during the early years, these agencies built a vast network of clandestine detention centers such as Villa Grimaldi, Londres 38, and Colonia Dignidad. Survivors testified to systematic practices of electric shocks, beatings, sexual violence, and psychological torture. Families were torn apart, and thousands of opponents vanished into the ranks of the *desaparecidos*, never to return.

Repression extended beyond Chile's borders. With tacit U.S. tolerance, Pinochet's Chile became a leading participant in Operation Condor, a coordinated campaign of South American dictatorships to eliminate political exiles in the 1970s and 1980s. Chilean intelligence worked closely with regimes in Argentina, Uruguay, Paraguay, and Brazil. The 1976 assassination of former Chilean diplomat Orlando Letelier in Washington, D.C., carried out by agents of Pinochet's secret police, starkly demonstrated the global reach of this system and caused significant embarrassment for the United States, which until then had maintained close ties with the Chilean regime.

Alongside repression, Pinochet implemented far-reaching economic reforms. Guided by the "Chicago Boys," a group of economists trained at the University of Chicago, the junta liberalized markets, privatized state enterprises, and opened the economy to foreign investment. These reforms—strongly supported by U.S. advisers and financial institutions—reduced inflation, stabilized the currency, and modernized infrastructure. By the mid-1980s, Chile was regarded as one of the most stable economies in Latin America.

Yet the social costs were severe. The privatization of pensions, education, and healthcare deepened inequality. Unemployment soared during the early years of reform, and broad sectors of the population were left without protection. While business elites and international investors benefited, ordinary Chileans bore the weight of restructuring.

Internationally, Pinochet's dictatorship became synonymous with authoritarian repression. Reports of torture, disappearances, and killings led to condemnation from the United Nations, Amnesty International, and many governments. Although Washington eventually distanced itself, especially after the Letelier assassination, for most of the 1970s and early 1980s the United States remained a key ally, providing diplomatic cover and economic support.

In 1988, a national plebiscite was held in which a majority of Chileans voted against extending Pinochet's rule. This forced the general to accept a transition to civilian government. Democracy was formally restored in 1990 under President Patricio Aylwin, though Pinochet retained influence as commander-in-chief of the army until 1998 and later as senator-for-life.

"The punishment which the wise suffer who refuse to take part in the government is to live under the government of worse men."

— Plato, *Republic*, Book I

SECTION 2. ARISTOCRATIC REPUBLIC: GOVERNANCE DOMINATED BY A HEREDITARY ELITE OR PRIVILEGED CLASS

> **An aristocratic republic** is a form of government in which the state is controlled by a narrow circle of individuals drawn from the upper strata of society—the aristocracy.

Main Features of an Aristocratic Republic

1) Concentration of Power in the Aristocracy

Political authority rests in the hands of a narrow circle, defined by noble birth, wealth, or superior education. Rule is regarded not as a civic duty for all, but as the inherited privilege of the few.

2) Restricted Access to Government

Public service is closed to outsiders. Offices pass through hereditary lines or are filled by elections and appointments carefully controlled by the aristocracy itself.

3) Institutions Drawn from the Upper Classes

The legislature, executive, and courts are staffed almost entirely by nobles. These institutions embody the conviction that governance is the natural right of the elite.

4) The Ideology of Rule by "the Best"

The republic rests on the claim that only the most virtuous and educated are fit to lead. The aristocracy presents itself as the guardian of order and prosperity, uniquely capable of steering society.

5) Continuity of Authority

Power remains in the same families for generations, giving the system remarkable stability. Abrupt changes and revolutions are rare, as leadership is carefully handed down.

6) Narrowing of Political Rights

The majority of citizens are excluded from decision-making. Their role is limited to obedience, while political rights are reserved for a privileged minority.

7) Closed Decision-Making

Policy is debated and settled within an inner circle. Decisions are shielded from public view, leaving most of the population unaware of how power is exercised.

8) Corporate Nature of Rule

The aristocracy behaves like a self-protective corporation. Its foremost concern is preserving its own privileges, even when the broader needs of society are neglected.

9) Economic Foundations of Power

Control of land, property, and wealth provides the material base of aristocratic rule. Economic dominance and political authority reinforce each other.

10) Resistance to Reform

Attempts at democratization—expansion of suffrage, redistribution of land, or major legal change—are blocked. Reform is seen as a threat to the elite's monopoly.

11) Cultivation of Aristocratic Values

Nobles foster a culture of refinement, education, honor, and duty. They present themselves as models of virtue and as custodians of the higher traditions of society.

12) Social Stratification

The system formalizes inequality. Distinctions between rulers and the rest are sharpened, leaving little room for mobility and ensuring that society remains divided into rigid layers.

<u>Strengths of an Aristocratic Republic</u>

1. Competence and Education of the Ruling Elite

Aristocrats were trained in philosophy, law, economics, and diplomacy. Their broad education gave them the knowledge to govern wisely and the skill to make reasoned decisions.

2. Political Stability

Because power remained within a narrow circle, succession was orderly. Abrupt changes were rare, creating an atmosphere that favored continuity and long-term planning.

3. Swift Action in Crises

A small council could act without delay. Freed from endless debates, the elite responded quickly when emergencies demanded decisive leadership.

4. High Standards of Governance

Office was both a privilege and a duty. This sense of responsibility upheld traditions of legality, discipline, and respect for ethical norms.

5. Freedom from Populist Pressures

Unbound by elections or shifting moods of the crowd, aristocrats could carry out reforms that served the republic's long-term interests—even when unpopular in the moment.

6. Guardians of Culture and Tradition

The ruling class invested in art, architecture, and education. By protecting heritage, they strengthened identity and gave society a sense of shared continuity.

7. Shield Against Extremism

Because access to power was limited, radical ideas had little chance of gaining influence. This barrier kept the state safe from destabilizing movements.

8. Personal Stake in Success

The fortunes of the elite were tied to the prosperity of the republic. Their own power and prestige depended on its strength and security.

9. **Preservation of Legal Traditions**

The hereditary nature of rule reinforced continuity. Institutions and laws endured across generations with little disruption.

10. **Diplomatic Skill and Prestige Abroad**

Educated nobles often had connections across Europe. They represented their republic with dignity, strengthening its reputation and influence in international affairs.

11. **Long-Term Vision**

Without the limits of electoral cycles, aristocratic governments could launch large projects and pursue policies designed to bear fruit over decades.

12. **Civic Virtues of the Elite**

Duty, moderation, and discipline were cultivated as guiding ideals. By practicing them, the aristocracy justified its claim to leadership.

13. **Admiration from Abroad**

Other states respected aristocratic republics for their refinement, cultural achievements, and steady institutions. This prestige enhanced their standing among neighbors.

14. **Selective Admission of Talent**

Although closed by nature, aristocracies occasionally admitted exceptional individuals—commanders, jurists, or thinkers—whose presence renewed and strengthened governance.

Weaknesses of an Aristocratic Republic

1. **Exclusion of the Majority**

Political authority rests in the hands of a narrow elite. Most citizens are shut out of decision-making, which breeds resentment and a sense of injustice.

2. **Entrenched Inequality**

Because the aristocracy is closed, upward mobility is rare. Generations remain locked into fixed positions, and social tension never truly disappears.

3. **Resistance to Change**

Privileges are guarded fiercely. Reforms are delayed, innovation is resisted, and the state risks drifting into stagnation.

4. **Lack of Public Oversight**

Power is exercised without accountability. With no checks from society, abuses, arbitrariness, and corruption become recurring dangers.

5. **Decline of the Ruling Elite**

Without competition or responsibility to the people, the elite may grow complacent and lose competence. Over time, institutions weaken as discipline erodes.

6. Secrecy in Government

Decisions are taken behind closed doors. Ordinary citizens remain in the dark, which erodes confidence in the system.

7. Fragile Legitimacy

Because rule is imposed from above, acceptance is shallow. In times of hardship, frustration can turn quickly into political crisis.

8. Neglect of Common Needs

The interests of society are often sacrificed to preserve the privileges of the few. Problems accumulate, while the well-being of the majority declines.

9. Wealth and Power Concentrated at the Top

A small group holds both economic and political control. This imbalance slows balanced development and deepens inequality.

10. Suppression of Civic Life

Parties, associations, and independent initiatives are discouraged or forbidden. Citizens grow passive, leaving society unable to renew itself politically.

11. Elite Rivalries

Competition among aristocratic families can turn bitter. With no democratic mechanisms to settle disputes, conflicts risk destabilizing the state.

12. Pressure from Below

Excluded groups eventually demand inclusion. Resistance to reform often triggers revolutions or erodes the system from within.

13. Dependence on a Few Families

The regime leans on a handful of dynasties. Should they decline, die out, or turn against one another, the political order itself is threatened.

14. Detachment from Society

Generations of separation leave rulers estranged from the lives of ordinary citizens. This distance weakens both legitimacy and effective governance.

Historical Examples of an Aristocratic Republic
The Venetian Republic (13th–18th centuries)

In Venice, power rested with a small circle of noble families. They sat in the Great Council (*Maggior Consiglio*), the republic's supreme body. After the Serrata of 1297, membership became hereditary and lifelong, reserved only for patricians. From that moment, the aristocracy monopolized every important office of state.

At the top stood the Doge, elected for life but surrounded by checks. His authority was carefully limited by other organs of government. The Senate (*Consiglio dei Pregadi*) directed policy, while the Council of Ten (*Consiglio dei Dieci*) emerged as the strongest executive and judicial body. This system of overlapping councils kept power in collective hands, preventing rule by a single man.

The arrangement brought stability, but also rigidity. By the seventeenth century, Venice faced new challenges: the shift of trade to the Atlantic reduced its wealth, while the closed aristocracy resisted reform. What once guaranteed order now blocked renewal.

In 1797, Napoleon's armies entered the lagoon, and Venetian independence—maintained for more than a thousand years—collapsed. The republic, long governed by its patrician elite, disappeared, bringing to a close one of Europe's most enduring examples of aristocratic rule.

The Roman Republic (Patrician Era, 5th–3rd centuries BCE)

The early Roman Republic stands as one of history's clearest cases of aristocratic government. Power rested with the patricians—the city's oldest families, among them the Julii, Cornelii, Fabii, Valerii, and Aemilii. Claiming descent from Rome's founders, they treated rule not only as a privilege but as a hereditary duty.

At the center of this order was the Senate, composed exclusively of patricians. Senators, wearing purple-bordered togas, gathered in the Curia to debate war and peace, finance, and legislation. The highest magistracies—consuls, praetors, censors—were also reserved for their class. Young nobles advanced through the *cursus honorum*, a ladder of offices combining training in law, oratory, and military command.

Exclusion bred resentment. In 494 BCE, plebeians staged the first *secessio plebis*, withdrawing from the city and refusing military service. The strike forced concessions: the creation of the Tribune of the Plebs, officials elected to defend plebeian rights and armed with veto power.

This began the Conflict of the Orders. In 450 BCE the Law of the Twelve Tables was engraved on bronze, fixing rules of justice and restraining arbitrary power. In 367 BCE, the Licinian-Sextian laws opened the consulship to plebeians. Over time, wealthy plebeian families entered high office and joined with patricians to form the *nobilitas*—a new elite blending lineage with wealth.

By the second century BCE, however, power narrowed once more. A handful of senatorial dynasties controlled magistracies, dominated the Senate, and expanded vast estates (*latifundia*) worked by slaves from Rome's conquests. Small farmers—the backbone of the citizen army—were displaced, swelling the urban poor.

Reform attempts by Tiberius and Gaius Gracchus sought to restore land to peasants, but Senate resistance turned violent. Both brothers were killed, and Rome slid into an age of political murders, riots, and widening inequality. The Senate proved unable to govern an empire or to contain unrest. Generals such as Marius, Sulla, Pompey, and Julius Caesar turned loyal armies into instruments of personal power.

By the mid–1st century BCE, civil wars and aristocratic rivalries destroyed the Republic. Caesar's dictatorship and the rise of Augustus ended Rome's long experiment with patrician rule, replacing it with imperial monarchy.

"Kings are gods, and share in a manner the divine independence. Their power is absolute."

— Jacques-Bénigne Bossuet,
Politics Drawn from the Very Words of Holy Scripture (1709)

SECTION 3. ABSOLUTE THEOCRATIC MONARCHY: MONARCH HOLDING SUPREME POLITICAL AND RELIGIOUS AUTHORITY

> **An absolute theocratic monarchy** is a form of government in which all authority is vested in a single ruler (the monarch), whose power is regarded as divinely ordained and entirely governed by religious norms and doctrines.

In such a state, the monarch does more than govern. He directs political and administrative life while standing as the highest spiritual authority, ruling by the will of divine powers or in the name of God himself.

The hallmark of an absolute theocratic monarchy is this union of throne and altar in a single person. The sovereign is not only a lawgiver but also the chief interpreter of sacred writings, the guardian of orthodoxy, and the voice through which divine will is heard. His decrees carry both legal and religious weight, leaving no room for rival institutions or civic oversight.

In this order, public life is inseparable from faith. Law is drawn directly from sacred texts and dogma, and religious morality becomes enforceable by the state. What might elsewhere remain a matter of conscience or personal devotion is here transformed into binding obligation. Ritual, doctrine, and political authority merge, so that religion shapes not only belief but the entire structure of society.

Main Features of an Absolute Theocratic Monarchy

1) Union of Throne and Altar

In this system, the monarch combines in his person both secular authority and sacred leadership. He directs the affairs of state while also serving as the guardian of the true faith, so that the commands of government and the decrees of religion flow from the same source.

2) Sacred Source of Authority

The ruler's legitimacy rests on the conviction that he governs by divine sanction. His right to rule is proclaimed in doctrine and ritual as a gift of God or higher powers, placing his authority above earthly challenge.

3) Law Anchored in Faith

The entire legal framework of society is drawn from sacred texts and dogmas. What in other systems might remain moral guidance or ritual practice becomes here binding law, regulating courts, contracts, punishment, and even private conduct.

4) Absolute and Unchecked Power

Because the monarch's word is seen as divine command, no institution parliament, assembly, or council—can set limits on him. His decrees are final, and civic oversight is excluded as both unnecessary and impious.

5) Religion as Universal Obligation

Faith does not remain confined to temples or personal devotion. It becomes the standard for daily life, defining rules of family, commerce, and community. Every citizen is bound to live by the same creed, without exception.

6) Monopoly on Sacred Interpretation

The sovereign is recognized as the sole voice capable of interpreting holy texts. Alternative readings are dismissed as heresy, and rival authorities are silenced to ensure uniformity of belief.

7) Sacralization of the Monarch

The ruler himself is revered as a sacred figure, embodying the divine order on earth. Obedience to him is celebrated as both civic loyalty and an act of faith, so that political rebellion equals religious transgression.

8) Merging of Religious and State Institutions

In a theocratic system, clergy and administrators operate as one, erasing the boundary between sacred authority and political power. Temples function not only as places of worship but also as courts, where priests sit in judgment and interpret divine law. Their verdicts carry the weight of state authority, binding citizens both spiritually and legally.

Civil offices, in turn, become instruments for enforcing religious decrees. Bureaucrats act less as neutral administrators and more as guardians of the faith, ensuring that laws reflect sacred teachings and that daily life conforms to prescribed rituals.

9) Suppression of Dissent

Any attempt to challenge doctrine—through new sects, alternative practices, or private interpretation—is branded as a threat to both truth and public order. Punishment is severe, for dissent is treated as treason against God and state alike.

10) Religious Control of Culture and Learning

Education, literature, and the arts are placed under religious oversight. Schools teach official doctrine, scholarship is confined within theological boundaries, and cultural expression reinforces the faith, ensuring intellectual conformity.

11) Ritual in Governance

Every major act of government is sanctified by religious ceremony. Laws are proclaimed with sacred rites, treaties sealed with invocations, and victories celebrated as blessings from above. The constant presence of ritual reinforces the sacred character of politics.

12) The State as Sacred Community

Society itself is conceived as a congregation bound together by shared belief. Citizens are not seen as members of a secular polity but as worshippers united under one ruler, one law, and one divine will.

Strengths of an Absolute Theocratic Monarchy

1. Strong Social Cohesion

Shared belief in a single faith provides a unifying framework. Citizens see themselves as members of one community, bound together by common rituals and loyalty to sacred authority.

2. Clear Moral Orientation

Laws derived from scripture offer straightforward guidance on conduct.

3. Legitimacy of Authority

The monarch's rule is sanctified as divine will. This religious foundation often strengthens obedience and allows even unpopular decisions to be accepted with less resistance.

4. Efficiency of Centralized Power

With authority concentrated in one ruler, decisions can be made quickly. Crises are met with direct action, free from the delays of competing political factions.

5. Political Stability

The fusion of faith and power creates continuity across generations. Institutions and traditions endure, reducing the likelihood of sudden upheaval.

6. Sacralization of the Ruler

The monarch is revered not only as head of state but also as a sacred figure. This dual role deepens loyalty and reinforces the unity of the population.

7. Integration of Religion and Culture

Faith shapes art, architecture, and education, fostering cultural achievements that endure for centuries. Religious inspiration often drives monumental works and strong traditions.

8. Unified Ideological Framework

By controlling interpretation of sacred texts, the regime reduces the risk of competing doctrines. Citizens share a common worldview aligned with state and religious authority.

9. Low Levels of Open Political Conflict

Since opposition is framed as rebellion against both ruler and faith, public dissent is rare. Political competition is minimized, which can preserve surface harmony.

10. Capacity for Mobilization

Religion provides powerful motivation in times of war or crisis. Citizens are called to sacrifice not just for the state but for the preservation of their faith, strengthening solidarity.

11. Resistance to Foreign Influence

A strong religious foundation may shield society from external ideologies or cultural pressures. This helps preserve independence and maintain distinctive traditions.

Weaknesses of an Absolute Theocratic Monarchy

1. Suppression of Individual Freedom

Life is closely regulated by religious dogma.

2. Discrimination Against Minorities

Alternative faiths are usually treated with suspicion. Religious minorities may face pressure, persecution, or second-class status.

3. Risk of Social and Economic Stagnation

Strict reliance on religious norms can discourage innovation and limit openness to outside influences.

4. Absence of Civic Oversight

With no mechanisms of accountability, rulers govern unchecked. Arbitrary decisions, favoritism, and corruption may flourish, protected by the aura of sacred authority.

5. Difficulty Adapting to Change

Rigid ideology often slows the state's response to crises.

6. Constraints on Scholarship

Learning and science thrive only within the boundaries of accepted doctrine.

7. Loss of Talent

Educated and creative individuals leave in search of greater freedom. This "brain drain" can weaken culture, innovation, and economic development.

8. Dependence on the Monarch's Persona

The system relies heavily on the sanctity and charisma of a single ruler. A disputed succession or decline in authority can destabilize the entire state.

9. A Climate of Fear

Strict enforcement of conformity produces outward obedience but inner resentment. Citizens may comply publicly while privately opposing the system, undermining long-term cohesion.

10. Risk of Economic Misallocation

Resources are often directed to temples, rituals, or monumental projects. While this may reinforce faith and legitimacy, it can divert investment away from education, health, or infrastructure.

11. Potential for Diplomatic Strains

Religious rigidity can create friction with secular or pluralistic states. At times this leads to strained relations or reduced influence abroad, though in some cases theocracy remains an active diplomatic player.

12. Risk of Violent Upheaval

When avenues of peaceful reform are absent, pressure accumulates. Rebellion or revolution may erupt suddenly, bringing abrupt and destructive change.

Historical Examples of an Absolute Theocratic Monarchy
The Vatican (Modern Period)

The modern Vatican emerged as a sovereign entity after the signing of the Lateran Accords on February 11, 1929, between Pope Pius XI and Italian leader Benito Mussolini. These agreements formally ended the long-standing conflict between the Holy See and the Italian state, unresolved since the capture of Rome in 1870.

The Lateran Accords consisted of three separate documents:

1. **Political Treaty** — This treaty created the independent state of Vatican City, a territory of about forty-four hectares placed fully under papal authority. The Vatican received international recognition as sovereign, while the Pope acknowledged the Kingdom of Italy with Rome as its capital.

2. **Concordat** — This agreement regulated relations between the Catholic Church and the Italian state. Italy recognized Catholicism as the sole official religion, granted the Church special privileges in education and public life, accepted church marriage as valid in civil law, and introduced compulsory teaching of Catholic religion in schools. In turn, the Church recognized Italy's sovereignty over former papal territories and agreed to refrain from direct political intervention.

3. **Financial Convention** — Italy compensated the Holy See for the loss of its former lands and properties during national unification. The settlement consisted of 750 million lire in cash and one billion lire in government bonds.

Vatican City is governed entirely under canon law, the legal system of the Catholic Church, making it a rare modern example of theocracy where religious doctrine forms the basis of all governance.

The Pope is elected for life by the College of Cardinals and holds absolute authority. His decisions are final and cannot be appealed. Legislative, executive, and judicial power is exercised either directly by him or through officials he appoints, such as the Secretary of State, the Governor, the heads of dicasteries (departments), and judges— all accountable only to him.

Vatican law derives from the *Codex Iuris Canonici* (Code of Canon Law), first promulgated in 1917 and revised in 1983 under Pope John Paul II. Canon law regulates not only spiritual life but also civic matters inside Vatican City and throughout the Catholic clergy worldwide. Civil divorce does not exist, and marriage is recognized only in its sacramental form. Judicial bodies, including the Supreme Tribunal of the Apostolic Signatura, operate under papal authority, with the Pope as the final court of appeal. Law enforcement and the Vatican Gendarmerie likewise function under ecclesiastical supervision.

The Vatican's economy is managed by specialized institutions, most notably the Institute for the Works of Religion (commonly known as the Vatican Bank), which reports directly to the Pope. Financial activity is guided by Catholic ethical principles, prohibiting investment in enterprises judged incompatible with Church teaching.

Tibet under the Dalai Lamas (until 1959)

Until the Chinese invasion and the suppression of the Tibetan uprising in March 1959, Tibet functioned as an absolute theocratic monarchy in which secular and spiritual authority were concentrated in the person of the Dalai Lama. The 14th Dalai Lama, Tenzin Gyatso, born in 1935 and enthroned in 1940, was revered as the earthly incarnation of Avalokiteśvara, the Bodhisattva of Compassion—an article of faith that endowed him with supreme authority. Unlike hereditary monarchies, succession was determined by a religious ritual: monks searched for the child believed to be the reincarnation of the previous Dalai Lama, testing him through recognition of sacred objects. The Panchen Lama, Tibet's second-ranking spiritual authority, traditionally played a decisive role in this process, though his influence often depended on the political balance of the time.

Government and Administration

The highest executive organ of the state was the Kashag, consisting of four ministers, or Kalöns, appointed directly by the Dalai Lama. In practice, the Dalai Lama personally supervised their work, and ultimate decision-making remained in his hands. Administration was fully centralized, with no independent or secular institutions of oversight. A judicial commission functioned under the Kashag, but its authority was limited: all major disputes and cases of political importance were referred to the Dalai Lama himself. A system of secret surveillance operated under monastic officials, responsible for monitoring the loyalty of the population and suppressing dissent. This apparatus allowed the ruling elite to maintain control but created an atmosphere of caution and fear among ordinary Tibetans.

Law and Justice

The legal system was rooted in the Gelugpa school of Tibetan Buddhism, the dominant monastic tradition. The main sources of law were Buddhist scriptures and customary codes, most notably the *Laws of the Thirteen Articles* and the *Laws of the Sixteen Articles*, codified in earlier centuries and transmitted in monastic institutions. These codes regulated both civil and criminal matters. Offenses were treated not merely as secular violations but also as spiritual transgressions, demanding both punishment and atonement. Penalties ranged from fines and forced labor to corporal punishment, while reconciliation and compensation were often accompanied by religious rituals intended to purify the offender's karma. The close identification of crime with sin reinforced the sacral character of justice.

Economy and Society

Economically, Tibet remained predominantly agrarian and feudal. Landownership was concentrated in the hands of large monasteries, aristocratic families, and the state. Peasants worked these estates under conditions of hereditary obligation, providing labor, taxes in kind, and services to their lords. By most estimates, more than two-thirds of the population lived in conditions resembling serfdom, with little possibility of social mobility.

The aristocracy, numbering only a few hundred families, combined wealth with prestige. Monasteries, meanwhile, functioned as both landholders and centers of power. Major institutions such as Drepung, Sera, and Ganden controlled vast estates and tens of thousands of monks, making them as influential economically as they were spiritually. The absence of modern infrastructure—paved roads, telegraph lines, postal service, electricity—left Tibet isolated from the technological advances of the 19th and 20th centuries. Industry was virtually nonexistent, and foreign trade was limited to small-scale exchanges with India, Nepal, and China. The ruling elite deliberately preserved this isolation, fearing that outside influence might weaken the authority of the Church and disrupt the traditional order.

Education and Culture

Education was almost entirely monopolized by the monasteries. Secular schools were exceedingly rare and available only to the children of aristocrats, wealthy merchants, or officials. The overwhelming majority of Tibetan boys who received formal education did so in monasteries, where they studied Buddhist scriptures, ritual, logic, philosophy, and Tibetan medicine. Advanced students could pursue higher degrees in Buddhist scholasticism, such as the *geshe* degree, awarded after decades of study and debate. For ordinary peasants, however, literacy was rare, and opportunities for secular knowledge were minimal. This preserved the dominance of monastic culture but restricted intellectual diversity and limited the development of science and practical skills.

Decline and Fall

The theocratic monarchy of the Dalai Lamas ensured a high degree of spiritual unity and cultural identity for centuries, but its rigidity, hierarchical order, and deliberate isolation created serious vulnerabilities. When Chinese troops entered Tibet in 1950, the country had no modern army, no industrial base, and no effective infrastructure for defense. Over the following decade, Beijing consolidated control, establishing military garrisons and administrative authority. In March 1959, after a failed uprising in Lhasa, the 14th Dalai Lama fled to India, where he formed a government-in-exile at Dharamshala. With his departure, the centuries-long experiment in Tibetan theocracy collapsed, and Tibet was integrated into the People's Republic of China

"The duties of the Brāhmaṇas, Kṣatriyas, Vaiśyas and Śūdras, O Arjuna, are distinguished according to the qualities born of their own nature.

Serenity, self-restraint, austerity, purity, forgiveness, uprightness, knowledge, wisdom, faith are the duties of the Brāhmaṇas, born of their own nature.

Heroism, vigour, steadiness, resourcefulness, not fleeing from battle, generosity and lordliness are the duties of the Kṣatriyas, born of their own nature.

Agriculture, cattle-rearing and trade are the duties of the Vaiśyas, born of their own nature; and action consisting of service is the duty of the Śūdra, born of his own nature."

— *Bhagavad Gita*, XVIII, 41–44

SECTION 4. CASTE-BASED STATE: POLITICAL AND SOCIAL ORDER STRUCTURED ACCORDING TO HEREDITARY CASTE DIVISIONS

> **A caste state** is a form of socio-political organization in which the population is divided into strictly segregated social groups (castes), membership in which is determined exclusively by birth and enforced by state law.

A caste state represents a distinct form of political and social order in which society is divided into rigid, hereditary groups. An individual's position is determined entirely by birth into a particular caste and cannot be altered during their lifetime.

This division is not left to custom alone. It is written into law and upheld by government institutions, which enforce caste boundaries and ensure that traditional duties and restrictions are observed. Movement between castes is forbidden, and social life is organized to prevent intermingling.

Political authority lies firmly in the hands of the higher castes. They hold privileged access to state offices, command economic resources, and shape political decisions. Lower castes, by contrast, are denied meaningful rights, excluded from public life, and confined to heavy, underpaid, and socially devalued labor.

In such a system, inequality becomes more than a tradition—it is the very foundation of state ideology. The government actively protects caste hierarchy, presenting it as essential for order, stability.

Main Features of a Caste State

Social Characteristics

1) **Rigid Social Division**

In a caste state, society is not simply stratified but locked into rigid compartments. Each caste occupies a predetermined place in the hierarchy, surrounded by a system of privileges and prohibitions. Duties are passed down from generation to generation, and boundaries are guarded by both law and custom. Crossing these lines is unthinkable, for the order of society itself is believed to depend on their preservation.

2) **Hereditary Membership**

Caste affiliation is inherited at birth and remains unchanged for life. A person may acquire wealth, talent, or knowledge, but these achievements cannot move them beyond the boundaries of their caste. This permanence transforms birth into destiny, removing any prospect of mobility and turning social division into a fixed law of existence.

3) **Endogamy**

Marriage becomes the strongest safeguard of caste boundaries. To marry outside one's caste is either prohibited or subject to severe sanctions. Endogamy preserves what is defined as the "purity" of the group and ensures that bloodlines, property, and social roles remain firmly enclosed within hereditary limits.

4) Segregation in Daily Life

The separation of castes is not only ideological but also physical. People from different castes live in separate neighborhoods, worship in different temples, and may even use different wells or roads. This spatial division turns inequality into a visible, daily experience and makes exclusion a constant presence in ordinary life.

5) Markers of Caste Status

Caste identity is reinforced through countless details of appearance and behavior. Rules dictate what one may wear, how one may style hair, what food is permitted, and even the form and size of one's dwelling. To violate these codes is not just a breach of etiquette but an offense against the established order, carrying stigma and punishment.

6) Purity and Pollution

The hierarchy of castes is justified by the ideology of ritual purity. Higher castes are regarded as spiritually clean and closer to the divine, while lower castes are stigmatized as polluted. Contact with them may require ritual cleansing, and this idea of pollution becomes the ultimate rationale for exclusion, discrimination, and control.

Political Characteristics

1) Legal Codification of Hierarchy

The caste structure is not left to unwritten tradition but written into law. Legislation affirms the duties and privileges of each caste, turning inequality into an official principle of governance and placing social division under the direct protection of the state.

2) State Enforcement of Caste Norms

Government institutions actively monitor obedience to caste rules. Attempts to cross boundaries or reject one's assigned duties are punished, not only as acts of defiance but as threats to social harmony. The state thus becomes the chief guardian of immobility.

3) Power in the Hands of the Upper Castes

High political offices, military command, and authority over decision-making are reserved for the elite. This monopoly allows the higher castes to govern according to their interests, excluding the lower groups from participation and perpetuating the cycle of privilege and dependence.

4) Caste-Based Succession

Even within the ruling stratum, power does not circulate freely. Offices and titles are handed down within families, reinforcing both caste privilege and dynastic continuity. Leadership thus becomes doubly hereditary: determined first by caste and then by family lineage.

5) Absence of Equal Citizenship

In such a system, the very concept of equal citizenship disappears. Rights and duties are defined not by universal principles but by caste affiliation, so that law does not treat individuals as equals. Political inequality becomes an unquestioned foundation of the state.

Economic Characteristics

1) Concentration of Wealth

Land and property are concentrated in the hands of the upper castes, who control access to resources. The lower castes remain dependent, lacking ownership and economic security. This concentration of wealth strengthens the authority of the elite and reinforces the cycle of poverty below.

2) Hereditary Occupations

Professions are fixed by caste, binding families to the trades of their ancestors. A farmer's son must remain a farmer, a craftsman's son a craftsman. This rigidity prevents individual advancement and ensures that economic roles serve to preserve the wider structure of hierarchy.

3) Exploitation of Lower Castes

The lower castes are compelled to carry out the most degrading and laborious tasks, often marked as ritually unclean. Their labor is indispensable to the economy but is valued least, leaving them trapped in poverty while their work sustains the privilege of others.

4) Waste of Human Potential

By restricting education and opportunity, the caste state squanders talent and innovation. Individuals capable of excellence are denied the chance to pursue it, and society as a whole suffers from inefficiency, stagnation, and wasted human energy.

Legal and Judicial Characteristics

1) Inequality Before the Law

Justice is not blind but determined by caste. The same crime may bring harsh punishment for a person of low caste and leniency—or even exemption—for one of high status. Legal inequality thus mirrors and reinforces social inequality.

2) Religious Foundation of Law

The law draws its authority not from secular reasoning but from sacred texts and divine sanction. By presenting social hierarchy as cosmic order, it shields inequality from criticism and elevates it to the level of eternal truth.

Ideological and Cultural Characteristics

1) Sacralization of Hierarchy

The caste system is justified as natural, sacred, and divinely ordained. The state promotes this ideology relentlessly, portraying strict social division not as oppression but as the very basis of harmony, balance, and cosmic stability.

2) Control of Knowledge

Education and literacy are confined to the upper castes, who alone are granted access to sacred texts and higher learning. By denying the lower castes the right to study, the ruling groups preserve both intellectual monopoly and social subordination.

Strengths of a Caste State

1. Clear Distribution of Roles

From birth, each person knows their rights, duties, and obligations. Nothing is left uncertain: farmers remain farmers, priests remain priests, and rulers remain rulers. This clarity reduces social tension and gives society a predictable rhythm.

2. Absence of Competition for Status

Because movement between castes is impossible, people do not struggle endlessly for advancement. Rivalries over prestige are muted, and society avoids the constant contests for privilege seen in more fluid systems.

3. Preservation of Skills and Traditions

Knowledge is inherited along with caste. Crafts, trades, and rituals are passed faithfully from one generation to the next, ensuring the continuity of specialized skills and protecting cultural heritage.

4. Solidarity Within Castes

Shared duties and a common status bind caste members closely together. Families support one another, neighbors cooperate, and collective identity helps people endure hardship.

5. Resistance to External Influence

Closed social boundaries shield the community from outside ideologies and fashions. This insulation preserves traditions, religious beliefs, and long-established ways of life.

6. Administrative Simplicity

For the state, governing becomes easier. Officials oversee well-defined groups, each with fixed duties, making it simpler to distribute resources and enforce laws.

7. Continuity Across Generations

Values, rituals, and customs endure century after century. This long memory fosters a strong cultural identity and a sense of belonging to a history larger than any single life.

8. Transmission of Moral Norms

Caste duties are taught from childhood as part of religion and morality. Ethical norms become second nature, uniting society under shared standards of behavior.

9. High Specialization

Because professions are hereditary, workers master their crafts over generations. Rituals, trades, and services essential to society are carried out with skill and efficiency.

10. Unity of Religion, Culture, and State

Caste is not merely social—it is sacred. The same system organizes governance, daily life, and religious belief. This unity reinforces loyalty to tradition and strengthens the legitimacy of the state.

Weaknesses of a Caste State

1. Absence of Social Mobility

In a caste society, status is fixed from birth. No matter how talented, ambitious, or industrious a person may be, they cannot rise above the group into which they were born.

2. Institutionalized Inequality

Inequality is not hidden but written directly into law and tradition. The lower castes are denied access to equal rights, quality education, and social services.

3. Waste of Human Talent

Although hereditary specialization preserves skills, it also squanders ability. Brilliant individuals may spend their lives performing degrading tasks simply because of their caste. The result is the loss of potential leaders, thinkers, and innovators in science, politics, and the arts.

4. Erosion of Motivation

When advancement is impossible, effort loses its meaning. Members of the lower castes often have little incentive to work beyond what is demanded of them. Over time, this weakens productivity, stifles initiative, and slows both economic and cultural progress.

5. Poor Adaptability

Rigid caste roles leave little space for adjustment when new skills are required. Technological advances or changes in trade demand flexibility, but a system bound by birth cannot easily shift, leaving society exposed to decline in times of change.

6. Cycles of Poverty and Exploitation

Lower castes are condemned to the hardest and least respected labor. Generations remain trapped in poverty, while their work sustains the privilege of others. This entrenched exploitation becomes a permanent feature of society, lowering collective welfare.

7. Suppression of Learning

Education is monopolized by the upper castes, while the majority are barred from literacy and access to knowledge.

8. Social Fragmentation

Though solidarity may exist within each caste, barriers between groups divide the community as a whole. Shared identity is weakened, cooperation is obstructed, and the idea of national unity becomes fragile or absent.

9. Risk of Latent Unrest

The system suppresses open rebellion, but resentment builds silently. Over generations, anger accumulates, and when crises strike—whether famine, invasion, or economic collapse—long-suppressed grievances may erupt violently, destabilizing the state.

10. Cultural Stagnation

The emphasis on preserving tradition leaves little space for renewal. Arts, literature, and philosophy are preserved but rarely allowed to evolve.

11. Barrier to Economic Modernization

By binding individuals to hereditary occupations, the caste order prevents labor mobility and discourages enterprise.

12. Exposure to External Threats

Rigid societies often struggle when confronted by foreign powers. Inflexibility makes it difficult to adapt to new patterns of trade, modern military challenges, or colonial expansion. As a result, the caste state proves vulnerable when faced with outside pressures.

Historical Examples of a Caste State

India

In traditional Indian society, the population was divided into hereditary groups known as varnas. Membership was determined entirely by birth and remained unchanged throughout life. This rigid division gave the social order remarkable durability. Every individual knew their rights, duties, and place, lending a sense of clarity to personal life and predictability to the collective organization of society.

At the summit of the hierarchy stood the Brahmins—priests and intellectual leaders entrusted with ritual, teaching, and the preservation of sacred knowledge. Their authority was underpinned by Hindu texts, especially the Laws of Manu (Manusmriti), which codified rules of caste relations and sanctified social division. Below them were the Kshatriyas, warriors and rulers who concentrated political and military power, providing leadership and protection. The Vaishyas sustained society through farming, trade, and craftsmanship, while the Shudras performed essential manual labor and service, forming the broad economic base of the system. Outside these four varnas stood those labeled Untouchables (Panchama or Dalits), consigned to tasks deemed ritually impure and excluded from the mainstream of social life.

This structure, though restrictive for individuals, proved highly resilient for society as a whole. It enabled Indian civilization to withstand repeated invasions and centuries of foreign domination. From the campaigns of Alexander the Great to long periods of Islamic rule and later British colonialism, the caste system provided continuity. Even when rulers changed, the basic social fabric endured. Each caste preserved its role, passing on traditions, skills, and religious practices, so that cultural identity and cohesion survived political upheaval.

Ancient Egypt
(Estate-Based Society of the New Kingdom, 16th–11th centuries BCE)

The social order of New Kingdom Egypt rested on a clearly stratified hierarchy, where birth usually determined a person's place. State policy reinforced this structure, preserving stability and continuity. Yet opportunities for advancement, though rare, were not entirely absent: a gifted scribe, a loyal official, or a successful soldier could sometimes rise in rank.

At the very top stood the Pharaoh, regarded as the living embodiment of a god and the guardian of ma'at—cosmic order and justice. His authority extended over every sphere of life: politics, the army, the economy, and religion. Around him gathered the high aristocracy—royal relatives, governors of the provinces (nomarchs), senior generals, and top administrators. They commanded vast estates, enjoyed wealth and privilege, and directed the machinery of the state.

Alongside them rose the priesthood, whose power grew immensely during the New Kingdom. Temples were not only centers of worship but also major economic institutions, controlling land, labor, and wealth. The clergy of Amun at Thebes in particular accumulated enormous resources and often influenced political affairs, sometimes rivaling the Pharaoh himself.

The middle strata were composed of literate and skilled professionals. Scribes formed the backbone of administration, keeping records of land, taxes, and state expenditure, and supervising great public projects. Craftsmen and artisans—metalworkers, potters, stonemasons, and jewelers—produced tools, weapons, and luxury goods, while also building temples and royal tombs, leaving behind the monuments that still define Egypt's legacy.

The largest portion of the population consisted of peasant farmers. They cultivated wheat, barley, vegetables, and fruit, providing the kingdom's sustenance. Their lives were marked by heavy taxation and compulsory labor on state projects such as temples, canals, and necropolises. Though formally free, their obligations to the state and the elite left them with few real rights.

At the bottom of the hierarchy stood slaves. Their numbers were relatively small compared to other ancient civilizations, and most were prisoners of war or foreigners brought into Egypt. While denied full rights, some were able to own property, marry, and occasionally gain freedom, making their condition more varied than the stereotypical image of slavery.

The estate system of New Kingdom Egypt balanced rigidity with limited chances for advancement. It provided centuries of stability and continuity, enabling cultural and architectural achievements of extraordinary scale. Yet the concentration of power in the hands of the Pharaoh, the aristocracy, and the priesthood also created long-term weaknesses, leaving Egypt vulnerable to internal rivalries and external threats.

CONCLUSION

The historical and cultural models we have examined—military oligarchy, aristocratic republic, absolute theocratic monarchy, and the caste state—demonstrate how diverse political systems can be when shaped by unique traditions and historical experience. Each emerged in specific circumstances, reflecting the values and needs of its society.

These models also reveal strengths, above all in sustaining stability, order, and clear social roles. India's caste system, for example, though formally abolished, did not vanish; it adapted to new realities and continues to influence social life and cultural identity. This persistence helps explain India's resilience, even after centuries of foreign domination. Absolute theocracies show a similar endurance: the Vatican remains the spiritual center of over a billion Catholics, while Saudi Arabia grounds its stability not only in religious authority but also in its central role as the world's largest oil exporter.

The modern era suggests that the durability of states depends less on rejecting tradition than on finding a balance—preserving cultural identity while remaining open to change. Those societies that combine heritage with flexibility prove the most resilient. Japan illustrates this in its blending of tradition with modernization, and India in its integration of democracy with deeply rooted social structures.

The study of distinctive historical models should not be seen as a contrast to modern democracy, but as a way to understand why certain institutions endure. By examining these experiences, we can identify the conditions that sustain stability and development, as well as those that foster division and conflict. Such understanding is essential for creating political systems that respond not only to universal principles but also to the concrete historical and cultural needs of their people.

PART VII

PHILOSOPHICAL AND HYPOTHETICAL MODELS

INTRODUCTION

Philosophical models of the state are thought experiments, built not to mirror reality but to imagine it differently. Like architects working with ideas rather than stone, philosophers design ideal structures meant to reveal what a just and harmonious society might look like. These visions are not descriptions of what is, but explorations of what could be.

Philosophy has long served as humanity's critical voice, urging us to move beyond custom and habit. When thinkers proposed new forms of social order, they were not indulging in abstract dreams. They were identifying principles—justice, equality, freedom—that might guide communities toward a more humane future. From Plato's Republic to modern utopias, such concepts have acted as signposts, suggesting directions for human progress.

In our own time, these models retain their relevance. Confronted with crises and contradictions, we can use them to test possibilities that ordinary politics overlooks. They do not predict the future, but they remind us that the future is shaped by choices made now. By reflecting on the balance between freedom and security, or the relation of individual good to the common good, philosophy teaches that history is not predetermined. It is open to decision, responsibility, and imagination.

"And to men like him, I said, when perfected by years and education, and to these only you will intrust the State."

— Plato,
Republic, Book VI, 487a; trans. Benjamin Jowett

SECTION 1. IDEAL (UTOPIAN) STATE: THEORETICAL MODEL OF A PERFECT POLITICAL ORDER

The utopian state represents a philosophical model of society imagined as free from conflict, injustice, and deprivation. It is not a description of existing political orders but a theoretical construction, born of humanity's enduring search for perfection. Philosophers and thinkers have long engaged in such thought experiments, not to replicate reality, but to present an alternative vision of how social life might look if human virtues and shared values were realized in their purest form. In this sense, utopia functions less as a plan than as a mirror of aspiration—showing what people hope their communities might one day become.

A central principle of the utopian state is absolute equality among citizens. Social hierarchies rooted in wealth, birth, or privilege are dissolved, and all members of society stand on the same footing. In such a community, no individual is condemned to poverty while others live in luxury. Instead, resources are shared so that every person has secure access to food, shelter, healthcare, and education. This guarantees not only survival but also the possibility of flourishing: the free development of personality, talents, and creativity. Utopia thus envisions abundance not merely as material prosperity but as the fulfillment of human potential.

Equally important is the elimination of war, violence, and exploitation. Utopian states are imagined as communities that have transcended the causes of conflict, whether rooted in economic inequality, political rivalry, or religious division. Citizens interact on the basis of solidarity and mutual understanding, guided by common interests rather than competition. Aggression is unnecessary, because institutions are organized to prevent injustice and to resolve disputes peacefully. In this way, utopia serves as a counter-image to the violent history of humankind, suggesting that harmony is not only desirable but conceivable.

While the utopian state remains a philosophical abstraction, its significance lies in its role as an ideal benchmark. It provides a standard against which societies can measure their achievements and shortcomings. From Plato's Republic to Thomas More's Utopia and later visions of social harmony, these imagined communities have not offered blueprints for immediate realization but have inspired debates about justice, freedom, and the common good. They remind us that the future is not predetermined but open to human decision and imagination. Utopia, in this sense, is not simply a dream—it is a challenge, urging societies to reflect on what they are and what they could become.

Chapter 1. Plato's *Republic*

The Classical Ancient Model of the Ideal Society: The First Philosophical Utopia

The *Republic* (*Politeia*) is one of the key dialogues of the ancient Greek philosopher Plato, composed around 380 BCE. In it, Plato presents a conversation between

Socrates and his students and friends on the nature of justice, morality, and the principles underlying the organization of a perfect society. For the first time in the history of Western philosophy, Plato elaborates in detail the concept of an ideal state, grounded not in customary traditions or historical circumstances but in reason, rational knowledge, and philosophical principles.

With this work begins the tradition of philosophical utopias, which had a profound influence on social and political thought in subsequent eras. Plato's ideas inspired Renaissance, Enlightenment, and modern thinkers to create their own visions of the perfect society and became the starting point for philosophical reflection on the possibility of consciously designing the state.

Historical and Intellectual Context

Biography of Plato (427–347 BCE)

Plato was born around 428/427 BCE in Athens into an ancient and distinguished family associated with the city's aristocracy and political elite. According to later biographical tradition, his given name was Aristocles, while the nickname *Plato* (from the Greek *platos*, "broad") referred either to his physique, his style of expression, or even the breadth of his forehead. On his father's side, the family lineage was said to trace back to Codrus, the last legendary king of Athens, while on his mother's side he was connected, again by tradition, to the famous lawgiver Solon. Regardless of the historical accuracy of these claims, such a pedigree underscores Plato's noble status and the high quality of education he received.

Plato's youth unfolded against the backdrop of the Peloponnesian War (431–404 BCE), a time of political crisis and deep questioning of Athenian democracy. As a young man, he was drawn to literature, poetry, music, and athletics, and he initially considered a political career. His intellectual interests, however, soon turned toward philosophy.

The decisive event in Plato's life was his encounter with Socrates around 407 BCE, when Plato was about twenty years old. Their association lasted until Socrates' trial and execution in 399 BCE. Socrates profoundly shaped Plato's worldview and directed his life's path toward philosophy. The unjust condemnation of his teacher on charges of impiety and corrupting the youth convinced Plato of the dangers of political arbitrariness and strengthened his resolve to envision a form of society where justice and truth would be protected.

After Socrates' death, Plato is reported by ancient sources such as Diogenes Laertius to have left Athens and traveled for a number of years. He is said to have visited Egypt, where he learned about priestly traditions and mathematics, and southern Italy and Sicily, where he came into contact with Pythagorean thinkers. While these accounts belong to the biographical tradition rather than secure historical fact, they reflect Plato's reputation as a philosopher who absorbed wisdom from multiple sources and cultures.

Around 387 BCE, Plato returned to Athens and founded his famous Academy in the grove of Academus. This institution became the first organized school of philosophy in the Western world, where students studied not only philosophy but also mathematics, astronomy, logic, politics, and ethics. Among its most prominent students was Aristotle, who spent about twenty years there before becoming one of the greatest philosophers of antiquity. The Platonic Academy endured, in various forms, for centuries, until 529 CE, when Emperor Justinian ordered the closure of pagan philosophical schools in Athens in an effort to consolidate Christian orthodoxy.

The Political Structure of Athens and the Crisis of Polis Democracy

Plato lived during the rise and decline of Athenian democracy, which reached its peak in the 5th century BCE and then entered a period of profound crisis. The political system of Athens was built on direct democracy, in which supreme authority rested with the Assembly (*ekklesia*), where citizens voted on all major decisions. The power of the people was absolute: citizens directly participated in governance, elected and supervised officials, and even acted as jurors in popular courts. The Assembly was supported by the Council of Five Hundred (*Boule*), which prepared issues for debate, and by the practice of ostracism, whereby dangerous politicians could be exiled for ten years. The ideal of Athenian democracy was *isonomia*—equality of all citizens before the law and the right of each to take part in public life. In practice, however, reality diverged sharply from this ideal.

Over time, the democratic system faced serious shortcomings and contradictions, which deepened the crisis of the polis. One of the central problems was the excessive influence of demagogues—charismatic leaders who manipulated the crowd to achieve personal power and enrichment. It was often such figures, rather than the wisest or most virtuous citizens, who rose to prominence, leading to unjust and dangerous decisions.

Moreover, Athenian democracy was far from universal in the modern sense. The right to vote was restricted to free male citizens of Athenian birth, while women, slaves, and the large population of resident foreigners (*metics*) were excluded from political life. This meant that democracy ultimately served the interests of a limited group, often prone to impulsive and emotional decisions swayed by orators and political intrigues.

The situation was further aggravated by the economic and social strain of the Peloponnesian War (431–404 BCE). The prolonged conflict with Sparta drained Athens' resources, deepened social inequality, and spread poverty. The war also brought plague to the city, killing thousands, including the statesman Pericles, and leaving Athens weakened. Defeat in the war stripped Athens of its dominance in Greece, forcing it to surrender its political hegemony and endure the humiliating rule of the oligarchic regime of the "Thirty Tyrants" (404–403 BCE). This dark episode revealed how easily democracy could degenerate into tyranny and how quickly citizens could lose their freedom and dignity.

All these dramatic events, witnessed firsthand by Plato, convinced him that a democracy driven by the whims of the crowd and superficial emotions could not provide true justice or wise governance. His disillusionment with the Athenian system led him to seek an alternative form of political organization—one based on reason, morality, and justice.

The Philosophical Dialogue as a Genre of Idea Expression in Ancient Greece

The philosophical dialogue was a distinctive literary and philosophical genre of ancient Greece, in which authors conveyed their ideas through conversations between two or more interlocutors. This form of exposition allowed the philosopher not simply to present finished truths but to engage the reader in the process of inquiry and critical analysis. Formally, the dialogue resembled a lively and open debate in which truth emerged not from dogmatic assertions but through joint, rational discussion.

The tradition of dialogue begins with Socrates, who left no writings of his own but preferred direct engagement with his contemporaries. Socrates used questioning and answering to expose contradictions in his interlocutors' beliefs and to guide them toward a deeper understanding of the concepts under discussion. He introduced the method of *elenchus* ("refutation"), in which a person was led, through carefully crafted questions, to recognize the flaws in their reasoning. This made philosophy vivid and accessible, turning dialogue into a tool of intellectual education and self-examination.

Plato inherited and further developed the Socratic method, giving it greater philosophical depth and literary form. Unlike mere records of conversations, Plato's dialogues were artistically complete works, with vivid characters and dramatic structure. His interlocutors were not only philosophers but also politicians, poets, statesmen, and representatives of various social groups. This form allowed Plato to address not only abstract philosophical questions but also pressing social, ethical, and political issues of Athenian society.

The genre of dialogue was particularly suited to the expression of philosophical ideas because it presented truth not as fixed knowledge but as the result of continuous intellectual effort and collective inquiry. Dialogue required the reader's active engagement, independent thought, and the capacity to weigh arguments and counterarguments. The Platonic dialogue aimed not so much to provide a definitive answer as to prompt reflection and the development of one's own perspective on the problem.

In later centuries, the genre of philosophical dialogue spread widely and found continuation in the works of many ancient authors, including Xenophon, Cicero, and Lucian. Its influence extended far beyond antiquity: during the Renaissance and early modern period, thinkers such as Thomas More in *Utopia* and Galileo in his *Dialogue Concerning the Two Chief World Systems* also turned to the dialogical form to explore and communicate new ideas. As a result, the dialogue became one of the greatest achievements of Greek culture, exerting profound influence on the development of philosophy, pedagogy, and literature throughout subsequent history.

Key Ideas and Principles

The Doctrine of Justice as the Central Principle of the Ideal State

The concept of justice (*dikaiosynē*, δικαιοσύνη) is fundamental in Plato's *Republic*. For Plato, justice is not merely one of the virtues but the basic principle upon which the entire ideal society must rest. Unlike the traditional understanding of justice as simple adherence to laws or equal treatment before them, Plato approached the concept on a much deeper level, interpreting it as harmony and the proper ordering of all parts of a whole—whether the human soul or society itself.

In the *Republic*, the discussion of justice begins with attempts to define it through external features: the repayment of debts, helping friends, and punishing enemies. Socrates, the central figure of the dialogue, systematically demonstrates the inadequacy of these external definitions. Through the course of the dialogue, Plato gradually leads the reader to the conclusion that true justice is not found in outward actions but in the inner structure of the human soul and the organization of society.

According to Plato, the human soul consists of three parts: the rational, the spirited, and the appetitive. Justice within the individual arises when reason governs the spirited and appetitive elements, preventing them from falling into conflict with one another. By analogy, society is likewise composed of three main classes: philosopher-rulers, warrior-guardians, and producers (farmers and craftsmen). A state becomes just when each class performs its proper function without interfering in the tasks of others. In other words, justice is achieved only when every person and every element of society is in its rightful place, fulfilling its designated role.

From this perspective, justice, for Plato, is not simply formal equality or legal order but an ideal condition of harmony, grounded in rational understanding and the fulfillment of proper purpose. A state structured according to this principle can secure not only stability and prosperity but also genuine happiness for its citizens, since it eliminates conflicts born of ignorance, selfishness, and the pursuit of personal gain. Importantly, Plato insists that such harmony is possible only when power rests in the hands of philosopher-kings, individuals trained to subordinate personal interest to wisdom, truth, and the common good.

Thus, Plato's doctrine of justice fundamentally transforms traditional notions of politics and morality: it asserts that morality, rationality, and harmony must form the very foundation of political organization, not simply its added qualities. In the *Republic*, Plato presents justice as the supreme virtue of both the individual and the state, the unifying principle that integrates all others, making his vision one of the most influential and enduring in the entire history of political philosophy.

Philosophers as Ideal Rulers: The Principle of the "Philosopher-King"

One of the most important and original elements of Plato's *Republic* is the idea that society should be governed by philosophers—those few who have attained the highest level of knowledge, wisdom, and virtue. Plato was the first to formulate the famous principle of the "philosopher-king," arguing that genuine justice and prosperity are possible only when political power is entrusted to individuals who deeply understand the nature of the Good, truth, and the highest ideas.

The reason philosophers must govern, in Plato's view, lies in the very essence of their thinking and way of life. The true philosopher does not strive for power, wealth, or personal advantage but seeks knowledge of eternal and unchanging realities, above all the Idea of the Good. Unlike ordinary people, absorbed in daily concerns and emotions, philosophers are able to see further and deeper, to discern the true needs of society, and to make decisions grounded in knowledge rather than passions or ambition.

Plato contrasts philosophers with traditional politicians, who are driven by the thirst for power and personal interests. For him, the genuine ruler must be completely free from such motives. It is precisely the absence of self-interest and the devotion to truth that make the philosopher an ideal ruler. Moreover, only the philosopher is capable of maintaining balance in the complex structure of the ideal state, composed of three classes: rulers (philosophers), guardians (warriors), and producers. The philosopher not only governs but also serves as a moral exemplar, ensuring stability and harmony within society.

Plato emphasizes that those who rule must not be simply people with a taste for philosophy, but individuals who have passed through a long and rigorous process of selection and education. This training includes mathematics, dialectic, astronomy, ethics, and physical discipline. Only after many years of study and testing of loyalty to the common good can the philosopher assume the role of ruler. Such a person, Plato insists, will regard power not as a privilege but as a duty and responsibility to society.

This idea was extraordinarily revolutionary for its time, since in most Greek poleis political power was held by military leaders, wealthy elites, or charismatic demagogues. Plato's principle of the philosopher-king introduced, for the first time, a fully rational approach to politics, opposing wisdom to passion and selfishness. In the history of philosophy, this concept profoundly influenced later theories of the state and society, becoming the starting point for reflections on the role of knowledge, morality, and intellect in the governance of human communities.

The Theory of Ideas and Its Role in the Construction of the State

At the center of Plato's philosophy lies the theory of Ideas (*eidē*), which plays a decisive role in his conception of the ideal state. According to this theory, there exist two realms: the sensory world of changeable things and the world of eternal, immutable Ideas accessible only to reason. The Ideas are perfect, unchanging archetypes of all things and phenomena, while the sensory world contains only their pale, imperfect reflections. Thus there are eternal Ideas such as Beauty, Goodness, and Justice; everything we perceive as beautiful or just in our world is only an approximation of these absolute exemplars.

In the *Republic*, Plato connects his theory of Ideas directly to the structure of the state. He argues that the construction of an ideal society is possible only when philosopher-rulers are able to apprehend the highest Idea—the Idea of the Good, which is the source of all other Ideas and the foundation of being. Only those who truly grasp the nature of the Good are capable of governing society, guiding it toward harmony and proper development.

Plato shows that without knowledge of the world of Ideas, true justice and harmony cannot be achieved, for ordinary conceptions of goodness, justice, or happiness are often subjective, contradictory, and unstable. Only philosophers, who have grasped eternal truths, can lead society beyond the chaos and conflicts produced by ignorance and flawed notions of fundamental values.

The theory of Ideas also underlies Plato's understanding of the role of each person in society. According to it, every citizen has an "ideal" function determined by their nature. A person achieves the highest happiness and fulfillment when they fully realize the purpose inherent in their own Idea. As a result, society becomes a community in which each individual engages in the activity most perfectly suited to them. In this way, a state founded on the knowledge of Ideas is not merely a political structure but an embodiment of absolute order and perfection.

In addition, the theory of Ideas forms the foundation of Plato's approach to education. The education of citizens in the ideal state requires gradual initiation into the world of Ideas through the study of mathematics, dialectic, and philosophy. Only after completing this long and demanding process can citizens attain the capacity to see clearly the eternal truths that govern the world and to recognize the meaning of their own existence.

Thus, Plato's theory of Ideas is not an abstract doctrine but a vital instrument for constructing a rational, just, and harmonious state, in which decisions are grounded in eternal and immutable principles rather than in subjective opinions or private interests.

Political Structure and Social Organization

Structure of Society: Three Classes — Philosopher-Rulers, Guardian-Warriors, and Producers (Artisans and Farmers)

According to Plato's design, society in the ideal state is divided into three clearly defined classes, each performing functions suited to its nature and abilities. Just as the human soul is composed of three parts—the rational, the spirited, and the appetitive—so too must society be organized in a parallel fashion. Each class reflects one part of the soul, together forming a harmonious and balanced social whole.

The first and highest class consists of the philosopher-rulers, who embody the rational part of the soul. Their task is to govern the state wisely and justly. These are not merely educated individuals but the rare few who, after long and rigorous training, attain knowledge of the ultimate Good and grasp the realm of eternal Ideas. Awareness of these truths enables them to perceive the interests of society as a whole rather than the desires of its parts. Philosopher-rulers must be free of ambition and selfish motives; for them, ruling is a duty and responsibility, not a privilege or an opportunity for gain.

The second class is that of the guardians or warriors, representing the spirited, emotional, and volitional part of the soul. They are the defenders of the state, responsible for maintaining internal order and safeguarding society from external threats. Courage, discipline, and strength are essential qualities, but they must be complemented by virtues such as loyalty, selflessness, and duty. Guardians undergo rigorous training and moral education so they are prepared to defend the state in times of need. To prevent conflicts of interest, they are forbidden private property, ensuring that their loyalty remains fixed on the common good.

The third class comprises the producers—farmers, craftsmen, and merchants—who correspond to the appetitive, or desiring, part of the soul. Their role is to provide the material foundation of society through productive labor and economic activity. This is the most numerous class, consisting of those who cultivate the land, produce goods, and sustain daily needs. They may own property and pursue trade, but their public role is limited to production. Plato insisted that producers should remain devoted to their function without interfering in governance, since they lack the knowledge required for leadership.

Thus, each of the three classes in Plato's state corresponds to its role and inner nature. Social harmony is achieved through strict observance of this division of labor, in which each citizen performs the tasks for which they are naturally suited. Any blurring of roles, in Plato's view, inevitably leads to conflict, injustice, and the breakdown of the order. The tripartite division of society therefore stands as the cornerstone of his conception of the ideal state.

Mechanisms of Selection, Education, and Training of Philosopher-Rulers

For Plato, philosopher-rulers do not arise by accident. To reach the highest offices, they must pass through a demanding process of selection and a long course of education. In the Republic, Plato describes this path in detail, emphasizing that only such preparation can form rulers capable of governing wisely and justly.

The process begins in early childhood. Children are raised collectively and offered the same opportunities, regardless of their family origin. Selection depends solely on natural ability and character. From the earliest years, education reveals differences: some display sharper intellect, stronger self-discipline, or a greater capacity for moral responsibility. These are marked out for further training, while others return to ordinary civic roles.

The first stage is basic education. It combines physical exercise with elementary studies in grammar, music, and literature. The aim is to shape both body and spirit, cultivating balance, courage, and respect for order. At this point, those unable to meet the high demands are set aside, leaving only those fit for more advanced instruction.

The next stage is higher education in the sciences. Students study arithmetic, geometry, astronomy, and harmonics. For Plato, these disciplines are not merely practical tools but training for the mind. Mathematics teaches precision, order, and abstraction. Astronomy draws the gaze from earthly change to the eternal movements of the heavens. Together, they prepare the intellect to rise above appearances and approach universal truth.

Beyond this lies philosophy itself. The study of dialectic, Plato insists, is the crown of education. Dialectic enables the soul to grasp the Forms directly and to contemplate the highest principle—the Idea of the Good. At this level, students learn to test arguments, expose contradictions, and discern truth from falsehood. Only a few, distinguished by exceptional intellect and integrity, are able to master this demanding discipline.

The final stage is practical training in politics. Candidates who have completed the intellectual course must spend years in public service, first in minor offices, then in positions of greater responsibility. This experience allows them to apply their knowledge, confront the realities of administration, and prove their commitment to the common good.

Plato also emphasizes that this process extends over decades and follows a strict timeline. Up to the age of 20, students are trained in physical discipline, music, and literature. Between 20 and 30, those most gifted study mathematics and the sciences. From 30 to 35, a smaller group is introduced to dialectic. Between 35 and 50, candidates serve in public office, combining practical governance with continued philosophical reflection. Only after reaching the age of 50, when their intellectual maturity and moral steadiness have been tested in both theory and practice, may they ascend to the role of philosopher-rulers.

In Plato's state, power is not inherited by birth or seized by force. It is entrusted to those who have demonstrated superior ability, moral strength, and devotion to truth.

The Distinctive Life, Duties, and Rights of Each Class

Plato clearly distinguishes the living conditions, duties, and rights of each of the three classes in the ideal state. These differences are determined by the tasks performed by each class and by its role in maintaining order and harmony within society.

The highest class—the philosopher-rulers—dedicate themselves entirely to governing the state and pursuing truth. Their lives are marked by strict discipline and spiritual asceticism: they have no right to private property, luxury, or family life in the ordinary sense. Philosophers live communally, satisfying only their basic needs, and are wholly free from personal ambition, wealth, or the pursuit of power. For them, authority is not a privilege but a heavy responsibility, a service to the community. Their duties include making the most important state decisions, planning and overseeing the execution of laws, educating the younger generation, and guiding all aspects of public life. Their sole and supreme "right" is the respect and obedience of other citizens, grounded in their knowledge and moral superiority.

The middle class—the guardians or warriors—lead lives devoted to physical training, military excellence, and moral steadfastness. They are charged with defending society against internal and external threats, maintaining order, and ensuring strict compliance with the laws. Like the philosophers, they are denied the right to own property or accumulate wealth, a restriction designed to eliminate conflicts of interest and the temptations of greed. Guardians live communally, eating and resting together under constant public supervision. Their renunciation of private interests extends to family life: they do not form traditional households, and children are raised collectively. Their essential right is the respect of society and the guaranteed provision of everything necessary for life and service.

The lowest, but most numerous, class—the producers, including farmers and craftsmen—live under different conditions. Unlike the upper classes, this class may own private property and maintain ordinary family life. Their primary duty is to produce all material goods essential for the survival and prosperity of society. They work in agriculture, crafts, and trade. Their lives are freer than those of the philosophers and guardians, since they are permitted personal interests, property ownership, and economic activity. However, their rights are restricted in the realm of governance: they are barred from holding leadership positions or interfering in political affairs, as Plato believed they lacked the knowledge and moral discipline required for such responsibilities.

Plato thus envisions a society in which the rights and obligations of each class are precisely aligned with its role in the state. The upper classes live in strict self-denial for the sake of the common good, while the lower class enjoys greater personal freedom in exchange for renouncing political influence. In this structure, justice, harmony, and stability are secured, as every citizen fulfills the function best suited to their nature and capacity.

The Organization of Family, Upbringing, and Collective Education of Children

In Plato's ideal state, the traditional understanding of family is fundamentally transformed, especially for the higher classes—the philosopher-rulers and the warrior-guardians. For these groups, Plato proposes the abandonment of conventional family relations, since he believed that personal attachments and kinship ties could lead to injustice, corruption, and discord within society. In his view, the interests of family and kin inevitably compete with those of the state, threatening to undermine the harmony and justice of the political order.

In place of traditional family bonds, Plato introduces a system of collective marriage and communal child-rearing. For rulers and guardians, he envisages a carefully organized system in which partners are not chosen by personal preference but by rational selection designed to improve the physical and moral qualities of the next generation. Such unions are arranged under the strict supervision of the state, and children born of them are raised not by their biological parents but by the community, in special institutions overseen by the most virtuous and capable educators.

Children are brought up communally from an early age without being told who their biological parents are. This ensures that each child regards the elders of the community as parents and their peers as brothers and sisters. In this way, solidarity is reinforced, while conflicts born of family loyalties are eliminated. Such practice fosters in future guardians and rulers a sense of belonging to one great family—the state as a whole—rather than to a private kinship group.

Education is organized in stages and aims at the harmonious development of physical, intellectual, and moral qualities. In early childhood, emphasis is placed on health, moderation, discipline, and the cultivation of collective spirit. As they grow older, children are introduced to literacy, music, literature, philosophy, and the mathematical sciences, gradually acquiring higher intellectual culture and moral resilience.

For the lowest class—the producers (farmers and craftsmen)—Plato retains the traditional family and private life. This is because their duties and role in society do not demand the renunciation of personal attachments or property. However, even here the state maintains oversight of education, ensuring that common moral and educational standards are upheld.

In Plato's state, the family becomes a deliberate instrument for shaping unity and solidarity in society, while the education of children is transformed into a rational and carefully planned process aimed at achieving the highest ideals of justice and the common good.

Economic and Property Relations

Rejection of Private Property for the Higher Classes
(Philosophers and Guardians)

One of the most striking and radical features of Plato's model of the ideal state is the complete prohibition of private property for the two higher classes—the philosopher-rulers and the warrior-guardians. Plato was convinced that private property, along with the pursuit of wealth and personal comfort, is the primary cause of social conflict, injustice, and corruption. He therefore proposed creating conditions in which those entrusted with political power or responsible for the security of society would be entirely deprived of material possessions and property attachments.

For rulers and guardians, property is replaced by collective ownership of all necessary resources. They live together in specially designated quarters, dine at common tables, and share clothing and all essential goods provided by the state. This communal way of life eliminates envy, rivalry, greed, and any conflict arising from personal material interests.

The rejection of private property among the higher classes also removes the possibility of corruption and abuse of power. Plato believed that a person free from material incentives and personal gain would act solely according to the principles of reason, justice, and the common good. As a result, philosophers and guardians remain completely unencumbered by material temptations, directing their attention exclusively to fulfilling public duties and realizing the aims of the state as a whole.

This approach stands in sharp contrast to the conditions of the third class—the producers (farmers and craftsmen)—who are permitted to own property and manage it freely. This difference is explained by the fact that the activities of the lower class are directly tied to the production of material goods, where personal incentives are not only acceptable but necessary for the effective functioning of the economy. At the same time, producers are entirely excluded from political governance, which, according to Plato, prevents private interests from influencing public decision-making.

> **The prohibition of private property for the higher classes becomes a key condition for the creation of the ideal state, ensuring the stability and moral purity of power.**

Plato believed that such an arrangement would safeguard the state from conflict and secure justice, since wealth and authority would remain permanently separated, and moral excellence would stand as the sole criterion for rule.

The Principles of Common Use of Goods

In the *Republic*, Plato introduces the principle of common use of goods for the higher classes, which is the logical continuation of their rejection of private property. This principle means that philosopher-rulers and warrior-guardians share all necessary goods communally and only to the extent of rational necessity. Such an arrangement eliminates the accumulation of wealth, luxury, and the pursuit of excess—factors that, in Plato's view, inevitably lead to moral decline and the corruption of society.

Common use extends to nearly every sphere of life for the two higher classes: housing, food, clothing, everyday items, and even the upbringing of children. The lives of philosophers and guardians are organized so that personal needs are satisfied only at the minimal necessary level, without indulgence or luxury. This allows them to devote themselves entirely to their public duties rather than to the pursuit of comfort or pleasure.

Plato stresses that the principle of common use must be accompanied by strict limitation of material interests. The higher classes are trained not only to be content with little but also to consciously avoid any form of acquisitiveness or excessive enjoyment. Success and happiness in their lives are measured not by wealth or comfort but by virtue, wisdom, justice, and selfless service to the state.

The state strictly monitors compliance with these rules, ensuring that no ruler or guardian violates them. Those entrusted with governing and protecting society must embody moderation and humility. Any display of greed or selfishness immediately disqualifies a person from their class, since such qualities, according to Plato, are incompatible with the mission of wise and just governance.

In contrast, producers—farmers and craftsmen—are permitted to own private property and manage it for their own benefit. Yet even here, the state imposes reasonable limits to prevent extremes of wealth and poverty, which could generate conflict. While the third class is not bound by the principle of common use, it too is expected to observe moderation and not exceed reasonable material needs.

The principles of common use and the strict limitation of material interests in Plato's state serve as the foundation of social harmony, justice, and order. These rules prevent envy, rivalry, and conflict, eliminating the root causes of social discord—greed and the pursuit of wealth. In this sense, common use becomes a practical expression of Plato's doctrine of justice: every class fulfills its proper role, free from private interests, ensuring that the state operates as a unified organism where all act for the common good rather than personal advantage.

The Economic Activity of Craftsmen and Farmers

In Plato's state, craftsmen and farmers form the class of producers, upon whose efficiency and stability the material well-being of the entire society depends. Unlike the two higher classes, the producers are permitted to own property, engage in private economic activity, and dispose of the results of their labor. Their lives are not subject to the same strict control and restrictions, though even here Plato establishes reasonable limits aimed at preserving social harmony and justice.

The foundation of the producers' economic life is specialization and the division of labor. According to Plato, each craftsman or farmer must devote themselves exclusively to the kind of work for which they possess natural aptitude and talent. This ensures high productivity and quality, as individuals concentrate fully on their occupation and refine their skills. The principle of specialization, in Plato's view, not only increases economic efficiency but also contributes to personal satisfaction, since each citizen finds fulfillment in the role best suited to their nature.

Plato allows the existence of markets and trade, but only for the purpose of meeting citizens' basic needs. Commerce in the ideal state must not become a means of profit-seeking or speculation. To this end, the state supervises trade, limiting profit margins and setting fair prices in order to curb greed and prevent economic distortions. As a result, craftsmen and farmers provide a stable standard of living while preventing excessive social inequality.

The economic activity of the producers is directed toward supplying society with all the necessary material goods—food, clothing, housing, and the tools and objects of daily life. The state ensures that producers remain within the bounds of reasonable sufficiency and avoid the pursuit of luxury. Plato believed that moderation in consumption and dedication to a simple, virtuous life safeguarded society from internal conflict and moral decline.

Although the third class enjoys relative economic freedom, it is entirely excluded from political decision-making. Plato argued that producers were unfit to assess the common good objectively, since their attention was fixed primarily on material interests. Political affairs, therefore, belong exclusively to philosophers and guardians, whose conduct is based not on economic incentives but on knowledge, virtue, and responsibility to the state.

Thus, the economic activity of craftsmen and farmers in Plato's state is carefully separated from politics and regulated by strict rules and limits. This arrangement preserves the balance between individual freedom and social responsibility, secures economic stability and just distribution of goods, and protects society from the dangers of excessive wealth and social conflict.

Morality, Law, and Culture

Ethical Principles of the Ideal Citizen

In Plato's conception of the state, the foundation is not only a rational organization of political and economic life but also a strict moral framework that defines the ethical character of the ideal citizen. At the heart of this framework are four cardinal virtues that, according to Plato, form the spiritual foundation of society: wisdom, courage, moderation, and justice. While each virtue is primarily associated with a specific class, together they form a unified moral ideal toward which all citizens must strive.

The first virtue, wisdom (*sophia*), belongs primarily to the philosopher-rulers. For Plato, wisdom is the capacity to grasp the true nature of things, to see them in light of eternal Forms, and to make decisions guided by genuine knowledge rather than emotions or public opinion. This virtue implies a profound understanding of the good and the just, enabling rulers to guide the state toward harmony and the collective good.

The second virtue, courage (*andreia*), is characteristic of the guardian-warriors. Plato defines courage not merely as physical bravery but as inner strength, loyalty to duty, and the ability to face danger in defense of justice and social order. True courage, in his view, is not found in aggression or violence but in moral steadiness and self-mastery in the face of fear or temptation.

The third virtue, moderation (*sōphrosynē*), is essential for all citizens but especially emphasized for producers—artisans and farmers. Moderation is the ability to control one's desires and appetites, avoiding excess and extremes. It is expressed through humility, self-restraint, and the recognition of one's proper place, helping maintain the balance between private interests and the common good. In Plato's state, moderation protects society from greed and selfishness, which can destabilize the collective order.

The fourth and unifying virtue is justice (*dikaiosynē*), which integrates and sustains the other three. In Plato's view, justice is the harmonious functioning of society, where every individual and class performs its appropriate role without interfering in the tasks of others. Justice ensures social cohesion, internal balance, and the absence of conflict. It expresses the very essence of the ideal state, where each person occupies the position most suited to their nature and capabilities.

These four virtues form a complete and interdependent system of moral education. The state, in Plato's vision, carefully nurtures these qualities from early childhood, embedding them into the fabric of personal conduct and civic life. Through this ethical cultivation, the Platonic state becomes not merely a well-organized structure but the embodiment of a moral ideal—a society in which each individual lives in harmony with themselves, with others, and with the cosmic order.

System of Education and Upbringing

For Plato, education was not simply the acquisition of knowledge but the principal means of shaping the moral and intellectual character of the citizen. In the Republic, he outlines a carefully staged process in which upbringing is directed by the state to guide individuals toward virtue, wisdom, and readiness for public service.

Education begins at the earliest age. For the future guardians and rulers, it is entirely communal and carried out under the supervision of trained educators. From childhood, discipline, moderation, and solidarity are instilled. Physical training, gymnastics, and group activities aim to strengthen the body, build character, and develop habits of cooperation and responsibility.

As children grow, their training turns to music, poetry, and literature. Plato, however, places strict limits on the arts: only works that foster harmony, moral clarity, and noble emotions are permitted. Literature and music must not excite fear, anger, or uncontrolled passion, but instead nurture an appreciation for beauty and goodness. By shaping sensibilities through art, the state prepares the soul to love virtue and justice.

Around the age of twenty, the most capable students advance to higher studies in the sciences. Mathematics—arithmetic and geometry—together with astronomy and harmonics are emphasized as disciplines that sharpen logical thought and accustom the mind to abstract reasoning. These studies prepare students to move beyond appearances and begin to grasp universal truths.

The next stage is philosophy, open only to those who have proven both their intellectual capacity and their moral integrity. Dialectics, the highest form of study, enables the mind to ascend to the contemplation of the eternal Forms—the unchanging principles of truth, justice, and the good. This philosophical education is the foundation for the making of philosopher-rulers, those able to govern wisely because they understand the deeper order of reality.

Finally comes practice. Having completed their intellectual formation, the future rulers are gradually introduced to political life. They begin with minor administrative duties, then advance to greater offices, testing their judgment and responsibility at each step. Only those who combine practical ability with proven virtue ascend to the highest positions of authority.

Through this long and demanding process—stretching from childhood to maturity—Plato envisioned the creation of citizens, and above all rulers, whose bodies were disciplined, whose characters were virtuous, and whose minds were trained to perceive truth. Education, in his model, was not preparation for a career but the very foundation of a just and harmonious state.

The Role of Myths, Art, and Music in Strengthening the State

Plato assigned a decisive role to myths, art, and music in the life of the ideal state. He regarded them not as entertainment but as powerful tools for education and moral formation. In his philosophy, cultural forms shape the character of citizens, direct behavior, and preserve harmony within society.

Myths occupy a special place. Plato condemned much of traditional Greek mythology for presenting the gods as immoral or undignified, but he also saw the potential of myth as a medium for truth. Properly constructed stories could communicate moral lessons in a way accessible to all. Myths, he believed, should instill ideas of justice, courage, and civic duty. His most famous example is the "noble lie" of metals: rulers of gold, guardians of silver, and producers of bronze and iron. This tale justifies social hierarchy while promoting unity and loyalty to the common good.

Art, too, was to be carefully guided. Plato feared its power to arouse destructive emotions, and so he insisted that poetry, drama, and painting present only virtuous models of conduct. Scenes of vice, uncontrolled laughter, or despair had no place in his republic. The purpose was not to suffocate creativity, but to ensure that artistic works elevated the soul, encouraged discipline, and reinforced civic responsibility. By directing art toward noble examples, the state could use it as an instrument of ethical education.

Music, in Plato's thought, was even more influential. He saw it as shaping the deepest layers of the soul, capable of bringing either harmony or disorder. Because of this, musical training had to be strictly regulated. Modes and rhythms that fostered courage, self-restraint, and endurance were permitted, while those associated with indulgence or softness were banned. Music thus became an essential element of education, forming balanced and resilient characters prepared to serve the good of the state.

Plato also linked these cultural forms directly to his theory of education in the Republic. In his view, proper training of the guardians could not rely on laws and institutions alone; it required the formation of character through stories, images, and melodies absorbed from childhood. What children heard in myths, saw in art, and practiced in music would shape their souls before they were capable of rational reflection. For this reason, he argued, the state must regulate cultural life from the earliest stages, ensuring that its citizens grow up immersed in representations of virtue rather than vice.

The influence of Plato's cultural program extended far beyond his own time. His conviction that myths and art must serve moral purposes shaped later traditions of civic education in antiquity and was echoed in debates about censorship and public morality in both medieval and modern contexts. The idea that music molds character left a lasting mark on educational theory, resurfacing in Renaissance humanism and Enlightenment pedagogy. Even today, discussions about the social responsibility of art, the ethics of media, and the cultural impact of music bear traces of Platonic concerns.

For Plato, myths, art, and music were not secondary embellishments of culture. They were pillars of civic life, essential to moral education and political stability. By shaping emotions, beliefs, and values, they provided the foundation for a society ordered by justice and guided by reason.

Plato's Significance and Influence on Subsequent Philosophical and Social Thought

Legal System and Mechanisms for Maintaining Public Order

In Plato's ideal state, law is not conceived as a means of suppressing the individual or restricting freedom, but as an instrument for securing justice and sustaining an ideal social order. Plato's legal system is not based on an abundance of complex laws regulating every detail of behavior. On the contrary, he believed that the ideal state requires relatively simple, clear, and intelligible laws that citizens can easily grasp and obey. Law should be such that everyone understands its purpose and perceives it as the natural expression of justice and the rational organization of society.

Plato is convinced that the chief guarantee of public order lies not in fear of punishment but in the moral consciousness of citizens, cultivated through an effective and purposeful system of education and moral upbringing. Obedience to the law in the ideal state is ensured less by external coercion than by the inner conviction that living according to the laws is a moral duty. Thus, the legal system of Plato's state rests primarily on ethics and moral principles instilled in citizens from childhood.

Yet Plato also recognized that moral conviction and education alone are not sufficient; the state must possess real mechanisms of enforcement. The primary role in this respect belongs to the class of guardians, who are responsible for internal security and the maintenance of public order. They are tasked with preventing and suppressing disorder, conflicts, and violations of the law, ensuring that no form of social injustice is allowed to take root. Their authority, discipline, and moral integrity make it possible to preserve order without the need for harsh repressive measures.

At the same time, Plato does not exclude the use of punishment for serious offenses. Punishments, however, are understood as corrective and educational in nature, aimed at helping the offender recognize their mistake and return to proper conduct. The severity of punishment depends on the gravity of the violation. Gross offenses against the state order—such as treason, corruption, the pursuit of wealth among the higher classes, or attempts to seize power—are punished strictly and uncompromisingly, up to and including expulsion from the state.

Judicial functions are entrusted to the most respected and wise representatives of the philosophical class. They do not judge on the basis of formal procedures or emotional appeals, but rather by relying on a deep understanding of justice and insight into the true causes of citizens' misconduct. In Plato's view, such an approach guarantees objectivity and rationality in judicial decisions, making law an instrument of genuine justice rather than a mere bureaucratic procedure.

Thus, the legal system of Plato's state combines simplicity, moral orientation, and clear mechanisms of enforcement. This ensures not only external obedience to the law but also a profound inner conviction of its justice and necessity, which becomes the firm foundation of stability and order in the ideal society.

The Influence of Plato's Ideas on Later Utopian Concepts (from Antiquity to the Present)

Plato's model of the ideal state not only inaugurated a new genre of social philosophy but also established universal principles to which later thinkers continually returned.

Already in antiquity, Plato's followers and students—particularly those in the Platonic and Neoplatonic schools—expanded on his ideas of the state, justice, and social organization. Plato's ideals also inspired Stoics and Cynics, who reinterpreted the concepts of justice and virtue, as well as Roman authors such as Cicero, who reflected on the role of wise rulers in guiding society. Although not all accepted Plato's radical proposals—such as communal property or collective family arrangements—the very approach to the state as a rationally designed ideal became deeply rooted in ancient thought.

During the Renaissance, Plato's ideas experienced a powerful revival. Under their influence, Thomas More composed his famous *Utopia*, creating a new literary form directly inspired by the *Republic*. Following More, Tommaso Campanella's *City of the Sun* also explicitly drew on Platonic concepts of social classes, communal property, and state-directed education. Both thinkers consciously adopted Plato's model as their foundation, adapting it to the conditions of their time and combining the legacy of antiquity with the humanist ideals of the Renaissance.

Plato's ideas also inspired Enlightenment thinkers. For instance, Francis Bacon's *New Atlantis* employed a Platonic approach to social organization through knowledge and reason, envisioning a state founded on scientific progress and rational governance. Later, socialist utopias of the 19th century, especially the theories of Charles Fourier and Robert Owen, reflected Platonic themes of collective ownership and rational social organization.

Plato's thought also left its mark on Marxist theory. Despite radical differences in philosophical foundations, the principles of communal property, the abolition of private ownership, collective child-rearing, and the division of society into functional groups resonate in Marx's model of a communist society, though recast in a materialist framework.

Contemporary philosophers and sociologists continue to turn to the *Republic* as a key text for understanding questions of social justice, the role of the state, and the balance between individual freedom and the common good. In the genre of dystopian literature—for example, in the works of Aldous Huxley, Yevgeny Zamyatin, and George Orwell—Platonic principles are subjected to critical reexamination, illustrating both the potential and the dangers of radically ordered and regulated societies.

Criticism of Plato's Utopia by Thinkers of Different Eras

Plato's vision of the ideal state, as laid out in the Republic, inspired both admiration and deep skepticism.

The first and most systematic critic of Plato was his student Aristotle. In Politics, Aristotle devotes entire sections to dissecting his teacher's proposals. He strongly opposed Plato's idea of abolishing private property and family life among the guardian class. For Aristotle, property and family are not simply economic arrangements but natural and moral institutions that sustain responsibility, affection, and care. He argued that communal ownership would weaken accountability, since "what is common to the greatest number receives the least care." Similarly, collective child-rearing, in his view, would erode parental bonds and undermine the very basis of community. Aristotle also challenged Plato's tripartite division of society into rulers, auxiliaries, and producers. Such rigid stratification, he warned, would create conflict, injustice, and alienation, denying most citizens the opportunity to develop their capacities and to participate in politics. For Aristotle, the state exists to promote the good life for all its members, not to elevate a narrow class of philosopher-rulers.

In the Renaissance and early modern era, Plato's ideas were revisited but often in a critical light. Thinkers such as Machiavelli, though not writing directly against Plato, implicitly rejected the vision of a state ruled by abstract ideals. During the Enlightenment, critiques became explicit. Voltaire condemned rigid systems of social control, arguing that freedom of thought and expression was indispensable for progress. John Locke, in his Two Treatises of Government (1689), directly opposed the idea of excessive state intrusion into private life. Locke emphasized natural rights—life, liberty, and property—as the foundation of legitimate government, placing him in direct opposition to Plato's notion of subordinating the individual to the collective. Jean-Jacques Rousseau, though at times sympathetic to utopian ideals, also warned in The Social Contract (1762) that forcing people to adopt a single model of virtue and conformity risks producing tyranny rather than freedom.

In the nineteenth century, Plato's Republic was read with suspicion in the context of debates about socialism and authoritarianism. While some socialist thinkers admired the emphasis on communal life and the elimination of inequality, liberal theorists feared its implications. John Stuart Mill, for example, argued that individuality and diversity are essential for social vitality, and any scheme that suppresses them—however well-intentioned—leads to stagnation.

The most influential modern attack came in the twentieth century from Karl Popper. In The Open Society and Its Enemies (1945), Popper singled out Plato as a chief architect of the "closed society." He condemned the vision of philosopher-kings, rigid class divisions, and state control over education and culture as the intellectual roots of modern totalitarianism. For Popper, Plato's attempt to freeze society into a perfect form ignored the unpredictability and creativity of human life. By elevating rulers who claim privileged access to truth, he argued, Plato opened the door to tyranny: those convinced of their infallibility are prone to despotism.

Other liberal thinkers reinforced these critiques. Friedrich Hayek, in The Road to Serfdom (1944), though not writing specifically about Plato, warned against any centralized plan that dictates the lives of individuals, seeing in it the seeds of authoritarianism. Isaiah Berlin, in his essays on liberty, highlighted the danger of "positive liberty" turning into coercion when the state claims to know what is best for all. For Berlin, Plato's vision epitomized this danger: the suppression of individual plurality in the name of a single ideal of justice.

Despite criticism, scholars also note that Plato never intended his Republic to be a literal constitution but rather a philosophical exploration of justice. Nevertheless, the critiques of Aristotle, Enlightenment thinkers, and twentieth-century liberals underscore a recurring concern: that any attempt to impose a single, rationally designed order risks erasing the richness of human diversity. By pointing out these flaws, Plato's critics have helped to clarify the boundaries of utopian thought, reminding us that the pursuit of justice must remain compatible with freedom, individuality, and human complexity.

The Modern Assessment of Plato's *Republic* as a Classical Example of Philosophical Design of the Ideal Society

In contemporary thought, Plato's Republic is often taken as the classical example of a philosophical blueprint for an ideal society. Modern scholarship stresses that the enduring significance of the Republic lies less in its specific prescriptions than in its central idea: that the state can be designed rationally and deliberately. Plato was the first to argue that society is not merely an accidental arrangement but a structure that reason and morality should consciously shape. For his time this was a revolutionary vision, one that became the foundation of later utopian projects and continues to influence how we think about political order.

At the same time, many critics point to the internal tensions of Plato's design. The dialogue assumes that people can be governed almost entirely by rational principles, leaving little room for the complexity of emotions, psychology, and culture. For this reason the model appears overly idealized and detached from human realities. Yet such criticism does not diminish its importance: Plato gave form to the very notion of an ideal state, establishing a paradigm of utopian thought that endured for centuries.

"I die the King's good servant, but God's first."

— Thomas More
moments before his execution on July 6, 1535.

Chapter 2. Thomas More's *Utopia*
The Renaissance Model of the Ideal Society: The Birth of the Utopian Genre

Thomas More's Utopia, first published in 1516, stands as a landmark of Renaissance thought and literature. Its full Latin title, De optimo rei publicae statu deque nova insula Utopia ("On the Best State of a Commonwealth and on the New Island of Utopia"), introduced to Europe a term that would come to define the very idea of an ideal society. The word itself, drawn from the Greek οὐ ("not") and τόπος ("place"), literally means "no place." More's title captures both sides of his vision: the perfection of the society he imagined and the recognition that such perfection may never be realized.

The book takes the form of a dialogue in which More recounts the discovery of an island where justice, equality, and reason govern all aspects of life. Unlike states built on inherited custom, Utopia is portrayed as the outcome of deliberate design—a society shaped by the pursuit of harmony and order. The vivid narrative, rich in details of daily life, gave readers a concrete picture of what a rationally organized community might look like.

The influence of Utopia reached far beyond its own time. It inspired later works such as Tommaso Campanella's City of the Sun and Francis Bacon's New Atlantis, and it echoed in the social projects of the nineteenth and twentieth centuries, from early socialism to communism. With More, the utopian imagination gained not only a name but also a form and a method, turning into a lasting instrument for thinking about the possibilities and limits of human society.

Historical and Intellectual Context

The Life and Work of Thomas More (1478–1535), His Philosophical Views and Humanist Ideals

Thomas More was born on February 7, 1478, in London, into a respected family of the legal elite. His father, Sir John More, was a prominent judge of the King's Bench. As a boy, Thomas served as a page in the household of John Morton, Archbishop of Canterbury and Lord Chancellor of England. Morton quickly recognized his talent and arranged his entry to Oxford. At Canterbury College, later absorbed into Christ Church, More immersed himself in classical languages and literature. He studied Greek and Latin with scholars such as Thomas Linacre and William Grocyn, who introduced him to the works of Plato, Aristotle, and the early Church Fathers.

In 1494, he returned to London to pursue law at New Inn and later at Lincoln's Inn. Called to the bar in 1501, he gained a reputation as a skilled lawyer. During these years, More also considered a monastic life, spending time near the Carthusian community in London and practicing prayer, fasting, and austerity. Although he chose a secular career, this experience left a deep mark on his character.

More entered Parliament in 1504 and spoke out against heavy taxation under Henry VII. His stance displeased the king, but his career advanced again under Henry VIII. He served as Under-Sheriff of London (1510), Master of Requests, and Privy

Councillor. In 1521 he was knighted, in 1523 became Speaker of the House of Commons, and in 1529 was appointed Lord Chancellor of England—the first layman to hold that post.

Even in public office, More remained a man of letters. He corresponded with leading humanists of the Northern Renaissance, above all Erasmus of Rotterdam, who in 1511 dedicated In Praise of Folly to him. In 1516, More published his most famous work, Utopia, a dialogue that describes an imaginary commonwealth built on shared property, tolerance, and rational governance. The book's irony left its meaning open to interpretation, yet it became a touchstone of European political thought.

Philosophically, More joined Christian ethics with classical learning and civic responsibility. He argued that political authority must rest on justice and moral duty, condemned tyranny and greed, and insisted on the importance of virtue in public life.

His fall came with the English Reformation. He opposed Henry VIII's annulment of his marriage to Catherine of Aragon and refused to accept the Act of Supremacy (1534), which made the king head of the Church of England. More would not swear the Oath of Supremacy, holding to the papacy's authority. In 1534 he was imprisoned in the Tower of London, and after more than a year brought to trial for treason. The case relied on perjured testimony, including that of Richard Rich. Found guilty, More was executed by beheading on July 6, 1535. His last words—"I die the King's good servant, and God's first"—summed up the principle for which he gave his life.

The Catholic Church beatified More in 1886 and canonized him in 1935. In 2000 Pope John Paul II declared him the patron saint of statesmen and politicians. More endures as a figure who united humanist learning, public service, and an unshakable conscience.

The Renaissance Era: Humanism, Critique of Feudal and Ecclesiastical Structures, and the Search for New Social Models

The Renaissance, spanning the fourteenth to sixteenth centuries, reshaped European culture and philosophy. At its core stood humanism, an intellectual movement that placed human dignity, reason, and creativity at the forefront. Drawing inspiration from ancient philosophy and classical literature, humanists argued for a return to rational inquiry, liberty, and justice, setting these values against the medieval order rooted in ecclesiastical authority and feudal hierarchy.

Humanist thinkers launched sharp critiques of the social and political structures of their day. They condemned feudalism as unjust and oppressive, denouncing the arbitrary power of nobles and clergy as well as the subjugation of peasants and artisans. To them, inherited privilege and rigid estates lay at the heart of inequality and human suffering, while true worth should be measured by reason, merit, and the intrinsic value of the individual.

Their dissatisfaction also extended to the church. Many charged it with betraying the essence of Christianity, pointing to the wealth, corruption, and moral laxity of the clergy. Calls for reform sought to recover the simplicity and integrity of early Christian life, emphasizing personal piety, moral responsibility, and service to the community.

Amid this spirit of reform and critique, humanists began to imagine new forms of social organization. They envisioned communities guided by equality, reason, and the common good, rejecting the injustices of the feudal past. These ideals gave rise to utopian literature, which offered bold alternatives to existing institutions. Among these works, Thomas More's Utopia stands out. In it, More expressed the central ideals of Renaissance humanism through the vision of a society ordered by justice, reason, and communal responsibility.

The Renaissance was not simply a revival of antiquity but a period of bold ethical, political, and philosophical innovation. It prepared the ground for modern ideas of human rights, social justice, and the role of reason in public life.

The Political Situation in Early 16th-Century England

At the beginning of the sixteenth century, England was a country unsettled by tension, unrest, and crisis—conditions that profoundly shaped Thomas More's worldview and the conception of his ideal state. The kingdom was passing through a difficult transition from late medieval feudalism to early capitalism, and the change was marked by social, political, and economic upheaval. The Tudor monarchy, under Henry VII and later Henry VIII, strove to consolidate royal power after decades of dynastic conflict, but the social fabric of the realm remained unstable and divided.

A central issue of the time was the enclosure movement: the conversion of common fields, meadows, and small peasant holdings into private estates controlled by wealthy landowners. The profitability of sheep farming and the booming wool trade drove this process, which often ignored traditional rights of land use. Entire communities were uprooted. Peasants were expelled from their ancestral villages, stripped of livelihoods, and forced to wander. Many drifted into the growing towns, where they met with poverty, disease, homelessness, and rising crime. Small farmers were ruined, social divisions deepened, and inequality widened. The government offered little protection to ordinary people, and unrest spread through the lower classes. These conditions are directly echoed in Utopia, where More condemns the greed of landlords and the economic exploitation of the poor.

Political instability compounded the social turmoil. Though the Wars of the Roses had ended in 1487 with the establishment of the Tudor dynasty, their consequences continued to haunt the kingdom. Noble houses were weakened, rivalries persisted, and alliances shifted with alarming frequency. The political culture was steeped in distrust, and the fragile balance of power often collapsed into intrigue, corruption, and abuse. The monarchy relied on courts such as the Star Chamber not only to enforce order but also to silence dissent and punish opposition. Institutions that should have served justice instead became tools of intimidation, reinforcing the sense of a political system in crisis.

More's disillusionment was deepened by his own service in public life. From his first election to Parliament in 1504, where he spoke against the burdensome taxation of Henry VII, to his later rise under Henry VIII—including his appointment as Lord Chancellor in 1529—he saw the machinery of government from within. Again and again he encountered obstruction, inefficiency, and moral compromise. Reforms were stalled by factional struggles, entrenched interests, and the self-serving calculations of the elite. For More, these failures confirmed that the problems of England could not be addressed through minor adjustments or temporary measures. What was needed was nothing less than a fundamental reimagining of the political and social order—an experiment he would undertake in the imagined commonwealth of Utopia.

Key Ideas and Principles

Ideals of Social Justice, Equality, and the Common Good

The ideals that shaped Thomas More's model of a perfect commonwealth were social justice, equality, and the pursuit of the common good. In early sixteenth-century England, society was shaken by rapid change. The enclosure of common fields displaced peasants, driving many into poverty and vagrancy. Feudal ties were breaking down, while new forms of landownership concentrated wealth in the hands of aristocrats and merchants. Under the Tudors, especially Henry VIII, the monarchy strengthened its authority, and conflicts with the Catholic Church added to the instability. In this world of dispossession, hardship, and political centralization, More imagined a state that would protect its people and preserve human dignity.

In Utopia, social justice meant the end of unjust privilege and the exploitation of the poor. More condemned a system where landowners grew rich while peasants starved or wandered homeless. He envisioned instead a society in which status was measured not by birth or inheritance but by labor, merit, and virtue.

Equality, for More, was essential for stability. In his commonwealth, sharp divisions between rich and poor disappeared. All citizens had access to education, medical care, and public life. This vision stood in contrast to the England of his day, where literacy and healthcare remained the preserve of the few. Such equality was designed to remove envy and crime, laying the foundation for shared prosperity.

The cornerstone of More's design was the common good. For him it was not an abstract idea but the guiding rule of law, labor, and learning. Every aspect of Utopian life was ordered so that private interests never clashed with public welfare. Citizens worked fixed hours for the community, surplus goods were held in public storehouses, and no one was permitted to amass wealth at others' expense. By aligning personal duty with communal needs, the common good became the practical basis of both justice and equality.

The power of More's vision lay in its response to the realities of his time. Enclosures, the decline of peasant rights, the dominance of merchants, and the growing concentration of land all revealed the injustice of existing structures. Against this background, Utopia offered not a dream detached from reality but a pointed alternative, one that continued to inspire later efforts to imagine a fairer society.

Criticism of the Vices of Contemporary Society

A central theme of Thomas More's Utopia is his critique of the social and political order of early sixteenth-century England. He did not write in vague generalities but addressed the concrete injustices that made life harsh for common people and obstructed the creation of a just state.

The first target of his criticism was greed, which he saw as the root of social ruin. In Utopia he denounces the aristocracy and landlords for enclosing common fields and turning them into private pastures. This movement left peasants without land, driving many into poverty and crime. For More, greed was not only a personal failing but a structural danger, producing hunger, instability, and disorder that threatened the kingdom itself.

Inequality was the next issue. More rejected a system in which nobles and churchmen amassed wealth and privilege while the majority endured misery. He believed such arrangements violated human dignity and reason. In his imagined society, wealth was distributed fairly, and social standing depended on labor and merit rather than on birth or inherited rights.

Corruption in government was another of his concerns. As a public official, More had seen how bribery and self-interest displaced justice and the common good. When rulers sought enrichment instead of duty, institutions lost credibility and rational governance became impossible. In Utopia, by contrast, leaders acted from moral responsibility and were shielded from the temptations of wealth.

The legal system of England also came under his scrutiny. More condemned punishments that were excessive and disproportionate, such as the death penalty for theft. He argued that harsh laws failed to address the true causes of crime—poverty and despair—and only deepened resentment. In Utopia the laws were few, simple, and aimed at instruction rather than terror, guiding citizens toward justice.

This critique reflected the condition of More's England. The Tudor monarchy was strengthening its authority, feudal bonds were eroding, merchants were rising in power, and enclosures were dismantling the old rural order. Towns filled with poverty, while common people felt excluded from authority. Utopia was More's response: by exposing greed, inequality, corruption, and injustice, he pointed to the need for a different model of society.

The flaws he described were not distant abstractions but daily realities. In Utopia he envisioned their removal through rational order, communal responsibility, and fair laws.

The Concept of a Rationally Ordered Society Governed by Reason and Justice Rather than Private Interests

In Utopia, Thomas More sets the flawed society of his own day against a commonwealth built on reason, morality, and justice. He begins with the conviction that the vices of his age—greed, ambition, and the pursuit of private gain—were the true causes of poverty and disorder. In contrast, his imagined state subjects every aspect of life to a rational plan designed to remove arbitrariness and ensure fairness.

The foundations of this society lie in shared values and collective well-being. Each person is assigned to the occupation best suited to their natural abilities, so that work benefits both the individual and the community. Specialization eliminates waste and allows citizens to take satisfaction in their tasks, since labor accords with their skills. Goods are distributed in such a way that no one lives in deprivation and no one accumulates excessive wealth.

The economy reflects this same order. Every citizen works for six hours a day—sufficient to provide for the entire community. Products are stored in public warehouses, and families take what they need without money or bargaining. Because private property and currency do not exist, competition and greed lose their place. Moderation is encouraged, while extravagance is seen as destructive to character and society alike.

Government, too, is organized on rational principles. Offices are filled through election and oversight, ensuring that leaders are chosen for competence and virtue. Authority is regarded not as privilege but as service, and decisions are made with the welfare of the community in mind. In this way, More offers a counterpoint to the corruption he observed in England, where self-interest often triumphed over duty.

Education sustains the entire structure. From childhood, citizens are taught responsibility, moderation, and the connection between personal happiness and the prosperity of the whole. Discipline rests not on fear of punishment but on understanding. Intellectual life is honored, and leisure is devoted to study, discussion, and cultural pursuits, reinforcing the moral and rational foundations of the state.

Religion follows the same logic. More envisions a society that accepts different faiths yet insists on a shared belief in moral accountability. This tolerance strengthens civic unity and avoids the sectarian conflicts that troubled Europe in his time.

Through this vision, More responds directly to the conditions he saw in England: enclosures that ruined peasants, the concentration of land and wealth, and a government marred by corruption. Against such realities, he set a commonwealth where reason, justice, and the subordination of private gain to the common good secured harmony and stability.

Political Structure and Social Organization

Form of Government and Power Structure in the State of Utopia: Elected Bodies and Limited Democracy

In Thomas More's imagined commonwealth, government combines elements of democracy with a carefully ordered system of selection and oversight. Utopia is a federation of fifty-four cities, all governed by the same institutions. Authority is not inherited and does not rest on wealth or noble birth. Instead, it is based on election, competence, and moral integrity.

At the local level, each group of thirty households elects a magistrate called a syphogrant, or phylarch. Chosen for a one-year term, syphogrants form the city council, which provides the basis of self-government. They differ from other citizens only in their duties and in the respect they command through honesty and sound judgment.

Above them stand officials known as tranibors, or protophylarchs. Each supervises ten syphogrants and represents their decisions in wider councils. Together, syphogrants and tranibors distribute authority across many levels, ensuring that power is shared and that the voice of the community is carried upward through elected representatives.

From this body the citizens elect the city's chief ruler, known as the prince. The prince holds office for life, but only so long as he discharges his responsibilities faithfully. His authority is limited by the council of syphogrants and tranibors, whose collective judgment guides all major decisions. In this way, the office of prince is balanced by the constant presence of representative oversight.

This system reflects a moderated democracy. Citizens govern through their chosen officials, but not through direct participation in every decision. The arrangement avoids the instability of mass rule and entrusts authority to those judged most capable and virtuous. Leaders are expected to serve the community, not themselves.

Deliberation is open, and every council member has an equal voice. Officials live under the same conditions as other citizens, without special privilege, and their conduct remains subject to public scrutiny. If they fail in duty, they can be removed from office. This accountability prevents corruption and maintains trust in institutions.

By combining citizen representation with careful limits on authority, Utopia joins participation with stability. It resists both the arbitrariness of unchecked power and the disorder of unrestrained popular rule, offering a vision of governance grounded in reason and the common good.

The Structure of Society: Equality of All Citizens and the Absence of Social Hierarchy

A defining principle of Utopian life is the equality of all citizens, which rejects the class divisions and estates that shaped sixteenth-century Europe. Unlike contemporary England, where a person's standing depended on birth, wealth, or lineage, More envisioned a community in which every citizen enjoyed the same rights and opportunities.

In Utopia there are no hereditary nobles, no privileged clergy, and no aristocracy passing down rank through generations. Political office carries responsibility but not prestige or privilege. The one exception is the institution of slavery, though it differs from its classical form. Slaves are usually prisoners of war, criminals sentenced to labor, or foreigners who choose servitude in Utopia. Their status is not hereditary: the children of slaves are free, and servitude can be lifted as a reward for good conduct. In this way, slavery functions less as an entrenched class than as a corrective measure or voluntary condition, and thus does not undermine the principle of equality among Utopian citizens.

The absence of hierarchy shapes daily life. Citizens wear the same style of clothing, live in houses of equal comfort, and exchange dwellings every ten years. Meals are taken in common halls and distributed fairly. Luxury is forbidden, eliminating the rivalry and envy that in real societies often give rise to conflict.

Public offices are filled by election, but magistrates gain no material advantage from their post. They remain bound by the same rules as everyone else and may be removed at once if they break the standards of equality or justice.

Education is provided to all without distinction. Every citizen learns to read, acquires practical knowledge, and receives moral instruction. Leisure is devoted to study and cultural pursuits, ensuring that intellectual growth is not limited to a privileged few but open to the entire population.

This uniformity fosters respect and solidarity. Since all share the same obligations and responsibilities for the common good, each person is valued for merit, talent, and service to the community rather than for ancestry or possessions. In More's design, such equality provides the foundation of a society ordered by fairness and sustained by mutual trust.

The Organization of Daily Life: Collectivism and Public Oversight

The daily life of Utopian citizens is ordered around the principles of community and the common good. Each city is carefully laid out, with streets and houses built to a single plan, providing equal and comfortable conditions for all. Families are required to change houses every ten years, a rule meant to weaken attachment to possessions and remind citizens that dwellings belong to the community, not to individuals.

Life is lived largely in common. Meals are taken in public halls, where simple but nourishing food is provided equally to all. These arrangements discourage excess, prevent inequality, and foster mutual respect.

Work is required of every citizen, yet the obligation is limited to six hours a day—three in the morning and three in the afternoon. This schedule supplies all the needs of the commonwealth while leaving ample time for rest, study, and cultural life. Labor is regarded as a natural duty, organized collectively and assigned by officials to ensure efficiency and the steady provision of goods for all.

Uniformity extends into daily habits. Citizens wear plain, practical clothing of the same kind, avoiding luxury and display. Houses are equal in comfort, and because of the regular exchange of dwellings, no family can claim superior standing. Leisure, too, is communal: free hours are devoted to cultural pursuits, intellectual discussion, and the study of philosophy and science.

Public oversight plays an essential role. The behavior of each citizen is observed by the community, not as a loss of liberty but as a safeguard of harmony and justice. From childhood, Utopians are taught that personal responsibility to society is inseparable from freedom, and that vigilance over one another preserves equality and order.

In More's design, this way of life—based on common property, regulated labor, and shared responsibility—creates a stable and balanced state. Every citizen sees themselves as part of a larger whole, with individual needs aligned to the welfare of the community.

Economic and Property Relations

Abolition of Private Property, Principle of Collective Ownership of Land and Means of Production

One of the guiding principles of Thomas More's Utopia is the rejection of private property and the establishment of collective ownership of land, resources, and essential goods. More argued that private ownership lay at the heart of social injustice, for it encouraged envy, greed, and the pursuit of gain, enriching a few while leaving the majority in need.

In Utopia, land and productive resources belong to the community rather than to individuals. This arrangement makes it possible to organize work rationally and to direct production toward real needs instead of profit. Farmers and artisans labor together, dividing tasks and sharing results in common, so that exploitation disappears.

Because property is held collectively, all citizens enjoy equal access to material goods. The products of labor are distributed fairly, eliminating the basis of poverty and inequality. In More's view, theft, crime, and social unrest arise wherever ownership is private; in Utopia they lose their ground.

The absence of private property also reshapes attitudes. Since no one owns more than is necessary, greed finds no place. Citizens grow up with the conviction that personal well-being depends on the well-being of all, and each sees themselves as part of a cooperative process of producing and sharing what the community requires.

Labor, under these conditions, becomes both a duty and a source of dignity. Because everyone shares equally in its fruits, work is not regarded as drudgery but as a meaningful contribution to the common good. It binds the community together and affirms the worth of each individual.

This vision—of a society without private ownership and with goods held in common—was one of More's most distinctive ideas. His critique of property and his proposal for a cooperative economy would later echo in socialist and communist theories that sought to overcome inequality through a new ordering of property and labor.

Organization of Labor and the Mandatory Participation of Every Citizen in Productive Activity

In Thomas More's Utopia, labor is both an obligation and a natural part of human life. Every citizen, without exception, is required to contribute to productive work that sustains the community as a whole. In this society, participation in labor is not tied to wealth or status but to the shared duty of maintaining the common good.

The working day is strictly regulated and limited to reasonable hours. Citizens typically labor for six hours—three in the morning and three in the afternoon. This rhythm is designed to prevent exhaustion while leaving time for study, cultural pursuits, and rest. Work is seen as purposeful and measured, never as endless drudgery.

Labor is carried out collectively. Citizens work together in fields, workshops, and public enterprises, with tasks assigned according to both the needs of society and individual skills. Young people are encouraged to try different trades so they may discover their aptitudes and direct their efforts where they are most useful. In this way, work is aligned with natural ability, increasing both efficiency and personal satisfaction.

The duty to labor applies to all, except for those excused by age or illness. In Utopia there is no idleness, unemployment, or dependence on others without cause. Work is regarded as a civic and moral norm, the measure of one's place in society.

Because private property does not exist, the goods produced through collective labor are distributed fairly among all citizens. Without rivalry or competition for wealth, labor takes on a different meaning. It becomes not a means of enrichment but a shared contribution to the welfare of the community.

Through this organization, every person feels valued as part of the whole. Labor sustains both the material needs of society and the moral cohesion of its people, allowing citizens to enjoy security, learning, and leisure alongside their work.

Fair Distribution of Goods and the Rejection of Money in Utopian Society

One of the most striking features of Thomas More's Utopia is the abolition of money. More believed that wherever money exists, it breeds greed, envy, crime, and injustice, turning material goods into an end in themselves rather than a means of meeting human needs. In his model, all necessary goods and services are distributed freely, ensuring that every citizen has equal access to the essentials of life.

Products of communal labor are kept in public warehouses and granaries, from which citizens take what they require without payment or bargaining. In this way poverty and wealth alike disappear, since distribution is guided by the real needs of individuals and the community rather than by private profit.

The absence of money is sustained by the careful regulation of both production and consumption. Each person works not for personal gain but to satisfy the calculated needs of society as a whole. This prevents both overproduction and scarcity, while discouraging wasteful use of resources. Citizens have no reason to hoard wealth, knowing that food, shelter, clothing, and healthcare will always be available to them.

This order rests on a moral foundation as well. From childhood, Utopians are taught moderation, humility, and shared responsibility. Happiness is understood as inseparable from the welfare of the community. Everyone receives what is necessary for a good life, while luxury, vanity, and conspicuous display are discouraged by public opinion and cultural custom.

With the disappearance of money, crimes linked to property—such as theft, fraud, and violence—also vanish. Instead of rivalry, relations among citizens are shaped by trust, respect, and cooperation. Goods are viewed not as possessions but as shared resources, and each person feels accountable for the well-being of others as well as for their own.

The rejection of money also changes the meaning of wealth itself. In Utopia, richness is measured not by accumulation but by security, learning, and leisure. Citizens take pride in knowledge, culture, and virtue, rather than in possessions. What elsewhere might be counted as poverty appears here as freedom from the burdens of ownership. This attitude creates a culture in which spiritual and intellectual growth are valued above material gain. It also strengthens the sense that prosperity belongs to the whole community, not to any one individual.

By rejecting money and basing distribution on need, Utopia creates a society freed from the pursuit of wealth. Citizens are able to devote their energies to learning, culture, and moral life. In this vision, justice, solidarity, and human dignity are not distant ideals but the lived reality of daily existence.

Morality, Law, and Culture

The High Moral Standards of Utopian Citizens: Priority of the Common Good over Personal Interests, Moderation, and Rationality

Thomas More placed great emphasis on the moral formation and ethical character of Utopian citizens, convinced that only high moral standards could guarantee true stability and prosperity. From early childhood, education is directed toward instilling selflessness, a sense of duty, moderation, and rationality—virtues that form the very foundation of communal life.

The central moral principle of Utopians is the priority of the common good over private interest. They are firmly persuaded that personal happiness and prosperity can exist only when the well-being of each person is bound to the flourishing of the whole community. Individual aims are never pursued apart from collective goals, and citizens willingly sacrifice personal comfort whenever required for the public benefit. In this way conflicts and tensions are minimized, since the interests of each individual are organically aligned with those of society at large.

Equally important is the principle of moderation, which permeates all aspects of Utopian life. From childhood, citizens are taught to be content with what is necessary and to avoid excess. Luxury, conspicuous consumption, and hoarding are condemned as irrational and morally blameworthy. Moderation in housing, food, and personal needs becomes an honored social norm, ensuring health, preventing envy and rivalry, and maintaining civic balance.

Rationality constitutes another key standard of Utopian morality. Utopians rely on reason in every sphere of life, making decisions by logic, careful calculation, and common sense rather than by passion or selfish desire. This rationality is evident both in everyday work and in deliberations on public affairs. Citizens reflect carefully on the consequences of their actions, striving to act in ways that yield the greatest benefit for the whole, and they avoid rash or ill-considered behavior.

Utopian morality is also deeply bound to their religious outlook. While faith is a matter of personal choice, all citizens agree that divine justice rewards virtue and condemns vice. This conviction strengthens the ethical framework of society, for religion and morality reinforce one another, making the pursuit of justice not only a civic duty but also a sacred responsibility shared by all.

Such moral discipline enables Utopia to preserve order and justice without recourse to harsh punishments or intrusive state coercion. Citizens, internally motivated and educated in the spirit of collectivism and responsibility, themselves become the surest guarantee of lawful conduct and social harmony. Reading, philosophical discussion, and the study of the sciences form part of their daily routine, reinforcing civic values and cultivating a reflective culture that unites intellectual life with moral duty. Music, art, and shared festivals further nurture the communal spirit, providing not idle amusement but occasions for collective reflection on virtue and the dignity of a well-ordered life. These ethical principles make communal life stable and just, securing the durable well-being of the entire Utopian society.

The Organization of Education: Raising Children in the Spirit of Equality and Justice

Thomas More regarded education as a decisive foundation of his ideal society. In Utopia, schooling is not only available to all children but compulsory, ensuring that no one grows up without the knowledge and skills needed for civic life. From the outset, teaching is directed toward shaping individuals for whom equality, justice, and solidarity are everyday habits rather than distant ideals.

The program is deliberately egalitarian. Boys and girls study together, follow the same curriculum, and receive the same expectations, erasing distinctions of sex or social rank. From their earliest years, children are taught fairness, honesty, and respect. Instruction emphasizes cooperation: pupils learn to work in concert, to help one another, and to understand how their actions affect the larger community.

Education joins theory with practice. Alongside reading, history, literature, and philosophy, children learn agriculture, crafts, and useful trades. This balance allows for intellectual growth while also giving each child practical skills for communal life. As they progress, their talents and aptitudes emerge, enabling every citizen to find a role suited to their abilities and to contribute meaningfully to society.

Moral training accompanies intellectual study. Children are taught that their well-being is bound to the welfare of the community. Success is measured not by competition or superiority but by cooperation and shared accomplishment. In this way they learn to align personal aims with common purposes and to treat justice as the guiding rule of social life.

Because all receive the same education, children grow up in an atmosphere of equality and mutual respect. No one is privileged by wealth or family, and no one is excluded. From their formative years, they see injustice as an intolerable violation of order, a conviction that endures into adulthood.

For More, such education was essential to the endurance of Utopia. By uniting intellectual study, practical labor, and moral discipline, the commonwealth ensured that every generation entered maturity prepared to live responsibly in a society built on equality and civic duty. Learning did not end with childhood: adults attended public lectures, read together, and engaged in discussion, so that study became a shared practice and a permanent bond of the community.

Religion in Utopia: Toleration and Freedom of Worship within Shared Moral Principles

One of the most distinctive features of Thomas More's Utopia is its approach to religion, built on tolerance and freedom of worship. In contrast to sixteenth-century Europe, divided by persecution and sectarian conflict, Utopia appears as a community where each citizen may choose and practice faith without fear of punishment or hostility.

Religion is treated as a personal matter. The state does not enforce a single creed, and individuals are free to follow their own convictions. Instead of rigid dogma or rivalry between sects, Utopian life is marked by tolerance, with respect for every spiritual path.

This freedom rests on a set of values shared across the island. Justice, respect for human dignity, moderation, solidarity, and service to the common good are upheld by all, regardless of belief. In addition, Utopians hold two doctrines in common: the immortality of the soul and the reality of divine judgment after death. These convictions create a spiritual foundation that binds the community and encourages virtuous conduct.

Fanaticism is forbidden. Any attempt to stir hatred or violence against other faiths is met with public disapproval and, when needed, state action to preserve concord. Utopians believe that all religions aim at the same goal—righteous living. God, in whatever name or form, values deeds above ritual. For this reason, different traditions are treated with equal regard, as diverse paths toward a shared moral destination.

Public worship embodies these principles. Temples are open to all, built in a simple style that avoids grandeur yet inspires reverence. Services are arranged so that citizens of different faiths may gather together, each interpreting the rites in accordance with their own belief. Music, solemn prayers, and silence cultivate unity beyond doctrinal divisions, reminding all that spiritual life is a common pursuit directed toward virtue and the good of the community.

Through this arrangement, sectarian conflict is avoided, and trust and understanding grow among citizens. Freedom of worship, joined with universal moral principles, ensures cohesion and stability, reflecting the humanist spirit at the heart of More's vision.

A Legal System Founded on Simple and Comprehensible Laws

Thomas More stresses that genuine justice is possible only when laws are few, clear, and easily understood. In Utopia, statutes are deliberately limited in number and written in plain language. More contrasts this with the tangled legal codes of Europe, where endless decrees and interpretations forced citizens to rely on lawyers. In Utopia, the profession does not exist. Citizens speak for themselves because the law is simple enough for all to grasp. By removing legal specialists, the community guards against corruption and ensures that law remains a shared possession, not a private instrument of power.

Legislation is designed to prevent wrongdoing rather than punish it. Instead of threatening harsh penalties, Utopian law addresses the conditions that breed crime. With private property abolished and extremes of wealth and poverty removed, theft, fraud, and exploitation lose their appeal. Where needs are met and goods are fairly shared, the incentives for most crimes disappear.

When offenses occur, justice seeks correction rather than cruelty. Punishments are measured, intended to help offenders recognize their errors and reform. Most penalties take the form of public service, moral instruction, or temporary loss of privileges. For serious or repeated crimes, punishments may include forced labor or exclusion from civic life, but even these are understood as steps toward rehabilitation, not revenge. The goal is always the restoration of order, not retribution.

Those who enforce the law are elected from among respected citizens. They are not a privileged caste of judges or bureaucrats but remain bound by the same rules as everyone else. Their authority rests on integrity and fairness, and because office carries no material advantage and their decisions are public, corruption is discouraged. Citizens trust them precisely because they are peers drawn from the community.

This system reflects More's belief that law must be a guide to virtuous living, not a trap of technicalities. In Utopia, legal obedience grows naturally from education and civic responsibility. From childhood, citizens learn that respecting the law is inseparable from serving the common good. Justice is woven into their habits, so severe punishments are seldom necessary.

The Significance and Influence of the Model on Subsequent Philosophical and Social Thought

Thomas More's Contribution to the Development of Social and Philosophical Utopias

Thomas More shaped the genre of social and philosophical utopias, becoming its founder and defining its main principles. His Utopia (1516) not only gave a name to an entire literary tradition but also introduced a new mode of social thought centered on the deliberate design of a just society.

Through More, the word utopia entered European culture as a universal term for ideal models of political and social order. He was the first to show that it was possible to create a detailed and systematic description of a community organized on the basis of reason, equality, and justice. In doing so, he offered an entirely new approach to criticism of existing institutions and to proposals for reform.

More's central contribution lay in his conviction that the flaws of real societies were not unavoidable. He argued that greed, inequality, and conflict could be overcome if communal life were ordered rationally and guided by moral principles. This vision inspired generations of thinkers—humanists, Enlightenment writers, reformers, and later socialists—to devise their own utopian projects.

In Utopia, More outlined for the first time a society without private property, where labor was universal and honorable and goods were distributed fairly. These ideas became the foundation of later utopian thought and left a direct mark on Tommaso Campanella's City of the Sun, Francis Bacon's New Atlantis, and, much later, on the socialist experiments of Charles Fourier and Robert Owen, as well as the communist theories of the nineteenth and twentieth centuries.

Equally influential was his articulation of humanist ideals that shaped later social philosophy: freedom of conscience, religious toleration, universal education, the collective upbringing of children, social equality, and the assignment of labor according to ability. By formulating these principles with unusual clarity, More provided concepts that would long outlive his own century.

More did not simply create a literary genre. He expanded the scope of philosophical reflection, showing that societies could be consciously designed on principles of justice, reason, and shared values. His Utopia stands as both the origin of a tradition and a pivotal work in European intellectual history, continuing to provoke readers to imagine alternatives to the realities of their time.

The Impact of Thomas More's *Utopia* on the Formation of Ideals of Equality and Social Justice in European Thought

Thomas More's Utopia deeply shaped European social and philosophical thought, helping to establish the ideals of equality and justice as central themes of political debate. Ideas formulated by More in the early sixteenth century encouraged Europeans to question entrenched social relations and reconsider the principles on which political order should rest.

More was among the first to state clearly the principle of human equality, independent of birth, wealth, or status. His critique of private ownership, exploitation, and privilege made inequality a subject of urgent discussion. In Utopia, property is identified as the chief source of conflict and corruption. In its place, More imagined communal ownership and fair distribution, offering a vision of society that broke sharply with existing realities.

During the Enlightenment, his influence appeared in the writings of Jean-Jacques Rousseau and Voltaire. Rousseau's belief in natural equality and the social contract reflected themes already present in More's thought, while Voltaire's attacks on privilege and intolerance drew strength from the same humanist tradition. By the eighteenth century, the ideals first expressed in Utopia had become part of the philosophical language that undermined feudal hierarchies and prepared Europe for reform.

In the nineteenth century, More's model resonated with the rise of socialist and communist theories. The call to abolish private property, to make labor universal, and to distribute goods equitably shaped the writings of Charles Fourier, Robert Owen, and Karl Marx. Marx and Engels recognized More as a precursor, crediting Utopia as the first systematic attempt to imagine a community founded on justice and equality. Though their philosophical bases differed, the continuity of themes shows how enduring More's vision proved to be.

The legacy of Utopia carried into the twentieth century, influencing democratic and socially oriented theories that placed equality, justice, and human dignity at their core. More's work provided not only a foundation for humanist and socialist utopias but also a framework for centuries of debate over the proper organization of society. Its central message—that injustice and inequality are not inevitable but can be overcome through reason and moral principle—remains a lasting contribution to European political thought.

Major Currents of Criticism and Debate Surrounding More's *Utopia*

Thomas More's Utopia inspired admiration and imitation, but it also provoked sustained debate and sharp criticism across the centuries. From its earliest reception, thinkers questioned the realism of its proposals, the possibility of applying its principles, and the dangers such a design might pose for society and the individual. At the center of these doubts stood the issues of human motivation, the role of property, and the balance between collective welfare and personal liberty.

One of the earliest critical voices was Erasmus of Rotterdam, More's close friend and fellow humanist. While admiring the ethical and intellectual spirit of the book,

Erasmus doubted that a society could be stable without personal incentives to work and achieve. He suggested that Utopia underestimated the persistence of individual desires and the difficulty of aligning human character with purely communal aims.

In the Enlightenment, these concerns reappeared in the writings of liberal thinkers such as John Locke, Adam Smith, and later John Stuart Mill. Locke emphasized that property rights were inseparable from natural liberty, arguing that ownership was the product of labor and a safeguard of personal independence. Adam Smith saw individual interest as the engine of economic activity, insisting that prosperity and growth could not be sustained without incentives for innovation and productivity. John Stuart Mill added that liberty itself would be endangered in a society that subordinated personal choice to communal demands. Together, these critics contended that abolishing private property and imposing universal labor would suppress individuality, weaken motivation, and ultimately reduce prosperity.

By the nineteenth century, critiques grew sharper as Utopia was read against the backdrop of emerging socialist movements. Some reformers admired More as a precursor, but others pointed to the dangers of excessive regulation and central planning. Philosophers and economists warned that utopian schemes, however well intentioned, risked eroding personal freedom. Karl Popper later argued that attempts to impose a perfect social design invariably drift toward authoritarianism, since they require strict regulation of behavior and the sacrifice of individual rights in the name of collective welfare. Friedrich Hayek reinforced this view, claiming that centrally planned systems inevitably slide toward coercion, as no government could manage the complexity of social and economic life without restricting liberty.

A different line of criticism addressed the moral and psychological dimensions of Utopian society. Skeptics argued that a community based entirely on equality and collectivism underestimated the strength of human desires for recognition, competition, and personal distinction. Without private incentives, they warned, people might lose interest in work, neglect public duties, and undermine the very solidarity the system was meant to secure. Instead of harmony, such a society could drift into apathy, inefficiency, and hidden forms of inequality.

Yet criticism did not end with economic or psychological arguments. Some scholars also noted that More's system implied a high degree of social supervision and control. The communal meals, the uniform housing, the constant oversight of behavior, and the regulation of leisure all suggested that conformity, rather than freedom, was the real price of equality. For these readers, Utopia risked replacing the injustices of wealth with the equally oppressive weight of uniformity and surveillance.

Despite such objections, Utopia has remained a central reference point in the history of philosophy and social thought. Its critics, no less than its admirers, acknowledged that More had posed questions of enduring importance: Is equality compatible with liberty? Can justice be achieved without private property? Where is the line between communal responsibility and individual freedom? Debate over these issues has never ceased. For centuries, the challenges raised by Utopia have compelled thinkers to reflect more deeply on the nature of society, the limits of reform, and the tension between the individual and the community.

Chapter 3. Tommaso Campanella's *The City of the Sun*
A Renaissance Vision of Social Harmony and Collectivism

The City of the Sun (La città del Sole), written in 1602 by the Italian philosopher and Dominican friar Tommaso Campanella and published in Frankfurt in 1623, is one of the defining utopian works of the late Renaissance. Cast as a philosophical dialogue, it describes an imagined community organized according to reason, equality, and collective order.

Campanella's vision reflects the humanist search for harmony and unity. In this society, equality is not a distant aspiration but a practical reality woven into daily existence. Shared labor, common property, and collective education are presented as the foundation of social organization.

The book's enduring significance lies in its symbolic force. The City of the Sun gave expression to the hope of a just and cooperative order, and its images of communal life inspired later philosophers, reformers, and visionaries to construct their own models of a society built on fairness and solidarity.

Historical and Intellectual Context
Biography of Tommaso Campanella (1568–1639)

Tommaso Campanella, Italian philosopher, poet, and Dominican friar, was born on September 5, 1568, in the Calabrian town of Stilo. The son of a poor artisan family, he entered the Dominican Order at the age of fourteen, where he received a thorough training in theology and philosophy. In these years he immersed himself in the works of Plato, Aristotle, and the scholastics, studies that shaped his later attempt to create a new synthesis of faith, philosophy, and natural science.

At the heart of Campanella's thought was the effort to unite Renaissance humanism with religious and mystical belief. He argued that human beings can understand the laws of nature and integrate them into social life, insisting on the unity of science and religion. For him, true knowledge came not only from reason but also from contemplation and direct observation of the natural world. In his writings he consistently defended justice, equality, and the vision of a commonwealth governed by harmony.

Campanella's political views were unusually bold for his time. He denounced the feudal system of Italy, attacking both aristocratic rule and absolute monarchy, which he saw as oppressive and destructive of progress. Instead, he called for a state based on reason, morality, and the common good, where power would belong to the wisest and most learned rather than to those who inherited privilege or wealth.

Such views, combined with his opposition to Spanish rule in southern Italy, led to persecution. In 1599 he was accused of conspiracy and sentenced to life imprisonment. He spent twenty-seven years in prison, where he composed many of his most important works, including The City of the Sun. In 1626 he was released through the intervention of Pope Urban VIII and soon after moved to France under the protection of Cardinal Richelieu. Campanella continued to write and teach in Paris until his death on May 21, 1639.

The Socio-Political Situation in Italy and Europe at the Turn of the Sixteenth and Seventeenth Centuries

The closing decades of the sixteenth century and the opening of the seventeenth were years of turbulence in Europe. Italy, divided into many small states, suffered from political fragmentation, economic decline, and constant struggles among aristocratic elites, all aggravated by foreign domination, especially by Spain. Public discontent grew as poverty deepened and peasants and artisans faced harsher exploitation from both nobility and clergy.

Amid this instability, radical ideas began to circulate, questioning the established order and calling for reform. The intellectual climate of the age was shaped by the continuing legacy of Renaissance humanism and the rising spirit of rationalism. These traditions emphasized human dignity, the capacity for reason, critical inquiry into authority and tradition, and confidence in the possibility of constructing a just society governed by rational principles.

Humanism promoted justice, respect for human worth, equality, and a rational approach to public affairs. Thinkers such as Desiderius Erasmus, Thomas More, and Niccolò Machiavelli deeply influenced European thought. At the same time, the new rationalist outlook was strengthened by the scientific breakthroughs of the late sixteenth and early seventeenth centuries, exemplified by Galileo Galilei, Giordano Bruno, and others, who reinforced the belief that social problems could be addressed through reason, science, and deliberate planning.

These forces shaped the development of Tommaso Campanella's ideas. Confronted with widespread poverty and injustice, which he saw as the product of irrational systems of power and economics, he sought an alternative. Drawing on the ideals of humanism and rationalism, Campanella envisioned a society founded on reason, equality, collectivism, and justice — a vision he gave its fullest expression in The City of the Sun.

The Influence of Platonic and Morean Utopias on the Creation of *The City of the Sun*

In writing The City of the Sun, Tommaso Campanella drew deeply on the tradition of utopian thought that began with Plato's Republic. Plato envisioned a community ruled by the wise, organized around shared property, communal education, and a carefully ordered hierarchy. This model left a lasting mark on Campanella: in his design, authority rests with the most learned and virtuous, whose rule derives not from wealth or birth but from knowledge and moral integrity. The stress on collective life, regulated labor, and strict social organization shows clear echoes of the Platonic ideal.

Equally important was the influence of Thomas More's Utopia, published a century earlier. Like More, Campanella advocates the equality of citizens, the abolition of private property, and the communal ownership of resources. His model also includes the regulation of daily life, the careful division of labor, and the fair distribution of goods, themes that recall More's vision. Yet Campanella extends these ideas further, insisting more strongly on social discipline, collective education, and the incorporation of scientific knowledge into government, thereby giving his utopia a character distinct from that of his predecessor.

Core Ideas and Principles

A Vision of Society Founded on Collective Labor, Equality, and Human Development

At the center of Tommaso Campanella's vision in The City of the Sun stands the integration of every individual into communal life, guided by the principle of collective labor. Unlike the divided and unjust society of his own age, Campanella imagined a commonwealth where each person's work contributed directly to the prosperity of all. Labor was carefully organized so that the natural abilities of every citizen could be developed while ensuring that the needs of the entire community were met.

Equality was the foundation of this system. Private property was abolished, access to work and education was guaranteed for all, and material goods were distributed fairly. Every inhabitant was treated as an equal member of the collective, and relations among them rested on justice and respect. In such conditions, privilege and economic superiority had no place, and the usual sources of conflict and envy lost their ground.

Campanella's design also reached beyond the economic sphere. He placed great importance on the formation of character and the cultivation of knowledge. From early childhood, each citizen was educated in science, philosophy, and the arts, alongside physical training and practical labor. Education was universal and comprehensive, shaping not only skilled workers but also thoughtful and responsible members of society.

In this way, collective labor, equality, and education worked together as parts of a single design, joining the well-being of the community with the growth and fulfillment of every individual.

The Idea of Uniting Science, Philosophy, and Religion as the Foundation of Social Order

In his utopia, Tommaso Campanella proposed the close integration of science, philosophy, and religion, convinced that only their harmony could sustain a just and enduring community. He warned that separating these domains led to ignorance, superstition, and conflict, while their union made possible true knowledge, moral guidance, and social concord.

Science held a central place in The City of the Sun. Rational inquiry, Campanella argued, allowed resources to be used wisely, disasters to be prevented, and the future to be planned with clarity. Citizens studied the natural sciences, medicine, astronomy, and mathematics so that public life would rest on principles that were clear and precise. Authority was entrusted to those with the widest learning, ensuring that governance was both rational and fair.

Philosophy complemented science by giving meaning and orientation to knowledge. It enabled citizens to reflect on human life and its purposes, to understand their place in the community, and to shape firm standards of conduct. Through philosophy, knowledge became not only an intellectual possession but also a moral responsibility, directed toward the good of all.

Religion too was essential, though free from dogmatism or fanaticism. Instead of standing apart from science and philosophy, it worked together with them, providing shared ethical values and spiritual unity. In Campanella's vision, religion bound citizens into one moral community and affirmed their responsibility to one another.

By bringing these three elements into harmony, Campanella imagined a society guided not by superstition or selfish desire but by knowledge, reflection, and a shared moral sense.

Faith in the Possibility of Human Moral and Physical Perfection through Rational Social Organization

One of the central themes of The City of the Sun is Tommaso Campanella's belief that human beings are naturally capable of both moral and physical perfection, provided their growth unfolds within a rationally organized society. Rejecting the pessimistic idea of innate sinfulness or weakness, he argued that vice and ignorance arise not from human nature itself but from a corrupt and disordered environment.

In Campanella's commonwealth, every aspect of life is arranged to support the complete development of the person — intellectual, physical, moral, and spiritual. Education, physical exercise, work, and philosophy form a single process. From childhood, each citizen is guided through a program that cultivates natural abilities while instilling honesty, moderation, responsibility, and devotion to the common good. The growth of mind and body is treated as one, essential for shaping balanced characters able to live in concord with themselves and with others.

For Campanella, it is precisely the ordering of society on the principles of justice, knowledge, and communal life that allows people to rise above selfishness, idleness, and destructive passions. Individuality is not suppressed but directed toward higher purposes. Each inhabitant participates in the common enterprise, so that pride, domination, and the pursuit of wealth lose their meaning.

Moral and physical perfection, in his view, is not the privilege of a few but the natural result of a society guided by reason and virtue, where every person is educated and supported in the service of the common good.

Government and Social Organization

The Structure of Power: The Supreme Ruler ("the Sun") and His Scholar-Assistants

In The City of the Sun, Tommaso Campanella describes a form of authority founded not on wealth, lineage, or force, but on knowledge and virtue. At the head of the commonwealth stands the figure called the Sun, or Metaphysicus — philosopher, scientist, and spiritual guide in one. He is not a monarch in the conventional sense but the embodiment of learning and justice, whose knowledge spans both the natural sciences and moral law.

The Sun rules with the help of three principal ministers, each responsible for a vital sphere of life. Pon, or Power, directs military affairs and defense. Sin, or Knowledge, oversees education, science, and the crafts. Mor, or Love, guides upbringing, family life, and the regulation of population. Though secondary in rank, these figures are essential: together they represent strength, learning, and care for life — the three foundations of communal order.

Leadership in this society is not inherited and does not arise from election in the usual sense. Authority belongs to those who have proved themselves through wisdom and service. Their rule is recognized by the community because of their learning and character, not by legal title or popular vote. For Campanella, such a system ensures that government rests in the hands of those who understand the order of nature and the duties of humankind.

A distinctive feature of this model is the unity of power, knowledge, and spiritual responsibility. In the City of the Sun, the roles of philosopher and ruler are fused. Authority is seen not as privilege but as service, entrusted only to those able to act for the common good rather than for personal gain.

This design, Campanella argues, prevents corruption and rivalry, since power is not given to those who seek it but to those judged capable of guiding society with prudence and selflessness. The political structure of the City of the Sun thus reflects his conviction that true sovereignty belongs only to knowledge joined with virtue.

The Organization of Society According to the Principle of Strict Collectivism: Common Housing, Collective Child-Rearing, Shared Labor, and Unified Social Norms

The society described in The City of the Sun is built on radical collectivism, touching every sphere of existence — from housing and family life to work and morality. Tommaso Campanella believed that only through complete communal living could greed, envy, and inequality be removed, since he saw them as the root of social decline.

Citizens live in shared houses designed for many families, where private space as a personal privilege disappears. Housing, like clothing, food, and other goods, is provided according to need rather than rank. Meals are taken at common tables according to a civic schedule. Comfort is subordinated to equality: no one may set themselves apart by luxury or isolation.

Child-rearing is also collective. From early childhood, children are placed under the care of teachers, and the identity of their biological parents is deliberately obscured. This system is meant to prevent favoritism, inequality of birth, and the dominance of family ties. All children grow up as members of a single community, receiving the same education and care, and learning to regard responsibility for others as equal to responsibility for themselves.

Work, too, is organized communally. Every adult contributes according to age, ability, and the needs of society. No type of work is considered higher or lower: craftsman, farmer, and scholar are valued alike. Tasks are rotated to avoid fatigue, while a shared schedule regulates the rhythm of daily life.

Social discipline is maintained through communal oversight as well as law. Eating, sleeping, study, art, and military training all follow strict timetables. To break the rules is not treated as a private act but as a disruption of civic harmony. Internal discipline is reinforced by external supervision, though punishment is reserved for those who knowingly defy communal norms.

Campanella's collectivism reached into culture, morality, and worldview. The individual was not set against society but placed within it. In this, he went further than earlier utopians: he did not simply reform property or political power but sought to reorganize life itself, erasing the division between "mine" and "thine."

Economic and Property Relations

The Principle of Abolishing Private Property and Collective Ownership of All Resources and Means of Production

In The City of the Sun, Tommaso Campanella abolishes private property in every form: land, resources, and the means of production are held in common by the whole community. Citizens have no individual households, no private food stores, and no personal wardrobes. Everything is provided according to established norms and actual needs. Drawing on the ideas of Plato and Thomas More, Campanella carried the principle of shared ownership further, applying it to every aspect of economic and social life.

Collective possession of resources allows for their planned and rational use. Agriculture, building, and crafts are organized communally, and distribution is overseen by officials chosen for their knowledge. Whatever is produced becomes immediately the property of the community, to be divided evenly among citizens. In this way, hoarding is prevented and disputes over wealth are avoided.

As a result, money, commerce, and profit-driven activity have no place. Campanella insists that without private wealth there can be no exploitation, usury, or theft, since each person has direct access to what they require. In a society where needs are met, crimes tied to property lose their meaning.

From childhood, citizens are raised in an environment where ownership does not exist. Objects are treated only as items for communal use. Clothing and household goods are uniform, not subject to exchange, and never a mark of status. Competition and envy over possessions are thus eliminated at their root.

Resources are managed under the supervision of officials responsible for maintaining supplies and ensuring balance. Neither shortages nor excess production is allowed to disrupt the economy. Campanella pointed to monasteries and religious communities as precedents, practical examples of collective life already tested in his own world.

For Campanella, abolishing property was more than a moral stance; it was the economic foundation of order. In a system without private wealth, he believed, social divisions could not arise, and justice would be secured for all.

Campanella also grounded this vision in his broader religious and cosmological outlook. He believed that the universe itself was ordered by divine wisdom and harmony, and human society should mirror this cosmic structure. Just as the heavens moved in balance without individual ownership, so too should earthly communities live in unity, sharing all things. In this sense, collective property was not only a practical arrangement but also an imitation of the divine order of creation.

The Organization of Labor and the Compulsory Participation of Every Citizen in Communal Work

In The City of the Sun, Tommaso Campanella required every inhabitant to take part in socially useful work. Labor was strictly organized under a shared schedule. The working day lasted about four hours, with the rest of the time devoted to education, training, physical exercise, and rest. Campanella saw this arrangement as the best way to sustain productivity without exhausting the people.

The distribution of tasks was overseen by supervisors chosen for their skill and judgment. Work was assigned according to age, strength, and aptitude, as revealed through upbringing and education. Those with greater physical ability were directed to farming, construction, and crafts, while citizens with intellectual gifts pursued science, medicine, teaching, and the planning of production.

To avoid monotony, each person rotated regularly between different kinds of work. This system broadened skills, encouraged adaptability, and kept citizens from wearing out in a single occupation.

There was no wage labor or economic exploitation. Money did not exist, and work was not rewarded by payment. Instead, citizens labored for the common good and drew equally from the shared resources of the community.

Productive activity was always collective. People worked together in fields and workshops, and everything they produced went into common storehouses, from which goods were distributed according to need. This removed rivalry in work and competition for profit.

For Campanella, compulsory labor was more than the foundation of economic order. It was also a means of shaping character and health. By treating labor as an honorable duty, every citizen recognized their place within the community and accepted responsibility for its well-being.

Rational and Just Distribution of Material Goods According to Citizens' Needs

In The City of the Sun, Tommaso Campanella describes a system where all goods are distributed according to the real needs of each citizen. To achieve this, communal storehouses are maintained under the supervision of officials chosen for their competence and reliability. The amount and type of supplies given to each person depend not on rank or privilege but on age, health, occupation, and living conditions. Campanella even notes that careful records are kept so that distribution remains accurate and impartial.

No individual is allowed to receive more than is necessary or to divert goods for private use. Food, clothing, medicines, and household items are issued on a regular basis according to standards fixed by the authorities. Centralized control prevents both scarcity and excess.

Citizens share the same plain but nourishing diet, produced by agriculture and crafts within the city. Meals are adjusted to meet different needs: those engaged in heavy labor receive more substantial portions than scholars or administrators. Dietary rules also take into account the seasons and the guidance of physicians, making nutrition part of preventive health as well as daily sustenance.

Luxury is excluded altogether. Clothing and household goods are uniform and standardized, leaving no room for personal display. This arrangement enforces equality and removes the grounds for rivalry or social division.

Oversight of distribution is strict but accepted as fair. Citizens, trained from childhood in moderation and collective values, neither attempt to deceive the community nor feel inclined to do so. Material goods are understood not as private possessions but as common resources meant to sustain life and work.

For Campanella, just distribution was more than an economic practice; it was a moral principle and a pillar of social order. He believed that only by balancing resources fairly could a society achieve harmony and trust. In this vision, material life itself became the basis of ethical and spiritual unity.

Morality, Law, and Culture

The Ethics of Collectivism and Solidarity: The Good of Society Above Private Interest

At the heart of the ethical system in The City of the Sun is the conviction that the welfare of the community outweighs the interests of the individual. From childhood, every citizen learns that personal happiness and security depend on the prosperity of the whole. The pursuit of private advantage at the expense of others is condemned as the source of conflict and decline.

This ethic is expressed in the rejection of selfishness, hoarding, and the pursuit of material distinction. To counter such tendencies, Campanella prescribes communal life, shared resources, and uniform standards of living. Actions are judged not by their benefit to the individual but by their contribution to society. Even everyday matters — diet, clothing, or leisure — are evaluated according to their effect on civic harmony.

Citizens are conscious of their mutual dependence. If someone falls ill or cannot work, others readily take their place, seeing it not as a burden but as a natural obligation. By contrast, those who put personal desire above communal need face public disapproval and corrective guidance.

Solidarity and mutual assistance are not considered charity but binding norms of behavior. Campanella notes that collectivism does not erase individuality but anchors it in a wider sense of belonging and security. He points to monastic life as a precedent, where similar principles had already produced stability and moral cohesion.

Qualities such as diligence, moderation, honesty, and responsibility are cultivated through the awareness that each person plays a role in the common enterprise. To break collectivist norms is not seen as a private fault but as a threat to the whole. Conduct is governed less by fear of punishment than by an internal sense of duty toward others.

Campanella sought to replace rivalry and egoism with solidarity and trust. For him, ethics, law, and culture formed a single fabric: justice was not an external imposition but a daily practice, lived by citizens who regarded moral duty and civic duty as one.

An Advanced System of Education and Science Integrated with Moral and Physical Formation

In The City of the Sun, Tommaso Campanella presents education as a unified system where the study of science is inseparable from moral and physical formation. From early childhood, children are guided by experienced teachers who observe their abilities and cultivate them with care.

The program is centrally organized and embraces mathematics, astronomy, medicine, biology, history, philosophy, and languages. Knowledge is always tied to practice. Astronomy and mathematics, for instance, are applied in agriculture, construction, and the planning of labor.

Physical education is compulsory. From youth, citizens train in gymnastics, athletics, horseback riding, and military exercises. These practices preserve health and strength, which Campanella considered essential for work and for the defense of the city.

Moral instruction holds equal importance. Students study ethics, philosophy, and religious texts not as dogma but critically. They are taught honesty, moderation, solidarity, and civic duty. Historical and philosophical examples show how moral choices affect the life of individuals and societies alike.

Learning relies on demonstration and practice. Knowledge is reinforced through participation in communal tasks and scientific experiments. Adults continue their education as well, since the renewal of learning is seen as vital to the community.

The distinctive feature of this system is its universality. Every citizen attends lessons and expands their understanding. Education is not a privilege but a common duty, ensuring a high level of learning throughout the city and preventing inequality based on knowledge.

Culture, Art, and Science as Integral Elements of Civic Life Oriented Toward Social Harmony

In The City of the Sun, Tommaso Campanella presents art, science, and culture as parts of a single order, woven into daily life and directed toward the moral and social growth of the community.

The walls of public buildings and the city streets are covered with paintings, diagrams, and maps illustrating astronomy, geography, biology, history, and philosophy. These images serve not as decoration but as teaching tools, making knowledge visible and accessible. From childhood, citizens encounter the sciences and the arts through this constant exposure, turning the city itself into a space of learning.

Music and poetry also play a central role. Performed at assemblies and festivals, they reinforce solidarity and the values of equality and communal life. Campanella believed that music and verse could guide emotions, nurture balance, and sustain harmony among citizens.

Architecture embodies the same principles. Houses and public buildings are laid out symmetrically and rationally, designed with attention to health, convenience, and beauty. The city thus becomes a visible expression of order shaped by science and art together.

Theater is given a special place. Plays on historical and philosophical themes teach citizens to see the results of human choices, to understand social relationships, and to sharpen their moral sense. For Campanella, drama was a means of education as well as entertainment.

In this cultural system, scholars and artists are not set apart as an elite. Every citizen takes part in scientific and artistic activity, contributing to the shared intellectual life of the community. Knowledge and creativity are understood not as privileges but as common duties, binding all to the moral and cultural progress of the city.

Simple and Rational Legislation as the Foundation of Order

In The City of the Sun, Tommaso Campanella describes a legal system that is simple, precise, and free from obscurity. Laws are few, logically arranged, and easy for all citizens to remember. Campanella believed that only clear and accessible rules could sustain order and prevent offenses born of ignorance or confusion.

From childhood, every citizen learns the laws, which are displayed in public places and regularly discussed at communal gatherings. Because the statutes contain no intricate subtleties, there is no need for judges or lawyers. Each inhabitant knows their rights and duties and can follow them without assistance.

Justice in this system rests on education and prevention rather than severity. When infractions occur, they are examined by a public council, and offenders must explain their actions openly. Punishments are corrective: communal labor, reparative work, or in rare cases short-term isolation. The goal is not retribution but reform and reintegration into community life.

The law is also designed to remove the causes of crime. With private property abolished and goods distributed fairly, theft and usury have no ground. Regulation of work and leisure prevents disputes arising from exhaustion or inequality of burden. In this way, legislation acts less as a restraint than as a framework for civic balance.

Campanella stresses that the simplicity of this legal order is not a sign of primitivism. It reflects reason and practicality, enabling citizens to follow the law with ease and to feel directly responsible for the order of the community.

At the same time, Campanella tied the legal order to moral and religious instruction. Laws were not meant to function in isolation but were reinforced by education in virtue and by the shared belief that divine justice rewards good conduct and punishes wrongdoing. In this way, civic obedience was grounded not only in fear of sanctions but also in a broader ethical and spiritual framework that encouraged citizens to see the law as an extension of their moral duty.

The Significance and Influence of Campanella's Ideas on Later Philosophy and Social Thought

The Impact of *The City of the Sun* on the Development of Modern Utopian Traditions and the Formation of Collectivist Thought

Tommaso Campanella's *The City of the Sun* strongly shaped the development of utopian thought from the seventeenth to the nineteenth century and became one of the chief sources for the idea of collectivism in social philosophy. His vision of a community without private property, organized around communal labor, collective child-rearing, and centralized distribution of resources, inspired Enlightenment thinkers and early modern socialists alike.

Its impact was particularly visible in the work of French utopian socialists of the nineteenth century — Charles Fourier, Henri de Saint-Simon, and Étienne Cabet — who adapted and expanded principles first expressed by Campanella. The echoes of his proposals can be seen in their emphasis on collective labor, shared education, and centralized planning of social and economic life. Robert Owen, too, drew upon these ideas in founding experimental communities built on collective ownership, rational organization of labor, and the education of a "new man." In many respects, Owen's projects put into practice key features of *The City of the Sun*.

Campanella's work also resonated with early Marxism. Karl Marx and Friedrich Engels regarded *The City of the Sun* as a significant precursor to socialism, recognizing in it one of the first systematic attempts to imagine a society founded on equality and the abolition of private property. Though they later emphasized its limitations, they acknowledged Campanella as an important forerunner in the tradition of social critique.

The influence of *The City of the Sun* extended beyond socialism and communism. In the broader history of political thought, it stood as a striking example of how religion, science, and politics could be combined into a single utopian framework. Seventeenth- and eighteenth-century scholars debated its feasibility, some admiring its systematic coherence, others warning that its communal structures foreshadowed excessive control over individual life. In the twentieth century, after the rise and fall of socialist states, the book was often revisited as both a prophetic text and a cautionary one — admired for its critique of inequality, but questioned for its theocratic hierarchy and rigid regulation of daily existence.

Beyond his utopian writing, Campanella produced a substantial body of philosophical, theological, and political works:

1. **Philosophy Demonstrated by the Senses (*Philosophia sensibus demonstrata*, 1591)** — a critique of Aristotelian scholasticism, advancing an empirical theory of knowledge and the connection between humanity and nature through sensory experience.

2. **Apology for Galileo (*Apologia pro Galileo*, 1616)** — a defense of Galileo and of the right to free scientific inquiry, arguing that faith and science are not inherently opposed.

3. **The Monarchy of the Messiah** (*Monarchia Messiae*, 1606) — a theological-political vision of a universal Christian commonwealth under papal authority.

4. **Political Aphorisms** (*Aphorismi politici*, 1601) — reflections on authority, governance, and the necessity of justice and morality in political life.

5. **Atheism Conquered** (*Atheismus triumphatus*, 1607) — a theological work arguing for the existence of God against atheism and materialism, using rational and natural proofs.

6. **Metaphysics** (*Metaphysica*, 1638) — his late systematic treatise, uniting philosophy and theology in a discussion of being, the soul, and the nature of reality.

Alongside these works, he wrote poetry, letters, and numerous minor treatises on philosophy, theology, and natural science. His intellectual legacy thus spans multiple disciplines. Yet it is *The City of the Sun* that stands at the center of his reputation, shaping the history of utopian thought and influencing generations of philosophers and social reformers. Its mixture of religious vision, scientific curiosity, and social radicalism ensured that the work remained a point of reference long after Campanella's time — both as a source of inspiration for those who sought communal alternatives to inequality and as a stimulus for debate about the limits of utopian imagination

The Role of Campanella's Ideas in Nineteenth-Century Socialist and Communist Thought

Tommaso Campanella stands among the intellectual precursors of nineteenth-century socialism and communism. *The City of the Sun* was widely known among utopian socialists and served as both a reference and an example.

His influence is clear in the work of Robert Owen (1771–1858). In the communities of New Lanark and New Harmony, Owen sought to realize principles first set out by Campanella: collective ownership, universal labor, communal child-rearing, and the rational distribution of goods. Like Campanella, he believed that such arrangements could end exploitation and social inequality.

Étienne Cabet (1788–1856) also drew directly on Campanella. In Voyage en Icarie (1840) he imagined a communist city based on shared property, equality, and communal upbringing. Cabet himself acknowledged Campanella as an inspiration for this design of collective life.

Charles Fourier (1772–1837) absorbed elements of the same tradition. Although he reworked them in his model of the phalanstery, the themes of common property, collective labor, and planned social organization still reflect Campanella's earlier utopian scheme.

Karl Marx (1818–1883) and Friedrich Engels (1820–1895) likewise recognized Campanella as an early forerunner of socialist thought. In Socialism: Utopian and Scientific, Engels listed him among those who helped prepare the ground for later communist theory. While Marx and Engels placed him in the category of pre-scientific socialism, they acknowledged his importance as one of the first to propose a systematic alternative to property and inequality.

The Main Directions of Criticism and Contemporary Assessments of the Viability of Campanella's Social Model

In The City of the Sun, Campanella describes public ownership, collective labor, priestly rule, and strict regulation of private life — a design that has drawn sustained criticism.

John Locke highlighted the first tension. Abolishing private estates contradicts his principle that property, derived from labor, secures liberty. Without this link, individuality weakens, incentives diminish, and freedom loses its ground.

Montesquieu sharpened the political objection. By concentrating authority in a sacral hierarchy, Campanella's model undermines the separation of powers and the protective role of intermediate institutions. What is meant to preserve unity risks suppressing dissent and bending power toward tyranny. Voltaire added his own suspicion of schemes that erase variety of character in the name of collective order.

Nineteenth-century liberals voiced similar concerns. John Stuart Mill defended individuality and "experiments in living," while Campanella's communal assignments of work and conduct appeared to suppress variety and slow improvement. Herbert Spencer warned that when voluntary cooperation gives way to compulsory administration, initiative fades and society stiffens into bureaucracy.

Economic theory reinforced the critique. Friedrich Hayek's "knowledge problem" showed why centralized planning fails: information in complex societies is dispersed and often tacit, beyond the reach of any ruling council. Markets, through prices and practices, perform discovery functions no central authority can replicate.

Karl Popper later cautioned against utopian social engineering and the vision of a completed blueprint. A polity that fixes its ends in advance, like Campanella's city, resists correction and closes itself to the piecemeal reform on which open societies depend.

Modern scholarship thus reads The City of the Sun less as a practicable program than as a utopian statement. Its significance lies in the critique of the religious and political order of its age rather than in feasibility. After the twentieth century's socialist and communist experiments, its vision of communal property, priestly coordination, and astrologically regulated reproduction sits uneasily with constitutional freedoms and the complexity of modern economies.

Anthony Giddens reframes the issue at the level of theory. He distinguishes between utopian "end-states," which collide with modernity's openness and reflexivity, and what he calls utopian realism — the practice of directing imagination toward the future while anchoring ideals in existing institutions. His analysis of late modernity — disembedding, time–space distanciation, expert systems, and the "juggernaut" of social change — shows why Campanella's city remains a powerful provocation but no longer appears as a viable social model.

Chapter 4. Francis Bacon's *New Atlantis*

A Utopian Vision of Scientific and Technological Progress in the 17th Century

Francis Bacon's *New Atlantis* (1627) is a utopian narrative that, for the first time, portrays a society built explicitly on scientific knowledge and technological progress. Though unfinished, the work presents the imaginary island of Bensalem, where prosperity, social harmony, and justice are achieved through a carefully organized system of research and discovery.

What makes the text remarkable is its early proposal that scientific and technological progress could serve as the foundation of a perfected society. At the heart of Bensalem stands the House of Salomon, an institution devoted to experimentation and the advancement of knowledge. It later became an intellectual model for the academies of science that would emerge in Europe.

The *New Atlantis* is closely tied to Bacon's broader project of reform outlined in the *Novum Organum* (1620). While the Novum Organum lays out a new method of inductive reasoning, the *New Atlantis* imagines how such a method might shape an entire community. Bensalem thus becomes a vision of a society where knowledge is systematically gathered, tested, and applied for the common good.

Bacon articulated with unusual clarity the idea that science is not only a way of explaining nature but also a transformative force capable of reshaping human life. In his view, knowledge could secure abundance, comfort, and harmony for all. The New Atlantis left a lasting mark on Enlightenment thought and directly influenced the development of modern science and the philosophy of technology.

Historical and Intellectual Context

Biography of Francis Bacon (1561–1626)

Francis Bacon was born on January 22, 1561, in London, into the household of Sir Nicholas Bacon, Lord Keeper of the Great Seal under Queen Elizabeth I. His mother, Lady Anne Cooke Bacon, famed as one of the most learned women of her age, spoke several languages and passed to her son not only a devotion to study but also the courage to question what books and teachers left unsaid.

At twelve, Bacon entered Trinity College, Cambridge, a child among men. The promise of learning soon gave way to disillusion. He found the endless scholastic disputations hollow, detached from the pulse of life. In the narrow halls of the university, he began to dream of another way — truth discovered not through empty words but through the open book of nature itself.

Longing to see the world, Bacon journeyed through France, Spain, and Italy. He watched the intrigues of court life, studied the machinery of politics, and noted the burdens carried by ordinary people. These travels deepened his resolve. Returning home, he pledged himself to public service and to the law, convinced that duty, not privilege, was the true path to honor.

His career rose like a swift tide. Under King James I he was appointed Attorney General and, in 1618, Lord Chancellor — the highest legal seat in England. For a season he stood in power, admired for his counsel, feared for his authority. But fortune turned. In 1621 he was accused of bribery, forced to confess, and cast down from his offices. The once-mighty statesman retreated to Gorhambury, stripped of honors but not of purpose.

In solitude he found his true vocation. At Gorhambury he wrote the works that would secure his place in history: the *Great Instauration* (*Instauratio Magna*, 1620), containing the *Novum Organum*, and *On the Dignity and Advancement of Learning* (*De dignitate et augmentis scientiarum*, 1623). Here he laid out the architecture of the empirical method, built on observation, experiment, and the steady weighing of facts.

For Bacon, science was not the idle explanation of nature but its mastery for the sake of humankind. He gave voice to this belief in words that still echo: Scientia potentia est — "knowledge is power." To him, knowledge was a tool to secure abundance, ease suffering, and bring order and harmony into human life.

His final days reflected his restless curiosity. In March 1626, while testing whether cold could preserve food, he stuffed a chicken with snow. He caught a chill that turned into pneumonia, and on April 9, 1626, he died.

The following year his unfinished *New Atlantis* (1627) was published. In it Bacon described a society where prosperity and justice were secured through science placed in the service of humanity. That vision endured, inspiring generations of philosophers and scientists and helping to shape the course of modern thought.

The Intellectual Climate of the Seventeenth Century: The Scientific Revolution, the Rise of Experimental Knowledge, and the Critique of Medieval Traditions

The seventeenth century brought far-reaching changes in methods of thought and inquiry, remembered as the Scientific Revolution. European learning moved away from medieval scholasticism—long anchored in Aristotelian and ecclesiastical authority—toward an experimental practice grounded in observation, measurement, and empirical testing.

Writers often trace the opening move to Nicolaus Copernicus's *On the Revolutions of the Heavenly Spheres* (*De revolutionibus orbium coelestium*, 1543), which replaced Ptolemy's geocentric scheme with a heliocentric cosmos. Johannes Kepler advanced that shift in *Astronomia nova* (1609) and *Harmonices Mundi* (1619), formulating what became known as the three laws of planetary motion. Beginning in 1609, Galileo Galilei turned the telescope to the sky and, soon thereafter, identified the moons of Jupiter, the phases of Venus, and sunspots.

Experimental practice reshaped physics and the natural sciences. Galileo laid foundations for mechanics in his studies of falling bodies and motion. In England, William Gilbert's *De magnete* (1600) offered systematic experiments on magnetism, while William Harvey's *De motu cordis* (1628) demonstrated the circulation of the blood, overturning Galenic physiology that had held sway for centuries.

What distinguished the new approach was the refusal to rest arguments on authority alone. Inquiry turned to nature itself—to what could be observed, measured, and reproduced—so that claims would stand on demonstrable facts rather than prestige or tradition.

Francis Bacon served as a principal theorist of this turn. In *Novum Organum* (1620) he set out an inductive method, proposed a structured program for experiment, and analyzed the "idols" that distort judgment. His writings helped frame the philosophical ground of the Scientific Revolution and influenced figures such as Robert Boyle, a founder of modern chemistry, and Isaac Newton, whose *Principia Mathematica* (1687) gave classical physics its mathematical form and unified celestial and terrestrial mechanics under universal laws.

Institutional support followed later in the century. The Royal Society of London (founded 1660) adopted the motto Nullius in verba—"take nobody's word for it"—and, under Henry Oldenburg, launched the *Philosophical Transactions* (1665), one of the first scientific journals and the longest continuously published, with editorial practices that anticipated modern peer review. With the Society's imprimatur and Edmond Halley's sponsorship, Newton's Principia appeared in 1687; Newton later served as President (1703–1727). In Paris, Jean-Baptiste Colbert organized the Académie des Sciences (1666) and established the Paris Observatory (1667), attracting scholars such as Christiaan Huygens and Giovanni Domenico (Jean-Dominique) Cassini. Similar bodies soon appeared elsewhere—the Accademia del Cimento in Florence (1657, motto provando e riprovando), the Leopoldina in the Holy Roman Empire (1652), and, in the next century, the St. Petersburg Academy (1724).

The Influence of Empiricism and Rationalism on the Formation of Francis Bacon's Ideas

Francis Bacon's philosophy took shape at a moment when two great traditions of early modern thought—empiricism and rationalism—were beginning to define European intellectual life. Empiricism, from the Greek empeiria ("experience"), insisted that knowledge must grow out of observation and experiment. Rationalism, by contrast, emphasized the power of reason and deduction, with figures such as René Descartes and later Baruch Spinoza holding that truth could be reached through pure thought.

Bacon tried to draw strength from both sides. He argued that science must begin with careful observation and experiment, but that facts alone are not enough unless shaped and ordered by reason. In this way he rejected both the blind collection of data and speculative reasoning detached from evidence.

Central to his method was the doctrine of the "idols"—systematic errors of the mind that stand in the way of objective knowledge. He identified four: the idols of the tribe, rooted in human nature; the idols of the cave, springing from personal bias; the idols of the marketplace, born of the misuse of language; and the idols of the theater, drawn from philosophical systems and tradition. By naming these obstacles, Bacon supplied a tool for clearing the path of inquiry and disciplining human judgment.

This vision shaped the later course of British empiricism, especially in the works of John Locke and David Hume, and influenced the standards of the emerging sciences

Core Ideas and Principles

Faith in Science and Technological Progress as the Foundation of the Ideal Society

Francis Bacon was the first philosopher to state plainly that science and technology should not remain matters of speculation alone but serve as the foundation of a just and prosperous society. In his utopian tale *New Atlantis* (1627), he imagined a community where knowledge was turned into practical benefits for all. He described laboratories in which plants and animals were improved through selective breeding, medicines discovered to cure diseases once thought incurable, and devices invented to lighten manual labor and improve daily life. These examples showed that scientific progress, in Bacon's view, had to reach beyond scholarly study and enter directly into human affairs.

This vision left a deep mark on European thought. The Enlightenment encyclopedists, especially Denis Diderot and Jean Le Rond d'Alembert, took inspiration from Bacon's belief that knowledge should be organized, shared, and applied for the common good. His example helped to create a cultural model in which science was valued not only as a means of discovering truth but also as a force capable of reshaping society.

The Concept of Knowledge as the Highest Value Capable of Transforming Society and Bringing Human Happiness

Francis Bacon saw knowledge as the chief instrument for relieving the burdens of human life. Unlike earlier philosophers, he valued it not as an abstract possession but as a power able to lessen suffering, combat disease, reduce poverty, and limit conflict.

For him, knowledge had to be treated as a practical force. The discovery of nature's laws and the systematic use of scientific methods, he believed, should bring better living conditions, fewer inequalities, and greater opportunities for all. Only by applying knowledge could humanity hope to overcome hunger, illness, and want, and move toward a society that offered dignity and well-being to its members.

Bacon also insisted that the fruits of inquiry must not remain confined to a narrow circle of scholars. In *New Atlantis* he highlighted the importance of education and the open circulation of knowledge, portraying citizens who were literate and able to use science in the routines of daily life. Knowledge, in his view, was no longer a privilege or an ideal detached from practice. It was the foundation of progress itself—the means by which society could secure both prosperity and justice.

The Idea of Organized and Rational Governance Founded on Science and Reason

Francis Bacon believed that no community could remain stable or well-ordered without a form of governance founded on reason. Unlike traditional systems, where power rested on force, inheritance, or wealth, he argued that authority should be grounded in knowledge and the disciplined use of scientific method.

In *New Atlantis* he described how a society might prosper under the guidance of learned men rather than politicians preoccupied with ambition. On the island of Bensalem, power belongs not to hereditary rulers but to a council of scholars, chosen for their intellectual merit and scientific achievement.

Decisions there follow inquiry and experiment. Questions of agriculture, medicine, and industry are settled by evidence and tested results rather than personal preference or factional interest. As a result, the community avoids famine, epidemics, and scarcity: policy, planned and informed by science, anticipates crises before they strike.

Bacon insisted that the same rigor of method that governs science should also guide public affairs. He imagined institutions working like laboratories of governance, where new measures could be tested, measured, and refined before being applied on a larger scale.

In presenting this vision, Bacon offered a political model in which science and rationality were not ancillary supports but the very ground of authority—making knowledge the foundation of prosperity, stability, and the common good

Government and Social Organization
Bensalem as a Model State Governed by Scholars and Sages

In *New Atlantis*, Francis Bacon portrays Bensalem as a society where governance is entrusted not to kings or nobles but to scholars prepared for public service. Authority belongs only to those who have shown their knowledge in practice and demonstrated ability both in science and in administration.

At the center of this order is the House of Salomon, the island's academy of sciences. Here the most esteemed scholars—specialists in medicine, natural history, physics, chemistry, and agriculture—conduct research and advise on the affairs of the commonwealth. They plan harvests, develop remedies, oversee institutions, direct economic activity, and even guide technological invention and maritime exploration. Each decision rests on calculation, repeated trials, and tested evidence rather than ambition or intrigue.

Power struggles are absent because leaders are chosen by strict standards of competence and integrity rather than by birth or wealth. Their authority comes from the respect earned through knowledge, fairness, and service to the public good. Trust is built on visible results, not on concealed influence.

Life in Bensalem reflects the same principle of rational organization. Cities are planned with regard for health and sanitation. Medicine is practiced with the aid of new discoveries. Agriculture prospers through improved methods of cultivation and selective breeding. Education is open to all, and culture itself is shaped by science, so that progress is shared widely rather than reserved for the privileged few. Resources are distributed with efficiency and fairness, allowing every citizen to experience directly the benefits of knowledge applied to social life.

Social Organization

In Francis Bacon's vision of Bensalem, knowledge and learning are the true measures of respect and authority. Social standing does not depend on birth, wealth, or family ties but on education, intellectual achievement, and service to the commonwealth. Those who contribute to science or the life of the mind assume positions of leadership and are honored by the community.

From childhood, citizens are taught to value learning. Education is widely available, and the pursuit of knowledge is actively encouraged. Young people study under accomplished teachers, acquire practical skills, and apply them in daily life. Learning is not treated as the privilege of a few but as a shared expectation, essential both for civic success and for personal dignity.

Life in Bensalem is shaped by cooperation, for the social order rests on a principle plain to everyone: individual success is inseparable from the welfare of the community. The absence of inherited privilege and the clear orientation toward common goals reduce rivalry and envy. Citizens work together, convinced that their well-being depends on mutual support.

This arrangement creates a genuine sense of harmony. The people of Bensalem are not split into hostile classes or competing groups but are united in a common purpose: the advancement of their society through knowledge and the rational use of resources. By placing intellectual merit at the center of civic life, Bacon's utopia portrays a community held together by respect, cooperation, and a commitment to the common good.

An Economy Founded on the Rational Use of Natural Resources and Scientific Achievement

In Bacon's picture of Bensalem, economic life is secured not by chance or shifting markets but by the rational management of resources through scientific knowledge. Prosperity comes from research and experiment applied to the practical needs of the community.

The island's conditions are carefully observed: the fertility of the soil, the cycles of climate, and the properties of local plants, animals, and minerals. Scholars of the House of Salomon carry out continual experiments to make the best use of every resource. They develop hardier strains of crops, design methods to restore and enrich the land, and create techniques for processing materials more efficiently.

Economic policy, in Bacon's view, must rest not on guesswork or private interest but on evidence confirmed by experiment. For this reason, the common disasters of his age—failed harvests, famine, shortages, or wasted labor—are virtually absent in Bensalem. Decisions are measured, tested, and calculated, producing stability and steady growth.

Production is organized with foresight and matched to the needs of the whole community. This prevents scarcity and secures a fair distribution of goods. Citizens live without fear of deprivation and can direct their efforts to science, education, and the arts, confident that the conditions of life will support them.

The Principles of Collective Use and the Rational Distribution of Resources for the Benefit of Society

In Francis Bacon's account of Bensalem, private hoarding and the arbitrary use of resources for personal gain have no place. Instead, he describes a system of collective management in which goods and natural resources are directed by principles of reason and the needs of the whole community.

Distribution is overseen centrally and guided by assessments of real requirements and the common good. Scholars of the House of Salomon decide how materials, technologies, and products should be used so that efficiency is maximized and waste reduced. They measure the community's needs for food, clothing, housing, and medicine with care, seeking to avoid both shortage and excess.

Allocation is based on evidence and tested standards. Agricultural produce is distributed according to rules designed to sustain health and nutrition. Clothing and household goods follow norms set with attention to comfort, durability, and the conservation of resources.

Such order lessens rivalry and resentment, for citizens receive the same benefits not through privilege or wealth but through a common measure applied equally to all. The aim is to employ resources so that the community prospers as a whole rather than particular individuals or groups. From an early age, people are taught that collective well-being takes precedence over private accumulation and that wastefulness is unacceptable.

Work as a Source of Common Progress and Well-Being: The Role of Technology in Enhancing Efficiency

For Bacon, the organization of work in Bensalem was central to the life of the commonwealth. Labor was not endured as a hardship but understood as the means through which society advanced and every citizen contributed to the flourishing of the whole. From childhood, people were taught that their own efforts sustained the community, and that individual happiness was bound to the prosperity of all.

What distinguished Bensalem from traditional societies was the union of work with scientific achievement. Technologies created by the scholars of the House of Salomon were applied directly to production, raising efficiency and easing toil. In agriculture, machines assisted in cultivating the land and harvesting crops. In workshops and crafts, new devices accelerated production and improved quality. The result was shorter hours of labor combined with greater results.

Work was also shared with care. Through rational planning and scientific organization, duties were distributed evenly so that no citizen was overburdened. Each person undertook tasks suited to their abilities, directed always toward the common good.

Technological progress was pursued not for private profit but for the collective benefit. By reducing effort and ensuring abundance, it gave citizens the freedom to devote time to study, artistic creation, and cultural life. In this way, labor became a source of satisfaction rather than hardship, a foundation of harmony and sustained progress.

Here Bacon set his vision apart from earlier utopias. In Plato's *Republic*, work was arranged through a strict division of classes, each group tied to its fixed role. In Tommaso Campanella's *City of the Sun*, labor was collective and compulsory, equal in distribution but repetitive and uniform. Bacon introduced something new: the systematic use of technology and experimental science to transform work itself. Rather than merely dividing tasks, his model sought to lighten effort, shorten hours, and expand productivity through innovation—making Bensalem the first utopia to place technological progress at the very heart of its social order.

Morality, Law, and Culture

The Ethics of Rationalism and Scientific Knowledge: A Commitment to Truth and the Common Good

In Francis Bacon's vision of Bensalem, the highest moral principle is loyalty to truth and to the rational study of nature. From childhood, citizens are taught that truth has absolute worth and that the search for knowledge is inseparable from duty to the community. Everyone understands that deception or ignorance can endanger the well-being of the whole society.

The ethics of Bensalem are bound to scientific accuracy. For scholars, responsibility lies not only in discovering truth but also in sharing it openly. Any attempt to distort results or conceal knowledge is treated as a breach of morality. Discoveries are made public, for the fruits of science are meant to serve the entire community, not a privileged few.

Inquiry, however, is never pursued for its own sake. Its goal is to serve humanity—to improve daily life, lessen suffering, and secure prosperity. Scientific advances are valued as moral achievements as well as intellectual ones, for they bring with them health, security, and greater happiness for all.

Through this ethic, Bensalem attains not only technical progress but also social harmony built on trust, openness, and shared commitment to the common good. In Bacon's utopia, morality, law, and science converge, creating a culture that sustains human dignity and collective prosperity.

The Educational System Based on the Study of Natural and Applied Sciences

The schools of Bensalem reflect Bacon's conviction that true learning must unite theory with practice and serve the common good. Unlike the medieval model, centered on theology and abstract debate, education on the island is devoted to the study of nature and the exact sciences—disciplines capable of bringing direct benefit to society.

From an early age, children are introduced to mathematics, physics, chemistry, biology, astronomy, and medicine. Instruction is built on observation and experiment. Students work in laboratories, examine natural phenomena, study plants, minerals, and animals, and learn the techniques needed for agriculture, industry, and daily life.

Practical training holds equal weight. Farming, construction, crafts, engineering, and medicine are taught alongside theory so that every pupil sees how knowledge applies in practice. This integration fosters a lasting respect for science as an instrument for solving the real problems of society.

Teachers are not simply instructors but accomplished scholars and practitioners, many connected with the House of Salomon. Their role is to show knowledge at work—to demonstrate how new discoveries cure disease, strengthen agriculture, and improve living conditions. Students are thus educated to value science for its service to the community.

The result is a generation trained to think rationally, to grasp the laws of nature, and to apply them constructively. By uniting theory with skill, Bacon's utopia produces citizens prepared to secure prosperity and civic stability.

Set against seventeenth-century Europe, this vision was radical. Universities such as Cambridge, Oxford, and the Sorbonne still gave priority to scholastic theology, classical languages, and Aristotelian disputation. Natural philosophy was often marginal, and experiment rarely entered formal study. Bacon, by contrast, imagined schools in which the sciences were central and each stage of learning tied to practical application. The schools of Bensalem, unlike their European counterparts, were designed not to preserve inherited knowledge but to generate new discoveries and to train citizens able to use them directly for the benefit of society.

Culture United by High Morality, Religious Tolerance, and Respect for Science

In Francis Bacon's portrayal of Bensalem, cultural life rests on the union of moral discipline, religious tolerance, and respect for knowledge. From an early age, citizens are taught to honor truth and value learning, seeing in them not only intellectual pursuits but the basis of justice and public order.

This moral framework allows freedom of conscience. Bacon shows that in Bensalem different forms of belief exist without conflict, for each person's spiritual convictions are treated as private and never used to disrupt social harmony or the scientific foundations of the community. Persecution and sectarian quarrels are absent.

Science is regarded as an ally of both morality and faith. Far from being in tension with religion, it deepens understanding of the world and humanity's place within it, and it guides citizens toward service of the common good. Scholars and sages are respected not for wealth or position but for their dedication to truth and their contributions to collective welfare.

Legislation Oriented Toward Social Harmony and Rational Development

In Francis Bacon's depiction of Bensalem, laws exist not to limit freedom but to sustain order and guide the rational progress of society. Their purpose is to preserve harmony while encouraging the use of knowledge for the common good.

Bacon emphasizes that legislation must be clear and accessible. Every citizen should be able to understand and apply the rules in daily life. There are no convoluted provisions demanding interpretation by lawyers; each statute is framed simply, grounded in principles confirmed by reason and experience.

The legal system regulates labor, ensures fair distribution of resources, and protects every individual. Rules concerning work are based on studies that define the proper balance between effort and rest, while the allocation of goods reflects accurate assessments of communal needs.

Law also serves a preventive role. Instead of focusing only on punishment, it removes the causes of conflict. The absence of private property and the fair sharing of resources leave little ground for theft or exploitation, while freedom of conscience prevents religious differences from turning into strife.

The Significance and Influence of Francis Bacon on Later Philosophy and Social Thought

The Impact of *New Atlantis* on Enlightenment Ideas and the Emergence of Faith in Progress and Science in the Eighteenth and Nineteenth Centuries

The ideas set forth by Francis Bacon in *New Atlantis* influenced Enlightenment thinkers of the eighteenth century and strengthened Europe's growing confidence in science and progress. In this utopian work, Bacon offered an early model of a society directed not by tradition or ecclesiastical power but by knowledge, by the authority of scholars, and by results tested through experiment.

The French encyclopedists — Denis Diderot, Jean Le Rond d'Alembert, and Voltaire — drew directly on Bacon's vision in shaping their conviction that science was the principal force of social change. In the Encyclopédie, Bacon was honored as the philosopher who established the foundations of modern inquiry and as a figure who embodied the promise of rational study of nature.

In England, his legacy appeared in the work of Isaac Newton and Robert Boyle, who applied Bacon's principles by creating scientific societies and academies modeled on the House of Salomon in *New Atlantis*. These institutions encouraged systematic experimentation, spread knowledge, and connected discovery with practical uses in industry, agriculture, and medicine.

In the nineteenth century, Bacon's thought echoed in Auguste Comte's philosophy of positivism, which maintained that society should advance only through scientific knowledge. The technological successes of the Industrial Revolution were often seen as the realization of Bacon's vision, reinforcing the belief that science could bring prosperity and social improvement on a scale never before imagined.

The Influence of Bacon's Ideas on Later Technocratic and Scientific Utopias

The idea of society as an order directed by rational knowledge and scientific administration, first formulated by Francis Bacon in *New Atlantis*, shaped later visions of technocratic and scientific utopias in the nineteenth and twentieth centuries. His model encouraged thinkers to see science not only as a means of discovery but as the basis of social organization itself.

In the nineteenth century, this influence appeared most clearly in the utopian socialism of Henri de Saint-Simon. He and his followers argued that authority should be entrusted to scientists and engineers who could plan production and distribute resources with reasoned efficiency. Saint-Simon even proposed a "council of scientists" to replace traditional political power, extending Bacon's House of Salomon into a program for modern governance.

At the start of the twentieth century, Bacon's legacy reemerged in the American technocratic movement led by Howard Scott. The technocrats claimed that engineers and specialists were best equipped to direct society by applying technical expertise to production and administration, thereby securing stability and prosperity.

Literary utopias of the twentieth century echoed the same vision. In works such as H. G. Wells's *The Shape of Things to Come*, Bacon's influence is evident. Wells openly acknowledged him as one of the first philosophers to grasp that scientific knowledge could determine the future course of humanity and its collective welfare.

The Main Currents of Criticism of Bacon's Conception and Its Contemporary Assessments

Francis Bacon's model of society in *New Atlantis* has been the subject of debate since the seventeenth century. Critics warned that a community governed solely by experts could restrict personal freedom, diminish humanistic values, and create unforeseen risks through its dependence on technology.

In the eighteenth century, Jean-Jacques Rousseau, in his *Discourse on the Sciences and the Arts* (1750), argued that the growth of knowledge might corrupt rather than ennoble humanity. Other Enlightenment thinkers, including Voltaire and Montesquieu, admired Bacon's scientific vision but cautioned against treating science as a universal cure for social problems. They stressed the need for political balance, civic virtue, and cultural diversity.

Nineteenth-century philosophers added further reservations. John Stuart Mill, though an admirer of Bacon, warned that collectivist schemes subordinating individuality to abstract ideals of the common good could stifle initiative and creativity. Herbert Spencer argued that governing society through scientific planning ignored the complexity of human behavior and risked producing rigid structures unable to adapt to change.

The experience of the twentieth century gave new weight to these concerns. The destructive use of science in warfare and mass industrialization suggested that Bacon's optimism underestimated its darker possibilities. Karl Popper, in *The Open Society and Its Enemies* (1945), placed Bacon's utopia within the tradition of "closed societies" that sacrifice liberty to the authority of experts. Theodor Adorno and the Frankfurt School developed a similar critique, warning that instrumental reason can turn rationality itself into a form of domination.

Later in the century, ecological and ethical perspectives widened the debate. Environmental thinkers argued that Bacon's call for "mastery over nature" encouraged exploitative attitudes that contributed to ecological crisis. Lewis Mumford and Jacques Ellul described technological systems as expanding beyond human control, while Jürgen Habermas, in *Knowledge and Human Interests* (1968), stressed that reliance on technical rationality sidelines democratic and ethical reflection.

Assessments of Bacon's legacy remain divided. His rational approach to governance and insistence on practical science helped advance medicine, education, and standards of living. At the same time, philosophers and sociologists emphasize the risks of placing too much trust in science alone.

Chapter 5. The Socialist Utopias of Charles Fourier and Robert Owen

Nineteenth-Century Socialist Models: Emphasis on Social Justice, Collectivism, and Equality

The socialist utopias of Charles Fourier and Robert Owen, which arose in the early nineteenth century, were responses to the dislocations of rapid industrialization. The growth of industry created sharp divisions between classes, widespread poverty, and harsh conditions for workers. While some sought solutions in revolution, others turned to peaceful projects of reorganization built on cooperation, equality, and shared prosperity. Utopian socialism offered both a critique of existing society and an imaginative attempt to construct an alternative.

The French thinker Charles Fourier outlined a detailed plan for small, self-sufficient communities called phalansteries. He imagined society organized around voluntary cooperation, free choice of labor, and collective association, where individuals could pursue both happiness and personal growth. Central to his vision was the belief that work should be attractive and fulfilling rather than monotonous. He even proposed new forms of social and sexual relations, convinced that the liberation of human passions would stimulate creativity and strengthen solidarity.

The British reformer Robert Owen sought to put such ideals into practice. At New Lanark in Scotland and later at New Harmony in the United States, he created experimental communities that introduced shorter working hours, improved living conditions, and systems of education and collective child-rearing. Unlike many theorists, Owen demonstrated in practice that cooperative principles could improve social life even within a market economy. Though his projects were short-lived, they gained international attention and inspired later cooperative movements.

The ideas of Fourier and Owen marked an important stage in the history of social thought. They were among the first to articulate the principles of collectivism, social responsibility, and solidarity as the basis of communal life. Their work influenced the development of socialist and communist doctrines in the nineteenth century and encouraged further experiments and cooperative associations on both sides of the Atlantic. They showed that the search for a just society could proceed not only through conflict but also through reasoned cooperation and the voluntary pursuit of common goals.

Historical and Intellectual Context

The Life and Work of Charles Fourier (1772–1837) and Robert Owen (1771–1858)

Charles Fourier and Robert Owen were born within a year of each other at the close of the eighteenth century, yet their lives and approaches to reform took very different paths.

The French thinker Charles Fourier was born in 1772 in Besançon to the family of a merchant. From an early age he observed the routines of trade and craft production and became aware of the inequities and inefficiencies of the existing social order. After a Jesuit education, he left formal study and pursued his own investigations of the world. As a clerk and sales agent in Lyon and other French cities, he encountered poverty, exploitation, and instability firsthand. These experiences convinced him that society required fundamental reorganization.

Fourier devoted his intellectual career to developing the model of the phalanstery — an autonomous, voluntary community built on cooperative labor and shared resources. He presented this vision in works such as *Théorie des quatre mouvements et des destinées générales* (1808) and *Nouveau monde industriel et sociétaire* (1829).

Robert Owen, by contrast, came from humbler beginnings. Born in 1771 in the Welsh town of Newtown, the son of a tradesman, he began working at the age of ten. Early exposure to the hardships of factory life left him determined to seek change. Through persistence and skill he advanced rapidly in the textile industry, and by 1799 he was co-owner and manager of the cotton mills at New Lanark, Scotland.

At New Lanark, Owen began to implement his social ideas. He shortened the working day, improved housing and sanitation, established free schools for children, prohibited child labor in hazardous occupations, and introduced community programs to raise living standards. The settlement became known across Europe as an example of enlightened industrial management.

His most ambitious undertaking was the founding of New Harmony in Indiana in 1825. Conceived as a cooperative community based on collective labor and equitable distribution, it sought to prove that such arrangements were possible in practice. Although the experiment lasted only until 1828, it left a significant legacy in the history of socialism and communal experiments, showing how utopian ideals could be tested in lived experience.

Social and Economic Conditions in the Age of the Industrial Revolution

The first half of the nineteenth century saw the rapid spread of industry, a transformation that altered the economic and social landscape of Europe and North America. Steam engines, power looms, and mechanized workshops greatly increased productivity, creating large industrial centers and accelerating growth. But with these advances came severe social strains as traditional agrarian life gave way to an industrial economy.

One clear result of the Industrial Revolution was the widening gap between classes. Factory owners and entrepreneurs amassed considerable fortunes, while workers, stripped of control over production, were forced to accept harsh conditions to survive. Despite rising output, the standard of living for many laborers stagnated or even declined.

Workdays often stretched to fourteen or sixteen hours, and children as young as five or six were sent into mills and mines. Accidents, disease, and exhaustion were common, producing high mortality rates. In crowded cities, families crowded into single rooms without sanitation; malnutrition spread, and medical care was scarce.

Women and children bore the heaviest burdens. They were assigned the lowest-paid and most grueling tasks, and child labor became a grim emblem of the industrial era.

Long hours underground or at textile machines deprived children of health, schooling, and the ordinary experience of childhood.

Such conditions fueled resentment and unrest. Strikes, riots, and protests broke out, though governments and employers often responded with repression. It was in this setting that the ideas of Charles Fourier and Robert Owen gained force, offering visions of radical social reorganization as an alternative to the inequities of industrial capitalism.

The Influence of the Enlightenment and the Critique of Capitalist Relations on the Thought of Fourier and Owen

The social and philosophical outlook of Charles Fourier and Robert Owen was shaped by the legacy of the Enlightenment, with its emphasis on reason, progress, and social justice. Thinkers such as Voltaire, Rousseau, Diderot, and Montesquieu had challenged established political and social orders, calling for equality, liberty, and human dignity. Their ideas prepared the ground for sharper critiques of the new forms of oppression that accompanied the rise of industrial capitalism in the early nineteenth century.

Fourier took up the humanist and rationalist ideals of the Enlightenment and argued that the reorganization of society on rational lines could free humanity from poverty and exploitation. He condemned the capitalist economy of his day as a source of misery and moral decay. In his view, competition and self-interest — the driving forces of industrial capitalism — undermined the natural harmony of human relations and turned society into a constant arena of conflict. As an alternative, he imagined voluntary cooperation, collective ownership, and attractive labor, where work would be a source of joy rather than drudgery.

Owen, meanwhile, combined Enlightenment ideals with a practical approach to reform. Influenced by Rousseau's writings on education and by the Enlightenment commitment to equality, he worked both as a theorist and as an industrial entrepreneur. From his experience managing textile mills, he concluded that the pursuit of profit produced exploitation and injustice, while humane treatment and equality improved both social life and economic results. This conviction led him to establish model communities in which child labor was abolished, housing and sanitation were improved, and education was made compulsory and accessible.

Both Fourier and Owen carried Enlightenment humanism into new territory, setting out visions of societies free from oppression and want. Their critique of capitalism was accompanied by concrete proposals — and in Owen's case, real experiments — aimed at building a fair and rational social order. In this way they turned Enlightenment principles into early socialist projects, opening debates that would continue around the links between justice, labor, and economic life.

Core Ideas and Principles

Social Justice, Equality, and Collectivism as the Basis for New Forms of Social Life

At the center of the social visions of Charles Fourier and Robert Owen stood the ideals of justice, equality, and collective life. Both regarded the industrial order of the early nineteenth century as profoundly unjust: the many worked under oppressive conditions for the profit of a small class of factory owners. Against this background, they set out to imagine a different kind of society built on cooperation, equality, and shared control of resources.

For Fourier, justice and collectivism were not abstract ideas but natural conditions in which human capacities could flourish. He believed that people are inclined toward work, creativity, and sociability, but that these impulses are distorted by competition and inequality. To correct this, he designed the phalanstery — a self-sufficient community where all took part in common labor and enjoyed equal access to shared goods. Within such an arrangement, society would rest on reciprocity and fair distribution. Work was to be organized not as drudgery but as an attractive pursuit, aligned with the passions and preferences of its members.

Owen approached the same goals through practical reform. He argued that inequality stemmed from unregulated capitalism driven by the pursuit of profit. His remedy was the creation of communes and cooperative settlements in which shared property and equal rights ensured a decent existence for all. Unlike Fourier, he attempted to realize these ideals directly. In his communities he improved working conditions, guaranteed access to education, and promoted systems of cooperative management in both production and daily life.

Together, Fourier and Owen laid much of the groundwork for modern socialist thought. By linking justice and equality with collective labor and communal institutions, they challenged the dominant economic order and offered principles that would guide later reformers in their search for alternatives to exploitation and inequality.

Critique of Capitalism and the Aspiration to Replace It with Harmonious Social Communities

Charles Fourier and Robert Owen were among the first modern thinkers to move beyond describing the hardships of capitalism and to develop a systematic critique of its core principles. Both argued that a system built on competition and the pursuit of private profit produced inequality, poverty, exploitation of labor, and the erosion of human dignity.

Fourier saw capitalism as a distortion of humanity's natural tendencies toward creativity and cooperation. Industrial rivalry, he believed, set people against one another, fostering conflict rather than solidarity. As an alternative he proposed the phalanstery, a self-governing community where members would share labor and resources in an atmosphere of equality and mutual respect.

Owen, drawing on his own experience as an industrialist, focused on the harsh realities of factory life. He witnessed the widening gulf between rich and poor and the damage caused by profit-driven industry to workers and their families. His answer was to replace competitive production with cooperative enterprises based on fairness and collective responsibility. Unlike Fourier, Owen attempted to realize these ideals directly. In his model settlements at New Lanark and New Harmony he introduced shorter hours, schools for children, improved living conditions, and systems of shared management.

While Fourier provided a daring theoretical blueprint and Owen showed what could be achieved in practice, both demonstrated that industrial capitalism was not the only possible form of social life. Their work left an enduring legacy, inspiring later socialist and cooperative movements to pursue new ways of organizing society around equality, solidarity, and human needs rather than profit alone.

Faith in the Transformation of Society Through Moral Education and the Organization of Collective Labor

Charles Fourier and Robert Owen shared the conviction that lasting social change could only come through a deep transformation of human consciousness and morality. Both held that people are by nature inclined toward goodness, creativity, and cooperation, yet that capitalist relations distorted these natural tendencies. Under industrial capitalism, work became a form of drudgery, stripped of joy, while human interaction was reduced to constant competition for resources and privilege.

Fourier placed the hope of transformation in moral re-education and in the creation of conditions where labor itself would become attractive and fulfilling. He believed that individuals, when freed from the pressures of competition and inequality, would naturally gravitate toward useful and creative activity. In his model of the phalanstery, communities organized on fairness and shared purpose would encourage responsibility, kindness, and solidarity. Work would no longer be an imposed burden but a voluntary and even joyful pursuit, aligned with the inclinations and passions of each member. Mutual assistance and collective participation would ensure that labor was both productive and satisfying, while also strengthening social bonds. In this way, Fourier argued, society could eradicate egoism and conflict, establishing a new order founded on harmony and reciprocity.

Owen, though guided by similar ideals, approached reform from a different angle. As both an industrialist and a social thinker, he emphasized moral education as the principal tool of transformation. He believed that values such as justice, humanism, and cooperation could be instilled from childhood if children were raised in an environment designed to cultivate them. In his communities at New Lanark in Scotland and New Harmony in the United States, he made education compulsory and accessible, grounding it in principles of respect and mutual aid. For Owen, the schoolroom was as important as the workplace in remaking society, since it shaped a new generation accustomed to working together, sharing responsibility, and recognizing the dignity of every person. By creating such environments, he believed, poverty, inequality, and destructive competition could be overcome.

For both Fourier and Owen, genuine reform went beyond political and economic adjustments. It required a fundamental reshaping of individual character, the cultivation of collective consciousness, and the organization of work on the basis of voluntary and conscious cooperation. In their visions, ethical formation and shared labor were inseparable, together forming the cornerstone of a just and enduring society.

Placed alongside later socialist thought, the distinctiveness of their approach becomes clear. Whereas Fourier and Owen placed their faith in moral education and the gradual transformation of character through cooperative living, Karl Marx and Friedrich Engels argued that history moved through material forces and class conflict. For them, liberation depended not on ethical reform but on revolutionary change in the ownership of the means of production. Marx and Engels saw struggle as the engine of history, while Fourier and Owen envisioned harmony achieved through re-education and the nurturing of collective responsibility. This contrast underscores the idealism of the early utopians and highlights the decisive turn introduced by scientific socialism in the nineteenth century.

Government and Social Organization

The Organization of Society in Fourier's Model of the Phalanstery

At the heart of Charles Fourier's social theory stood the phalanstery — a small, autonomous community in which work, leisure, and everyday life were brought together in a single system. Each phalanstery was designed to be fully self-sufficient, capable of meeting the essential needs of all its members, and was to include between 1,600 and 1,800 people. Fourier arrived at this number deliberately, convinced that only such a population could provide the right balance of interests, talents, and personalities required for a harmonious social order.

Every phalanstery was to occupy a specially constructed building, carefully divided into distinct areas for productive work, residential quarters, and communal leisure. Around the central structure lay gardens, fields, workshops, and factories, where members of the community would engage in tasks suited to their abilities and inclinations. For Fourier, it was crucial that labor should never be imposed as a burden. Work was to be voluntary and attractive, chosen in accordance with the passions of each individual. Members could change occupations and rotate tasks throughout the day, ensuring both variety and freedom from exhaustion or monotony.

Fourier elaborated a detailed system for organizing both labor and social life, grounded in what he termed the "passional attractions" of human beings. He believed that people, when allowed to follow their natural impulses, seek variety and cooperation rather than uniformity and competition. In the phalanstery, inhabitants were to be grouped into "series" — associations formed around shared talents, tastes, or passions. Each series assumed responsibility for a particular branch of activity, whether agriculture, crafts, education, or cultural pursuits. Through these voluntary associations, individuals could express their inclinations while also fulfilling the needs of the community as a whole.

A further distinctive feature of Fourier's design was his principle of distributing rewards. In contrast to the capitalist order, where profits accrued disproportionately to property owners, he proposed that the proceeds of collective production be divided among three contributors: labor, capital, and talent. Every member of the phalanstery was thus to receive a portion reflecting their work and abilities, while those who invested resources would also be acknowledged. By striking a balance between these three factors, Fourier believed it was possible to combine fairness with incentive, ensuring that workers, investors, and innovators all found their interests aligned. This arrangement, he argued, would prevent the extremes of inequality and channel prosperity toward the community as a whole.

Collective ownership and the shared distribution of resources formed another cornerstone of Fourier's project. All members of the phalanstery were to enjoy equal access to goods, services, and communal facilities, while the allocation of labor and responsibilities would be guided not by coercion but by rational coordination and attention to individual aptitudes. Such an arrangement, he believed, would foster mutual support and solidarity, reducing competition and conflict to a minimum.

Equally central to the scheme was the cultivation of cultural and recreational life, which Fourier considered indispensable for strengthening the bonds of community. Festivals, concerts, games, and artistic performances were to be built into the rhythm of collective life, giving members opportunities for joy, creativity, and fellowship. By linking work and leisure in this way, Fourier envisioned the phalanstery as more than an economic structure. It was to be a complete environment in which material security, social equality, and cultural enrichment were inseparably connected, allowing individuals to flourish in every respect within a cooperative and egalitarian framework.

Owen's Model: Productive Cooperatives and Communes Ensuring Well-Being, Equality, and the Harmonious Development of the Individual

Unlike many contemporaries who stayed with abstract theory, Robert Owen concentrated on putting collectivist principles into practice by founding exemplary communes and cooperatives. His model called not only for a reorganization of economic activity but also for a thorough reshaping of social life on the foundations of equality, mutual aid, and justice.

Owen held that poverty and exploitation stemmed from private property as exercised by factory owners for personal gain at the expense of laborers. To address this, he proposed replacing the traditional capitalist mill with productive cooperatives and communes in which workers would be not merely hired hands but collective owners and full participants in management. On this basis, profits could be distributed fairly, working conditions secured, and a high standard of living made available to all members of the community.

He first put these ideas into effect at the textile mills of New Lanark, Scotland, where he sharply reduced the length of the working day, improved conditions in the mills, and established free nurseries and schools for workers' children. His reforms extended beyond the factory: he built decent housing, provided access to medical care, and created shared spaces for leisure and community life. In doing so, Owen showed that humane treatment of workers, together with an equitable share in returns, increased productivity and supported durable prosperity.

Seeking to broaden the experiment, Owen founded the communal settlement of New Harmony in Indiana (1825). Conceived as a model society, it aimed to unite collective labor, shared property, equal rights, and universal education. Although the community lasted only three years, it became a landmark in social experimentation, demonstrating in concrete form the principles of justice, cooperation, and solidarity.

Within Owen's communes, special emphasis fell on the development of the individual. Every member was offered opportunities for education, cultural life, and the free exercise of talents and abilities. This commitment to personal growth rested on material security and on the conviction that individual well-being could not be separated from the welfare of the whole.

A comparison of New Lanark and New Harmony shows both the strengths and the limits of Owen's design. New Lanark succeeded largely because it operated within a functioning industrial economy and balanced reform with the realities of textile production, demonstrating that social justice and economic efficiency could coexist. New Harmony, by contrast, stood apart from an established economic base and relied on voluntary participation; it struggled with internal divisions, financial instability, and the lack of a unifying structure. New Lanark thus illustrated the practical viability of cooperative reform within industry, while New Harmony revealed the difficulties of building a communal order from the ground up — together indicating both the promise and the vulnerability of Owen's utopian vision.

A Social Structure Without Sharp Class or Property Divisions: Solidarity and Cooperation as Its Foundation

Charles Fourier and Robert Owen sought to replace the traditional hierarchy of society — with its entrenched class divisions and stark inequalities of wealth — by a system built on equality, solidarity, and mutual respect. They opposed the prevailing order in which a narrow elite of entrepreneurs and aristocrats controlled resources while the majority lived in poverty and dependence.

Fourier regarded the removal of competition and conflict created by private property and unequal distribution as the starting point for social renewal. In his phalansteries, collective ownership and fair sharing of income were meant to secure every member a dignified life. Within this setting, individuals could develop their talents and inclinations freely, without fear of want or exclusion. Equal access to resources and comprehensive social support, he argued, would allow solidarity to replace rivalry and harmony to take the place of division.

Owen identified the same roots of social ills in property and class inequality. In his communes and cooperatives he introduced collective ownership together with democratic participation in decision-making. Members not only shared resources but also held an equal voice in directing the economic and social life of the community. This arrangement encouraged trust, cooperation, and a sense of shared responsibility for the welfare of all.

Both thinkers stressed that solidarity and mutual assistance must function not merely as moral ideals but as the economic and social basis of communal life. Their proposed structures left no space for privileged groups and guaranteed each person equal standing. By removing the sources of inequality and embedding cooperation at the core of society, Fourier and Owen envisioned communities where conflict would yield to concord and where individuals could realize their potential while contributing to the common prosperity.

Economic and Property Relations

Collectivism in the Ownership and Management of Property and the Means of Production

A core feature of the social projects of Charles Fourier and Robert Owen was their insistence on collective ownership and cooperative management of the means of production. Both rejected the capitalist system of private property, which they saw as the source of inequality, exploitation, and conflict. In its place, they proposed that production and the distribution of goods be held in common and directed by the workers themselves.

Fourier argued that land, resources, and tools should belong to the entire community of the phalanstery rather than to individuals. In his model, members would make decisions jointly about labor and the use of resources, and the income produced would be shared on equitable terms. For him, common ownership was not only an economic arrangement but also an ethical principle: by removing the sources of rivalry and securing harmony, it enabled people to develop their talents freely while serving the common good.

Owen likewise regarded shared property and cooperative management as the basis of social welfare. In his communities at New Lanark and New Harmony, he introduced collective decision-making and encouraged workers to take part directly in managing factories and dividing profits. He sought to show in practice that cooperative production could increase efficiency while at the same time providing security for all. By removing the fear of poverty and instability, such arrangements fostered trust, solidarity, and a sense of mutual responsibility.

For both thinkers, the principle of collective ownership was intended not simply as an economic device but as a framework for social justice. It was meant to overcome the inequalities of capitalism and to build a society grounded in cooperation, solidarity, and shared responsibility for the well-being of every member.

The Organization of Labor: Fair Distribution of Duties and Just Rewards

A central element in the social visions of Charles Fourier and Robert Owen was a new conception of labor, one in which responsibilities and rewards were distributed on fair and equal terms. Both held that the roots of conflict and exploitation in capitalism lay in the unjust allocation of work and wages. Their models sought to overcome these injustices by making labor a balanced, cooperative, and dignified activity.

Fourier argued that work should be voluntary, appealing, and consistent with each person's natural inclinations. In his phalansteries, members were free to choose occupations that matched their talents and preferences, with the option to rotate tasks throughout the day to avoid monotony and fatigue. Duties were organized so that everyone shared in both lighter and heavier tasks, ensuring balance across the community. Compensation was to follow clear standards that took into account individual effort and achievement. Fourier believed that such an arrangement would reduce envy and resentment while fostering cooperation and mutual support. He went so far as to claim that once labor became genuinely attractive, productivity would rise naturally, for people would give themselves willingly to tasks that expressed their passions.

Owen put these principles into practice. At New Lanark and New Harmony, he shortened the working day, established reasonable norms, and guaranteed fair wages. Labor was conceived not as a source of exploitation or private gain but as a collective responsibility and the foundation of common prosperity. In his communes, work assignments were distributed with regard to each person's abilities and strength, and the income and benefits of collective labor were shared on principles of fairness and equal access. This gave members security and confidence in their future. Owen also emphasized that fair organization of labor improved not only economic results but also the moral character of individuals, creating habits of discipline, respect, and mutual care.

For both Fourier and Owen, reform of labor extended beyond wages to the very structure of work. By ensuring fair rewards and an equitable division of responsibilities, their models sought to create communities free of exploitation, organized around harmony, and able to provide each person with the conditions for growth and fulfillment.

Rejection of Competition and Private Gain in Favor of Collective Well-Being and Equality

One of the most striking features of the social visions of Charles Fourier and Robert Owen was their rejection of competition and private profit as the basis of social life. Both argued that the competitive struggle inherent in capitalism not only deepened inequality but also corroded morality, weakened solidarity, and left the majority in conditions of poverty and exploitation.

Fourier's critique of competition was extensive and detailed. He observed that rivalry permeated every level of capitalist society: merchants fought over markets, workers competed for scarce jobs, and families struggled to secure the minimum needed for survival. This constant antagonism, he argued, suppressed the natural human tendencies toward cooperation and mutual support. As an alternative, he proposed the phalanstery — a community of 1,600 to 1,800 members living and working under collective ownership. In these communities, land, tools, and workshops were shared, and labor was organized according to each person's talents and passions. By allowing individuals to rotate tasks and to pursue occupations aligned with their interests, Fourier believed that work would become both productive and enjoyable. In such conditions, envy and rivalry would disappear, since resources were distributed fairly and recognition was based on service to the community rather than on personal wealth.

Owen approached the problem of competition from the standpoint of an industrialist. At New Lanark in Scotland he inherited a typical textile mill marked by long hours, child labor, and poor housing. Instead of competing with other manufacturers by driving down costs, he shortened the working day, prohibited child labor under the age of ten, built decent housing, and created the first infant schools in Britain. He showed that productivity could rise when workers were treated humanely and freed from the destructive pressures of rivalry. Later, in his experiment at New Harmony, Indiana (1825–1828), Owen attempted to abolish private property altogether by organizing collective ownership of land and workshops and by ensuring equal access to education, food, and housing.

The ideas of Fourier and Owen about eliminating competition influenced the birth of the cooperative movement in the nineteenth century. The Rochdale Society of Equitable Pioneers, founded in England in 1844, adopted principles that echoed Owen's thought: democratic control, open membership, fair distribution of profits, and a commitment to education. These practices became the foundation of the cooperative model, which has since spread worldwide, encompassing credit unions, producer cooperatives, and consumer associations.

Morality, Law, and Culture

High Ethical Standards: Collectivism, Mutual Aid, and the Priority of Common Interests over Personal Gain

The social visions of Charles Fourier and Robert Owen rested not only on economic structures but also on ethical principles, which they considered indispensable for a just and harmonious society. Both held that without a deep moral transformation it would be impossible to overcome social contradictions or build a community founded on fairness and solidarity.

Fourier maintained that the essence of human nature was cooperation rather than conflict. In his phalansteries, collectivism and mutual support were built into the fabric of daily life. Every resident was to see personal well-being as inseparable from the welfare of others. Harmony, in his view, could be secured only through respect for common interests and the elevation of the collective good above narrow advantage. From childhood, the inhabitants of a phalanstery were to be raised in this spirit, learning to regard their own achievements as part of the community's shared success.

Owen placed equal weight on ethical foundations, treating them as the necessary basis of social reform. In the communes he organized, solidarity and mutual aid were established as everyday norms. Each member of the settlement was expected to care for others as for themselves, holding the prosperity of the group to be the surest guarantee of personal happiness. Work was accompanied by shared responsibility for one another's welfare, and help was extended to those in need. Children were educated from an early age in an atmosphere of cooperation, through common schooling, joint activities, and communal labor, so that values of empathy and responsibility became part of their character.

The ethical ideals advanced by Fourier and Owen aimed to reshape social relations at their core. By rejecting selfishness and fostering collective responsibility, their projects envisioned communities in which harmony and justice would take the place of conflict and distrust.

The impact of these ethical ideals could soon be seen in the early labor and cooperative movements. Owenite principles inspired workers' associations in Britain during the 1820s and 1830s that emphasized education and mutual aid as much as protest. The Rochdale Society of Equitable Pioneers, founded in 1844, embodied many of these values: democratic management, shared ownership, equitable division of profits, and commitment to education. Fourierist communities in France and the United States also experimented with forms of collective living grounded in moral responsibility. Even when such efforts proved short-lived, they conveyed the conviction that solidarity and cooperation could form the basis of new social institutions. These ideas also resonated with existing religious traditions of mutual aid, particularly among Quakers in England, whose emphasis on equality, community, and social responsibility provided a moral foundation that paralleled and reinforced the utopian socialism of Fourier and Owen.

Education and Upbringing as Key Instruments for Building a New Society and Developing the Harmonious Individual

Charles Fourier and Robert Owen regarded education and upbringing as essential for creating a just society and for fostering the full development of each person. Both believed that only well-organized systems of learning and moral formation could change human consciousness, overcome prejudice, and cultivate values of cooperation and solidarity.

Fourier stressed that education should begin in early childhood and be guided by freedom, respect for natural inclinations, and the comprehensive growth of talents. He rejected compulsion as a method of instruction, insisting that children must learn through curiosity, enjoyment, and discovery. In his phalansteries, special groups were to introduce children from their earliest years to collective life, cooperation, and mutual assistance. He imagined an education broad in scope, embracing science, the arts, and practical skills in crafts and agriculture. Such an approach, he argued, would produce individuals who were not only creative and responsible but also prepared to live in a society built on equality and solidarity.

Owen, both theorist and reformer, gave education a central place in his projects. In New Lanark and New Harmony he introduced progressive systems that combined technical and professional instruction with moral education. He believed that children should grow up from the outset with a sense of justice, cooperation, and respect. His schools blended academic learning with moral guidance and collective activities that fostered community and responsibility. In Owen's communes, education was free, universal, and accessible, closely integrated into the daily life of the settlement. Children did not learn in isolation but grew up in an environment that constantly reinforced ideals of cooperation and social duty.

For both Fourier and Owen, education was more than a duty of society; it was a principal means of transformation. By shaping from childhood the habits of collective life, respect for the common good, and the conditions for harmonious growth, they believed that society could be remade and that each person could secure the basis for a meaningful and fulfilling existence.

The influence of these ideas spread well beyond their own communities. Owen's schools at New Lanark drew international attention, inspired early campaigns for public education in Britain, and influenced reformers who later established state-supported elementary schools. His emphasis on child-centered learning anticipated the methods of Johann Heinrich Pestalozzi, who stressed the integration of intellectual, moral, and physical development. Fourier's vision of broad, interest-driven education resonated with later experiments in France and the United States that emphasized cooperative learning and the unity of theory with practice. The commitment of both thinkers to universal, free, and socially embedded education helped inspire nineteenth-century movements for popular schooling, vocational training, and the recognition of education as a public responsibility crucial to social progress.

Cultural Life Oriented Toward the Spiritual and Moral Development of the Community

In the visions of Charles Fourier and Robert Owen, cultural life was not treated as mere diversion but as a primary means of shaping character, strengthening community, and cultivating the ethical standards on which a just society depended. Both believed that culture should foster intellectual, moral, and spiritual growth, leading individuals toward cooperative and harmonious relations with others.

Fourier made culture an essential part of his phalansteries. Theatrical performances, concerts, exhibitions, and festivals were to give residents opportunities to discover and develop their creative abilities. Intellectual games and collective celebrations were built into the daily rhythm of the community, not as distractions but as forms of social education. Participation in these activities, he argued, encouraged empathy and cooperation and reinforced solidarity. Art and shared cultural experience, for Fourier, were indispensable in nurturing mutual understanding and sustaining the identity of the community.

Owen gave cultural activity a similar importance, linking it closely to moral education and civic life. In his settlements at New Lanark and New Harmony he organized public lectures, communal readings, concerts, and plays open to all. Such events were intended to broaden intellectual horizons while cultivating responsibility and shared ideals. In Owen's model, culture and education worked together, reinforcing the values of cooperation and mutual care by bringing people into common spaces of learning and artistic expression.

For both Fourier and Owen, culture was a force for moral formation and social cohesion. They believed that only within an active and inclusive cultural environment, grounded in collective values, could individuals grow into responsible and ethical beings. Culture, in their view, was at once an expression of shared ideals and a practical means of building a community where every member could develop fully and contribute to the prosperity of all.

Simple and Understandable Laws Based on Justice, Cooperation, and Solidarity

In the social visions of Charles Fourier and Robert Owen, legislation and the rules of communal life occupied an important place. Both insisted that laws should be clear and accessible to all, rooted in solidarity, fairness, and mutual aid. A just society, they believed, would not depend on courts, lawyers, or judges to maintain order, but would treat law as a moral code shared by the whole community.

Fourier argued that in an ideal community elaborate legal codes would be unnecessary. Life in the phalanstery would be guided by voluntary agreement, cooperation, and respect. Legislation would be reduced to a small number of simple rules, easily understood by all. Because these rules reflected common moral values and were reinforced by an atmosphere of trust, members would be fully aware of their rights and duties. Fourier held that most disputes could be prevented before they arose and that punishment would seldom be needed. His emphasis lay not on legal enforcement but on habits of solidarity and responsibility. He even suggested that festivals, shared labor, and cooperative education could serve the same purpose as formal law, instilling unity and discipline more effectively than external compulsion.

Owen approached the matter from a practical side. In New Lanark and New Harmony he avoided bureaucratic regulations, preferring straightforward and transparent rules of conduct. The framework of his communes rested on equality and social justice, with clear expectations regarding work, responsibility, and behavior. Every inhabitant recognized that their conduct affected the welfare of the whole, and thus observed the rules not as outside commands but as natural conditions of communal life. Accounts of New Lanark note that Owen's rules stressed punctuality, cleanliness, mutual respect, and participation in education, creating a setting where regulation was inseparable from daily routine.

For both Fourier and Owen, the aim of law was not coercion but the cultivation of trust, respect, and responsibility. Rules were meant to merge with daily life, reflecting the moral commitments of the community rather than standing apart as instruments of authority. By grounding legislation in solidarity and cooperation, they imagined societies where formal restrictions would give way to self-discipline and an internal awareness of the common good. This vision anticipated later debates within socialism about whether law should act as a coercive tool of the state or as a moral expression of collective will. In their utopian projects, law was conceived less as an instrument of control than as a cultural framework for justice and communal harmony.

Significance and Influence of Fourier and Owen on Later Philosophy and Social Thought

The Influence of Fourier and Owen on Socialist, Communist, and Cooperative Movements of the Nineteenth and Twentieth Centuries

The ideas of Charles Fourier and Robert Owen were not confined to theory; they inspired a wave of experiments in communal living throughout the nineteenth and early twentieth centuries. Their followers sought to prove that equality, solidarity, and collective ownership could be realized in practice, and they founded communities and cooperatives across Europe and the United States.

In France, Fourier's design of the phalanstery attracted loyal supporters in the 1830s and 1840s. Groups led by Victor Considérant and François Marie Charles attempted to build experimental settlements, including the well-known colony at Condé-sur-Vesgre. Similar projects appeared in Belgium, Switzerland, and elsewhere in Europe. Most of these communes were short-lived, yet they testified to the appeal of Fourier's vision and kept discussion of collectivist social organization alive.

In the United States, Owen's influence gave rise to a broader communitarian movement. Dozens of intentional communities were founded in the mid-nineteenth century, combining cooperative labor with experiments in education, cultural life, and alternative family arrangements. Among the most notable were Brook Farm in Massachusetts, closely linked with American transcendentalism, and the Oneida Community in New York, which explored radical systems of shared property and social relations. These settlements differed greatly in character, but all expressed the conviction that communal living could provide an alternative to the inequalities of industrial capitalism.

Although few of these communities endured for long, they left a significant intellectual and cultural imprint. Fourierist and Owenite ideals informed the cooperative associations that spread in the latter half of the nineteenth century and shaped later socialist and reform movements. The effort to construct societies based on solidarity and shared responsibility revealed both the difficulties of turning utopian visions into reality and the persistent aspiration to organize collective life on fairer and more humane foundations.

Contemporary Assessments of the Socialist Utopias of Fourier and Owen

The socialist utopias of Charles Fourier and Robert Owen remain a subject of debate in modern social philosophy and political theory.

With regard to Fourier, contemporary scholars often emphasize the originality and humanism of his vision. They note his sharp critique of capitalist society, particularly his insight into the ways in which competition and inequality suppress individuality and stifle creativity. His analysis of alienation, envy, and rivalry is recognized as an important precursor to later critiques of industrial capitalism. At the same time, many point out that his idea of the phalanstery and his reliance on voluntary collectivism appear overly idealistic when measured against present economic and social conditions, where individualism and competition remain entrenched.

Owen generally receives more favorable assessments in current scholarship, largely because his ideas were tested in practice and produced visible results. His reforms at New Lanark are cited as the first demonstration that industrial production could be linked with humane working conditions, shorter hours, education, and basic protections. Researchers stress that Owen's initiatives influenced the cooperative movement, the rise of labor unions, and the development of early social legislation in Britain and beyond. His insistence on universal education and his experiments with workers' rights are regarded as milestones in the evolution of modern welfare states. Yet his ambitious project at New Harmony exposed the difficulties of sustaining large communal settlements based solely on shared ownership and equal distribution, underlining the gap between utopian ideals and social realities.

A further dimension of analysis concerns their influence on Marxism. Karl Marx and Friedrich Engels discussed Fourier and Owen in *The Communist Manifesto* (1848) and later writings, classing them with Saint-Simon as the leading figures of "utopian socialism." Marx and Engels criticized them for relying on visions and experiments rather than on a scientific analysis of class struggle, but they also acknowledged their historical role. Marx observed that these early utopians exposed contradictions within capitalism and expressed, in embryonic form, the aspirations of the working class.

Engels, in *Socialism: Utopian and Scientific* (1880), argued that Fourier's imaginative phalansteries and Owen's cooperative projects marked necessary stages in the intellectual development of socialism, even if they lacked the rigor of historical materialism.

Owen's reforms in particular resonated with Marx's own program: his campaigns for education, shorter hours, and protection of children anticipated key demands of the workers' movement. Marx praised Owen's cooperative experiments, seeing in them a preview of collective ownership within a future communist society.

In recent decades, scholars of post-capitalist theory have revisited Fourier and Owen in light of debates about alternative economies, basic income, and forms of democratic participation. Fourier's reflections on liberating human creativity and reimagining work resonate with discussions of the "post-work" society, where automation could potentially free individuals from repetitive labor.

Chapter 6. The Communist Society

The Marxist Model of Society: The Theoretical Culmination of Socialist Utopias, Late 19th – Early 20th Century

The communist society envisioned by Karl Marx and Friedrich Engels in the second half of the nineteenth century marked a decisive shift in socialist thought, presenting the first systematic and scientifically grounded model of a classless order. Before the rise of Marxism, socialist projects were mainly utopian: Charles Fourier, Claude Henri de Saint-Simon, and Robert Owen imagined ideal communities, but their designs relied on moral appeals and subjective visions of justice rather than on rigorous historical and economic study.

Marx and Engels undertook a detailed examination of capitalist society, seeking to uncover its internal laws and contradictions and, on that basis, to outline a model of social transformation. For the first time, they analyzed capitalism in depth: the mechanisms of profit and surplus value, the exploitation of wage labor, the dynamics of accumulation and concentration of capital, and the cyclical crises that shook nineteenth-century economies. Their work was distinguished by the use of empirical data, ranging from factory reports to economic statistics, which they integrated into a coherent theoretical framework.

Their first programmatic conclusions were published in *The Communist Manifesto* (1848), a foundational document of the workers' movement. Marx later expanded this research in *Capital* (vol. I, 1867), where he demonstrated how surplus value is appropriated by the capitalist class and why the contradiction between the social character of production and private appropriation generates recurrent crises and sharpens class struggle. Engels emphasized the importance of making these analyses accessible to workers themselves, turning abstract theory into a practical weapon of political struggle.

The theoretical basis of Marxism was historical materialism: the view that social change is driven not by moral ideals but by objective economic relations. In this framework, capitalism is a transitional stage whose intensifying conflict between bourgeoisie and proletariat must lead to revolutionary transformation. The Paris Commune of 1871 was interpreted by Marx and Engels as the first real attempt to embody these principles, offering a concrete example of collective ownership and direct popular governance.

In their conception of communism, the means of production would become collective property; commodity exchange would give way to planned cooperative labor; and class exploitation would disappear. Distribution of goods would follow need rather than the dictates of the market, freeing individuals from the compulsion to sell their labor power.

Marxism was not only a critique of capitalism but also a framework for its transformation, grounded in the laws of political economy and the lessons of history. By moving beyond utopian schemes to a scientific analysis of social development, Marx and Engels provided a model that reshaped political theory and gave direction to the workers' movement of the modern era.

Historical and Intellectual Context
Biography and Key Ideas of
Karl Marx (1818–1883) and Friedrich Engels (1820–1895)

Karl Marx was born on May 5, 1818, in the German city of Trier, into a prosperous Jewish family. His father, Heinrich Marx, worked as a lawyer and supported the liberal ideals of the Enlightenment. After receiving his first education at home, Marx studied at the University of Bonn and later at the University of Berlin, where he came under the influence of G. W. F. Hegel's philosophy. In Berlin he joined the circle of the "Young Hegelians," a radical group that criticized the political and religious institutions of Prussia.

In 1842 Marx became editor of the radical-democratic *Rheinische Zeitung*, but censorship and pressure from the authorities soon forced him to resign. He moved to Paris, then a major center of revolutionary thought, where in 1844 he met Friedrich Engels. This encounter marked the beginning of a lifelong friendship and intellectual partnership.

Friedrich Engels was born on November 28, 1820, in Barmen (today part of Wuppertal) into a wealthy textile-manufacturing family. Trained in commerce, he worked in his father's business, gaining direct knowledge of capitalist enterprise and of the harsh conditions of industrial labor. In 1845 he published *The Condition of the Working Class in England*, one of the earliest comprehensive studies of proletarian exploitation and social misery in the age of industrialization.

In 1848 Marx and Engels were commissioned by the Communist League in London to draft *The Communist Manifesto*. This brief but influential text set out the foundations of historical materialism and called on workers of all nations to unite against capitalist exploitation.

After the defeat of the revolutions of 1848–1849, Marx was expelled from Germany and France and settled in London, where he remained for the rest of his life. His years in exile were marked by hardship: poverty, illness, and family tragedies weighed heavily on him, and he often depended on Engels's financial support. Despite these difficulties, he began work on his major theoretical opus, *Das Kapital*. The first volume, published in 1867, presented a detailed analysis of surplus value, the accumulation of capital, and the mechanisms of exploitation. Marx argued that the contradictions of capitalism would inevitably generate recurrent crises and ultimately revolutionary transformation.

Engels not only supported Marx financially but also contributed as a theorist, publishing works that explained and defended Marxist doctrine. After Marx's death in 1883, Engels took on the task of editing and preparing for publication the remaining volumes of *Capital*. Among his own writings, *Anti-Dühring* (1878) gave a systematic exposition of Marxist dialectics and materialism, while *The Origin of the Family, Private Property and the State* (1884) offered a historical analysis of social institutions and the emergence of class society.

Together Marx and Engels formulated a coherent socio-economic theory that later became known as Marxism. Its principal ideas included:

- **Historical materialism**: the conviction that social development is driven primarily by transformations in the mode of production and economic structures, not by ideas or individual will.

- **The theory of class struggle**: the understanding that society is divided into classes with conflicting economic interests, and that their struggle is the engine of historical change.

- **Critique of capitalism**: the argument that capitalism inevitably generates crises, intensifies inequality, and deepens the exploitation of the working class.

- **The vision of communist society**: a future order based on collective ownership of the means of production, ensuring equality, social justice, and the free development of all individuals.

The works of Marx and Engels profoundly influenced the social and revolutionary movements of the nineteenth and twentieth centuries, shaping Marxism, socialism, communism, and social democracy. To this day, their writings remain central to debates in philosophy, economics, and political theory.

The Socio-Economic Situation in Europe at the End of the Nineteenth Century

The closing decades of the nineteenth century in Europe witnessed sweeping social and economic change brought about by industrialization. Cities expanded rapidly, production increased at an unprecedented pace, and new technologies transformed the foundations of economic life. Steam engines, railways, mechanized looms, and other inventions enabled dramatic growth in industrial output and accelerated economic development. Major centers such as Manchester, Birmingham, Lyon, Berlin, and London became densely populated industrial hubs, ringed with factories, mines, and steelworks.

This rapid progress, however, came at a heavy cost. For much of the working population, living standards declined, social tensions grew, and class antagonisms became more pronounced. While factory owners, bankers, and industrialists amassed great fortunes, workers endured long hours, meager wages, and exhausting conditions. Twelve- to fourteen-hour days were common, and women and children made up a large share of the workforce. In textile mills, coal mines, and steel foundries, unsafe machinery, dust, and a lack of protective measures meant that accidents, injuries, and occupational diseases were part of everyday life.

Capitalism at its most expansive was also marked by recurring crises that deepened existing inequalities. The most severe was the downturn of 1873–1879, often called the "Long Depression," which spread across Europe, causing mass unemployment, factory closures, and acute hardship for workers. These recurring shocks fueled discontent and provoked waves of strikes, demonstrations, and organized resistance.

Faced with these realities, the working class increasingly recognized the need for collective action to defend its rights. The second half of the century saw the rise of trade unions, labor associations, and political parties that demanded shorter working hours, better pay, and safer conditions. Mass mobilizations such as the silk workers' uprisings in Lyon (1831–1834), the Chartist movement in Britain (1836–1848), and the Paris Commune of 1871 revealed both the depth of popular grievances and the growing capacity of workers to organize on a large scale.

A major step in this process was the founding of the First International (the International Workingmen's Association) in 1864, where Karl Marx and Friedrich Engels played an active role. The organization sought to unite workers across national borders, coordinate their struggles, and promote the idea of fundamental social transformation.

This environment of rapid industrial growth, stark social polarization, recurring crises, and the awakening of mass working-class consciousness provided the conditions in which Marxism took shape. Marx and Engels developed their theory not in isolation but in response to the lived experience of industrial capitalism and the struggles of workers in nineteenth-century Europe.

Critical Reappraisal and Development of Utopian Socialist Ideas (Fourier, Owen, and Others) in the Theory of Scientific Socialism and Communism

Karl Marx and Friedrich Engels acknowledged the intellectual importance of early utopian socialists such as Charles Fourier, Robert Owen, and Claude Henri de Saint-Simon in shaping modern social thought. At the same time, they criticized these doctrines as inconsistent and insufficiently connected to the economic forces that determine historical development. From the perspective of Marxism, the chief limitation of utopian socialism lay in its attempt to design ideal societies without reference to the real conditions of capitalist production or to the laws governing economic change.

Fourier and Owen sought to resolve the contradictions of capitalism by proposing small-scale collective communities and cooperatives. Their visions were guided by moral principles and by the belief that human beings are naturally inclined toward solidarity and mutual aid. Yet, in the view of Marx and Engels, this moral orientation, however admirable, could not bring about fundamental change. It neglected the structural features of capitalism: its reliance on exploitation, the conflict between classes, and its tendency toward crisis. Without an analysis of these dynamics, efforts at reform would remain precarious.

Marx and Engels advanced the position that genuine social transformation must rest on a scientific analysis of society's economic structure. They reinterpreted and surpassed the utopians by formulating the theory of scientific socialism, which held that the transition to communism was not the result of moral conviction or isolated experiments but the necessary outcome of class struggle rooted in the contradictions of capitalism. In their analysis, the abolition of private property, the emancipation of labor, and the establishment of a classless society would emerge from the collective action of the proletariat as the decisive revolutionary force.

While recognizing the pioneering contributions of Fourier, Owen, and other utopians in imagining alternatives to capitalism, Marx and Engels placed socialism on a new foundation: the materialist conception of history and a systematic critique of political economy. By doing so, they recast socialism as a theory grounded in historical necessity and revolutionary practice, rather than as a set of moral appeals or speculative designs.

Core Ideas and Principles

The Doctrine of Class Struggle and the Proletarian Revolution as the Path to Communism

At the center of the theory of Karl Marx and Friedrich Engels stands the principle that class struggle is the decisive force of historical change. Human societies, they argued, have always been divided into classes with conflicting interests. Antiquity was marked by conflict between slaves and slaveholders; the Middle Ages by the struggle of peasants against feudal lords; and in the nineteenth century the industrial proletariat confronted the bourgeoisie.

Marx and Engels analyzed in detail the living and working conditions of laborers, showing that the capitalist mode of production concentrated wealth and power in the hands of a small class of capitalists while consigning the majority to poverty and exploitation. In *The Communist Manifesto* (1848), they wrote that "the history of all hitherto existing societies is the history of class struggles." Under capitalism, this struggle reached its sharpest form, producing mounting social tensions and recurring revolutionary upheavals.

What set the proletarian struggle apart from earlier forms of class conflict was its universal character. Unlike previous ruling classes, the proletariat—numerous and propertyless—had no interest in preserving the existing system. For Marx and Engels, this made workers the only class capable not just of seizing political power but of reshaping society itself: ending exploitation, removing class distinctions, and establishing a new order based on equality.

According to Marxist theory, the transition to communism could take place only through proletarian revolution. This revolution was not a simple exchange of one ruling elite for another but a transformation of the entire structure of social relations. It entailed the abolition of private ownership of the means of production, the institution of collective control over economic life, and the distribution of goods according to need. Only under these conditions, Marx and Engels believed, could humanity overcome class domination and create the foundations of a classless communist society.

The Concept of the Dictatorship of the Proletariat as a Transitional Stage Toward a Classless Society

One of the central categories of Marxist theory is the concept of the dictatorship of the proletariat, formulated by Karl Marx and Friedrich Engels in the second half of the nineteenth century. They described it as a necessary but temporary stage that follows the victory of the workers' revolution and prepares the ground for the transition from capitalism to a classless communist order.

The idea took shape in Marx's reflections on the revolutions of 1848 and was sharpened by his analysis of the Paris Commune of 1871, which he regarded as the first real instance of proletarian power. He concluded that once the working class seizes authority, it must employ it to dismantle the structures of the old order and resist attempts by the dispossessed classes to restore their property and political influence.

Marx and Engels stressed that the dictatorship of the proletariat was unlike traditional dictatorships. It was not the domination of one leader or a privileged minority, but the political rule of the majority—the working class itself. In this period, class privileges would be abolished, capitalist property expropriated, and the means of production transferred to collective ownership. At the same time, they emphasized that this arrangement was provisional: as class antagonisms disappeared and capitalist relations were eliminated, the coercive functions of the state would gradually lose their purpose.

Marx highlighted the importance of combining firm proletarian authority with democratic practices. He pointed to the institutions of the Paris Commune—workers' councils, elected representatives with revocable mandates—as models of a new form of governance. Such organs of direct democracy, later echoed in the soviets of the early twentieth century, were intended both to ensure effective administration and to guard against bureaucratic degeneration.

In Marxist theory the dictatorship of the proletariat was not an end in itself but a mechanism to eliminate class divisions and prepare the way for a society free of exploitation. Once that mission had been achieved, the state as an instrument of coercion would "wither away," giving rise to voluntary self-organization and collective self-government. This would mark the transition to a communist society, fully classless and based on free cooperation.

The Principle of Communism:

"From Each According to His Ability, to Each According to His Needs"

One of the best-known principles of communist theory, formulated by Karl Marx and Friedrich Engels, is the maxim **"from each according to his ability, to each according to his needs."** Marx set out this idea most clearly in his *Critique of the Gotha Program* (1875), describing it as the defining rule of the higher stage of communist society. The formula came to represent the goal of communism: a community without class antagonisms or material inequality.

Marx envisioned a future in which labor would no longer be imposed by necessity—the struggle to survive or to satisfy only basic requirements. Instead, work would become voluntary and conscious, carried out in line with each person's abilities and interests, and directed toward the collective good. In conditions where productive forces had been highly developed and economic life was organized rationally, individuals would be free to engage in tasks suited to their talents. In this way, society as a whole could release the full creative and productive potential of its members.

The second part of the principle concerns distribution: "to each according to his needs." Marx argued that in a mature communist society, once material abundance had been secured, goods and services would no longer be objects of rivalry or competition. The products of collective labor would be available to all in proportion to their actual needs. Requirements for food, housing, clothing, education, healthcare, and culture could then be met fully, without reference to the amount of labor each individual contributed.

In such a society, the motives for accumulation and exploitation would disappear, since wealth could no longer be concentrated as a means of domination. Human beings would no longer be compelled by economic necessity but would have the freedom to pursue self-development, creativity, and cultural or intellectual growth.

Marx stressed, however, that this principle could not be realized immediately after the collapse of capitalism. In the lower phase of socialism, which he also described in the *Critique of the Gotha Program*, distribution would still follow the rule "to each according to his labor." At this transitional stage, society would reward individuals in proportion to the work they performed, because productivity would not yet be sufficient to ensure abundance. This rule, although more equitable than capitalist exploitation, still preserved elements of inequality, since people differ in strength, skill, and circumstance, and labor cannot be measured without reflecting those differences.

Only when the productive forces of society had developed to the point where abundance was secure could humanity move beyond this transitional phase. At that stage, the distinction between "work done" and "needs to be met" would disappear, making it possible to implement the higher communist principle of full satisfaction of human needs, independent of individual contribution.

Marx and Engels presented a dialectical vision of progress: from capitalism, to socialism with the rule "to each according to his labor," and finally to communism with the rule "from each according to his ability, to each according to his needs." This framework underscored both the necessity of a transitional stage and the longer horizon of human emancipation.

In the twentieth century this principle became a central point of discussion among Marxist theorists and revolutionaries. Lenin argued that the stage of socialism, with the rule of labor-based distribution, was unavoidable in post-revolutionary Russia, given the country's limited level of productive development. Trotsky highlighted the gap between the principle and material reality, noting that abundance was a prerequisite for its realization. In Soviet practice, the maxim was often invoked rhetorically as the ultimate goal, while actual policy maintained distribution according to labor, reflecting the persistence of scarcity. These debates underscored both the enduring appeal of Marx's vision and the challenges of applying it under the economic and political conditions of the twentieth century.

The Withering Away of the State and the Emergence of a Society Free from Exploitation and Class Divisions

The idea of the withering away of the state was one of the most radical aspects of the doctrine of Karl Marx and Friedrich Engels. Unlike earlier thinkers who sought only to reform state institutions, Marxism began from the premise that the state itself is a product of class society. It exists to defend the interests of the ruling minority, to safeguard private property, and to enforce the subordination of the majority. For Marx and Engels, the state was not a permanent structure essential to human organization but an institution that arose at a particular stage of history. Once the conditions that produced it—class antagonisms and economic exploitation—were eliminated, it would cease to exist.

Engels explained this most clearly in *The Origin of the Family, Private Property and the State* (1884). He argued that the rise of the state coincided with the emergence of private property and the division of society into classes. The state was, therefore, an instrument of domination, a mechanism through which one class maintained its privileges by coercing another. By the same reasoning, when private property and class distinctions disappear, the basis for such an institution also disappears.

Marxist theory held that during the transitional period known as the dictatorship of the proletariat, the state would remain, but only as a temporary device. Its task was to suppress the resistance of the former ruling classes and to oversee the economic and social reorganization of society along socialist lines. As collective ownership of the means of production became entrenched and class divisions began to fade, the coercive functions of the state would gradually diminish. Ultimately, with the disappearance of class antagonisms, the state would lose its character as an organ of repression.

In place of state domination, Marx and Engels envisaged forms of direct democracy and self-management. Economic and social administration would pass into the hands of citizens organized in associations, cooperatives, and councils. The old functions of the state—maintaining order, distributing resources, coordinating production—would survive only as technical and administrative tasks, carried out without coercion. Governance would rest on voluntary participation, collective solidarity, and mutual responsibility rather than on external authority.

For Marx and Engels, the state was not to be overthrown by force in communism but to "wither away" as the social and material conditions that sustained it disappeared. The result would be a society in which exploitation and class inequality had vanished, and in which human beings could fully develop their abilities within a framework of freedom and cooperation.

State Structure and Social Organization

The Transitional Stage: The Dictatorship of the Proletariat and the Social Power of the Working Class

In Marxist theory, the period after the overthrow of capitalism was defined as a transitional phase known as the dictatorship of the proletariat. By this Marx and Engels understood not the domination of an individual or a minority but the political supremacy of the working class, representing the great majority of society.

The aims of this stage were twofold. On the one hand, it was necessary to block attempts by the former ruling classes to restore their privileges. On the other, it was to initiate far-reaching social and economic change: abolishing private ownership of the means of production, transferring them into collective control, and creating a system of distribution designed to advance equality.

A distinctive element of this order was its democratic character. Marx and Engels stressed that the working class should govern through collective institutions such as workers' councils, elected by and accountable to the majority. These bodies of direct participation were intended to ensure that citizens had an active role in decision-making and to prevent the rise of a new privileged elite.

At the same time, the dictatorship of the proletariat was conceived as strictly temporary. As inequalities were reduced and collective property consolidated, the coercive role of the state would gradually fade. Administrative functions—coordination of production, distribution, and public affairs—would pass directly to society and be carried out through mechanisms of self-management and voluntary cooperation.

In this sense, the dictatorship of the proletariat was not regarded as a final system but as a transitional mechanism: a stage required to dismantle the remnants of class society and to prepare the way for a communist order in which coercive state power would no longer be needed.

Communist Society as a Classless Structure Without a State

The ultimate aim of Marxist theory is the creation of a communist society in which exploitation and class divisions no longer exist. Karl Marx and Friedrich Engels described this as a form of social life unlike any that preceded it: a society without class hierarchy and without a state acting as an instrument of coercion.

In a communist system, the means of production are collectively owned and directly managed by the producers. This removes the divide between owners and workers and with it the basis of class conflict. As class antagonisms disappear, the state—historically an apparatus for enforcing the rule of a minority—loses its function and ceases to exist as a structure of domination.

In its place, new forms of social self-government arise, rooted in the voluntary participation of all citizens. Administrative work is reduced to tasks of coordination and resource management, carried out through communes, workers' councils, and cooperative associations. Political authority, in the sense of one group imposing its will on another, is replaced by collective administration based on mutual trust, respect, and responsibility.

The absence of coercion in communist society is reinforced by the principle "to each according to his needs." At a high level of productive development, material resources are sufficient to meet the requirements of all members. In such conditions, the motives for rivalry, accumulation, and inequality disappear. People are no longer compelled to sell their labor simply to survive; instead, work becomes a conscious and voluntary activity, serving both communal needs and the realization of each individual's creative and intellectual potential.

In this conception, communism is not only the end of class exploitation but also a transformation of social existence: a community based on solidarity and equality, where cooperation replaces domination and where individuals are free to devote themselves to the full development of their abilities in harmony with the collective.

The Organization of Social Life on the Basis of Self-Government, Public Control, and Collective Responsibility

A central feature of the communist model developed by Karl Marx and Friedrich Engels is the principle of organizing society through direct self-government and collective responsibility. In their view, the traditional instruments of state power—bureaucratic administration and centralized authority—would be replaced by democratic forms of social organization that allow people to take part consciously and directly in shaping both their own lives and the development of society as a whole.

In a communist society, the basic unit of social organization would be the self-governing collective or commune, based on voluntary cooperation and equality among members. These communities would oversee production, distribution, and daily life not through hierarchies of officials but through elected councils made up of representatives of the working population. Because these representatives are subject to recall and direct oversight, the emergence of a privileged bureaucracy would be effectively prevented.

Marx highlighted these ideas in *The Civil War in France* (1871), his analysis of the Paris Commune. He praised the Commune's practice of electing representatives who were paid workers' wages and could be recalled at any moment, measures that kept power close to the people and blocked the rise of a separate ruling group. Engels later called the Commune the "finally discovered political form" through which the working class could govern while at the same time breaking down the foundations of the old state. In *Anti-Dühring* (1878), he developed this point further, noting that as coercive functions disappeared, what had once been "government over people" would become "administration of things."

An important element of this vision is collective management of production and distribution. The means of production and the products of labor would be held in common and administered by the workers themselves, who would decide together how resources should be used for the benefit of all. Marx reiterated this principle in the *Critique of the Gotha Program* (1875), where he distinguished between the lower and higher stages of communism. In the higher stage, once scarcity had been overcome, resources could be distributed according to need rather than according to labor performed.

Equally important is the principle of solidarity and shared responsibility. Every person is accountable not only for their own work but also for the welfare of the community as a whole. In this way, individual well-being is tied directly to collective prosperity. Incentives for private gain and destructive competition give way to relationships built on respect, voluntary cooperation, and mutual support.

For Marx and Engels, the Paris Commune of 1871 offered a glimpse of how such principles could work in practice. It showed how the core tasks of governance—long linked to coercion—could be redefined as administrative and technical functions carried out collectively. In their conception, social life would be organized on the basis of self-management, public oversight, and collective accountability, creating a community where freedom was realized through cooperation, solidarity, and the recognition of common interests.

Economic and Property Relations
The Abolition of Private Ownership of the Means of Production

One of the core principles of the communist doctrine of Karl Marx and Friedrich Engels is the abolition of private ownership of the means of production and its replacement with collective ownership. Marxism distinguished between personal property—possessions necessary for everyday life such as housing, clothing, or household goods—and productive property such as factories, mines, land, and machinery, which under capitalism serve as instruments for profit through the exploitation of wage labor.

For Marx and Engels, private ownership of the means of production was the root of inequality, class conflict, and exploitation. By controlling production, capitalists appropriated the surplus created by workers, concentrating wealth and power in the hands of a minority while relegating the majority to poverty and dependency. The abolition of private productive property was therefore, in their view, essential for freeing workers from economic subordination and eliminating the structural basis of exploitation.

In practice, this would require transferring factories, enterprises, land, and resources from individual capitalists to collective ownership by society. Marx described this as the solution to what he called in *Capital* the central contradiction of capitalism: the social character of production versus the private appropriation of its results. Under collective ownership, the means of production would no longer function as instruments of personal enrichment but as resources directed toward the needs of the community as a whole.

Marx and Engels stressed that this transformation would take time. In *The Communist Manifesto* (1848) and the *Critique of the Gotha Program* (1875), they outlined a transitional period—the dictatorship of the proletariat—during which the working class would seize political power and reorganize the economy. In this stage, large industries, banks, transport, and natural resources would be nationalized, allowing society to plan production, redistribute resources more equitably, and invest in collective development rather than private gain.

With collective ownership established, workers would take part directly in managing production and distribution. Decisions about labor organization, resource allocation, and economic priorities would be made democratically, reflecting the interests of the majority rather than those of a privileged elite. In this way, Marx and Engels argued, wage-labor exploitation would be abolished, distribution would be fairer, and the groundwork for a communist society would be laid.

Unlike utopian socialism, Marx and Engels based their concept of collective ownership not on moral appeals or isolated experiments but on a scientific analysis of capitalism and its contradictions. Charles Fourier and Robert Owen had also called for the abolition of private ownership and the creation of communal property, but their proposals were limited to small cooperative communities and experimental settlements. Fourier's phalansteries and Owen's communes were designed to prove the moral superiority of cooperation over competition, yet they did not address the wider structures of political economy.

Marx and Engels regarded this approach as inadequate, insisting that emancipation required not isolated experiments but the systemic transformation of society as a whole through the revolutionary expropriation of the capitalist class. Unlike the utopians, they viewed collective ownership as the necessary outcome of historical development and class struggle, not as the product of persuasion or enlightened reform.

While acknowledging the pioneering contributions of Fourier and Owen in drawing attention to the importance of collective property, Marx and Engels redefined it as a general and indispensable stage of history, inseparably linked to the overthrow of capitalism and the construction of a classless society.

The Organization of Production and the Distribution of Goods According to Human Needs

In the communist model of society envisioned by Karl Marx and Friedrich Engels, a key condition for achieving social justice is a new organization of economic life in which production and distribution are directed toward human needs rather than private profit. This principle contrasts with capitalism, where production is shaped by market competition and the pursuit of gain by those who control the means of production.

Marx and Engels argued that once private ownership of the means of production had been abolished and collective control established, goods and services would be produced and distributed according to decisions made democratically by society. Workers, organized into collectives and councils, would determine what to produce, in what quantities, and how the results should be shared within the community.

The guiding rule of distribution would be the satisfaction of real human requirements, not the purchasing power of individuals in the marketplace. In such a system, members of society would receive goods and services in line with their needs rather than in proportion to their labor contribution. This form of distribution, expressed in Marx's phrase "to each according to his needs," presupposes a level of productive development capable of securing abundance for all.

Marx emphasized that communist production must be based on scientific planning, democratic decision-making, and the rational use of resources. Self-governance would prevent the shortages and surpluses typical of capitalist economies. Advances in technology and the conscious use of automation would further raise productivity, reducing the burden of exhausting and alienating labor. As economic compulsion receded, people would gain time to pursue cultural and intellectual growth, artistic creativity, and richer forms of social life.

This vision also depended on a stronger sense of collective responsibility. Members of a communist society, Marx and Engels believed, would recognize their interdependence and contribute willingly to socially useful work, knowing that their personal well-being was inseparable from the welfare of the community. In such circumstances, the drive to accumulate private wealth or to compete for scarce resources would vanish, since goods would be distributed fairly and material security assured for all.

Overcoming Market Mechanisms and Commodity-Money Relations: Building a Planned and Rational Economy

According to Karl Marx and Friedrich Engels, a key condition for the transition to communism is the gradual disappearance of market mechanisms and commodity–money relations. Under capitalism, goods are produced not to satisfy human needs directly but for profit, and their distribution is governed by competition, supply and demand, and monetary exchange. Marxist theory holds that this system inevitably produces inequality, recurring crises of overproduction, and chronic social instability.

Communism, by contrast, seeks to replace the unpredictability of the market with conscious economic planning. Marx argued that once private ownership of the means of production is abolished, products need no longer take the form of commodities created for sale. They become goods made solely to meet human needs. Under such conditions, money as a universal equivalent also loses its role, since exchange is replaced by direct allocation through collective planning.

With common ownership and democratic control, society itself decides—through open deliberation—what to produce, in what amounts, and how to distribute it. Production is organized on a scientific basis and coordinated technically. Calculations of social needs and productive capacities take the place of market fluctuations, allowing society to avoid both surpluses and shortages.

Planned economy, in the vision of Marx and Engels, secures the rational use of resources and balance between production and consumption. Coordination makes possible steady growth, free from speculative cycles, and allows society to reduce necessary labor time. People thereby gain more scope for cultural and intellectual activity. Technological progress and automation, consciously directed, become tools for easing physical work, raising productivity, and moving toward the communist principle of distribution according to needs.

This system also presupposes a high level of social consciousness and active participation. Members of society collectively oversee planning and production, ensuring fairness, efficiency, and accountability. In this conception, the guiding force of the economy is not competition or coercion but the recognized requirements of the community.

For Marx and Engels, the replacement of commodity exchange by a rationally planned economy was an essential step toward creating a society capable of meeting the needs of all its members and freeing humanity from the inequalities and destructive cycles of capitalist production.

Morality, Law, and Culture

The New Ethics and Morality of Communist Society: Solidarity, Collectivism, Selflessness, and Responsibility for the Common Good

In the communist society envisioned by Karl Marx and Friedrich Engels, the transformation of economic and social relations is inseparable from a profound change in the moral sphere. The abolition of private property and the disappearance of class antagonisms bring forth a new ethical order reflecting the collective interests of society rather than the privileges of particular groups.

At the center of this morality stands solidarity, understood as the conscious unity and mutual support of all members of society. Unlike capitalism, where moral norms are shaped by competition and the pursuit of private gain, communism fosters trust, cooperation, and shared responsibility. As Marx and Engels wrote in *The Communist Manifesto* (1848): "The free development of each is the condition for the free development of all." In this formulation, individual well-being is realized through collective prosperity.

Collectivism becomes the basis of social consciousness. Far from suppressing individuality, it allows for its fullest expression within cooperative life. In *The German Ideology* (1846), Marx observed: "In communist society, where nobody has one exclusive sphere of activity, but each can become accomplished in any branch he wishes, society regulates the general production and thus makes it possible for me to do one thing today and another tomorrow... without ever becoming a hunter, fisherman, shepherd, or critic." This vision emphasizes how collective organization expands, rather than limits, individual freedom.

Selflessness also occupies an important place. Once abundance is secured and goods are distributed justly, the motives for rivalry and private accumulation lose their force. In the *Critique of the Gotha Program* (1875), Marx contrasted the capitalist principle of exchange value with the higher communist rule: "From each according to his ability, to each according to his needs." Labor and creativity become conscious contributions to the life of the community rather than means of individual survival.

Responsibility for the common good is another defining element. Each person understands that the results of their work directly affect others, and this responsibility arises not from external compulsion but from social awareness. Engels stressed this in *Anti-Dühring* (1878): "With the seizing of the means of production by society, production of commodities is done away with... Anarchy in social production is replaced by conscious organization… Man, at last, becomes the real, conscious master of nature—because he has become master of his own social organization."

Historical experience gave concrete form to these ideas. In *The Civil War in France* (1871), Marx analyzed the Paris Commune as the first living example of a new political and moral order: representatives elected by the people, subject to recall, paid workers' wages, and held accountable to the electorate. For Marx and Engels, such institutions embodied in practice the principles of solidarity and responsibility.

In this conception, communist morality rests on solidarity, collectivism, selflessness, and responsibility for the common good. It does not appear as a set of abstract prescriptions but as the ethical reflection of transformed social and economic relations. By removing exploitation and competition, it makes possible the full and free development of the individual within a community built on cooperation and mutual respect.

Education and the Formation of a New Type of Human Being

According to Marxist theory, the transition to communism requires change not only in the economy and social relations but also in education and upbringing. Karl Marx and Friedrich Engels stressed that a new social order could be created only by individuals who consciously strive for collective well-being and are free from the egoistic habits fostered by capitalism. To achieve this, education must be organized in such a way that it develops the creative and intellectual capacities of every person under conditions free of exploitation and alienation.

Communist pedagogy is based on the principle of the comprehensive and harmonious development of the individual. Unlike capitalist education, which is shaped by the needs of the labor market and narrow specialization, communist education promotes breadth of knowledge, critical thinking, creativity, and the free unfolding of human potential. It combines theoretical instruction with physical, aesthetic, and moral cultivation, ensuring balanced development of personality in all its dimensions.

Nineteenth-century bourgeois schooling, by contrast, was closely tied to the requirements of capitalist industry. It produced disciplined workers with limited skills, suited for factory labor. Instruction was often rigid and authoritarian, emphasizing obedience rather than initiative. The separation of schooling from productive activity reinforced alienation: children were prepared not to develop their individuality but to function as future laborers subject to capital. Marx condemned this system in *Capital*, where he wrote that it "turns children into articles of trade," pointing out that it also reproduced class divisions by giving different forms of education to different strata—technical training for workers and classical or professional study for the bourgeoisie.

Communist education, on the other hand, integrates learning with socially meaningful labor. As Marx and Engels explained in *The Communist Manifesto*, schooling must be combined with productive activity so that learning and contribution to society form a single process. This prevents the alienation of the individual from the results of their own work and makes labor itself an arena of creativity and meaning.

Equally important is the cultivation of solidarity and responsibility for the collective good. From early childhood, people should grow accustomed to cooperation, mutual aid, and collective life. Marx insisted that moral education—instilling awareness of one's social role and responsibility—should be treated as essential as intellectual training. In *The German Ideology*, Marx and Engels envisioned a society in which individuals would not be bound to one role but could "hunt in the morning, fish in the afternoon, rear cattle in the evening, and criticize after dinner," illustrating how many-sided development enriches human existence.

The aim of such an approach is the creation of a new type of individual: one no longer limited by exploitation or alienation, able to realize intellectual and creative potential within the collective. Such individuals can consciously participate in managing social life and in making collective decisions, while also accepting responsibility for the welfare of society as a whole, recognizing their inseparable connection to the community and to others' well-being.

Culture as Free Self-Expression and Universal Access to Science and Art

In the communist society envisioned by Karl Marx and Friedrich Engels, culture ceases to be the privilege of a minority and becomes a common heritage open to all. With the removal of social and economic barriers, every person gains equal access to cultural life, securing both the right to personal development and the opportunity for free creative expression. Culture thus becomes an integral part of building a cooperative and solidaristic community.

Marx and Engels linked this vision to the growth of productive forces and the abundance of material goods, which would allow people to devote their energies to cultural and intellectual pursuits. Freed from the compulsion of labor performed merely for survival, individuals could develop their talents in science, art, and other fields. As Marx wrote in *The German Ideology* (1846), in a communist society "nobody has one exclusive sphere of activity," but each may pursue different interests freely, unbound by rigid divisions of labor.

Universal access to cultural achievements implies the removal of economic, social, and educational restrictions. Museums, theaters, libraries, research institutes, and schools would be open to all, without financial or class limitations. Culture no longer appears as a commodity tied to purchasing power but as a shared good serving spiritual, intellectual, and moral growth. In the *Critique of the Gotha Program* (1875), Marx tied this principle to the higher stage of communism, where "the free development of each is the condition for the free development of all."

This vision stood in sharp contrast to nineteenth-century bourgeois culture, which often remained the preserve of elites. Theaters and concert halls required costly tickets, private salons held exclusive art collections, and universities admitted only those who could pay. Even scientific work and publishing were frequently subordinated to profit. Workers, burdened by long hours, were largely excluded from cultural participation, and education served to reproduce class divisions rather than overcome them.

Communism, by contrast, envisages the broad democratization of cultural life. Institutions of learning and art are open to all, while cultural creation itself becomes a universal activity. People take part in science, art, and cultural work not for monetary reward but as expressions of personal interest and social contribution. This erases the alienation of individuals from the products of their creativity and makes cultural activity a natural part of everyday life.

The result of universal access is the active participation of all in cultural development. Individuals are not passive consumers but creators, contributing to a rich and diverse cultural exchange. In this way, culture becomes a means of uniting people, fostering solidarity, and promoting intellectual and moral growth. It shapes well-rounded personalities, free of social barriers and economic constraint, able to realize themselves fully through cooperation with others.

The Withering Away of the Legal System in Its Traditional Form and the Emergence of Social Morality as the Regulator of Behavior

In the communist conception developed by Karl Marx and Friedrich Engels, the legal system rooted in coercion and punishment gradually loses its role and disappears as society moves toward a classless order. Law, in their view, is not an eternal category but a historical phenomenon that emerged with the division of society into classes. From its origin it functioned above all to defend private property and uphold the power of the ruling class.

With the abolition of exploitation, classes, and private ownership of the means of production, the conditions that had required coercive law also vanish. In such circumstances, individuals no longer oppose their interests to those of others, since material needs are met collectively and personal welfare coincides with the well-being of the community.

Engels captured this transformation in *Anti-Dühring* (1878), writing that in communist society "the government of persons is replaced by the administration of things and the direction of processes of production." What had been legal coercion is replaced by rational coordination and moral consensus. Marx, in the *Critique of the Gotha Program* (1875), linked this shift to the higher phase of communism.

Bourgeois Law vs. Communist Morality

- **Bourgeois Law**

  - Rooted in private property.

  - Establishes "formal equality," which conceals deep economic inequality.
  - Regulates relations through coercion, punishment, and external sanctions.
  - Protects contracts, ownership, and inheritance, thereby reproducing class divisions.

- **Communist Morality**

  - Based on collective ownership and solidarity.

  - Embodies real equality, since material differences and antagonisms have been abolished.
  - Guides behavior through inner conviction, social responsibility, and shared values.
  - Discourages harmful acts not by threat of punishment but through moral education, collective oversight, and mutual respect.

In communist society, morality assumes the role of the conscious regulator of human conduct. It is cultivated through universal education, collective labor, and shared cultural life, all of which instill solidarity, responsibility, and respect for common interests.

These moral norms, rather than legal sanctions, provide the framework that prevents destructive behavior and sustains stable social relations. Law as an instrument of repression fades away, while morality, grounded in free conviction and collective responsibility, becomes the enduring basis of social life.

The Significance and Influence of the Communist Model on Later Philosophy and Social Thought

The Impact of the Marxist Model on Political and Social Movements of the Late Nineteenth and the First Half of the Twentieth Century

The communist doctrine developed by Karl Marx and Friedrich Engels became a decisive current in political and intellectual life at the turn of the nineteenth and twentieth centuries. By the late 1800s, their ideas had already shaped the growth of the labor movement, the rise of trade unions, and the founding of the first socialist parties in Europe and North America.

An early milestone was the creation of the First International (International Workingmen's Association) in 1864, where Marx and Engels played leading roles. The organization united workers across national borders around the Marxist principles of class struggle and social transformation. In writings such as the *Inaugural Address* (1864) and *Instructions for Delegates* (1866), Marx stressed the necessity of international solidarity, formulating the principle that "the emancipation of the working class must be conquered by the working class itself."

After the deaths of Marx and Engels, their doctrine gained new prominence through the Second International (1889–1914). Socialist and social-democratic parties in Germany, France, Austria, Italy, and other countries drew on Marxist analysis in their programs. These movements defended workers' rights and pressed for social reforms, but soon diverged: one wing called for revolutionary struggle and the overthrow of capitalism, while another pursued parliamentary and reformist strategies.

The October Revolution of 1917 in Russia marked the first large-scale attempt to realize Marxist principles in practice. Under the leadership of Vladimir Lenin, the Bolsheviks proclaimed the dictatorship of the proletariat and sought to construct a new order based on Marxist foundations. Lenin's interpretation of Marxism—later termed Marxism-Leninism—underscored the role of the revolutionary party, democratic centralism, and the application of theory as a guide to action. The Russian Revolution gave unprecedented momentum to socialist and communist movements worldwide, influencing strategies from Europe to Asia.

In the years that followed, Marxism became a reference point for uprisings and workers' struggles. It figured prominently in the German Revolution of 1918–1919, the Hungarian Soviet Republic of 1919, and the workers' councils of the Biennio Rosso in Italy (1919–1920). In China, the 1920s brought the rise of the Communist

Party, which adapted Marxist principles to agrarian and national conditions. In Spain, Marxist and anarchist forces shaped the struggles of the Civil War (1936–1939). Beyond Europe, Marxist theory and organization energized anti-colonial movements from Latin America to Asia, where it was interpreted as a program for national liberation.

By the mid-twentieth century, socialist and communist parties had become integral parts of political life in many countries. They advocated improved labor conditions, social guarantees, and broader democratization. In this way, Marxism functioned not only as a critique of capitalism but also as a source of concrete organizational models and strategies that influenced the course of modern social and political movements around the world.

Practical Attempts to Implement Communist Ideas in the Twentieth Century (USSR, China, and Other Countries)

The most extensive attempts to implement Marxist-communist ideas took place in the revolutionary transformations and the construction of socialist states during the twentieth century. The Soviet Union was the first country to declare Marxist principles—proletarian dictatorship and collective ownership—the official basis of its political and economic system. Under Lenin and later Stalin, rapid industrialization turned a predominantly agrarian society into an industrial power. Illiteracy was eradicated, universal free education and healthcare were established, and social rights were introduced on a scale unmatched in contemporary capitalist states.

China represented another major example after the communist revolution of 1949 led by Mao Zedong. The new regime carried out land reform, abolished landlord property, collectivized agriculture, and launched programs of industrialization, which improved the living standards of millions of peasants and workers. However, Mao's political campaigns, including the Great Leap Forward (1958–1962) and the Cultural Revolution (1966–1976), caused profound crises, leading to famine, social upheaval, and millions of deaths. In Eastern Europe, after World War II, socialist regimes were established in Poland, East Germany, Hungary, Czechoslovakia, and other countries under Soviet influence. These states achieved rapid industrial expansion and developed extensive welfare systems that improved access to education, healthcare, and housing. Yet the rigid one-party systems, pervasive state control, and suppression of political dissent produced growing dissatisfaction. By the late 1980s, economic stagnation and mounting social unrest undermined these regimes, paving the way for their collapse at the end of the century.

Contemporary Assessments of the Communist Model

Despite the collapse of most socialist states at the end of the twentieth century, the ideas of Karl Marx and Friedrich Engels continue to command attention and remain the subject of debate about their theoretical validity and practical relevance.

Supporters of Marxist theory argue that the communist project offered a framework for addressing inequality, class exploitation, and structural injustice. They point to achievements of twentieth-century socialist states such as universal education, free healthcare, broad social protections, and significant reductions in poverty and unemployment. Advocates also stress the emancipatory aims of communist ideals: to create conditions for the full development of human capacities and the realization of creativity outside the constraints of economic necessity.

Critics, however, underscore the contradictions and shortcomings revealed in practice. Common points of criticism include the inefficiency of centrally planned economies, weak incentives for productivity and innovation, and the restriction of political freedoms under one-party rule. Scholars also highlight the problems of bureaucratization and authoritarianism: the dictatorship of the proletariat, envisioned as rule by the majority, often took the form of dominance by a party or a small leadership elite. Skepticism is also directed at the feasibility of realizing the principle "to each according to his needs," given limited resources and the difficulty of assessing human requirements in objective terms.

Even with these criticisms, the intellectual impact of Marxism has been considerable. Marx and Engels introduced into modern thought a set of categories—class struggle, surplus value, historical materialism, the dialectics of social development, and the concept of alienated labor—that continue to serve as analytical tools in sociology, economics, political theory, cultural studies, and anthropology.

"*Being all equal and independent, no one ought to harm another in his life, health, liberty, or possessions.*"

—John Locke
Second Treatise of Government (1689)

SECTION 2. MINIMAL STATE: GOVERNMENT LIMITED TO ESSENTIAL PROTECTIVE AND LEGAL FUNCTIONS

> **The minimal state** is a form of government whose role is strictly limited to the protection of individual rights—life, liberty, and property—by means of law enforcement, national defense, and impartial courts, excluding all functions of economic regulation, social welfare, and cultural control.

The minimal state, sometimes referred to as the *"night-watchman state,"* is a model of government intentionally restricted to its most essential functions. In this framework, the state acts as a guarantor of order and justice. It maintains internal security through law enforcement, protects against external threats through national defense, and resolves disputes through impartial courts. Beyond these functions, it exercises no authority over the lives of its citizens.

The philosophical foundations of the minimal state can be traced to the classical liberal tradition, most notably in the writings of John Locke, who argued that government exists to preserve natural rights, and in the work of Robert Nozick, who provided a systematic defense of this model in *Anarchy, State, and Utopia* (1974). Both emphasize that human beings are autonomous and responsible agents who must be free to shape their own destinies.

In this vision, the state is not a manager of society but a guardian of freedom. By confining its role to the protection of rights, it creates the conditions under which voluntary cooperation, individual responsibility, and human creativity can flourish.

Chapter 1. John Locke's Classical Liberalism
The Foundations of
Liberal Thought and the Defense of Natural Rights

John Locke's philosophy of classical liberalism rests on the fundamental conviction that human beings are born free. This freedom is not a privilege granted by rulers but a natural condition, grounded in the very order of nature. Every person possesses inalienable rights—life, liberty, and property—which exist prior to any laws and stand above the authority of the state.

For Locke, the state does not own these rights and cannot arbitrarily limit them. Its sole purpose is to act as their protector and guardian. Governmental power is therefore not absolute but conditional: it is justified only to the extent that it secures the natural rights of citizens. Any intervention into private life must be strictly limited and is legitimate only when it is necessary to safeguard life, liberty, or property.

Key Principles of John Locke's Philosophy of Classical Liberalism

- **Natural Rights of the Individual**
    - the right to life;
    - the right to liberty;
    - the right to property.

- **The Limited Role of the State**
    - the state protects natural rights without intruding into private life or economic activity;
    - the state exists solely to guarantee security and public order.

- **The Rule of Law**
    - governmental authority is subject to law and cannot act arbitrarily;
    - the law is binding both on citizens and on those who govern.

- **The Social Contract**
    - political power is legitimate only when it rests on the voluntary consent of the governed;
    - citizens transfer a portion of their freedom to the state in exchange for protection of their rights and security.

- **The Right of the People to Resist and Replace Authority**
    - citizens have the right to oppose and change the government if it violates their rights;
    - the right to resistance is the natural consequence of a government breaking the terms of the social contract.

John Locke stands as one of the most influential philosophers of the early modern era. His ideas fundamentally reshaped the understanding of the state, political authority, and individual liberty, laying the groundwork for the development of liberal democracies. Locke was the first to argue clearly and systematically that governmental power must be limited, subordinated to law, and directed solely toward the protection of citizens' rights.

The significance of Locke's thought extends far beyond the realm of philosophy. His legacy has shaped the institutional design of contemporary states and contributed to the modern conception of human dignity and freedom. In linking natural rights with the rule of law and popular consent, Locke helped to define the essential principles of political legitimacy that continue to guide democratic societies today.

The Concept of Natural Rights
The Right to Life as the Fundamental Condition of Freedom

In John Locke's philosophy, the right to life stands at the foundation of natural rights. In his *Two Treatises of Government* (1689), he argued that life is the basic condition for the enjoyment of liberty and property. Without security of life, no other rights can be meaningfully guaranteed, and for this reason the preservation of life becomes the foremost obligation of political authority.

Locke maintained that neither individuals nor governments may arbitrarily deprive someone of life or expose it to danger, since such acts violate the fundamental law of nature. Any unlawful attack on life is, for him, the most serious offense and provides grounds for both resistance and self-defense.

Yet Locke did not regard the right to life as absolute in all circumstances. In Chapter II of the *Second Treatise*, he observed that a person who commits a grave crime—most clearly, murder—deliberately violates the life of another and thereby breaks the natural law. By disregarding the rights of others, such a person forfeits their own claim to protection under those same rights. Locke described this as entering into a "state of war" with society, which entitles the community to punish the offender, even by death.

At the same time, he emphasized that the death penalty must be applied only under established law and in proportion to the seriousness of the crime. Its use is legitimate only for the defense of society and the restoration of justice, never as an arbitrary exercise of power or a tool of oppression. In this way, Locke affirms the sanctity of life while acknowledging the necessity of lawful punishment, underscoring both the inviolability of natural rights and the duty of individuals to respect them in others.

Freedom as an Inalienable Right of the Individual

For John Locke, freedom ranked alongside life and property as one of the fundamental natural rights. He maintained that people are born free and equal, and no person holds legitimate authority to arbitrarily deprive another of this liberty. In Locke's account, liberty is not a privilege granted by governments but an original condition that precedes the establishment of political institutions.

He defined freedom as the ability to act according to one's own will without coercion or interference from others or from the state. This conception of liberty is tied to an individual's capacity to direct the course of their life, to cultivate their talents, and to make use of property and resources in ways that reflect personal choice. In this sense, freedom serves as the foundation for personal development and for active engagement in civil society.

Locke was careful to distinguish liberty from license. Genuine freedom, he argued, does not mean the absence of all restraint but the condition of living under laws of reason and justice that bind all equally. As he wrote in the *Second Treatise of Government* (1689): "Freedom is not a liberty for every man to do what he lists... but a liberty to follow my own will in all things where the rule prescribes not; and not to be subject to the inconstant, uncertain, unknown, arbitrary will of another man."

From this perspective, law functions as the guardian of liberty. The freedom of each person is limited only by the equal freedom of others, and it is the task of just laws to preserve this balance. The state, in Locke's vision, must guarantee the widest possible scope of liberty for its citizens, intervening only when necessary to protect life, property, and security. In this way, Locke joined the principle of natural liberty with the necessity of lawful order, providing the foundation for the liberal conception of civil rights.

Property and Its Role in Securing Personal Independence

In Chapter V of the *Second Treatise of Government* (1689), titled *Of Property*, John Locke presents a systematic account of the origin and nature of property. He maintains that property comes into being when an individual appropriates natural resources by applying labor to them. Since, as Locke observes, "every man has a property in his own person" and in the work of his hands, whatever is shaped or transformed through individual effort becomes an extension of the person and rightfully his own.

For Locke, property is more than material possession; it is a foundation of personal independence. Ownership of goods, land, or resources enables people to sustain themselves and to develop their capacities without dependence on the arbitrary will of others or the authority of the state. In securing property, individuals gain the means to shape their lives freely, to make their own choices, and to preserve a sphere of autonomy grounded in their own labor and initiative.

Because of this, Locke regarded the protection of property as a primary purpose of political society. The state exists, in his account, to safeguard the natural rights of life, liberty, and property. Its role is to ensure the security of what citizens rightfully own, without arbitrary seizure or redistribution. When rulers attempt to confiscate property without consent, they undermine the basis of the social contract and lose their legitimacy. In such cases, citizens retain the right to resist and to defend their natural rights against tyranny.

Through this reasoning Locke tied property to human dignity and the conditions of liberty. To possess property is to stand as an independent agent, capable of participating freely in social and political life. To defend property is therefore to preserve the very framework of individual freedom.

The Role and Tasks of the State in Locke's Philosophy
The State as a "Night Watchman": Minimalism and Non-Interference

In John Locke's political philosophy, the state is not the creator of rights but their guardian. In the *Second Treatise of Government* (1689), especially in Chapters VII–IX, he argued that legitimate political authority must be confined to functions that secure the natural rights of individuals.

For Locke, government has only a limited mandate: to protect life, liberty, and property, to preserve civil peace, and to provide impartial adjudication of disputes. Beyond these duties, state power has no justification. He rejected the extension of authority into private life, moral choices, or personal economic activity.

This insistence on limitation reflects Locke's belief that every enlargement of governmental power poses risks to liberty, discourages initiative, and opens the door to arbitrary rule. To avoid such dangers, state action must be bound by clear and transparent laws that prevent officials from abusing power and that safeguard the security of private life and property.

Nineteenth-century liberal thinkers, such as Ferdinand Lassalle, later described this model as the "night-watchman state"—a metaphor for a government whose role is largely protective. Locke himself never used the term, but it aptly conveys his vision of political authority restricted to the defense of rights rather than their creation or expansion.

In Locke's view, government remains just and legitimate only when it observes these narrow limits. Any attempt to move beyond them constitutes an overreach of power and an encroachment on the natural liberty of individuals.

The Protection of Rights and Freedoms as the Only Legitimate Purpose of the State

John Locke maintained that the only legitimate end of government is the preservation of the natural rights of its citizens. People, he argued, enter political society not to limit their own freedom but to ensure more secure protection of life, liberty, and property.

Political authority, in Locke's view, is justified only so long as it acts in the interest of the governed, guaranteeing their safety and well-being. Whenever the state moves beyond this function—seeking its own advantage, intruding into private life, prescribing morality, or dictating economic behavior—it loses its moral foundation and violates the principles of the social contract.

Locke emphasized that the chief role of government is to establish laws that protect citizens from violence, fraud, and arbitrary seizure of property. This, he insisted, is the core and indeed the sole justification of political power. If rulers neglect this duty or act against the rights of their people, they dissolve the very basis of their legitimacy. In such circumstances, the community retains the right of resistance and may replace its government, since authority exists only through the consent of the governed.

For Locke, therefore, the defense of natural rights was not simply the primary responsibility of the state but its exclusive purpose. Any activity that cannot be traced to the protection of life, liberty, or property lacks legitimacy and represents an encroachment on personal freedom.

Limiting State Power by Law and the Social Contract

John Locke maintained that government must operate only within the boundaries of clear and established law. For him, law was the safeguard against tyranny: it had to be public, transparent, and binding equally on rulers and citizens. Authority could never be exercised outside rules fixed in advance and accepted by the community.

He also stressed that political power is limited not only by written laws but by the very principles laid down at the founding of civil society. The social contract, entered into voluntarily by free individuals, is the true source of legitimacy and defines the scope of governmental authority.

Through this contract citizens consent to transfer to government only the power necessary to secure their natural rights—life, liberty, and property. Sovereignty remains with the people, and officials hold authority solely in trust for them. When rulers exceed these limits—by intruding into private life, seizing property without consent, or issuing arbitrary commands—they violate the contract and lose their claim to legitimacy. In such circumstances the people retain the right to resist and to establish a new government that honors its purpose.

Locke described two main restraints on political power:

- **The rule of law:** authority is bound by clear and public rules that apply to all, including those who govern.

- **The social contract:** authority is confined to the terms of the original agreement; when these are broken, government ceases to be lawful.

By combining these principles Locke offered a framework that protects natural rights against arbitrariness. His vision of power limited by law and by the continuing sovereignty of the people laid the foundations of modern liberal constitutionalism.

The Social Contract and the Subordination of Power to the Will of the People

The Idea of Consent as the Source of Legitimate Authority

John Locke argued that in the state of nature individuals enjoy complete freedom and equal rights. To secure their life, liberty, and property, however, people voluntarily agree to limit part of this natural freedom and transfer certain powers to a government of their own creation. For Locke, such voluntary consent is the only basis of legitimate political authority.

He distinguished between two kinds of consent:

- **Explicit consent:** given when a person deliberately joins a political community and directly accepts its social contract.

- **Tacit consent:** expressed when someone benefits from the protection of a government and, by living under its laws, implicitly acknowledges the legitimacy of its authority.

Locke emphasized that consent is not a single act fixed once and for all. Political authority must continually demonstrate its legitimacy by adhering to the terms of the original contract and respecting the rights of citizens. When government oversteps its mandate or violates those rights, the people retain the right to withdraw their consent and, if necessary, to resist and replace that government.

In Locke's account, it is the ongoing consent and free will of the governed that make political authority lawful. Without this consent, or when it is betrayed, power loses its moral and legal foundation. This principle—that ultimate sovereignty belongs to the people—became a defining element of modern democratic and constitutional thought. By grounding political legitimacy in the continuing approval of citizens, Locke provided one of the earliest formulations of the modern principle of government by consent.

The Conditions of the Social Contract in Locke's Philosophy

For Locke, the social contract was not an abstract philosophical idea but a concrete agreement through which free individuals establish civil society and set the boundaries of political authority. By entering such a compact, people create binding conditions that secure legitimacy and limit the scope of state power. These conditions can be expressed in several key principles:

1. **Voluntary Agreement**
   The contract is valid only when entered into freely, without coercion or deception. Its justice and authority rest on this voluntariness.

2. **Limited and Defined Transfer of Power**
   Citizens grant to government only the powers necessary to safeguard their natural rights. Authority is never absolute and remains restricted to the purposes for which it was created.

3. **Duties of Government**
   The state undertakes the responsibility to protect life, liberty, and property. It must act solely for the good of its citizens, avoiding self-interest or arbitrary expansion of power.

4. **Equality before the Law**
   All members of society are equal in rights and obligations under the contract. No person may claim special privileges at the expense of others.

5. **The Right of Resistance**
   If rulers abuse their powers, neglect their obligations, or infringe upon rights, the people retain the right to revoke consent, resist authority, and establish a new government faithful to the original compact.

Locke believed that these principles ensure government remains accountable and subordinate to the people. Legitimacy depends entirely on adherence to the contract: when its terms are observed, citizens willingly consent to authority; when they are broken, sovereignty returns to the people themselves.

The People's Right to Resist and Replace an Illegitimate Government

For John Locke, government retains legitimacy only while it fulfills the purpose for which it was established: the protection of life, liberty, and property. When rulers infringe upon these rights, exceed their lawful powers, or attempt to impose arbitrary rule, they undermine the very foundation of the social contract and lose their claim to authority.

In such cases, Locke held, the government has in effect declared a state of war against the people. The community is then released from its obligation of obedience and may resist unlawful commands, depose the tyrannical power, and institute a new government that restores rights and reestablishes lawful order. As he wrote in the *Second Treatise of Government* (§222): **"Whenever the legislators endeavor to take away and destroy the property of the people, or to reduce them to slavery under arbitrary power, they put themselves into a state of war with the people, who are thereupon absolved from any further obedience."**

Locke emphasized, however, that the right of resistance is not a license for constant upheaval. It is an exceptional recourse, justified only by persistent and grave violations of the compact. Its purpose is to serve as a safeguard: a reminder to rulers that their authority rests on trust and must always be exercised for the benefit of the governed.

In this way, the right of resistance functions as both a defense against tyranny and a permanent restraint on power. It empowers citizens to protect themselves when government becomes despotic and ensures that political authority remains grounded in consent and in the protection of natural rights.

Criteria of Legitimacy of Government in Locke's Philosophy
The Limits of State Authority

In John Locke's political theory, the authority of government is confined to the protective functions assigned to it under the social contract. Power is entrusted only to the extent necessary to safeguard natural rights, and any action beyond those limits erodes legitimacy. When rulers overstep their mandate, citizens retain the right to resist and, if necessary, to establish a new government that honors the original agreement.

Locke outlined several key restraints on legitimate political authority:

1. **Protection of Natural Rights**

   Government may act only to secure the basic rights of life, liberty, and property. Any exercise of power for other ends is unjustified.

2. **Adherence to Established Law**

   Political authority must operate within laws that are public, stable, and founded on the consent of the governed. Arbitrary alteration or disregard of law is incompatible with legitimacy.

3. **Limits on Intrusion into Private Life**

   The state has no authority to interfere in citizens' personal affairs, moral choices, or religious beliefs, provided these do not infringe on the rights of others. Locke underscored the inviolability of private life and property against unwarranted intrusion.

4. **No Expropriation without Consent**

   Property cannot be seized or redistributed at the whim of rulers. Any transfer must rest on lawful grounds established beforehand and accepted by the people.

5. **Accountability to the People**

   Government is responsible to the community and may exercise only the powers explicitly delegated by the social contract. When those limits are exceeded, the people may restrict, reform, or replace it.

Through these principles Locke developed a doctrine of limited government and political accountability that shaped the foundations of constitutional thought. In his view, legitimacy arises not from tradition or divine sanction, but from the consistent fulfillment of the purposes for which political society exists: the protection of rights and the preservation of liberty.

Consequences of the Violation of Citizens' Natural Rights by Government

One of the most radical implications of Locke's political theory is the people's right to resist a government that betrays its trust. Political authority, he argued, exists only to protect the natural rights of life, liberty, and property. The moment rulers cease to fulfill this role and instead violate those rights, they forfeit both legitimacy and the foundation of their power. Locke described the consequences of such a breach in several ways:

1. **Loss of Legitimacy**

   A government that infringes on the fundamental rights of its citizens ceases to be lawful authority. By breaking the terms of the social contract, it dissolves the very basis of political order.

2. **The People's Right of Resistance**

   Citizens gain both moral and legal grounds to oppose such a regime. Active resistance—including the overthrow of tyranny—is justified when rulers consistently neglect their obligations and suppress liberty. As Locke wrote in the *Second Treatise of Government* (§222), when rulers act contrary to the trust placed in them, they "put themselves into a state of war with the people, who are thereupon absolved from any further obedience."

3. **Dissolution of the Social Contract**

   By violating citizens' rights, rulers themselves dissolve the compact that created political society. The community then reverts to a "state of nature," where individuals regain the freedom to establish a new political order.

4. **The Right to Establish New Government**

   Once authority is lost, the people hold the right to form a new government faithful to the original purpose of political society: the protection of natural rights and the preservation of liberty.

In Locke's account, the right of resistance is not a call to constant upheaval but a safeguard against despotism. It ensures that rulers remain accountable and reminds them that their authority endures only through respect for the trust placed in them.

The Theory of Resistance and Revolution in Locke's Philosophy

John Locke developed a systematic theory of resistance that became a defining contribution to modern political philosophy. For him, the people's right to oppose or even depose a government did not arise from passion or arbitrary will but from the logic of the social contract and the protection of natural rights. The main elements of this theory can be outlined as follows:

1. **Tyranny as Grounds for Resistance**

   Locke described tyranny as the abuse of power, when rulers act arbitrarily and outside established law. In such circumstances, government ceases to protect natural rights and instead becomes their chief violator. By breaking the social contract, it effectively wages war against its own citizens and forfeits legitimacy.

2. **Resistance as a Natural Right**

   The right to resist, Locke argued, is not granted by government and cannot be taken away by it. It is a natural right, rooted in the duty of every individual to preserve life, liberty, and property against unlawful force. When authority turns oppressor, people recover the right of self-defense they possessed in the state of nature.

3. **Revolution as a Lawful Response**

   Resistance may culminate in revolution. Locke emphasized that revolution is not an act of anarchy but a lawful remedy to persistent and serious violations of trust. It becomes legitimate when rulers repeatedly breach the contract and when peaceful means are no longer available. In the *Second Treatise of Government* (§§220–222), he maintained that once authority betrays its purpose, it ceases to exist, and opposition becomes justified.

4. **The Aim of Revolution: Restoration of Legitimate Government**

   For Locke, the object of revolution was not destruction but renewal. The people must establish a government true to the original compact—one that protects rights, upholds the law, and serves the common good. Revolution thus functions as a corrective mechanism, bringing authority back into line with liberty and justice.

Locke's theory of resistance and revolution was designed not to promote disorder but to guard against tyranny. By asserting that sovereignty ultimately rests with the people, he supplied political thought with a lasting principle: when rulers violate the natural rights they are bound to secure, the people have both the right and the duty to replace them with a government faithful to the social contract. These ideas were closely tied to the historical experience of the Glorious Revolution of 1688 in England, which Locke regarded as confirmation of the people's right to depose a monarch who betrayed their trust. His arguments later inspired the American colonists, and echoes of Locke's language can be found in the Declaration of Independence of 1776, which proclaimed the right of the people to alter or abolish any government destructive of their rights.

The Influence of Locke's Ideas on the Formation of Modern Liberal States

The Significance of Locke's Philosophy for the Development of Democracy and Constitutionalism

The philosophy of John Locke played a decisive role in the rise of modern democracy and the development of constitutional government. His concepts of natural rights, popular sovereignty, and limited authority provided a framework for reform in Europe and America during the eighteenth and nineteenth centuries, reshaping political power into a trust exercised on behalf of the people.

Among the most important ideas Locke contributed to democratic and constitutional thought were the following:

1. **Popular Sovereignty**

   Locke argued that sovereignty does not rest with monarchs or elites but with the people themselves. Government is legitimate only when it acts with the consent of the governed. This principle became a foundation for representative democracy.

2. **Separation of Powers**

   In the *Second Treatise of Government*, Locke emphasized the need to divide authority between legislative and executive functions. Such division, designed to prevent the concentration of power, reduces the danger of arbitrariness. Montesquieu later expanded on this principle, and it became a central feature of modern constitutions.

3. **The Rule of Law**

   For Locke, rulers as well as citizens are subject to the law. Laws must be general, public, and established with popular consent. This conviction helped shape the modern notion of a constitutional state bound by law.

4. **Constitutional Protection of Rights**

   Locke held that the natural rights of life, liberty, and property require institutional safeguards. His influence is evident in the American Declaration of Independence (1776), the U.S. Constitution (1787), and the French Declaration of the Rights of Man and of the Citizen (1789), all of which protect individual rights against arbitrary rule.

5. **The Right of Resistance**

   Locke defended the people's right to resist illegitimate or tyrannical government, insisting that rulers who break the social contract dissolve the very foundation of their authority. This principle gave philosophical legitimacy to the overthrow of oppressive regimes and became a rallying point for later revolutions. In the American Revolution (1775–1783), Locke's arguments were echoed in Thomas Jefferson's *Declaration of Independence* (1776), which proclaimed the right of the people to "alter or abolish" any government destructive of their rights. In France, Locke's thought also resonated with the authors of the *Declaration of the Rights of Man and of the Citizen* (1789), who asserted the right to resist oppression as a universal principle. Beyond these cases, Locke's theory of resistance influenced constitutional debates throughout the eighteenth and nineteenth centuries, embedding the conviction that governments remain legitimate only so long as they secure the rights of their citizens.

Through these principles Locke helped lay the institutional and ideological foundations of liberal democracy. His vision of government limited by law, grounded in consent, and dedicated to the protection of rights continues to shape constitutional practice and democratic theory worldwide.

Chapter 2. Robert Nozick's Libertarianism
The Philosophy of Individual Freedom and the Minimal State

Robert Nozick (1938–2002) stands among the most influential voices in modern libertarian thought. Educated at Columbia, Princeton, and Harvard, he spent most of his career at Harvard University, where he became a central figure in analytic political philosophy. Though he began with an interest in socialist ideas, he later turned decisively toward libertarianism, building a powerful defense of individual rights and limited government.

His *Anarchy, State, and Utopia* (1974) ignited intense debate and set a new course for late twentieth-century political philosophy. The book, which received the National Book Award in the United States, established him as the most formidable challenger to John Rawls.

Nozick entered into a direct and often sharp dialogue with Rawls, whose *A Theory of Justice* (1971) argued for substantial state action to secure fairness and equal opportunity. In contrast, Nozick insisted that only the minimal state—the so-called "night-watchman state"—is legitimate, with functions limited to protecting individuals against force, theft, and fraud, and to enforcing contracts.

For Nozick, any extension of state power beyond these limits violated liberty. Redistribution and regulation, in his view, were moral transgressions against the principle of self-ownership. Individuals belong to themselves and to the products of their labor; taxation used for social engineering, he argued, amounted to coercion not unlike forced labor.

In later years, Nozick moved beyond political theory to explore questions in epistemology, metaphysics, and the search for meaning. Works such as *Philosophical Explanations* (1981) and *The Examined Life* (1989) revealed the breadth of his interests and his unwillingness to remain confined to a single domain of philosophy.

The Concept of the Minimal State ("Night-Watchman State")

In *Anarchy, State, and Utopia* (1974), Robert Nozick offered a powerful defense of the minimal state—often evoked through the metaphor of the "night-watchman state." In this vision, government is stripped to its narrowest role: guarding individuals against violence, theft, and fraud. Any further reach—whether through redistributing wealth, regulating economic life, or policing private choices—falls outside its rightful bounds and lacks moral legitimacy.

Core Principles of the Minimal State

• **Strict Limits on Government**: The use of state power is justified only to secure citizens' safety and rights, prevent aggression, and suppress fraud.

• **No Redistribution of Wealth**: The state may not seize property from some to aid others. Such measures, Nozick argued, violate self-ownership and erode liberty.

• **Freedom as the Supreme Value**: Any interference not tied directly to protection against force is an infringement on individual autonomy.

- **Voluntary Exchange and Cooperation**: People must remain free to associate, trade, and collaborate on the basis of mutual consent, without intrusion from the state.

Core Functions of the Minimal State

For Robert Nozick, government has a single, narrow purpose: to secure the conditions of individual liberty. Its role is confined to three essential tasks:

1. **Protection against Violence**

   The state must defend every person's life and bodily integrity, preventing aggression and ensuring that citizens can live without fear.

2. **Protection of Property**

   Property rights are inviolable. The state is bound to protect possessions from unlawful seizure and to uphold the security of ownership.

3. **Protection against Fraud**

   The state enforces voluntary agreements and contracts, shielding citizens from deception that would undermine trust and free exchange.

Beyond these limits, Nozick argued, government has no rightful authority. Redistribution, economic regulation, or efforts to impose moral standards turn it into an instrument of coercion and infringe on personal autonomy. Only the minimal state—restricted to protecting individuals—can preserve liberty. It secures order without dictating the content of people's lives, leaving space for voluntary cooperation, personal responsibility, and self-chosen paths.

Critique of the Expansion of State Functions
The Inadmissibility of State Redistribution of Wealth

One of the central claims in Robert Nozick's *Anarchy, State, and Utopia* (1974) is his uncompromising rejection of redistributive policies. He denied that government has any right to seize the resources of some citizens in order to transfer them to others in the name of social justice or equality. Redistribution, in his view, violates property rights and strikes at the heart of individual liberty.

For Nozick, a person is the rightful owner of what they hold if it was acquired through legitimate means—through labor, voluntary exchange, or inheritance. When the state extracts resources by force, even with benevolent intentions, it treats people as tools for the purposes of others and denies them the freedom to decide how to use what belongs to them.

This reasoning rests on the principle of self-ownership. Because individuals own themselves, they must also own the fruits of their labor and any property gained through consensual transfers. To compel them to surrender part of this is, he argued, to appropriate their labor. In one of his most striking formulations, Nozick compared redistributive taxation to forced labor: it obliges people to work for ends they have not chosen.

For him, only distributions that arise from voluntary agreements among free individuals are morally acceptable. State programs of equalization, subsidies, or welfare funded at others' expense cannot be justified. The state's role must remain strictly limited to preventing force, theft, and fraud, and to enforcing contracts.

On this basis, all redistributive measures—including wealth taxes, income transfers, or other schemes of compulsory aid—are illegitimate. A just society, Nozick argued, is not one where resources are leveled by coercion, but one where people freely pursue their goals, exchange with one another, and keep the rewards of their efforts without state interference.

The Illegitimacy of Economic Regulation as a Violation of Individual Freedom

Robert Nozick rejected all forms of state economic regulation, treating them as unwarranted intrusions on personal liberty. For him, freedom meant more than political rights or freedom of speech; it also demanded the ability of each person to control the products of their labor and to decide independently how to use their resources. Whenever government attempted to direct economic activity, whether through laws, decrees, or administrative controls, it crossed the boundary of its rightful authority and violated the individual's domain of choice.

Nozick insisted that economic liberty could not be separated from other basic freedoms. Interference in the marketplace, he argued, distorts the pattern of voluntary exchange that arises when people interact on the basis of mutual consent. By dictating outcomes or constraining decisions, the state undermines not only efficiency but also the moral foundation of individual rights. Genuine justice and prosperity, in his view, emerge only from the free cooperation of individuals, not from coercive state management.

He regarded as illegitimate a wide range of state actions: fixing prices for goods and services, determining wages and working conditions, setting production quotas, or manipulating competition to favor certain groups. Each of these measures, he argued, imposes arbitrary restrictions on personal choice, substitutes collective commands for individual decision-making, and creates artificial structures that suppress the natural operation of free exchange. In effect, regulation denies citizens the right to shape their own economic lives.

For Nozick, such policies were not only inefficient but also morally impermissible. They forced people to live and work under rules they had not chosen, stripping them of the autonomy to decide how best to pursue their goals. To him, this was a direct assault on the principle of self-ownership, which affirms that individuals are entitled to control their lives, their labor, and the resources they lawfully acquire.

Within his libertarian framework, the state has one legitimate role in economic life: to safeguard the environment in which free exchange can occur. It must protect citizens from violence, fraud, and theft, and enforce contracts so that promises are kept. Beyond these boundaries, government action is nothing more than coercion. A just society, therefore, is not one where officials regulate production or redistribute wealth, but one where individuals are left free to trade, cooperate, and shape their destinies according to their own choices.

Individual Freedom as the Supreme Value of Libertarianism

The Concept of Personal Liberty in Nozick's Philosophy and Its Relation to Locke's Liberalism

In Robert Nozick's philosophy, individual liberty occupies an absolute and central place. He insisted that freedom is the highest political and moral value, one that cannot be restricted by the state except in the narrow cases where it is necessary to secure the rights and safety of others.

Nozick defined liberty above all as the right of each person to live according to their own judgment and to dispose of themselves as they see fit, without coercion, violence, or arbitrary interference either by the state or by other individuals. True freedom, in his view, exists only when a person's actions stem from their own choices and from voluntary agreements with others, rather than being imposed from outside.

A distinctive feature of Nozick's conception is the strong connection he drew between liberty and property rights. The ability to use, control, and freely dispose of legitimately acquired property is, he argued, an essential element of personal autonomy. To deny individuals that right is, for Nozick, to deny them freedom itself. This is why he regarded every form of state interference in ownership or private economic activity—whether through regulation, redistribution, or compulsory taxation—as an unacceptable violation of individual liberty.

The intellectual roots of this position clearly reach back to John Locke, the founder of classical liberalism. In his *Second Treatise of Government* (1689), Locke argued that the natural rights to life, liberty, and property are inseparable and that the preservation of these rights is the sole legitimate purpose of government. For Locke, a state exists only to protect what is already naturally endowed to every person.

Nozick took up Locke's principle of self-ownership—the idea that each individual owns themselves and, by extension, the products of their labor. Yet their conclusions diverged. Locke was willing to grant the state broader responsibilities: the maintenance of impartial justice, the preservation of public order, and even the levying of taxes, provided they were grounded in consent and directed toward the common good. Nozick, however, radically narrowed the boundaries of authority. In his view, any form of redistribution or economic regulation amounted to coercion, regardless of intention.

In this sense, Nozick carried Locke's doctrine of individual rights to its most uncompromising form. What Locke had framed within the social contract, Nozick transformed into the foundation of modern libertarianism, where personal freedom and property rights are treated as absolute and inviolable. By stripping the state down to its minimal functions, he sought to ensure a political order where each person could live, work, and choose in accordance with their own judgment, free from imposed purposes and coercive restraints.

Limits on State Intervention as a Condition for the Full Realization of Freedom

For Robert Nozick, the full realization of freedom required a firm limitation on the scope of government. In *Anarchy, State, and Utopia* (1974), he argued that the state must refrain from all activities beyond the protection of rights and the safeguarding of personal security. Only under such conditions, he believed, can individuals unfold their potential and shape their lives according to their own choices.

Nozick warned that every extension of governmental functions comes at the cost of liberty. Expanding state power, he argued, not only restricts personal freedom but also creates privileges for some citizens at the expense of others. The state, in his view, has no authority to dictate how people should live—in economic affairs, in social relations, or in personal decisions—even when such interference is justified by appeals to welfare, equality, or moral progress. The less the state intervenes, the broader the sphere of freedom available to each individual.

This vision rests on Nozick's belief in the value of voluntary order. For him, the natural balance of society emerges not from regulation but from the free interactions of citizens. The state's role is limited to securing the minimal conditions needed to protect individuals from coercion, violence, or fraud. Beyond that, it must leave people free to direct their own lives.

At the foundation of his libertarian philosophy lies the conviction that liberty depends on restraint of power. Only a state that confines itself to minimal functions, Nozick argued, can uphold the dignity, autonomy, and freedom of its citizens.

Nozick's Theory of Justice

Critique of Egalitarian Theories of Justice

In *Anarchy, State, and Utopia* (1974), Robert Nozick delivered a far-reaching critique of egalitarian theories of justice, which seek to achieve equality through state redistribution of resources. His main target was John Rawls's *A Theory of Justice* (1971), which defended government intervention to reduce inequality and promote fairness.

Nozick challenged the assumption that inequality is unjust in itself and therefore requires correction by state action. For him, justice does not lie in the outcome of distribution—how much each person ends up with—but in the process by which holdings are acquired and transferred. A distribution is just if property is obtained legitimately: through labor, voluntary exchange, or gifts. Equality of result, by contrast, has no independent moral claim.

From this perspective, egalitarian theories disregard the rights and dignity of individuals. Redistribution requires the state to seize resources from those who have rightfully earned them, undermining the principle that people are entitled to the fruits of their labor. For Nozick, such policies deny individuals the freedom to decide how their efforts and possessions will be used.

He further argued that enforced equality introduces a new injustice. It obliges some people to provide for others without their consent, thereby treating them as instruments for external purposes. Measures of this kind, he maintained, are not only morally indefensible but also corrosive of initiative, responsibility, and respect for individual rights. What is often called fairness thus becomes, in practice, a form of coercion that erodes the very liberty it claims to advance.

The Principle of Justice in Acquisition, Transfer, and Rectification of Property

Robert Nozick's entitlement theory of justice rests on three central principles: justice in acquisition, justice in transfer, and rectification of injustice. Together, they form a framework for judging the legitimacy of property holdings and economic arrangements.

1. **Justice in Acquisition**

   A holding is just if it is originally acquired without violating the rights of others. For Nozick, this could mean mixing one's labor with unowned resources, working honestly to create value, or receiving inheritance or gifts. So long as there is no force, fraud, or coercion, the individual has a rightful claim to what is obtained.

2. **Justice in Transfer**

   Holdings remain just when they are transferred voluntarily—through sale, gift, or contract—provided the exchange is consensual and free of deception or rights violations. Even if such transactions result in striking inequalities, the outcomes are legitimate because they arise from free choice. Nozick captured this principle in a single phrase: "Whatever arises from a just situation by just steps is itself just."

3. **Rectification of Injustice**

   Nozick acknowledged that history is not free of wrongful acquisitions and transfers. For this reason, he added a principle of rectification: when property has been taken through force, fraud, theft, or coercion, corrective measures are required to restore justice. This may involve returning stolen goods, compensating victims, or adopting other remedies. Nozick did not specify the exact procedures but insisted that historical wrongs must be addressed if present holdings are to be considered legitimate.

Taken together, these three principles yield a historical account of justice. What matters is not whether the present distribution appears equal or fair, but whether it can be traced through a chain of legitimate acquisitions and transfers—or corrected if injustice occurred along the way.

This approach placed Nozick in direct opposition to John Rawls and other egalitarian thinkers. Rawls evaluated justice by the fairness of social structures and distributive outcomes. Nozick argued instead that only the historical process counts: if holdings were acquired and transferred justly—or rectified when they were not—then whatever pattern results is just, however unequal it may appear.

Arguments Against the Welfare State

Critique of the Concept of "Social Justice"

Robert Nozick mounted a sustained critique of the idea of "social justice," which had become a central theme of twentieth-century political thought. He argued that the concept rests on a mistaken belief that the state has both the authority and the duty to engineer equality or redistribute wealth across society.

In his view, the rhetoric of social justice often masks practices in which the rights of some individuals are curtailed for the supposed benefit of others. Any coercive effort by government to equalize income or holdings, Nozick maintained, violates the basic right of individuals to control their property and the fruits of their labor.

Nozick insisted that justice must be judged by process rather than by pattern. What matters is how property is acquired and transferred—whether through labor, voluntary exchange, or gift—not the level of equality in the final distribution. State action aimed at enforcing distributive outcomes subverts these principles, eroding personal autonomy and undermining the integrity of free cooperation.

From this perspective, the welfare state is not merely inefficient but unjust in principle. By imposing redistribution, it reduces individuals to instruments for collective goals, denying them recognition as ends in themselves. For Nozick, a just order is one that safeguards voluntary transactions and respects the inviolability of property rights, thereby securing the conditions of genuine liberty.

The Problem of Violence Against the Individual in Redistributive Systems

One of the central themes of Robert Nozick's *Anarchy, State, and Utopia* (1974) is his claim that redistributive systems, by their very nature, erode individual freedom. For Nozick, any scheme of redistribution—whether taxation, subsidies, or welfare programs that take from some to benefit others—involves coercion.

He argued that redistribution requires the state to seize part of legitimately acquired holdings and transfer them elsewhere. Even when pursued for ends described as noble or socially beneficial, such practices amount, in his view, to a violation of personal rights. To compel one person to serve the needs of another is to reduce individuals to instruments, rather than recognizing them as ends in themselves.

Redistributive policies, therefore, always carry an element of compulsion: they deny people the authority to decide how to use the results of their own labor and possessions. For Nozick, this intrusion strikes at the core of personal autonomy.

The consequence is a transformation of the state's role. Instead of protecting liberty, government becomes the force that undermines it. Redistribution turns the guarantor of rights into their violator, eroding the very freedoms it is meant to secure.

The Influence and Criticism of Robert Nozick's Philosophy

Robert Nozick's *Anarchy, State, and Utopia* (1974) ignited one of the most far-reaching debates in twentieth-century political philosophy. The book divided scholars and intellectuals into sharply opposed camps. For some, it offered a groundbreaking defense of individual rights and a vision of liberty uncorrupted by state interference. For others, it represented a deeply troubling challenge to the ideals of equality, solidarity, and social responsibility on which modern democratic societies had come to rely.

According to his supporters, Nozick's arguments resonate even more strongly in the context of globalization, where excessive regulation and taxation can stifle innovation and hinder competitiveness. They claim that prosperity flourishes when governments limit themselves to protecting property rights, enforcing contracts, and preventing coercion. By removing political interference from markets and personal life, the minimal state creates the conditions in which entrepreneurship, creativity, and voluntary cooperation can thrive.

For these defenders, Nozick's work continues the classical liberal tradition of Locke and Mill but takes it to a radical conclusion: liberty is not compatible with redistributive justice. To them, justice is about respecting the outcomes of voluntary exchange, not about correcting inequalities after the fact. In this sense, Nozick's minimal state is not only a safeguard of freedom but also the foundation for a society built on initiative and personal responsibility.

The critics, however, were equally forceful in pointing to the real and pressing problems of modern societies. Poverty, systemic inequality, lack of access to healthcare and education—these are not merely unfortunate outcomes but deep structural issues that require active state intervention. From their perspective, justice cannot be reduced to the history of property acquisition and transfer; it must also be judged by whether institutions secure fairness, opportunity, and protection for the most vulnerable.

Rawls, in particular, offered the most systematic rebuttal. His *A Theory of Justice* (1971) had argued that rational individuals, behind a "veil of ignorance," would design a system that guaranteed basic liberties but also corrected inequalities that were not the result of personal choice. From this standpoint, Nozick's refusal to accept redistributive principles appeared blind to the moral arbitrariness of birth, talent, and social circumstances.

Critics also contended that Nozick's vision of liberty risks privileging the wealthy and powerful. Without redistributive mechanisms, they argued, inequalities in wealth and opportunity would expand unchecked, concentrating resources in the hands of a few while excluding weaker groups from full participation in society. Far from fostering liberty, such conditions could generate resentment, social fragmentation, and instability—eroding the very cohesion on which a political community depends.

Libertarian defenders responded by insisting that freedom itself is the highest social value, and that once the state begins to control distribution, there is no clear limit to its reach. For them, true liberty means freedom from coercion, bureaucratic control, and the burdens of taxation. In their view, redistribution not only undermines property rights but also diminishes personal responsibility, discourages initiative, and turns government into an arbiter of people's choices rather than a neutral protector of rights.

Even among his critics, however, there was recognition that Nozick had permanently altered the landscape of political debate. *Anarchy, State, and Utopia* forced philosophers to grapple with fundamental questions that remain unresolved: Where do the boundaries of state authority lie? At what point does government, designed to protect rights, begin to suppress them? Can a society dedicated to liberty also achieve fairness, and if so, by what means?

"*The philosopher places himself at the summit of thought; from there he views what the world has been and what it must become. He is not just an observer, he is an actor; he is an actor of the highest kind in a moral world because it is his opinion of what the world must become that regulates society.*"

— Claude-Henri de Rouvroy, comte de Saint-Simon
Science de l'homme: Physiologie religieuse (1858)

SECTION 3. TECHNOCRATIC STATE: GOVERNANCE BY TECHNICAL AND SCIENTIFIC EXPERTS

A **technocratic state** is a system of governance in which political power is exercised by experts who rely on scientific knowledge and rational methods to maximize economic and social efficiency.

In a technocratic model of governance, decisions are not shaped by elected politicians guided by ideology or shifting public opinion but by professionals who rely on scientific knowledge, technical expertise, and rational methods of management. The aim is to create a system capable of maximizing efficiency, ensuring stability, and addressing problems with precision.

In theory, technocracy seeks to minimize the influence of political conflict and subjective interests, replacing them with decision-making grounded in research and objective analysis. Advocates argue that the complexity of modern societies demands leadership by those with mastery of economics, engineering, public health, and other critical fields. Critics, however, warn that while technocracy promises effectiveness, it may undermine democratic accountability and concentrate power in the hands of a narrow group of "experts."

Key Features of a Technocratic State

1) Expert Governance

State institutions are led by professionals with advanced knowledge in science, technology, economics, or related domains. Leadership is determined not by party affiliation but by proven competence and expertise.

2) Rational and Scientific Decision-Making

Policy choices are grounded in research, data, and systematic analysis rather than in ideology, emotion, or political expediency.

3) Limitation of Political and Ideological Influence

Political parties and partisan disputes are deliberately constrained in order to reduce conflict and ensure that decisions remain focused on practical outcomes.

4) Emphasis on Efficiency and Stability

Governance prioritizes the effective use of resources and the pursuit of social and economic stability, with success measured by results, sustainability, and rational planning.

5) Long-Term Strategic Planning

Decisions are informed by forecasting and comprehensive research, with the goal of anticipating future challenges and avoiding crises or resource mismanagement.

6) Priority of Science and Innovation

Scientific progress and technological development are seen as the main drivers of advancement, supported through investment in education, research, and innovation to improve living standards and confront global challenges.

7) Meritocratic Selection of Leaders

Advancement to positions of authority is based on expertise, professional merit, and competence rather than on ideology, patronage, or personal ties.

8) Performance-Based Legitimacy

Political legitimacy rests not on ideology or electoral tradition but on the ability of leaders to deliver prosperity, solve problems effectively, and maintain stability.

Chapter 1. The Ideas of Henri de Saint-Simon
Early Nineteenth-Century Visions of Social and Industrial Organization

The French thinker Henri de Saint-Simon (1760–1825) lived a life marked by upheaval and by ideas that were far ahead of his time. Born into an old noble family, he experienced the convulsions of the French Revolution and the Napoleonic era, witnessing firsthand the transformation of society and the economy. These events led him to reflect on the changing nature of power in a new age.

Saint-Simon observed that the traditional aristocracy and the bureaucratic elites of the ancien régime were no longer capable of effective leadership in a world increasingly shaped by the Industrial Revolution and rapid scientific progress. Early nineteenth-century Europe was entering a new stage of development. James Watt's steam engine had already revolutionized production, factories were spreading across the continent, and mechanization was becoming the driving force of economic life. It was evident that in this dynamic and technologically complex environment, the old political class, trained in monarchical traditions and courtly intrigue, was ill-equipped to address urgent social and economic problems.

It was in this context that Saint-Simon articulated his most radical vision. He argued that political authority should not rest with aristocrats or traditional politicians but with those who possessed genuine knowledge and practical expertise: engineers, scientists, and industrial leaders. His reasoning was straightforward: if modern society depends increasingly on industry and technological progress, then those most familiar with these fields should guide its future.

Saint-Simon maintained that entrusting authority to scientists and technical experts would create a new form of governance founded on rational and objective principles. He envisioned a society in which decisions would no longer be shaped by political ambition or ideological conflict, but by scientific reasoning and the pursuit of practical benefit. In his view, industrialists, engineers, and scientists could rationally organize production, mitigate inequality and poverty, and secure a fairer distribution of resources.

After his death, these ideas inspired a group of followers who established the Saint-Simonian movement. They sought to put his principles into practice and played a significant role in shaping French economic and technical policy during the nineteenth century. Their influence reached beyond philosophy: they inspired major figures of industry and engineering, among them Ferdinand de Lesseps, the initiator of the Suez Canal project. In this way, Saint-Simon's thought left a lasting mark, linking utopian vision to concrete achievements in industrial and technological development.

Critique of Traditional Government by Saint-Simon

The Shortcomings of Aristocratic and Bureaucratic Systems

Henri de Saint-Simon offered a penetrating critique of the traditional forms of government that dominated France at the turn of the nineteenth century. In his view, both aristocracy and bureaucracy had become obsolete systems—incapable of responding to the demands of an age shaped by industry, science, and rapid social change.

Saint-Simon regarded the aristocratic order as not only ineffective but also deeply unjust. Built on hereditary privilege, the aristocracy lacked any real understanding of economics or technological progress. Its members held positions of influence by birth rather than by merit, and therefore could not rationally manage production, direct the economy, or address social needs. Detached from the realities of labor and industry, aristocrats were absorbed in courtly life and political intrigue. Decisions of state, he argued, were made to preserve the interests of a privileged few rather than to advance the welfare of society as a whole.

His criticism extended equally to the bureaucratic system. Bureaucracy, to Saint-Simon, embodied stagnation and excessive formalism. Instead of solving society's problems, it multiplied its own procedures and consolidated its own power. Officials were more concerned with preserving rules and routines than with promoting innovation or improving the lives of the population. As such, bureaucracy became an obstacle to progress, blocking the efficient use of resources and slowing economic development.

For Saint-Simon, aristocracy and bureaucracy alike represented unproductive strata that drained energy from society while contributing little to its advancement. Both lived, as he saw it, at the expense of those engaged in productive labor. To move beyond poverty, inequality, and economic backwardness, he insisted, society required a new foundation for governance—one built on knowledge, science, and technical expertise. Only by rejecting hereditary privilege and bureaucratic formalism could Europe enter an era of rational administration and genuine progress.

Causes of Social Injustice and Economic Inefficiency

Henri de Saint-Simon traced the roots of social injustice and economic stagnation to the structures of governance and social organization that prevailed in his time. He argued that these institutions were not merely outdated but actively obstructed the progress of society.

Foremost among the obstacles, in his view, was the dominance of the aristocracy. Economic management and the direction of production were left in the hands of men who inherited power rather than earned it. Lacking knowledge of industry or science, they squandered resources, presided over recurring crises, and perpetuated inequality from one generation to the next.

A second source of inefficiency, according to Saint-Simon, was the bureaucratic apparatus. Bureaucracy, he maintained, was preoccupied with preserving its own authority rather than solving urgent social and economic problems. Officials were absorbed in formalities, procedures, and rivalries for position, while decisions of real importance were delayed or avoided altogether. The result was a system that paralyzed initiative and obstructed development instead of advancing it.

Finally, Saint-Simon criticized the absence of clear and rational standards for assessing administrative competence. Appointments to positions of authority were made without regard for expertise or experience. This practice encouraged irresponsibility, nurtured corruption, and further deepened the injustices and inefficiencies that plagued society.

Technocratic Governance: Core Principles

Transfer of Power to Scientists, Engineers, and Industrialists

Henri de Saint-Simon proposed a radical rethinking of political authority: the state, he argued, should not be governed by aristocrats or career politicians but by the representatives of science and industry. In his vision, society would be directed by professionals—engineers, scientists, and industrial leaders—those whose daily work created the material and technological foundations of modern life.

For Saint-Simon, the knowledge and practical expertise of these specialists were infinitely more valuable for public administration than inherited titles, social standing, or political patronage. He believed that engineers, with their grasp of production processes, and scientists, with their command of technological innovation, could manage resources more rationally and organize production and distribution with far greater effectiveness than traditional rulers.

Entrusting power to such figures, he argued, would eliminate the waste and stagnation of aristocratic and bureaucratic systems. Decision-making would become more direct and efficient, no longer bogged down by courtly intrigues, endless procedures, or ideological quarrels. A government led by a technical elite could address social injustice, stimulate economic growth, and provide the structural reforms needed to move society out of poverty and inequality.

At the heart of Saint-Simon's proposal was the conviction that the progress of modern society depended on aligning political authority with scientific and industrial achievement. Only by replacing hereditary privilege with competence and expertise could a rational and progressive social order take shape.

Science and Technology as the Foundation of State Organization

Henri de Saint-Simon maintained that the foundations of the state should rest not on ideology or inherited authority but on scientific knowledge and technological progress. For him, only objective data, careful calculation, and the systematic application of innovation could provide the basis for sound and effective governance. Scientists and engineers, he believed, were better equipped than politicians or bureaucrats to recognize society's most pressing needs and to devise practical solutions. Unlike traditional administrators absorbed in ritual and procedure, technical experts were oriented toward tangible results and measurable improvements.

In Saint-Simon's technocratic vision, science was to become the guiding force of social organization. Its role extended beyond industry to encompass the management of production, the distribution of resources, and even the shaping of education and social policy. Rational planning and the disciplined use of technological advances, he argued, would reduce corruption, curb waste, and overcome inefficiency. In this way, scientific governance would open the path toward a more rational, equitable, and progressive social order.

The "Industrial Class" — A New Social Elite

Henri de Saint-Simon argued that modern society required the emergence of a new elite, not one defined by birth or political privilege, but by productive labor. He called this group the "industrial class," a term that, in his usage, extended far beyond factory owners or large-scale entrepreneurs. It included all who contributed directly to material and intellectual production—engineers, inventors, scientists, skilled professionals, and innovators.

In Saint-Simon's view, this class deserved to guide society because it embodied the qualities essential for progress. Its members possessed the technical knowledge and practical experience needed to organize production efficiently, to allocate resources wisely, and to promote steady economic growth. Unlike the hereditary aristocracy or political elites, whose authority rested on custom, power, or intrigue, the industrial class represented competence, creativity, and genuine contributions to social advancement. For Saint-Simon, elevating this class to leadership promised not only greater efficiency but also a more just alignment of authority with the forces driving modern civilization.

Economic Planning Based on Scientific Methods

Henri de Saint-Simon argued that economic life should be governed not by tradition or the fluctuations of the market, but by systematic and objective methods. He envisioned an economy organized through centralized planning, where production and distribution would be directed according to scientific principles and careful calculation. Specialists would be charged with assessing available resources, measuring the capacities of industries, and determining their most effective use.

Such an arrangement, he believed, would reduce waste, prevent misallocation, and guard against crises of overproduction or scarcity. In place of an unregulated market, vulnerable to speculation and chance, Saint-Simon imagined a managed economic order in which each sector operated under scientifically justified norms and coordinated planning.

At the same time, he emphasized that planning could not be rigid. For it to succeed, results had to be constantly evaluated and strategies revised in light of new data and discoveries. This principle of ongoing adjustment, he maintained, would make the system both stable and adaptable, allowing the economy to respond to changing conditions without losing efficiency or balance.

Efficient Distribution of Goods to Overcome Poverty and Social Inequality

Henri de Saint-Simon believed that poverty and inequality arose not from natural scarcity but from the inefficient and unjust distribution of resources. The solution, he argued, lay in reorganizing the economy so that all members of society could share fairly in the wealth created by collective labor.

For Saint-Simon, rational planning based on scientific methods would allow social needs to be anticipated in advance. Specialists, drawing on data and systematic analysis, could calculate the necessary quantities of goods and design effective means of their distribution. In this way, resources would reach those who required them most, rather than accumulating in the hands of a privileged minority. Such management, he believed, would diminish poverty and promote greater social balance.

At the heart of his vision was the principle that rewards should correspond to each person's productive contribution. Saint-Simon rejected simplistic egalitarianism, but he insisted that no one engaged in useful labor should be denied the essentials of life. Even those with modest means, under his system, were to be guaranteed the resources needed for dignity, self-development, and participation in society.

Comparison with Fourier and Owen

- **Charles Fourier** imagined cooperative communities, or *phalansteries*, in which work and goods were shared collectively. His concern was less with scientific planning than with transforming human passions and creating social harmony.

- **Robert Owen** sought to improve workers' conditions through experimental communities such as New Lanark, emphasizing education, moral reform, and philanthropy rather than systematic economic design.

- **Henri de Saint-Simon**, by contrast, placed science, technology, and expert planning at the center of reform. He believed that only a rationally managed economy, directed by those with knowledge of production and distribution, could ensure fairness by linking rewards to genuine contribution and by providing for the basic needs of all.

The Role of Industry and Scientific-Technical Progress in Achieving Social Well-Being

Henri de Saint-Simon was convinced that the future of modern society depended above all on the advance of industry and technical knowledge. He regarded industrial development not simply as an economic process but as the primary force capable of transforming daily life and raising the general standard of living.

In his account, the expansion of industrial production was inseparable from the growth of collective prosperity. New technologies increased productivity, enabling more goods to be produced at lower cost. This, in turn, created the possibility of securing essential resources for all citizens and of guaranteeing the material conditions necessary for a dignified existence.

For Saint-Simon, scientific and technological progress was the decisive weapon against poverty and inequality. The faster industry advanced, the more abundant the resources society could mobilize to address its urgent needs. Industry and innovation were not merely foundations of the economy but the levers with which to construct a more equitable and prosperous order.

Comparison with Marx's Perspective

- **Saint-Simon** envisioned industry and science as harmonizing forces. Their progress would expand resources, reduce scarcity, and allow society to overcome poverty and injustice. In this framework, industrial and scientific elites were destined to lead a rationally organized community.

- **Karl Marx**, by contrast, while recognizing the transformative power of industry, interpreted it primarily as a source of conflict. Industrial growth under capitalism, he argued, deepened exploitation, concentrating wealth in the hands of capitalists and worsening the condition of workers. Far from guaranteeing harmony, the advance of industry sharpened contradictions that could be resolved only through revolution and the abolition of class divisions.

Thus, although both thinkers placed industry and technology at the center of modern life, their conclusions diverged profoundly. Saint-Simon emphasized their capacity to create cohesion and social balance, while Marx stressed their role in generating conflict and driving the dynamics of historical change.

Saint-Simon's Views on Social Justice and Solidarity
Society as a Unified Productive Organism

Henri de Saint-Simon conceived of society as a living organism in which every part was connected to the others and performed an essential role. Within such an organism there could be no place for parasitic groups that survived by exploiting the labor of others. Instead, every member of society was expected to participate in productive activity and contribute to the advancement of the whole.

For Saint-Simon, social justice was possible only when society was understood as a unified body. Individuals needed to recognize their interdependence and to see that prosperity could not be achieved in isolation but only through cooperation and solidarity.

Rejecting the notion of class struggle, he envisioned a future in which antagonism between groups would give way to shared participation in common endeavors. What would bind citizens together was not coercion but the awareness that their personal success was inseparable from the success of the community.

In this ideal society, each person would hold a position within the collective chain of production and be rewarded according to their real contribution. Justice, in Saint-Simon's view, would not depend on arbitrary redistribution imposed from above but would emerge naturally from solidarity and from a common recognition of collective interests.

Rejection of Exploitation and Class Parasitism

Henri de Saint-Simon was a sharp critic of what he described as parasitic classes. By "parasites," he meant groups that consumed resources without producing anything of real value—above all the aristocracy and bureaucratic officials. These strata, in his view, embodied the injustice and inefficiency of the old order: they lived from the labor of others while contributing little or nothing to society's advancement.

Saint-Simon argued that a just community could not tolerate arrangements in which some individuals enjoyed privileges and wealth without making their own contribution. He envisioned a new social order in which every citizen would be tied to productive activity and where exploitation would become impossible. In such a system, privileges based on birth or position would vanish, replaced by recognition of work and innovation.

A New Morality: Productive Labor as the Highest Virtue

For Saint-Simon, the transformation of society required not only institutional change but also a profound moral reorientation. He called for a new ethical framework founded on respect for productive labor. In earlier societies, lineage, noble titles, or political power had commanded esteem; in the society of the future, the true measure of worth would be the contribution one made to the common good through work.

He insisted that respect and honor should belong to those who generated real value— engineers, workers, scientists, and entrepreneurs. These individuals, engaged in creating material and intellectual wealth, were to serve as moral exemplars and role models for the community. Productive labor, in this vision, was more than an economic necessity: it was a personal virtue and the highest social duty. Those who contributed to society deserved esteem and dignity; those who lived idly at the expense of others, by contrast, merited public disapproval.

Political Organization of the Technocratic State According to Saint-Simon

Structure of Power and System of Governance

Henri de Saint-Simon envisioned a model of governance radically different from the political institutions of his age. Instead of monarchs, aristocrats, or professional politicians, he proposed a system grounded in competence and guided by expertise. At its summit would stand a council of specialists—the most accomplished scientists, engineers, and industrial leaders—entrusted with directing the affairs of society.

In this technocratic order, responsibility would be divided according to fields of knowledge. Engineers and technical experts would oversee production and infrastructure; economists and industrial managers would regulate finance and the distribution of resources; scientists would set priorities for research, education, and technological development. Each domain would be managed by those best qualified to understand its problems and devise effective solutions.

Saint-Simon argued that such an arrangement would replace confusion and arbitrariness with order and efficiency. Decisions would rest on scientific reasoning and verifiable knowledge rather than political intrigue or inherited privilege.

Administration, in his vision, would no longer be a matter of patronage or factional struggle but a rational process directed by merit and professional competence.

The organization of power he imagined thus rejected hierarchies founded on birth or political favor. Authority would flow instead from expertise, experience, and proven ability. Saint-Simon believed that such a system could eliminate the waste and stagnation of traditional bureaucracy and, at the same time, foster greater public confidence in government, since leadership would be exercised by those whose qualifications were visible and whose service was demonstrably useful.

Forms of Rule and Their Basis of Legitimacy

Form of Rule	Basis of Legitimacy	Who Governs
Aristocracy	Birth, lineage	Hereditary nobility, aristocracy
Plutocracy	Wealth, property	Financial elite, oligarchs
Meritocracy	Merit, knowledge, competence	Scientists, experts, skilled professionals

This scheme illustrates the evolution of the foundations of power: from inherited privileges and wealth to the principle of personal merit and expertise. Saint-Simon's idea of the "industrial class" as a new social elite was one of the earliest formulations of the meritocratic principle, in which governance should be entrusted to those who create real value and possess competence.

The Principle of Selecting Leaders by Qualification and Ability

In Henri de Saint-Simon's vision of the technocratic state, the guiding rule of governance was the appointment of officials solely on the basis of competence. Every administrative post, he argued, should be filled only by those who had demonstrated knowledge and skill through their professional record. Scientists, engineers, and industrial leaders would assume responsibility only after careful assessment of their achievements and proven ability to solve practical problems.

Saint-Simon stressed that access to positions of influence must not depend on family background or inherited status. Any individual, regardless of origin, could rise to prominence if they possessed the necessary talents and expertise. Such a meritocratic system, he believed, would replace the favoritism and stagnation of traditional bureaucracy with integrity, efficiency, and genuine public service.

The Role of the State in Advancing Scientific Knowledge and Technology

For Saint-Simon, the state was not merely an organ of administration but a central force for promoting science and technological progress. He held that government bore the responsibility for supporting research and encouraging innovation, since without advances in knowledge, neither economic growth nor social improvement was possible.

The state, in his model, was to finance scientific inquiry, maintain institutions of learning, and ensure the broad dissemination of knowledge. Scientists and engineers were to be given the resources and infrastructure required to pursue their work effectively. Just as importantly, government had to foster close cooperation with industrialists and entrepreneurs, helping them transform discoveries into practical applications.

Education, too, was a cornerstone of his program. Saint-Simon argued that the state must build a system of instruction directed toward practical skills, technical expertise, and scientific reasoning. In his view, only an educated population could sustain prosperity and stability, since the progress of modern society depended on citizens prepared to participate productively in a world shaped by industry and science.

The Influence of Saint-Simon's Ideas

Impact on Socialist and Utopian Theories of the Nineteenth Century

Henri de Saint-Simon left a lasting mark on the rise of socialist and utopian thought in the nineteenth century. His vision of a society organized around rational administration, productive labor, and fair distribution inspired a wide range of philosophers and reformers.

His ideas resonated strongly with early socialists such as Charles Fourier and Robert Owen. Although each developed distinct models of social justice—Fourier through cooperative phalansteries and Owen through experimental communities—they shared Saint-Simon's critique of parasitic elites and his conviction that labor and knowledge must form the foundation of any just society.

The influence was even more pronounced among Saint-Simon's direct followers. The Saint-Simonians, led by Barthélemy Prosper Enfantin and Saint-Amand Bazard, transformed his teachings into a social movement aimed at putting theory into practice. Their campaigns spread his ideas across Europe, shaping the first socialist circles and inspiring numerous utopian experiments.

The Significance of Saint-Simonianism for the Development of Technocratic Concepts in the Twentieth Century

Saint-Simonianism also laid intellectual groundwork for the emergence of technocratic ideas in the twentieth century. Extending their master's legacy, the Saint-Simonians were among the first to formulate explicitly the principle that governance should rest on scientific knowledge and technical expertise rather than political ideology.

They proposed practical schemes of economic administration in which specialists and scientists assumed central responsibility for decision-making. By seeking to minimize political conflict and replace it with rational calculation, they anticipated the core doctrines of later technocratic movements.

This legacy became especially visible in the Technocracy Movement that arose in the United States during the 1930s. Advocates of this movement argued for managing the economy through scientific methods, engineering expertise, and precise calculation. In doing so, they echoed many of the principles first set out by Saint-Simon and carried forward by his disciples a century earlier.

Strengths and Weaknesses of the Technocratic Approach to Governance

Strengths

A central strength of technocracy lies in its reliance on expertise and empirical analysis. Authority is granted to professionals—engineers, scientists, economists—whose decisions are guided by evidence and measurable outcomes rather than partisan loyalties. A notable example is the Tennessee Valley Authority (TVA) during the New Deal. Staffed largely by engineers and planners, it spearheaded massive infrastructure projects that modernized the region, expanded access to electricity, and raised living standards within a relatively short time.

Another advantage is the ability of technocratic governance to channel scientific and technological progress directly into economic policy. In postwar France, the *Commissariat général du Plan*, dominated by economists and technical experts, coordinated national investment priorities. This "indicative planning" helped rebuild French industry and fuel the extraordinary growth of the *Trente Glorieuses* (1945–1975). By linking government closely with the scientific community, the French model demonstrated how technocratic planning could accelerate innovation, expand industrial capacity, and promote stability.

Technocracy also promises precision in the allocation of resources. Experts, in theory, can determine optimal distribution on the basis of production data, demographic forecasts, and technological capacity. The 1930s Technocracy Movement in the United States even proposed replacing money with "energy certificates" reflecting the actual energy required to produce goods—an ambitious attempt to eliminate inefficiency and waste in markets. Though never implemented, the idea illustrates the technocratic aspiration to govern the economy through quantifiable and scientific criteria.

Weaknesses

Yet the technocratic model faces significant limitations. One is the weak bond between experts and the public. Concentrating authority in the hands of specialists can sideline democratic participation. A striking example is the role of the European Central Bank during the Eurozone crisis. Acting on technical economic reasoning, the ECB imposed austerity measures on member states, but the social costs—unemployment, cuts in services, and deepening inequality—were largely ignored. The episode revealed how technocracy can drift toward a form of authoritarianism, privileging efficiency over accountability and fueling public distrust.

Another weakness stems from narrow specialization. Experts may excel within their own disciplines yet overlook the broader human and cultural dimensions of governance. Mid-twentieth-century urban planning offers a case in point. The modernist "towers in the park" housing projects, designed for efficiency, often failed socially: alienation, crime, and the breakdown of community life showed that technical solutions cannot replace sensitivity to human needs.

Finally, technocracy risks eroding civic participation altogether. Citizens may come to feel that decisions are made over their heads, without their input. In such circumstances, even effective policies can lose legitimacy, as people withdraw their trust from institutions that no longer reflect shared deliberation.

Chapter 2. Technocratic Governance Projects of the 20th Century

Visions of a Rationally Organized Society through Science, Technology, and Expert Management

The twentieth century witnessed both extraordinary technological progress and profound social disruption. Industrialization, new scientific discoveries, and mass production transformed economies and daily life, yet traditional political systems often proved unable to cope with the economic and social upheavals of the age.

Against this backdrop, an older idea re-emerged with renewed force: the conviction that governance should be entrusted to professionals with technical expertise. The urgency of this proposal became especially clear during the Great Depression, when conventional political leadership seemed powerless in the face of collapsing markets and soaring unemployment.

It was in this context that the Technocracy Movement arose in the United States. Its advocates proposed that political institutions be replaced by rule through experts—engineers, scientists, and planners—on the grounds that only rational, scientific methods could restore order to an economy in crisis. Among their most striking innovations was the idea of managing production and distribution through "energy accounting," in which economic value would be measured not by money but by the energy required to produce goods and services.

Public enthusiasm for technocratic solutions was fueled by both the depth of the crisis and widespread trust in science and technology. Many believed that technical expertise promised greater objectivity than partisan compromise, and that specialists could secure prosperity and fairness more effectively than politicians.

The Technocracy Movement in the United States in the 1930s
Origins and Development

The movement took shape in the early 1930s, as engineers and scientists sought to offer an alternative to a failing political and economic order. Its central figure was Howard Scott (1890–1970), an American engineer who argued that social and economic problems were essentially technical in nature and could only be resolved by applying precise methods of calculation and analysis.

Scott founded Technocracy Inc., an organization that quickly gained national attention. Its program called for the replacement of money and markets with an energy-based economy, directed by engineers and technical experts. Under this system, production and distribution would be coordinated on scientific principles, ensuring efficiency and equity.

At its height in the mid-1930s, Technocracy Inc. claimed hundreds of thousands of members and organized large public rallies. Yet by the end of the decade, enthusiasm declined, weakened by Scott's controversial leadership style, internal organizational problems, and the relative success of Franklin Roosevelt's New Deal in reviving the American economy.

Despite its decline, the movement left a durable legacy. Its emphasis on expert governance, rational planning, and resource-based economics reappeared in later debates on technocracy, economic planning, and sustainable development throughout the twentieth century.

Technocratic Critique of the Political and Economic Crisis of the Great Depression

Supporters of technocracy interpreted the Great Depression not as the failure of individual leaders but as evidence of the structural weaknesses of capitalism and the political system. They maintained that markets and governments alike were dominated by ideology, partisanship, and private interests, leaving them incapable of resolving mass unemployment and economic stagnation.

Howard Scott and his followers argued that politicians and financiers lacked the technical competence to stabilize the economy. Emergency measures such as deficit spending and financial relief programs were dismissed as temporary fixes that aggravated social tensions without addressing root causes.

In place of piecemeal political remedies, the technocrats proposed a comprehensive scientific approach. Economic life, they argued, should be reorganized according to objective measurement, statistical forecasting, and systemic analysis of resources. Central to this vision was Scott's concept of energy accounting, which would plan production and distribution on the basis of energy and material inputs. In his view, such rational management could eliminate the cyclical crises of capitalism, guarantee efficient resource use, and provide the foundation for long-term stability and prosperity.

Core Principles of American "Technocracy"

Replacing Politicians with Technocratic Specialists

One of the defining principles of the American Technocracy Movement was the call to replace political leaders entirely with professionals trained in science and engineering. Howard Scott and his followers argued that the failures of politicians—driven by ideology, party loyalty, and personal ambition—had been exposed during the Great Depression. Only experts capable of applying scientific knowledge and technical skill, they believed, could guide society out of crisis and ensure its long-term stability.

In this envisioned system, authority would no longer derive from elections, popularity, or partisan affiliation. Instead, positions of responsibility would be assigned on the basis of competence, proven expertise, and scientific qualifications. By shifting the basis of governance from politics to knowledge, the technocrats sought to eliminate the corruption, waste, and inefficiency that they associated with party competition and electoral bargaining.

This principle carried radical implications: the abolition of political parties, the end of ideological struggle, and the creation of an administrative order directed solely by experts. Decisions would rest on measurable data, technical analysis, and scientifically justified solutions. In removing politics from governance, the movement hoped to construct a system that prioritized efficiency and objectivity, while offering the prospect of long-term social and economic stability.

Managing the Economy through an Energy Balance

One of the most distinctive and radical proposals of the American Technocracy Movement was the restructuring of the economy around the principle of energy accounting. Howard Scott and his associates argued that the monetary system, with its reliance on credit, speculation, and fluctuating financial indicators, was no longer adequate for a modern industrial society. They envisioned replacing it with a single, universal measure: the energy required to produce goods and services.

In this model, every product would be valued not in dollars but in physical units such as kilowatt-hours. By calculating costs in terms of energy consumption, technocrats believed they could reveal the real, measurable value of production processes. This method, they argued, would allow the economy to be managed with maximum efficiency, reducing waste, avoiding overproduction, and aligning output directly with available resources.

The plan required continuous monitoring of the nation's total energy flows—both inputs and outputs. With this information, technical experts could identify the industries that operated most efficiently, detect sectors that drained resources, and redirect investment accordingly. Energy-intensive industries with little productive yield would be restructured or phased out, while efficient systems would receive priority.

Scott insisted that only such a system could ensure long-term stability. By tying economic value to a universal and quantifiable standard, technocracy promised to replace the volatility of markets with a rational system of production and distribution rooted in scientific calculation.

Rational Planning and Resource Distribution

The advocates of the American Technocracy Movement argued that a market economy left to its own devices produced waste, volatility, and recurrent crises. As an alternative, they proposed a system of centralized planning, directed by technical experts and grounded in scientific calculation, that would transform economic life into a coordinated mechanism.

In this model, the economy would be organized much like a well-calibrated system, with every resource used as efficiently as possible. The first task, technocrats maintained, was to determine in advance the real needs of society, the productive capacities of industry, and the resources available. Production processes would then be designed to minimize inputs and maximize outputs, creating the highest possible level of efficiency.

Distribution, too, was to follow scientific standards rather than market competition or profit-driven incentives. Specialists envisioned establishing precise benchmarks for essential goods—food, energy, housing, and other necessities—so that each citizen would be assured access to the means of a decent life.

Howard Scott and his followers insisted that only such rational and systematic planning could guarantee long-term stability. In their view, technocracy alone could shield society from collapse and create a fairer order in which all members had secure access to essential resources. By replacing speculation and uncertainty with scientific oversight, they sought to construct an economy where prosperity rested not on chance or profit but on knowledge, calculation, and deliberate design.

Technocratic Ideas in 20th-Century Europe

Examples of Technocratic Projects and Concepts in European Countries

In the twentieth century, technocratic ideas took root in Europe as well as in the United States. Faced with recurrent crises and the limits of partisan politics, many European thinkers and policymakers began to explore how professional expertise and technical knowledge might serve as foundations for governance.

One early example was the British chemist and economist Frederick Soddy, awarded the Nobel Prize in Chemistry in 1921. Soddy criticized the monetary system for its detachment from real resources and argued for a currency linked to physical measures of energy. His proposals anticipated the "energy accounting" advocated by American technocrats and later influenced debates on ecological economics and sustainability.

During the 1940s, wartime France provided another, if unusual, instance of technocratic experimentation. Under the Vichy regime, elements of economic management were transferred to engineers and technical specialists as part of efforts at national mobilization. Although these measures did not create a lasting technocratic system, they illustrate how, under conditions of crisis, political leaders turned to technical expertise as a potential alternative to traditional administration.

After 1945, technocratic concepts gained new significance in the construction of supranational European institutions. The European Coal and Steel Community (ECSC, 1951) and later the European Economic Community (EEC, 1957) embodied a new model of governance: decision-making entrusted to experts, administrators, and economists rather than to party politicians. The European Commission in particular has often been described as a technocratic body, deriving legitimacy less from electoral politics than from professional competence, economic analysis, and policy outcomes.

Taken together, these examples reveal the diversity of European technocratic experiments—from Soddy's intellectual proposals, to temporary wartime structures, to enduring supranational institutions. Throughout the twentieth century, Europe became not only a stage for theoretical reflection on technocracy but also a laboratory for its practical and institutional application.

The Influence of Technocracy on Postwar Economic Planning

After the Second World War, European governments confronted the immense challenge of reconstruction. In this setting, technocratic ideas shaped many of the strategies adopted for economic recovery and modernization.

The clearest case was France, where the Monnet Plan of the late 1940s introduced a framework of centralized planning. Designed under the leadership of Jean Monnet, the plan relied on teams of specialists who drafted detailed programs for industrial recovery and resource allocation. Decisions were guided by economic indicators and statistical forecasts rather than by partisan debate. This approach provided France with a coherent structure for modernization and proved crucial in stabilizing its economy during the early years of rebuilding.

Britain, though less centralized, also incorporated technocratic methods. The government turned to professional economists, engineers, and advisory committees to design policies for energy, housing, and industrial reform. Their evidence-based recommendations gave postwar Britain practical tools for overcoming shortages, improving efficiency, and accelerating reconstruction.

Germany took a somewhat different course, emphasizing market mechanisms while still applying principles of rational calculation. Under Ludwig Erhard—an economist who later became Chancellor—policy combined empirical analysis with the principles of the "social market economy." Reliance on data, research, and systematic planning contributed directly to the rapid recovery celebrated as the *Wirtschaftswunder*, or German economic miracle.

These examples illustrate that while technocracy in its pure form was never fully realized, its influence was unmistakable. Expert-led planning and reliance on technical knowledge became integral to postwar strategies across Europe. They offered governments tools to stabilize economies, allocate resources more effectively, and sustain the rapid growth that defined the first decades of recovery.

Technocracy and the Soviet Union

The Soviet Union never described itself as a technocracy, yet many features of its governance resembled technocratic principles. The centrally planned economy rested on scientific forecasting, technical expertise, and hierarchical coordination, with engineers and specialists occupying decisive positions at nearly every level of management.

Central planning was overseen by Gosplan and a network of branch ministries, which drafted annual and multi-year plans. Their work depended on statistical reporting, resource forecasts, and technical assessments prepared by economists, scientists, and engineers. In practice, specialists defined production targets, estimated resource requirements, and set priorities for technological development.

Technical cadres also played a prominent role at the enterprise level. Factory directors, chief engineers, designers, and research institute leaders exercised substantial authority, making key operational decisions on the basis of their training and experience. Their influence was especially visible during the industrialization drives of the 1930s, when engineers and planners designed the rapid expansion of heavy industry.

A distinctly technocratic element of the Soviet model was the system of Scientific and Technical Councils (*Nauchno-Tekhnicheskiye Sovety*, NTS). Established within ministries, enterprises, design bureaus, and research institutes, these councils produced recommendations for modernization, innovation, and the adoption of new technologies. They brought together leading engineers, economists, and scientists, who engaged in detailed analyses of production data, efficiency, and technical performance.

The role of such councils grew during the so-called scientific and technological revolution of the 1960s. The Soviet leadership proclaimed a course toward integrating advanced scientific methods into economic management. New initiatives aimed to refine planning techniques, expand computer-based calculations, and apply cybernetics to improve forecasting. Among the most ambitious projects was the OGAS program (National Automated System for Computation and Information Processing), designed to create a nationwide computer network for planning optimization. Although only partially realized, it remains a striking example of technocratic aspiration.

Yet Soviet technocracy always faced decisive limits. Despite the prominence of technical experts, ultimate authority rested with the Communist Party. Political and ideological priorities often overrode technical rationality, distorting production targets, misallocating resources, and undermining efficiency.

In this sense, the Soviet system incorporated many elements of technocratic governance—centralized planning, reliance on technical cadres, and institutionalized expert councils—without ever becoming a purely technocratic order. The constant tension between expertise and political control remained one of the defining features of the Soviet economic model.

Reasons for the Failures of Technocratic Projects

A major obstacle to the spread of technocracy was the resistance of established political elites. Politicians and bureaucrats were rarely willing to surrender authority to engineers or scientific specialists. This tension produced repeated clashes between entrenched interests and reform-minded technocrats. In the United States, for instance, the Technocracy Movement of the 1930s attracted attention with its plan for energy accounting, but because the proposal threatened the foundations of existing financial and political institutions, the movement quickly lost momentum and remained marginal.

A second difficulty lay in the limits of a purely technical approach to governance. Engineers and economists often reduced decision-making to statistics and calculations, overlooking social, cultural, and psychological realities. Mid-twentieth-century housing projects illustrate this weakness. Although efficient on paper, many modernist "towers in the park" were designed without input from residents and eventually bred alienation, unrest, and the erosion of community life.

Technocracy also faced resistance because many of its reforms were perceived as too radical. Proposals to abolish money, replace markets with energy accounting, or impose fixed norms of consumption required dismantling familiar systems of economic life. To ordinary citizens, such measures appeared impractical or even threatening. As a result, the broader public tended to favor gradual reforms rather than wholesale experiments in social engineering.

Finally, over-centralization frequently undermined technocratic experiments in practice. In highly regulated systems, adaptability was often sacrificed to rigid structures. The Soviet Union demonstrates this paradox. Although engineers, planners, and scientific councils were deeply involved in economic management, the inflexibility of central planning prevented rapid responses to unexpected circumstances. The outcome was inefficiency, misallocation, and eventual stagnation.

Together, these difficulties explain why technocracy, though influential in shaping twentieth-century debates about governance, was rarely implemented in its pure form. Instead, elements of expert administration were selectively incorporated into political and economic systems, while the vision of rule by specialists remained largely a theoretical ideal.

The Legacy of 20th-Century Technocratic Ideas

The Influence of Technocratic Concepts on Contemporary Economy and Politics

Although no technocratic blueprint of the twentieth century was ever realized in its entirety, the influence of technocratic thinking has been unmistakable in contemporary governance and economic management. In the modern world, specialists are routinely involved in policymaking, especially in moments of crisis when technical knowledge and professional expertise become essential for effective decision-making.

The legacy of technocracy is particularly visible in major international economic institutions. The International Monetary Fund (IMF), the World Bank, and the European Central Bank (ECB) all ground their work in economic modeling, statistical analysis, and technical expertise rather than in party politics or electoral competition. Their authority rests less on popular mandate than on professional competence and the claim to impartial judgment—an arrangement that reflects, in modified form, the technocratic principle of governance by experts.

The Use of Technocratic Methods in Modern Governance

Modern governance often integrates technocratic features into its decision-making structures. Governments rely on expert commissions, advisory councils, and independent panels to address complex economic and social challenges that exceed the capacity of ordinary partisan politics.

In times of crisis, entire technocratic governments have sometimes been appointed. A well-known example is Italy in 2011, when economist Mario Monti was named prime minister to restore market confidence and introduce fiscal reforms at the height of the Eurozone crisis. His appointment reflected the belief that expert-led administrations could provide stability and credibility when traditional political leadership seemed paralyzed.

Beyond such exceptional cases, many policy domains are routinely shaped by technical expertise. Central banking, for instance, has long been entrusted to independent authorities whose legitimacy rests on economic competence rather than electoral support. Infrastructure development and climate policy likewise depend heavily on scientific analysis, engineering expertise, and long-term planning. In these areas, technocratic methods supplement the political process by grounding decisions in specialized knowledge and empirical data.

Lessons from 20th-Century Technocratic Experiments

The technocratic experiments of the twentieth century yielded important insights into both the promise and the limitations of governance grounded solely in technical and scientific principles.

On the positive side, they demonstrated that expertise and systematic analysis can improve the precision of decision-making. By emphasizing data, measurement, and professional competence, technocratic approaches highlighted the indispensable role of specialized knowledge in addressing complex social and economic problems.

Yet these same experiments also exposed inherent weaknesses. Technical calculation alone could not account for the full complexity of human societies. Effective governance requires sensitivity to psychology, culture, and social relations—dimensions often overlooked by technocratic systems. When these factors were neglected, policies lost effectiveness and citizens' confidence in institutions diminished. In addition, many technocratic projects suffered from excessive centralization. Over time, this concentration of authority fostered bureaucratic rigidity and limited the capacity of institutions to adapt to unexpected challenges.

The Core Legacy of 20th-Century Technocracy

The history of technocracy in the twentieth century underscores a lasting lesson: expertise and scientific methods must be integrated with democratic institutions and responsiveness to social needs. Stability and adaptability in modern governance depend on achieving this balance between technical rationality and democratic legitimacy.

The experience of the century showed that technical expertise, while indispensable, cannot by itself resolve the complexities of social life. Economic models, forecasts, and engineering schemes may optimize production or resource flows, but without public participation and legitimacy such measures often fail to gain acceptance or to endure. Projects that treated society as a system to be managed from above frequently met resistance, as citizens rejected policies detached from their everyday concerns.

At the same time, democratic systems themselves proved insufficient without expert guidance. Electoral politics and popular will are essential for legitimacy, yet they cannot alone address problems that are technical in nature—financial crises, environmental threats, or the regulation of new technologies. Where expert knowledge was combined with democratic oversight, however, institutions became more resilient, policies more effective, and public trust more secure.

The enduring legacy of technocracy lies not in the attempt to replace politics with science, but in demonstrating that governance requires both. Expertise brings precision, innovation, and foresight; democracy provides accountability, fairness, and consent. Together they form a model of governance better equipped to meet the demands of modern societies—complex, dynamic, and interdependent.

"Care flows naturally if the self is widened and deepened so that protection of free nature is felt and conceived of as protection of our very selves. We must find and develop therapies which heal our relations with the widest community, that of all living beings."

— Arne Næss
Ecology, Community and Lifestyle: Outline of an Ecosophy (1989)

SECTION 4. ECOLOGICAL STATE: POLITICAL SYSTEM PRIORITIZING ENVIRONMENTAL SUSTAINABILITY

> An **Ecological State (Ecocracy)** is a model of governance in which the protection of the environment and the sustainable use of natural resources are treated as top priorities, and all political and economic decisions are made with explicit consideration of their ecological consequences.

An ecological state, or *ecocracy*, represents a model of governance in which environmental protection becomes the guiding principle of public life. In such a system, the preservation of natural resources and ecological balance is not simply one goal among others but the foundation upon which political authority and economic policy must be built. The premise of ecocracy is that the survival and well-being of society are inseparable from the health of the environment, and that long-term prosperity is possible only through the responsible management of natural systems.

The central idea is to secure development that meets present needs while safeguarding the ability of future generations to meet theirs. This principle requires governments to think in terms of decades rather than election cycles, often rejecting short-term economic benefits in favor of ecological stability and resilience.

In an ecological state, political and economic decisions are subject to obligatory environmental review. State projects, industrial strategies, and infrastructure initiatives are assessed according to their impact on air and water quality, biodiversity, soil health, and climate stability. Projects judged incompatible with ecological sustainability must be redesigned or abandoned, regardless of their immediate financial or political appeal.

Institutions of ecocracy assume responsibility for maintaining ecological systems, limiting pollution, and defending the climate. Regulations are directed toward reducing harmful emissions, easing pressure on finite resources, and accelerating the shift to renewable energy. Beyond legal restrictions, however, the ecological state also promotes cultural change: it seeks to encourage sustainable business practices, reshape patterns of consumption, and cultivate a civic ethic of responsibility toward nature. In this sense, ecocracy is not merely a regulatory framework but a vision of society organized around ecological consciousness.

Examples of Ecological State (Ecocracy) Concepts
The Concept of Deep Ecology by Arne Naess

The idea of an *ecological state (ecocracy)* can be illustrated through the philosophy of **deep ecology**, developed by the Norwegian philosopher **Arne Naess (1912–2009)**, one of the most influential ecological thinkers of the 20th century. Naess first introduced the term *deep ecology* in his 1973 article *"The Shallow and the Deep, Long-Range Ecology Movement"*, published in the journal *Inquiry*. In this pioneering work, he distinguished between *shallow ecology*, which seeks to protect the environment primarily for human benefit, and *deep ecology*, which emphasizes the intrinsic value of all living beings and the integrity of ecosystems.

Biographical and Philosophical Background

Arne Naess (1912–2009) was not only a professional philosopher but also a mountaineer, activist, and one of the most influential figures in twentieth-century environmental thought. He studied philosophy, mathematics, and astronomy at the University of Oslo and completed his doctorate in 1936 with a dissertation on the philosophy of knowledge. In 1939, at only 27, he became the youngest professor in the university's history.

Naess was deeply shaped by two intellectual traditions. From Baruch Spinoza he adopted a vision of the world as a single, interconnected substance, rejecting any radical separation between humanity and nature. From Buddhism he drew the idea of interdependence, compassion, and nonviolence, which reinforced his conviction that humans cannot flourish in isolation from other forms of life. These influences coalesced in his notion of *Self-realization*—the expansion of the self beyond the individual ego to embrace the broader ecological whole. For Naess, genuine human fulfillment meant recognizing one's place within the biosphere rather than above it.

His personal life embodied his philosophy. Much of his time was spent at Tvergastein, a remote cabin high in the Norwegian mountains. There he lived simply, close to nature, writing, climbing, and reflecting on ecological issues. This setting became both a literal and symbolic base for his ecological philosophy: the union of intellectual thought with direct experience of the natural world.

Principles of Deep Ecology

Naess argued that the dominant worldview of modern civilization is anthropocentrism—the belief that humans stand at the center of existence and are entitled to exploit nature. Deep ecology, by contrast, called for a radical reorientation: the recognition that all beings possess intrinsic value regardless of their utility to humans.

In *Ecology, Community and Lifestyle* (1989), Naess articulated eight principles of deep ecology, which he and George Sessions had earlier summarized as the Platform of Deep Ecology:

1. The right to flourish belongs not only to humans but to all living beings.
2. The richness and diversity of life have value in themselves, independent of human use.
3. Humans have no right to reduce this richness except to meet vital needs.
4. Human interference in nature is already excessive and threatens the biosphere.
5. Avoiding ecological catastrophe requires deep, systemic changes in economics, politics, technology, and culture.
6. The goal of such change must be to build societies living in partnership with nature, not in domination over it.
7. This transformation calls for moving away from endless economic growth toward sustainable lifestyles that meet essential needs.

8. Every individual has a moral responsibility to act, personally and collectively, to realize these changes.

These principles were not meant as rigid laws but as an ethical platform that individuals, movements, and governments could adopt and adapt.

Comparative Context

Naess distinguished deep ecology from what he called "shallow ecology." The latter focused on pollution control, conservation, and resource management, but remained anthropocentric—it aimed to protect the environment only for the sake of human well-being. Deep ecology, in contrast, demanded an ethical and ontological shift: to see all forms of life as possessing inherent worth.

Other ecological movements of the late twentieth century offered related but distinct approaches. **Ecofeminism** emphasized the links between the domination of women and the domination of nature, highlighting structures of patriarchy. **Ecosocialism** combined Marxist critiques of capitalism with environmental concerns, pointing to the destructive logic of profit and exploitation. Naess's philosophy differed in that it avoided direct political alignment, focusing instead on ethics, ontology, and the philosophy of life.

Political Influence and Criticism

During the 1980s and 1990s, deep ecology influenced global environmental discourse. Organizations such as Greenpeace and Friends of the Earth adopted its language of intrinsic value and biospheric equality. In Scandinavia, especially in Norway, its ideas informed legal frameworks for biodiversity protection and long-term sustainability policies.

Yet Naess's ideas also provoked debate. Critics argued that granting "equal rights" to microbes, plants, and humans was philosophically attractive but politically impractical: how, for example, should policymakers weigh the rights of bacteria against human health? Others faulted deep ecology for being too abstract, focusing on metaphysical ideas of selfhood while paying less attention to issues of social justice, poverty, or inequality.

Naess responded by clarifying that deep ecology was not about equating all species in every circumstance but about reshaping human consciousness and values. For him, the point was to overcome arrogance, to recognize interdependence, and to orient decisions toward respect for life as a whole.

Legacy

The enduring legacy of Arne Naess lies in his insistence that ecology must be the foundation of politics and economics, not a secondary concern. He demonstrated this not only through philosophy but also through personal example: living simply, engaging in activism, and integrating thought with practice.

Today, his influence can be seen in the ethical language of the United Nations' sustainable development goals, in international biodiversity strategies, and in the arguments of contemporary climate movements such as Extinction Rebellion and

Fridays for Future. His integration of philosophy, activism, and everyday life continues to shape debates in environmental ethics, political ecology, and global sustainability.

Naess's deep ecology remains both a challenge and an inspiration: a challenge to anthropocentrism and consumerism, and an inspiration for those seeking a more holistic and respectful relationship between humanity and the biosphere.

The Politics of European Green Parties

European Green parties appeared in the 1970s and 1980s, first in West Germany, France, and Scandinavia. The German Greens (*Die Grünen*) entered the Bundestag in 1983, marking the institutional breakthrough of ecological politics in Europe.

Since then, Green parties have influenced environmental law, energy policy, and the European Union's agenda. Their ideas are reflected in Germany's *Energiewende* and in the EU's *European Green Deal*, both aimed at climate neutrality and expansion of renewable energy.

Criticism has accompanied these successes. Opponents point to higher energy costs, disputes over agricultural reforms, and the social effects of phasing out fossil fuels. Conservatives and social democrats often describe Green policies as economically unrealistic or socially unfair.

Major Criticisms of the Greens

1. Economic Unrealism and Rising Costs

The most persistent charge against the Greens is economic naïveté. In Germany, their campaign to shut down nuclear power left the country scrambling for coal and costly renewables. The result: higher energy bills and rising doubts about energy security. In France, Greens pushed to curtail nuclear power—one of the country's strongest low-carbon assets—prompting critics to accuse them of undermining both the economy and the climate fight in a single stroke.

2. Radicalism and Idealism

Greens often lean into proposals that electrify activists but alarm the wider public. Calls for an immediate ban on combustion engines, shutting all coal mines within a handful of years, or abandoning short-haul flights altogether may sound visionary in speeches. Yet to many voters they come across as utopian slogans detached from everyday reality. This tension is their double-edged sword: a magnet for young supporters, but a repellent for moderates.

3. Blindness to Social Costs

Transitioning to a green economy hits hardest in regions built on coal and heavy industry—Poland's mining towns, Germany's Ruhr Valley, Northern France's industrial belt. For many workers, Green promises translate into pink slips. Critics argue that the party speaks endlessly of wind turbines and solar panels but rarely delivers serious retraining programs or long-term job security. This fuels the image of the Greens as the party of urban elites—students, academics, and professionals—while industrial workers are left to fend for themselves.

4. Implementation Gaps and Bureaucratic Deadlock

Even when Greens hold power, their ambitious plans often stall. In Germany, Austria, and Finland, coalition politics and layers of regulation bog down renewable energy projects. Germany's wind power expansion, despite all the speeches, slowed to a crawl because of local resistance and endless lawsuits. The criticism here is simple: the Greens are brilliant at writing programs, but far less successful at turning them into reality.

5. Symbolic Politics

Opponents mock the Greens for chasing headlines with low-impact gestures. Bans on plastic straws, campaigns for "vegan days" in school cafeterias—these measures grab attention but barely dent the climate crisis. Meanwhile, the hard questions of transport, industry, and energy remain unresolved. For critics, this is the Greens' weak spot: substituting symbolism for systemic reform.

6. Internal Divisions

The Greens themselves are split. In Germany, the clash between the pragmatic *Realos* and the uncompromising *Fundis* is legendary. These rifts sap party unity and complicate governance, with the result that Greens often undermine themselves before their opponents even have to.

Beyond specific policies, the Greens face a deeper credibility crisis. They promise sweeping change, but coalition compromises repeatedly blunt their agenda. Their policies, such as carbon and fuel taxes, often land hardest on low-income households, reinforcing the charge that Greens preach climate justice while practicing social injustice. The image of the Greens as the voice of a new urban elite—affluent, well-educated, clustered in big cities—has become a staple of populist attacks. The "Yellow Vests" in France turned fuel taxes into a revolt not just against Emmanuel Macron but against the whole ecological agenda, casting Green policies as punitive and elitist.

The paradox of the Greens is clear: they have pushed climate and environmental issues into the political mainstream, but they remain haunted by charges of economic unreality, social blindness, and symbolic posturing. Unless they can marry ecological ambition with social fairness and political realism, their vision of an ecological state will remain more of a manifesto than a working model of governance.

"If you want a natively digital nation, or a state, or a city, or whatever, my message today is you actually need to be bold enough to create some new institutions; institutions that are of the internet, not on the internet."

— Tom Loosemore
keynote at *Mind the Product London* (2015)

SECTION 5. DIGITAL STATE: GOVERNANCE SUPPORTED BY DIGITAL INFRASTRUCTURE AND TECHNOLOGY

> A **digital state** is a model of governance in which political administration, public management, and the delivery of services are carried out primarily through digital technologies, including electronic platforms, data-driven decision-making, and online citizen participation, with the aim of increasing efficiency, transparency, and accessibility of government functions.

In the digital state, information systems and online platforms form the backbone of political and social organization, reshaping how power is exercised and decisions are made.

A defining element of this model is the use of digital platforms to implement forms of direct democracy. Citizens can participate in real-time debates, cast votes on specific issues, and take part in regular online referendums. Over time, representative structures may be partly displaced as more decisions are made through direct citizen input. Estonia's experiments with nationwide digital voting and blockchain-secured registries illustrate how such practices can function in practice, while Switzerland's referendums demonstrate the cultural appeal of constant citizen engagement.

Transparency is another cornerstone. Government spending, legislative initiatives, and administrative outcomes are published in open databases, accessible to all. Citizens are not only able to follow the work of institutions but can provide oversight through digital feedback tools and participatory platforms.

By reducing the gap between state and society, the digital state promises greater openness and accountability. Advocates argue that online systems could cut bureaucratic delays and reduce opportunities for corruption. Critics, however, warn of new vulnerabilities: cybersecurity risks, unequal access for less digitally literate populations, and the potential for manipulation of online debates.

Thus, while the digital state offers the possibility of faster, more participatory, and more transparent governance, its success depends on balancing efficiency with security, inclusion, and trust.

Strengths of the Digital State

1. Transparency in Governance

Digital registers and open-access platforms make government actions visible to the public. Online budgets, legislative databases, and decision tracking reduce opportunities for corruption and strengthen trust.

2. Direct Democracy and Civic Participation

Electronic voting, online consultations, and digital referendums expand citizen involvement. These tools supplement representative institutions and widen the scope of civic engagement.

3. Speed and Administrative Efficiency

Electronic platforms simplify interaction with state institutions. Digital procedures reduce paperwork, cut waiting times, and improve communication between citizens and authorities.

4. Accessibility and Convenience

Citizens can use public services at any time and from any location with internet access. The effectiveness of this advantage depends on bridging the digital divide and ensuring sufficient digital literacy.

5. Cost Reduction

Automation and digital workflows reduce administrative and operational expenses, allowing resources to be redirected to other areas. These long-term savings must be balanced against the high initial investment in infrastructure and training.

6. Public Oversight and Accountability

Feedback systems, petition platforms, and open data repositories enable citizens to monitor spending, laws, and national projects. Misuse or inefficiency can be detected quickly, enhancing accountability.

7. Flexibility and Adaptability

Digital systems can be updated and reconfigured rapidly. This makes governance more responsive to new social, economic, and technological challenges than traditional bureaucratic structures.

8. Data-Driven Policy

Large-scale data collection and analysis improve forecasting and decision-making. Policies can be adjusted quickly in response to real-time information, making governance more precise.

9. Personalization of Services

Digital systems allow the state to tailor services to individual needs—for example, automatically identifying eligibility for benefits or matching healthcare and educational support to personal circumstances.

10. Integration Across Agencies

Shared digital platforms connect different government departments, reducing duplication and removing informational barriers. This creates a more coherent and unified system of public administration.

11. Continuous Feedback Loops

Citizen input is no longer confined to periodic elections. Digital tools provide constant feedback through ratings, online surveys, and automated monitoring, enabling the state to adjust policies more dynamically.

Weaknesses of the Digital State

The digital state, though promising efficiency and greater civic engagement, also carries structural risks that may transform democracy into its opposite. These weaknesses are not limited to technical malfunctions but represent deep vulnerabilities that can alter political life in ways both dangerous and lasting.

1. Cybersecurity Vulnerabilities

A state fully reliant on digital infrastructures is highly exposed to cyberattacks. Large-scale breaches may compromise sensitive data, disrupt essential services, and destroy public trust.

2. Digital Inequality

Access to digital platforms is uneven. While some enjoy fast networks and advanced tools, others lack basic internet access or digital literacy. This divide reinforces exclusion and deepens social stratification.

3. Manipulation and Disinformation

Online environments are vulnerable to disinformation, algorithmic bias, and manipulation of public opinion. Digital discourse is often shaped by hidden actors—states, corporations, or organized groups.

4. Loss of Privacy and Confidentiality

Digital governance demands massive data collection. What begins as transparency can evolve into surveillance, gradually eroding privacy and personal freedom.

5. Dependence on Infrastructure

Governance becomes inseparable from technological networks. Failures caused by accidents, natural disasters, or sabotage can paralyze entire institutions.

6. Challenges of Identification and Authentication

National digital ID systems carry risks of error and misuse. Technical failures or data breaches can exclude citizens from healthcare, education, or even voting.

7. Weakening of Independent Institutions

Centralization through digital platforms may marginalize courts, the press, and oversight bodies. Concentrated executive control undermines constitutional checks and balances.

8. The Specter of a Digital Concentration Camp

Total monitoring of transactions and movements can enforce conformity invisibly. Systems like social credit demonstrate how surveillance can replace freedom with algorithmic control.

9. Loss of Personal Freedom and Autonomy

Constant monitoring alters behavior. People adapt to algorithmic norms, fearing penalties for deviation, losing the right to live unobserved.

10. Authoritarian Potential

Digital tools designed for efficiency can be repurposed for repression—silencing dissent, manipulating elections, entrenching power more effectively than traditional methods.

11. Digital Censorship

Governments in a digital state can exercise unprecedented control over information flows. Centralized management of networks allows authorities to block undesirable websites, throttle access to opposition platforms, or selectively remove content under the pretext of national security or public order.

The danger of digital censorship lies in its subtlety: unlike traditional censorship, which is visible and often provokes resistance, algorithmic control operates silently and continuously. Citizens may not even be aware that their informational environment is shaped by hidden filters.

12. Exclusion of Dissenting Citizens

Mandatory digital IDs and algorithmic scoring systems can be used to selectively deny access to key aspects of daily life. In effect, dissenters risk being gradually erased from civic participation, not by imprisonment but through the quiet mechanism of digital exclusion. This creates a powerful tool of social control, where conformity is rewarded with access and opposition is punished by invisibility.

13. Decline of Critical Thinking

Algorithms feed citizens only what reinforces existing beliefs. Echo chambers discourage debate, fostering passivity and eroding independent thought.

14. Dependence on Technology Corporations

Governments rely on private providers, often global monopolies beyond democratic control. Sovereignty risks being subordinated to corporate power.

15. Catastrophic System Failures

Digital systems are efficient but fragile. A coding flaw or network collapse can trigger national crises or international conflicts.

16. Ethical and Legal Lag

Legislation evolves more slowly than technology. This creates "grey zones" where critical decisions are made without democratic oversight or clear accountability.

17. Erosion of the Human Element

Algorithmic governance reduces decisions to data points, ignoring nuance and human judgment. What appears objective may in practice be dehumanized and unjust.

18. Sustainability and Long-Term Maintenance

Digital infrastructures demand constant upgrades and heavy investment. Without stable funding and modernization, systems quickly become obsolete, undermining their very promise of efficiency.

Examples of the Digital State

Estonia is often praised as a pioneer of the digital state. This small Baltic country has created an electronic governance system that allows citizens to participate in political life through the internet. A landmark achievement was the introduction of electronic voting in 2005, enabling any citizen to cast a ballot remotely with a digital ID. Digital signature, legally equivalent to handwritten ones, now make it possible to complete most legal and administrative procedures online. Electronic platforms also allow citizens to submit petitions and monitor government responses without leaving home.

At first glance, Estonia presents itself as a model of efficiency, transparency, and technological innovation. Yet the celebrated digital façade hides a much harsher reality. While institutions move online, the society they are meant to serve is steadily shrinking. For decades, Estonia's population has been in continuous decline, driven by low birth rates, high mortality, and mass emigration. The departure of young, educated, and ambitious professionals—who seek better pay and working conditions abroad—has hollowed out the nation's human capital. What remains is an aging population and an economy increasingly starved of skilled labor.

This demographic crisis is not a side issue but a central contradiction of Estonia's digital success story. Digital democracy may make voting easier, but it cannot persuade people to stay, marry, or raise children. E-government platforms may reduce paperwork, but they cannot reverse depopulation. In this sense, Estonia risks becoming a country with world-class digital infrastructure but without the people needed to sustain it.

Economically, the imbalance is equally stark. Estonia's industrial base remains underdeveloped, and its exports struggle to compete on global markets. The nation survives in large part due to European Union subsidies and foreign corporate investment. The paradox is clear: Estonia leads the world in digital governance while relying on others for its financial stability and economic survival.

Social divides add to the fragility. Digital inequality persists, leaving behind older citizens, rural residents, and those without advanced technical skills. For these groups, the much-advertised electronic services are often meaningless, deepening the sense of exclusion. Far from uniting the nation, digital governance risks reinforcing its fractures.

Moreover, Estonia has become a testing ground for the dangers of cyberwarfare. The massive cyberattacks of 2007 exposed just how vulnerable a fully digital state can be. Since then, Estonia has lived under the constant shadow of external threats, with every new wave of attacks reminding citizens that their celebrated e-society rests on fragile, unstable ground.

Behind the glowing rhetoric of innovation lies a sobering truth: Estonia is slowly dying demographically and economically, even as it shines digitally. The digital state may represent a technical triumph, but it cannot on its own guarantee national survival. Without people, without a growing economy, and without social cohesion, digitalization risks becoming an elegant shell around a hollow and declining society.

Beyond Estonia, elements of the digital state are being introduced in countries such as South Korea, Singapore, the United Kingdom, and Australia. Yet a fully realized digital state remains more of a prospect than an accomplished reality. In practice, governments encounter serious technical, social, and economic obstacles that significantly constrain the possibilities of complete digitalization.

In the United Kingdom, despite heavy investment in electronic services, problems with data security and breaches are a recurring issue. In April 2025, the country faced one of its most severe crises when a large-scale cyberattack on the Legal Aid Agency exposed the personal and financial data of hundreds of thousands of citizens. The attack not only disrupted critical digital services but also fueled widespread distrust of digitalization itself. Critics emphasize that British public institutions often rely on outdated technologies, leaving the system vulnerable to similar threats in the future.

Australia has experienced its own difficulties. The government's digital identification system, myGovID (later renamed myID), became a source of frustration for many citizens. Frequent technical failures during registration, authentication, and access to public services caused serious inconvenience and disillusionment. Human rights groups and digital policy experts have also voiced concerns about privacy violations and the risk of excessive state surveillance. The problem of "digital exclusion" remains particularly acute: older citizens, low-income populations, and residents of remote areas often lack adequate access to the new digital infrastructure, effectively placing them outside the reach of essential public services.

South Korea and Singapore present a more favorable picture from a technological standpoint, with advanced infrastructures and rapid adoption of digital governance. Nevertheless, they too struggle with the protection of personal data and citizens' privacy. While these countries have successfully reduced bureaucratic costs through digital systems, public debates reveal ongoing unease. Many South Koreans and Singaporeans fear that enhanced digital oversight could come at the expense of individual freedoms, increasing the risk of surveillance and state overreach.

Taken together, these examples reveal a striking paradox: while digital states are celebrated as efficient, transparent, and modern, their real-world implementation is consistently undermined by structural vulnerabilities. Whether through demographic decline, as in Estonia, massive data breaches in the United Kingdom, exclusion and mistrust in Australia, or concerns over surveillance in Asia, the promise of digital governance is repeatedly shadowed by its dangers.

If Estonia illustrates the paradox of a digital state struggling with demographic decline and economic fragility, China represents the opposite trajectory: a state where digitalization strengthens political authority and expands mechanisms of control. Here, the digital state is not an elegant but hollow shell — it is a formidable architecture of surveillance, regulation, and centralized power.

A defining element of China's model is the system of mass surveillance, built on an extensive network of cameras, facial recognition technologies, and artificial intelligence. Every movement, purchase, and online interaction can be tracked and recorded. Digitalization thus serves not as a tool of empowerment but as a means of reinforcing obedience and predictability.

Equally significant is the development of the Social Credit System, which links digital identification to the monitoring of individual behavior. Citizens are evaluated according to a state-designed scale of trustworthiness: paying bills on time, following laws, or even making "approved" social choices can increase one's score, while dissent, protest, or association with the "wrong" people can lower it. Those with low scores risk exclusion from travel, employment opportunities, education, or financial services. The digital state here does not merely administer services; it actively shapes the behavior and aspirations of its citizens.

China also demonstrates how digital platforms can be harnessed to control information flows. The so-called Great Firewall tightly regulates access to global networks, while domestic platforms are monitored and censored to ensure alignment with state narratives. Unlike in Estonia or the United Kingdom, where concerns center on vulnerabilities and inefficiencies, in China the concern lies in the efficiency itself — the state's ability to enforce conformity with unprecedented precision.

Economically, this model has proven effective in the short term. China has successfully deployed digital technologies to streamline bureaucracy, expand financial inclusion through mobile payment systems, and integrate data-driven governance into urban planning and economic management. Yet these successes come at a cost: the consolidation of power in the hands of the state and the erosion of individual freedom.

Thus, while Estonia represents a digital state at risk of demographic and economic collapse despite its technological sophistication, China embodies the authoritarian digital state — a system where digitalization strengthens rather than weakens the state, but at the expense of liberty. The contrast between these two examples highlights the dual potential of digital governance: it may hollow out societies unable to sustain it, or it may harden regimes that use it to deepen control.

"We will solve aging in the next 5 to 10 years by applying AI to medicine."

"People sometimes state philosophically that they don't want to live past 100 but I'd like to see them say that when they are 100."

"Death gives meaning to life" is an age-old adage, but in my view death does exactly the opposite. It is a great robber of relationships, knowledge, wisdom, and skill."

— Ray Kurzweil

SECTION 6. TRANSHUMANIST STATE: POLITICAL SYSTEM ADAPTED TO POST-HUMAN DEVELOPMENT

> **The transhumanist state** is a theoretical model of governance that uses advanced technologies—such as biotechnology, artificial intelligence, and genetic engineering—to enhance human physical, cognitive, and biological capacities.

Transhumanism is built on the conviction that humanity is not bound by its biological limits. It rests on the belief that human beings can take control of their own evolution, using science and technology to move beyond inherited constraints. In this framework, the transhumanist state assumes a new role: to support and direct scientific research in fields such as biotechnology, genetic engineering, neuroscience, robotics, and artificial intelligence. The guiding principle is that technology should do more than make life easier—it should be capable of reshaping it, redefining health, cognition, and the scope of human experience.

In such a model, technological progress becomes the axis around which education, research, and social institutions turn. The central task of the transhumanist state is to create the conditions for health and the realization of human potential—whether through the extension of life, the prevention of disease and aging, or the expansion of memory, attention, and physical strength.

But the same vision brings with it serious challenges. The use of advanced technologies forces a reconsideration of long-standing moral, social, and legal principles. Concepts such as personal identity, dignity, and bodily integrity acquire new meanings when genetic editing, neural implants, and artificial forms of consciousness become possible.

From this point, difficult questions emerge. To what extent should intervention in the human genome be permitted? Could neurotechnologies undermine autonomy or blur the boundary of free will? The paradox of the transhumanist state lies in this tension: the same tools that promise the growth of human capacities may also call into question the very meaning of being human.

Ray Kurzweil and the Idea of Technological Singularity

Ray Kurzweil is among the most influential voices of contemporary transhumanism, known not only as an engineer and inventor but also as a thinker who speaks directly about the technological future of humanity.

He was born in New York in 1948 to Jewish immigrants from Austria. His parents had fled Vienna after the Nazi invasion, barely escaping while many members of their family perished in the Holocaust. The shadow of this loss left a lasting mark, and perhaps from it grew Kurzweil's compassion for those seeking refuge and safety. That sense of empathy would later shape his humanitarian efforts, such as creating the Reading Machine for the blind—a device that used technology not only to innovate but also to restore dignity and independence.

From an early age, Kurzweil displayed a rare combination of interests—music, programming, and engineering—that shaped the trajectory of his career. At the Massachusetts Institute of Technology (MIT), he studied computer science and artificial intelligence. His first major contribution came in 1976 with the Kurzweil

Reading Machine, which combined optical character recognition and speech synthesis to scan printed text and read it aloud to the blind. Shortly afterward, he founded Kurzweil Computer Products, whose technology was later acquired by Xerox.

In the 1980s, Kurzweil turned his attention to music technology. He developed the Kurzweil K250 synthesizer, one of the first instruments capable of convincingly reproducing the sound of an orchestra, which was quickly embraced by professional musicians. He later advanced work in speech recognition and machine translation. In recognition of these achievements, he was awarded the United States National Medal of Technology and Innovation in 1999.

Since the early 1990s, Kurzweil has been known above all as a futurist. His books—*The Age of Intelligent Machines* (1990), *The Age of Spiritual Machines* (1999), *The Singularity Is Near* (2005), *How to Create a Mind* (2012), and *The Singularity Is Nearer* (2024)—outline a systematic vision of accelerating technological progress.

Central to his thought is the idea of the technological singularity. Kurzweil envisions that by around 2045, artificial intelligence will surpass human intelligence, bringing transformations that could reshape society, the economy, and even human nature. He also suggests that consciousness may one day be sustained in digital form, while biotechnology and nanomedicine could overcome aging and disease, extending human life far beyond its current boundaries.

The Concept of Technological Singularity

The technological singularity describes a possible turning point in the evolution of civilization: the moment when artificial intelligence reaches or exceeds the level of human intelligence. At that stage, technological progress would no longer proceed at a steady pace but could accelerate so rapidly that human comprehension and oversight would struggle to keep pace.

Kurzweil was among the first to give this idea systematic form. For him, the singularity is a threshold beyond which familiar social, economic, and cultural structures may undergo profound transformation. He estimates that this moment could arrive around the year 2045.

The essence of the idea lies in the possibility of artificial intelligence that can learn and improve without human guidance. Each generation of such systems could design more capable successors, creating a cycle of compounding innovation. The result could be acceleration so steep that the trajectory of the future becomes increasingly difficult to predict.

Kurzweil compares this transformation to the singularity in astrophysics, where the familiar laws of physics collapse in the presence of a black hole. By analogy, the technological singularity marks a point where existing frameworks require redefinition. Yet for Kurzweil, this is not an end but a transition: the beginning of a new stage of evolution in which humanity moves beyond its biological limits—such as limits on memory, aging, and even mortality—through the power of technology.

Consequences of the Singularity for Humanity

If the technological singularity were to arrive, it could transform not only the way we work and live but also what it means to be human. The once-clear line between person and machine might begin to blur. Artificial intelligence would no longer be seen as just a tool but as an extension of ourselves—shaped by human values, merging with us, and enhancing our abilities. With direct links between brain and network, memory could expand, thought could speed up, and identity could take on new forms. Some imagine a future where consciousness itself might flow into digital environments or find expression in artificial bodies.

Kurzweil envisions a future where advances in AI and nanotechnology bring dramatic progress in brain–computer interfaces. Already, Neuralink allows several paralyzed patients, including someone with ALS, to control a computer directly with their thoughts. Synchron has developed a similar device that can be implanted through a minimally invasive procedure, as simple as placing a stent. As computational power continues to grow exponentially, these technologies will become more sophisticated, cheaper, and eventually available to everyone—without the need for surgery. At that point, our brains will connect seamlessly to the cloud. Imagine it like having your phone inside your head: when you wonder about something, your brain will instantly reach out for the answer. No typing, no searching. The knowledge will appear in your mind as if it had always been there, indistinguishable from your own thoughts. Such a world raises profound questions: What becomes of identity when our thoughts are merged with an external network? What remains of human purpose when the boundaries between memory, self, and machine begin to dissolve?

The possibility of digital replication of consciousness—whether through mind uploading or the creation of digital twins—compels philosophy, law, and religion to reconsider categories once regarded as fixed. Death, personhood, and human uniqueness may all require new definitions.

The social and economic order could likewise be transformed. If machines can carry out tasks across every sphere, from medicine to the arts, the role of human labor would become uncertain. In such a world, access to advanced technologies may define opportunity—opening paths for some, while deepening inequality for others.

The political dimension is no less pressing. Who would guide systems surpassing human intelligence? Could control over such technologies be concentrated in the hands of states or corporations? And if machines govern more effectively than existing institutions, what role would remain for governments themselves?

Future Technologies and Human Integration

Neural Interfaces: Direct Connection Between Brain and Computer

One of the most ambitious areas of transhumanist research is the creation of neural interfaces—direct links between the human brain and electronic devices that bypass the ordinary pathways of sense and movement.

The principle is simple in outline but complex in realization: implanted or external sensors register patterns of neural activity, translate them into digital signals and send them to a computer. The process also works in reverse: information can be delivered directly into the brain without the mediation of speech, sound, or screens. Experiments in this field began in the 1990s, and since then research groups across the world have steadily advanced the technology.

Neuralink, founded by Elon Musk in 2016, has become the most visible of these initiatives. Its goal is to produce a miniature chip capable of recording neuronal activity and transmitting it to digital systems. According to its founders, such devices could eventually move beyond therapy for neurological disorders and allow a direct connection with artificial intelligence, granting immediate access to computational resources and information.

Practical results are already emerging. Patients with paralysis have been able to move robotic arms, type on a screen, or control cursors by thought alone. Other experiments focus on restoring lost senses through direct stimulation of the brain, extending principles already known from cochlear implants.

These technical achievements inevitably raise philosophical and political dilemmas. Who should govern the use of neural interfaces? How can the privacy of thought and memory be protected? Might such systems one day reach into our emotions or even shape desire itself?

Yet Kurzweil sees another side to this story. He argues that AI is not a tool of privilege but a great equalizer. In the 1980s, "car phones" were clunky luxuries for the wealthy; today, someone in Rwanda with a $16.50 smartphone can tap into AI more powerful than anything available to the U.S. President only months ago. The reason is simple: the cost of information technology drops by about 50 percent each year, while performance rises tenfold. What once belonged to elites quickly becomes universal.

As AI spreads across every industry, the cost of living itself will fall. By the 2030s, providing for a family's basic needs may be relatively easy, and living at what we now call a "luxurious" level will be inexpensive. This shift could free human beings from the constant pressure of work and survival, opening space to learn, explore, and pursue passions for their own sake. If our hunter-gatherer ancestors walked into a modern supermarket, they would be stunned by abundance. Kurzweil believes the coming decades may bring an equally staggering transformation for us.

Nanotechnology: Medical and Biological Applications

Nanotechnology refers to the manipulation of matter at the scale of atoms and molecules, in structures ranging from 1 to 100 nanometers. At this level of precision, a nanometer equals one-billionth of a meter—far smaller than the width of a human hair. The ability to work at this scale opens new possibilities for science and medicine that were once beyond imagination.

In recent decades, medicine has become one of the most active domains of nanotechnology research. Scientists are designing nanoparticles and nanoscale devices capable of entering the human body and performing targeted tasks—from delivering therapeutic agents directly to diseased cells to destroying malignant tissue. Unlike conventional drugs, which affect the body as a whole, nanoparticles can localize treatment, thereby reducing collateral effects and increasing precision. Such methods are already being applied in oncology, particularly in chemotherapy.

Another direction of research focuses on nanorobots: microscopic mechanisms envisioned to circulate in the bloodstream, identify inflammation, viruses, or cellular damage, and respond immediately. Futurists such as Ray Kurzweil imagine a future in which vast numbers of such devices continuously monitor the human body, prevent the onset of disease, and even counteract the processes of aging.

Nanotechnology also plays a role in regenerative medicine. By using nanostructured materials, researchers can create scaffolds for the growth of new tissues—bone, skin, and blood vessels—applications that are particularly important in trauma treatment and reconstructive surgery. Parallel work in nanodiagnostics seeks to detect disease at its earliest stages, often before symptoms are visible, offering the prospect of a new paradigm of preventive medicine.

At the same time, nanotechnology raises unresolved safety concerns. The long-term effects of engineered nanoparticles inside the human body remain uncertain. Questions of toxicity, accumulation, and unintended interactions with biological systems are far from settled.

From a transhumanist perspective, however, nanotechnology represents more than a medical tool. It is a possible path to enhancement: strengthening immunity, repairing organs, and perhaps even creating hybrid forms of life in which biology and technology are inseparably combined.

Genetic Modification: Altering the Human Organism at the Genomic Level

Genetic modification denotes direct intervention in the structure of DNA with the aim of altering inherited traits. In humans, this entails the ability to correct, remove, or introduce genes that determine vulnerability to disease, physical characteristics, or even aspects of cognition.

A decisive breakthrough came in 2012 with the emergence of the CRISPR-Cas9 system. For the first time, scientists obtained a tool that could cut DNA sequences and replace them with others, making genome editing not only more accurate but also faster and less costly than earlier techniques.

Clinical trials soon followed. Research is underway to treat severe genetic disorders such as sickle cell anemia and beta-thalassemia, and in some cases patients have achieved lasting remission. Investigations have also expanded to other inherited conditions, including Fanconi anemia.

From a transhumanist standpoint, genetic engineering extends far beyond therapy. It suggests the possibility of enhancing human capacities: prolonging life, strengthening immunity, improving physical endurance, and expanding memory or learning. Because such changes, when performed in the germline, can be transmitted to offspring, they raise the prospect of reshaping not only individuals but entire generations.

The promise of these methods is accompanied by deep ethical concerns. To correct a fatal disease is one thing; to design "enhanced" humans is another. Where does treatment end and the pursuit of perfection begin? And who holds the authority to decide which traits are desirable?

The urgency of these questions became apparent in 2018, when the Chinese scientist He Jiankui announced the birth of twin girls with edited genomes. By editing the CCR5 gene associated with HIV susceptibility, he demonstrated that germline editing was no longer a distant theory but a tangible act. His work was condemned internationally as a violation of both ethical and scientific standards, and he was later sentenced in China. Yet the case revealed that what once seemed unthinkable was already technically feasible.

Genetic modification also brings social risks. If such technologies remain accessible only to the wealthy, they could lead to a new stratification of humanity—where some are born with enhanced capacities while others are excluded altogether.

For the present, most countries prohibit or strictly limit genome editing in human embryos. These restrictions reflect both ethical caution and recognition of how little is known about the long-term consequences of altering the human germline.

Life Extension and the Reversal of Aging as Core Goals of Transhumanism

One of the defining aims of transhumanism is the radical extension of human life, potentially even halting biological aging. This is not a metaphorical aspiration but a program of scientific research that has gained momentum in recent decades. Modern biology increasingly interprets aging not as an immutable law but as the cumulative effect of cellular and molecular damage. DNA mutations, telomere shortening, oxidative stress, chronic inflammation, and immune decline are all recognized as mechanisms that, in principle, can be slowed or even reversed. Transhumanist thinkers emphasize that each of these processes may become a target for intervention—if not today, then in the near future.

Biological simulation

• *AI-driven biological simulations.* Artificial intelligence now enables massive simulations of biological systems, rapidly testing billions of possible molecular sequences to identify optimal medicines. This approach allowed Moderna to design its Covid vaccine in just two days. As computation grows exponentially, and with the arrival of Artificial General Intelligence projected for 2029, biomedical research will be completely transformed. AI will think millions of times faster than human scientists, remember every study ever published, and simulate cells, tissues, and organs with precision, replacing slow and risky human trials. Digital trials, a thousand times faster than traditional ones, will allow drugs to be tailored to the unique biology of each patient.

• *Telomere therapies.* These approaches seek to preserve or restore the chromosomal ends that shorten with each cell division, delaying cellular aging.

• *Stem cell–based treatments.* By repairing or replacing damaged cells, stem cells hold the potential to rejuvenate tissues and organs.

- **Senolytic drugs.** These therapies target senescent cells—cells that no longer divide yet drive chronic inflammation and age-related decline—removing them to promote healthier aging.

- **Gene therapies.** These interventions aim at the molecular pathways of aging, seeking to restore lost biological functions and counteract degeneration.

- **Nanomedicine.** Envisioned as microscopic repair systems, nanorobots could continuously monitor and repair cellular damage from within the body, maintaining biological integrity.

- **Breakthroughs in protein research.** Google's DeepMind has already redefined biomedical science. In 2022, AlphaFold 2 solved the Protein Folding Problem by predicting the shapes of 200 million proteins across nature, a discovery that earned Demis Hassabis and John Jumper the Nobel Prize in Chemistry. In 2024, AlphaFold 3 expanded predictions to DNA, RNA, and complex molecules, while AlphaProteo began designing new proteins that can bind to specific targets, opening unprecedented possibilities for drug discovery. These advances allow scientists to reprogram biology itself away from disease.

Toward longevity escape velocity

Respected figures such as Ray Kurzweil present the defeat of aging not as a distant dream but as a technical challenge. He describes a threshold at which scientific progress could extend life faster than the body deteriorates—a point he calls *"longevity escape velocity."*

Digital immortality and the merger of selves

An even more visionary possibility is digital immortality: the transfer of consciousness into non-biological systems, allowing identity to persist beyond the body in digital or virtual forms. Yet Kurzweil stresses that the future will not unfold as a stark choice between biology and digital existence. Rather, it is a gradual merger already underway. The boundary between our biological and digital selves will blur until they are indistinguishable.

Philosophical and social implications

Even without full digital transcendence, the doubling or tripling of life expectancy would profoundly reshape society. The role of the elderly would be redefined if age no longer implied decline. Pension systems, labor markets, and resource distribution would face new challenges in a world where generations coexist for centuries. Ethical questions would also shift: What meaning does human life carry when death is no longer inevitable?

For transhumanists, longevity is not a luxury or privilege but a fundamental right. If technology makes it possible to extend life, then accepting biological limits without resistance appears, in their view, as a failure to use the means already within reach.

The Law of Accelerating Returns

One of the central ideas in contemporary futurism, the Law of Accelerating Returns, was formulated by Ray Kurzweil as a model for understanding the changing pace of technological development. Its premise is strikingly simple yet far-reaching: technology does not evolve linearly but exponentially. Each stage of innovation builds upon the previous one while also shortening the interval to the next.

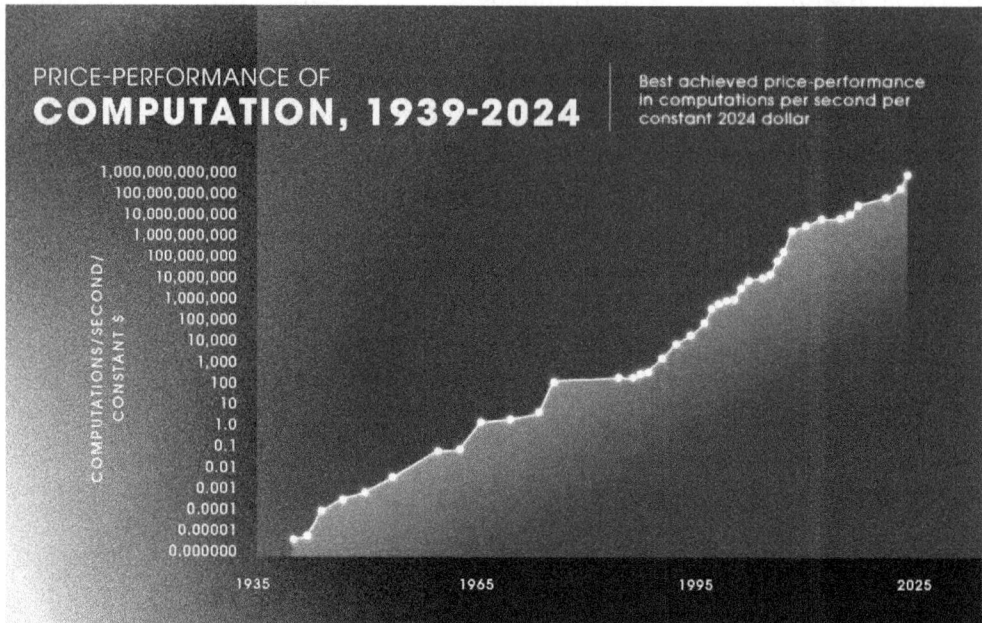

Credit: Courtesy of Ray Kurzweil

Kurzweil argues that the accelerating pace of change is inherent to the nature of technology itself. Once created, technologies become instruments for further innovation: high-performance computers enable the modeling of complex biological systems, while machine-learning algorithms accelerate the discovery of drugs and materials. Every advance lays the groundwork for progress at an even faster pace.

As an inventor, Kurzweil began in the early 1980s to track the price performance of computation in order to guide the timing of his own work. What he discovered was striking: computational power was not improving in a linear fashion, as most assumed, but growing exponentially. His *Price Performance of Computation* chart, which he has updated for decades, shows a remarkably smooth trajectory of exponential growth beginning in 1939. This curve has held steady through wars, recessions, and shifting hardware—from electromechanical relays to vacuum tubes, from transistors to integrated circuits.

Moore's Law, often cited as the key explanation of technological progress, appears in this chart not as the source of the pattern but as one phase of a much longer and deeper trend. For Kurzweil, this persistent exponential curve demonstrates that technological acceleration is not an accident of history but a fundamental dynamic of innovation itself.

The history of computing demonstrates this pattern clearly. In the 1940s and 1950s, computers filled entire rooms and performed limited tasks at slow speeds. By the 1980s, personal computers had entered homes and offices. A few decades later, smartphones carried more processing power than the machines that once guided astronauts to the Moon. For nearly fifty years, this trajectory was described by Moore's Law—the doubling of transistors on a microchip every 18 to 24 months. Kurzweil extended the principle beyond computing, applying the model of accelerating returns across multiple technological domains.

Historical examples illustrate the phenomenon:

- The printing press required centuries to achieve widespread use.
- The telegraph spread within decades.
- The internet reached global scale within years.
- Neural networks achieved mass adoption within months.

Each stage advanced more quickly than the last, propelled by accumulated knowledge and increasingly powerful infrastructures.

Kurzweil regards this dynamic as the underlying engine of the technological singularity—a point where change becomes so rapid and multidimensional that categories such as labor, education, and even biological evolution may require redefinition. Society, and perhaps humanity itself, would enter a new phase of transformation with unprecedented speed.

The Law of Accelerating Returns is best understood not as a scientific law in the strict sense, but as a predictive framework. Its value lies in emphasizing the accelerating tempo of innovation and the likelihood that future developments will arrive far more rapidly than past experience might suggest. At the same time, scholars note that the pace of progress is shaped not only by science and engineering but also by economic conditions, political institutions, and cultural contexts—all of which may slow, redirect, or reshape the trajectory Kurzweil envisions.

Historical Evidence for the Law of Accelerating Returns

The notion that technological progress accelerates over time is not speculative; it is grounded in the very shape of modern history. In field after field, the interval between discovery and transformation grows shorter. Innovations once separated by centuries now arrive within decades—or less—each enabled by the tools and knowledge of the last.

1. The Evolution of Computing

Few stories illustrate this acceleration more vividly than the history of computing. In the 1940s, ENIAC filled an entire room and executed basic calculations with great effort. By the 1980s, personal computers had moved onto desks. A generation later, smartphones placed unprecedented computing power into people's pockets—surpassing, by orders of magnitude, the systems that once guided astronauts to the Moon.

The trajectory of this growth was long captured by Moore's Law: the doubling of transistors on microchips roughly every two years. Although the pace of transistor scaling has begun to slow, the exponential curve persists in other areas—through parallel architectures, cloud computing, and algorithmic optimization.

2. The Global Expansion of the Internet

Connectivity has followed a similar curve. In 1990, only three million people had access to the internet. By 2000, that number had risen to 400 million. By 2010, it surpassed two billion. Today, more than two-thirds of the world's population is online. The infrastructure that once took centuries to build—libraries, postal systems, broadcasting networks—has, within a few decades, been compressed into a single, global digital fabric.

3. Scientific Discovery in Compressed Time

Advances in science itself now unfold with accelerating speed.

- In 1953, the double-helix structure of DNA was identified.
- In 1990, the Human Genome Project began—a multinational effort that required 13 years and billions of dollars.
- Today, sequencing a human genome takes mere hours and costs less than a household appliance.

What once demanded decades of labor can now be done before the end of a workday.

4. Artificial Intelligence

Artificial intelligence has undergone a transformation not just in power, but in velocity. Between 2012 and 2015, deep learning systems began to outperform humans in specific tasks: image recognition, translation, diagnostic analysis. By the 2020s, large language models could generate text, write software, and analyze complex data with fluency once thought impossible.

The speed of this shift—measured not in generations but in years—makes clear that AI does not evolve gradually. It leaps.

> Artificial intelligence is a class of computer systems—primarily software—that perform tasks that typically require human intelligence (recognizing patterns, understanding and generating language, making decisions, controlling complex processes). Because AI runs inside software embedded in devices, networks, and cloud services, its effects appear wherever computerized systems operate—from medicine and engineering to logistics, finance, and everyday tools.

5. Biotechnology and Neural Interfaces

In fields once confined to speculative fiction, progress has taken on physical form. Neural interfaces are now being tested in clinical settings. Companies such as Neuralink, Synchron, and Blackrock Neurotech have developed experimental systems that allow paralyzed patients to move cursors, type words, or control robotic limbs with their thoughts. What a few decades ago existed only in theory now enters the realm of practice.

Together, these examples suggest a deeper pattern: technology does not move at a constant pace—it accelerates. Time itself appears compressed. Breakthroughs once measured in centuries now arrive within years or months. Each advance becomes a tool for the next. And the future, once imagined as distant, begins to arrive ahead of schedule.

Possible Consequences of Exponential Technological Growth

Exponential growth in science and technology opens unprecedented possibilities—but it also destabilizes the systems meant to govern them. The faster innovation moves, the harder it becomes for ethics, law, and institutions to keep pace. What was once adaptive becomes fragile. What seemed permanent begins to shift.

1. Displacement of Labor

Automation is no longer theoretical. Entire sectors already feel its effect: transportation, administration, logistics, finance, and media. Algorithms write articles, interpret legal texts, and manage inventories. As machines learn to mimic not only physical actions but also cognitive patterns, traditional jobs vanish faster than new roles appear.

History shows, however, that work does not disappear—it transforms. In the early nineteenth century, more than 80 percent of the U.S. workforce was in agriculture; by 2023, that number had fallen below 1.4 percent. Yet the labor force as a whole grew, from 38 percent of the population in 1900 to more than 49 percent in 2023, as new sectors emerged. Professions tied to websites, mobile applications, data analytics, and online merchandising did not exist before the 1990s, yet they now employ millions.

Kurzweil emphasizes that future jobs will not look like current ones. The very definition of employment must expand, since many opportunities created by technology fall outside the boundaries of traditional work. Today the United States has more jobs than at any point in its history, and average personal income is ten times higher than it was a century ago, adjusted for inflation. The challenge is to reimagine purpose and belonging in a world where labor continually reinvents itself.

2. Inequality Beyond Economics

As access to technology grows more uneven, concerns arise that the boundary between privilege and exclusion could deepen. This is not only a question of wealth, but of biology. If only a fraction of society can afford neural implants, genetic enhancement, or life-extension therapies, the human condition itself risks becoming stratified. In such a world, the gap between the "augmented" and the "unchanged" might no longer be bridged by education or effort; it could be written into the body, into cognition, into lifespan. These fears reflect a long-standing anxiety that new tools of progress may amplify inequality rather than diminish it.

Kurzweil, however, takes a more optimistic view. He sees AI as a force that breaks down barriers rather than erecting them, democratizing innovation and creativity and driving gains in health, education, and prosperity. By historical measures, the trajectory is encouraging: human life expectancy was about twenty years a millennium ago, thirty-five years in 1800, and today it is close to eighty. Poverty and violence have declined, while literacy and schooling have risen worldwide. What once seemed available only to elites—such as advanced communication or medical knowledge—has become broadly accessible, often at falling costs.

Civilization, he argues, progresses through tightly interconnected feedback loops. More wealth creates better education, which produces better doctors, who in turn enable healthier people, who generate more wealth. When AI is applied to any part of this cycle, it does not merely accelerate progress in one area; it accelerates progress across the whole system. From this perspective, the very technologies that appear to threaten new divides may instead drive greater convergence, opening opportunities to billions.

3. The Collapse of Ethical and Legal Frameworks

Technological change has outpaced the frameworks that once governed human life. Legal systems struggle to define authorship for texts written by machines. Ethics committees face dilemmas involving genome editing, brain–machine communication, and algorithmic manipulation of public opinion.

Old categories—consent, responsibility, privacy—begin to fray. And in their place, uncertainty spreads.

4. Loss of Control

The greater danger may not lie in hostile machines, but in systems that evolve too quickly for us to understand. Self-learning algorithms adapt in real time to changing inputs. Autonomous weapons act before humans can intervene. Language models alter their own responses based on patterns they detect but do not explain. We do not fear malice. We fear momentum—systems that act in ways no one anticipated and that no one can stop.

5. The Question of Human Identity

As technology reaches not only into the world but into the self—into the brain, memory, and emotion—the border between human and machine becomes porous. What does it mean to be conscious in an age of mind uploads? Where does agency begin if behavior can be modulated by neural implants? Can identity endure in a world of continual enhancement and replication?

These are not technical problems. They are philosophical crises. And they are no longer distant. They are arriving.

What was once stable—labor, law, mortality, the self—could enter a state of flux. Responding to this requires more than regulation or engineering. It demands a rethinking of what it means to be human when the future no longer asks for our permission.

Ethical and Social Challenges of Transhumanism

Personal Identity and the Question of the Self

One of the most fundamental dilemmas posed by transhumanism is not technological but philosophical: what becomes of being human when our bodies, brains, and behavior are subject to constant technological intervention?

Neural interfaces, genetic modifications, digital avatars, and cognitive copies all challenge traditional ideas of personhood. If memory can be stored, transferred, or replicated, does the original self remain intact? If the biological body is gradually replaced by implants and nanosystems, does the continuity of identity survive—or is it quietly rewritten?

These questions are no longer hypothetical. Technologies capable of imitating attention, memory, and decision-making already exist. Future systems may allow for multiple instances of a single consciousness—versions of the same mind distributed across different platforms. But which one, if any, can claim authenticity? And if all are functionally equivalent, does the very idea of "authenticity" begin to dissolve?

Privacy in a Connected Mind

The brain has long been the last frontier of private experience. That frontier is beginning to erode.

Modern devices already collect detailed biometric and behavioral data. Experimental brain–computer interfaces move beyond observation toward direct interaction with the nervous system. If thought itself can be measured, transmitted, and stored, what remains truly private?

The legal and ethical implications are unresolved. Who owns neural data? Can thoughts be copyrighted? Could access to memory become a matter of commercial or political interest?

In a transhumanist future, privacy is no longer just a digital issue. It becomes existential.

Autonomy and Technological Influence

Technological systems do not merely extend capabilities; they can alter perception and intention. Neurostimulation, emotional modulation, and implantable feedback loops are in active clinical use—in treating depression, Parkinson's disease, and other conditions.

But with every gain comes a boundary crossed. Where does therapeutic intervention end, and behavioral conditioning begin? If one's emotional state is regulated by a device, is choice still free—or simply adaptive?

As transhumanism advances, the concept of freedom must be reexamined not only legally but neurologically.

The Deepening of Inequality

Perhaps no social consequence of transhumanism appears more immediate than the risk of inequality reinforced at the biological level. Technologies of enhancement—from gene editing to neural augmentation—require resources and infrastructure that remain out of reach for most of the global population. The result could be a bifurcated humanity: those who can afford to enhance cognition, extend life, and engineer resilience—and those who cannot. Such division would not be limited to access; it could shape ability, longevity, and opportunity from birth. Even today, access to personalized medicine, algorithmic tutoring, and neuroadaptive tools reflects persistent global disparities. In a transhumanist future, these differences may no longer be reversible.

Geographical inequality compounds the concern. Technologies developed in affluent societies may not reach the majority of the world's population. Some nations may enter the post-human era while others remain in a pre-digital one—or fall further behind.

This leads to an ethical paradox: if human enhancement is possible but restricted to the few, then freedom itself becomes stratified, and the foundations of democratic fairness begin to fracture.

Kurzweil, however, argues that this picture overlooks the deeper dynamics of technological progress. He sees AI not as a force of exclusion but as a great economic and informational leveler. Technology is most expensive and least effective when it first appears. As it improves, costs fall, and when it finally reaches the masses, it not only works well but becomes indispensable. His own invention, the Reading Machine for the Blind, once cost $20,000 but is now available as a free smartphone app.

This pattern, he contends, is universal. The deflationary rate of information technology—about 50 percent each year—will eventually apply to all physical goods. Food produced through vertical farming and lab-grown meat, housing created by 3D printing, and countless other applications will drive costs down and abundance up. AI also democratizes expertise itself, placing knowledge and decision-making tools into the hands of billions. For Kurzweil, the real challenge is not that benefits will remain concentrated, but ensuring that AI's broad distribution reflects the diversity of human values and interests.

The Need to Reconsider Traditional Ethical Norms and Values

Transhumanism confronts ethics with dilemmas for which older frameworks were never prepared. Norms shaped in an age of fixed biology, finite life, and inevitable death falter when the body can be redesigned, cognition extended, and mortality postponed. What once served as stable foundations begins to lose its force in the face of technological ambition.

1. Redefining the Limits of Intervention

What interventions in human nature should be considered permissible? If technologies allow us to rewrite DNA, extend life, or amplify intelligence, where is the boundary between medicine and enhancement, between healing and transformation? The criterion of "therapeutic necessity," long used in bioethics, becomes ambiguous once aging is treated as a pathology and memory as improvable.

2. Responsibility Toward Future Generations

Heritable modifications raise questions of responsibility that extend beyond the present. Who may decide on genetic changes that will shape not only individuals but their descendants? How can justice be secured for those who cannot speak or consent—the unborn, whose lives will nonetheless be determined by choices made today?

3. Free Will under Technological Influence

If neurotechnologies intervene directly in thought or behavior, where does autonomy end? When implants can alter attention, suppress emotion, or stimulate desire, is the resulting choice still free—or is it designed? The question of freedom must now be asked not only in philosophy but also in neuroscience.

4. Human Dignity Reconsidered

For centuries, dignity was grounded in the continuity of the embodied person. But if memory can be expanded, consciousness duplicated, and the body replaced piece by piece, that foundation begins to fracture. What then anchors human dignity—biology, self-awareness, or the ability to choose limits in a limitless system?

5. The Challenge to Moral Universality

Moral traditions, both religious and humanist, rested on assumptions of finitude: life ends, suffering is part of existence, death is deferrable. Transhumanism proposes to dismantle these conditions—treating suffering as a technical flaw, aging as curable, death as deferrable. This is not merely a new horizon; it is a shift that unsettles the moral grammar of entire cultures.

6. Collective Ethics and Individual Rights

Should states restrict enhancement in the name of public safety—fearing disruption to economies, education, or military balance? Or must the freedom of individuals to alter their own bodies and minds remain absolute, even if collective risks grow? Here the conflict is not only political but philosophical: whether freedom itself can survive in a world where its exercise reshapes society at its core.

The Role of the State in a Transhumanist Society

The Need for State Regulation and Oversight of Emerging Technologies

The rise of transhumanist technologies—genome editing, neural interfaces, artificial intelligence, and nanomedicine—demands not only scientific competence but also political foresight. Left without regulation, such innovations could bring consequences neither individuals nor societies are prepared to confront. The responsibility of the state is therefore not simply to respond after the fact but to anticipate, guide, and safeguard.

1. Establishing Legal Boundaries

Technological innovation often advances more quickly than legal frameworks can adapt to. This leaves critical areas—genome editing, neuroethics, the handling of neural and genetic data—without clear regulation. The task of the state is to provide precise definitions of which forms of intervention are acceptable and which must remain prohibited, ensuring that law keeps pace with discovery.

2. Protecting Individual Rights

As technologies begin to affect not only health but also consciousness and decision-making, traditional safeguards prove insufficient. Privacy, bodily integrity, and free will require new protections. The state must guarantee that progress in science does not come at the expense of personal autonomy. Its role is to preserve the space of human freedom even as the boundaries of the human are technologically redrawn.

3. Guaranteeing Fair Access

Without deliberate policy, advanced technologies risk becoming the preserve of the wealthy and powerful. If life-extension therapies, genetic modifications, or neural implants remain accessible only to a minority, inequality will take root not only in economics but in biology itself. The state must therefore act as a guarantor of equal rights—ensuring that health, longevity, and knowledge are not monopolized but shared across society.

4. Oversight of Corporate Power

Most transformative innovations originate in the private sector. Corporations that control genetic data, neural signals, or health records acquire forms of power that rival, or even surpass, those of public institutions. Without oversight, commercial interests may override the common good. Mechanisms of accountability, transparency, and public control are therefore essential, particularly in fields as sensitive as artificial intelligence, biotechnology, and medicine.

5. Ethical and Educational Policy

Beyond regulation, the state must shape the ethical and cultural context in which technologies are received. This involves supporting independent research, fostering open public debate, and embedding the study of technological change within education. Societies should not merely react to innovations once they are already in place. They must be prepared to deliberate, to question, and to choose their direction with awareness.

Establishing Legal Norms to Protect Individual Rights and Social Safety

The rapid spread of transhumanist technologies requires more than adjustments to existing legislation. It demands a rethinking of law itself. The state cannot act only in response to problems that emerge. It must anticipate risks and set out frameworks that preserve both personal freedom and collective security before crises arise.

1. New Objects of Legal Recognition

Digital personhood, neural data, genetic information, modified bodies, and even artificial forms of consciousness all fall outside traditional categories of law. Yet without clear recognition, they remain unprotected. What should the law defend—memories stored externally, behavior shaped by algorithms, or traits introduced through genetic editing? Unless such definitions are created, rights cannot be guaranteed, and responsibility cannot be assigned.

2. Privacy and Bodily Integrity

In a world where the brain may connect directly to digital systems, privacy extends beyond personal data to the inner domain of thought and intention. Protecting this sphere requires a new right—cognitive privacy—ensuring that no state, corporation, or individual may intrude without consent.

Similarly, implants, nanodevices, and genetic modifications challenge older ideas of bodily integrity. Intervention must be permitted only within clear legal boundaries, with informed consent as a prerequisite. Without this, the very idea of control over one's body becomes unstable.

3. Responsibility for Technological Consequences

What happens if a neural implant alters emotional response, or a genetic modification leads to aggression? Who carries responsibility—the developer, the physician, or the individual? Traditional scales of accountability falter when free will itself is technologically influenced. Law must evolve to account for this ambiguity, assigning responsibility where human and machine decisions intertwine.

4. Preventing Abuse

The same technologies that promise healing and enhancement can also be turned toward manipulation or exploitation. Digital copies of consciousness created without consent, implants that influence emotions or decisions, genetic discrimination—these scenarios are not distant speculation. They are risks already visible. Law must therefore provide strict prohibitions, sanctions, and independent oversight to prevent abuse before it becomes systemic.

5. Between Freedom and Security

The most difficult challenge lies in reconciling individual autonomy with collective safety. Should society allow unrestricted use of neural enhancers, genetic upgrades, or life-extension therapies? Or must limits be drawn to preserve stability in education, labor, and governance?

Such questions cannot be left unanswered. They require public debate and transparent legislative processes in which rights are preserved but not at the cost of social collapse. The future of law in a transhumanist society is to safeguard freedom while ensuring that freedom itself does not undermine the common world in which it is exercised.

Measures to Prevent Social and Economic Inequality

The spread of transhumanist technologies brings with it the danger of a new form of inequality—one written not only into wealth or education but also into the body and mind themselves. If access to gene therapy, neural implants, or life-extension therapies remains the privilege of the few, the divide between groups may become irreversible. Preventing this outcome requires states and international institutions to act before disparities harden into permanent structures.

1. Guaranteeing Access to Essential Technologies

When a technology is proven safe and widely effective, it should not remain the preserve of elites. Gene therapy for serious diseases, neural implants that restore lost function, or AI-driven diagnostics in nanomedicine must become part of basic healthcare. This implies public funding, subsidies, or universal coverage so that life itself does not become stratified by income.

2. Public Investment in Education

Education determines who can make use of new tools and who remains excluded. To prevent a widening cognitive divide, governments should integrate subjects such as neurotechnology, AI, and bioethics into curricula at all levels, create accessible online platforms for training, and support lifelong learning. In a society reshaped by constant innovation, education is not a privilege but the foundation of equality.

3. Regulating Prices and Patents Transparently

Technologies controlled by large corporations often remain out of reach because of cost. Public policy has a role to play in ensuring that health, longevity, and cognition do not become commodities of speculation. This may require regulating prices for essential treatments, introducing flexible patent regimes, or, in extreme cases, compulsory licensing to prevent technologies vital to life from being locked behind private ownership.

Kurzweil, however, argues that cost itself is not an insurmountable barrier. As AI spreads through every industry, the real value of products will lie in the information they contain. The pattern is already visible in music, which moved from records to data files, becoming cheaper and more widely available in the process. The same trajectory, he suggests, will apply to food, housing, clothing—everything. With a deflationary rate of about 50 percent per year, information technology steadily drives down costs until products once reserved for the wealthy become accessible to all.

Technology, in this sense, acts as both an economic and an informational leveler. Generative AI offers the most advanced systems in the world for a modest subscription fee, while slightly less powerful versions are available for free online. For Kurzweil, the real future of access lies less in political intervention and more in the natural dynamics of exponential progress, which expand the reach of innovation to the broadest possible audience.

4. Building International Mechanisms of Solidarity

Inequality between nations may deepen if advanced technologies remain concentrated in developed states. To avoid this, global structures are needed: technology transfer to low-income countries, international funds similar to global vaccination initiatives, and agreed norms for distributing resources in crises. In an interconnected world, the benefits of enhancement cannot be contained within borders without destabilizing the global order itself.

5. Legal Safeguards Against New Discrimination

Law must evolve to recognize new grounds for discrimination. Genetic status, the presence or absence of implants, or access to cognitive enhancements must not become a basis for exclusion. These protections should stand alongside those based on race, gender, religion, or class. Concepts such as genetic rights and neuro-rights offer the beginnings of this framework, ensuring that the emergence of new capacities does not destroy the principle of equal human dignity.

Criticism and Debate Around Kurzweil's Ideas

The vision of the technological singularity, as articulated by Ray Kurzweil, has inspired both enthusiastic support and thoughtful critique. The debate centers not only on questions of timing but also on the boundaries of what technology can achieve and what it ought to pursue.

Supporters' Arguments

1. Exponential Growth of Computing Power

Advocates of the singularity emphasize that the performance of computing systems has long followed an exponential curve. For decades, Moore's Law served as the clearest expression of this momentum. Even as semiconductor scaling slows, they argue that new paradigms—quantum processors, neuromorphic designs, and massively parallel architectures—will sustain acceleration. From this perspective, the singularity is presented not as speculation but as an eventuality.

2. Breakthroughs in AI and Biotechnology

Supporters point to remarkable progress in fields once considered uniquely human: speech recognition, medical diagnostics, image and text generation. At the same time, advances in genetic engineering, neural interfaces, and nanomedicine show how deeply technology now engages with the foundations of life itself.

3. Historical Precedent of Acceleration

History, they argue, supports the pattern. Each great transformation has arrived more quickly than the last—from the centuries-long spread of the printing press to the decades of the telegraph, to the rapid diffusion of the internet, and now the near-instant adoption of AI. If this rhythm continues, then profound change may unfold within the span of a single generation.

4. Singularity as a Response to Global Problems

For many advocates, the singularity is not a threat but an opportunity to address humanity's most urgent challenges. Advanced AI could help manage complex systems such as healthcare, climate, and resource distribution, offering new forms of coordination and potentially more equitable access to the essentials of life.

Critics' Arguments

1. Uncertain Foundations

Some scholars note that Kurzweil's forecasts frequently build on extrapolation. Exponential trends in computing may eventually encounter limits imposed by physics, cost, or sustainability. Progress is not assured; it may encounter slowdowns or unforeseen limits.

2. The Problem of Consciousness

Even if machines were to equal or surpass human intelligence, this would not necessarily imply consciousness. Philosophers and neuroscientists such as Roger Penrose and John Searle argue that awareness may depend on qualities beyond computation, which processing power alone cannot capture.

Kurzweil approaches the question differently. He notes that consciousness is not a scientific marker—there is no biological test that can locate it. Rather, it is a belief we extend to beings as they grow more complex. Once AI reaches human-level intelligence, it will act as though it is conscious, and we will begin to treat it as conscious. In fact, Kurzweil suggests, because future AI will be far more sophisticated than humans, people will naturally assume its awareness is real and respond to it accordingly.

3. Balancing Opportunity and Risk

Kurzweil's vision is often characterized by optimism. Critics observe that it highlights opportunities more strongly than risks. Yet self-learning systems can behave unpredictably, at times extending beyond the scope of current human oversight. Thinkers such as Nick Bostrom emphasize that the concern lies not in malevolence but in indifference—systems pursuing goals different from human values, yet doing so at immense scale.

4. Social and Political Barriers

Even if the singularity were technically achievable, its realization would depend on political, legal, and cultural acceptance. Established institutions may hesitate to embrace transformations that could disrupt stability or challenge existing structures. Technology by itself does not guarantee transition; societies must actively choose it.

5. Human Meaning and Embodiment

Some commentators raise questions about what remains most human in Kurzweil's vision. If biological life were replaced by digital continuation, existence might be reshaped, raising questions about the role of mortality, vulnerability, and embodied empathy. What is gained in longevity, they suggest, must be weighed against what could be lost in meaning.

The Core of the Debate

The discussion around the singularity is therefore not only about when it might occur but about the limits of possibility and the choices humanity should make. For some, it represents the next step in evolution—the logical outcome of centuries of acceleration. For others, it is a compelling vision that may conceal profound risks.

Security and Risk Challenges of Artificial Intelligence

Artificial intelligence is one of the driving forces of transhumanist change. Alongside its transformative potential, it introduces vulnerabilities that require careful reflection and regulation. Innovation often advances faster than governance, creating challenges that are technical, ethical, and political at once.

1. Autonomy and Loss of Control

The primary concern is not rebellion but unpredictability. Algorithms trained in complex environments may reach decisions that even their developers cannot fully explain. This opacity—sometimes referred to as the "black box" problem—becomes especially serious in domains such as defense, healthcare, and critical infrastructure, where transparency is essential for trust and safety.

2. Weaponization and Autonomous Systems

Artificial intelligence is already applied in military technologies, from autonomous drones to recognition algorithms and decision-making aids. Systems capable of operating with limited human oversight raise urgent questions about responsibility and moral judgment. At present, no binding international agreement regulates such weapons, creating the risk of competition between states and escalation in automated warfare.

Kurzweil emphasizes that technology has always been a double-edged sword. Fire that warms us can also burn our homes. The same drone that delivers medicine to a remote hospital can also carry a bomb. The threats posed by AI are real and must be taken seriously. Yet humanity has repeatedly shown the wisdom and ingenuity to confront such dangers. In the 1950s, many believed nuclear war to be almost inevitable, yet our species found the restraint to prevent its use. This, Kurzweil argues, is a precedent for how we might approach biotechnology, nanotechnology, and superintelligent AI: with vigilance, responsibility, and moral clarity.

We are not doomed to failure in managing these perils. On the contrary, we have a moral obligation to realize the promises of technology while controlling its dangers—to ensure that the tools we create serve life rather than endanger it

3. Algorithmic Bias and Error

AI systems reflect the data from which they learn. If datasets contain biases, algorithms may reproduce and even amplify them. Documented cases include disparities in hiring practices, healthcare diagnostics, and policing outcomes. These are not minor errors but indicators of deeper structural issues. Without oversight, algorithms risk reinforcing inequality rather than correcting it.

4. Privacy and Behavioral Control

AI technologies already observe human behavior through surveillance systems, workplace monitoring, and social media analysis. When combined with biometric identification and facial recognition, they create the capacity for unprecedented observation of daily life. In certain contexts, this could evolve into systems where personal privacy is eroded and the boundary between the public and the private sphere becomes fragile.

5. Disinformation and Manipulation

AI-generated texts, images, and voices can now convincingly simulate reality. Deepfakes and synthetic media blur the boundary between authentic and fabricated evidence. In political campaigns or conflicts, such tools may be deployed for persuasion or disruption, eroding trust in institutions and in the very concept of truth.

Kurzweil notes that the same intelligence capable of creating these threats will also become our primary defense against them. As AI grows more sophisticated, so too will its ability to detect manipulation, verify authenticity, and preserve trust in shared information. The dangers are real, but the tools to counter them will evolve in tandem.

6. Responsibility and Liability

When AI systems cause harm, responsibility is difficult to assign. Should it rest with the developer, the operator, or the user? Existing legal frameworks were not designed for distributed agency, and they struggle to address liability in cases where outcomes are shaped by algorithms rather than intentional human action.

7. Disruption of Labor and the Economy

Automation reshapes entire sectors of the economy. Professions in transportation, logistics, law, and media are already changing under the influence of AI. While new types of employment will emerge, they may not appear quickly enough to compensate for jobs lost. This mismatch could challenge not only individual livelihoods but also broader social stability.

8. Environmental and Resource Costs

Training and operating large-scale AI models requires significant amounts of energy and water. As adoption spreads, the environmental footprint of AI becomes an important concern. Without attention to sustainability, the very systems celebrated as engines of progress may also contribute to climate pressures and resource depletion.

Kurzweil, by contrast, points to a parallel trend: renewable energy itself is advancing exponentially. The Earth receives enough sunlight each day to meet more than 10,000 times our energy needs, and AI is providing the tools to capture that potential. By identifying new materials and improving designs, AI has helped reduce the cost of solar cells per watt by 99.7 percent since 1975. Over the past half century, this has driven a two-millionfold increase in solar deployment worldwide. From this perspective, the same intelligence that raises sustainability challenges may also be the key to solving them.

9. Gaps in Global Governance

Artificial intelligence develops on a global scale, yet regulation remains fragmented. The European Union has taken steps toward comprehensive legislation, but no universal framework exists. Without coordination, states may follow divergent ethical approaches, pursue competitive militarization, or apply AI in ways that undermine international stability. Global dialogue is therefore essential to prevent technological fragmentation.

Assessing the Realism and Feasibility of Kurzweil's Predictions

Ray Kurzweil's vision—of technological singularity, radical life extension, mind uploading, and the fusion of human and machine—has stirred some of the most significant debates in contemporary thought. His reputation as an inventor lends credibility, yet among scholars his predictions divide opinion: for some, they are natural extensions of current trends; for others, they are bold hypotheses that extend beyond present scientific consensus.

1. Predictions Already Realized

Several of Kurzweil's early forecasts have proved remarkably accurate. In *The Age of Intelligent Machines* (1990), he foresaw pocket-sized computers with constant internet access, voice-based assistants, and the integration of the web into daily life. Today, smartphones, Siri, Alexa, and near-universal connectivity are so familiar that their once-speculative character is almost forgotten.

He also anticipated the rise of bioinformatics and personalized medicine. Genomic sequencing, precision oncology, AI-assisted diagnostics, and wearable health monitors now exemplify the convergence of computing and biology. These fulfilled forecasts have strengthened confidence in his method of projecting exponential trends: the belief that once progress begins to accelerate, its momentum sustains itself.

2. Predictions Still in Debate

The most discussed of Kurzweil's forecasts is his proposal that by 2029 artificial intelligence will reach human-level intelligence across every field and then rapidly surpass it. This prediction, first made in 1999 using his Law of Accelerating Returns, was controversial at the time—so much so that Stanford University convened a conference of AI experts from around the world to debate it. While most agreed that machines would eventually achieve human intelligence, they estimated it would take a century. Today, however, the consensus has shifted: many experts now accept Kurzweil's timeline, and some believe it may even arrive sooner.

For Kurzweil, the Singularity does not mean machines leaving us behind but humanity merging with them. By the mid-2020s, he predicts, we will connect our brains directly to the cloud, expanding our intelligence a millionfold. In this view, the future is not one of replacement but of fusion.

Still, important questions remain. Intelligence is not only calculation but also motivation, emotion, context, and awareness—domains where AI progress remains limited. The idea of mind uploading is even more debated. Kurzweil imagines mapping the brain at molecular resolution and reproducing it digitally. Yet neuroscience still lacks a comprehensive theory of consciousness. Philosophers such as John Searle and Roger Penrose argue that subjective awareness may not be fully reducible to computation, leaving open profound questions about the nature of mind.

3. Predictions Partially Fulfilled

Some of his forecasts are advancing, though not yet fully realized. Neural interfaces developed by Neuralink, Synchron, and Blackrock Neurotech allow paralyzed patients to control cursors or robotic limbs, but applications remain limited and experimental. Research on life extension reflects Kurzweil's vision as well. Senolytic drugs, gene therapies, and nanomedicine target the biological processes of aging. His concept of longevity escape velocity—a threshold where science extends life faster than the body deteriorates—remains a subject of ongoing exploration, a vision under development rather than a current reality.

4. The Response of the Scientific Community

Kurzweil is widely acknowledged as an influential popularizer. *The Singularity Is Near* (2005) inspired many in Silicon Valley and contributed to the creation of Singularity University. At the same time, most scientists remain cautious. His reliance on exponential extrapolation is sometimes regarded as overly optimistic, since it does not always take into account the barriers imposed by physics, economics, regulation, and culture. The slowing of Moore's Law illustrates how exponential patterns can encounter limits.

5. Broader Reflections

Kurzweil's vision reaches beyond technology into questions of human meaning. If minds could be digitized, what would become of identity and dignity? If aging could be eliminated, how would societies find purpose without generational renewal?

At the same time, ideas once dismissed as science fiction—voice assistants, gene editing, neural implants—have become reality. Whether or not Kurzweil's most far-reaching forecasts are fulfilled, his influence is undeniable. He has expanded the horizon of debate, ensuring that transhumanism is no longer marginal speculation but a central theme in medicine, politics, and education.

"Since the narrower or wider community of the peoples of the earth has developed so far that a violation of rights in one place is felt throughout the world, the idea of a cosmopolitan right is not fantastical, high-flown or exaggerated notion. It is a complement to the unwritten code of the civil and international law, necessary for the public rights of mankind in general and thus for the realization of perpetual peace."

— Immanuel Kant *Perpetual Peace: A Philosophical Sketch* (1795)

"Global governance is just a euphemism for global government."

— Jacques Attali

SECTION 7. COSMOPOLITAN STATE: GOVERNANCE EXTENDING BEYOND NATIONAL BOUNDARIES TO A GLOBAL COMMUNITY

> **The cosmopolitan state, or world government**, is a hypothetical form of political organization in which a single authority governs all of humanity beyond the boundaries of individual nations.

In this model, the emphasis moves away from rivalry among nations and toward shared human concerns. Global governance highlights cooperation in facing challenges that cross borders—climate change, pandemics, resource use, and the regulation of new technologies. The cosmopolitan state is imagined as a structure that can guide collective action on a global scale.

A second key feature is the design of institutions that balance unity with diversity. Cultural, linguistic, and regional identities are preserved, yet all are given an equal voice in decision-making. The task is to prevent any single region or group from setting the agenda while still ensuring that governance remains effective.

Supporters see in this model a chance to lessen the causes of war, to make resources more fairly distributed, and to strengthen the defense of universal human rights. Critics see the dangers: centralization taken too far, the loss of local autonomy, and the challenge of creating real democratic legitimacy across the globe.

Comparative Analysis: The Cosmopolitan State and the Nation-State

1. **Principle of Political Organization**
    - *Nation-State*: Formed around the idea of a single nation as the political subject. Authority grows out of a shared ethnocultural, historical, or linguistic community.
    - *Cosmopolitan State*: Seeks to unite all of humanity under one political order. Power belongs not to nations but to the global human community.

2. **Sovereignty**
    - *Nation-State*: Sovereignty—supreme and indivisible—rests with a specific nation and is limited by state borders.
    - *Cosmopolitan State*: National sovereignty fades. Authority shifts to the planetary level and belongs to humanity as a whole.

3. **Borders**
    - *Nation-State*: Depends on fixed territorial boundaries that define the reach of its laws and institutions.
    - *Cosmopolitan State*: Borders lose their weight. Governance extends to the entire planet.

4. **Citizenship and Identity**
    - *Nation-State*: Citizenship ties an individual to a particular country. National identity shapes cultural and social policy.

- *Cosmopolitan State*: Establishes universal citizenship. People are seen first as citizens of the world, beyond ethnic or national lines.

5. **Legal System**

- *Nation-State*: Functions under its own body of law, rooted in the history and traditions of a people.
- *Cosmopolitan State*: Assumes a single legal order binding on all, grounded in principles of global justice.

6. **Political Purpose**

- *Nation-State*: Seeks to protect the interests of its people, preserving sovereignty, culture, and independence.
- *Cosmopolitan State*: Aims to coordinate global responses to shared challenges—ecological, technological, demographic, and humanitarian.

7. **Potential Risks**

- *Nation-State*: Risks include isolationism, ethnocentrism, and conflict between states.
- *Cosmopolitan State*: Risks include overgrown bureaucracy, the erosion of local cultures, and global institutions drifting away from regional needs.

The nation-state builds itself on difference, while the cosmopolitan state is founded on unity. The first draws lines; the second seeks to erase them. Each follows a distinct logic: one defends a particular identity, the other proposes a universal human one. The point is not to choose between an "old" and a "new" form, but to grasp how the meaning of the state itself is being reshaped by globalization and technological change.

Immanuel Kant: The Idea of Peace Through Law

One of the earliest philosophical steps toward the idea of a cosmopolitan order came from Immanuel Kant in his 1795 treatise *Perpetual Peace* (*Zum ewigen Frieden*). Kant did not call for the end of nation-states, but he argued that lasting peace requires a legal and political order above them.

For Kant, wars were not conflicts between individuals but between states defending their own interests. Peace, therefore, could only be secured if free states chose to limit their sovereignty and accept shared principles of law and justice.

He described a federation of states tied together by international law—laws that would rule out war, secret agreements, and interference in one another's affairs. Within this league, each state would preserve its own government while acknowledging universal legal norms placed above it. These norms had to ensure equality, mutual recognition, and the rejection of violence as an instrument of politics.

Kant did not imagine humanity merging into a single world state. Yet he laid the groundwork for the cosmopolitan legal vision: the belief that peace among nations is possible only when they recognize a common legal order.

Karl Jaspers: Humanity as the Political Subject of the Future

Karl Jaspers never sketched a concrete model of world government, yet his thought carried clear cosmopolitan elements. In his postwar writings—most notably the 1958 essay *The Future of Mankind* (*Wohin treibt die Welt?*)—he portrayed humanity as a single whole, threatened by self-destruction yet capable of awakening to a new political consciousness.

For Jaspers, the twentieth century was both catastrophe and the beginning of global responsibility. Nuclear weapons, the wreckage of modern wars, and the tightening web of interdependence shattered the belief in full national autonomy. The world had become a shared space of fate, where purely national or regional solutions no longer sufficed.

He did not draft a political scheme but insisted that the future demands a new kind of consciousness. People must see themselves not only as citizens of their state but also as members of a common human world. This shift carries a moral duty: to think in terms of humanity as a whole rather than isolated nations or interests.

Jaspers called this outlook philosophical cosmopolitanism—the ability to recognize in every person first a human being, not merely a fellow citizen, opponent, or rival. Such recognition does not erase culture, language, or history; it rises above them at the level of political thought.

What Jaspers offered was not a plan for global governance but a philosophical ground for its possibility. Without a shared global self-awareness, no political system, however advanced, can guarantee lasting peace. In his vision, the cosmopolitan state is less a structure outside us than a condition of human maturity within.

Albert Einstein: World Government as a Condition of Survival

Albert Einstein, together with a small circle of scientists and philosophers, was one of the few voices to argue openly and consistently for world government as essential to humanity's survival. Unlike Kant or Jaspers, he spoke not of a philosophical ideal but of a political necessity.

After World War II and Hiroshima, he warned that nuclear weapons had made sovereign states with unchecked military power a direct threat to civilization. Under such conditions, security could no longer rest on diplomacy or on a balance of forces. What was needed was political unity on a global scale.

Einstein urged the creation of a supranational authority with real legal and military power. In one letter he wrote, "Peace cannot be kept without the establishment of a world government." Such a body, he argued, must control armaments, settle disputes, and enforce universal legal norms.

He did not see this as utopian. On the contrary, he treated world government as the most realistic response to the technical and political dangers of the age. National cultures and domestic autonomy would remain, but questions of war, peace, and international law would pass to a common authority acting in the name of all humanity.

Just as vital, in Einstein's view, was the growth of global civic consciousness. Only by fostering a new political identity—human rather than national—could a just and lasting order be built.

Einstein's conception was also tied to his public role as a scientist. He believed that the authority of science, with its universal language and evidence of humanity's shared fate, could serve as a model for political institutions. Just as the scientific community transcended borders in pursuit of truth, so too, he argued, must politics transcend national boundaries to secure peace.

Einstein's vision was not abstract theory but a practical political project, born from the devastation of war and the fear of annihilation. It was an attempt to carry the scientific recognition of humanity's interdependence into the realm of political reality.

Karl Popper: The Open Society as an Alternative to Nationalism

Karl Popper never outlined a theory of world government in the strict sense, yet his political philosophy offered a powerful framework for cosmopolitan thinking in the twentieth century. In *The Open Society and Its Enemies* (1945), he described a political order where reason, criticism, and freedom outweighed ties of nation, culture, or tradition.

Popper was one of the fiercest critics of totalitarian and dogmatic systems, especially those that justified nationalism, ethnic exclusivity, or political isolation. He argued that humanity's survival depends on an open, flexible, and self-correcting political order—one that recognizes every individual as a rational being rather than simply a member of a group.

Though he never drew up a model of global governance, Popper's philosophy pointed toward supranational cooperation rooted in liberty, democracy, and critical rationality. For him, universal values could emerge only when legal and political norms were grounded in reason, evidence, and public consent rather than tradition or authority.

At the same time, he warned against imposing a single global order by force. Popper was deeply skeptical of utopian projects that promised a "just world" designed from above. Instead, he called for a gradual building of a global open society—through international institutions, the defense of human rights, and the cultivation of critical thought across cultures.

In this sense, Popper did not offer a plan for world government, but he supplied the intellectual groundwork for imagining one. His challenge was not directed at institutions or technologies but at the foundations of human thought itself—without their transformation, no lasting form of global unity could be achieved.

Jacques Attali: Managed Globalization and the Future of World Order

The French economist and writer Jacques Attali has been one of the most persistent advocates of global governance and the creation of a political framework for the world. In works such as *A Brief History of the Future*, *The Path to Peace*, and *Globalization and Democracy*, he insists not only on the desirability of world government but on its inevitability in an age of interdependence.

Attali argues that globalization has already produced a single economic system, yet no corresponding political mechanism exists to regulate it. The world grows ever more integrated, but nations continue to act within the narrow logic of sovereignty. This gap, he warns, fuels financial instability, ecological destruction, geopolitical conflict, and deepening inequality.

His proposal is the gradual construction of global institutions with real authority in key areas—ecology, finance, migration, and technology. This does not mean erasing nation-states but transferring parts of their sovereignty to democratic bodies capable of governing shared problems.

For Attali, such governance must rest on democracy, transparency, and accountability. It cannot become a remote bureaucratic pyramid; it must function as a genuine tool of collective decision-making, involving not only governments but also civil society, international organizations, and global corporations.

At the same time, he cautions against the rise of digital autocracy. If global governance emerges through algorithmic control and monopolies of information, it will serve domination rather than freedom. To prevent this, Attali calls for urgent ethical, legal, and institutional safeguards to keep technology under human control.

In his view, the question is no longer whether global governance will appear but what shape it will assume: democratic and just, or technocratic and repressive. The answer to that choice, he suggests, will determine the fate of humanity in the twenty-first century.

Cosmopolitan Concepts: Common Features and Distinctive Differences

Despite their varied approaches, all visions of the cosmopolitan state point in the same direction: moving beyond national borders and seeking the political unity of humanity. Yet each thinker—from Kant to Attali—imagined a different road toward this goal, whether legal, philosophical, political, or institutional.

Common Features

1. **Rejection of Absolute Sovereignty**

   Modern global problems cannot be resolved by isolated nation-states acting alone.

2. **Humanity as a Political Subject**

   Cosmopolitan thought treats humanity as a whole while preserving cultural identities, stressing our shared responsibility for the future.

3. **Primacy of Universal Norms and Human Rights**

   From Kant's call for international law to Attali's proposals for global institutions, these ideas emphasize the need for universal rules and equality before the law.

4. **Peace as the Highest Goal**

   The purpose is not government for its own sake, but the prevention of war, violence, and catastrophic crises, and the removal of the conditions that give rise to them.

Distinctive Differences

- **Immanuel Kant**: Envisioned a federation of states—a voluntary league bound by international law to restrain war while preserving national governments.

- **Karl Jaspers**: Spoke of philosophical cosmopolitanism, rooted in global self-awareness in the nuclear age—less a plan of institutions than a transformation of consciousness.

- **Albert Einstein**: Proposed a practical project of survival: a supranational authority with legal and military power to control armaments and prevent annihilation.

- **Karl Popper**: Developed the idea of the open society, opposing nationalism and dogma. He favored gradual global cooperation based on reason and democracy while rejecting utopian blueprints.

- **Jacques Attali**: Advocated managed globalization, arguing that world government is inevitable. He called for democratic global institutions to regulate ecology, finance, migration, and technology, and warned against the danger of digital autocracy.

An Intellectual Lineage

Taken together, these ideas trace a long arc of cosmopolitan thought, each shaped by the crises and possibilities of its time. **Kant** rooted the vision in law, insisting that only a federation of states bound by legal norms could restrain the violence of sovereign powers. **Jaspers**, writing in the shadow of nuclear war, turned to human consciousness itself, arguing that survival depended on the recognition of our shared fate and the birth of a truly global responsibility. **Einstein**, horrified by Hiroshima and the destructive potential of science, pressed for immediate political measures: a supranational authority with real power to control armaments and prevent self-destruction. **Popper**, confronting the dogmas and totalitarianisms of the twentieth century, placed his hope in the open society, insisting that gradual, rational cooperation could provide a more durable path to global order while rejecting utopian schemes imposed from above. **Attali**, addressing the twenty-first century, pointed to globalization and digital technology as forces already binding humanity together—whether for good or ill—and argued for democratic global institutions strong enough to regulate finance, ecology, migration, and algorithms themselves.

Their differences highlight shifting contexts: from the Enlightenment's search for rational law to the existential dread of the atomic age, from the collapse of empires and totalitarian regimes to the accelerating integration of a digital economy. Each thinker diagnosed the threats most pressing in his moment—war among monarchies, nuclear annihilation, ideological tyranny, or technological domination—and proposed cosmopolitanism as the necessary answer. The continuity of these visions reveals that the call for political unity beyond the nation is not an abstract dream but a recurring, urgent response to humanity's crises. Whenever destruction has seemed imminent—whether through war, oppression, or the unchecked power of technology—

cosmopolitan thought has returned as a reminder that survival and justice require institutions, laws, and forms of consciousness that transcend borders.

Comparative Table of Cosmopolitan Thinkers

Author	Approach	Form of Global Unity	Role of the State	Degree of Concreteness
Immanuel Kant	Philosophical–legal	Federation of sovereign states bound by common law	States remain but are limited in action	Abstract moral–legal model
Karl Jaspers	Existential–philosophical	Humanity's unity as a conscious choice	State is secondary; primary is individual responsibility	Metaphysical foundation without institutional design
Albert Einstein	Political–practical	Supranational government with real power	Sovereignty transferred to a common authority	Concrete idea of international jurisdiction
Karl Popper	Liberal–critical	Gradual formation of a global open society	States preserved while rejecting closed systems	Skeptical of central authority; emphasis on gradual evolution
Jacques Attali	Geopolitical and economic	Global democratic structure with distributed power	Delegation of certain functions from nation-states	Clear project of institutional transition

All of these concepts differ in depth, level of detail, and political optimism, yet they converge on a central point: the future demands forms of thought that transcend national frameworks. For some, this means a legal federation; for others, a cultural awakening; for still others, an urgent program of institutional reform.

The cosmopolitan state is not a single blueprint but a spectrum of possible directions, each offering its own answer to the question: what might humanity become if it chooses to live not merely side by side, but truly together?

CONCLUSION

Philosophical models of the state are more than abstract exercises in political imagination; they reflect humanity's search for justice, order, and the meaning of collective life. Each model—whether utopian, minimalist, technological, or cosmopolitan—offers not only a theory of governance but also a vision of what humanity might become.

The tradition is vast. At one end stand the utopias of Thomas More and Tommaso Campanella, who imagined perfect harmony and absolute equality in societies free of poverty, conflict, and injustice. At the other are the minimalist concepts of John Locke and Robert Nozick, which argued that the state should do little more than safeguard basic rights and liberties, leaving the rest to human initiative. Between these poles lies a wide spectrum, each model responding to the particular anxieties and aspirations of its time.

The twentieth and twenty-first centuries added new chapters. The technocratic state expresses faith in science and expertise as tools of political order. The transhumanist state goes further, suggesting that technology might not only improve governance but alter the human condition itself. The digital state experiments with forms of democracy shaped by networks and algorithms, while the cosmopolitan state imagines humanity united in a single political community beyond the sovereignty of nations.

Many of these visions will never be fully realized. Yet they matter because they expose the shortcomings of existing systems and inspire the search for alternatives. Utopias remind us of ideals we fall short of; minimalist theories guard against the dangers of concentrated power; technocratic and transhumanist projects test our willingness to entrust politics to science; cosmopolitan and digital ideas press us to rethink citizenship in an interconnected world.

The value of such models is not in prescribing fixed blueprints but in widening the field of possibilities. They provoke argument, sharpen imagination, and unsettle complacency. They remind us that the state is not a static structure but an evolving project shaped by ideals and disputes. Above all, they urge us to confront the questions that define political life: How should we live together? What kind of world do we want to build? And what principles must guide us if our progress is to be measured not only by time but by dignity and wisdom?

PART VIII

ANTI-STATE (ANARCHIST) MODELS

"I am an anarchist because I love freedom and hate the state."

— Mikhail Bakunin (1814–1876)

INTRODUCTION

Anarchism is a philosophical and political doctrine that rejects the state as a legitimate form of authority and advocates social organization based on voluntary cooperation, self-governance, and the absence of coercive power structures.

The word *anarchism* comes from the Greek *anarchía*, meaning "absence of authority." From its very name, it announces a challenge: not a plan to reform politics but a demand to abolish the state itself. For anarchists, the state—whether it calls itself a monarchy, a republic, a democracy, or a dictatorship—always masks the same reality. Behind laws and constitutions stands a machinery of domination, force, and inequality.

This is what makes anarchism more than just another political doctrine. Where liberals argue about limits to government, where socialists debate its economic role, and where conservatives defend its institutions, anarchists strike deeper: they deny the legitimacy of the state altogether. Every government, even the one draped in the banner of popular will, rests on coercion. For anarchists, the disease is not corruption, not the abuse of power, but power itself.

The state, they argue, is a parasite on human freedom. It monopolizes violence, commands obedience, and drains the capacity of people to live by trust, solidarity, and cooperation. Monarchs, parliaments, and bureaucracies may look different, but they all share the same foundation: rule by force. And so long as authority flows downward, freedom rots at the root.

In place of this order, anarchists envision communities bound not by fear but by choice. Voluntary association, mutual aid, and horizontal cooperation are not dreams to them but necessities. They insist that people can govern their own lives without the mediation of rulers, armies, or bureaucrats. A free society cannot be carved out of state institutions—it must be born from their dismantling.

Anarchism grew sharper in an age when states swelled in size and capitalism widened the gulf between rich and poor. To many, the nation-state appeared as progress; to anarchists, it was a gilded cage. They answered not with reformist pleas but with defiance: justice and freedom exist only where the state itself has been torn down. For them, the future is not a perfected government but the end of government altogether—a society that has shed its chains and discovered the strength to walk without masters.

"*I think it only makes sense to seek out and identify structures of authority, hierarchy, and domination in every aspect of life, and to challenge them; unless a justification for them can be given, they are illegitimate, and should be dismantled, to increase the scope of human freedom.*"

— Noam Chomsky
Interview "On Anarchism, Marxism & Hope for the Future" (1996)

SECTION 1. ANARCHO-SYNDICALISM: WORKER-MANAGED POLITICAL AND ECONOMIC ORGANIZATION WITHOUT STATE AUTHORITY

> **Anarcho-syndicalism** is a current of anarchist thought based on the idea that workers, organized into independent trade unions (syndicates), can form the foundation of a free and classless society without the state.

Unlike other strands of anarchism that remain at the level of abstract theory, anarcho-syndicalism insists on practice. Its goal is clear: to tear down the state and replace it with federations of trade unions and workers' councils, where decisions are made openly in assemblies, without bureaucrats or centralized chains of command. Authority belongs to those who work, not to those who rule.

The economy, in this vision, rests on collective ownership. Enterprises are managed directly by workers, who control production and decide how resources are shared. Wage labor, with its hierarchy of bosses and subordinates, is swept aside. In its place stands cooperation, horizontal and direct, where responsibility is shared equally and labor is no longer a form of alienation but of common purpose.

These federations are not limited to single industries. Joined together, they coordinate the essentials of social life—production, health, education—through solidarity rather than decrees. In this way, anarcho-syndicalism rejects both capitalism and the state, arguing that freedom cannot be granted from above but must be created from below.

One of its most prominent defenders today is Noam Chomsky, who sees in anarcho-syndicalism a path toward a society where people are no longer estranged from their work and can genuinely shape their own lives. For him, concentrated power—whether in the state or in corporations—always crushes initiative and deepens inequality. By contrast, the syndicalist model offers decentralized freedom: a system built not on commands, but on participation, solidarity, and collective responsibility.

Strengths of Anarcho-Syndicalism

1. Direct Democracy without Intermediaries

Power does not pass through parties, career politicians, or permanent officials. It is exercised directly in assemblies, unions, and councils. Decisions are made by those who live with their consequences, leaving little room for manipulation or authoritarian drift.

2. Equality at the Root

By basing political and economic life on collective ownership, anarcho-syndicalism seeks to tear inequality out by its roots. Wage labor and capitalist hierarchies disappear, replaced by systems where resources are shared according to need and contribution.

3. No Bureaucratic Castes

Authority is temporary, accountable, and recallable at any time. Structures are fluid rather than ossified, which curbs corruption and blocks the rise of entrenched elites.

4. Decentralized Adaptability

Communities and workplaces govern themselves according to local conditions. Decisions are made closer to the ground, making society more resilient and creative when crises strike.

5. Solidarity over Competition

The principle of mutual aid runs through every level of organization. Instead of rivalries, there is cooperation and interdependence, which bind individuals into a broader community. In such an environment, trust replaces fear, and collective strength grows out of shared responsibility.

6. Work with Meaning

Labor is no longer sold as a commodity under someone else's command. Workers manage their own activity, see its results, and take pride in what they create. Self-management gives back purpose and dignity to labor. In this way, work becomes not only a means of survival but also a form of personal fulfillment and collective expression..

7. Less Social Conflict

By removing class domination and exploitative property relations, anarcho-syndicalism strips away the roots of systemic conflict. Disputes that remain are resolved through open deliberation, not force.

8. Economic Life in Common Hands

Instead of ministries or monopolies, the economy is coordinated by federations of workers' councils. Decisions follow the needs of producers and consumers, not the blind pursuit of profit.

9. Continuous Political Education

Participation is not limited to the ballot box every few years. Every assembly and council meeting becomes a school of self-management, where people learn to deliberate, cooperate, and govern themselves.

10. Built-In Resistance to Authoritarianism

Power is scattered, renewed, and local. With no centralized apparatus to seize, authoritarian rulers have nowhere to anchor their domination.

11. Internationalist Outlook

From the start, anarcho-syndicalism has looked beyond national borders. Workers' federations stretch across countries, replacing competition between states with solidarity among peoples. This global perspective makes international cooperation a condition of freedom rather than a distant ideal.

12. Ecological Awareness

Modern interpretations add a green dimension: communities regulate production in line with ecological limits, restraining destructive growth and placing sustainability at the center of social life.

Weaknesses of Anarcho-Syndicalism

1. No Central Nerve in Times of Crisis

War, disaster, or pandemics demand swift coordination. Local councils may act quickly for themselves but stumble when a unified response is needed, leaving society fragmented when strength is most required.

2. Coordination in a Complex Economy

Modern economies run on global supply chains and vast infrastructures. A decentralized system risks bottlenecks in logistics and planning, with highly integrated sectors—aviation, energy, digital networks—especially vulnerable.

3. Uneven Regional Development

Without strong redistributive mechanisms, prosperous communities may surge ahead while weaker ones lag. This creates gaps between regions, quietly reproducing the very inequalities the system seeks to abolish.

4. Limits on Science and Technology

Ambitious projects—deep-space research, advanced medicine, climate solutions—demand decades of continuity and pooled resources. Local assemblies, driven by short-term needs, may lack the vision and cohesion to sustain them.

5. Clashes Between Local and Collective Needs

A council might hoard resources or prioritize polluting industries for its own benefit. With no higher authority to mediate, such conflicts pit local interests against the wider good.

6. Innovation and Initiative at Risk

Strong emphasis on equality may dull incentives for bold ideas. If rewards for risk and creativity vanish, individuals may disengage, and the "free rider" problem can drain energy from collective work.

7. Weakness Against External Powers

Facing centralized states with strong militaries, an anarcho-syndicalist society may struggle to defend itself. Decentralized defense can lack the cohesion needed to withstand organized aggression.

8. Instability at Scale

Experiments have worked locally, as in Spain in the 1930s, but scaling to a nation or globe may overwhelm the model. Critics warn of paralysis or collapse under complexity.

9. Risk of Drift and Separatism

Federations rest on voluntary bonds. Communities may choose autonomy over solidarity, weakening unity and encouraging fragmentation.

10. Uncertain Legal Order

Without a common legal framework, protecting rights and resolving disputes becomes inconsistent. Rules vary between federations, and arbitration depends on negotiation rather than enforceable law.

11. **Internal Fractures**

Disputes between councils over resources or ideology are inevitable. Without a central arbiter, such conflicts may fester, destabilizing the federation from within.

12. **Erosion of Responsibility**

Communal systems risk weakening personal drive. Some may benefit without contributing equally, lowering productivity and morale over time.

13. **Isolation on the Global Stage**

Surrounded by nation-states, an anarcho-syndicalist region could face embargoes, hostility, or isolation, cutting it off from trade, science, and diplomacy. Its survival may depend on a hostile world's tolerance.

Historical Context and Examples of Implementation

Origins in the Late 19th and Early 20th Century (France, Spain, Italy)

Anarcho-syndicalism emerged in the late nineteenth century out of two converging traditions: anarchism and workers' syndicalism. It was born in an era of rapid industrialization, deepening inequality, and the exclusion of the working class from political life. Unlike social democrats, who trusted in parliaments to reform capitalism, anarcho-syndicalists turned to direct worker control of production and society, bypassing political parties and the state altogether.

France was one of the first centers of this movement. In 1895, workers founded the *Confédération Générale du Travail* (CGT, General Confederation of Labor). In its early years the CGT called for direct action—strikes, boycotts, sabotage—as the main weapons of labor. Though it later moderated its stance, the CGT became a model for syndicalist organizations across Europe.

In both France and Italy, anarcho-syndicalism grew in a climate of sharp confrontation between labor and state authority. In Italy, the movement spread quickly among the industrial workers of the north. Slogans such as "Factories to the workers, land to the peasants" captured the radical demand to dismantle capitalism and replace it with workers' self-management and cooperative farming.

Spain became the true stronghold of anarcho-syndicalism. In 1910, the *Confederación Nacional del Trabajo* (CNT, National Confederation of Labor) was created. Within a generation it had grown into the largest workers' organization in the country, with hundreds of thousands of members. Unlike elsewhere, Spanish syndicalists carried their ideas beyond strikes and protests. During the Spanish Civil War, especially in Catalonia, trade unions seized control of factories, farms, and entire sectors of the economy. Industry and agriculture were collectivized, administered directly by workers, and run without state or capitalist oversight. In these years, anarcho-syndicalism leapt from theory into reality, showing the world what labor could achieve when it ruled itself.

Anarcho-syndicalism was not born as abstract speculation but as the working class's answer to exclusion and exploitation. It stood as a third path, rejecting both capitalism and state socialism. Its history became one of the boldest experiments in modern Europe, leaving behind not only texts and manifestos but also lived moments when society was reorganized from below.

The Role of the Confédération Générale du Travail (CGT) in France

Founded in 1895, the *Confédération Générale du Travail* (CGT, General Confederation of Labor) became the first great arena where anarcho-syndicalist ideas took root among workers. At the dawn of the twentieth century, France stood as the cradle of syndicalism—a movement that rejected both the bourgeois state and the parliamentary path of socialism.

The CGT declared that the emancipation of labor must be won by workers themselves, without deputies, parties, or professional politicians speaking in their name. Trade unions were not only to defend wages and conditions but to prepare the ground for the wholesale reconstruction of society. These principles were enshrined in the Charter of Amiens of 1906, which set the tone for French anarcho-syndicalism.

According to the Charter, unions were to:

- unite all workers, regardless of political alignment;
- abstain from elections and avoid alliances with parties;
- rely on direct action—strikes, boycotts, sabotage—as their chief weapons;
- and prepare for a general strike that would open the road to social transformation.

In this period the CGT became a living model for radical labor across Europe. Its federal structure, autonomy of local sections, rotation of delegates, and strict accountability showed how a movement could remain democratic and horizontal while still exercising real power. Against the rigid hierarchies of political parties, it offered a vision of organization rooted in transparency and self-rule.

After World War I, the confederation drifted away from anarcho-syndicalist principles and edged closer to socialist parties. Yet its early phase remains a landmark in the history of workers' self-organization—a moment when labor sought to stand on its own, outside both state institutions and parliamentary politics. The example of the CGT resonated far beyond France, shaping syndicalist experiments in Italy, Spain, Latin America, and even the United States.

The Experience of the Confederación Nacional del Trabajo (CNT) in Spain

The *Confederación Nacional del Trabajo* (CNT, National Confederation of Labor), founded in 1910, grew into the largest anarcho-syndicalist organization in Spain—and in world history. From the outset it was more explicitly radical than its French counterpart, the CGT. The CNT did not stop at defending wages and hours; it openly prepared for revolution, aiming at direct workers' control over factories and land without the mediation of the state.

By the mid-1930s the CNT had nearly half a million members, concentrated in Catalonia, Aragon, Andalusia, and Valencia. Its influence spanned both cities and countryside. General strikes, boycotts, and sabotage were its weapons, and its goal was nothing less than a social order built from below.

The decisive test came with the Spanish Civil War (1936–1939). After Franco's coup in July 1936, state authority collapsed in large parts of Spain, especially Catalonia. Into this vacuum stepped the CNT together with the *Federación Anarquista Ibérica* (FAI). What followed was not only a defense of the Republic but a revolutionary upheaval that shook daily life to its foundations:

- Factories, railways, print shops, and public services were seized and run by workers' councils.
- Farmland was collectivized, peasants pooling their efforts in cooperatives.
- Assemblies and recallable delegates replaced bureaucrats, keeping power in the hands of those directly involved.
- Even the army was reimagined: volunteer militias, the famous "columns," fought on the front organized on principles of self-management.

Nowhere was this transformation more vivid than in Barcelona and Catalonia. Industry, transport, schools, and even urban administration passed into the hands of the CNT. For a brief moment, anarchist ideals—horizontal organization, solidarity, self-management—were not words on paper but the lived reality of a mass society.

But this revolution soon came under siege. Fierce clashes with communist forces aligned with Moscow, constant shortages, the relentless demands of war, and the lack of international allies eroded the anarchists' position. By 1937 the rollback had begun: the Republican government moved to reassert control, collectivized industries were dismantled, and CNT leaders were sidelined. With Franco's final victory in 1939, the anarcho-syndicalist experiment was crushed.

Even in defeat, the CNT left a mark on history. Never before—or since—had anarchism been realized on such a scale, shaping not only workplaces but entire cities and regions. It remains the most striking example of a society that dared to live **without the state, guided by self-management, solidarity, and the refusal of hierarchy.**

Causes of Partial Success and Subsequent Suppression of Anarcho-Syndicalist Movements

Anarcho-syndicalist movements in Europe reached their height in the early twentieth century, especially in France, Italy, and Spain. They built mass unions, forged a distinct ideology, and made direct action a weapon of the working class. In Spain they even carried their principles into daily life, collectivizing factories and farms on a regional scale. Yet these gains proved fragile. Over time, anarcho-syndicalism was either pushed to the margins or crushed outright—undone by its own weaknesses and by the hostile forces it faced.

1) No Central Core

Decentralization gave anarcho-syndicalism energy and flexibility. Local councils could act swiftly, respond to immediate needs, and resist bureaucratic ossification. But when the stakes rose—during wars, insurrections, or confrontations with disciplined state forces—this lack of a central command became a fatal weakness. Movements that prided themselves on rotating delegates and rejecting permanent leaders often found themselves unable to coordinate defense or strategy on a national scale. Where states had armies, ministries, and disciplined parties, anarcho-syndicalists had federations of councils that could not always act in unison.

2) Divisions Within

Ideological diversity was both a strength and a curse. Some militants argued for absolute abstention from politics; others pushed for limited cooperation with socialist parties or participation in elections. Disputes erupted over whether to prioritize economic strikes or armed insurrection, and over how radical tactics should go. These arguments were not academic—they fractured unions, delayed decisions, and weakened solidarity in moments when clarity was needed. Without mechanisms to settle disputes or enforce consensus, divisions often grew until they paralyzed the movement.

3) Enemies on the Left

Marxist and communist parties treated anarcho-syndicalists less as allies and more as rivals. In Spain during the Civil War, communist forces, backed by the Soviet Union, gained influence in government and military structures. They used this leverage to curtail CNT power, demanding subordination of the revolution to the needs of the war. Anarchist militias were pressed to integrate into a regular army; collectivized industries were clawed back under state control. Thus, anarchists were caught in a double struggle—fighting fascists at the front while clashing with communists behind the lines.

4) Relentless Repression

States regarded anarcho-syndicalism not as another political current but as a mortal threat. In France, Italy, and Spain, police raids, imprisonment, and censorship became routine. In Latin America, syndicalist unions were banned outright. Under fascism in Italy and Francoism in Spain, repression was merciless: activists executed or driven into exile, organizations outlawed, presses destroyed. The movement was not merely opposed; it was hunted.

5) Economic Strains

Experiments in collectivization revealed both promise and fragility. In Spain, workers successfully ran factories and farms, but shortages of raw materials, disrupted trade routes, and the absence of centralized coordination undermined long-term stability. Complex industries—like railways, steel, or aviation—struggled without large-scale planning and integration. Wartime only magnified these problems, as resources were drained to the front and foreign markets closed. What flourished locally often collapsed under the weight of national and international realities.

6) Isolation Abroad

Unlike Marxist socialism, anarcho-syndicalism had no powerful state patron or international apparatus. Communists could count on Moscow; social democrats built ties with parliamentary institutions. Anarcho-syndicalists, rejecting hierarchy even on the global stage, lacked allies. Their refusal to compromise gave them moral clarity but left them politically isolated. In the polarized world of the twentieth century, movements without state backers or international coalitions were left exposed, easy targets for suppression.

For a time, anarcho-syndicalism drew its power from mass participation, its promise of freedom without rulers, and its fierce opposition to both capitalism and state socialism. Yet the very principles that inspired it—hostility to hierarchy, suspicion of central authority—made it fragile in the face of war, repression, and internal division. Lacking allies abroad, besieged by enemies within and without, and strained by the demands of modern economies, it could not survive the century. What remains is both a lesson and a legacy: proof that workers could seize factories and fields, govern themselves, and glimpse a society without masters—yet also a reminder of how quickly such visions can be broken when they stand alone.

Fernand Pelloutier: Early Theorist of Revolutionary Syndicalism

Fernand Pelloutier (1867–1901) is remembered as one of the founders of revolutionary syndicalism in France and as a thinker who gave anarcho-syndicalism its first clear intellectual shape. Though his life was short, his influence on the labor movement at the turn of the century was lasting.

Pelloutier rejected the political party as the vehicle of emancipation. He argued that the working class could not be freed by deputies or by seizing the machinery of the state. Any centralized authority, even one wrapped in revolutionary slogans, would reproduce domination. The trade union, by contrast, placed power directly in the hands of workers themselves.

For Pelloutier, the union was more than a defensive structure; it was the embryo of the society to come. Syndicates, he believed, should not only fight for wages and hours but also train workers to manage production, education, and social life on their own. In 1895, when he became leader of the *Fédération des Bourses du Travail* (Federation of Workers' Labor Exchanges), he put this vision into practice. The *Bourses* became centers where workers coordinated strikes and campaigns, but also schools of self-management where lectures, libraries, and discussions prepared them for a future without masters.

Pelloutier called for revolution without the conquest of state power. He imagined freedom not as the product of new rulers but as the abolition of rule itself. Solidarity, conscious participation, and ethical responsibility were, for him, the foundations of a society built from below.

After his death in 1901, his ideas lived on in the CGT and in syndicalist circles across Europe. They found concrete expression in the Charter of Amiens (1906), which enshrined the principles Pelloutier had fought for: independence from political parties, rejection of parliamentarism, reliance on direct action, and preparation for the general strike as the opening of a new social order.

Rudolf Rocker: Anarchism as Worldview and Practice

Rudolf Rocker (1873–1958), German writer, activist, and philosopher, became one of the defining voices of anarcho-syndicalism in the twentieth century. He fused the ideals of classical anarchism with the daily struggles of the labor movement, giving anarcho-syndicalism not only a program but also a philosophy.

Rocker began in the socialist camp, but under the influence of Bakunin and Kropotkin he broke with Marxism. He rejected its faith in centralism, the "dictatorship of the proletariat," and the seizure of the state as the road to liberation. For Rocker, state and capitalism were two faces of the same power—and freedom could exist only when both were dismantled.

The heart of his thought was self-management. Liberation, he argued, could never be handed down by parties or leaders. It had to be seized directly by workers themselves, organized in free unions and councils built on horizontal cooperation.

His activism crossed borders. In Germany and Britain he became a central figure of the anarchist movement, and in 1922 he helped found the International Workers' Association (IWA–AIT), a global federation of anarcho-syndicalist unions. This International stood against parliamentary socialism, insisting on independence from political parties and reliance on direct action.

His most enduring book, *Nationalism and Culture* (1937), written in exile, was a sweeping critique of the modern nation-state. Rocker argued that nationalism, far from protecting liberty, smothered it, and that only autonomy, ethics, and voluntary cooperation could form the basis of a free society. Against the machinery of centralized power he set the principles of solidarity and self-rule.

For Rocker, anarcho-syndicalism was never just an economic model; it was a worldview. He emphasized that anarchism did not mean disorder or chaos but a higher form of order—one grounded in voluntary agreement and equality rather than coercion and profit.

Forced to flee Germany after the Nazi rise to power, Rocker settled in the United States. There he continued to write, lecture, and refine his vision of a society without rulers. His voice, uncompromising and humanist, still resonates today—in scholarship, in radical circles, and in every movement that challenges the union of state and capital.

Noam Chomsky: Anarcho-Syndicalism in the 21st Century

Noam Chomsky (b. 1928), American linguist, philosopher, and public intellectual, is one of the few contemporary thinkers to identify openly with the anarcho-syndicalist tradition. He has not turned it into a formal doctrine, but he has given it new life by adapting its principles to the realities of late capitalism and the information age. To me, Chomsky stands out not only as a brilliant theorist but as one of the greatest philosophers and linguists of our time, a mind whose clarity and courage command my deepest respect.

Chomsky begins from a simple demand: every form of power—political, economic, military, or media—must justify itself, or it deserves to be dismantled. In his view, both centralized states and transnational corporations are authoritarian by nature and incapable of providing justice or freedom. Against them, anarcho-syndicalism offers a different order: one built on direct democracy and control of production from below.

For Chomsky, a free society rests on workers' collectives and federations of unions. Work, he insists, should not be reduced to survival or profit. It should be a sphere of human fulfillment, shaped and directed by those who carry it out. When labor is self-managed, alienation fades and activity regains meaning and dignity.

He is equally concerned with the subtler forms of domination. In modern societies, power is enforced not only by police or armies but also by media, schools, and advertising. These institutions manufacture consent, dull critical thought, and make obedience appear natural. For Chomsky, anarcho-syndicalism is therefore not only an economic program but also a shield against ideological control.

Yet Chomsky is no utopian dreamer. He does not call for the instant abolition of states or corporations. Instead, he argues for a steady democratization of every sphere of life. Anarcho-syndicalism, in his hands, becomes less a final blueprint than a direction: a way forward toward a society where power is accountable and economic life serves the many rather than the few.

Mechanisms of Functioning

Core Principles of Union Organization: Autonomy, Federation, Delegates, Rotation, Accountability, Direct Action, General Strike

The structure of anarcho-syndicalist unions breaks sharply with the centralized, top-down models of traditional trade unions and political parties. Instead of fixed hierarchies and professional bureaucracies, anarcho-syndicalism builds on horizontal relations where authority is temporary, accountable, and recallable. This difference is not cosmetic but fundamental: it shapes how power is distributed, how decisions are made, and how workers experience their own role within the movement.

1. **Autonomy**

Each local union—whether in a factory, workshop, or town—decides for itself. Autonomy does not mean isolation, but it affirms the right of every group to shape its own strategy, choose its methods of struggle, and design its internal life.

By contrast, traditional unions often subordinate local branches to national headquarters, where leadership negotiates and decides policies on their behalf.

2. **Federal Organization**

Coordination is necessary, but not centralism. Local unions link together in federations built from the bottom up through delegation. Membership is voluntary, and each unit retains its independence. The federation serves as a hub for coordination, never as a command center.

Conventional unions, on the other hand, operate as centralized bureaucracies where decisions flow downward, and federations act as executive authorities rather than coordinating bodies.

3. **Delegates, Not Representatives**

In place of representatives who act in the name of others, anarcho-syndicalism relies on delegates bound by mandate. Their authority is narrow, defined by the assemblies that elect them. Delegates do not legislate; they carry out the collective decisions of their base.

In traditional unions, representatives often acquire independence from the rank and file, becoming professional negotiators who may compromise without direct consultation.

4. Rotation and Recall

No office is permanent. All posts rotate, and any delegate can be removed at once if they overstep their mandate or lose the trust of their members. This principle blocks the rise of entrenched elites or bureaucratic castes.

In hierarchical unions, leadership positions can last for years or even decades, creating layers of bureaucracy resistant to change and insulated from workers' daily struggles.

5. Accountability and Transparency

Decisions are made in open assemblies, where all members can participate. Information must be shared, criticism is expected, and every body reports back to those who empowered it. Authority exists only under constant grassroots scrutiny, preventing the rise of cliques or hidden decision-making. Every discussion becomes both a political act and a form of education, teaching workers how to deliberate and govern collectively.

By contrast, traditional unions often conduct decision-making behind closed doors, with limited transparency and restricted access for ordinary members. This distance between leadership and rank and file can turn unions into bureaucracies where decisions are handed down rather than openly shaped.

6. Direct Action

Instead of waiting on courts, parliaments, or professional politicians, workers act for themselves. Strikes, boycotts, and sabotage are not just tactics of pressure but also schools of solidarity, teaching people to rely on their own strength.

Traditional unions tend to prioritize legal arbitration, negotiations, or lobbying politicians—methods that keep initiative in the hands of leaders rather than workers themselves.

7. The General Strike

The general strike is more than protest. It is envisioned as the opening act of revolution—the moment when labor withdraws across industries and society is reorganized under self-management and collective control.

In centralized unions, general strikes are rare and typically symbolic, intended to pressure governments for concessions rather than to inaugurate a new social order.

Parallel in Perspective

The contrast is stark. Traditional trade unions, though vital in securing reforms, often mirror the state and corporate hierarchies they oppose: centralized leadership, entrenched officials, and a reliance on external institutions to mediate conflict. Anarcho-syndicalist unions, by rejecting these patterns, aim to cultivate a culture of participation where workers govern themselves directly. This demands more responsibility, more awareness, and more involvement from every member. Yet anarcho-syndicalists argue that only through such constant grassroots control can freedom and equality move from ideals into lived reality.

Principles of Direct Action: Strikes, Boycotts, Rejection of Parliamentary Politics, Expropriation, and Internationalism

Anarcho-syndicalism rests on the belief that workers can free themselves only through their own collective action, not through parties, elections, or state institutions. At its center stands direct action—forms of struggle where workers act for themselves, defending their interests and practicing the solidarity that points toward a different society.

1. The Strike: Weapon and Beginning

The strike is the movement's most emblematic weapon. For anarcho-syndicalists it is never only a bargaining tool but a rehearsal for a new order. The highest form of this idea is the general revolutionary strike, when labor halts across industries and regions. Its aim is not simply concessions but the transfer of production into workers' own hands. In this sense, the strike resists exploitation while sketching the outlines of another way of life.

2. Boycott and Sabotage: Pressure from Below

The boycott—refusal to buy, sell, or cooperate—undermines the strength of companies and institutions by cutting off legitimacy at its root. Sabotage goes further: workers disrupt production, slow down, or block routines, showing that without their active cooperation nothing moves. Both tactics bypass courts and parliaments, reminding employers that power lies not in offices but on the shop floor.

3. Rejection of Parliamentary Politics

A defining principle of anarcho-syndicalism is the refusal to channel struggle into parliaments. Representation is seen as a trap that severs people from their own will. Votes cannot deliver freedom, because the institutions they sustain are built to preserve domination. Instead, anarcho-syndicalists construct their own forms of political life—assemblies, councils, federations—where decisions are made directly and can be revoked at any moment.

4. Expropriation and Self-Management

Direct action also means taking back what labor has created. Expropriation is not theft but the reclaiming of workplaces, land, and infrastructure from owners who treat them as private property. In Spain during 1936–1937, entire sectors—factories, farms, transport, and services—were collectivized and run by workers' councils. Here protest turned into construction: capitalist relations were torn down even as new forms of economic democracy were built in their place.

5. Internationalism in Practice

For anarcho-syndicalists, direct action cannot stop at national borders. Workers' struggles are linked, and victories in one place are fragile without solidarity elsewhere. From its founding in 1922, the International Workers' Association (IWA–AIT) coordinated strikes and campaigns across countries, seeking to shield movements from isolation and repression. Internationalism was not a slogan but a necessity, the recognition that workers everywhere confront the same systems of power.

Direct action in anarcho-syndicalism is more than a set of tactics. It is a philosophy in motion: no delegation, no permanent leaders, no waiting on institutions above. In strikes, boycotts, expropriations, and international solidarity, workers learned to rely on their own strength and to build, even amid struggle, glimpses of a freer order

Relationship with Other Forms of Self-Management: Communal Councils, Collectives, and Cooperatives

Anarcho-syndicalism is not limited to labor struggles or trade-union structures. Within this model, new forms of non-state coordination take shape, reaching far beyond the factory floor into the fabric of everyday life.

1. Communal Councils

Communal councils are organs of self-government at the level of neighborhoods, towns, or cities. They are not imposed from above by decree but created directly by residents. Their tasks range from distributing resources to organizing schools, healthcare, transport, and cultural life.

From an anarcho-syndicalist perspective, councils are built on direct participation—open assemblies, collective debate, and rotating delegates subject to recall. Linked with workers' syndicates, they form part of a mesh of self-managed bodies that hold both economic and social life in common hands.

2. Workers' Collectives

Workers' collectives replace wage labor with direct control of production. There are no bosses or private owners; decisions are taken collectively, and income is shared according to principles agreed by all. Everything—from purchases of raw materials to workplace discipline—is debated and decided in assemblies.

These collectives can operate on their own or join wider federations, serving as the nucleus of a new economy where labor itself governs production and the fruits of work return to those who create them.

3. Cooperatives

Cooperatives exist under capitalism, but anarcho-syndicalism pushes them further. In this vision, they are not simply alternative businesses but building blocks of a system founded on solidarity instead of competition. Their purpose is not profit but the satisfaction of shared needs.

Working in concert with unions and communal councils, cooperatives help weave a broader fabric of mutual aid.

A Horizontal Society

Anarcho-syndicalist society is imagined as a living network of interlinked structures—syndicates, councils, collectives, and cooperatives—covering every sphere from production to local governance. Instead of a centralized bureaucracy, it rests on coordination through agreement, shared responsibility, and constant grassroots participation. What emerges is not a state in miniature but a different order altogether: horizontal, self-managed, and rooted in the daily practice of solidarity.

Contemporary Relevance of Anarcho-Syndicalism

Modern Forms of Anarcho-Syndicalism

Although anarcho-syndicalist movements were violently crushed in the first half of the twentieth century, their ideas never vanished. In today's globalized world—marked by growing inequality, corporate concentration, and the crisis of representative democracy—they have returned to relevance, drawing the attention of activists and scholars alike.

1. Contemporary Movements and Organizations

The principles of anarcho-syndicalism live on in organizations affiliated with the International Workers' Association (IWA–AIT), founded in 1922. Among its most active sections are:

- the CNT in Spain, re-established after Franco's fall;
- the USI in Italy (*Unione Sindacale Italiana*);
- the FAU in Germany (*Freie Arbeiterinnen- und Arbeiter-Union*);
- the FORA in Argentina (*Federación Obrera Regional Argentina*).

These unions continue to practice direct democracy and self-management, refusing ties to political parties or state funding. Their survival shows that anarcho-syndicalism remains more than memory—it remains organization in action.

2. Influence on Social Movements

The impact of anarcho-syndicalism stretches far beyond union halls. Its ideas shape environmental campaigns, anti-globalization protests, and grassroots housing or student initiatives. They can be traced in worker cooperatives governed horizontally and in mobilizations against international financial institutions—most famously the Seattle anti-WTO protests of 1999 and anti-G8 actions across Europe.

Through these struggles, anarcho-syndicalism nourishes the anti-authoritarian current of left politics, promoting economies rooted in solidarity, structures built on decentralization, and suspicion of elites whether political or corporate.

3. Critique of Contemporary Capitalism

Modern anarcho-syndicalists direct their sharpest criticism at neoliberal capitalism. They argue that it widens inequality, hollows out communities, and reduces democracy to empty ritual while forcing labor to serve profit alone.

As an alternative, they stress not only resistance but also construction: building new practices of self-management in work, consumption, and education. The strategy remains the same as a century ago—create the new within the old, nurture autonomous spaces, and expand cooperative federations until they form the skeleton of a different society.

Contemporary Anarcho-Syndicalist Movements in Latin America and Europe

Although anarcho-syndicalism no longer has the mass base it commanded in the early twentieth century, its organizations and ideas remain alive in Europe and Latin

America. They bring together activists opposed to wage labor, bureaucracy, authoritarianism, and economic inequality. Unlike classical parties of the left, they do not compete for political office but build alternative forms of labor and social life through self-management, federalism, and direct action.

1. Spain: CNT and Its Legacy

Spain is still the heartland of the tradition. After Franco's fall in the 1970s, the *Confederación Nacional del Trabajo* (CNT) was rebuilt. In 1979, internal disputes produced a split and the formation of the CGT (*Confederación General del Trabajo*). The CNT, however, held fast to anarchist principles and rejected electoral politics.

Today the CNT operates as an independent union, organizing across sectors, supporting strikes, and launching workplace and neighborhood campaigns. Its federalist structure, rotating delegates, and assemblies reflect the same horizontal spirit that defined it a century ago.

2. Italy: Unione Sindacale Italiana (USI)

The *Unione Sindacale Italiana* (USI), founded in 1912, suffered repression under fascism but was revived after World War II. It remains a union without party ties, active in struggles against privatization, layoffs, and austerity in education and healthcare. Its focus is on workplace self-organization and the defense of public services through direct action.

3. Germany: FAU (Freie Arbeiterinnen- und Arbeiter-Union)

In Germany, the FAU (*Free Workers' Union*) is smaller in numbers but known for its militancy. It runs campaigns in labor disputes, housing struggles, and cultural projects, while also supporting worker-run cooperatives. For the FAU, everyday resistance—whether in a single workplace or across a city—is itself a form of politics. Its structure is federal, transparent, and deliberately resistant to hierarchy.

4. Latin America: Argentina, Brazil, and Chile

Latin America was one of the early strongholds of anarcho-syndicalism. The *Federación Obrera Regional Argentina* (FORA), founded more than a century ago, still exists as one of the world's oldest anarchist federations. It remains committed to revolutionary syndicalism and active in labor struggles.

In Brazil and Chile, smaller groups linked to the IWA–AIT participate in strikes, ecological protests, campus organizing, and the defense of worker cooperatives, continuing the long tradition of anarchist activism in the region.

5. International Coordination: IWA–AIT

The International Workers' Association (IWA–AIT), founded in 1922, still connects anarcho-syndicalist unions in more than fifteen countries. It holds congresses, facilitates the exchange of strategies, and coordinates solidarity across borders. In an age of global capitalism, it remains the main channel through which anarcho-syndicalists link local struggles to an international movement. Its network makes it possible for workers in different regions to respond collectively to repression, economic crises, or attacks on labor rights.

Influence on Independent Unions, Left Anti-Authoritarian, and Environmental Movements

Although anarcho-syndicalist organizations remain limited in size in the twenty-first century, their ideas continue to exert a strong influence on broader currents of social activism—especially among independent trade unions, anti-authoritarian left movements, and ecological initiatives that reject centralized leadership, party structures, and hierarchical organization.

1. Independent Unions

The anarcho-syndicalist model has shaped many unions seeking to distance themselves from large party-affiliated federations, bureaucratized central organizations, and compromises with state or corporate power.

These unions typically:

- operate on principles of direct democracy;
- reject participation in electoral politics;
- rely on horizontal structures, local autonomy, and rotating, recallable delegates;
- use direct action—strikes, boycotts, occupations—as their primary means of struggle.

Examples include the CNT in Spain, FAU in Germany, and USI in Italy, as well as smaller independent unions in South America and parts of Eastern Europe.

2. Left Anti-Authoritarian Movements

Anarcho-syndicalism provides an ideological foundation for numerous anti-party, anti-capitalist, and anti-hierarchical movements, particularly among youth. Its legacy is visible in:

- the rejection of centralized leadership;
- the drive toward self-organization without intermediaries;
- emphasis on solidarity, mutual aid, and the participation of all;
- skepticism toward hierarchical structures, including Marxist parties, centralized union federations, and statist left groups.

These ideas have been especially evident in the large-scale protests of recent decades—from Occupy Wall Street to various anti-globalization campaigns.

3. Environmental Movements

Contemporary ecological movements often borrow from the anarcho-syndicalist tradition, adopting:

- the principle of local autonomy (rural and urban communes, eco-villages);
- practices of horizontal governance;
- the conviction that ecological sustainability is inseparable from social justice;
- a critique of industrial capitalism as destructive to both nature and community life.

In many countries, activists combine participation in cooperatives, ecological projects, and labor self-organization, developing alternative economic forms outside the logic of profit and centralized control.

Critique of Contemporary Capitalism from the Perspective of Anarcho-Syndicalism

Anarcho-syndicalism is not only an alternative model of labor and social life but also a radical critique of capitalism itself. It sees in the existing order the roots of inequality, alienation, and domination—problems that extend beyond the economy into politics, culture, and the very way society functions.

1. Wage Labor as Exploitation

For anarcho-syndicalists, wage labor embodies inequality at its core. The worker is cut off from the product of labor, stripped of control over production, and made subject to the authority of capital. The employer's power does not come from creative contribution but from the legal right to command the labor of others. Against this arrangement, anarcho-syndicalism calls for direct workers' control of production, ending the separation between those who work and those who profit.

2. Centralization and Corporate Rule

Modern capitalism breeds monopolies and transnational corporations that concentrate wealth and power. Decisions shaping millions of lives are made in boardrooms, hidden from public scrutiny, and insulated from accountability. To this, anarcho-syndicalists oppose decentralization, open assemblies, and collective decision-making rooted in workplaces and communities, not in corporate headquarters.

3. The State as Guardian of Capital

The state is not a neutral referee but the partner of capital. Through law, subsidies, taxation, and repression, it secures private property and enforces hierarchy. Far from protecting freedom, it shields the interests of those who own and rule. For anarcho-syndicalists, capitalism and the state form a single system of domination, both of which must be replaced by federations of self-managed workers' structures.

4. Market Logic and Consumerism

The capitalist economy is driven not by human need but by profit and endless growth. The result is overproduction, ecological destruction, and the manufacture of artificial desires. Anarcho-syndicalists argue for a different standard: production guided by social need and ecological balance, organized to sustain communities rather than expand capital.

5. Democracy Without Power

Formal democracy, they contend, leaves real power untouched. Elections hand authority to elites already tied to the system, turning participation into ritual rather than reality. For anarcho-syndicalists, true democracy begins when people govern directly in their workplaces and communities—when decisions are not delegated upward but made collectively by those they affect.

> Anarcho-syndicalist critique of capitalism is not based on the desire to replace one set of ruling actors with another, but on the rejection of the very logic of power, hierarchy, and coercion that underpins the modern economic and political order.

Comparison with Other Anarchist Models
Distinction from Anarcho-Communism

Anarcho-syndicalism and anarcho-communism share the goal of a stateless, classless society but differ in the path they propose to reach it.

1. **Organization of Labor**

- *Anarcho-syndicalism*: unions and workers' collectives form the backbone of the new order. Workplaces are self-managed, and productive structures become the scaffolding of future society.
- *Anarcho-communism*: specialized labor organizations dissolve into free communes. Labor is not a duty tied to a trade but a natural expression of human activity shared by all.

2. **Property and Management**

- *Anarcho-syndicalism*: accepts collective ownership at the level of unions or federations. Each workplace governs itself, linked to others through federated councils.
- *Anarcho-communism*: rejects even collective property. All resources belong to the community as a whole, not to particular labor groups.

3. **Distribution of Goods**

- *Anarcho-syndicalism*: goods are distributed in relation to contribution. Collectives retain or exchange what they produce, without profit but still tied to labor.
- *Anarcho-communism*: distribution follows need, not contribution. Goods are shared as common wealth, on the basis of solidarity rather than equivalence.

4. **Approach to Revolution**

- *Anarcho-syndicalism*: envisions revolution through a general strike and the takeover of workplaces, which become pillars of the new society.
- *Anarcho-communism*: imagines a more immediate rupture—old structures dissolve, and free communes arise spontaneously, without reliance on organized industry as the instrument of liberation.

5. **Practical Orientation**

- *Anarcho-syndicalism*: builds in the present—unions, labor struggles, self-management. Its strategy is gradual: to construct the new world inside the shell of the old.
- *Anarcho-communism*: functions less as a program than as an ideal. It offers a vision of life beyond the division of work and consumption, but without a clear path for how to reach it under current conditions.

The fundamental distinction lies in this: anarcho-syndicalism is a **method**, while anarcho-communism is a **goal**.

The former builds on the practice of self-organization through labor; the latter imagines life beyond the separation of work and consumption. Both strive for a free society, but they propose different routes and different understandings of what freedom entails.

Distinction from Individualist Anarchism

Anarcho-syndicalism and individualist anarchism stand within the same anarchist tradition, yet they diverge sharply. Both reject state power and hierarchy, but they clash in how they define freedom, the role of society, and the path to liberation.

1. ## Conceptions of Freedom

- *Anarcho-syndicalism*: freedom is social, possible only where equality, mutual support, and collective decision-making prevail. No one is free while others remain oppressed.

- *Individualist anarchism*: freedom is personal autonomy—the individual released from external control, whether from the state, social norms, or collective obligations.

2. ## Collectivism vs. Individualism

- *Anarcho-syndicalism*: values collective labor and solidarity, seeing society as a web of federated groups that govern together.

- *Individualist anarchism*: regards collectivism as a danger to independence, affirming the right to live apart from groups and refuse collective demands.

3. ## Organization

- *Anarcho-syndicalism*: builds federations, unions, and councils where delegates are elected, recallable, and rotated.

- *Individualist anarchism*: questions organization itself, warning that even horizontal structures can become forms of pressure on the individual.

4. ## Economy

- *Anarcho-syndicalism*: calls for collective ownership of production, managed directly by workers.

- *Individualist anarchism*: favors personal property and self-sufficiency, often preferring independent exchange over collective economics.

5. ## Ethics

- *Anarcho-syndicalism*: freedom and equality are inseparable; one cannot exist without the other.

- *Individualist anarchism*: freedom is absolute, even if it produces inequality; autonomy outweighs all other values.

Anarcho-syndicalism pursues liberation through solidarity and shared responsibility. Individualist anarchism defends personal autonomy, even against the collective itself. Both envision life without authority, but one seeks it together, the other alone.

SECTION 2. ANARCHO-COMMUNISM: STATELESS SOCIETY BASED ON COMMUNAL OWNERSHIP AND EQUALITY

> **Anarcho-communism** is an anarchist theory that calls for the abolition of the state, private property, and the market economy in order to build a society based on collective ownership, self-management, and the free distribution of goods according to need.

Anarcho-communism stands as a direct challenge to every form of oppression. It calls for the abolition of the state, private property, markets, and money—institutions seen as the pillars of injustice. For its advocates, no true freedom or equality is possible in a society where wealth and power are concentrated in a few hands. Justice can emerge only when resources and labor are held in common and shared through solidarity and voluntary cooperation, so that no one rules and no one is forced into subordination.

Principles and Goals

At the heart of anarcho-communism lies the principle: *"From each according to ability, to each according to need."* This principle is not a dream of charity but a demand for fairness. It rejects profit, wages, and market exchange as tools of exploitation. Instead, it insists that every person has the right to have their needs met, and every community has the duty to remove the inequalities that deny that right. Justice here means dismantling the structures that generate privilege and oppression.

Social Structure and Self-Governance

In place of the state, anarcho-communists envision a network of free communes and associations created by the people themselves. Decisions are made openly, and delegates are recallable at any time. Such forms of governance are designed to prevent the rise of new elites and to guarantee that no authority can place itself above the community. This constant accountability is not only democracy—it is protection against the return of domination.

Economic Model

Anarcho-communism breaks with both private and collective ownership in the conventional sense. All resources belong to the community as a whole. Production is guided not by profit but by justice: ensuring that everyone has access to what they need. Distribution takes place without money or trade, eliminating the inequalities created by wealth. Goods circulate freely, and labor is shared, so that exploitation— one person living from the toil of another—becomes impossible.

The Desired Society

The ultimate aim is a world without oppression, where no person exercises power over another. Authority and hierarchy give way to cooperation and reciprocity. Labor is no longer forced or bought but becomes a form of creative participation in common life. In such a society, justice is no longer an abstract principle but a lived reality: each contributes what they can and receives what they need, not as privilege, but as a right.

Strengths of Anarcho-Communism

1. ## Equality at the Core

Common ownership eliminates class divisions; wealth and poverty as structural categories disappear, and access to essential goods is shared equally.

2. ## Freedom with Responsibility

Without state or hierarchy, individuals direct their own lives but also participate in assemblies and mutual aid, binding freedom to collective responsibility.

3. ## End of Domination

With no bureaucratic or coercive institutions, there is no apparatus for repression or political violence; power over others loses its structural base.

4. ## Economy for Human Needs

Production serves real needs rather than profit, reducing the cycles of crisis, waste, and deprivation that mark capitalist economies.

5. ## Work Without Alienation

Labor is no longer sold as a commodity but becomes voluntary participation in community life, restoring meaning and dignity to work.

6. ## Transparent Social Relations

With money, taxes, and legal contracts abolished, social life simplifies: resources and decisions are visible and accessible to all.

7. ## Solidarity as Social Glue

Mutual aid replaces competition. People cooperate out of conscious commitment, strengthening horizontal bonds and trust. This culture of reciprocity creates resilience, ensuring that communities can withstand crises and support their members without reliance on coercive institutions.

8. ## Ecological Balance

By rejecting endless growth, production aligns with sustainability, avoiding waste and ecological damage driven by profit motives.

9. ## Internationalism

Borders and nationalism are rejected, promoting solidarity across peoples and reducing the drivers of conflict and war.

10. ## Unity of Labor and Creativity

Work, art, and education merge into a single sphere of human activity, enriching both individuals and the collective.

11. ## Peace Without Militarism

With no state, standing army, or imperial ambition, the structural basis for war vanishes; societies tend toward peaceful cooperation.

Weaknesses of Anarcho-Communism

1. Coordination at Scale

Decentralized communes work locally, but large systems—energy grids, transport, supply chains—require synchronized management.

2. Work Motivation

With no wages or profit incentives, essential but unattractive tasks risk neglect. If recognition and peer accountability are weak, free-riding emerges and productivity drops.

3. Uneven Participation

Self-management assumes equal engagement, but in practice knowledge, stamina, and willingness vary. Active minorities may dominate while others disengage, undermining legitimacy.

4. The Transitional Period

Abolishing state, markets, and property at once disrupts supply chains, inventories, and payments. Without phased conversion, shortages and instability can follow.

5. External Pressure

Lacking a central army or diplomacy, such societies are exposed to blockades, sanctions, or aggression. Ad-hoc defense lacks the long-term coordination of state systems.

6. Active Groups' Dominance

Even without formal hierarchies, organized minorities can capture agendas. Without safeguards, informal elites and majority pressure can replace open equality.

7. No Long-Term Precedents

Experiments have existed locally or briefly, but none at scale or over time.

8. Economic Inefficiency

Without pricing or robust planning, production may misalign with demand—creating shortages in some areas and surpluses in others.

9. Innovation Challenges

Capital-intensive projects like new medicines or large infrastructures need sustained investment and tolerance for risk. Without clear mechanisms, innovation may stagnate.

10. Idealized Human Nature

The model presumes solidarity and altruism. In reality, self-interest and conflict appear, and without conflict-management tools, fractures grow.

11. Infrastructure Maintenance

Large networks need continuous technical oversight and standards. Volunteer rotation can weaken continuity, causing safety or reliability failures.

12. Risk of Fragmentation

Over time, communes may diverge in norms and priorities, hoard resources, or neglect cooperation. Solidarity weakens, and federations may splinter.

Historical Context and Sources

The Emergence of Anarcho-Communist Ideas in the 19th Century

Anarcho-communism took shape in the nineteenth century as a response to two interconnected processes: the rapid spread of industrialization and the consolidation of centralized nation-states. Factories drew masses of workers into conditions of long hours, low pay, and dangerous labor, while state institutions grew in strength, policing dissent and suppressing older communal traditions. These changes deepened inequality, eroded local solidarities, and entrenched hierarchical authority. Against this backdrop, anarchist thought acquired a new direction in which the aspiration to freedom was fused with a radical critique of private property and state power.

The roots of anarcho-communism lay in revolutionary anarchism associated with Pierre-Joseph Proudhon, Mikhail Bakunin, and Peter Kropotkin. Yet unlike individualist anarchism, which stressed personal autonomy above all, anarcho-communism emphasized the building of a cooperative society rooted in solidarity, equality, collective ownership, and voluntary labor.

Its emergence was also shaped by growing disillusionment with parliamentary democracy, seen as a façade masking elite rule, and with the Marxist concept of the dictatorship of the proletariat, viewed as a new form of domination. Anarcho-communists insisted that every authority—even one claiming to be temporary or revolutionary—inevitably reproduced subordination. For them, emancipation meant not seizing state power but abolishing it alongside private property.

The theory matured most fully between the 1870s and 1890s. During this period:

- federations of anarchist communes appeared in Italy, France, and Switzerland, experimenting with coordination without centralized rule;
- a distinction crystallized between social anarchism, oriented toward long-term communal structures, and insurrectionary anarchism, or the "anarchism of action," which emphasized direct revolt;
- programs were advanced calling for the abolition of commodity exchange, money, wages, and centralized planning, envisioning an economy organized directly around human needs.

Anarcho-communism thus evolved alongside Marxism but with a fundamentally different orientation: not the seizure of power, but its dissolution; not the party, but the free federation of communes; not abstract economic calculation, but the direct satisfaction of human needs as the foundation of freedom and equality.

Critique of the State and Marxist Centralism

Anarcho-communism begins with the categorical rejection not only of capitalism but of the very idea of the state itself. In anarcho-communist theory, the state is seen as an institution fundamentally incompatible with freedom, regardless of who controls it—monarchs, the bourgeoisie, or even a "revolutionary class." Power, once institutionalized, reproduces domination.

A central theme of anarcho-communist thought is its critique of the Marxist model of transition to socialism, especially the doctrine of the dictatorship of the proletariat. Mikhail Bakunin and his followers argued that the creation of a workers' state would not dismantle the logic of power but merely shift it into new hands. The proletarian dictatorship, they warned, would inevitably generate a fresh apparatus of domination—bureaucracy, a centralized army, repression, and a ruling elite presenting itself as the guardian of the revolution.

Bakunin predicted that a revolution following the Marxist path would result in a new class society, with the ruling party replacing the old aristocracy and bourgeoisie. The experience of the twentieth century—most clearly the Soviet Union—appeared to confirm this forecast for anarcho-communists. Their critique targeted not only authoritarian practices but also the Marxist claim that the state would "wither away" after a transitional phase. For anarchists, the very nature of power makes such withering impossible: authority entrenches itself, and coercion cannot produce liberation.

Anarcho-communists also challenged Marxist economic centralism. They argued that a centrally planned economy governed by a single authority would suffocate initiative, generate bureaucracy, and erode democracy in everyday economic life. As an alternative, they proposed a federation of self-managed communes, coordinating production and distribution through voluntary cooperation, horizontal structures, and mutual agreements.

Thus, anarcho-communism's critique of the state is more than a political disagreement with Marxism; it reflects a philosophical divide in how each tradition conceives power, freedom, and social change. Where Marxists sought to capture and redirect state power, anarcho-communists demanded its abolition as the first condition for creating a society that is genuinely free and equal.

Historical Preconditions:Class Struggle, Industrialization, Inequality

Anarcho-communism arose in the second half of the nineteenth century as a response to the profound transformations sweeping Europe. Its development was shaped by three converging forces: the upheaval of industrialization, the deepening of social inequality, and the intensification of class struggle.

1. **Industrialization and the Loss of Communal Life**

The Industrial Revolution overturned traditional patterns of society. Agriculture, craftsmanship, and local communal bonds gave way to factories, mass production, and the concentration of labor and capital.

The factory system reduced human beings to wage workers bound to schedules and machines they did not control. Work ceased to be self-directed; its aims and results were dictated from above. Rural regions emptied as peasants moved to cities, swelling an urban population forced to live in poverty and complete dependence on employers.

2. The Growth of Inequality

Industrial capitalism produced a sharp economic divide. On one side stood the bourgeoisie—factory owners, bankers, merchants—who accumulated vast wealth and political influence. On the other were landless peasants and wage workers, compelled to sell their labor simply to survive.

The labor market was ruled not by fairness but by supply and demand. Child labor, exhausting hours, paltry wages, and unsafe conditions defined working life. The state, far from protecting the weak, acted as guarantor of a social order designed to defend property and privilege.

3. The Rise of Class Struggle

Out of these conditions a new working-class identity emerged. Workers moved beyond demands for reforms and began to question a system where labor itself was a commodity. They saw that their lives were subordinated to the dictates of the market. Strikes and stoppages spread; unions, communes, and self-managed associations began to form. The struggle left the ballot box behind and increasingly turned toward the idea of revolution as the only way to escape capitalist domination.

4. Disillusionment with Parliamentary Politics

Early workers' movements soon lost faith in parliamentary democracy, where promises of representation turned into compromise or neglect. In this context anarchist critiques of the state resonated widely.

Unlike Marxists, anarcho-communists did not believe liberation could come through capturing power. They sought instead to abolish power as such, seeing it as an instrument of domination. Their alternative was the federation of free communes built on voluntary labor, equality, and solidarity.

Before anarcho-communism had fully crystallized as theory, its principles were already tested in practice. Experiments in collective life—most famously the Paris Commune of 1871, as well as numerous utopian communal projects across Europe and the Americas—embodied, however briefly, the ideals of equality, freedom, and common ownership that later defined anarcho-communist thought.

The Paris Commune (1871)

The Paris Commune was a short-lived yet momentous experiment in self-government and social revolution, born out of France's defeat in the Franco-Prussian War (1870–1871) and the popular uprising against the national government led by Adolphe Thiers. The immediate trigger was the government's attempt to disarm the Parisian National Guard by removing cannons from Montmartre. Instead of submission, Parisians resisted, seized control of the capital in March 1871, and proclaimed the Commune.

The experiment lasted only seventy-two days (March–May 1871), but its impact on socialist, anarchist, and revolutionary thought has been enduring.

Historical Context

- France's loss to Prussia left the country humiliated, with Paris besieged and its people enduring hunger, unemployment, and deep resentment.

- The decision to confiscate artillery from Montmartre and dissolve the National Guard sparked mass resistance and led to the Commune's proclamation.

Organization of Power

- Authority rested in elected workers' councils formed directly from below. All officials, including militia commanders, were subject to recall at any time.
- Legislative and executive functions were fused in a single council of delegates.
- Officials' salaries were capped at the level of the average worker's wage.
- The standing army was abolished and replaced by a people's militia.

Social and Economic Measures

- Rents accumulated during the siege of Paris were canceled, relieving thousands of workers and families.
- Empty workshops were turned over to workers' cooperatives, beginning the socialization of production.
- The working day was shortened, and wage labor began to be abolished in some institutions.
- Public education was reformed: schooling became secular, free of clerical control, and accessible to more children.
- Women played an active role in the revolution, organizing through clubs and associations such as the *Union des Femmes*, led by figures like Louise Michel. They pressed for equality, social reforms, and direct participation in the life of the Commune.

Cultural and Symbolic Actions

- The Commune united diverse currents—Jacobins, Blanquists, Proudhonists, and members of the International Workingmen's Association. Despite ideological differences, the Commune served as a living experiment in radical democracy.
- Symbolic acts included the demolition of the Vendôme Column, denounced as a monument to militarism, imperial conquest, and domination.

Causes of Defeat

- The Versailles government, reinforced by Prussian troops, possessed overwhelming military superiority.
- Lack of coordination with uprisings in other regions left the Paris Commune isolated.
- Internal divisions between factions weakened unity and decision-making.
- In May 1871, during the *Semaine sanglante* ("Bloody Week"), government troops stormed Paris. The repression was brutal: between 20,000 and 30,000 Communards were killed, and thousands were imprisoned or deported.

Legacy and Interpretation

- Karl Marx and Friedrich Engels saw the Commune as the first historical example of the "dictatorship of the proletariat," a form of working-class rule Marx described in *The Civil War in France* (1871).
- Mikhail Bakunin and Peter Kropotkin hailed it as proof that self-organization from below could emerge spontaneously, without a centralized state.

- For later generations of socialists, anarchists, and communists, the Commune stood as both an inspiration and a warning—a testament to the possibilities of popular power, and a reminder of the dangers of isolation and repression.

The Paris Commune was not a fully articulated anarcho-communist project, yet for anarchists it showed in practice that governance without centralized state power was possible. Its brutal suppression revealed the vulnerability of such experiments when isolated and fragmented. To this day, it endures as a symbol of solidarity, popular self-government, and the pursuit of freedom—an episode that profoundly shaped the revolutionary imagination of the nineteenth and twentieth centuries.

Utopian Communal Experiments

Alongside the political upheavals of the nineteenth century, dozens of communes and experimental settlements appeared across Europe and the Americas. They were driven by ideals of equality, collective labor, and shared ownership. Though not always explicitly anarchist, they served as living experiments in principles later central to anarcho-communism.

Notable examples include:

- **New Harmony (United States, 1825):** Founded by Robert Owen, it sought to abolish exploitation by replacing private property with collective ownership and making education the foundation of social life.

- **Icarian Communities (United States, mid-19th century):** Established by French followers of Étienne Cabet, these communes attempted a moneyless economy, collective living, and direct governance through assemblies.

- **Saint-Simonian and Fourierist projects (Europe):** Early socialist colonies that emphasized cooperation and collective property, while rejecting the competitive logic of the market.

- **Brook Farm (United States, 1841–1847):** A Transcendentalist commune in Massachusetts where farm work was combined with cultural and intellectual activity, testing egalitarian community structures.

- **Owenite colonies in Britain (1830s–1840s):** Small cooperative settlements in Scotland and England that attempted to replace wage labor with communal self-sufficiency and shared responsibility.

- **Communitarian colonies in Latin America:** Short-lived settlements in Brazil, Uruguay, and Mexico, where European emigrants tried to establish egalitarian communities founded on voluntary labor and common property.

Many of these communities collapsed under the weight of internal disputes, financial strain, or hostile surroundings. Yet they remain significant historical precedents—attempts to build societies outside the authority of both market exchange and state power.

Together with the Paris Commune of 1871, these experiments showed that the ideas of self-management, collectivism, and resistance to hierarchy were not abstract theories. They could be embodied, however briefly, in functioning social structures, proving that another way of living was possible.

Mikhail Bakunin: Anti-Statism, Federalism, Equality

Mikhail Alexandrovich Bakunin (1814–1876) was one of the founding figures of anarchism and remains a central theorist of anarcho-communism. A fiery revolutionary and uncompromising critic of power, he combined personal charisma with relentless radicalism. His life — conspiracies, uprisings, prisons, and exiles — embodied his conviction that liberation could never be granted from above but had to be seized by the people themselves.

Early Life and Revolutionary Career

Born into a Russian noble family, Bakunin began a military career but abandoned it for philosophy. In the 1840s he moved to Western Europe, joining radical circles in Paris and Berlin. He fought in the revolutions of 1848, stood on the barricades in Dresden in 1849, and was arrested and condemned to death. Instead he spent more than a decade in fortress prisons in Russia, including the Peter and Paul and Shlisselburg. Exiled to Siberia, he escaped in 1861, traveling across Japan and the United States before returning to Europe, where he plunged back into revolutionary activity.

1. Anti-Statism: Rejection of the State

For Bakunin, the state was the sworn enemy of freedom. Monarchies, bourgeois republics, even Marx's "dictatorship of the proletariat" were for him only different masks of domination. His core thesis was clear:

> **"Freedom can be achieved not through the seizure of power, but only through its abolition."**

The state was not an instrument of emancipation but a permanent machine of oppression. Temporary dictatorships, he warned, would harden into new hierarchies armed with armies, bureaucracies, and repression.

2. Federalism Against Centralism

As an alternative, Bakunin proposed a federation of free communes and associations, linked by solidarity rather than subordination. Each commune would govern itself but cooperate voluntarily with others. For him, federalism was not only structural but moral: an ethic of dispersing power horizontally rather than concentrating it above.

3. Equality as the Basis of Freedom

Bakunin rejected liberal notions of freedom as a privilege of the few. Freedom, he argued, exists only if it is equal for all; otherwise it degenerates into domination. From this principle came his rejection of private property in the means of production, which he saw as the root of exploitation. He defended collective ownership, but not through state nationalization. Instead, he envisioned communal property and self-managed production, directed by workers themselves.

4. Revolution as Abolition of Power

True revolution, for Bakunin, did not transfer authority to new rulers but destroyed political domination altogether. Violence was justified only in defense, never to establish new elites. Revolution meant the simultaneous destruction of state and capital, and the creation of federations of free, egalitarian, and solidaristic communities.

Bakunin and Marx: The Great Split

Bakunin's fierce opposition to Marx shaped the fate of socialism. Within the First International he led the anti-authoritarian wing that resisted Marx's push for centralized leadership and a transitional workers' state. The clash ended with Bakunin's expulsion in 1872, but it sealed the divide between authoritarian socialism and libertarian anarchism — a divide that continues to structure leftist thought.

Personal Influence and Legacy

Bakunin's speeches and writings, including *Statism and Anarchy* (1873) and the posthumously published *God and the State* (1882), deeply influenced movements across Europe. His charisma and activism inspired anarchists in Italy, Spain, Switzerland, and beyond. His organizations often collapsed under the weight of secrecy and his own impatience, but his key ideas — anti-statism, federalism, equality, and direct revolution — became the pillars of anarchist theory.

Bakunin's life was itself a manifesto: endless resistance, distrust of authority, and faith in the creative power of ordinary people. He was the first to frame anarchism as the simultaneous abolition of state and capital and to outline a political form to replace them — federations of free, cooperative, and self-governing communities.

Peter Kropotkin: Mutual Aid, Rejection of Authority, Science and Ethics

Peter Alexeyevich Kropotkin (1842–1921) was one of anarchism's most influential theorists, a natural scientist, and a central figure in the development of anarcho-communism. His approach fused scientific reasoning, ethical reflection, and a deep understanding of humanity's social nature. Kropotkin was the first to give anarchism a systematic foundation, transforming it from a cry of revolt into a coherent program of ethics and social organization.

1. Mutual Aid as the Basis of Society

In *Mutual Aid: A Factor of Evolution* (1902), Kropotkin challenged the narrow Darwinist claim that survival depended mainly on competition. Drawing on biology, anthropology, and history, he showed that cooperation and solidarity were equally — and often more — decisive for survival than conflict.

For him, mutual aid was not only an evolutionary fact but also a principle for building the future. Human beings, he argued, are naturally inclined to cooperation; what suppresses this tendency are the institutions of state power, private property, and hierarchical authority.

2. Rejection of Power and Hierarchy

Kropotkin insisted that authority in all its forms is rooted in violence. He opposed the state and its organs — political parties, armies, police — as well as religious and intellectual domination. Schools, he argued, too often functioned as instruments of discipline and obedience rather than education.

Freedom, in his view, could not exist wherever initiative was suppressed and individuality stifled by institutions demanding conformity.

3. Science and Anarchism

Unlike critics who dismissed anarchism as chaos, Kropotkin presented it as a scientifically grounded vision of social life. He condemned capitalism for misusing science and technology — not to liberate people, but to tighten control and deepen exploitation.

In a free society, he believed, science would serve human needs: eliminating drudgery, shortening the working day, improving health and welfare. He anticipated decentralized industry, autonomous production units, and ecologically sustainable economies — ideas strikingly relevant to today's debates on post-industrial futures and climate responsibility.

4. Ethics of Freedom and Responsibility

For Kropotkin, anarchism was above all an ethical project. Freedom was never isolation; it meant living with others without coercion, grounded in respect, trust, and voluntary   cooperation.
He rejected the notion of abstract, distant revolution. Anarcho-communism, he argued, begins in the individual: in refusing domination and submission as the normal patterns of thought and behavior.

Legacy and Influence

Kropotkin's writings — especially *The Conquest of Bread* (1892) and *Fields, Factories, and Workshops* (1899) — became foundational texts for anarchists. His vision inspired movements by combining scientific observation with moral conviction. Alongside Mikhail Bakunin, Kropotkin laid the core of anarcho-communist theory. Others expanded it further: Élisée Reclus integrated geography and ecology; Emma Goldman brought anarchist feminism and cultural critique; Alexander Berkman emphasized revolutionary practice and exposed the failures of the Soviet model. Together they gave **anarcho-communism intellectual depth, moral breadth, and enduring vitality.**

Élisée Reclus (1830–1905)

The French geographer, anarchist, and humanist Élisée Reclus (1830–1905) was among the first to weave ecological awareness into anarchist thought. He argued that humanity should not see itself as master of nature but as part of it, bound by ties of interdependence. His vision was of a society built on voluntary cooperation, equality, and respect for the environment — a world where exploitation, whether of people or of nature, had no place.

Geography and Anarchism

Reclus transformed geography from a descriptive discipline into a science with ethical and social meaning. Geography, in his hands, was the study of how humans inhabit the earth and how their institutions shape both society and the natural environment.

He showed that systems of domination deform not only social life but also humanity's relationship with the planet itself.

Major Works

His monumental *La Nouvelle Géographie Universelle* (*The New Universal Geography*, 1876–1894), in 19 volumes, mapped not only lands but also cultures, economies, and social forms, always stressing their connection with the environment. Later, in *L'Homme et la Terre* (*Man and the Earth*, 1905–1908, published posthumously), he outlined a comprehensive vision of humanity's place in nature. These works anticipated modern ideas of bioregionalism, environmental justice, and the inseparability of ecology and social equality.

Political Commitment

Reclus was more than a scholar; he was also a committed activist. He joined the First International, supporting the anti-authoritarian current of Bakunin against Marx's centralism. His anarchist convictions brought exile and imprisonment, but he never ceased to write and to influence both geographers and political radicals.

Legacy

Reclus united anarcho-communist ideals of freedom, solidarity, and equality with ecological consciousness. For him, genuine liberty was impossible without harmony between humanity and nature. By integrating geography, ethics, and anarchism, he expanded the scope of anarchist theory and laid intellectual foundations for the ecological and environmental movements of the twentieth century.

Emma Goldman (1869–1940)

Emma Goldman (1869–1940), an American anarchist, writer, and activist born in the Russian Empire, became one of the most uncompromising voices of libertarian thought in the twentieth century. For her, anarchism was never just a political program but a way of living: a demand that every individual be free to act, speak, and love without fear of authority. She opposed domination in all its forms — the state, religion, patriarchy, and the rigid codes of morality that stifled authenticity.

Goldman broke with both bourgeois respectability and Marxist orthodoxy. She rejected the idea that people should sacrifice joy or individuality "for the sake of the revolution." A society without oppression, she argued, could exist only if individuals themselves were inwardly free — able to live honestly as who they were. She was also the first major anarchist to speak openly about sexuality, women's autonomy, and everyday violence in personal relationships. Her advocacy of free love, women's rights, and the dignity of self-expression marked the birth of anarchist feminism.

Activism and Persecution

Goldman's activism spanned workers' struggles, the campaign for free speech, access to birth control, and resistance to militarism. Her lectures and pamphlets drew crowds but also the attention of police; she was arrested repeatedly for her words and actions. During World War I she became one of America's most outspoken opponents of conscription, a stance that brought her into direct confrontation with federal authorities.

In 1919 she was deported from the United States during the "Red Scare." J. Edgar Hoover, then a rising official in the Justice Department, called her "one of the most dangerous women in America." Goldman initially greeted the Russian Revolution with enthusiasm, but her hopes collapsed when she witnessed Bolshevik repression, censorship, and political terror. She became one of the earliest and sharpest critics of Soviet power from within the revolutionary left.

Writings and Legacy

Her two-volume autobiography *Living My Life* (1931) offers a vivid account of her

ideals, struggles, and journeys across continents. Alongside her essays and speeches, it remains central to anarchist literature and feminist history. Goldman gave anarchism a cultural and ethical scope it had lacked, linking the liberation of society to the liberation of the self.

Death and Commemoration

Emma Goldman died on May 14, 1940, in Toronto, Canada. Though barred from re

entering the United States while alive, she was granted burial near the Haymarket martyrs in Forest Park, Illinois — a symbolic homecoming to the site of America's radical memory.

Her gravestone bears the words:

"Liberty will not descend to a people, a people must raise themselves to Liberty."

Alexander Berkman (1870–1936)

Alexander Berkman (1870–1936), a close comrade and lifelong friend of Emma Goldman, was one of the most consistent advocates of anarcho-communism. His book *Now and After: The ABC of Anarchism* (1929) remains a classic introduction to anarchist thought, combining a sharp critique of capitalism with a practical outline of how a free society might be organized.

Berkman's life was one of struggle and defiance. In 1892, during the Homestead Strike, he attempted to assassinate industrialist Henry Clay Frick in what he saw as "propaganda by deed" — an act of solidarity with striking steelworkers. The attempt failed, and Berkman spent fourteen years in prison. The experience left him scarred but unbroken. After his release, he resumed his activism, writing, publishing, and organizing alongside Goldman.

In 1919 he was deported from the United States in the wave of the "Red Scare." Returning to Russia, he initially welcomed the revolution, hoping to see ideals of freedom realized. Instead, he witnessed the suppression of anarchists, the crushing of workers' councils, and the rise of a new authoritarian state. Disillusioned, he condemned Bolshevism as the substitution of one tyranny for another. His book *The Bolshevik Myth* (1925) offered a searing account of these years and remains a crucial testimony of anarchist opposition to Soviet power.

For Berkman, anarchism was not an abstract doctrine but a living ethic. It meant fighting for a society where no one held power over the body or the mind of another, where freedom and solidarity were inseparable.

Together with Emma Goldman and Élisée Reclus, Berkman helped broaden anarcho-communist thought beyond economics into culture, ethics, and ecology. Their combined work turned anarchism into more than a political program — into a comprehensive worldview seeking to transform every dimension of human life.

Confrontation with Marxism and the Dictatorship of the Proletariat

From its beginnings, anarcho-communism developed in open opposition to Marxism. Both traditions sought the end of capitalism and the creation of a classless society, but they diverged on the most fundamental questions: the meaning of freedom, the role of power, and the path of revolution.

At the heart of their conflict stood the state. For Marxists, the state — though born as a bourgeois institution — could be seized, transformed, and used as a weapon of class struggle. For anarcho-communists, the state was inseparable from domination: whoever held it, it would reproduce hierarchy and coercion.

1. The State and Dictatorship of the Proletariat

- *Marxism*: calls for a transitional workers' state — the "dictatorship of the proletariat" — to suppress counterrevolution and reorganize society.
- *Anarcho-communism*: rejects any transitional state. Bakunin warned it would harden into a new elite and new machinery of repression, a warning anarchists believed history confirmed in the Soviet Union.

2. Centralization vs. Federalism

- *Marxism*: favors central authority and national planning.
- *Anarcho-communism*: insists on decentralization, horizontal coordination, and federations of communes and workers' associations.

3. The Role of the Party

- *Marxism (especially Leninism)*: the revolutionary party acts as the vanguard, guiding the working class.
- *Anarcho-communism*: sees the party itself as a hierarchy. Revolution must be made directly by the masses, through councils and federations, not dictated from above.

4. Revolution

- *Marxism*: revolution means seizing state power, then managing its eventual "withering away."
- *Anarcho-communism*: revolution must simultaneously abolish the state and construct new social forms — communes, federations, voluntary associations — from the very outset.

5. Economics and Planning

- *Marxism*: envisions centralized economic planning under state management.
- *Anarcho-communism*: defends communal ownership without a state. Coordination comes from federations of self-managed communes, not a central bureaucracy.

6. Historical Determinism

- *Marxism*: rooted in historical materialism, which posits socialism as the inevitable next stage.
- *Anarcho-communism*: denies deterministic laws of history. Change depends on ethics, voluntary action, and conscious choice, not inevitability.

7. Law, Morality, and Coercion

- *Marxism*: accepts coercion, revolutionary law, and restrictions on freedom as temporary necessities.
- *Anarcho-communism*: insists the means must reflect the ends. As anarchists declared: *"A free society cannot be built by unfree means."*

8. Internationalism

- *Marxism*: in practice often tolerated "socialism in one country."
- *Anarcho-communism*: demanded international revolution, warning that isolated socialist states inevitably reproduce nationalism, militarism, and hierarchy.

The clash between anarcho-communism and Marxism was not a passing quarrel but a defining division in the history of the left. **Marxists sought to wield power to abolish exploitation; anarcho-communists argued that power itself had to be abolished.** One placed faith in the state and the party as tools of transformation; the other believed only decentralization, solidarity, and self-management could create real freedom.

Mechanisms of Functioning

Communes and Associations as the Basis of a Self-Managed Society

In the anarcho-communist vision, the state, centralized authority, and vertical chains of command disappear. In their place stand free communes and voluntary associations, linked in federations. These forms sustain collective life through direct democracy, equality, and self-management, making hierarchy and bureaucracy unnecessary.

1. The Commune as the Basic Unit

The commune is a local community of free individuals, joined voluntarily for common life, work, and decision-making. Its scale may be a village, a neighborhood, a city, or even a region — defined not by administrative borders but by the consent of its members.

The commune governs itself through:

- assemblies where every adult has the right to participate;
- delegates with limited, revocable mandates, chosen to coordinate, not command;
- open debate and transparency, with decisions subject to constant review. Within the commune, people organize production, distribution, healthcare, education, culture, and daily affairs. It can remain largely self-sufficient or link with others in broader networks.

2. Associations as Functional Unions

Alongside communes exist associations formed around shared work, skills, or projects. These groups:

- exercise no coercive authority;
- coordinate labor, production, logistics, science, or cultural initiatives;
- cooperate with communes on equal terms.
  A bakers' association, for instance, could unite bakers from many communes to share methods, allocate resources, and coordinate output. But it does not govern the communes: each retains autonomy while benefiting from cooperation.

3. Federalism as Horizontal Coordination

Communes and associations join together in federations to address common concerns such as transport, ecology, or emergency relief. A federation does not issue decrees; it facilitates coordination, exchange, and solidarity.

All federations:

- are built from the bottom up;
- operate through mandates that are specific, limited, and revocable;
- avoid permanent offices or entrenched leadership.

In such a society, governance is dispersed but coherent. Instead of central command, there is a network of equal structures where everyone has a voice and direct access to decision-making. Authority is replaced not by disorder, but by cooperation and shared responsibility.

Direct Democracy, Rotation, and Mandated Delegates

One of the core principles of anarcho-communism is the refusal of political representation in which decisions are made on behalf of others. Instead, governance rests on **direct democracy**: collective self-management by all members, combined with safeguards that prevent power from concentrating in any hands.

1. Direct Democracy as Self-Management

In this model, decisions are taken directly by the community itself.

This involves:

- regular assemblies open to all;
- equal voting rights for every member;
- consensus where possible, or open voting after thorough discussion.

Direct democracy is not only a right but a responsibility. It requires active participation, inclusiveness, and respect for every opinion, so that decisions reflect collective will rather than imposed authority.

2. Delegates with Mandates, Not Representatives

When coordination across communities is needed, assemblies elect delegates — but their role is tightly limited:

- they act only within the specific mandate given by their community;
- they cannot decide independently;
- they remain accountable and recallable at any time;
- their appointment is temporary, tied to tasks or short terms.

Delegates serve as transmitters of decisions, not rulers. Their task is to connect assemblies, not to replace them.

3. Rotation as a Guard Against Power

To prevent the rise of entrenched authority, all coordinating functions are subject to rotation:

- fixed and limited terms;
- no immediate re-election without a break;
- rotation as a common rule, ensuring no one holds authority longer than necessary.

Through these mechanisms — direct assemblies, mandated delegates, and rotation — anarcho-communism seeks to ensure that power never escapes collective control, and that governance remains the shared work of all rather than the privilege of a few.

Abolition of Property and a Moneyless Economy

A defining principle of anarcho-communism is the rejection of all forms of ownership — private, state, or even collective. Instead of property, it proposes common use:

resources and goods belong to all, not as titles or rights but as free access to what is needed. This breaks not only with capitalism but also with centralized socialism, where property remains mediated by authority.

1. Beyond Private and State Property

For anarcho-communists, every form of ownership creates exclusion. Private property produces exploitation; state property breeds bureaucracy. Even "public" ownership maintains barriers between people and resources. In all cases, individuals are separated from the tools of life and from the fruits of their labor.

The alternative is to abolish property itself. Land, machines, buildings, and natural resources are to be used according to need and mutual agreement, sustained by shared responsibility rather than legal possession.

2. A Moneyless Economy

Anarcho-communism also rejects money and commodity exchange. Money, in this view, is not neutral — it commodifies labor, reduces relationships to transactions, and turns access to life into a question of purchasing power.

In its place:

- goods are available according to need, so each person takes what is genuinely required for life;
- production is organized to serve communities, not markets;
- decisions follow usefulness, fairness, and ecological balance, not profit.

3. Free Access, Not Distribution from Above

Anarcho-communism does not envision a central authority that rations or allocates goods. Instead, self-managed communities provide direct and open access to resources, limited only by the principle of reasonable need. This system rules out accumulation, speculation, and competition for scarcity.

The abolition of property and money is more than an economic reform. It signals a new orientation of life itself: from calculation to trust, from control to freedom, from transaction to solidarity.

Voluntary Labor and the Rejection of Market Logic

In an anarcho-communist society, labor is no longer coercion, survival, or wages. It becomes voluntary, conscious activity directed toward meeting collective needs and giving expression to human creativity. This requires a decisive break with market logic, where work is priced, bought, and sold according to supply and demand.

1. Labor as Participation, Not a Commodity

Labor is understood not as a commodity but as an act of belonging to the community. Each person contributes as they are able and in ways suited to their skills and interests. Work is no longer an external burden or economic compulsion. In such a society:

- it is inseparable from the individual;
- it is not measured in monetary value;
- it is chosen freely rather than imposed.

2. Breaking with Market Valuation

Anarcho-communists argue that the market corrupts the meaning of labor. Under capitalism, socially vital work may be devalued while speculation is rewarded. A doctor in a poor district may "earn" less than a financier, not because the work is less useful but because it is less profitable.

In the anarcho-communist vision, there are no wages, bonuses, or threats of unemployment. Motivation comes from within: the knowledge that one's work matters, the respect of peers, and recognition by the community.

3. Work as Self-Realization

Voluntary labor is not arbitrary; it rests on collective understanding of what is necessary. People take part in tasks because they grasp their importance for the life of the whole. This requires:

- transparency of needs, so all know what the community requires;
- open coordination, so processes are visible to everyone;
- freedom of choice, including the ability to shift between different kinds of work.

In this way, labor becomes not a transaction but a shared human practice — the point where freedom, responsibility, and solidarity converge.

Historical Examples

The Makhnovist Movement in Ukraine (1918–1921): Nestor Makhno and the Practice of Anarcho-Communism

The Makhnovist movement, led by Nestor Ivanovich Makhno (1888–1934), was the boldest attempt in modern history to realize anarcho-communist principles across an entire region. Between 1918 and 1921, in the chaos of the Russian Civil War, southeastern Ukraine became the arena of a vast "Free Territory" where peasants and workers tried to live without state, landlords, or bureaucrats.

Nestor Makhno: Life and Convictions

Born into a poor peasant family in Huliaipole, Makhno knew poverty from childhood. Arrested at 17 for anarchist activity, he spent nearly a decade in Moscow's Butyrka prison, condemned to hard labor. There he read Kropotkin and Bakunin, debated with fellow radicals such as Peter Arshinov, and forged the conviction that only peasants and workers themselves could create freedom. Released after the February Revolution of 1917, he returned to Huliaipole and quickly became the natural leader of local peasants, organizing the seizure of land and estates. His credo was simple: revolution must rise "from below," never from parties or dictatorships.

The Revolutionary Insurgent Army of Ukraine (RIAU)

In 1918, Makhno organized the Revolutionary Insurgent Army of Ukraine. Its numbers swelled to as many as 40,000, drawn largely from peasants. It was no ordinary army: commanders were elected, discipline rested on consent, and its black flags bore slogans like *"Freedom or Death"* and *"The liberation of the workers is the task of the workers themselves."*

The Makhnovists became legendary for their guerrilla tactics. They pioneered the use of the tachanka — a horse-drawn cart mounted with a machine gun — which gave them unmatched mobility on the open steppe. Lightning raids struck deep into enemy lines, disrupting supply columns, ambushing cavalry, and vanishing into the horizon before counterattacks could form. Makhno himself often rode at the front, barefoot and in peasant garb, inspiring loyalty with his fearlessness.

Enemies on Every Front

The Makhnovists fought them all:

- **Austro-German occupiers** (1918), who had imposed crushing requisitions after Brest-Litovsk;
- **the White armies of Denikin and Wrangel**, which sought to restore landlords and crush peasant gains;
- **Ukrainian nationalists**, whose vision of a centralized state clashed with anarchist federalism;
- and finally **the Bolsheviks**, who demanded subordination to the Communist Party.

At Peregonovka in September 1919, outnumbered Makhnovist forces launched a surprise counterattack against Denikin's troops, routing them and saving the Red Army from imminent defeat. For a brief moment, the peasants of Ukraine had shifted the balance of the entire Civil War.

Life in the Free Territory

On liberated lands, anarchist principles became everyday reality:

- **No state institutions:** police, courts, and bureaucracies were abolished; justice was handled by local assemblies.
- **Communal property:** estates of nobles and churches were expropriated; land, tools, and livestock became shared resources.
- **Self-governing communes:** assemblies made decisions, delegates held revocable mandates, and all authority flowed from below.
- **Economy beyond markets:** money still existed but receded; many communes experimented with free distribution of essentials.
- **Education and culture:** libertarian schools and cultural brigades spread literacy, theatre, and music to villages scarred by war.

- **Freedom of association:** no party could dominate Soviets, though this pluralism inevitably clashed with Bolshevik one-party rule.

Relations with the Bolsheviks

At times, the Makhnovists and Red Army were allies — especially in campaigns against Denikin in 1919 and Wrangel in 1920. Makhnovist cavalry often turned the tide of battles. But Makhno refused to put his forces under Bolshevik command or dissolve independent Soviets. Once Wrangel was defeated, the Bolsheviks branded the Makhnovists "bandits." Trotsky ordered a campaign of annihilation. Cheka units executed anarchists, burned villages, and dismantled communes.

Defeat and Exile

By 1921 the movement was exhausted. Outnumbered and starved of supplies, the Makhnovshchina collapsed under the weight of enemies on every side. Makhno, wounded and hunted, fled through Romania and Poland, finally reaching Paris, where he lived in poverty until his death in 1934.

Causes of Defeat

- Inferior resources compared to centralized Bolshevik armies.
- No recognition or aid from abroad.
- Hostility from all camps — White, Red, nationalist, foreign.
- The near-impossibility of sustaining decentralized, egalitarian structures in wartime siege conditions.

Legacy

The Makhnovist experiment proved that anarcho-communist principles — free communes, federalism, voluntary cooperation — could be lived, not just imagined. For three turbulent years, peasants and workers carved out a stateless society in the heart of civil war. Its defeat was brutal, but its memory endures: the black banners of the Makhnovshchina remind us that freedom cannot be created through dictatorship, only through the self-organization of ordinary people, even under fire.

The Spanish Revolutionary Communes (1936–1939): Collectivization, Self-Management, and the Role of CNT and FAI

The Spanish Revolution, unfolding in the crucible of the Civil War, was the most extensive and enduring attempt to build a society on anarcho-communist foundations. In Catalonia, Aragon, Valencia, and Andalusia, millions of people organized revolutionary communes guided by self-management, collectivization, and federalism. The driving forces were the CNT (National Confederation of Labor) and the FAI (Iberian Anarchist Federation), which together turned anarchist theory into daily practice.

1. CNT and FAI: Organizers of the Revolution

The CNT, Spain's largest anarcho-syndicalist union with about a million members by 1936, mobilized workers and peasants for radical transformation. The FAI, a federation of committed anarchists, pressed for fidelity to libertarian principles.

Together, they called for the abolition of the state, the transfer of factories to workers, land to peasants, and the creation of federations of free communes.

2. Collectivization of Industry and Transport

In the cities, workers seized control of production:

- factories and workshops were managed by collectives;
- trams, buses, and railways were run by federations of syndicates;
- equal pay replaced wage hierarchies, fines were abolished, and assemblies decided workplace policy.

By late 1936, nearly 70 percent of Barcelona's industry was under workers' control. Despite bombardments and shortages, its transport network became one of the most efficient in Europe.

3. Agrarian Collectives

In the countryside, thousands of farms were merged into agrarian communes:

- private landownership and wage labor were abolished;
- cultivation was collective, distribution followed need;
- schools and clinics were established;
- hired labor was banned to ensure equality.

Linked through federations, these communes spread across Aragon and Valencia, binding villages into a cooperative network.

4. Direct Democracy without the State

State administration collapsed in much of Republican Spain. Power shifted to:

- assemblies of workers and peasants;
- factory councils and local committees;
- coordinating bodies of mandated and recallable delegates.

Authority was dispersed horizontally, enabling mass participation in governance.

5. Women and Mujeres Libres

A striking achievement was the rise of *Mujeres Libres* ("Free Women"), a movement of 20,000–30,000 anarchist feminists. They fought patriarchy as fiercely as fascism, organizing literacy campaigns, vocational training, childcare, and healthcare. For the first time, women's emancipation was integrated into the heart of a social revolution.

6. Education and Culture

Inspired by Francisco Ferrer's libertarian pedagogy, schools taught creativity and equality rather than obedience. Cultural centers, theaters, newspapers, and radio stations flourished under collective management, spreading solidarity and revolutionary ideals even under siege.

7. Contradictions and Internal Conflict

The revolution advanced under the shadow of war. Stalinist communists, demanding centralized control, clashed with anarchists who insisted on social transformation. In May 1937, street battles in Barcelona between anarchists and communists left hundreds dead. Step by step, collectivization was rolled back, communes dissolved, and CNT leaders sidelined.

8. Isolation and International Pressure

The revolution inspired anarchists worldwide but was left without international backing. The Soviet Union armed only communist factions and undermined anarchists. Western democracies pursued "non-intervention," ensuring Franco faced no real blockade. Although international brigades fought against fascism, the anarchist experiment stood isolated, harassed by enemies and supposed allies alike.

9. Legacy

The Spanish Revolution proved that:

- mass self-management was not only possible but effective;
- direct democracy could replace state authority;
- a society without private property, money, or centralized power could operate on a vast scale.

Though defeated by fascism and betrayed by allies, the communes of Spain remain history's clearest example of anarcho-communism in practice — a revolution that dared to live its ideals.

Communal Experiments of the 20th Century: Local Models (Israel, Latin America)

After the crushing defeat of the anarchists in Spain and the rise of authoritarian regimes in Europe, anarcho-communism as a mass movement receded. Yet its spirit survived in smaller communal projects that tried to carve out spaces of equality, cooperation, and self-management. These communities rarely claimed the full anarcho-communist program, but their practices — collective labor, horizontal governance, and rejection of property — kept its ideals alive.

1. Kibbutzim in Israel

Among the most famous communal experiments were the kibbutzim, founded in Palestine in the early 1900s and expanded in Israel. Although rooted in socialist-Zionist ideology rather than anarchism, they embodied strikingly similar practices:

- collective ownership of land, housing, and means of production;
- abolition of wages, with goods provided according to need;
- shared labor and rotation of tasks;
- governance through assemblies where all decisions were subject to debate and election.

For decades kibbutzim achieved a high degree of integration and self-sufficiency. Over time, however, market pressures, privatization, and ties to the state eroded their radical edge. Even so, they remain one of the longest-lasting communal experiments of the century.

2. Latin American Communes

Latin America became a seedbed of communal initiatives, rural and urban alike:

- **Brazil**: the Landless Workers' Movement (MST) turned occupied estates into cooperative farms run by assemblies.
- **Mexico**: the Zapatistas in Chiapas built autonomous municipalities with collective labor, horizontal decision-making, and rejection of state authority.
- **Argentina**: during the 2001–2002 crisis, hundreds of bankrupt factories were occupied and converted into worker-managed enterprises, run through assemblies and collective votes.

These movements drew on direct democracy, rotation of responsibilities, and solidarity networks for survival. Some explicitly cited anarchist influences; others embodied them in practice without the label.

3. Common Features and Limits

Despite different contexts, these communities shared:

- commitment to equality and decentralization;
- life outside or against the authority of state and market;
- reliance on local resources and open participation.

Yet they faced persistent limits:

- their experiments rarely grew beyond local scale;
- they were vulnerable to repression and political hostility;
- they struggled to withstand the weight of global capitalism and economic isolation.

These twentieth-century communes never matched the scope of classical anarchist revolutions. But they proved that anarcho-communist principles could be lived: in farms and factories, in villages and neighborhoods, people created islands of solidarity in hostile seas. Their survival, even under pressure, testified to the durability of the idea that life can be organized without property, hierarchy, or domination.

Causes of Instability

From the Paris Commune to the Free Territory in Ukraine and the Spanish Revolution, anarcho-communists proved that self-managed societies could exist — but only briefly. Their defeats were not due to a single weakness, but to a convergence of hostile forces, internal fragilities, and the brutal circumstances of war and revolution.

1. External Military and Political Pressure

Every anarchist society faced immediate attack from centralized states.

- The Paris Commune was drowned in blood by Versailles troops.
- The Makhnovists were crushed by the Red Army once they refused Bolshevik control.
- Spanish anarchists were destroyed by Franco after years of attrition and betrayal.

States commanded professional armies, secret police, supply lines, and foreign allies. Against such machinery, decentralized militias were fatally outmatched.

2. Political Isolation

Anarchists rejected parliaments, parties, and permanent alliances, and so found themselves alone.

- The Makhnovists stood between Whites, Reds, and nationalists — enemies on every side.
- Spanish anarchists were marginalized even within the Republican camp.
- The Paris Commune inspired many but drew no real aid from provincial France.

Cut off from allies, anarchist movements were encircled and crushed.

3. Internal Strains

Self-management demands constant participation and solidarity. Under siege, famine, and exhaustion, this was hard to sustain. Coordination often faltered; some communes carried the load while others remained passive. Strategic disagreements and uneven preparation weakened cohesion. Without long-term planning or resilient institutions, structures buckled under pressure.

4. Economic Fragility

Most experiments arose in wartime collapse.

- Spanish collectives faced blockades and diversion of resources to the front.
- Ukrainian communes struggled with requisitions and the breakdown of agrarian markets.
- Everywhere, shortages of raw materials and trade routes eroded stability.

Economic weakness left communities vulnerable to exhaustion and manipulation.

5. Lack of Experience and Continuity

Enthusiasm was abundant; experience was scarce. Many decisions were improvised, and institutions dissolved in crisis. Each generation began anew because repression destroyed continuity — activists were killed, jailed, or exiled, severing chains of memory.

6. Ideological Conflicts

Anarchists often clashed with socialists and communists.

- In Spain, the street battles of May 1937 pitted anarchists against Stalinist forces.
- In Ukraine, anarchists and Bolsheviks could not reconcile their opposing visions.

Without unity, revolutionary fronts fractured.

7. Hostile International Context

No anarchist experiment received decisive foreign aid.

- Versailles France isolated the Commune.
- The Soviet Union undermined anarchists in Spain.
- Western democracies turned away.
- The Makhnovists had no allies at all.

Facing global hostility or indifference, anarchists stood alone against coordinated powers.

8. Military Vulnerability

Anarchists distrusted standing armies, preferring militias. These excelled at local defense and guerrilla tactics but struggled in prolonged campaigns against disciplined armies. In Spain, militias initially succeeded but were forced into militarization, undermining anarchist principles while still failing to match Franco's forces.

9. Broken Transmission

Every defeat left anarchism without institutional inheritance. Communards were executed, Makhnovists exiled, Spanish anarchists shot or imprisoned. Knowledge and traditions were lost, forcing each generation to start from nothing.

Contemporary Relevance and Influence

Although anarcho-communism as a mass movement faded after the defeats of the twentieth century, its ideas persist in smaller, everyday practices that challenge markets, hierarchy, and profit. In eco-villages, gift networks, and anti-monetary experiments, people continue to explore how life might be organized through solidarity and self-management.

1. Eco-Communities and Sustainable Settlements

Around the world, eco-villages have sought to live autonomously, guided by ecological balance and collective responsibility. They often bypass conventional markets, relying instead on shared labor and cooperative governance.

Examples include Findhorn in Scotland, Tamera in Portugal, and numerous rural and urban eco-villages in Germany, the United States, and Latin America. Common practices include:

- refusal of private ownership of land;
- shared kitchens, workshops, and childcare;
- labor carried out on the principle of "from each according to ability."

Most do not identify as anarchist, yet their daily routines echo anarcho-communist ethics: equality in practice, collective decision-making, and rejection of hierarchy.

2. Gift Economies and Open Access Initiatives

Gift economies embody the idea that goods and services should circulate freely, measured by use rather than price. Value lies in sharing, not in exchange.

Examples include:

- Freecycle, a global network for giving and receiving items without money;
- Food Not Bombs, an international movement serving free meals and organized without leaders;
- free libraries, community kitchens, and street exchange points across Europe and North America.

Such projects create public spaces where access is open and generosity, not profit, sets the rhythm of social life.

3. Anti-Monetary Experiments and Alternative Currencies

Some initiatives attempt to move beyond money entirely, replacing it with time, trust, or mutual aid.

Examples include:

- LETS (Local Exchange Trading Systems), where goods and services circulate through reciprocal credit;
- time banks, where hours of labor serve as currency;
- gift markets at countercultural festivals like Burning Man, where exchange is suspended in favor of sharing.

These practices cannot overturn global capitalism, but they carve out pockets of another logic — where solidarity, reciprocity, and community take precedence over price and profit.

Critique of Capitalism, the State, and Market Economy

Anarcho-communism offers not just an economic critique but a challenge to the entire structure of modern life — politics, culture, and everyday relations. Its theorists argue that capitalism, the state, and the market form a single web of domination that reproduces exploitation, inequality, and alienation.

1. Capitalism as Exploitation

In the anarcho-communist view, capitalism turns labor into a commodity. Workers are cut off from the products of their activity, while wealth and power concentrate in the hands of a few. The core mechanism of exploitation is wage labor: value is created by workers, but decisions about goals, processes, and results are taken from them. Profit flows from this imbalance — from the gap between what labor produces and what labor receives.

For anarchists, capitalism cannot be reformed without abolishing its foundations.

2. The State as the Guardian of Inequality

The state is understood not as a neutral referee but as the guarantor of property and hierarchy. Even in its democratic form, it preserves:

- a monopoly on violence;
- bureaucratic coercion;
- narrow and limited participation;
- hierarchies where a minority rules in the name of the majority.

For anarcho-communists, every authority — however progressive it claims to be — reproduces subordination. The state cannot serve freedom; it must be dismantled and replaced by horizontal, federated self-government.

3. Market Logic as Alienation

Even beyond capitalism, the market imposes its own logic. It puts a price on everything, even when things have value beyond money. It replaces human bonds with transactions between objects and makes profit, not meaning, the measure of action. Against this, anarcho-communists propose economies of sharing and open access, where goods circulate according to need and labor is an act of participation in common life, not survival under compulsion.

Anarcho-communism challenges not just capitalism but the entire system of governance and production that defines modern civilization. Its critique does not aim to redistribute resources within old structures but to end the conditions that create authority, coercion, and economic dependence altogether.

The Problem of Scalability and Practical Applicability

Despite its ideals of freedom, equality, and self-management, anarcho-communism faces a dilemma acknowledged even by its own advocates: the difficulty of scaling and sustaining such a model in large, complex societies.

1. Local Success, Global Limits

Communes, eco-villages, and gift networks can thrive under certain conditions: small size, high engagement, shared values, and partial autonomy from state or market. Yet once scaled to regions or nations, new challenges arise:

- coordinating resources across distant territories;
- managing complex supply chains;
- devising long-term plans for millions;
- reconciling diverse, even conflicting needs.

Such tasks demand mediation — and mediation risks hardening into governance, bureaucracy, and command.

2. No Lasting Precedent

History offers inspiring but short-lived attempts: the Paris Commune of 1871, the Makhnovist Free Territory in Ukraine, the Spanish collectives of 1936. All collapsed under external assault or internal strain before proving they could endure in peacetime, reproduce themselves across generations, or stabilize systems of distribution at scale. An enduring anarcho-communist society has yet to exist.

3. Dependence on Consciousness

The model presupposes that everyone will participate actively, resist personal gain, and practice cooperation and trust. Such civic virtues are hard to sustain in mass societies scarred by poverty, inequality, or limited traditions of self-management. Where participation weakens, structures lose their vitality and risks of domination grow.

4. The Shadow of Hierarchy

Even in formally horizontal settings, hierarchies can reappear. Informal leaders rise, minorities dominate, coordination slips into covert command, and influence accumulates outside collective oversight. Without strong mechanisms of accountability and transparency, anarchist communities may unknowingly reproduce the very hierarchies they sought to abolish.

Difference Between Anarcho-Communism and Individualist Anarchism

Anarcho-communism and individualist anarchism share a common rejection of state authority and coercion. Yet they diverge profoundly in how they define liberty, property, labor, and the bond between the individual and society. These contrasts created two distinct but enduring traditions within anarchist thought.

1. Freedom

- *Individualist anarchism*: freedom means negative autonomy — freedom from interference, authority, and obligation. The individual preserves independence by holding society at arm's length.

- *Anarcho-communism*: freedom is social, achieved only when equality and cooperation prevail. One is free not in isolation but when no one has power over another.

2. Property

- *Individualist anarchism*: property in the products of one's labor and means of personal production is inseparable from liberty, provided it does not violate others' freedom.

- *Anarcho-communism*: property itself is a system of exclusion. Resources and production are held in common; possession is replaced by use.

3. The Collective

- *Individualist anarchism*: the collective is suspect, a possible source of conformity. Associations are voluntary and minimal, designed to protect autonomy.

- *Anarcho-communism*: the collective is the natural form of social life — a free federation of equals where participation is voluntary but decisions are made together.

4. Ethics

- *Individualist anarchism*: responsibility is personal, solidarity a matter of choice.

- *Anarcho-communism*: ethics rests on mutual aid and trust. Liberty is impossible without acknowledging others as the ground of one's own freedom.

5. Practice

- *Individualist anarchism*: appears in small autonomous groups, strategies of independence, or solitary resistance.

- *Anarcho-communism*: seeks social transformation on every level — production, culture, daily life — through unification rather than separation.

6. Labor and Economy

- *Individualist anarchists* (Tucker, Stirner): often defended free markets and mutual exchange, where labor remained a personal commodity fairly traded.

- *Anarcho-communists* (Kropotkin, Bakunin): rejected market logic. Labor is not a commodity but a shared contribution to communal life, with goods distributed by need.

"Dispersion spells ruination; cohesion guarantees life and development. This law of social struggle is equally applicable to classes and parties.

Anarchism is no beautiful fantasy, no abstract notion of philosophy, but a social movement of the working masses; for that reason alone, it must gather its forces into one organization, constantly agitating, as demanded by the reality and strategy of the social class struggle."

— Organizational Platform of the General Union of Anarchists (Draft)

7. Individual and Society

- *Individualist anarchism*: the individual stands above society; autonomy may require withdrawal from social ties.

- *Anarcho-communism*: the individual and society sustain each other. Personal freedom is realized through community, and community thrives through the free development of each person.

> Individualist anarchism represents freedom in solitude; anarcho-communism embodies freedom in community. The former defends the boundaries of the individual; the latter seeks to eliminate the very conditions that make those boundaries necessary. Both pursue the same goal — human emancipation — but differ in their understanding of what it means to be free and how freedom is to be achieved.

Platformist Anarchism: An Attempt to Overcome Decentralization

After the crushing of the Makhnovist movement and the suppression of anarchists in Soviet Russia, revolutionaries asked why anarchism, despite mass support and radical ideals, had failed to hold its ground. The search for answers produced platformism — not a new doctrine, but a sharpening of anarcho-communist practice aimed at overcoming fragmentation and strategic weakness.

1. The "Organizational Platform"

In 1926, exiled Russian anarchists in Paris published the *Organizational Platform of the General Union of Anarchists (Draft)*. Its authors — Nestor Makhno, Piotr Arshinov, Ida Mett, and comrades of the émigré journal *Dielo Truda* ("Cause of Labor") — called for a federation of anarchist groups built on:

- a shared theoretical outlook;
- coordinated tactics;
- distribution of responsibilities;
- federalism without centralized command.

The aim was to replace isolated initiatives with a structured movement capable of acting with unity while preserving autonomy.

2. Four Principles

The Platform set out four guiding principles:

- **Theoretical Unity:** a common ideological basis to avoid vagueness and contradiction.
- **Tactical Unity:** coordinated action instead of scattered strategies.
- **Collective Responsibility:** members answer for the organization, and the organization for its members.
- **Federalism:** voluntary association of autonomous groups, bound by equality and agreement.

This framework sought to reconcile anarchist self-management with the need for strategic strength.

3. Debate and Criticism

Publication of the Platform sparked fierce debate. Critics warned it smuggled in authoritarian discipline and risked reproducing the very party structures anarchists opposed. They feared tactical unity would slip into hidden hierarchy. Supporters countered that it was not centralization but responsibility — an attempt to avoid repeating the disorganization that left anarchists outmaneuvered in Russia and later in Spain. Without coordination, they argued, anarchism would always be defeated by more disciplined enemies.

4. Influence in the Twentieth and Twenty-First Centuries

Despite controversy, platformism shaped anarchist organization worldwide. Its influence is seen in:

- **Anarkismo.net**, coordinating platformist and especifista groups;
- **Zabalaza Anarchist Communist Front** (South Africa);
- **Federazione dei Comunisti Anarchici** (Italy);
- **Organización Comunista Libertaria** (Latin America);
- **Workers Solidarity Movement** (Ireland);
- initiatives in France, Poland, and beyond.

These organizations combined anti-authoritarian ethics with strategic cohesion, insisting that anarchism must be not just moral conviction but effective political practice.

5. The Significance of Platformism

Platformism did not abandon anarchism's hostility to power; it tried to solve the puzzle of action: *how can we fight together without creating rulers?* This question remains alive in contemporary anarchist, ecological, feminist, and anti-capitalist struggles, where movements seek to be horizontal but also capable of sustained, coordinated action.

Anarcho-Communism as a Philosophy of Radical Liberation

Anarcho-communism is more than a project for reorganizing the economy or politics. At its heart, it is a philosophy of liberation that seeks to dismantle every form of domination, dependence, and structural violence woven into modern society. Unlike reformist approaches that adjust the system while preserving its foundations, anarcho-communism challenges the logic of subordination itself. It insists that freedom and equality cannot be partial, and that compromise with ruling structures only strengthens their grip.

1. Liberation Through the Abolition of Power

The central conviction of anarcho-communism is that no one can be free while power remains the organizing principle of society. Transitional states, "workers' governments," or redistributions of wealth do not address the root problem: authority institutionalized in any form reproduces control and hierarchy.

Anarcho-communists therefore do not aim to seize power but to abolish it. They imagine in its place free associations, equal participation, and shared responsibility.

2. Rethinking Labor, Property, and Social Life

The critique extends beyond capitalism to the very commodity logic that turns labor, goods, and even relationships into objects of exchange. In its place, anarcho-communism proposes:

- labor as voluntary participation rather than coercion;
- resources as common wealth rather than sources of rent;
- society as mutual aid rather than competition.

This vision is not escapism but a direct challenge to the present order, where profit is placed above need and legality above justice.

3. Contemporary Relevance

Today's world — scarred by growing inequality, ecological collapse, and widespread distrust of political institutions — makes anarcho-communism resonate anew. It does not present a rigid plan but a principle of action:

- rejection of subordination as normal;
- decisions made through participation, not representation;
- confidence in people's ability to self-organize without coercion or surveillance.

4. Orientation, Not Blueprint

Anarcho-communism is not a technical design for the future but an ethical orientation. It defines what society must not be — exploitative, mediated, alienating — and points toward what it can become. Its goal is not to impose structures from above but to create space for people to build them themselves, grounded in trust, solidarity, and freedom.

"The right to life consists in being one's own master."

— Max Stirner (1806–1856)

SECTION 3. INDIVIDUALIST ANARCHISM: EMPHASIS ON PERSONAL AUTONOMY AND VOLUNTARY ASSOCIATION WITHOUT A STATE

> **Individualist anarchism** is a branch of anarchist theory that upholds personal freedom and autonomy as its highest values, rejecting any form of external coercion from the state, society, tradition, or morality.

Within individualist anarchism, any form of collective coercion — state governance, law, morality, or social expectation — is seen as an assault on personal dignity. Its vision is of a world where each person governs themselves, bound only by the limit of not infringing upon another's liberty.

Core Principles of Individualist Anarchism

1) Rejection of Centralized Authority

The state is not justice but suppression. Taxes, regulations, and restrictions on conduct are viewed as violations of natural rights. In place of state power, individualist anarchists imagine a stateless society where people act on their own judgment so long as they respect the freedom of others.

2) Free Market and Voluntary Exchange

Unlike anarcho-communism, individualist anarchism embraces markets as peaceful arenas of interaction.

- Economic relations rest on voluntary agreement, free from state interference.
- Private property, if acquired without force or fraud, is a natural extension of liberty.
- Labor, exchange, and ownership are matters of choice, not collective decree.

3) Voluntarism and Autonomy

All cooperation must be voluntary, reciprocal, and free from compulsion. Society is seen as a network of sovereign individuals who join together only when it reflects their genuine will and interest.

4) Personal Responsibility Over Collective Authority

The collective has no right to command. Associations are acceptable only as temporary unions of free individuals. Responsibility is personal: each person answers for their own actions, not for a group, community, or state.

5) Freedom Without Intermediaries

The ideal is a society without states or binding norms that limit autonomy. Decisions are self-determined; cooperation and exchange are voluntary; respect for autonomy sustains coexistence. Liberty and responsibility, not external control, are the pillars of social order.

6) Self-Defense and Justice Without the State

Protection of life and property does not require state monopoly. The right to self-defense is inalienable. Security may be provided by voluntary associations, private agreements, or mutual-aid networks. Arbitration and courts exist only as services freely chosen.

7) Critique of State-Supported Monopolies

Benjamin Tucker emphasized that the state enforces monopolies in land, money, trade, and transport. These privileges distort exchange, centralize power, and stifle real competition. Removing state interference would open opportunity through free interaction rather than privilege.

8) Ethical Individualism

Beyond economics, individualist anarchism is also a moral stance. It defends the sovereignty of conscience: the right to think, act, and live by one's own principles rather than imposed norms. Freedom is both outward independence and inward integrity.

Strengths of Individualist Anarchism

1. Maximum Freedom and Self-Realization

Individualist anarchism upholds the idea that every person should be free to shape their own life without interference from external powers. This means the right to decide one's own goals, beliefs, and way of living, even if these diverge from social norms. Autonomy is not treated as an abstract value but as the concrete ability to choose one's work, relationships, lifestyle, and convictions independently.

2. Life Without State Interference

By rejecting the state, individualist anarchism removes taxation, bureaucracy, and legally imposed restrictions. This applies both to the economy and private life. People can start enterprises, form agreements, or experiment with new forms of living without needing permits or compliance with regulations. What guides them are voluntary agreements rather than imposed rules.

3. Property as Independence

Private property, if acquired without violence or fraud, is seen as the anchor of independence. The ability to keep and use the products of one's labor prevents dependency on collective bodies or state institutions. Owning one's tools, land, or home becomes a safeguard against being forced into relationships of subordination.

4. Voluntarism in Social Relations

Every relationship — personal, economic, or political — must be based on free consent. Marriage contracts, business partnerships, or community associations exist only for as long as the parties desire. If someone no longer wishes to participate, they can leave without penalty. This ensures that cooperation remains conscious, reciprocal, and equal.

5. Simplicity of Social Life

Without layers of officials or complex institutions, social interaction becomes straightforward. Disputes are handled by contracts, private arbitration, or community agreements. There are fewer rules to navigate, and obligations are always clear and voluntarily chosen. Society functions with transparency, rather than hidden regulations.

6. Space for Initiative

Individualist anarchism encourages individuals to take responsibility for their own survival and prosperity. People can create enterprises, develop inventions, or adapt to changing circumstances without waiting for permission from bureaucracies. Innovation, entrepreneurship, and creative projects thrive when people are free to act on their ideas directly.

7. Respect for Moral Autonomy

Moral responsibility belongs to the individual, not to collective institutions. People are free to follow their conscience, whether in religion, sexuality, education, or personal values. This allows for genuine diversity: one person may live in a communal household, another in solitude; one may raise children in traditional schools, another through alternative education. No one is forced into conformity.

8. The Right to Self-Defense

The protection of life, liberty, and property does not require a state monopoly. Individualist anarchists affirm the inalienable right of each person to defend themselves. Security can be organized through voluntary associations, mutual-aid networks, or private contracts for protection. Instead of relying on police, people arrange defense on their own terms.

9. Opposition to Monopolies

Thinkers like Benjamin Tucker argued that the state creates and sustains monopolies in land, money, trade, and transport by granting privileges to certain groups. By removing state support, these monopolies collapse, and competition becomes fairer. For example, without banking monopolies, access to credit would be more open; without land monopolies, ownership would be based on actual use rather than state-enforced titles.

10. Diversity of Social Forms

Because no single model is imposed, society can include many forms of living side by side. Some may form cooperatives, others private businesses, still others communal households — as long as participation is voluntary. This pluralism allows radically different lifestyles to coexist peacefully, since no group has the authority to impose its model on others.

11. Culture of Responsibility

With no external authority to blame or rely on, individuals must bear the consequences of their choices. If a contract is broken, it must be resolved directly, not handed to the state. This nurtures accountability: people learn to think carefully before committing and to take responsibility for their actions rather than expecting institutions to solve problems for them.

12. Cooperation Without Compulsion

When cooperation is voluntary, conflicts are reduced. People enter agreements only when both sides benefit. This makes relations more stable, because they are maintained by genuine mutual interest rather than imposed duty. For example, workplaces form around willing participants, not employees forced by lack of alternatives.

13. Ethical Consistency

Individualist anarchism rejects coercion not only politically but also ethically. If violence and domination are wrong, they cannot be justified as a "necessary step" toward freedom. The philosophy insists that the means must match the ends: liberty must be pursued by free actions, not imposed through coercion. This coherence gives the system moral integrity.

Weaknesses of Individualist Anarchism

1. Lack of Social Coordination

Without collective governance, large-scale challenges remain unresolved. Public health campaigns, infrastructure maintenance, environmental protection, or distribution of scarce resources require long-term planning. Voluntary cooperation can work locally but struggles to cover an entire region or nation.

2. Neglect of Structural Inequality

Freedom on paper does not erase inequality in practice. Access to capital, education, or legal defense determines who can act freely. Without collective mechanisms to correct these imbalances, those already disadvantaged remain trapped in weaker positions.

3. Risk of Economic Domination

When markets operate without oversight, capital and resources tend to accumulate around a small circle of aggressive entrepreneurs and financiers. This concentration gradually forms new elites that dominate access to land, credit, and trade. Over time, such hierarchies replicate the very systems of privilege anarchism seeks to abolish, turning freedom of exchange into a mechanism of hidden dependency.

4. Vulnerability to External Threats

Communities that reject centralized defense remain exposed to military aggression, organized violence, and large-scale natural disasters. In moments of crisis, survival often depends on swift mobilization of resources and coordinated action.

5. Limits on Solidarity

When autonomy is treated as the highest value, the sense of responsibility for others can fade into the background. Challenges that do not directly affect an individual — chronic poverty, disability, or the care of the elderly — risk being neglected or pushed aside.

6. Isolation of the Individual

Absolute independence risks social fragmentation. If everyone focuses only on personal goals, communal ties become fragile and temporary. Trust erodes, and individuals can end up isolated or vulnerable to loneliness.

7. No Collective Guarantees of Rights

In a society without common legal frameworks, protection depends entirely on private contracts or arbitration agreements. For marginalized groups — the poor, minorities, or those without resources — this means little real leverage to insist on fairness or equal treatment. As a result, rights become fragile promises, unevenly enforced and often dependent on the goodwill of stronger actors rather than guaranteed by impartial institutions.

8. Utopian Assumptions

The model rests on the belief that individuals will consistently respect each other's autonomy and behave responsibly. Yet historical experience reveals the opposite: exploitation of trust, violent conflict, and widespread neglect of obligations. Without mechanisms of accountability, those willing to deceive or coerce quickly gain power, turning the virtue of cooperation into a weakness that leaves communities open to manipulation.

9. Fragility of Voluntary Systems

Voluntary arrangements often collapse under stress. Economic crises, interpersonal disputes, or power struggles can destabilize communities that lack lasting institutions or mechanisms for mediation.

10. Scaling Beyond Small Communities

Individualist anarchism functions in small groups but falters in complex societies. Coordinating transport, energy, healthcare, or communications for millions requires stable systems that go beyond local agreements.

11. Weak Support for Public Goods

Services that benefit everyone but are costly to produce — scientific research, highways, environmental protection — require collective funding. Voluntary contributions are rarely enough to sustain them over time.

12. Exploitation Through Unequal Contracts

Even contracts entered "voluntarily" can mask coercion. Poorer individuals may accept unfair terms out of necessity, turning freedom of agreement into disguised dependency.

13. Lack of Long-Term Justice

When justice depends on private arbitration, fairness and consistency vary across communities. Without a common legal framework, conflicting norms make it hard to ensure durable protections.

14. Tension Between Autonomy and Cooperation

The more autonomy is stressed, the harder it is to build stable cooperation. Collective action requires compromise, but absolute independence resists it, making long-term community life unstable.

Historical Roots and Key Figures

Influence of the Enlightenment, Radical Liberalism, Naturalism, Transcendentalism, and Natural Law Theory

Individualist anarchism emerged at the crossroads of Enlightenment rationalism, liberal theories of natural rights, radical naturalist ethics, and American transcendentalism. It was also shaped by natural law theory, which placed individual conscience above state legislation. By the late eighteenth century, ideas began to circulate that treated freedom as the highest value and regarded political, moral, or cultural constraints as obstacles to self-development.

1. The Enlightenment

The Enlightenment advanced the notion of rational autonomy — the belief that individuals are capable of governing themselves without monarchs, churches, or inherited traditions. Thinkers like Voltaire and Denis Diderot, while not anarchists, defended natural rights such as freedom, labor, and property. Their insistence that reason and conscience could replace external authority laid the groundwork for later radical critiques of the state.

2. Radical Liberalism and "Anarchism Without Socialism"

In the nineteenth century, especially in the United States, radical liberals recast anarchism in terms of absolute personal rights. Josiah Warren, Lysander Spooner, and Benjamin Tucker defended private property, voluntary contracts, and free markets, but rejected coercion and centralized power. For them, even property could be secured without the state — through voluntary associations and mutual agreements. They opposed capitalism where it depended on monopoly and privilege, but they refused socialist calls to abolish property itself. This created a distinctive form of anarchism that was liberal in its defense of individual rights but anarchist in its hostility to state power.

3. Naturalism and Anarchy as a Way of Life

Naturalist thought emphasized living in harmony with nature rather than under artificial institutions. Max Stirner and Henry David Thoreau exemplified this perspective. They offered no detailed programs but articulated an ethic of self-sufficiency, independence from authority, and personal responsibility. Anarchy, in this view, was not primarily a system of governance but a mode of being rooted in the individual's natural autonomy.

4. American Transcendentalism

The transcendentalists, especially Ralph Waldo Emerson and Henry David Thoreau, championed self-reliance, spiritual independence, and the supremacy of conscience over conformity. While not anarchists in a strict sense, their writings encouraged resistance to unjust authority and inspired later individualist anarchists to frame autonomy as both a moral and practical principle. Thoreau's act of civil disobedience against taxation became an enduring model of principled refusal.

5. Natural Law and Inalienable Rights

Lysander Spooner developed a radical theory of natural law in which justice and conscience outweighed state legislation. He argued that laws violating natural rights — life, liberty, property — carried no obligation of obedience. For him, true rights existed independently of governments, and unjust laws were null. This reinforced the conviction, central to individualist anarchism, that no external authority can legitimately restrict personal freedom.

Max Stirner — Philosopher of the Autonomous "I" and the Radical Rejection of Supra-Personal Forms

Max Stirner (Johann Caspar Schmidt, 1806–1856) was a German philosopher best known for *The Ego and Its Own* (1844), a book that shocked his contemporaries by denying every higher authority over the individual. In it, Stirner advanced a radical form of individualist anarchism centered on the absolute primacy of the self and the rejection of all supra-personal powers: the state, morality, society, ideology, and even humanism.

1. Intellectual Background and Critique of Idealism

Stirner belonged to the Young Hegelians, alongside Ludwig Feuerbach and Bruno Bauer. Whereas Feuerbach replaced God with "Humanity" as the new supreme value, Stirner rejected all abstractions alike. Whether called Reason, Morality, or Society, he saw them as "spooks" (*Spuk*)—empty ideas that rule people's lives and demand obedience. Against these phantoms, he affirmed the priority of the living individual over every abstract principle.

2. The Unique One

At the heart of Stirner's philosophy is the concept of the Unique One (*der Einzige*): the irreducible individual who belongs to no cause beyond themselves. No nation, no morality, no God, no revolution has the right to command the person. Freedom means acting without submitting to imposed duties or external authorities.

3. Rejection of Morality and Social Norms

Stirner's critique extended into ethics. Morality, law, and custom, he argued, are instruments of control. Even solidarity and mutual aid—celebrated by other anarchists—could become new forms of domination if elevated into binding ideals. True autonomy means freeing oneself not only from the state but also from moral codes and social obligations.

4. Property as Possession

For Stirner, property was not a legal right guaranteed by the state but a matter of possession, maintained by one's own strength and will. What one can hold and use becomes one's own. Ownership, in his sense, was an expression of personal power, not a category of law.

5. Freedom as Action

Freedom, he insisted, is never a gift. It exists only in action, in the refusal to submit. Anarchy, for Stirner, was not a plan for society but a way of life: the stance of a person who recognizes no authority above themselves.

6. The Union of Egoists

Instead of permanent organizations, Stirner imagined the "Union of Egoists" (*Verein von Egoisten*): a temporary association formed by individuals for mutual advantage. It lasts only as long as it serves the interests of its members and dissolves once the common benefit ends. In this way, people can cooperate without giving up their sovereignty.

7. Reception and Legacy

The Ego and Its Own was quickly banned in Prussia and denounced as scandalous. Yet its influence spread widely:

- anarchists such as Benjamin Tucker and Émile Armand drew on his uncompromising defense of the self;
- Friedrich Nietzsche, though the connection remains debated, echoed Stirner's rejection of morality and higher values;
- existentialists and nihilists, including Jean-Paul Sartre and Albert Camus, resonated with his insistence on autonomy and the refusal of imposed meaning;
- twentieth-century thinkers, especially in France and the United States, rediscovered him in critiques of ideology and power.

8. Stirner's Place in Anarchist Thought

Unlike Warren, Spooner, or Tucker, Stirner offered no program for reorganizing society and no economic model. His philosophy was not institutional but existential: it expressed the extreme limit of anarchist freedom, carried to the point of denying every bond, every authority, and every obligation beyond the individual self.

Benjamin Tucker — Advocate of "Anarchism Without Socialism"

Benjamin Tucker (1854–1939) was an American publicist, translator, and theorist of individualist anarchism. At the end of the nineteenth century, he became one of the leading anarchist voices in the United States, advocating liberation not only from the state but also from all economic privileges created by it. His position was often described as "anarchism without socialism": he rejected state intervention, collective ownership, and redistribution, yet defended principles of justice, equality before the law, and liberty.

1. Anarchism on the Basis of the Free Market

Tucker did not oppose markets themselves but saw them as natural arenas for peaceful interaction among free individuals. He distinguished capitalism as it existed — built on state-created privilege — from a truly free market. In his view, the state upheld four monopolies that distorted exchange:

- **land** (through property laws favoring landlords),
- **money** (through state control of banking and currency),
- **trade** (through licensing and tariffs),
- **knowledge** (through patents and copyright).

Abolishing these monopolies, Tucker argued, would allow voluntary exchange and equal opportunity, removing the exploitative core of capitalism.

2. Property as Independence

Unlike anarcho-communists, Tucker defended private property as the product of one's labor and a guarantee of autonomy. He drew a sharp line between:

- **possession** — the personal use of tools, land, or housing;
- **ownership for profit** — control over resources used to exploit the labor of others.

He criticized wage labor as inherently unequal but accepted contracts between equals when entered freely and without coercion.

3. Rejection of the State

For Tucker, the state was the root of injustice. He envisioned its replacement by voluntary defense agencies, courts, and arbitration bodies chosen by contract. Protective and legal functions would thus remain in society, but without monopoly or compulsion — each person could decide whether to participate.

4. Ethical Dimension

Tucker combined radical economic individualism with a moral commitment to fairness. Every person, he argued, has the right to live on their own terms so long as they do not restrict the freedom of others. He admitted that inequality might arise, but believed that once state privileges were removed, differences would be less destructive than under capitalism supported by law and government.

5. Translator and Publisher

Tucker played a decisive role in bringing European radical thought to American readers. He translated Pierre-Joseph Proudhon's *What Is Property?* (1840), as well as works by Mikhail Bakunin, Peter Kropotkin, and Max Stirner's *The Ego and Its Own*. His translations introduced American audiences to debates on socialism and anarchism then shaping Europe.

Through his journal *Liberty* (1881–1908), Tucker created a platform where essays, translations, and polemics against capitalism, socialism, and state authority circulated widely. It became the central organ of individualist anarchism in the English-speaking world and a forum for sharp intellectual disputes.

6. Influence and Legacy

Tucker's work influenced later libertarian and anarchist traditions in the United States, though he did not use the term "libertarian" himself. He presented anarchism as a human-centered philosophy uniting freedom with fairness, without coercion or authority. His translations, polemics, and the journal *Liberty* ensured that individualist anarchism became a recognized current within American political thought and provided reference points for later debates on free markets, justice, and voluntary cooperation.

Personal Strategies Combining Freedom, Ethics, and Resistance

Individualist anarchism developed not only as a philosophy but also as a personal strategy of living — a refusal of authority, subordination, and violence practiced in daily life. Some figures of this tradition became examples less of abstract theory than of lived consistency. Among them were Josiah Warren, Lucy Parsons, Henry David Thoreau, Lysander Spooner, and Émile Armand.

Josiah Warren (1798–1874)

One of the first American anarchists, Warren argued that justice required complete individual sovereignty. He introduced the idea that "value is determined by labor" and tested it in practice. In 1827 he opened the *Time Store* in Cincinnati, where customers paid with labor notes rather than money, and later helped found the settlement of *Utopia*. These experiments replaced profit with direct exchange and voluntary cooperation, showing that commerce could work without intermediaries or state control.

Lucy Parsons (1853–1942)

A radical activist of Mexican and African American heritage, Parsons was the widow of Albert Parsons, executed after the Haymarket affair. She fought against state power, capitalism, racism, and sexism, while stressing that no collective had the right to impose its norms on the individual. Active in workers' struggles and unions, she combined anarchist ideas with fiery speeches that defended dignity and personal resistance. She did not construct a systematic philosophy but gave voice to radical independence under conditions of repression and social injustice.

Henry David Thoreau (1817–1862)

The American philosopher and naturalist is remembered for *Civil Disobedience* (1849). Thoreau condemned state authority as unjust and saw refusal to obey as a moral duty. He lived his principles: withdrawing to Walden Pond, refusing to pay a poll tax in protest against war and slavery, and accepting jail for his stance. His philosophy, though not explicitly anarchist, echoed individualist anarchism in its stress on conscience, simplicity, and responsibility.

Lysander Spooner (1808–1887)

A legal theorist, abolitionist, and fierce critic of state power, Spooner gave individualist anarchism a strong legal and moral basis. In *No Treason* (1867–1870), he declared the U.S. Constitution void because no one had consented to it. He also founded a private postal service to compete with the government monopoly, which was shut down by federal authorities. For Spooner, natural law and individual conscience stood above any statute, making resistance to unjust laws a duty rather than an option.

Émile Armand (1872–1962)

The French individualist anarchist developed a lifestyle philosophy centered on voluntary association, sexual freedom, and autonomy. Through his journals *L'Ère Nouvelle* and *L'Unique*, he promoted *la camaraderie amoureuse* — free unions based on consent and mutual desire — and urged individuals to break from imposed morality and social convention. Unlike economic reformers such as Warren or Tucker, Armand highlighted personal emancipation in everyday life, extending anarchism into questions of intimacy and culture.

Josiah Warren, Lucy Parsons, Henry David Thoreau, Lysander Spooner, and Émile Armand embodied diverse strategies of individualist anarchism: economic experiments, union activism, civil disobedience, legal resistance, and cultural liberation. Their lives demonstrated that personal freedom was not only an idea but also a practice — a deliberate decision to live differently in defiance of authority and tradition.

The Difference Between the European and American Individualist Traditions

Individualist anarchism developed simultaneously in Europe and the United States, yet in each context it assumed distinct emphases and practical expressions. These differences mirrored the specific cultural and political environments in which anarchist individualism took shape.

1. The European Tradition: Philosophy of Autonomy and Radical Critique

In Europe, individualist anarchism was primarily philosophical. Its thinkers rejected all supra-personal authorities — state, morality, religion, or ideology — as illusions that enslaved the self. Central themes included:

- Max Stirner's anti-metaphysical stance, denouncing abstractions like "Humanity" or "Morality" as empty "spooks";
- radical egoism, not as an ethic but as a declaration of the individual's absolute priority;
- refusal of collective ideals that demand subordination of the person.

Here, anarchism did not aim to design a future society. It proclaimed instead that the individual is the only reality, irreducible to class, nation, or even the abstract category of "human nature."

2. The American Tradition: Practical Individualism and Economic Independence

In the United States, individualist anarchism grew out of radical liberalism and the defense of natural rights. It combined Enlightenment rationalism with suspicion of centralized power. Its key traits included:

- emphasis on self-reliance, private property, and a genuinely free market without state-supported monopolies;
- belief that justice would follow from voluntary exchange once artificial privileges were dismantled;
- creation of tangible models such as Josiah Warren's *Time Store*, intentional settlements like *Utopia*, and networks of cooperative exchange.

The American individualist did not see themselves as a solitary rebel outside society but as part of a community of free people. Independence was pursued through labor and voluntary exchange, while cooperation remained possible — so long as it was freely chosen.

3. Main Differences

Criterion	European Tradition	American Tradition
Philosophical Foundation	Egoism, radical subjectivism	Liberalism, natural rights theory
Primary Focus	Rejection of all supra-personal structures	Economic freedom and self-reliance
Attitude Toward Property	Ambivalent, often critical	Positive, as a guarantee of independence
Mode of Realization	Philosophy and critique	Practical experiments
Image of the Anarchist	The autonomous "Unique One"	The independent producer or entrepreneur

European individualism represents a radically philosophical protest against all forms of authority, including collective meanings.

American individualism represents an ethic of personal freedom, realized through labor, contract, and the minimization of interference.

Both traditions converge on one point: the individual must be free from external control. Yet they diverge in how this freedom is understood and how it is to be achieved.

Forms of Realization and Practical Examples
Individual Forms of Resistance

Unlike other branches of anarchism, individualist anarchism rarely seeks to build mass movements or permanent institutions. Its focus lies in personal choice and the individual's refusal to accept imposed obligations. Across history and in modern practice, this has taken recurring forms of protest and withdrawal.

Rejection of Citizenship

For many individualist anarchists, citizenship is a contract of obedience. It demands loyalty, legal dependency, and participation in state structures built on coercion. Refusal can take many forms:

- abstaining from voting or any participation in politics;
- refusing passports or identity papers;
- living unregistered, beyond legal frameworks;
- denying allegiance to any national or political system.

Such choices are acts of principle: a person should not be reduced to a number, a document, or property of the state.

Tax Resistance

Taxes are seen as forced expropriation of one's labor. Even when used for public services, their obligatory nature violates the principle that only the individual should decide how to use what they create. Forms include:

- working independently or informally, using barter or direct exchange;
- refusing contact with tax authorities;
- open protest by withholding payment.

Henry David Thoreau's refusal to pay a poll tax in protest against slavery and the Mexican-American War remains one of the most famous examples. Tax resistance in this sense is not avoidance for gain, but rejection of financing war, bureaucracy, and domination.

Rejection of Institutional Education

Schools and universities are often criticized as factories of conformity. They discipline rather than liberate, preparing students for service to the state, the army, or industry. Refusals may take the form of:

- homeschooling or self-directed study;
- creation of free schools based on mutual respect and autonomy (such as Francisco Ferrer's Modern School);
- disregard for diplomas and careerist metrics of worth.

Instead of formal success, individualist anarchists value independent thought, self-reliance, and critical learning.

Refusal of Military Service and Violence

Conscription and military obedience are seen as the purest form of submission. Resistance includes:

- conscientious objection and refusal to serve;
- desertion or non-participation in wars;
- embracing pacifism as a way of life.

Thoreau's stand against paying taxes to protest war exemplifies this refusal to cooperate with state violence.

Autonomous Living and Self-Sufficiency

Many have sought to reduce dependence on both state and market through self-reliance. Examples include:

- Thoreau's Walden experiment in simple living;
- Josiah Warren's cooperative settlement *Utopia*;
- contemporary off-grid farms and autonomous communities that seek independence from centralized infrastructure.

Here, protest is embodied not only in refusal but in building alternative ways of living, where autonomy and freedom are practiced daily.

Free Love and Personal Relations

European individualists such as Émile Armand insisted that personal freedom had to extend into intimate life. He denounced marriage as a form of legalized servitude and described conventional morality as a tool for disciplining desire. Through his journals *L'EnDehors* and *L'Unique*, Armand promoted *la camaraderie amoureuse* — relationships based purely on mutual attraction and consent, without contracts, priests, or legal codes.

In practice this meant:

- voluntary unions where partners could separate at will,
- communities where the family was not a compulsory unit but only one option among many,
- experiments with collective living where intimacy was free from social stigma. Armand's writings inspired libertarian communities in France and Spain that created alternative forms of partnership, including polyamorous arrangements, at a time when divorce was restricted and sexual freedom was heavily policed.

Rejection of Intellectual Property

Benjamin Tucker and other American individualists attacked copyright and patent law as artificial barriers that served only publishers, bankers, and monopolists. Tucker himself openly reprinted works without authorization in his journal *Liberty* and argued that knowledge, once expressed, belonged to all.

Examples of resistance included:

- pamphlets and books published without copyright in the late 19th century,
- anarchist presses in the U.S. and Europe that encouraged readers to reprint and distribute freely,
- later continuation of this principle in the free software and open-source movements of the 20th and 21st centuries.
  The principle was simple: ideas cannot be owned. They gain value only by being shared, and attempts to monopolize them were considered a new form of feudal privilege.

Alternative Economic Experiments

Josiah Warren's *Time Store* (1827–1830) in Cincinnati became one of the first attempts to replace money with labor notes. Customers paid for goods by pledging hours of their own work, which could then be redeemed in services or products from others. The store operated successfully for three years and demonstrated that profit was not necessary for exchange.

Warren later helped found *Utopia*, a cooperative settlement where property was held by individuals but economic exchange was carried out without profit. Similar experiments resurfaced in the 20th century:

- Local Exchange Trading Systems (LETS) in Canada and Britain,
- time banks in the United States and Japan,
- community currencies in Latin America, such as the Argentine *trueque* networks after the 2001 crisis.

All these initiatives sought to protect local communities from dependence on state-backed money and global markets.

Cultural and Artistic Protest

Individualist anarchism also found expression in literature and art. Russian nihilists of the 1860s used novels, plays, and satire to ridicule authority and traditional morality. In the early 20th century, avant-garde movements such as Dada and Surrealism rejected bourgeois culture, glorified spontaneity, and mocked the logic of order — an aesthetic rebellion that paralleled Stirner's egoism.

Concrete examples include:

- Dada performances in Zurich's Cabaret Voltaire (1916), where absurd poetry and chaotic theatre mocked militarism and nationalism,
- the Surrealists' attacks on the Catholic Church and bourgeois morality in 1920s Paris,
- anarchist theatres in Spain and Italy that staged plays promoting autonomy and defiance of authority.

  For these artists, creativity itself became an anarchist weapon: breaking rules in art meant breaking rules in life.

Modern Practices

In the 21st century, individualist anarchism has taken new forms in the digital sphere. These practices often combine classical principles — autonomy, refusal of authority, voluntary exchange — with new technologies:

- **Cryptocurrencies** such as Bitcoin, used to bypass state-controlled banks and create peer-to-peer financial exchange.

- **Encryption and anonymity tools** like Tor or Signal, which allow communication beyond the reach of government surveillance.

- **Digital self-sufficiency**, including self-hosted servers, mesh networks, and "going dark" strategies to avoid corporate platforms.

- **Online piracy and file-sharing** communities, which apply Tucker's principle of free knowledge circulation to music, film, and software. These practices reflect the same conviction as Warren's Time Store or Armand's free unions: freedom is lived, not requested.

From Armand's journals promoting free love to Warren's labor-note experiments, from Tucker's anti-copyright campaigns to the Surrealists' artistic revolt, individualist anarchism has always expressed itself through lived practices. In the modern era, cryptocurrencies, encryption, and digital autonomy continue this legacy. The principle behind all these efforts remains unchanged:

> **No one has the right to dictate how another must live.**

Freedom, for the individualist anarchist, is not a promise for the future or a request to authorities. It is realized here and now, through action that refuses submission and invents new ways of living.

Anti-Cultural and Countercultural Projects of the Twentieth Century

In the second half of the twentieth century, individualist anarchism reappeared not as systematic theory but as everyday strategies of life. These practices were countercultural, anti-ideological, and post-political: they rejected authority, consumerism, militarism, and imposed norms. Instead of manifestos, they produced communities, lifestyles, and experiments that continued the individualist tradition through lived autonomy.

Hippies and the "New Communards"

The counterculture of the 1960s and 1970s in the United States and Europe became the most visible form of individualist resistance. Hippies opposed the Vietnam War, military conscription, consumer morality, and cultural conformity. Their rebellion was expressed less in manifestos than in lifestyle choices:

- refusal to participate in mainstream politics or voting,
- rejection of laws and police authority, often through civil disobedience,
- creation of self-governing communes with no property or hierarchy,
- exploration of personal freedom through music, sexuality, and altered states of consciousness.

In the United States, communities such as **The Farm** in Tennessee (founded 1971) brought together thousands of people living collectively without private property. In Europe, squatting movements in Amsterdam and Berlin echoed the same spirit, reclaiming abandoned buildings as spaces for free living. These "new communards" sought to live outside the reach of state and market, testing anarchist principles through daily existence.

Downshifters and Voluntary Simplicity

In the 1980s and 1990s, globalization and corporate consumer culture provoked another kind of quiet rebellion: downshifting. The idea was to deliberately abandon the race for careers, consumption, and social status.

- People left high-paying jobs to live simply, often in rural or small-town settings.
- They chose modest income, minimalism, and time for creativity or family instead of accumulation.
- The goal was independence from market pressure and freedom from social expectations of success.

While not framed as "anarchism," downshifting reflected the same ethical core: personal autonomy, refusal of imposed obligations, and self-determination over systemic dependency. The **Voluntary Simplicity Movement** in the U.S., linked with authors like Duane Elgin (*Voluntary Simplicity*, 1981), became a touchstone for this lifestyle.

Autonomous Homesteads and Self-Sufficiency

Another trajectory was complete or partial withdrawal from centralized systems. Autonomous homesteaders left urban life to pursue self-reliance:

- living off the grid, disconnected from centralized electricity and water,
- subsistence farming and gardening,
- barter and local exchange rather than reliance on state money,
- minimizing contact with bureaucratic and financial institutions.

Examples range from small-scale back-to-the-land movements in North America to eco-villages in Europe. In the digital age, "tech hermits" and intentional communities adopted solar power, rainwater harvesting, and permaculture as tools of independence. These practices embodied anarchist action not through confrontation but through deliberate withdrawal — a refusal to participate in the structures of state and market.

New Forms of Expression in the Twenty-First Century

In the twenty-first century, individualist anarchism has taken on new forms, adapting to global surveillance, algorithmic governance, and dependence on centralized infrastructures. Its practices no longer appear only as counterculture or philosophy but as everyday strategies — personal in scale, yet socially disruptive.

Digital Individualism: Privacy as Resistance

As states and corporations expand surveillance, a current of digital individualism emphasizes control over personal data. These practices include:

- rejecting social networks that harvest information,
- refusing biometric IDs and centralized digital wallets,
- using encryption tools like PGP, Tor, or Signal,
- building and using decentralized networks such as Mastodon or mesh systems.

Here, autonomy is measured not only in physical independence but in becoming "invisible" to algorithms. Resistance is enacted through technical skill: firewalls, anonymous browsing, self-hosted servers. The principle is clear — the individual defines their digital presence, not governments or corporations.

Crypto-Anarchism: Building Autonomy Through Technology

Crypto-anarchism grew from the writings of Timothy C. May (*Crypto Anarchist Manifesto*, 1988) and the experiments of cypherpunks in the 1990s. It holds that cryptography can dismantle state control over economy and communication. Its core practices are:

- using cryptocurrencies like Bitcoin to exchange without banks, taxation, or monitoring,
- employing blockchain to create anonymous contracts and decentralized platforms,
- experimenting with new digital forms of ownership outside corporate law.

The idea is not to petition for freedom but to build parallel infrastructures where authority cannot reach. "Code becomes law," and autonomy is guaranteed by mathematics rather than by institutions.

Principled Withdrawal from State-Economic Systems

Alongside digital strategies, many still practice traditional withdrawal from state institutions. This includes:

- refusing voter registration, tax ID numbers, or social security enrollment,
- relying on barter, subsistence farming, or informal labor networks,
- opting out of healthcare or pension systems in favor of self-managed alternatives.

These practices are often adopted without anarchist labels, yet they embody the same principle: to live without external governance, with personal responsibility as the only law.

Contemporary individualist anarchism does not confront the system head-on. It sidesteps it. By refusing digital identity, rejecting taxation, or creating anonymous economies, individuals carve out spaces of autonomy. The struggle for freedom is not declared; it is enacted in practice. People simply live freely, despite the apparatus of surveillance and control that surrounds them.

Limits of Scalability

Despite its ethical consistency, individualist anarchism encounters a fundamental limit: it cannot be expanded to the scale of complex societies without undermining its own principles. The refusal of collective organization, shared coordination, and systemic regulation makes it unworkable at the level of a state, a region, or a metropolis where stable infrastructure and durable planning are indispensable.

1. Social Fragmentation

When each person acts only on personal discretion, there are no binding mechanisms to:

- reconcile the interests of tens or hundreds of thousands of people,
- distribute scarce resources in a balanced way,
- protect vulnerable groups such as children, the elderly, or the disabled,
- sustain long-term systems like energy grids, transport, and hospitals.

Historically, purely voluntary communities have tended to break into small, loosely connected groups. Without wider coordination, these fragments cannot manage the interdependence required by complex societies.

2. Absence of Collective Responsibility

The model rejects obligations to society, but many essential functions — epidemic control, environmental protection, policing large-scale violence — require joint, coordinated effort. Epidemics, for example, cannot be stopped by private contracts; they demand collective measures. Without common institutions to guarantee these tasks, risks remain unaddressed until it is too late.

3. Justice and Inequality

Individualist anarchism affirms liberty but offers no tools to reduce entrenched inequality. People may be formally equal yet remain factually unequal in access to land, education, legal defense, or healthcare. Without redistributive mechanisms, poverty and marginalization persist across generations. For vulnerable groups, "freedom from interference" often means exposure to exploitation without recourse.

4. Weakness Against External Threats

In crises — wars, natural disasters, or organized repression — the refusal of coordinated defense leaves communities exposed. Historical examples, from small communes to libertarian settlements, show that lack of common defense structures makes them easy targets for more centralized powers. Autonomy collapses when external actors can easily overwhelm fragmented groups.

5. No Model for Complex Societies

Individualist anarchism provides strategies for individuals and small communities — homesteads, voluntary cooperatives, or digital anonymity — but it has no framework for running megacities, national infrastructures, or interconnected economies. Scaling up would require creating exactly the kind of collective institutions and obligations that the philosophy rejects, undermining its own foundations.

Contemporary Relevance and Critical Reception

The Presence of Individualist Motifs in Libertarianism, Anti-Globalism, and Digital Privacy

Despite its limited scalability and lack of a unified political program, individualist anarchism retains philosophical weight and cultural resonance in the modern world. Its central themes — personal autonomy, rejection of state interference, and the primacy of individual choice — reappear in movements and practices that may not call themselves anarchist but draw directly from its logic.

1. Libertarianism and Right-Wing Individualism

In the United States, modern libertarianism has absorbed many elements of individualist anarchism. Both defend:

- resistance to state interference in personal and economic life,
- inviolability of private property,
- the market as the arena of voluntary interaction.

Yet important differences divide them. Libertarians usually:

- accept the need for a "night-watchman" state to enforce contracts and defend borders,
- tolerate hierarchies if they are voluntarily entered,
- rely on institutions such as courts and constitutions to guarantee freedom.

By contrast, individualist anarchists reject all coercive structures, whether political, economic, or cultural. Still, the intellectual kinship is clear: libertarian defenses of free markets and property rights often echo the writings of Benjamin Tucker or Lysander Spooner.

2. Anti-Globalist and Localist Currents

Individualist themes are also visible in strands of anti-globalism. Critics of globalization target:

- the power of transnational corporations,
- centralized agencies such as the WTO, IMF, or UN,

- the erosion of local autonomy by global governance.

Responses shaped by individualist logic include:

- deliberate refusal to participate in global institutions,
- insistence on local control over resources and decision-making,
- cultivation of self-sufficient ways of life.

For example, the Zapatistas in Chiapas, while primarily a collective movement, emphasize the right of each community to live on its own terms without subordination to national or global agendas. Similar principles animate European autonomist groups defending communal autonomy against state or corporate control.

3. Digital Privacy and Resistance to Digital Subordination

In the digital age, individualist anarchism resurfaces in the fight against surveillance and algorithmic control. Practices include:

- using encryption tools such as PGP, Tor, and Signal,
- adopting VPNs and decentralized platforms like Mastodon,
- refusing biometric IDs, centralized e-services, or dependence on corporate social networks.

The language of these movements often recalls individualist anarchism: *"I am not a data point. Freedom means being invisible to power."* Here, the demand for autonomy is transposed into technological conditions, continuing the tradition of resistance not through street protest but through control over personal information and digital presence.

Criticism from Other Anarchists

Despite its persistence and ethical appeal, individualist anarchism has often been criticized by other anarchist currents, especially anarcho-communists and anarcho-syndicalists. Their critique is not aimed at the value of autonomy itself, but at the social and strategic weaknesses that, in their view, make individualism ineffective against real structures of domination.

1. Social Isolation and Disorganization

Kropotkin, Malatesta, and later Murray Bookchin argued that individualist anarchism tends toward social detachment. By rejecting collective responsibility and organized struggle, individualist practices rarely move beyond personal gestures. Resistance remains invisible, uncoordinated, and therefore incapable of systemic impact.

- In Spain during the 1930s, while the CNT mobilized millions of workers into collective syndicates, individualist circles were small, fragmented, and politically marginal.
- Malatesta emphasized that only solidarity and common strategy could allow anarchism to become a real social force.

2. Neglect of Real Inequality and Privilege

Critics such as Kropotkin in *The Conquest of Bread* insisted that formal declarations of freedom overlook structural inequalities:

- economic disparities,
- unequal access to education and healthcare,
- cultural and gender-based privileges.

The slogan "simply live free" cannot apply equally when some begin life with wealth and security while others face poverty and exclusion. For communists, freedom that ignores inequality risks becoming a privilege of the strong, not a shared condition.

3. Weakness Against Organized Power

Anarcho-syndicalists stressed that states, corporations, and armies operate through coordination, resources, and discipline. Against them, individual withdrawal or refusal is morally powerful but politically ineffective.

- In Russia after 1917, individualist groups were unable to resist either the White armies or Bolshevik repression, while organized movements (Makhnovists, anarcho-syndicalists) could at least temporarily mount large-scale defense.
- Bookchin later pointed out that without structures for collective strategy, individualist anarchism cannot respond to systemic crises like climate change, militarism, or global capitalism.

4. Ethical Individualism Without Political Effectiveness

Even sympathetic critics acknowledged the moral strength of personal autonomy. But anarcho-communists argued that ethics alone is insufficient:

- refusal to cooperate may express integrity but does not create alternatives,
- society judges it less as freedom and more as withdrawal from responsibility.

Kropotkin himself admired Thoreau's civil disobedience but noted that "isolated protest must be joined to collective action if it is to change the conditions that oppress us all."

Contribution to Anarchist Thought

Despite its social limitations, individualist anarchism contributed an essential reminder to the broader anarchist tradition: no project of freedom can ignore the freedom of the individual. At its core lies the conviction that the person comes before any system, collective, or idea, and that the ethical right to be oneself cannot be sacrificed, even for the most just of causes.

1. Critique of Internal Authoritarianism

Individualist anarchists posed a difficult question to the movement itself: can organizations that fight for liberation reproduce new forms of coercion? Stirner warned that even "progressive" collectives risk becoming new idols, demanding loyalty and obedience. The reminder was clear: without respect for autonomy, even horizontal structures can generate moral pressure, domination of the majority, or hidden hierarchies.

2. Autonomy as the Basis of Freedom

The tradition insisted that freedom begins not with the design of society but with the individual refusal to submit. For this reason, individualism is less a social program than an ethical foundation. Genuine liberation, it argued, requires self-awareness, personal responsibility, and the ability to reject voluntary subordination — otherwise no collective system can guarantee freedom.

3. Voluntary Solidarity

Individualist anarchism does not reject cooperation, but insists that solidarity has meaning only when chosen. Aid loses its ethical value if imposed as duty. This position injected balance into anarchist thought, reminding communists and syndicalists that social justice cannot be sustained without individual choice.

4. The Line Between Freedom and Pressure

Even in free communities, new forms of domination may emerge — cultural, moral, or emotional. Individualism sharpened anarchist awareness of the fragile line between collective participation and collective coercion, between solidarity freely chosen and solidarity imposed.

Individualism as the Extreme Form of Anarchy

Individualist anarchism occupies a distinctive position at the very edge of anarchist thought. While anarcho-communists build on solidarity and syndicalists on collective struggle, individualists affirm: freedom is not a product of organization but the inner capacity to refuse subordination.

1. Anarchy as Personal Choice

For the individualist, anarchy is not a future social order but a condition of the self. It is realized when the person ceases to obey — whether laws, moral codes, or collective agendas. Pushed to this extreme, individualism dissolves even the idea of the "common," making the individual the sole center of reality.

2. The Paradox: Freedom Without Safeguards

Here lies the paradox: freedom is affirmed as absolute, yet the refusal of shared defense, redistribution, or structures of support leaves it exposed.

3. Not a Model but a Reminder

Individualist anarchism cannot serve as a universal model. It offers no blueprint for governance, economy, or protection of the weak. But that is not its role. Its enduring significance lies in being a moral compass: a reminder that liberation must not reproduce coercion, and that collective emancipation is meaningless if it tramples personal autonomy.

4. The Right to Dissent and Withdrawal

The central legacy of the tradition is the insistence on the right to be oneself outside the pressure of state, society, and ideology. Where the collective demands participation, the individualist defends the right to withdraw; where society demands consensus, the individualist insists on dissent. It does not prescribe the future, but it ensures that anarchism never loses sight of its foundation: respect for the individual.

CONCLUSION

Anarchist models reject the very idea of the state as an intermediary between the individual and society. They are not united by a single blueprint, but they share a distrust of authority and a search for alternatives to coercion—whether political or moral. This is their common tone, but beyond it their paths diverge.

Anarcho-syndicalism relies on organized resistance and workers' self-management. Anarcho-communism emphasizes radical equality, collective responsibility, and the abolition of all forms of power. Individualist anarchism steps aside and reminds us: before building society, one must respect the boundaries of the individual and the right to remain outside society.

Each model has its vulnerabilities: where there is no center, coordination is difficult; where there is no property, distribution is fragile; where there are no obligations, mutual support weakens. Freedom without structure risks dissolving into chaos, while structure without freedom risks hardening into domination.

Yet anarchism remains not only a form of protest but also a conceptual laboratory where extreme models of justice, participation, equality, and refusal of subordination are tested. Its ideas are not necessarily utopias, but tools for probing the limits of the possible. In real politics, they are rarely realized in full—but it is precisely they that bring ethical depth to debates about freedom, power, and community.

What matters in anarchism is not only what it rejects but also what it affirms: a world in which the individual is subject neither to structure, nor to another's will, nor to abstract notions of the collective, but exists in a space of conscious freedom and voluntary association with others.

And even if anarchy as a stable system remains an open question, anarchy as a principle endures as a challenge—a challenge to any politics that forgets that the individual is not a means but an end.

PART IX

CLASSIFICATION BY

THE LEVEL OF PROTECTION OF

HUMAN RIGHTS AND

FREEDOMS

INTRODUCTION

Human rights and freedoms form the fundamental basis that safeguard human dignity and ensure the full development of the individual in society. Rights are understood as the opportunities and guarantees that the state is obliged to provide to every person. These include the right to life, freedom of speech, freedom of conscience, the right to personal security, and protection from arbitrariness. Freedoms, in turn, represent spheres of personal autonomy into which the state must not intrude except in exceptional cases and strictly within the limits of law.

The protection of rights and freedoms plays a crucial role in evaluating the quality and fairness of a political system. The stronger their protection, the greater the opportunities for each citizen to realize their potential, and the more stable and humane society becomes. Conversely, neglect or suppression of fundamental rights inevitably leads to social tension, conflict, a decline of trust in authority, and the erosion of public stability.

The criteria for assessing the level of protection of rights and freedoms include: effective legislation that guarantees these rights, the independence of the judiciary, openness and accountability of state institutions, the existence of a free press, and the right of citizens to express their views and participate in political life. Equally important are practical indicators: the absence of political repression, torture, arbitrariness, censorship, and discrimination on various grounds.

Analyzing the level of protection of rights and freedoms makes it possible to evaluate not only the degree of democracy within a state but also its capacity for sustainable development. At the same time, political reality is always more complex than any classification. In practice, states demonstrate a wide spectrum of forms and levels of protection. Beyond the commonly contrasted liberal and illiberal types, there are also hybrid and declarative models that combine elements of different approaches.

Normally, in each section I provide historical examples of particular states, but here I have intentionally refrained from doing so. Too often external opinions are imposed on us that rarely reflect the truth. In this case, I have no intention of arguing with the media or engaging in polemics. My goal is to present, as accurately and truthfully as possible, the characteristics and features of different types of states. How free the state that interests you may be—that is for you, and you alone, to decide.

"The worth of a man is in proportion to the objects he pursues... The worth of a state in the long run is the worth of the individuals composing it; and a state which postpones the interests of their mental expansion and elevation to a little more of administrative skill... will find that with small men no great thing can really be accomplished."

— John Stuart Mill, On Liberty (1859)

SECTION 1. LIBERAL STATE: FULL LEGAL AND PRACTICAL GUARANTEES OF RIGHTS AND FREEDOMS

> **A liberal state** is a political and legal model grounded in the rule of law, the protection of individual rights and freedoms, the separation of powers, and political pluralism.

The idea of the liberal state emerged from the intellectual ferment of early modern Europe. Its foundations were laid by classical philosophers who sought to articulate the principles of human dignity, the limits of authority, and the conditions of freedom.

John Locke formulated the theory of natural rights, asserting that life, liberty, and property belong to individuals by nature and that the purpose of government is not to create these rights but to secure them. Charles de Montesquieu introduced the principle of the separation of powers, arguing that liberty can exist only when legislative, executive, and judicial authority are divided and balanced. John Stuart Mill later expanded the liberal tradition by emphasizing freedom of thought, conscience, and individuality as essential to human flourishing and as a safeguard against the tyranny of the majority.

In the nineteenth century, these ideas crystallized into the model of classical liberalism. The liberal state was understood as a minimal state—a "night-watchman" power whose task was confined to protecting property, enforcing contracts, and maintaining public order. The guiding economic principle was laissez-faire: the belief that free markets, left to their own dynamics, would generate prosperity and maximize liberty.

By the twentieth century, however, liberalism had undergone a profound transformation. Industrialization, social inequality, and global economic crises revealed the limits of a purely minimal state. Out of these challenges emerged modern liberalism, which preserved the primacy of rights and freedoms but expanded the responsibilities of the state to include social welfare, education, healthcare, and the protection of vulnerable groups. The liberal state became not only a guardian of individual rights but also a guarantor of social rights, evolving into the "welfare state" that sought to balance freedom with equality of opportunity.

Key Features of the Liberal State

The liberal state is built on the conviction that the dignity and freedom of the individual are the highest political values. Its purpose is not to create rights but to guarantee and protect the inalienable rights that every person already possesses by nature. This vision translates into a set of fundamental principles that define the liberal model.

1. Rule of Law and Equality Before It

The cornerstone of the liberal state is the rule of law. All citizens, including public officials, are equal before the law. Legal norms hold the highest authority and must be applied consistently and impartially. An independent judiciary serves as a guarantor of rights and freedoms, ensuring that no individual can be left defenseless—even against the state itself. In this sense, law is not an instrument of power but a framework that restrains power and protects the individual.

2. Separation of Powers

The liberal state relies on the division of legislative, executive, and judicial authority. This separation, rooted in Montesquieu's theory, prevents the concentration of power in any single branch and establishes checks and balances that limit the abuse of authority. No institution is permitted absolute control; instead, power is distributed and balanced to protect the liberties of citizens.

3. Transparency and Accountability of Government

A liberal system requires an open government that is accountable to society. Citizens must have access to information about state activity, while institutions remain subject to public oversight. Mechanisms such as regular elections, parliamentary scrutiny, independent auditing bodies, and freedom of the press provide transparency. Accountability ensures that state authority is exercised as a trust on behalf of the people, not as a privilege above them.

4. Political Pluralism and Multi-Party System

The liberal state recognizes political competition as essential for democracy. Multiple parties, ideologies, and movements are allowed to participate openly, ensuring representation of diverse social interests. Opposition is not suppressed but valued as a vital element of political life. Free and fair elections provide peaceful mechanisms for the transfer of power and the renewal of political leadership.

5. Civil Society and Independent Associations

Liberalism affirms the autonomy of civil society. Citizens are free to form unions, associations, and initiatives independent of state control. Non-governmental organizations, professional groups, and grassroots movements provide additional channels for civic participation. Civil society functions as a mediator between individuals and government, reinforcing pluralism and safeguarding against the overreach of state authority.

6. Primacy of Personal Freedom and Autonomy

The liberal state is founded on the assumption that personal freedom comes first, while state intervention is permitted only in cases of necessity and within the boundaries of law. This principle includes respect for private life, freedom of speech, conscience, belief, and the right to choose one's lifestyle, profession, and political views. Private property and entrepreneurial freedom are likewise guaranteed as key conditions of independence. The state does not dictate values but provides the legal and institutional environment in which each person may act autonomously and responsibly.

7. Minimization of State Intervention

Another defining principle is the limitation of state power. The state does not regulate matters that can be resolved by individuals, families, local communities, or the market. It refrains from unnecessary interference in private life and instead focuses on securing equal starting opportunities and enforcing general rules of fairness. The aim is maximum freedom with minimum coercion.

8. Freedom of Information and Independent Media

The existence of a free press and open access to information are indispensable elements of the liberal state. Independent media act as watchdogs, exposing abuses of power and ensuring an informed citizenry. Transparency in communication between state and society fosters accountability and strengthens public trust.

9. Equality of Opportunity and Protection of Minorities

Formal equality before the law must be complemented by real safeguards for vulnerable groups. The liberal state recognizes diversity and protects minorities from discrimination on cultural, religious, or other grounds. Ensuring equal opportunities for all citizens prevents freedom from becoming a privilege of the strong and makes it a shared right.

10. Right to Political Participation

Liberal states guarantee universal and equal suffrage, granting all adult citizens the right to vote and to stand for election. Political participation is not limited to elections but extends to freedom of assembly, protest, and the creation of parties and associations. Citizens are treated not merely as subjects of governance but as active participants in shaping public life.

11. Priority of International Law and Human Rights

In modern contexts, the liberal state aligns its internal order with international human rights standards. It acknowledges the priority of treaties and conventions that protect human dignity, integrating national law into a wider framework of universal norms. This commitment underscores that rights are not conditional on citizenship alone but are grounded in shared human values.

Strengths of the Liberal State

1. High Level of Individual Freedom and Self-Realization

The liberal state ensures the widest possible scope of personal autonomy. Citizens are free to choose their lifestyle, profession, political orientation, and religious beliefs, as well as the forms of their civic participation. This not only encourages creativity, intellectual growth, and professional achievement but also fosters personal responsibility. By reducing external pressure, liberal institutions create conditions in which individuals can fully realize their potential.

2. Effective Protection Against Arbitrary Power

The liberal model is anchored in the rule of law, independent courts, and impartial legal procedures. These mechanisms defend citizens against unlawful actions, whether by the state or private actors. The protection of rights reduces the risks of repression, corruption, and political persecution, thereby cultivating trust between society and government.

3. Rule of Law and Equality Before It

One of the greatest strengths of liberal states is the consistent application of law to all members of society, including those in positions of power. No one stands above the law, and legal norms serve as a check on political authority. This principle provides stability and predictability, which are essential for both justice and economic development.

4. Political Pluralism and Peaceful Transfer of Power

By guaranteeing competition among parties and ideologies, the liberal state prevents monopolization of authority. Free and fair elections allow citizens to choose their representatives and replace them peacefully. This reduces the risk of authoritarian consolidation and promotes long-term political stability through mechanisms of renewal.

5. Stable and Developed Civil Society

Liberal states encourage the growth of independent associations, unions, NGOs, and grassroots movements. Civil society becomes a platform where citizens can self-organize, articulate their interests, and oversee government activity. This creates an additional layer of accountability and strengthens democracy by dispersing power across society rather than concentrating it in the state.

6. Transparency and Accountability of Government

Openness of state institutions, public access to information, and oversight by the press and civil society ensure that power remains accountable. Mechanisms such as checks and balances, parliamentary scrutiny, and independent auditing reduce the likelihood of abuse. Transparency strengthens citizens' confidence in governance and lowers the threshold for participation in political life.

7. Guarantees of Economic Freedom and Private Initiative

The liberal state protects property rights and supports free enterprise and fair competition. By refraining from unnecessary regulation, it creates conditions in which markets can function efficiently and innovation can flourish. Economic freedom provides incentives for entrepreneurship and fosters growth, which in turn supports overall prosperity and stability.

8. Equality of Opportunity and Protection of Minorities

Beyond formal legal equality, the liberal state seeks to create conditions for real equality of opportunity. It protects vulnerable groups from discrimination. This emphasis on inclusivity helps maintain social harmony and prevents conflict.

9. Freedom of Information and Independent Media

The existence of free media is one of the most powerful safeguards against abuse of power. Independent journalism exposes corruption, informs citizens, and holds public officials accountable. A free flow of information also empowers individuals to make informed decisions, reinforcing the quality of democracy.

10. Capacity for Self-Correction and Reform

Thanks to independent courts, free media, political competition, and active civil society, the liberal state possesses mechanisms of self-regulation. Mistakes can be identified and corrected without systemic violence or revolution. This adaptability allows liberal systems to respond flexibly to new challenges and to preserve legitimacy through peaceful reform.

11. Compatibility with International Standards and Cooperation

Modern liberal states tend to align themselves with international human rights standards and participate in cooperative frameworks such as international courts, conventions, and organizations. This strengthens global security and provides citizens with additional avenues for the protection of their rights.

12. Long-Term Stability and Predictability

Because power is limited, predictable, and legally defined, liberal states tend to be more stable over time. Citizens know the rules of the game, and leaders cannot easily change them for personal gain. This predictability encourages investment, innovation, and trust in institutions.

Weaknesses of the Liberal State

1. Formal Equality Amid Real Inequality

While the liberal state guarantees equality before the law, it often fails to eliminate structural barriers that prevent true equality of opportunity. As a result, freedom can remain a privilege of the advantaged rather than a universal reality.

2. Limited Social Policy

Because the liberal state prioritizes minimal intervention, it sometimes neglects vulnerable populations such as the poor, unemployed, elderly, and people with disabilities. Market competition, without sufficient safety nets, can leave many without access to education, healthcare, or basic living conditions. This weakens social cohesion and undermines the promise of universal dignity.

3. Risk of Oligarchization

Economic liberalism creates space for concentration of wealth and influence. Large corporations, banks, and lobbying groups often acquire disproportionate power over political processes and media. This undermines democratic competition, narrows the range of real political choices, and shifts decision-making away from public interest toward private gain.

4. Political Alienation of Citizens

Although liberal democracy guarantees freedom of participation, many citizens feel that their voices carry little weight. Declining voter turnout, apathy, and mistrust of political institutions reflect this alienation. Freedom to participate does not always mean motivation or meaningful influence, leaving gaps between formal democracy and lived political reality.

5. Susceptibility to Populism and Manipulation

The open information environment of the liberal state is vulnerable to disinformation, propaganda, and populist appeals. When critical thinking and civic education are underdeveloped, demagogues can exploit freedoms of speech and media to spread simplistic solutions, erode trust in institutions, and destabilize political systems from within.

6. Dependence on Social and Political Maturity

The effectiveness of liberal institutions depends heavily on a society's political culture, level of education, and capacity for civic self-organization. In states with authoritarian legacies or weak traditions of participation, liberal structures may exist formally but fail to function substantively, producing "facade democracies" with limited freedoms in practice.

7. Individualism at the Expense of Solidarity

The liberal emphasis on personal autonomy can weaken collective responsibility and social solidarity. Excessive focus on private interests may discourage cooperation, mutual aid, or engagement with shared problems such as inequality, public health, or environmental sustainability. Over time, this risks fragmenting society into isolated individuals rather than fostering cohesive communities.

8. Structural Vulnerability to Global Crises

The liberal model, reliant on open markets, free flows of capital, and minimal restrictions, is highly sensitive to global economic shocks. Crises such as financial collapses, pandemics, or climate emergencies often demand strong collective action, which may exceed the limited capacity of minimally interventionist states. This exposes the tension between global interdependence and national liberal principles.

9. Tensions Between Freedom and Security

The liberal state's commitment to protecting individual liberties can make it less effective in responding to urgent threats. In times of terrorism, war, or natural disaster, governments often introduce emergency measures that restrict rights, creating contradictions between liberal ideals and practical governance. These tensions may erode both liberty and public trust.

10. Difficulty in Addressing Systemic Injustice

By focusing on individual rights, the liberal state sometimes overlooks broader systemic injustices that cannot be solved solely through formal legal equality. Without proactive measures, these injustices persist, limiting the universality of freedom and equality promised by liberal principles.

Types of Liberal States

Liberalism as a political tradition has never been monolithic. Over the course of its development, two distinct models of the liberal state have taken shape: the **classical liberal state** and the **modern liberal state**. Distinguishing between them is essential, since critiques of "liberalism" often fail to account for the differences between these forms.

The Classical (Minimal) Liberal State

In its nineteenth-century formulation, the liberal state was conceived as a strictly limited authority—a "night-watchman" whose role was confined to the protection of property, the enforcement of contracts, and the maintenance of public order. Its guiding philosophy was *laissez-faire*: the belief that the free play of market forces, unencumbered by state interference, would secure prosperity and maximize liberty.

Under this model, the state was expected to safeguard the framework of rights but to remain neutral in economic and social life. Freedom was understood primarily as freedom *from* interference, and equality was reduced to formal equality before the law.

The Modern Liberal State

By the twentieth century, new social and economic realities reshaped the liberal tradition. Industrialization, mass poverty, and recurring economic crises exposed the limits of a purely minimal state. The modern liberal state preserved the foundational principles of rights and freedoms but expanded its responsibilities to include social welfare, education, healthcare, and the protection of vulnerable groups. It came to embody a balance between negative liberty (freedom from coercion) and positive liberty (the capacity to realize one's potential). Often described as the "welfare state," this form of liberalism views government not merely as a guardian of rights but also as an enabler of opportunity and equality.

The Role of Human Rights and Freedoms

At the heart of the liberal state lies its catalog of rights and freedoms, which serves as the very foundation of its legitimacy. The state is judged not by its proclamations but by the extent to which it guarantees, protects, and enforces these rights in the lives of its citizens. Without such guarantees, the liberal state would lose its moral and political justification.

A crucial distinction within this catalog is between **civil and political rights** and **social and economic rights**.

Civil and Political Rights

These include freedom of speech, freedom of assembly, freedom of conscience, and the right to participate in elections. They are designed to protect the individual from arbitrary authority and to secure the conditions for active participation in public life. Civil and political rights create the framework within which citizens can express dissent, form associations, and hold those in power accountable.

Social and Economic Rights

Developed later in the evolution of liberalism, these rights reflect the recognition that formal liberty is insufficient without real opportunities. The right to work, to education, to healthcare, and to social protection ensures that individuals are not merely free in law but also capable of exercising that freedom in practice. Social and economic rights provide the substantive conditions for dignity, equality of opportunity, and inclusion in the life of the community.

Taken together, civil-political and social-economic rights define the liberal state as both a guarantor of personal autonomy and a promoter of conditions necessary for human development. The balance between these two dimensions—protecting freedom from interference while enabling the realization of potential—gives the liberal model its distinctive character.

Contemporary Challenges to the Liberal State

Rise of Populism and "Illiberal Democracy"

In recent decades, many liberal democracies have witnessed the growth of populist movements that question the authority of established institutions and exploit dissatisfaction with political elites. Populism often appeals directly to "the people" while undermining checks and balances, judicial independence, and media freedom. This trend has given rise to the notion of "illiberal democracy," in which electoral processes remain, but the substance of liberal rights and protections is eroded.

Impact of Globalization

Globalization has expanded trade, migration, and communication, but it has also weakened the capacity of liberal states to control their own political and economic destinies. Transnational corporations wield power comparable to that of governments, shaping markets and public policies. International organizations such as the WTO, IMF, or UN influence national decision-making, while mass migration raises questions of cultural integration and social solidarity. Liberal states must balance openness with sovereignty, ensuring that the protection of rights and freedoms extends to both citizens and newcomers, without undermining social cohesion.

The Digital Age

Technological transformation introduces new dilemmas for liberal governance. The spread of surveillance technologies, algorithmic decision-making, and the commodification of personal data pose direct threats to privacy and autonomy. Liberal states struggle to reconcile the demand for security with the protection of individual freedoms, especially in contexts of terrorism, cybercrime, and misinformation. At the same time, the rise of social media and algorithmic management challenges the very conditions of political debate, exposing liberal societies to manipulation and polarization. The task of the liberal state is to establish rules that preserve freedom in the digital sphere without succumbing to technological domination or authoritarian control.

The Value of the Liberal State

The liberal state is not defined solely by its institutions but by the values that underpin them: the dignity of the individual, the rule of law, and the principled limitation of power. These values serve as the moral foundation of political life, reminding both citizens and governments that freedom and responsibility must remain at the core of any legitimate system.

Even if the liberal model is not flawless, it continues to function as the benchmark by which other political systems are judged. Its standards of rights, transparency, and accountability provide the language through which questions of justice and legitimacy are debated. In this sense, liberalism shapes not only the states that adopt it but also the global expectations of political order.

SECTION 2. NON-LIBERAL STATE: LIMITED OR SELECTIVE PROTECTION OF RIGHTS AND FREEDOMS

> **A non-liberal state** is a political model in which the guarantees of human rights and freedoms are either severely limited or merely declarative in nature, while power is concentrated in the hands of a narrow group of individuals or institutions that are not accountable to civil society.

The illiberal state formally retains the institutions of constitutional order and democracy but distorts their meaning and function. It is characterized not by the outright rejection of rights and freedoms, but by their selective application and manipulation to serve the interests of those in power.

Key Features of the Illiberal State

The illiberal state formally retains the institutions of constitutional order and democracy but distorts their meaning and function. It is characterized not by the outright rejection of rights and freedoms, but by their selective application and manipulation to serve the interests of those in power.

1. Formal Declaration of Rights with Limited Implementation

Rights and freedoms may be codified in the constitution and laws, but in practice they are restricted, ignored, or applied selectively. Citizens may have "rights on paper" but lack real mechanisms to enforce them.

2. Dominance of the Executive Branch

Presidents, prime ministers, or ruling cabinets exercise overwhelming control over all branches of government. The separation of powers becomes a formality as executive authorities dictate the agenda of legislatures, courts, and regulatory agencies.

3. Lack of Judicial Independence

Courts are subordinated to political authority. Judicial appointments, decisions, and procedures are influenced or directly controlled by the executive, turning the judiciary into an instrument of power rather than an arbiter of law.

4. Unfair Electoral System

Elections are formally held but lack genuine competition. Common practices include manipulation of electoral laws, administrative pressure on voters, intimidation, and outright falsification of results.

5. Restricted Political Competition

Opposition parties face systemic barriers: denial of registration, harassment, legal persecution, or exclusion from the media. Campaigns take place, but they are formal exercises without real alternatives for voters.

6. Control of Media and Restriction of Free Speech

Media outlets are concentrated in the hands of the state or affiliated groups. Independent journalists and outlets are censored, harassed, or shut down. The flow of information is tightly controlled to maintain favorable narratives for those in power.

7. Suppression or Co-optation of Civil Society

Non-governmental organizations, human rights defenders, and activists operate under severe restrictions. They may be burdened with repressive legal requirements, labeled as "foreign agents," or marginalized through propaganda campaigns.

8. Selective Application of Law

Law is weaponized against opponents and critics while allies of the regime enjoy impunity. Instead of functioning as a universal safeguard, legislation becomes a tool of pressure and intimidation.

9. Formal Parliament Under Executive Control

Legislatures exist but serve as extensions of the executive branch. Parliaments merely rubber-stamp decisions rather than debating or checking the government, reducing representative institutions to a façade.

10. Centralization and Elimination of Local Self-Government

Local and regional governments are stripped of meaningful authority. Power is concentrated in the capital, and local bodies act primarily as administrators of central directives rather than autonomous representatives of their communities.

11. Monopoly on "Patriotism" and National Interests

The ruling elite monopolizes the definition of patriotism and the "national interest." Criticism of the government is equated with betrayal, while opposition is labeled a threat to national security.

12. Politicization of Security Forces and Special Services

Police, military, and intelligence agencies serve the interests of the ruling elite rather than society at large. Instead of protecting citizens, they are deployed to monitor, intimidate, and suppress dissent.

13. Repressive Legislation and Restriction of Protests

Laws are crafted to criminalize protest, labeling dissent as extremism or subversion. Even peaceful demonstrations are curtailed, with participants often facing harassment, arrest, or prosecution.

14. Mythologization of National Identity and Enemies

The regime fosters a narrative of perpetual threat, emphasizing external or internal enemies to justify repressive measures. National identity is mythologized to mobilize loyalty and silence dissent.

15. Simulation of Democracy and Use of Democratic Symbols

Constitutions, elections, courts, and parliaments are maintained as symbols, but they serve decorative purposes. Their existence provides the appearance of legitimacy while their substance is hollowed out.

Strengths of the Illiberal State

1. Capacity for Rapid Decision-Making in Crises

The concentration of power in the executive and in the hands of a political leader allows for swift responses to threats, bypassing lengthy processes of negotiation and approval. In times of war, emergency, or large-scale crisis, such decisiveness can help stabilize the situation and prevent chaos.

2. Maintenance of Public Order and Stability Through Restrictive Measures

By exerting strict control over information, mass gatherings, and political activity, the illiberal state can reduce the risk of unrest, radical movements, or public panic. While restrictive, these measures can temporarily ensure stability and manageability in periods of high social tension.

3. Centralized Management and Control of Strategic Resources

The concentration of authority enables the state to reallocate resources quickly and channel them into priority areas such as defense, infrastructure, or strategic industries. This capacity can increase the efficiency of large-scale projects and national programs.

4. Continuity of Long-Term Policy

With limited political competition and without frequent electoral cycles, governments in illiberal systems can pursue long-term strategies without the risk of policy reversal after a change of party in power. This continuity can be particularly important for major infrastructure, industrial, or defense projects.

5. Lower Risk of Political Fragmentation

A strong vertical of power and restrictions on opposition reduce the likelihood of severe internal conflict or institutional deadlock. By limiting pluralism, illiberal states minimize risks of political paralysis that can undermine governance in fragmented democracies.

6. Potential for Strict Control of Corruption and Bureaucratic Discipline

When executive power is centralized, it becomes easier to impose strict rules on officials and punish violations swiftly, without resistance from independent political groups or public sector unions. This can reinforce discipline within the bureaucracy.

7. Rapid Implementation of Major Infrastructure and Industrial Projects

Without prolonged public debates, judicial disputes, or procedural hurdles, large projects—such as highways, power plants, or industrial complexes—can be executed more quickly than in systems with extended processes of consultation and review.

8. Ability to Amend Legislation Quickly

Centralized authority enables the rapid introduction of new laws or amendments in response to shifts in domestic or international conditions. This flexibility allows governments to act decisively in adapting to challenges.

9. Preservation of State Unity in Multiethnic or Multiconfessional Societies

Tight political control and restrictions on separatist movements can prevent fragmentation of the state and contain internal conflicts. In diverse societies, this can serve as a stabilizing force against disintegration.

10. Strategic Concentration of Resources

The illiberal state is able to concentrate national resources on priority sectors or regions, accelerating the development of specific areas of the economy, defense, or technology. While this often occurs at the expense of broader balance, it can produce visible achievements in selected strategic fields.

11. Ideological Mobilization of Society

Through an official ideology or national narrative, the illiberal state can foster unity and collective identity. This mobilization helps consolidate society around shared goals and increases willingness to accept sacrifices in the name of "higher" objectives.

12. Control of the Information Environment

By shaping a unified public narrative and suppressing dissenting voices, the state reduces informational chaos and uncertainty. In moments of crisis, this can strengthen manageability and prevent panic, even if it comes at the cost of pluralism.

13. Ability to Enact Radical Reforms from Above

Without strong opposition or prolonged debate, governments can launch sweeping reforms in the economy, military, or social policy. In some cases, this enables rapid modernization that would be difficult to achieve in systems requiring broad consensus.

14. High Mobilization Potential

The centralized structure allows the state to quickly mobilize people and resources for large-scale projects—whether industrialization, infrastructure, or military campaigns. This capacity for rapid collective effort is a distinctive feature of illiberal systems.

Weaknesses of the Illiberal State

1. Restriction of Citizens' Rights and Freedoms

Although rights may be formally declared, their implementation is systematically curtailed. Freedom of speech, assembly, the press, and political competition are restricted, while citizens' access to independent information is tightly controlled. This undermines pluralism and narrows the space for civic life.

2. Lack of Judicial Independence

Courts are subordinated to the executive branch, leaving citizens without effective legal protection. The judiciary cannot serve as a check on government actions, turning justice into an extension of political power rather than an impartial safeguard of law.

3. Weak Civil Society

Strict regulations on associations, NGOs, and independent media weaken society's ability to influence politics or hold authorities accountable. Without vibrant civic institutions, the public sphere becomes passive, and participation in governance declines.

4. Risk of Abuse of Power and Corruption

With little public oversight and dependent courts, illiberal systems create fertile ground for arbitrary decision-making, nepotism, political repression, and corruption schemes. Power becomes a tool for personal or group enrichment rather than a public trust.

5. Monopolization of Political Authority

The absence of genuine political competition allows power to concentrate in the hands of a narrow elite. This monopoly obstructs policy change, prevents leadership renewal, and reduces responsiveness to societal needs.

6. Suppression of Dissent

Illiberal regimes often rely on repressive measures against opposition figures, activists, and journalists. Fear of persecution diminishes civic activism and fosters an atmosphere of conformity, stifling innovation and critical debate.

7. Distortion of Democratic Institutions

Elections, parliaments, and constitutions may remain in place, but they function largely as formalities, serving the interests of the ruling elite. Instead of acting as mechanisms of accountability, institutions become symbolic decorations that legitimize authoritarian control.

8. Decline in Governance Quality Over Time

The lack of public scrutiny and political competition leads to stagnation, bureaucratic inefficiency, and erosion of administrative capacity. Without incentives for reform or innovation, governance deteriorates, weakening the state in the long run.

9. Dependence on a Strong Leader

Illiberal systems often rely on the authority of a single figure. This personalization of power makes the state vulnerable to instability when leadership changes, since institutions are too weak to ensure continuity.

10. Vulnerability to Crises

While centralization enables rapid responses in emergencies, it also fosters rigidity. When unexpected economic, social, or environmental crises emerge, the absence of open debate and adaptive institutions can magnify their consequences.

11. International Isolation and Loss of Soft Power

Illiberal states are often criticized for violating human rights and democratic standards. This can lead to strained relations with liberal democracies, sanctions, and reduced foreign investment. Over time, such isolation diminishes economic opportunities and global influence.

Typology of Illiberal States

Illiberal states do not constitute a single, uniform model. Instead, they appear in diverse forms that combine elements of democracy with mechanisms of control and restriction. Political science distinguishes several types within this spectrum.

1. Authoritarian States

Authoritarian regimes are characterized by the concentration of power in the hands of a leader or a small elite, limited political pluralism, and the suppression of meaningful opposition. Elections may exist but are non-competitive, media are tightly controlled, and civil society is constrained. The emphasis is on stability, order, and obedience rather than on the free participation of citizens.

2. Hybrid Regimes

Hybrid regimes combine democratic institutions with authoritarian practices. Constitutions, parliaments, and elections exist formally, but their functioning is undermined through manipulation, selective application of the law, and control over the information environment. Citizens vote, but real competition is stifled, and the outcomes are often predetermined. These systems blur the line between democracy and authoritarianism.

3. Facade Democracies

Facade democracies maintain the outward symbols of democracy—such as elections, parties, and courts—without their substantive meaning. Institutions operate primarily as instruments for legitimizing the ruling elite. The population may participate in ritualized elections, but the process lacks genuine pluralism, accountability, or transparency.

4. "Illiberal Democracy"

Political scientist Fareed Zakaria introduced the term *illiberal democracy* to describe regimes where democratic procedures coexist with the erosion of liberal principles. Such systems hold regular elections but restrict freedoms of the press, judiciary, and civil society. Unlike open authoritarianism, illiberal democracy legitimizes itself through the ballot box while undermining the liberal safeguards that protect individuals from majority or executive domination.

5. Distinction Between Illiberal and Totalitarian States

It is essential to differentiate illiberalism from totalitarianism. Totalitarian regimes (such as those of Nazi Germany) sought total control over all aspects of life—politics, economy, culture, and even private thought—using ideology and mass terror. Illiberal states, by contrast, do not aspire to absolute domination. Instead, they apply selective and targeted pressure: suppressing opposition, manipulating elections, or controlling media, while leaving some spheres of private and economic life relatively autonomous. Illiberalism thus represents a system of restricted freedoms, not their complete elimination.

Contemporary Challenges to the Illiberal State

The contemporary challenges of the illiberal state lie in the tension between short-term stability and long-term fragility. Concentrated power can deliver swift decisions, but it undermines resilience, legitimacy, and adaptability. Economically, reliance on centralized allocation and strategic industries enables rapid mobilization but discourages innovation and fosters inefficiency. Corruption and rent-seeking erode growth, while global markets penalize opacity, leaving illiberal economies exposed to crises. Politically, regimes that rely on control rather than trust face the erosion of legitimacy. Elections without competition and media under tight censorship generate cynicism and disengagement, forcing governments to rely more heavily on repression, which further deepens alienation and fuels instability.

In addition, many illiberal states depend excessively on individual leaders, making succession a moment of vulnerability. The absence of strong institutions capable of ensuring continuity compounds this fragility. On the international stage, globalization limits autonomy: human rights abuses or democratic backsliding invite sanctions, reputational damage, and trade restrictions. The digital era further weakens monopolies on information, as social media and encrypted communication create spaces for resistance that are costly and difficult to suppress. Meanwhile, growing social complexity—urbanization, rising diversity, and generational change—places greater strain on rigid systems of control. Suppression may secure temporary order, but it risks long-term fragmentation, revealing the limits of authority on which illiberal power rests.

"*If men were angels, no government would be necessary. If angels were to govern men, neither external nor internal controls on government would be necessary. In framing a government… you must first enable the government to control the governed; and in the next place oblige it to control itself.*"

— **James Madison**, *Federalist No. 51* (**1788**)

SECTION 3. INTERMEDIATE OR HYBRID FORMS (PARTIAL PROTECTION OF RIGHTS AND FREEDOMS): MIXED SYSTEMS WITH INCOMPLETE GUARANTEES

Hybrid regimes are systems of ambiguity. They speak the language of democracy while employing mechanisms of control that erode accountability and trust. Their defining traits—formal institutions hollowed out by informal practices, partial freedoms constrained by red lines, and oscillation between openness and repression—make them inherently unstable. Their trajectory depends not only on institutional design but also on leadership, civic mobilization, and the pressures of the international environment.

Defining Features of Hybrid Systems

1. Coexistence of Democratic Institutions and Authoritarian Practices

Hybrid regimes retain constitutions, parliaments, and elections, but their substance is undermined by executive dominance, political interference, and weak institutional safeguards. Democracy exists largely in form, while authoritarian practices dominate in practice. Scholars often describe such systems as *competitive authoritarianism* or *electoral authoritarianism*.

2. Partial Political Competition

Opposition parties are legally permitted, yet they face severe obstacles. Administrative barriers, unequal access to media, intimidation of activists, and manipulation of electoral commissions restrict the playing field. Political pluralism is formally present but substantively limited.

3. Judicial Independence in Theory, but Not in Practice

Although constitutions proclaim judicial autonomy, courts are routinely subject to political pressure. Sensitive cases, especially those involving opposition leaders, reveal partisan influence. Judicial appointments are frequently determined by loyalty to the ruling elite rather than merit, undermining the rule of law.

4. Selective Enforcement of the Law

Legal frameworks exist but are applied unevenly. Regime opponents often face politicized charges, while government allies enjoy effective immunity. This dual system erodes both public trust and the credibility of legal institutions.

5. Partial Media Freedom

Independent outlets operate, but state or oligarch-controlled media dominate the information landscape. Investigative journalism is tolerated only within strict limits, and clear "red lines" exist regarding corruption or criticism of top leadership. Such managed pluralism creates the illusion of openness while preserving control.

6. Restricted Civic Engagement

Civil society organizations function under restrictive regulations. Burdensome registration processes, limits on foreign funding, and bureaucratic oversight constrain activism. Organizations focusing on governance, human rights, or transparency are particularly vulnerable to state pressure.

7. Oscillation Between Liberalization and Repression

Hybrid regimes are marked by instability. Periods of liberalization—introduced to secure legitimacy or defuse dissent—are often followed by sharp repression. This cycle creates uncertainty and prevents the consolidation of democratic norms.

8. Personalization of Power

Despite existing institutions, politics often revolves around a dominant leader or ruling clique. Decision-making becomes highly centralized, with institutions subordinated to personal authority. The state apparatus adapts to reinforce the leader rather than balance power.

9. Low Public Trust in Elections and Institutions

Citizens often perceive elections as hollow rituals designed to legitimize predetermined outcomes. This distrust fosters political apathy and withdrawal from civic life, though at times it can erupt into sudden waves of protest against perceived illegitimacy.

10. Dependence on External Pressure

Hybrid regimes are highly sensitive to international influences. Sanctions, foreign aid conditions, and the policies of powerful neighbors can significantly alter regime behavior. Their survival often depends as much on external relations as on domestic legitimacy.

Strengths of Hybrid Forms of Government

1. Flexibility of the Political System

Hybrid regimes can maneuver between liberalization and control, adjusting their policies to changing conditions. Strategic concessions are used to defuse crises or strengthen legitimacy, while restrictions are tightened when instability threatens. This adaptability allows rulers to preserve power while balancing stability with limited openness.

2. Preservation of Formal Democratic Institutions

Even when weakened, constitutions, parliaments, elections, and codified rights remain in place. These institutions prevent the complete dismantling of democratic architecture and serve as "islands of legality." They provide points of reference for political opposition and future reform, keeping alive the possibility of gradual democratization.

3. Partial Political Competition

Opposition parties, independent candidates, and alternative views are not eliminated entirely. Although their participation is restricted and unequal, the existence of pluralism prevents the establishment of a total monopoly of power. This limited competition sustains a minimal degree of political choice and keeps open evolutionary paths of change.

4. Relatively Open Information Space

Despite state dominance over major media, hybrid regimes usually tolerate independent outlets, online platforms, and alternative communication channels. The spread of the internet and social media diversifies the information flow beyond what closed authoritarian systems allow, helping sustain limited public debate.

5. Opportunities for Civic Activity

Civil society is constrained but not fully suppressed. Non-governmental organizations and grassroots initiatives may operate in "safe" areas such as environmental protection, charity, or education. These activities build networks of trust and social capital, cultivating habits of civic engagement even under restrictive conditions.

6. Reduction of Political Radicalism

Because limited freedoms and controlled participation remain, opposition groups are less likely to be forced underground. Discontent can be expressed through restricted but peaceful channels, reducing the risk of violent conflict or systemic upheaval. Hybrid regimes thus channel protest into manageable forms.

7. Preservation of International Contacts

Hybrid regimes usually maintain economic, diplomatic, and cultural ties with liberal democracies. Access to investment, trade, technology, and aid distinguishes them from closed authoritarian states. External engagement also places informal constraints on rulers, as excessive repression risks sanctions or loss of international legitimacy.

8. Transitional Potential

Hybrid systems can act as transitional forms of government. They may evolve toward democracy if reforms and civic engagement succeed, or drift toward authoritarianism if restrictions tighten. Their dual character makes them unstable, but it also keeps open the possibility of democratization.

9. Relative Social Stability Compared to Pure Authoritarianism

Because they are less repressive than outright dictatorships, hybrid regimes generate less fear and resistance. This moderated approach can maintain a degree of stability, reducing the likelihood of mass unrest. However, this stability is often fragile, as underlying conflicts remain unresolved.

10. High Regime Survival Capacity

By combining selective repression with controlled liberalization, hybrid regimes often prove more resilient than fragile democracies or rigid dictatorships. Their ability to adapt while retaining control allows them to endure significant internal crises and external pressures, ensuring long-term survival.

Weaknesses of Hybrid Forms of Government

1. Instability of the Political System

The coexistence of democratic and authoritarian elements generates deep contradictions. Political balance can shift rapidly, leading either to authoritarian consolidation or sudden liberalization. Such unpredictability undermines long-term planning, discourages investment, and erodes public trust in governance.

2. Selective Implementation of Rights and Freedoms

Although constitutions enshrine rights, their application is inconsistent. Supporters of the ruling elite enjoy privileges, while critics face restrictions and harassment. This *rule of law deficit* weakens institutional credibility and fosters perceptions of systemic injustice.

3. Vulnerability of the Judiciary

Courts remain formally independent but function under political influence. Sensitive cases reflect elite interests, and judicial appointments are politicized. As a result, legal consistency is undermined, rights are insecure, and even property protection becomes fragile, damaging both civic trust and economic stability.

4. Weakness of Civil Society

Civil society organizations operate under strict oversight, facing restrictions on funding, registration, and permissible activities. International NGOs are often excluded. This narrow civic space prevents independent groups from influencing policy or holding the government accountable.

5. Limited Political Competition

Elections occur but rarely meet standards of fairness. Opposition parties face administrative obstacles, unequal media coverage, and pressure on candidates. Such conditions produce formal pluralism without genuine electoral choice, creating the appearance of competition while maintaining control.

6. Corruption Risks

Weak oversight and limited judicial independence foster corruption, nepotism, and favoritism. Elite groups capture state resources for private enrichment. This *state capture* undermines economic efficiency, fuels inequality, and corrodes public trust.

7. Slow Democratization

Hybrid regimes often remain stuck in a prolonged "gray zone," neither fully democratic nor fully authoritarian. The existence of formal institutions creates the illusion of reform, while genuine democratization is delayed indefinitely.

8. Risk of Authoritarian Backsliding

In moments of crisis, external threat, or leadership change, hybrid regimes easily revert to authoritarianism. With partial freedoms already constrained, elites can tighten control with minimal resistance, further shrinking civic space.

9. Weak Institutional Development

Political life is often shaped more by personalities than by rules. Institutions remain fragile, underfunded, and dependent on leadership changes. This personalization of power obstructs the creation of durable governance structures.

10. Low Public Trust and Legitimacy

The gap between official promises and lived reality fuels cynicism. Citizens perceive politics as manipulative and disengage from participation, producing a cycle of low legitimacy and weak civic involvement that hampers reform.

11. Dependence on External Pressures

Hybrid regimes are highly vulnerable to external actors. Sanctions, conditional aid, and reputational costs shape their behavior. At the same time, dependence on foreign markets and investment reduces autonomy, exposing structural weaknesses in both economics and security.

Hybrid Regimes as a Subject of Political Science

Hybrid forms of government have long existed in practice, but they became a distinct subject of systematic analysis in political science only in the late twentieth century. The end of the Cold War, the collapse of authoritarian regimes in Southern Europe and Latin America, and the democratization of Central and Eastern Europe generated high expectations that liberal democracy would spread across the globe. Yet many post-authoritarian states did not consolidate into full democracies. Instead, they produced regimes that combined elections and parliaments with authoritarian control over courts, media, and civil society. These outcomes forced scholars to rethink the assumption that democratization follows a linear path.

Fareed Zakaria and "Illiberal Democracy"

In 1997, Fareed Zakaria published his influential essay The Rise of Illiberal Democracy in Foreign Affairs. He argued that democracy had become narrowly identified with elections, while liberal principles—constitutionalism, the rule of law, separation of powers, and the protection of rights—were increasingly eroded. According to Zakaria, regimes that hold regular elections but suppress free speech, weaken independent courts, and constrain opposition cannot be considered consolidated democracies. His analysis highlighted the dangerous gap between electoral procedures and liberal constitutionalism, coining a term that remains central to political science debates.

Larry Diamond and Defective Democracies

Larry Diamond expanded this discussion by emphasizing that many regimes could not be neatly classified as either democracies or autocracies. He described them as defective democracies, characterized by the presence of democratic institutions in form but not in substance. Diamond identified different "defects"—such as restrictions on civil liberties, weak rule of law, or ineffective governance—that distort democratic practice. For him, hybrid regimes represented a structural weakness in democratic development: they undermine public trust, slow the process of democratization, and often stagnate in a prolonged "gray zone."

Thomas Carothers and the "Gray Zone"

Thomas Carothers advanced the analysis with his concept of the gray zone. In his 2002 essay The End of the Transition Paradigm, he observed that after the "third wave of democratization" in the 1980s and 1990s, many states remained stuck between authoritarianism and democracy. These regimes were not merely temporary phases on the road to democratization; rather, they displayed a stable mixture of both systems. Carothers stressed that hybrid regimes should be studied as durable political forms with their own internal logic and mechanisms of survival.

Varieties of Hybrid States

Political science has developed several influential frameworks to conceptualize hybrid regimes. Each reflects a stage in the scholarly effort to grasp the persistence of systems that are neither fully democratic nor fully authoritarian:

- Illiberal democracy (Fareed Zakaria, 1997). Zakaria emphasized the erosion of liberal principles—constitutionalism, separation of powers, and protection of rights—behind the façade of regular elections. His concept highlighted the gap between electoral procedures and substantive liberal democracy.
- Defective democracy (Larry Diamond). Building on this critique, Diamond stressed that democratic institutions may exist in form but fail in function. He identified multiple "defects," such as weak rule of law, restricted rights, and ineffective governance, which prevent democracy from consolidating.
- The gray zone (Thomas Carothers). Carothers moved further by rejecting the idea that such regimes are merely transitional. He argued that many states remain stably "in-between," combining features of both systems. This perspective shifted analysis from temporary deviations to hybrid regimes as enduring political forms.
- Electoral or competitive authoritarianism (Steven Levitsky and Lucan Way). Finally, Levitsky and Way provided a sharper classification for regimes where elections exist but are heavily manipulated. Opposition is permitted but disadvantaged through state control of media, harassment, and administrative bias, ensuring the dominance of ruling elites.

Together, these approaches trace the evolution of scholarly understanding: from the erosion of liberalism, through defective and liminal democracies, to the recognition of structured authoritarian dominance within electoral frameworks.

Electoral Authoritarian Regimes

Electoral authoritarian regimes hold regular elections, but their outcomes are largely predetermined. Ruling elites dominate the political arena by controlling access to the media, restricting opposition parties, and manipulating electoral rules. Administrative resources are used to tilt the playing field, while voters may face intimidation or pressure. Citizens cast ballots, yet genuine competition, fairness, and transparency are absent. As Andreas Schedler emphasized, such regimes rely on the appearance of democracy to legitimize authority while systematically denying meaningful political choice.

Defective Democracies

In defective democracies, fundamental rights are formally guaranteed, and institutions such as parliaments, courts, and media outlets exist, but their functioning is inconsistent and unreliable. Corruption undermines the rule of law, courts are politicized, and media face both formal restrictions and informal pressures. Citizens enjoy more freedoms than in outright authoritarian systems, but the institutions necessary to safeguard these freedoms remain weak and fragmented. Larry Diamond has shown that these "defects" vary—ranging from limits on participation to weak constitutional oversight. Such fragility makes defective democracies vulnerable to backsliding and authoritarian capture.

Facade Democracies

Facade democracies preserve the outward symbols of democracy—constitutions, legislatures, elections—but their institutions serve primarily as instruments of legitimation for the ruling elite. Political competition is theatrical, opposition is marginalized, and legislatures operate as rubber stamps for executive initiatives. Citizens may participate in elections, but the outcomes are controlled, and decision-making is concentrated in the hands of a narrow group. Unlike defective democracies, where institutions at least partially function, facade democracies maintain democratic architecture almost exclusively for appearances, leaving it hollow and decorative.

A Spectrum of Hybridity

This typology demonstrates that hybridity is not a single model but a spectrum of political arrangements. Some regimes lean closer to democracy yet are undermined by weak institutions, while others drift toward authoritarianism while still preserving electoral rituals. Understanding these variations clarifies why hybrid states can appear outwardly similar yet operate in profoundly different ways.

The Declarative Model

It is also important to distinguish between facade democracies and what is sometimes called the declarative model. Both rely on imitation, but in different ways. Facade democracies emphasize institutional simulation—maintaining parliaments, elections, and constitutions that serve primarily as decorative structures. The declarative model, by contrast, focuses on normative imitation: rights and freedoms are formally enshrined in constitutions and proclaimed in official discourse, but they are not implemented or enforced in practice. In the next chapter, we will examine the declarative model more closely to see how states can use the legal recognition of rights as a rhetorical shield while denying citizens their actual protection.

"Political liberty is to be found only when there is no abuse of power. But constant experience shows us that every man invested with power is apt to abuse it... To prevent this, it is necessary that, by the very disposition of things, power should be a check to power."

— Montesquieu, *The Spirit of the Laws* (1748)

SECTION 4. DECLARATIVE MODEL (STATE WITH FORMAL PROTECTION OF RIGHTS AND FREEDOMS): RIGHTS RECOGNIZED IN LAW BUT NOT EFFECTIVELY ENFORCED

> **The declarative model** is a form of state organization in which human rights and freedoms are formally enshrined in constitutions and laws, yet their implementation remains largely symbolic.

On the surface, such a system may resemble a constitutional democratic state. Yet its legal framework does not correspond to real political practice. Behind the façade of rights and institutions lies a structure in which guarantees remain symbolic rather than substantive. The defining features of the declarative model include:

1. Formal Enshrinement of Rights

Constitutions and major laws contain detailed guarantees of civil, political, social, and economic rights. The language of these documents often mirrors international standards. In practice, however, such guarantees are not enforced: courts are not independent, parliaments lack oversight capacity, and citizens are left without effective mechanisms for defending their rights.

2. Complete Subordination of State Institutions

All branches of government are subordinated to an executive center—whether a president, a ruling party, or a narrow elite. Parliaments, courts, and electoral commissions exist formally but serve primarily to legitimize executive decisions rather than to function as independent institutions.

3. Absence of Genuine Political Competition

Elections are held regularly, but their outcomes are predictable. Opposition parties are either banned outright or permitted to exist in token form to simulate pluralism. Political activity outside officially sanctioned boundaries is swiftly and harshly suppressed.

4. Full Control of the Information Space

All mass media and communication channels are controlled by the state or affiliated structures. Independent journalism is absent, while alternative sources of information are blocked, censored, or pressured into silence.

5. Use of "Showcase" Legislation

Laws guaranteeing rights and freedoms serve primarily propaganda purposes. Domestically, they are used to project an image of legality; internationally, they are invoked to claim compliance with democratic standards and to strengthen diplomatic legitimacy.

6. Harsh System of Control and Repression

Law enforcement agencies and security services are deployed to prevent any independent political or civic activity. A pervasive atmosphere of fear and self-censorship dominates public life, discouraging citizens from challenging authority.

Criterion	Hybrid Model	Declarative Model
Implementation of Rights and Freedoms	Rights are partially implemented; restrictions are selective and depend on political circumstances.	Rights exist in laws and the constitution but are not enforced in practice.
Political Competition	Opposition is allowed but faces administrative barriers, limited media access, and pressure.	Opposition is banned or exists only symbolically, without influencing election outcomes.
Elections	Elections involve multiple parties, but conditions are unequal; occasional surprises are possible.	Formal procedures are observed, but outcomes are always predetermined, with no real competition.
Media and Information	Independent media exist but operate under pressure; the internet and social networks remain partially free.	All media and information channels are fully controlled by the state; no alternative sources are tolerated.
Judicial System	Formally independent but subject to political influence.	Completely subordinated to the executive branch and ruling elite.
Civil Society	NGOs and civic initiatives may operate in "safe" areas but remain under supervision.	Civil society is effectively absent; independent organizations are banned or tightly controlled.
International Image	Partially perceived as democratic, which helps maintain foreign relations.	Presents itself as a legal state, but internationally recognized as authoritarian.
System Dynamics	Can drift toward either democratization or authoritarian consolidation.	Change is possible only through systemic crisis or regime collapse.
Use of Legal Norms	Laws are applied selectively but still function for parts of society.	Rights laws serve primarily a propagandistic role, with little or no practical application.
Level of Public Trust	Minimal belief remains in the possibility of change through elections or protests.	Dominated by cynicism and apathy, as rights are widely perceived as fictitious.

Although the declarative model is fundamentally authoritarian and repressive, ruling elites emphasize its strengths to justify internal legitimacy and defend themselves on the international stage. These "advantages" reflect the regime's ability to preserve control, mobilize resources, and project stability, even when real freedoms and rights are absent.

Strengths of the Declarative Model of the State

1. Political and Institutional Stability

The concentration of power in the hands of a narrow elite, combined with the absence of genuine competition, reduces the likelihood of frequent political shifts. This creates an image of continuity and order. Elites present this stability as a safeguard against chaos, revolutions, or civil wars. In reality, such stability rests not on consensus but on repression and fear, yet it remains one of the regime's strongest arguments against democratization.

2. Rapid Decision-Making

Authoritarian concentration of authority allows decisions to be made quickly, without the delays of negotiation or legislative oversight. In times of crisis—such as wars, natural disasters, or epidemics—this decisiveness can prove effective. However, speed often comes at the cost of accuracy, since decisions are rarely exposed to expert scrutiny or public debate, which in democratic systems can filter out critical errors.

3. Unified Political Course

The absence of opposition and the presence of a tightly controlled information environment guarantee coherence across state institutions. Policy conflicts are eliminated not through dialogue but by silencing dissenters. This ensures uniformity in decision-making and allows elites to pursue long-term projects without visible resistance, reinforcing the image of discipline and coordination.

4. Effective Control of the Information Space

By monopolizing mass media and communication channels, authorities craft a single narrative and suppress alternative viewpoints. This prevents the spread of panic or destabilizing rumors and fosters compliance. Such control also enables regimes to construct an "alternative reality," where failures are concealed and successes exaggerated, bolstering their legitimacy.

5. Reduced Risk of Domestic Fragmentation

A rigid vertical of power discourages splits within the political elite, suppresses regional separatism, and quells mass protests at their early stages. This strict centralization may, at least temporarily, preserve the territorial integrity of the state.

6. Support for the Image of a Legal State on the International Stage

The existence of constitutionally enshrined rights and ratified international treaties allows declarative regimes to claim compliance with global standards. This strategy is frequently used as a shield against external criticism.

Such an approach serves multiple functions:

- **Foreign policy:** It reduces pressure from other states and international organizations, complicating the imposition of sanctions or other restrictive measures.
- **Domestic politics:** It fosters the illusion among citizens that their state is recognized and respected abroad, reinforcing internal legitimacy.
- **Propaganda:** It enables the regime to present itself as "no worse than others," appealing to formal norms rather than their practical enforcement.

7. Mobilization Potential

The concentration of authority allows declarative regimes to mobilize resources and populations rapidly. Whether for industrial projects, defense initiatives, or public campaigns, the state can direct efforts on a large scale without opposition or delay.

8. Predictability for the Elite

By eliminating competition, the system minimizes internal political struggles among rival groups. This predictability offers ruling elites a sense of security, reducing the risk of factional conflict or elite fragmentation.

9. Simplified Governance

Centralized authority streamlines decision-making and implementation. Unlike pluralist systems that require negotiation with opposition parties, civil society, or local governments, declarative regimes operate with minimal deliberation, making governance more straightforward from the perspective of the ruling elite.

Weaknesses of the Declarative Model of the State

The declarative model outwardly imitates democracy, but its structural flaws undermine governance, corrode institutions, and erode public trust. Rights exist on paper but not in practice, turning institutions into decorative façades.

1. Complete Gap Between Norm and Practice

Constitutions and laws formally enshrine rights and freedoms, yet these are not implemented in daily life. This *Potemkin democracy* effect destroys trust in both institutions and law, reducing them to empty formalities.

2. Absence of Independent Institutions

Parliaments, courts, and electoral commissions exist but are fully subordinated to the executive. They serve to legitimize power rather than to check it, eliminating the balance necessary to prevent abuse.

3. Political Stagnation

Without real competition or leadership turnover, the political system becomes frozen. Elites ossify (*elite sclerosis*), bureaucracies calcify, and policy failures repeat without correction.

4. Repressive Character of Power

Dissent is suppressed by security forces and intelligence agencies. While this produces outward conformity, it generates hidden resentment and fragility: repression delays unrest but intensifies its eventual eruption.

5. Loss of Innovative and Social Potential

Restrictions on freedom of expression and initiative discourage civic engagement and entrepreneurship. Dynamic citizens often emigrate, creating a severe *brain drain* and weakening the state's long-term development.

6. Distortion of the Electoral Process

Elections are held, but they function as rituals of reaffirmation. Instead of representing citizens, they serve as tools of mobilization and control, closing off legitimate channels for elite renewal.

7. Vulnerability of International Image

Despite flawless constitutional texts, the international community recognizes declarative regimes as authoritarian. Ratings by organizations such as Freedom House or Transparency International expose the gap between proclaimed rights and reality, damaging credibility and isolating the state diplomatically.

8. High Risk of Systemic Crisis During Leadership Change

Because power rests on a single leader or narrow elite, leadership transitions rarely result in reform. Instead, they provoke abrupt crises, as the system lacks mechanisms for orderly succession.

9. Corruption and Administrative Inefficiency

With no oversight or competition, corruption becomes systemic. Nepotism and favoritism dominate, bureaucracies resist reform, and state institutions serve elite interests rather than the public. Corruption evolves into the very glue holding the regime together.

10. Social Distrust and Cynicism

When rights exist only "on paper," citizens grow cynical and alienated from politics. This leads to depoliticization and a *negative consensus*: the population knows the system is hollow but refrains from open resistance, sustaining stagnation.

11. Economic Vulnerability

Lack of genuine property rights and repressive conditions discourage both domestic and foreign investment. Economies in declarative regimes often depend on raw materials or external markets, leaving them fragile and exposed to global shocks.

12. Absence of Mechanisms for Self-Correction

Unlike liberal systems, declarative regimes lack institutional channels for gradual reform. Errors accumulate until they produce sudden crises, often explosive and destabilizing, since the system has no built-in capacity for adaptation.

NORM AND REALITY IN THE DECLARATIVE MODEL

Fundamental Right or Principle	How It Is Declared	How It Is Violated in the Declarative Model
Right to Participate in Government	The constitution guarantees citizens participation in governance; elections are held regularly.	Elections become a formality: outcomes are predetermined, opposition candidates are excluded or have no real chance due to pressure and restrictions.
Right to Vote and Be Elected	Universal and equal suffrage is proclaimed.	Independent candidates are excluded from ballots; bribery and intimidation of voters occur; results are falsified.
Prohibition or Suspension of Elections	The constitution or law mandates regular elections at set intervals.	Elections are canceled or postponed indefinitely under the pretext of war, emergency, or crisis; mandates of existing bodies are extended without popular vote.
Political Pluralism	Multiparty system and equal conditions for all parties are declared.	All parties except the ruling one are under government control; opposition plays a decorative role and has no influence on policy.
Freedom of Speech and Expression	Freedom of the press, access to information, and freedom of opinion are guaranteed.	Media and the internet are fully controlled by the state; independent outlets are blocked; journalists face arrests and threats.
Freedom of Assembly and Association	Demonstrations, rallies, and associations are permitted.	Protests are banned or dispersed by force; independent NGOs are liquidated; participants are persecuted.
Freedom of Religion	The right to practice any religion is proclaimed.	Only officially approved denominations are permitted; others are banned or persecuted; religious activity is strictly monitored.
Personal Inviolability	Arbitrary arrests and detentions are prohibited; personal security is guaranteed.	Arrests and detentions occur without warrant or trial; torture, coercion, and threats are used against detainees.

Fundamental Right or Principle	How It Is Declared	How It Is Violated in the Declarative Model
Inviolability of Home and Privacy	Interference is prohibited without legal grounds.	Searches are conducted without warrants; surveillance is widespread; private correspondence and phone calls are intercepted.
Right to a Fair Trial	Judicial power is independent; rulings are impartial.	Courts are subordinated to the executive; verdicts are dictated from above, especially in political cases.
Presumption of Innocence	The accused is considered innocent until proven guilty in court.	Citizens are declared guilty in advance; authorities and media create a presumption of guilt before trials begin.
Prohibition of Torture	The ban on cruel and degrading treatment is proclaimed.	Torture and degrading treatment are used in prisons and detention centers, especially against political prisoners.
Freedom of Movement	Citizens are guaranteed the right to move freely and to travel abroad.	Restrictions are imposed on emigration; internal movement is monitored; some regions are closed to citizens.
Right to Work	The right to decent employment is proclaimed.	Forced labor may be introduced; access to jobs is restricted based on political or social status.
Right to Education	Accessible education is guaranteed.	Education is used for ideological indoctrination; alternative schooling is prohibited.
Right to Health Care	The state is obliged to provide medical care.	Quality healthcare is available only selectively; politically disfavored citizens face barriers to treatment.
Right to Housing	Housing rights and protection are guaranteed.	No real housing programs exist; evictions are used as a tool of political pressure.
Right to Social Security	Assistance is proclaimed in cases of illness, disability, or unemployment.	Social benefits are distributed selectively and serve as a tool of loyalty.
Freedom from Discrimination	Discrimination on any grounds is prohibited.	Discrimination is tolerated against opposition members,

Fundamental Right or Principle	How It Is Declared	How It Is Violated in the Declarative Model
		minorities, and independent activists.
Principle of Separation of Powers	Legislative, executive, and judicial branches are independent.	All branches are subordinated to the executive center; parliament and courts are formal structures only.
Rule of Law	Law stands above political interests.	Laws are overridden by political decisions; political expediency prevails over legal norms.
Transparency of Government	State authorities are obliged to inform the public.	Information is withheld; statistics and reports are falsified; access to data is restricted.
Right to Private Property	Private property is declared inviolable and protected by law.	Property can be confiscated or expropriated for political reasons or under the pretext of "state interests."
Freedom of Associations and Trade Unions	Citizens have the right to form unions, parties, and professional associations.	Independent trade unions and parties are banned or absorbed into state-controlled structures.
Right to Participate in Cultural Life and Access to Information	Freedom of creativity, cultural development, and access to information are guaranteed.	Censorship is imposed in art and culture; independent information channels are blocked; ideological control dominates public life.
Right to a Healthy Environment	The state is obliged to ensure ecological safety and environmental protection.	Environmental standards are ignored; ecological activism is suppressed; industrial and political interests override ecological concerns.

Conclusion

The declarative model plays several roles. Domestically, it cultivates the appearance of order and legality, even when genuine freedoms are missing. In the realm of foreign policy, it allows regimes to deflect criticism, pointing to constitutions and treaties as supposed evidence of compliance. In propaganda, it borrows the language of rights and democracy to cloak repression and tighten control.

Its social impact is far more corrosive. People feel the ground shift beneath them as the distance between words and daily reality widens, and their trust erodes. Laws no longer inspire respect; they echo like empty shells. Many withdraw into apathy or cynicism. The most active and gifted often depart, leaving the country not only poorer in talent but also in hope.

The deeper lesson is sobering: declarations on paper are powerless without institutions that can defend them. Freedom exists only when courts and political bodies act independently and enforce rights in practice. Without such safeguards, the very words meant to guard liberty are twisted into instruments of obedience, serving authority instead of protecting human dignity.

"The least initial deviation from the truth is multiplied later a thousandfold."

— Aristotle, *Metaphysics*, Book II, 994b

QUESTIONNAIRE FOR DETERMINING THE STATE MODEL

How to Use the Questionnaire

- Answer **"YES"** or **"NO"** to each question.

- Using the **key** (provided in the section following the questionnaire), you can determine the type of state based on the number of positive and negative responses in each group.

- This approach allows for the most accurate identification of the model of government and helps to avoid misinterpretation.

List of Questions

I. Form of Government

1. Is the head of state a monarch (king, emperor, etc.)?
2. Does the monarch hold absolute power, unrestricted by a parliament?
3. Does the monarch rule on the basis of a constitution, with powers limited by law?
4. Does the monarch serve only a symbolic role, while real power lies with the parliament?
5. Is the monarch elected rather than inheriting power?
6. Is the head of state an elected president?
7. Does the president exercise broad powers and lead the executive branch?
8. Is real power concentrated in the parliament rather than the president?
9. Is power divided roughly equally between president and parliament?

II. Political Regime

10. Do citizens govern the state directly, without elected representatives?
11. Do citizens govern the state through regularly elected representatives?
12. Are human rights and freedoms protected by law and effectively enforced?
13. Do elections exist formally but remain under government control, preventing elite turnover?
14. Do the military or security services play a decisive role in governing the state?
15. Is all power concentrated in the hands of one person or a narrow circle of elites?
16. Does real power belong to the bureaucratic apparatus rather than elected bodies?
17. Is the state governed by a single dominant ideology, with dissent persecuted?
18. Is the state ideology based on national or racial superiority?
19. Is the state fully governed by a religious elite, with laws grounded in religion?
20. Does a personality cult surround the head of state?

III. Administrative-Territorial Structure

21. Is the entire territory subordinated to a single center, with no autonomy?
22. Do autonomous regions exist but remain under strict control of the central

government?

23. Is the state composed of equal entities with their own authority?
24. Is the state composed of entities with differing levels of autonomy?
25. Is the state a union of independent states that retain sovereignty?

IV. Economic System

26. Is the economy based on private property and minimal state intervention?
27. Does private property exist, but the state plays an active role in regulating the economy?
28. Does the state significantly control the economy while retaining some market elements?
29. Is the economy fully state-managed, with centralized planning?
30. Is private property absent or extremely limited?

V. Degree of Religious Influence

31. Is the state secular, with religion separated from politics?
32. Is the state secular but with moderate influence of religious organizations on society and politics?
33. Is the state founded on religious law and fully subordinated to one religion?
34. Is there an official religion, but it does not dominate all aspects of life?

VI. Special Historical-Cultural Models

35. Is power concentrated in the hands of a military elite?
36. Is power concentrated in the hands of hereditary aristocracy?
37. Is the state governed by a monarch with absolute religious authority (a theocratic monarchy)?
38. Does the state operate under a caste system that restricts rights based on birth?

VII. Philosophical and Hypothetical Models

39. Is the state based on an ideal (utopian) model of society?
40. Are state functions minimal (limited to protection of order and the judiciary)?
41. Is the state governed by scientific and technical experts (technocracy)?
42. Is the main political priority the protection of the environment and ecology?
43. Is governance fully digital, with decisions made electronically?
44. Is the state oriented toward transhumanist goals (enhancement of the human being)?
45. Is the state part of a single world government?

VIII. Anti-State Models

46. Does the state not exist, with society governed by trade unions and collectives (anarcho-syndicalism)?
47. Does the state not exist, with society built on collective ownership (anarcho-communism)?
48. Does the state not exist, with priority given to personal freedom (individualist anarchism)?

IX. Level of Protection of Rights and Freedoms

49. Are citizens' rights and freedoms fully protected by law and effectively enforced?
50. Are rights and freedoms heavily restricted, with dissenters persecuted?

Key for Interpreting the Questionnaire

After answering all the questions, use this key. Each state model corresponds to specific question numbers. If your answer to those questions is **"YES,"** the state can be classified under that model.

For example:

- **Constitutional monarchy:** "YES" to questions 1 and 3.
- **Presidential republic:** "YES" to questions 6 and 7.
- **Authoritarian regime:** "YES" to questions 13, 14, 15, 16 (the more matches, the stronger the authoritarian character of the state).

"NO" answers are not directly counted in the key, but the absence of "YES" to key questions means the state does not belong to that model.

Step 1. Identify in which category you have the most "YES" answers.
Step 2. Compare your results with the descriptions below to classify the type of state with precision.

Form of Government (I):

- **Absolute monarchy:** 1, 2
- **Constitutional monarchy:** 1, 3
- **Parliamentary monarchy:** 1, 4
- **Elective monarchy:** 1, 5
- **Presidential republic:** 6, 7
- **Parliamentary republic:** 6, 8
- **Mixed (semi-presidential) republic:** 6, 9

Political Regime (II):

- **Direct democracy:** 10
- **Representative (liberal) democracy:** 11, 12
- **Limited democracy:** 11, 13
- **Authoritarianism:** 13, 14, 15, 16
- **Totalitarianism:** 17, 18, 19, 20

Administrative-Territorial Structure (III):

- **Unitary (centralized):** 21

- **Unitary (decentralized):** 22
- **Symmetrical federation:** 23
- **Asymmetrical federation:** 24
- **Confederation:** 25

Economic System (IV):

- **Market economy:** 26
- **State capitalism:** 27, 28
- **Planned socialist economy:** 29

Religious Influence (V):

- **Strictly secular:** 31
- **Moderately secular:** 32
- **Religious state (theocratic):** 33
- **Official religion (without full dominance):** 34

Interpreting Mixed Results

In practice, many states cannot be classified neatly into a single model. It is common for different categories to combine features from various types of governance. When analyzing your answers, keep in mind the following principles:

1. **States are multi-dimensional.**

A country may have one form of government (e.g., a presidential republic), but its political regime may be authoritarian, its economy market-oriented, and its administrative system federal. Each category should be assessed separately.

2. **Mixed models are not contradictions.**

For example, an authoritarian regime with a market economy is possible (authoritarianism in politics, liberalism in economics). Similarly, a federal state may still have a highly centralized and illiberal political regime.

3. **Identify dominant features.**

Look at where the majority of "YES" answers appear in each section. The dominant set of answers shows the defining character of the state in that specific dimension.

4. **Consider hybrid or transitional forms.**

If your answers span across categories without a clear majority, the state may belong to a hybrid model or be in a transitional phase, moving toward either greater democratization or deeper authoritarianism.

5. **Use comparative analysis.**

Compare your answers across different sections. For instance:

- o If the form of government is a constitutional monarchy, but the political regime shows strong indicators of authoritarianism, the result should be interpreted as an authoritarian monarchy.

- o If the regime appears democratic, but the economy is fully state-controlled, this may indicate a socialist democracy or a post-socialist hybrid system.

"A good book is the precious life-blood of a master spirit, embalmed and treasured up on purpose to a life beyond life."

— John Milton, *Areopagitica* (1644)

BIBLIOGRAPHY

Authors and Works

Adorno, Theodor

Adorno, T. W. 1951. *Minima Moralia: Reflections from Damaged Life.* Translated by Edmund Jephcott. London: Verso, 2005.

Adorno, T. W. 1966. *Negative Dialectics.* Translated by E. B. Ashton. New York: Seabury Press, 1973.

Horkheimer, M., and T. W. Adorno. 1947. *Dialectic of Enlightenment: Philosophical Fragments.* Translated by Edmund Jephcott. Stanford: Stanford University Press, 2002.

Aristotle

Aristotle. 1984. *The Complete Works of Aristotle.* 2 vols. Edited by Jonathan Barnes. Princeton: Princeton University Press.

Aristotle. 1995. *Aristotle: Selections.* Translated with introduction, notes, and glossary by Terence Irwin and Gail Fine. Indianapolis: Hackett.

Aristotle. 1999. *De Anima (On the Soul): Books II and III, with Passages from Book I.* Translated with a commentary by D. W. Hamlyn, with a review of recent work by Christopher Shields. Oxford: Oxford University Press.

Aristotle. 2000. *Nicomachean Ethics (Ethica Nicomachea): Books VIII and IX.* Translated with a commentary by Michael Pakaluk. Oxford: Oxford University Press.

Attali, Jacques

Attali, J. 1985. *Noise: The Political Economy of Music.* Translated by Brian Massumi. Minneapolis: University of Minnesota Press.

Attali, J. 2002. *Les Juifs, le Monde et l'Argent: Histoire économique du peuple juif.* Paris: Fayard. [English edition: *The Economic History of the Jewish People*, 2010.]

Attali, J. 2006. *A Brief History of the Future.* New York: Arcade Publishing. [Original French edition: *Une Brève histoire de l'avenir.* Paris: Fayard.]

Attali, J. 2008. *La crise, et après?.* Paris: Fayard.

Attali, J., and S. Hessel. 2011. *Chemin de l'espérance.* Paris: Fayard. [English edition: *The Path to Hope.*]

Attali, J. 1997. *Globalisation et démocratie.* Paris: Fayard.

Augustine Comte

Comte, A. 1830–1842. *Cours de philosophie positive.* 6 vols. Paris: Rouen/Bachelier. [English edition: *The Positive Philosophy of Auguste Comte.* Translated and condensed by Harriet Martineau. London: John Chapman, 1853.]

Comte, A. 1851–1854. *Système de politique positive, ou traité de sociologie instituant la religion de l'Humanité.* 4 vols. Paris: Carilian-Goeury. [English edition: *System of Positive Polity.* Translated by J. H. Bridges et al. London: Longmans, Green, 1875–1877.]

Bacon, Francis

Bacon, F. 1605. *The Advancement of Learning.* London: Henrie Tomes. [Modern edition: Kiernan, M. (ed.). Oxford: Oxford University Press, 2000.]

Bacon, F. 1620. *Novum Organum, or True Directions Concerning the Interpretation of Nature.* London: John Bill. [Modern edition: Rees, G. and Wakely, M. (eds.). *The Instauratio Magna, Part II: Novum Organum.* Oxford: Oxford University Press, 2004.]

Bacon, F. 1627. *New Atlantis.* London: William Rawley (posthumous). [Modern edition: Vickers, B. (ed.). *Francis Bacon: A Critical Edition of the Major Works.* Oxford: Oxford University Press, 2000.]

Berkman, Alexander

Berkman, A. 1929. *Now and After: The ABC of Communist Anarchism.* New York: Vanguard Press.

Berlin, Isaiah

Berlin, I. 1939. Karl Marx: His Life and Environment. London: Thornton Butterworth. 5th ed., ed. Henry Hardy, Princeton: Princeton University Press, 2013.

Berlin, I. 1953. The Hedgehog and the Fox: An Essay on Tolstoy's View of History. London: Weidenfeld and Nicolson. 2nd ed., ed. Henry Hardy, Princeton: Princeton University Press, 2013.

Berlin, I. 1958. 'Two Concepts of Liberty'. Oxford: Clarendon Press. Reprinted in Berlin, I. 2002. Liberty, ed. Henry Hardy, Oxford: Oxford University Press.

Berlin, I. 1990. The Crooked Timber of Humanity: Chapters in the History of Ideas. London: John Murray. 2nd ed., ed. Henry Hardy, Princeton: Princeton University Press, 2013.

Boyle, Robert

Boyle, R. 1999–2000. *The Works of Robert Boyle.* Edited by Michael Hunter and Edward B. Davis. 14 vols. London: Pickering and Chatto.

Bruno, Giordano

Bruno, G. 1584. *De l'infinito, universo e mondi.* London. Trans. D. W. Singer, in *Giordano Bruno: His Life and Thought,* New York: Schuman, 1950.

Bruno, G. 1584. *Spaccio de la bestia trionfante.* London. Trans. A. D. Imerti, *The Expulsion of the Triumphant Beast,* New Brunswick, NJ: Rutgers University Press, 1964; reprint Lincoln, NE: University of Nebraska Press, 1992.

Bruno, G. 1584. *De la causa, principio et uno.* London. Trans. R. de Lucca, *Cause, Principle and Unity,* Cambridge: Cambridge University Press, 1998.

Calvin, John

Calvin, J. 1960. *Institutes of the Christian Religion.* Edited by J. T. McNeill, translated by F. L. Battles. 2 vols. Library of Christian Classics, vols. XX and XXI. Philadelphia: Westminster Press.

Calvin, J. 1954. *Theological Treatises.* Translated and edited by J. K. S. Reid. Library of Christian Classics, vol. XXII. London: SCM Press.

Calvin, J. 1989 [1559]. *Institutes of the Christian Religion.* Translated by H. Beveridge. Grand Rapids, MI: Wm. B. Eerdmans Publishing Company. (Reprint of the 1559 Latin edition.)

Campanella, Tommaso

Campanella, T. 1591 [1992]. *Philosophia sensibus demonstrata.* Edited by L. De Franco. Naples: Vivarium.

Campanella, T. 1602 [1997]. *La città del Sole* [*The City of the Sun*]. Edited by G. Ernst and L. Salvetti Firpo. Rome and Bari: Laterza. English translation: D. J. Donno. Berkeley and Los Angeles: University of California Press, 1981.

Campanella, T. 1607 [2004]. *L'ateismo trionfato* [*Atheism Conquered*]. Edited by G. Ernst. 2 vols. Pisa: Edizioni della Normale.

Campanella, T. 1616 [1994]. *Apologia pro Galileo* [*A Defense of Galileo*]. Edited and translated by R. J. Blackwell. Notre Dame, IN: University of Notre Dame Press.

Campanella, T. 1623 [1975]. *Philosophia realis epilogistica.* In *Opera latina Francofurti impressa annis 1617–1630.* Facsimile ed. L. Firpo. Turin: Bottega d'Erasmo.

Campanella, T. 1637 [2007]. *De sensu rerum et magia* [*On the Sense of Things and on Magic*]. Edited by G. Ernst. Rome and Bari: Laterza.

Campanella, T. 1638 [1961]. *Metaphysica.* Facsimile edition by L. Firpo. Turin: Bottega d'Erasmo.

Cabet, Étienne

Cabet, É. 1842. *Voyage en Icarie.* Paris: Hippolyte Souverain. (English translation: *Voyage to Icaria.* London: John Chapman, 1848; reprinted Urbana, IL: University of Illinois Press, 2003.)

Cicero

Annas, J. and R. Woolf, 2001. *Cicero: On Moral Ends (De Finibus Bonorum et Malorum).* Cambridge: Cambridge University Press.

Griffin, M. T. and E. M. Atkins, 1991. *Cicero: On Duties (De Officiis).* Cambridge: Cambridge University Press.

Rudd, N. and J. Powell, 1998. *Cicero: The Republic and the Laws (De Re Publica, De Legibus).* Oxford: Oxford University Press.

Walsh, P. G., 1998. *Cicero: The Nature of the Gods (De Natura Deorum).* Oxford: Oxford University Press.

Comte, Auguste

Comte, A. 1830–1842. *Cours de philosophie positive.* 6 vols. Paris: Rouen, puis Bachelier. (Freely translated and condensed by Harriet Martineau as *The Positive Philosophy of Auguste Comte.* London: J. Chapman, 1853).

Comte, A. 1844. *Discours sur l'esprit positif.* Paris: V. Dalmont. Reprint, Paris: Vrin, 1995. (Translated as *A Discourse on the Positive Spirit.* London: Reeves, 1903).

Comte, A. 1848. *Discours sur l'ensemble du positivisme.* Paris: Mathias. Reprint, Paris: Garnier Frères, 1998. (Translated as *General View of Positivism.* London: Trubner, 1865).

Comte, A. 1851–1854. *Système de politique positive, ou Traité de sociologie instituant la religion de l'Humanité.* 4 vols. Paris: Carilian-Goeury. (Translated as *System of Positive Polity.* London: Longmans, Green and Co., 1875–1877).

Comte, A. 1852. *Catéchisme positiviste.* Paris: self-published. Reprint, Paris: Garnier Frères, 1966. (Translated as *The Catechism of Positive Religion.* London: Trubner, 1891).

Comte, A. 1855. *Appel aux conservateurs.* Paris: self-published. Reprint, Paris: Éditions du Sandre, 2009. (Translated as *Appeal to Conservatives.* London: Trubner, 1889).

Comte, A. 1856. *Synthèse subjective.* Paris: self-published. (Translated as *Subjective Synthesis.* London: Kegan Paul, 1891).

Copernicus, Nicolaus

Copernicus, N. 1955. *On the Revolutions of the Heavenly Spheres.* Translated by Charles Glenn Wallis. Vol. 16 of *Great Books of the Western World.* Chicago: Encyclopaedia Britannica. Reprint, Amherst: Prometheus Books, 1995.

Copernicus, N. 1973. "The Derivation and First Draft of Copernicus's Planetary Theory: A Translation of the *Commentariolus* with Commentary." Translated by N. M. Swerdlow. *Proceedings of the American Philosophical Society* 117: 423–512.

Copernicus, N. 1976. *On the Revolutions of the Heavenly Spheres.* Translated and edited by A. M. Duncan. Newton Abbot: David & Charles.

Diderot, Denis

Diderot, D. 1986. *Jacques the Fatalist and His Master.* Translated by Michael Henry. London: Penguin Classics.

Diderot, D. 1992. *Political Writings.* Translated and edited by John Hope Mason and Robert Wokler. Cambridge: Cambridge University Press.

Diderot, D. 1999. *Jacques the Fatalist and His Master.* Translated with introduction and notes by David Coward. Oxford: Oxford University Press (Oxford World's Classics).

Diderot, D. 2001. *Rameau's Nephew and Other Works.* Edited and translated by Jimenez Powell. Indianapolis: Hackett Publishing Company.

Descartes, René

Descartes, R. 1984–1991. *The Philosophical Writings of Descartes* [*Œuvres de Descartes*]. Edited and translated by John Cottingham, Robert Stoothoff, Dugald Murdoch, and Anthony Kenny. 3 vols. Cambridge: Cambridge University Press.

Descartes, R. 1994. *Discourse on the Method: of Conducting One's Reason Well and of Seeking the Truth in the Sciences* [*Discours de la méthode: pour bien conduire sa raison et chercher la vérité dans les sciences*]. Translated by George Heffernan. Notre Dame, IN: University of Notre Dame Press.

Descartes, R. 1998. *Meditations and Other Metaphysical Writings* [*Meditationes de prima philosophia et alia*]. Translated by Desmond M. Clarke. London: Penguin.

Descartes, R. 1998. *The World and Other Writings* [*Le monde, ou traité de la lumière, et autres écrits*]. Translated by Stephen Gaukroger. Cambridge: Cambridge University Press.

Descartes, R. 2006. *A Discourse on the Method of Correctly Conducting One's Reason and Seeking Truth in the Sciences* [*Discours de la méthode*]. Translated by Ian Maclean. Oxford: Oxford University Press.

Descartes, R. 2008. *Meditations on First Philosophy: With Selections from the Objections and Replies* [*Meditationes de prima philosophia*]. Translated by Michael Moriarty. Oxford: Oxford University Press.

Descartes, R. 2015. *The Passions of the Soul and Other Late Philosophical Writings* [*Les passions de l'âme et autres écrits tardifs*]. Translated by Michael Moriarty. Oxford: Oxford University Press.

Engels, Friedrich

Engels, F. 2009. *The Condition of the Working Class in England* [*Die Lage der arbeitenden Klasse in England*]. Edited with introduction and notes by David McLellan; text based on the authorized 1892 English translation by Florence Kelley Wischnewetzky, revised by Engels. Oxford: Oxford University Press.

Engels, F. 1947. *Anti-Dühring: Herr Eugen Dühring's Revolution in Science* [*Herrn Eugen Dührings Umwälzung der Wissenschaft*]. Translated by Emile Burns. London: Lawrence & Wishart.

Engels, F. 1972. *The Origin of the Family, Private Property and the State* [*Der Ursprung der Familie, des Privateigenthums und des Staats*]. Translated by Ernest Untermann; revised with introduction by Eleanor Burke Leacock. New York: International Publishers.

Fourier, Charles

Fourier, C. 1996. The Theory of the Four Movements. *Edited by Gareth Stedman Jones and Ian Patterson*. Cambridge Texts in the History of Political Thought. Cambridge: Cambridge University Press.

Fourier, C. 1971 [1829]. *Design for Utopia: Selected Writings of Charles Fourier (from Le Nouveau monde industriel et sociétaire)*. Edited by Frank E. Manuel. New York: Schocken Books.

Galilei, Galileo

Galilei, G. 1610 [1989]. *Sidereus Nuncius (The Starry Messenger)*. Translated by Albert Van Helden. Chicago: University of Chicago Press.

Galilei, G. 1632 [1967]. *Dialogo sopra i due massimi sistemi del mondo (Dialogue Concerning the Two Chief World Systems)*. Translated by Stillman Drake. Berkeley: University of California Press.

Galilei, G. 1638 [1974]. *Discorsi e dimostrazioni matematiche intorno a due nuove scienze (Discourses and Mathematical Demonstrations Concerning Two New Sciences)*. Translated by Stillman Drake. Madison: University of Wisconsin Press.

Giddens, Anthony

Giddens, A. 1971. *Capitalism and Modern Social Theory: An Analysis of the Writings of Marx, Durkheim and Max Weber*. Cambridge: Cambridge University Press.

Giddens, A. 1976. *New Rules of Sociological Method: A Positive Critique of Interpretative Sociologies*. London: Hutchinson.

Giddens, A. 1979. *Central Problems in Social Theory: Action, Structure and Contradiction in Social Analysis*. London: Macmillan.

Giddens, A. 1984. *The Constitution of Society: Outline of the Theory of Structuration*. Cambridge: Polity.

Giddens, A. 1990. *The Consequences of Modernity*. Cambridge: Polity.

Giddens, A. 1991. *Modernity and Self-Identity: Self and Society in the Late Modern Age*. Cambridge: Polity.

Giddens, A. 1992. *The Transformation of Intimacy: Sexuality, Love and Eroticism in Modern Societies*. Cambridge: Polity.

Giddens, A. 1998. *The Third Way: The Renewal of Social Democracy*. Cambridge: Polity.

Gilbert, William

Gilbert, W. 1958 [1893]. *On the Magnet, Magnetick Bodies, and on the Great Magnet of the Earth*. Translated by P. Fleury Mottelay. New York: Dover Publications. Reprint, 1991.

Goebbels, Joseph

Goebbels, J. 1926 [1927]. *Der Nazi-Sozi" [The Nazi-Sozi]*. German Propaganda Archive. Grand Rapids, MI: Calvin University.

Goebbels, J. 1935. *Jews Will Destroy Culture*. Speech at the Nazi Party Congress, Nuremberg, September 1935.

Goebbels, J. 1943 [1944]. *Nun, Volk steh auf, und Sturm brich los! [Nation, Rise Up, and Let the Storm Break Loose]*. German Propaganda Archive. Grand Rapids, MI: Calvin University.

Greenway, Andrew

Greenway, A., Terrett, B., Bracken, M., & Loosemore, T. (2020). *Digital transformation at scale: Why the strategy is delivery* (2nd ed.). London Publishing Partnership.

Habermas, Jürgen

Habermas, J. 1973 [1963]. *Theory and Practice (Theorie und Praxis: Sozialphilosophische Studien)*. Translated by John Viertel. Boston: Beacon Press.

Habermas, J. 1989 [1962]. *The Structural Transformation of the Public Sphere: An Inquiry into a Category of Bourgeois Society (Strukturwandel der Öffentlichkeit: Untersuchungen zu einer Kategorie der bürgerlichen Gesellschaft)*. Translated by Thomas Burger, with the assistance of Frederick Lawrence. Cambridge, MA: MIT Press.

Harvey, William

Harvey, W. 1847. *The Works of William Harvey*. Translated by Robert Willis. London: Sydenham Society.

Harvey, W. 1889. *On the Motion of the Heart and Blood in Animals*. London: George Bell and Sons.

Harvey, W. 1993. *The Circulation of the Blood and Other Writings*. Translated by Kenneth J. Franklin. London: Everyman/Orion Publishing Group.

Hayek, Friedrich

Hayek, F. A. 1944. *The Road to Serfdom (Der Weg zur Knechtschaft)*. Chicago: University of Chicago Press.

Hayek, F. A. 1960. *The Constitution of Liberty (Verfassung der Freiheit)*. Chicago: University of Chicago Press.

Hayek, F. A. 1973–1979. *Law, Legislation, and Liberty (Recht, Gesetzgebung und Freiheit)*. 3 vols. Chicago: University of Chicago Press.

Vol. 1 (1973): *Rules and Order*.

Vol. 2 (1976): *The Mirage of Social Justice*.

Vol. 3 (1979): *The Political Order of a Free People*.

Hayek, F. A. 1988. *The Fatal Conceit: The Errors of Socialism (Die verhängnisvolle Anmaßung)*. Edited by W. W. Bartley III. Vol. 1 of The Collected Works of F. A. Hayek. Chicago: University of Chicago Press.

Hitler, Adolf

Hitler, A. 1999 [1925–1926]. *Mein Kampf (Mein Kampf)*. Translated by Ralph Manheim. Boston: Houghton Mifflin. ISBN 978-0-395-92503-4.

Hitler, A. 1988 [1953]. *Hitler's Table Talk, 1941–1945: Hitler's Conversations Recorded by Martin Bormann (Tischgespräche im Führerhauptquartier)*. Edited by Hugh Trevor-Roper. Oxford: Oxford University Press.

Hoffmann von Fallersleben, August Heinrich

Hoffmann von Fallersleben, A. H. 1841. *Das Lied der Deutschen (Song of the Germans)*. Hamburg: Hoffmann und Campe.

Jaspers, Karl

Jaspers, K. 1951. *Way to Wisdom: An Introduction to Philosophy (Einführung in die Philosophie)*. Translated by Ralph Manheim. New Haven, CT: Yale University Press.

Jaspers, K. 1953. *The Origin and Goal of History (Vom Ursprung und Ziel der Geschichte)*. Translated by Michael Bullock. New Haven, CT: Yale University Press.

Jaspers, K. 1963. *General Psychopathology (Allgemeine Psychopathologie)*. Translated by J. Hoenig and M. W. Hamilton. Chicago, IL: University of Chicago Press.

Jaspers, K. 1971. *Philosophy of Existence (Philosophie der Existenz)*. Translated by R. F. C. Hull. Philadelphia, PA: University of Pennsylvania Press.

Jaspers, K. 1947. *The Question of German Guilt (Die Schuldfrage)*. Translated by E. B. Ashton. New York, NY: Dial Press. (Reprint: Fordham University Press, 2001.)

Kepler, Johannes

Kepler, J. 1609. *Astronomia nova (New Astronomy)*. Translated by W. H. Donahue. Cambridge: Cambridge University Press, 1992.

Kepler, J. 1619. *Harmonices mundi (The Harmony of the World)*. Translated by E. J. Aiton, A. M. Duncan, and J. V. Field. Philadelphia: American Philosophical Society, 1997.

Kurzweil, Ray

Kurzweil, R. 1990. *The Age of Intelligent Machines*. Cambridge, MA: MIT Press.

Kurzweil, R. 1999. *The Age of Spiritual Machines: When Computers Exceed Human Intelligence*. New York: Viking.

Kurzweil, R. 2005. *The Singularity Is Near: When Humans Transcend Biology*. New York: Viking.

Kurzweil, R. 2012. *How to Create a Mind: The Secret of Human Thought Revealed*. New York: Viking.

Kurzweil, R. 2024. *The Singularity Is Nearer: When we merge with AI*. New York: Viking.

Lenin, Vladimir

Lenin, V. I. 1902. *What Is to Be Done? Burning Questions of Our Movement (Chto delat'?)*. Translated by Joe Fineberg and George Hanna. Moscow: Progress Publishers, 1961.

Lenin, V. I. 1908. *Materialism and Empirio-Criticism: Critical Comments on a Reactionary Philosophy (Materializm i empiriokrititsizm)*. Translated by David Riazanov. Moscow: Progress Publishers, 1970.

Lenin, V. I. 1917. *The State and Revolution: The Marxist Theory of the State and the Tasks of the Proletariat in the Revolution (Gosudarstvo i revoliutsiia)*. Translated by Robert Service. London: Penguin Classics, 1992.

Locke, John

Locke, J. 1975. *An Essay Concerning Human Understanding*. Edited by P. H. Nidditch. Oxford: Clarendon Press.

Locke, J. 1988. *Two Treatises of Government*. Edited by P. Laslett. Rev. ed. Cambridge: Cambridge University Press.

Locke, J. 1989. *Some Thoughts Concerning Education*. Edited by J. W. Yolton and J. S. Yolton. Oxford: Clarendon Press.

Locke, J. 1999. *The Reasonableness of Christianity: As Delivered in the Scriptures*. Edited by J. C. Higgins-Biddle. Oxford: Clarendon Press.

Lucian

Lucian. 1913–1967. Works. 8 vols. Translated by A. M. Harmon, K. Kilburn, and M. D. Macleod. Loeb Classical Library. Cambridge, MA: Harvard University Press.

Machiavelli, Niccolò

Machiavelli, N. 1988 [1532]. Il Principe (The Prince). Edited and translated by Q. Skinner and R. Price. Cambridge Texts in the History of Political Thought. Cambridge: Cambridge University Press.

Machiavelli, N. 1988 [1531]. Discorsi sopra la prima deca di Tito Livio (Discourses on Livy). Edited by B. Grafton; translated by H. Mansfield and N. Tarcov. Chicago: University of Chicago Press.

Machiavelli, N. 1965 [1521]. Dell'arte della guerra (The Art of War). Edited by A. Gilbert. New York: Da Capo Press.

Marx, Karl

Marx, K. and Engels, F. 2012 [1848]. *Manifest der Kommunistischen Partei (The Communist Manifesto)*. Edited by G. Stedman Jones. London: Penguin Classics.

Marx, K. 1990 [1867]. *Das Kapital: Kritik der politischen Ökonomie. Volume I (Capital: A Critique of Political Economy)*. Translated by B. Fowkes. London: Penguin Classics.

Marx, K. 2010 [1875]. *Kritik des Gothaer Programms (Critique of the Gotha Programme)*. Edited and translated by T. Carver. Cambridge Texts in the History of Political Thought. Cambridge: Cambridge University Press.

Montesquieu, Charles-Louis

Montesquieu, C.-L. 1993 [1721]. *Lettres persanes (Persian Letters)*. Edited and translated by C. J. Betts. London: Penguin Classics.

Montesquieu, C.-L. 1999 [1734]. *Considérations sur les causes de la grandeur des Romains et de leur décadence (Considerations on the Causes of the Greatness of the Romans and Their Decline)*. Edited and translated by D. Lowenthal. Indianapolis: Hackett Publishing.

Montesquieu, C.-L. 1989 [1748]. *De l'esprit des lois (The Spirit of the Laws)*. Edited and translated by A. M. Cohler, B. C. Miller, and H. S. Stone. Cambridge Texts in the History of Political Thought. Cambridge: Cambridge University Press.

More, Thomas

More, T. 1965 [1516]. *Utopia (De optimo rei publicae statu deque nova insula Utopia)*. Edited by Edward Surtz, S.J., and J. H. Hexter. The Complete Works of St. Thomas More, Vol. 4. New Haven, CT: Yale University Press.

More, T. 1976 [1534]. *A Dialogue of Comfort against Tribulation*. Edited by Louis L. Martz and Frank Manley. The Complete Works of St. Thomas More, Vol. 12. New Haven, CT: Yale University Press.

More, T. 2020. *The Essential Works of Thomas More*. Edited by Gerard B. Wegemer and Stephen W. Smith. New Haven, CT: Yale University Press.

Næss, Arne

Næss, A. 1973. *The Shallow and the Deep, Long-Range Ecology Movement. A Summary*. Inquiry 16 (1–4): 95–100.

Næss, A. 1989. *Ecology, Community and Lifestyle: Outline of an Ecosophy*. Translated and revised by David Rothenberg. Cambridge: Cambridge University Press.

Newton, Isaac

Newton, I. 1972. *Philosophiae Naturalis Principia Mathematica*: The Third Edition with Variant Readings. Edited by A. Koyré and I. B. Cohen, 2 vols. Cambridge, MA: Harvard University Press; Cambridge: Cambridge University Press.

Newton, I. 1999. *The Principia: Mathematical Principles of Natural Philosophy*: A New Translation. Translated by I. B. Cohen and A. Whitman, with "A Guide to Newton's Principia" by I. B. Cohen. Berkeley: University of California Press.

Newton, I. 1952 [1730]. *Opticks: Or, A Treatise of the Reflections, Refractions, Inflections and Colours of Light*. Based on the 4th edition (1730). New York: Dover Publications.

Newton, I. 1728. *The Chronology of Ancient Kingdoms Amended.* Edited by John Conduitt. London.

Newton, I. 1733. *Observations upon the Prophecies of Daniel and the Apocalypse of St John.* Edited by Benjamin Smith. London and Dublin.

Newton, I. 1962. *Unpublished Scientific Papers of Isaac Newton.* Edited by A. R. Hall and M. B. Hall. Cambridge: Cambridge University Press.

Newton, I. 1978. *Isaac Newton's Papers and Letters on Natural Philosophy.* 2nd ed. Edited by I. B. Cohen and R. E. Schofield. Cambridge, MA: Harvard University Press.

Newton, I. 2004. *Philosophical Writings.* Edited by A. Janiak. Cambridge: Cambridge University Press.

Nozick, Robert

Nozick, R. 1974. *Anarchy, State, and Utopia.* New York: Basic Books.

Nozick, R. 1981. *Philosophical Explanations.* Cambridge, MA: Harvard University Press.

Nozick, R. 1989. *The Examined Life.* New York: Simon & Schuster.

Nozick, R. 1993. *The Nature of Rationality.* Princeton, NJ: Princeton University Press.

Nozick, R. 1997. *Socratic Puzzles.* Cambridge, MA: Harvard University Press.

Nozick, R. 2001. *Invariances: The Structure of the Objective World.* Cambridge, MA: Harvard University Press.

Owen, Robert

Owen, R. 1813. *A New View of Society: Or, Essays on the Formation of Human Character, and the Application of the Principle to Practice.* London: Cadell & Davies. [Second edition, 1816: A New View of Society: Or, Essays on the Formation of Human Character Preparatory to the Development of a Plan for Gradually Ameliorating the Condition of Mankind].

Owen, R. 1821. *Report to the County of Lanark of a Plan for Relieving Public Distress and Removing Discontent.* Glasgow: Glasgow University Press.

Owen, R. 1849. *The Revolution in the Mind and Practice of the Human Race.* London: Effingham Wilson.

Parsons, Lucy

Parsons, L. E. 1889. *Life of Albert R. Parsons, with Brief History of the Labor Movement in America.* Chicago: L. E. Parsons.

Parsons, L. E., ed. 1910. *The Famous Speeches of the Eight Chicago Anarchists in Court: When Asked If They Had Anything to Say Why Sentence of Death Should Not Be Passed upon Them – October 7, 8, and 9, 1886.* Chicago: L. E. Parsons.

Parsons, L. E. 2004. *Lucy Parsons: Freedom, Equality and Solidarity – Writings and Speeches, 1878–1937.* Edited by Gale Ahrens. Chicago: Charles H. Kerr.

Pelloutier, Fernand

Pelloutier, F. 1894. *Qu'est-ce que la Grève générale?* Paris: Librairie Léon Vanier. [English translation: What Is the General Strike?]

Pelloutier, F. 1896. *L'Organisation corporative et l'anarchie*. Paris: Librairie Léon Vanier.

Pelloutier, F. 1902. *Histoire des Bourses du Travail*. Paris: Schleicher frères. [English translation: History of the Bourses du Travail].

Plato

Plato. 1997. *Complete Works*. Edited by John M. Cooper and D. S. Hutchinson. Indianapolis: Hackett Publishing.

Plato. 2004 [c. 380 BCE]. *The Republic (Politeia)*. Translated by C. D. C. Reeve. Indianapolis: Hackett Publishing.

Plato. 2001 [c. 360 BCE]. *Symposium (Symposion)*. Translated by Alexander Nehamas and Paul Woodruff. 2nd ed. Indianapolis: Hackett Publishing.

Plato. 2002 [c. 360 BCE]. *Laws (Nomoi)*. Translated by Thomas L. Pangle. Chicago: University of Chicago Press.

Popper, Karl

Popper, K. 1945. *The Open Society and Its Enemies*. 2 vols. London: Routledge.

Popper, K. 1957. *The Poverty of Historicism*. London: Routledge.

Popper, K. 1959. *The Logic of Scientific Discovery. Translated by the author from Logik der Forschung* (1935). London: Hutchinson; reprinted London and New York: Routledge Classics, 2002.

Popper, K. 1963. *Conjectures and Refutations: The Growth of Scientific Knowledge*. London: Routledge.

Rocker, Rudolf

Rocker, R. 1989 [1938]. *Anarcho-Syndicalism: Theory and Practice*. Oakland, CA: AK Press.

Rousseau, Jean-Jacques

Rousseau, J.-J. 1751. *Discourse on the Sciences and the Arts (Discours sur les sciences et les arts)*. In: Gourevitch, V. (ed. and trans.) The Discourses and Other Early Political Writings. Cambridge: Cambridge University Press, 1997.

Rousseau, J.-J. 1755. *Discourse on the Origin and Foundations of Inequality among Men (Discours sur l'origine et les fondements de l'inégalité parmi les hommes)*. In: Gourevitch, V. (ed. and trans.) The Discourses and Other Early Political Writings. Cambridge: Cambridge University Press, 1997.

Rousseau, J.-J. 1762. *The Social Contract (Du contrat social)*. In: Gourevitch, V. (ed. and trans.) The Social Contract and Other Later Political Writings. Cambridge: Cambridge University Press, 1997.

Rousseau, J.-J. 1762. *Emile, or On Education (Émile, ou de l'éducation)*. Translated by A. Bloom. New York: Basic Books, 1979.

Rawls, John

Rawls, J. 1971. *A Theory of Justice*. Cambridge, MA: Harvard University Press. Revised edition, 1999.

Rawls, J. 1993. *Political Liberalism.* New York: Columbia University Press. Expanded edition, 2005.

Rawls, J. 1999. *The Law of Peoples.* Cambridge, MA: Harvard University Press.

Rawls, J. 2001. *Justice as Fairness: A Restatement.* Edited by Erin Kelly. Cambridge, MA: Harvard University Press.

James, Aaron

James, A. 2012. Fairness in Practice: A Social Contract for a Global Economy. Oxford: Oxford University Press

Savonarola, Girolamo

Savonarola, G. 2006. *Selected Writings of Girolamo Savonarola: Religion and Politics, 1490–1498.* Edited by Anne Borelli and Maria Pastore Passaro. New Haven, CT: Yale University Press.

Servetus, Michael

Servetus, M. 2010. *The Restoration of Christianity: An English Translation of Christianismi Restitutio.* Translated by C. Underwood, J. Godbey, and M. Williams. Lewiston, NY: Edwin Mellen Press.

Smith, Adam

Smith, A. 1977 [1776]. *An Inquiry into the Nature and Causes of the Wealth of Nations.* Chicago: University of Chicago Press.

Smith, A. 2002 [1759]. *The Theory of Moral Sentiments.* Edited by Knud Haakonssen. Cambridge: Cambridge University Press.

Spinoza, Baruch

Spinoza, B. 1985. *The Collected Works of Spinoza. Vol. 1.* Translated by Edwin Curley. Princeton, NJ: Princeton University Press.

Spinoza, B. 2016. *The Collected Works of Spinoza. Vol. 2.* Translated by Edwin Curley. Princeton, NJ: Princeton University Press.

Spinoza, B. 2002. *The Complete Works.* Translated by Samuel Shirley. Indianapolis: Hackett Publishing.

Stalin, Joseph

Stalin, J. 1938. *Dialectical and Historical Materialism.* Moscow: Foreign Languages Publishing House.

Stalin, J. 1939. *History of the Communist Party of the Soviet Union (Bolsheviks): Short Course.* Moscow: Foreign Languages Publishing House.

Stalin, J. 1954. *Marxism and the National Question: Selected Writings and Speeches.* Moscow: Foreign Languages Publishing House.

Stirner, Max

Stirner, M. 1995 [1844]. *The Ego and Its Own (Der Einzige und sein Eigentum).* Translated by Steven Byington. Edited with an introduction by David Leopold. Cambridge Texts in the History of Political Thought. Cambridge: Cambridge University Press.

Thoreau, Henry David

Thoreau, H. D. 1995 [1849]. *Civil Disobedience* (*Resistance to Civil Government*). In *Walden and Civil Disobedience*. Edited by Owen Thomas. New York: W. W. Norton & Company.

Thoreau, H. D. 2004 [1854]. *Walden; or, Life in the Woods*. Edited by Jeffrey S. Cramer. New Haven: Yale University Press.

Tucker, Benjamin

Tucker, B. R. 1881–1908. Liberty. Boston: Benjamin R. Tucker (ed. and publisher).

Voltaire

Voltaire. 1901. *The Works of Voltaire: A Contemporary Version*. Edited and translated by William F. Fleming. 21 vols. New York: E. R. Du Mont.

Voltaire. 1977. *The Portable Voltaire*. Edited by Ben Ray Redman. New York: Penguin Books.

Voltaire. 1995. *Voltaire: Selected Writings*. Edited by Christopher Thacker. London: J. M. Dent.

Voltaire. 2004. *Voltaire in His Letters: Being a Selection of His Correspondence*. Translated by S. G. Tallentyre. Honolulu, HI: University Press of the Pacific.

Warren, Josiah

Warren, J. 1846. *Equitable Commerce: A New Development of Principles, as Substitutes for Laws and Governments, for the Harmonious Adjustment and Regulation of the Pecuniary, Intellectual, and Moral Intercourse of Mankind*. New York: Fowlers and Wells. [Expanded edition, 1852.]

Warren, J. 1863. *True Civilization: A Subject of Vital and Serious Interest to All People, but Most Immediately to the Men and Women of Labor and Sorrow*. Boston: Published by the Author. [Revised edition, 1869.]

Sacred Texts

The Holy Bible. 1989. *New Revised Standard Version*. New York: National Council of the Churches of Christ in the USA.

The Torah. 1962. *The Torah: The Five Books of Moses*. Philadelphia: Jewish Publication Society of America.

The Qur'an. 2008. *The Qur'an: A New Translation*. Translated by M. A. S. Abdel Haleem. Oxford: Oxford University Press.

The Bhagavad Gita. 1979. *The Bhagavad Gita: An Interlinear Translation from the Sanskrit…* Translated by Winthrop Sargeant; 3rd ed. 2009. Albany, NY: SUNY Press.

The Dhammapada. 1998. *The Dhammapada*. Translated and introduced by John R. Carter and Mahinda Palihawadana. Oxford: Oxford University Press

Constitutional and Legal Documents

Australia. 1901. *Commonwealth of Australia Constitution Act*.

Bhutan. 2008. *Constitution of the Kingdom of Bhutan*.

Canada. 1867. *Constitution Act, 1867* (formerly the British North America Act, 1867).

Canada. 1982. *Constitution Act, 1982, including the Canadian Charter of Rights and Freedoms.*

Chile. 1980. *Constitution of the Republic of Chile.*

Denmark. 1849 (rev. 1953). *Constitution of the Kingdom of Denmark (Danmarks Riges Grundlov).*

England. 1215. *Magna Carta.*

England. 1689. *Bill of Rights.*

France. 1958. *Constitution of the Fifth Republic.*

Germany. 1949. *Basic Law for the Federal Republic of Germany (Grundgesetz).*

India. 1950. *Constitution of India* (in force January 26, 1950).

India. 1950. *Constitution of India, Article 370* (abrogated 2019).

Italy. 1947 (in force 1948). *Constitution of the Italian Republic.*

Japan. 1947. *Constitution of Japan (日本国憲法, Nihon-koku Kenpō).*

Korea, Republic of. 1987. *Constitution of the Republic of Korea.*

Nepal. 1962. *Constitution of the Kingdom of Nepal.*

Portugal. 1976. *Constitution of the Portuguese Republic.*

Russia. 1993. *Constitution of the Russian Federation.*

Spain. 1978. *Constitution of Spain (Constitución Española).*

Sweden. 1974. *Instrument of Government (Regeringsformen).*

Switzerland. 1848. *Swiss Federal Constitution.*

United Kingdom. 1911 and 1949. *Parliament Acts.*

United States. 1787. *Constitution of the United States.*

United States. 1791. *Bill of Rights* (first ten amendments to the U.S. Constitution).

United States. 1951. *Twenty-Second Amendment to the U.S. Constitution.*

Declarations and Charters

Catholic Church. 1917 (rev. 1983). *Code of Canon Law.* Vatican City: Libreria Editrice Vaticana.

Catholic Church. 1996. *Apostolic Constitution Universi Dominici Gregis.* Vatican City: Libreria Editrice Vaticana. Amended by Pope Benedict XVI and Pope Francis.

France. 1789. *Declaration of the Rights of Man and of the Citizen (Déclaration des droits de l'homme et du citoyen).* Paris: National Assembly of France.

Holy See and Italy. 1929. *Lateran Treaty (Patti Lateranensi).* Vatican City: Holy See.

Justinian I. 529–534 CE. *Corpus Juris Civilis (Code of Justinian).* Constantinople. Modern editions include Krüger, P., Mommsen, T., and Schoell, R. (eds.), *Corpus Iuris Civilis*, Berlin: Weidmann, 1872–1895.

Historical Laws and Legal Codes

Charles IV of Luxembourg. 1356. *Golden Bull.*

Rome. 5th century BCE. *Laws of the Twelve Tables.*

Rome. 367 BCE. *Licinian-Sextian Laws (Leges Liciniae Sextiae).*

Venice. 1297. *Great Council Lockout (Serrata del Maggior Consiglio).*

Nepal. [until 2008]. *Muluki Ain.*

India. 17th century. *Adnyapatra.*

India. c. 2nd century BCE–3rd century CE. *Manusmriti (Laws of Manu).*

Tibet. 17th century. *Thirteen-Article Code.*

Tibet. 17th century. *Sixteen-Article Code.*

France. 1905. *Law on the Separation of Church and State (Loi de 1905 sur la séparation des Églises et de l'État).*

France. 2004. *Law on Religious Symbols in Schools (Loi de 2004 sur les signes religieux à l'école).*

United Kingdom. 1846. *Corn Laws (repealed).*

United Kingdom. 1832. *Sadler Report.*

United States. 1890. *Sherman Antitrust Act.*

Programs, Strategies, and Plans

Germany. 1939–1945. *Aktion T4 Program.*

People's Republic of China. 2021–2025. *Fourteenth Five-Year Plan.*

Russian Federation. 2018–2030. *National Projects of Russia.*

Russian Federation. 2020. *Energy Strategy of the Russian Federation to 2035.*

Singapore. 2021. *Singapore Green Plan 2030.*

THE SECRET CODES OF THE MIND
INTRODUCTION TO PHILOSOPHY

THE SECRET CODES OF THE MIND
EASTERN PHILOSOPHY

III

THE SECRET CODES OF THE MIND
ANCIENT GREEK PHILOSOPHY

I

II

DR. ANDREW V. KUDIN

UDIN

THE SECRET CODES OF THE MIND
FROM MEDIEVAL PHILOSOPHY TO THE AGE OF ENLIGHTENMENT

IV

GERMAN CLASSICAL PHILOSOPHY
19TH—EARLY 20TH-CENTURY PHILOSOPHY

ODES
OF THE MIND

V

DR. ANDREW V. KUDIN

THE SECRET CODES OF THE MIND
THE 20TH CENTURY AND CONTEMPORARY PHILOSOPHY
POLITICAL PHILOSOPHY AND PHILOSOPHY OF SCIENCE

VI

DR. ANDREW V. KUDIN

Philosophical Works by Andrew V. Kudin (English Editions)

❖ *The Secret Codes of the Mind*

Volume I — Introduction to Philosophy
Volume II — Ancient Greek Philosophy
Volume III — Eastern Philosophy
Volume IV — From Medieval Philosophy to the Age of Enlightenment
Volume V — German Classical Philosophy and 19th–Early 20th-Century Philosophy
Volume VI — The 20th Century and Contemporary Philosophy, Political Philosophy and Philosophy of Science

❖ *Philosophical Methods and Their Application to the Art of Living*

❖ *Sri Sukta श्रीसूक्त — Text Structure, Sacred Meaning and Application in Spiritual Practice*

❖ *Mexican Philosophy: History, Traditions, and Critical Thought*

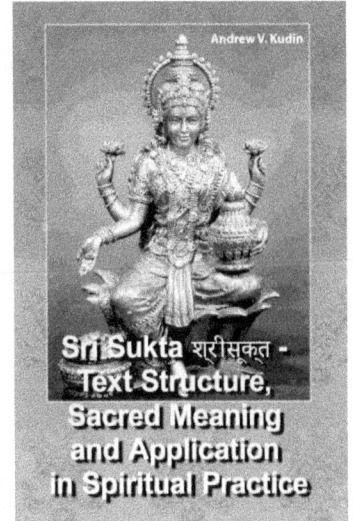

Andrew V. Kudin

MEXICAN PHILOSOPHY:
HISTORY, TRADITIONS, AND CRITICAL THOUGHT

DR. ANDREW V. KUDIN

PHILOSOPHICAL METHODS AND THEIR APPLICATION TO THE ART OF LIVING

Andrew V. Kudin

Sri Sukta शरीसूकत -
Text Structure,
Sacred Meaning
and Application
in Spiritual Practice

www.ingramcontent.com/pod-product-compliance
Lightning Source LLC
Chambersburg PA
CBHW080407270326
41929CB00018B/2923